AF816503

Trade Outside the Box

Advanced thinking for professional traders

Brent Donnelly

For more information, please visit

www.spectramarkets.com

Special thanks to **TradingView** for letting me use their excellent charts in this book. TradingView is the best in the business, by a mile. Not a paid endorsement; I just like their product. I use it every day!

Copyright © 2026 Brent Donnelly

All rights reserved. No part of this book may be reproduced or used in any manner without written permission of the copyright holder.

Cover design: Steve Donnelly and Brent Donnelly

Editing and layout: Stephen K. Donnelly

Index: Teri Greenberg

ISBN 978-1-7367398-4-6 (softcover)
ISBN 978-1-7367398-5-3 (e-book)
ISBN 978-1-7367398-6-0 (hardcover)

This book is dedicated to:

Christine, the one who sticks with me, despite and because.

And in celebration and memory of:

RS 1972—2025

CONTENTS

Foreword by Sam Rines 1
FIVE QUICK STORIES BEFORE WE START 3
PART ONE: NEW WAYS TO THINK ABOUT MARKETS 17
Introduction 17
Markets are the universe, you are a grain of sand 20
The science of creativity 21
Perspective 23
The illusion of control 24
Geo-, ego-, and chronocentrism 28
Seeing around corners 38
High school derivatives refresher 44
Second-order thinking 46
Keynes' beauty contest 47
Guess 2/3 of the average 49
Smarties or pencils? 52
Second-order use of technical analysis 54
What multi-level thinking is not 60
Conclusion 62
New tools 63
AI & LLMs 63
r/wallstreetbets 73
Prediction markets 79
Conclusion 108
PART TWO: INSPIRATION FROM OTHER DOMAINS 109
Introduction 109
Psychology and mental health 111
The DSM-5 111
ADHD 112
Side quest: stop losses 117
Generalized Anxiety Disorder 119
Insomnia 126
Gambling Disorder 127
Conclusion 148
Better trading through poker 149
The psychology of the game 149

When the market eats an Oreo 154
Market tell #1: Good news/bad price 155
Market tell #2: Everybody's tilting 157
Market tell #3: Correlation breakdown and regime change 160
Market tell #4: Volume spike with price reversal 172
Market tell #5: Gaps 176
Market tell #6: Falling volatility 178
Mental stamina 179
Probability and expected value (EV) 180
Variance 181
Side quest: Do good traders vary bet size? 188
Conclusion 197
Concepts I wish I'd learned earlier 198
Ergodicity 198
Skew 208
Initial conditions 211
Good forecasts 216
Narrative contagion 220
Adverse selection 227
The multiverse 241
Conclusion 245
Choosing the right game 246
What does "metagame" mean? 246
The too-hard pile 255
The institutional metagame 257
The hedge fund metagame 258
The market maker metagame 263
Retail day trader metagame 269
Event trading 273
Career risk, rationality and EMH 279
The calendar metagame 281
Conclusion 281
Short selling, the hardest game of all 282
The math of short selling 282
The politics and history of short selling 288
Conclusion 290
PART THREE: FRAMEWORKS 291

Introduction 291
Nine ways to sound smart and lose money 292
Faulty Framework #1: Time horizon mismatch 293
Faulty framework #2: Overreliance on models 304
Faulty framework #3: The one trick pony 306
Faulty framework #4: Disregard for mental capital 308
Faulty framework #5: Single variable frameworks 321
Faulty framework #6: Bad breadth is bearish 323
Faulty framework #7: Underestimating gap risk 325
Faulty framework #8: Don't fight the Fed 326
Faulty framework #9: Fade Jim Cramer 327
Conclusion 333
Choose your weapon 334
Decision-making and good thinking 334
Execution and tactics 339
Trade structuring 355
Conclusion 375
What are we doing here? 376
Build and protect your reputation 383
Humility 384
Self-awareness 391
Growth is slow and linear 393
Nice guys finish first 394
Final thoughts on getting rich 395
Conclusion 396
The 21 Principles 397
Acknowledgements 398
Index 399
About the author 418

FOREWORD BY SAM RINES

There is a porch in nowhere Maine forever etched into my psyche. Not memory—psyche. The yearly Camp Kotok gathering begins, and largely ends, on a giant deck overlooking a lake. That deck—and others like it—are where I came to know the man behind the trades. Yes, Camp Kotok is ostensibly a retreat where conversations orbit the macro outlook and market structure. But that is the beauty of Brent: we almost never talked markets.

And—believe it or not—that is precisely what makes *Alpha Trader* so enduring. Superficially, Brent and I have little in common. He's Canadian. I am a Bruins fan. From a markets perspective, there would seem to be little to no overlap. Different time frames? Check. Different asset classes? Check. Wildly different processes? Check. Yet *Alpha Trader* was never about the trades. It was about curiosity, process, and the discipline of constantly interrogating one's own assumptions.

The logical question, then and now, is why Brent would ever want to talk to someone like me. The answer is simple: Brent is insatiably curious—a trait that sits at the core of *Alpha Trader*. Our conversations revolved around what made us curious. He studied magazine covers for narrative signals. So, we debated their relevance for FX and equities. We talked about shifts in musical preferences and even exploding hay bales. The relevance to investing? Knowing thyself and understanding that the past leaves an indelible imprint on how we construct processes and interpret markets. (It partially explains why Brent claims he does not specialize in EM currencies yet writes incessantly about the Loonie.) At one point, the discussion even veered toward writing a graphic novel centered on cryptocurrencies. No topic was ever off-limits. Get better. Learn.

To be clear, Brent is annoyingly talented. That daily note—am/FX—forces readers to go a layer deeper. There is almost always an Easter egg buried in the prose, an idea that migrates from FX to rates, equities, or crypto. You never quite know what you are going to learn. *Alpha Trader* has the same quality: it rewards attentiveness. We may both write. But Brent does it better.

One of the most important moments on that deck at Kotok came when Brent said, almost offhand, "you need to know who to call." I was ranting about something, and Brent had solved the issue in his typical fashion. Your best asset is knowing what you do not know. The second best is knowing who does know. A benign statement on the surface, but one carrying Brent-level insight. Have something you need to understand to grasp a narrative? Know that you need to ask. Then know who to ask. I have thought about that line for years. In a sentence, Brent had given a lifetime of homework.

Knowing is a double-edged sword. Know why people will call you—and be honest with yourself about when the phone should be your friend. Years later, many of the people who populate the deck at Camp Kotok are precisely those phone-a-friends. This ethos—network, humility, curiosity—runs straight through *Alpha Trader*.

Of course, being an Alpha Trader is not all fun and fishing in northern Maine. There is also the conundrum of how to lose. Losing is never the desired outcome, but it is inevitable. And if you read Brent, you immediately understand how to deal with it: admit it, learn from it, and move on. That may be the hardest lesson to internalize. The lessons leave scars. The scars are not something to hide or shy away from in this business. They are real world lessons in being humble and being able to laugh after a lesson learned.

That lesson was driven home on a long car ride with Brent. For reasons still unclear, he had driven his new BMW to Maine. He offered me a ride back to civilization, and we embarked on a six-hour journey. We traded war stories—mostly our worst moments—and how those experiences shaped our processes and biases. Was that how we framed it at the time? Of course not. It was simply two people talking about being right for all the wrong reasons, or being wrong when we were convinced there was no way to lose. Needless to say, the trip went by quickly (and not strictly because of the conversation).

Alpha Trader is not, and never was, just a book about trading. It is a guide to the mindset required to survive—and thrive—in an inherently stressful, outcomes-based business. It forces introspection, evolution, and learning—not as a one-off exercise, but as a commitment to constant improvement. That is why the book matters, and why this follow-up is so timely.

Sam Rines, Macro Strategist at WisdomTree, 2026

Throughout this book, examples, hypothetical scenarios, and anecdotes are in grey boxes (like this). These tidbits provide additional width, depth, or nuance to the topic and are highlighted for ease of reference.

FIVE QUICK STORIES BEFORE WE START

Hi. Thanks for grabbing my new book. I know everyone has limited cash and limited time and I hope you find this will be a good use of both. My plan here is to expand on some of the ideas and themes in *Alpha Trader*—and go in some entirely new directions. I will share how I make money trading, how I think about markets, and how my thinking has evolved over time.

Before we start, let me share five super short trading stories, each with an important takeaway.

Short story #1

Old dog, new tricks

It's early morning. The last day of 2025. As I finish up my coffee and work on my final am/FX of the year, I see a headline:

***CORCEPT SAYS FDA REJECTED RELACORILANT NDA**

Three years ago, that headline would have meant nothing to me. I would have thought:

> "That headline sounds bad, but I have no idea what it actually means. I have no edge trading biotechs. Corcept could have 50 products in the pipeline, and that's just one of them. Or Relacorilant could be their only product in development and they're completely pooched. No clue."

I would have gone back to my coffee and my writing, and CORT would have done whatever it was going to do without me. But this is late 2025. There are new tools. The stock is halted, so I have time to query an LLM. I fire up Gemini…

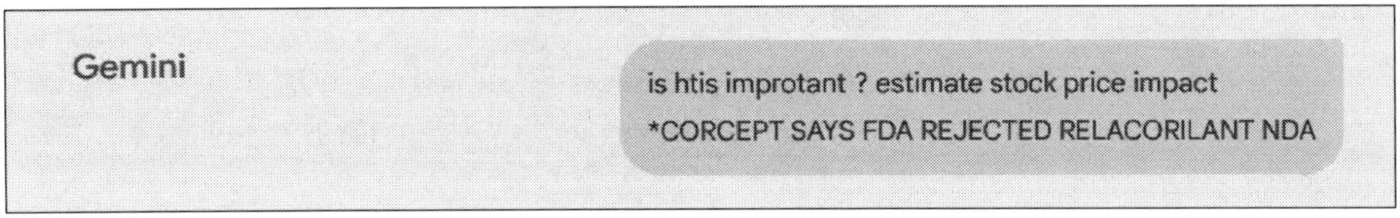

… and seconds later, I have this.

Yes, this is **critically important** news for Corcept Therapeutics (CORT).

The FDA issuing a "Complete Response Letter" (CRL) essentially means they have **rejected the application** in its current form. This is a major setback for the company.

Here is a breakdown of why this matters and an estimate of the stock price impact.

I quickly see this is a big deal. The stock was $70 pre-halt, so some quick mental math tells me that if this assessment is correct, it should trade down to something between $42 and $56. I read on:

1. Why is this so important?

Single-Product Risk: Corcept currently relies almost entirely on one product, Korlym, for its revenue. Relacorilant was supposed to be the "next generation" drug—safer and more selective than Korlym.

Pipeline Failure: Relacorilant is the company's most advanced pipeline asset. A rejection here delays diversification and growth plans by years.

The Reason is Concerning: The FDA stated they need "additional evidence of effectiveness." This is often the worst-case scenario for a rejection because it typically implies the company may need to run another Phase 3 clinical trial, which is expensive and takes years to complete.

2. Estimated Stock Price Impact

Based on how biotech stocks with single-asset dependency react to CRLs (rejections), you should expect a severe negative reaction.

Immediate Impact: Expect a drop of 20% to 40%.

Context: The stock was trading at a high valuation (P/E ~60+) because investors had "priced in" this approval. That premium will now be wiped out.

Price Targets:

Before this news, the stock was trading in the $70–$80 range.

Downside Support: Analysts and historical data suggest a fall toward the $45–$50 level is possible in the near term as the market removes the value of Relacorilant from its models.

3. What happens next?

Management Response: Corcept will likely request a "Type A" meeting with the FDA to clarify exactly what "additional evidence" is needed.

Timeline Shift: Instead of a 2026 launch, we are likely looking at a delay of 1-3 years if a new trial is required.

THESIS-BREAKING! That sounds juicy. I run the same query in ChatGPT to confirm that Gemini isn't on mushrooms, and it offers a similar response. There is no such thing as free money, so I think about the worst-case risk management scenario.

Let's say I sell at $55, and the market just thinks this is a nothingburger. It's instantly back at $70 again. That's probably my main risk. It's doubtful the stock will go higher than it was trading prior to the halt but let's say end of the world crazy days scenario maybe it goes to $80. It's important to think about worst-case scenarios when measuring risk.

Good traders think more about what they might lose than how much they're going to win.

You can leave limit orders in a stock that is halted. When the stock reopens, the auction will proceed and if a bid better than your ask comes in post-open, you will get filled.

I leave a limit order to sell 2,000 shares at $55 to go short the stock when it reopens.

My worst case is a $50,000 loss—but that's a tail risk. My base-case loss is more like $10,000 or $20,000. If the stock goes to $42, I make $26,000. Maybe I get lucky and extract even more. Assigning probabilities to these outcomes, I whip up an expected value grid that looks something like the table at right.

Short 2000 shares of CORT at $55

		P&L	Probability
Exit price	80	(50,000)	2%
	75	(40,000)	5%
	70	(30,000)	10%
	65	(20,000)	5%
	60	(10,000)	5%
	55	-	10%
	50	10,000	10%
	45	20,000	20%
	40	30,000	20%
	35	40,000	8%
	30	50,000	5%
		Expected Value	**9,200**

That's a nice positive expected value and I feel confident enough about the probabilities. I wait patiently for the market to reopen…

DING! Filled at $56, and it's instantly trading below $50. I am instantly in the money $16,000. I load up a bid for 1,000 at $42 and I am filled less than two minutes after I sold. I decide to run the other 1,000 shares into the open (9:30 a.m.) and see what happens.

Here's the 1-minute chart:

CORT 1-minute chart, December 31, 2025

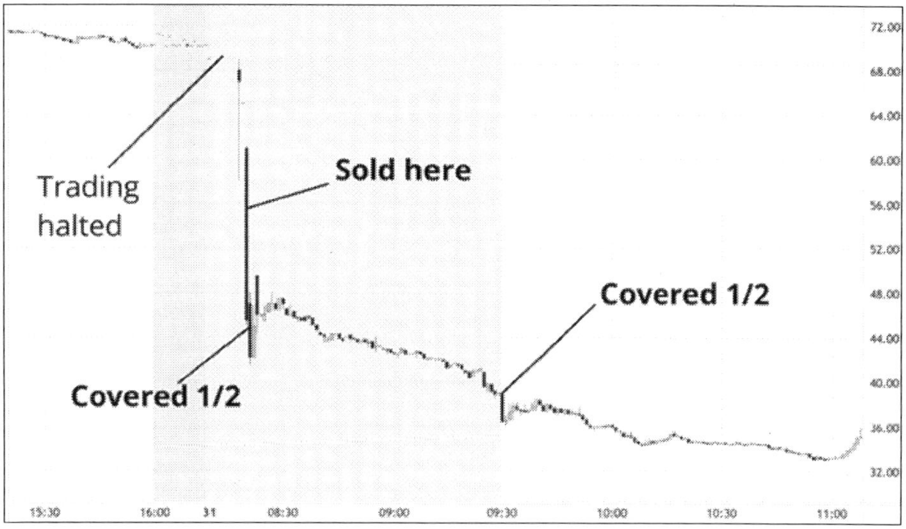

I figured that by the open, the juice would be squeezed out of this trade, so I bid on the open at 9:30 a.m. and covered around $38.80. Good trade!

Could I have sold higher than $56? Yes.

Could I have covered lower than $38? Definitely.

I don't care. The goal is not to be perfect; it's to win. If you obsess over selling the top tick and buying the bottom tick, you're going to be miserable all the time. Catch the juicy part of the move, be happy, and move on.

This was a good trade, and I bring it up because it's a good example of how trading changes over time. In 1999, I was sitting with headphones listening to live trading from the S&P futures pit and front running retail favorites whenever paper buyers came in on the floor. As you probably know, this is not a way to make money in 2026!

Principle 1: The way you make money today is not how you will make money tomorrow.

By definition, the market sniffs out profitable trades and gradually or quickly arbitrages them away. The juicier your edge now, the more likely it is to be discovered and eliminated in the future. High Sharpes pull in money like ants to sugar. No matter how profitable your methodology is today, you should always be looking for new ways to make money.

Whatever your current edge, assume that it will expire—sooner or later.

Short story #2

I sold the hole, and the hole won

The 2025 low in EchoStar (ticker: SATS) was $15.00

I sold 5,000 shares at $11.50.

Here's what happened.

The period from 5 p.m. to 7 p.m. can be a great time to trade stocks because not everyone is paying attention and there are plenty of random headlines. Fridays can be particularly spicy (and dangerous) because you have to either get in and out super-quick or hold risk over the weekend. My bias is to avoid these weekend headline trades because

a) there is gap risk, and
b) I don't want to spend my weekend worrying about a random position or scanning for headlines that might reinforce or offset the headline I traded late on Friday.

On Friday, June 6, 2025, at 6:21 p.m. this headline dropped:

*EchoStar Preps Potential Bankruptcy Filing, Sources Say – WSJ

Normally when you see a headline about a company going bankrupt, the stock has already priced it in and it's trading at $2 or lower. When I brought up SATS, I saw it was trading at $17. What?! *Insane*! At this point, I had no clue about the company—I honestly would have assumed EchoStar (which ran the DISH Network) went bankrupt ten years ago given the number of DISH Network mini satellite dishes rusting away on rooftops across Middle America.

But here was EchoStar, still limping along at $17, and their CEO talking about bankruptcy.

Naturally, I sold; but liquidity was bad, and I went a bit wild with excitement, hitting all the way down to $10.55. I ended up short 5,000 shares at an average of $11.50 and the stock was instantly trading $13.50/$15.00.

Hmm. Maybe I'm missing something here. If the stock goes back to $20, I'm down $50,000, which isn't really what I am hoping for going into the weekend!

EchoStar (SATS) common stock, 5-minute chart, early June 2025

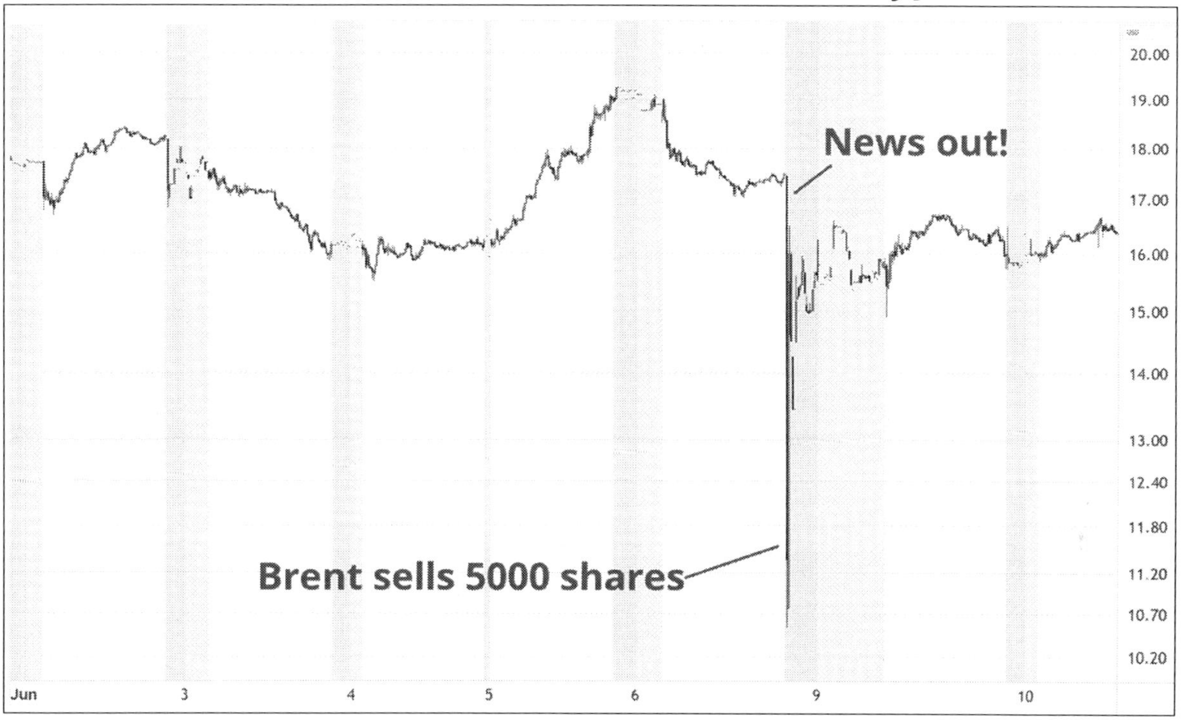

For the next 30 minutes I read everything I could, pumped the info into various LLMs, and kept a radically open mind. The whole situation was mega-confusing. SATS had no functioning business but owned a bunch of bandwidth with potentially enormous value. The problem was, since the business wasn't doing much, the bandwidth was sitting unused and the government threatened to take it away; if that were to happen SATS would be bankrupt.

A lot of if/then statements there! The stock was trading at $15 and could be worth zero. I decided to hold the short and spent the entire weekend hitting refresh on Bloomberg, SATS US equity CN to get updated company news. The same story kept repeating and there was no new information at all. The stock opened Sunday night at $16/$17.

When more than 24 hours of trading have passed and something has not reacted to news, that's a massive red flag. Either it's a bad news/good price setup, or you are misreading the news. Either way, I would need to set an extremely high bar to stay short at this point. The market had two days to interpret the news and the stock was unchanged. At this point, it was much more likely I was wrong, and not the market.

Given that I was pretty confused by both the price action and the story itself, I decided to cut. But surely the stock wouldn't rip higher right away with the negative news overhang, so I got on the bid at $16.10, hoping to save some money. If I crossed the spread in after-hours trading on Sunday night, it would cost me an extra $5,000.

While I waited for the bid to get filled (or not filled), I did another deep dive into SATS, read everything I could and pumped it all through ChatGPT. I started to get a pretty good idea of the situation. It was a political story, not an economic one. After a few hours, I realized the CEO of SATS was bluffing to put pressure on the FCC and Trump, and this was not a bankruptcy play. Now that I had a full understanding of the story, I plugged my nose and covered the stock at $17.

Here's what happened next:

SATS common stock, June to September 2025

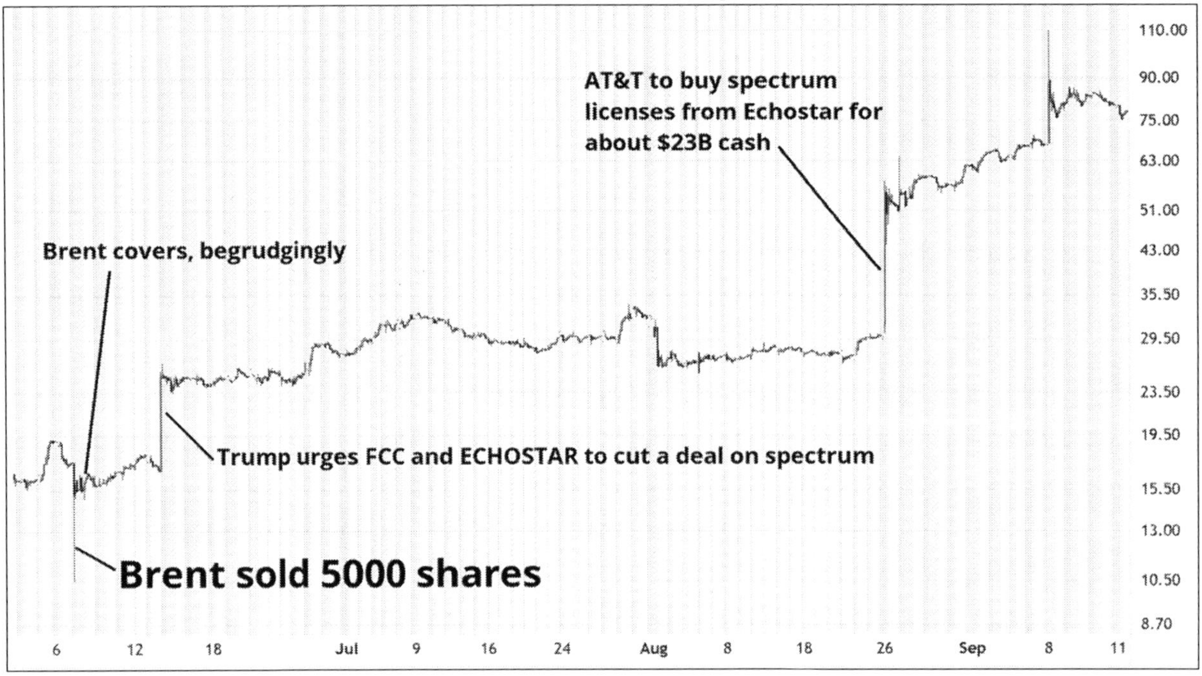

One of the key lessons I've learned in my 30 years of trading is that I need to trust my internal pattern-recognition machine. I need to note the times when the market does not do what it "should" be doing. When the market does something weird—that's information.

Principle 2:
When the market does something weird—pay attention.

My $30,000 loss could have been an $80,000 loss and then a $270,000 loss if I kept holding. The awesome thing was that because I was well-versed in the story by the time the AT&T

deal happened, I knew that SATS had exactly $23B in debt. When I saw the headline, I knew that the remaining licenses would probably be worth way more than $40 per share and I managed to get long at $43 that day and sell at $62 a week later. I am net profitable on SATS for 2025, despite selling a chunk 30% below the low, which is a huge win!

If you make a mistake, get out ASAP. Don't pray or double down. Often, the market's reaction tells you more than the news itself.

Twenty years ago, I would have held the short for way too long and stopped out only when I could no longer take the financial pain. I would have had a vendetta against the stock and found it impossible to go long, regardless of the news flow. And I would have been too lazy to dig into all the details of the broadband story. I would have lost way more money and learned nothing.

Principle 3: Study your mistakes and they'll pay you back double.

Short story #3

Brexit 2016

It's early February 2016, and I'm running the spot FX (currency) trading desk at Citibank New York. The UK is on edge over Brexit and there is high drama as forecasters call for a possible collapse of the pound in the "extremely unlikely" event that the British populace votes to leave the EU. It sets up to be one of the great moments in currency trading, on par with Black Wednesday in 1992, or the SNB floor break of 2015. The referendum date hasn't been announced yet, but the market is already buzzing in anticipation.

We salivate over the prospect of a 10% one-day move in the pound (up, or down… doesn't matter!) as the head of the options desk compulsively hits Shift-F9 to make sure no short vol has appeared around any of the prospective dates for the yet-to-be-announced vote.

Meanwhile, my life is pretty good. I survived an abysmal first year at Citi in 2014. In 2015, my New York team outperformed the London spot desk (an extremely rare feat at any bank because London sees way more flow and nearly double the active trading hours of NY). This year has started out okay, and there's lots to look forward to: I'm going away to Cayman with my family in March and I have an awesome fishing trip in Maine planned with my eldest son in June.

I have two sons and traveling alone with one or the other is a special opportunity that comes along every few years at most. Kids are just different when they're alone with you. They don't have to compete with a sibling for airtime, and it's easier for both the kid and the parent to be present. It's the best. A headline drops on Bloomberg:

*BREXIT REFERENDUM DATE SET FOR JUNE 23

My gut drops. I open Outlook, but I already know the answer. The Brexit vote is the day after I am supposed to leave for my fishing trip in Maine.

A few times in my life, I had to make a decision like this, and I made the wrong one. In this case, there was only one answer. I made the right decision, and I did not cancel the fishing trip, and I did not trade the pound the night of the referendum. I checked the market a few times and had some pretty bad FOMO as the pound collapsed from 1.50 to 1.30 that night.

I never regretted the decision for one second. The fishing was awesome. My son and I still talk about the crazy video game idea we came up with out on the lake and all the details we got into because we were out in the silence on the water four hours at a time. The game was called "Werld". It was a massive open-sea world full of islands where you start alone on an empty island with nothing and try to build towards a civilized empire of united city-islands, via negotiation or force.

Anyway, I digress.

With the benefit of hindsight, it has become increasingly clear to me that moments like that define your values and your priorities. Much as I still feel guilty for skipping my grandmother's funeral when I was 25 because I was too lazy to get on a plane from NY back to Canada, I am proud of skipping Brexit to go fishing with my son. These decisions stick with you for the rest of your life, so make the right one as often as you can.

Sure, this is a book about how to get rich(er) through trading. But you can get rich and do the right thing, or you can get rich and be a selfish prick. You get to decide. If there is a choice between markets and health or family, I advise you to choose health and family. Every time. The people you work for will either accept and admire your choice, or they will not. It doesn't matter. Fifteen years from now, that old boss that gave you a hard time about missing Brexit isn't going to be in your life.

Your family will be.

Principle 4: Choose family and health over markets.

Short story #4

Rags to riches to rags to riches to rags

I worked with a woman whose story went something like this:

Graduated from a random, mid-level U.S. college in 1981, got a bit lucky at age 40 as an early employee at a B2B company in the Dotcom bubble. She was a multimillionaire on paper as of January 2000. Her stock was fully vested, but everyone at the company wanted to stay loyal and they told her to hold onto the stock because "it's definitely going to keep going up". The Dotcom bubble collapsed, her stock went to zero and she was bankrupt.

She clawed her way back, working in the back office of a bank from 2000 to 2007, and accumulated enough money via savings (and a medium-sized inheritance) that she could retire again. Her liquid net worth at that point was around $3 million. Her financial advisor had her almost fully invested in bank stocks because "that's the safe place to be" and "the dividends are good", and "they've been doing well" and yada yada.

In October 2008, she panicked and sold everything down 80% as the banks collapsed.

When I first met her in 2012, she was in her early 50s, working reception at a different bank. She had no savings despite twice being in a position to comfortably retire.

This story is not about diversification, bad financial planning, or incompetent financial advisors, although they all obviously played a role. The lesson from this story is much broader and simpler:

Principle 5: You only need to get rich once.

As you achieve greater wealth, your risk preferences should change. There is no point making life-changing money if you're not going to change your life. If you grow a crypto trading account from $100,000 to $2,000,000... Take some money out and put it in low-risk investments where you can't touch it!

It's the moral of the story above and it's one of the threads from Jesse Livermore's life all the way to the altcoin pumpfun bros in the 2020s. Risk it all if you have $25,000. But don't trade your entire net worth, with leverage, if you have seven figures.

As you gain more wealth and as you age, your investments should become increasingly risk-averse. You don't need to make 20% returns if you have $5 million in the bank. Lock it in and live a fun life. Write books, ski, or become a teacher. Whatever you do, don't risk it all in an effort to maximize returns. You're rich! You don't need to maximize returns anymore! The marginal utility of your first million dollars is exponentially higher than the marginal utility of the second or third or fourth.

Sure, you can worry about trying to beat inflation so your money maintains its real purchasing power. That's smart. But take steps to set yourself up so that literally no matter what happens, once you get rich the first time, you don't need to ever do it again.

People love to read about the ups and downs of guys like Jesse Livermore, Victor Niederhoffer, and John Meriwether. Those are fun stories because they are full of drama, devastation, and disaster: things that are fun to read, but are not fun in real life. You don't need to fill your story with drama, destruction, and disaster. Learn the meaning of the word 'enough.'

Short story #5

Stoney goes mad

It's mid-September 1996, and oddly enough, I work at Citibank in this story too. I worked there from 1995 to 1998 and again from 2014 to 2017. Anyhoo. My boss at the time, known as Stoney, was a madman in the best possible way. He became a great friend of mine, almost instantly, and I still keep in touch with him 30 years later.

In the 1990s, currency markets worked differently. There were no electronic brokers. Trades went through human voice brokers and specialized bank-to-bank, hard-wired computers in the OTC or direct market. If I worked as the USDCAD trader at Citibank, any major bank could call me on a dedicated Reuters electronic dealing platform and ask me for a price in 10 million USDCAD and I had to show five pips wide. A pip in USDCAD is 0.0001.

If USDCAD is trading 1.3821, and UBS calls me for a price in 10 million USDCAD, I can show them 1.3819/1.3824, or 1.3817/1.3822, etc. They don't have to tell me whether they are buyers or sellers; I show a bid and an offer and they can choose to trade on either side. In the last example, they can sell to me at 1.3817 or buy from me at 1.3822.

The entire direct calling process was famously chaotic as it could erupt out of the blue at any time. A client comes in at some random moment to sell 200 million USDCAD, and the USDCAD trader leaps up and screams "USDCAD CALLS!"

Every other trader on the desk (at that time, the Citi spot desk was 30 people) has a list of other banks to call on Reuters. When the prices start to come in, each trader yells them out and the main trader responsible (the USDCAD trader) yells out "SELL!" or "PASS!" In FX, the first three digits are understood, so if the price is 1.3819/1.3824, you simply yell "19/24!".

So, the trading floor would erupt with shouts, like:

"19/24!"	"SELL!"
"20/25!"	"SELL!"
"12/17?"	"*Shit*. PASS!"

After each callout, a junior would run around and add up all the trades, calculate a rough average price, and relay the information to the senior trader. It was incredibly stressful for all involved (and super fun)!

As soon as you dealt with a few banks, the market would start to move, and it would become obvious what you were doing. So, you had to be coordinated and fast and deal with as many banks as possible, all at once. You could even buy from a particularly aggressive bank if you were truly a seller, in the hope that he would jam the broker market higher, and you could slam all the other banks at some ridiculously high rate. This was known as spoofing, and it's illegal now. Those were good times.

Here's roughly how things played out that day in 1996.

```
INT. CITIBANK TRADING FLOOR - DAY

A salesman tells Stoney his client needs to sell 100 million
AUDUSD (aka "Aussie"). Stoney explodes out of his chair.

                          STONEY
                        (screaming)
                  AUSSIE CALLLLLLSSSSS!!!!!!

Traders are shaken from their stupor by Stoney's terrifying yell.
Everyone is badly hungover. They press the required buttons to
automatically contact counterparty banks via the Reuters
electronic dealing system.

                         TRADER 1
                          20/25?

                          STONEY
                           SELL!

                         TRADER 1
                       I MISSED IT!

                         TRADER 2
                          21/26?
```

STONEY
SELL! Yes! Sell at 21! I told Brent to sell at 20! What the fuck is wrong with you??

TRADER 2
Sold 10 at 21!

TRADER 3
22/27?

STONEY
(Shakes his head in disbelief)
SELL, for fuck sake. Sell.
Is 22 a higher number than 21, mate?

TRADER 3
Oh, shit. I bought at 27! What should I do?

TRADER 5
07/12??

Stoney is red-faced, fuming, unable to speak.

TRADER 5
I sold at 07! Is that OK?

The market was 20/25 when we started. Now, it's 01/06 and Stoney tells me to go around and sum the trades and get the average. He was hoping to sell maybe 50 or 60 million at an average somewhere around 18.

I check the trades:

- Sold 10 at 21
- Bought 10 at 27
- Sold 10 at 07

For a net average… We sold 10 at 01. *Absolute disaster.*

STONEY
(screaming)
Rosey's kindergarten class could do a better job than you idiots! What is wrong with you? What the bloody hell is wrong with everyone? Jesus. H. [redacted].

Stoney is red-faced as he smashes his fist down on the Reuters number pad. Number keys fly like popcorn. He smashes his fist down again on the Reuters keypad and a few more buttons fly off. The trading floor is completely silent. Everyone stares at Stoney, waiting to see what happens next. There is an air of terror on our team, and the rest of the trading floor looks on with morbid curiosity.

BEEP BEEP BEEP.

"GSNY AUD 10" appears on Steve's Reuters screen, which means Goldman Sachs is asking for a quote in 10 million AUDUSD. It is common that a bank you just traded with reverts back to you right after a trade. Goldman was the bank we just sold to at 21. Stoney hits ACCEPT and prepares to make Goldman a standard rate, five points wide. The market is 02/07 now, so something like 01/06 would make sense.

Stoney looks down at his keypad and sees all the keys are gone except the ACCEPT button, the 5 and the 9.

I look at him. He looks at me.

He hits ACCEPT and types the only price he can to Goldman: 59/95.

Goldman responds with: ????.

Honestly, for about seven seconds, I am too scared to laugh. The trading floor is still in complete silence. Then Stoney cracks, and starts laughing hard, and the tension dissolves. I laugh, and then everyone runs over to see what happened and soon everyone else is laughing too. Best job in the world.

Stoney was a ruthless competitor who got ferociously angry when people did a bad job. Working with Stoney was crazy and emotional (and sometimes scary) but he was also hilarious, open-minded, and smart. Fundamentally, he understood that trading is a big job, but it's not open-heart surgery. The stakes in trading feel high, but they are not life or death.

People that didn't know him thought he might be a psychopath, meanwhile he was reading *Don't Sweat the Small Stuff (And It's All Small Stuff)* on the train and inviting me to share Christmas Day with his family one year because I couldn't make it back to Ottawa due to an insane ice storm. He was a hard competitor with a brilliant sense of perspective.

If you can take the job seriously while maintaining perspective and humility, you will come out the other side in better shape than if you think every day is a zero-sum game where you *gotta get yours*.

Principle 6: Take the job, but not yourself, seriously.

Alright… Let's start the book.

PART ONE: NEW WAYS TO THINK ABOUT MARKETS

Introduction

If you work in accounting, construction, or air traffic control, you should consistently use the standard methods everyone else uses because you want standard results. If everyone approaches accounting in the same way, results will be comparable across companies and industries, and results will be uniform and professional.

But think about how this works in markets. If everyone applied the same methodology to markets, everyone would have the same view. We'd all be bullish Palantir at the same time and there would be no sellers. Everyone would think the euro is going to zero; there would be no buyers. A functioning market requires differing methodologies and dissenting views.

But if you read the best-known books on trading (including mine!), you will see a box containing four disciplines:

Fundamentals	**Technicals**
Valuation & Cash Flow Models	Trend
Earnings Forecasting	Chart Patterns
Industry Analysis	Momentum
Economics	Volume
Global Macro	Volatility
Behavioral	**Quantitative**
Sentiment	Systematic Strategies
Positioning	Backtesting & Modeling
Reflexivity	Derivatives
Cognitive Bias	Algorithmic Trading
Bubbles & Crashes	Machine Learning & AI

A solid knowledge of these four quadrants is crucial. There are many books, including *Alpha Trader*, that cover them in depth. I will be going wider and deeper on those four categories throughout this book, adding to my thoughts from *Alpha Trader*.

But what if you want to go outside the box? What if you want to look at the market from new angles? What if you prefer to think different(ly)? That is the main idea behind this book. As a degenerate polymath, I tend to stick my mental fingers into many intellectual pies. I'm interested in a diverse range of fields, and most relate directly or tangentially to trading and investing.

Whether I'm watching a YouTube video about the physics of avalanches, reading a book about military tactics, or studying reruns of the World Series of Poker, I see trading lessons the way Haley Joel Osment sees dead people. And because of my lifelong obsession with trading, I am forever test-driving new ways to navigate financial markets. I am always looking for new frameworks that might help me make more money trading. Whether you see markets as a machine, an organism, or an insane group of drunk, gambling-addicted teenagers, different frameworks and perspectives help you to see things you might not see otherwise.

Principle 7: If you think like everyone else, you'll perform like everyone else.

The book is split into three parts.

Part One discusses creativity, and why it's a critical X-factor that contributes to trading success. Then we look at humility and perspective. Whether you are trading like a god or you can barely put one foot in front of the other, it helps to know your place in the universe. Then we get into second-derivative and multi-order thinking to help you go beyond the obvious and see around corners. We close with a discussion of some relatively new phenomena: AI and LLMs, WSB raids, and prediction markets. I'll explain how I use them to trade traditional financial markets more profitably.

Part Two looks at scientific and other domains for lessons about trading, narrative propagation, risk management, and non-linearity. We look at clinical psychology, professional poker and ergodicity. We talk about which trading and investing games are winnable, which are worth playing, and why short selling is the hardest game of all.

Part Three explores frameworks: how to choose them, which ones to reject, and which ones I have seen destroy the most capital over the years. To make money, you need practical frameworks that apply to real markets in real life. You need to use the right frameworks at the right times and distinguish between cyclical and structural factors.

I go through specific frameworks and approaches and discuss which ones I find indispensable—or useless. I expand on some ideas introduced in *Alpha Trader,* with new real-world examples. Finally, we close with some quick thoughts on humility, ethics, and the meaning of life (!).

Mixed in are war stories, case studies, and fun facts. The idea is not to simply lay out a bunch of approaches that might work for you, though that is certainly a primary objective. The hope is to pry open your mind and show you different ways I look at the market so that you are inspired to discover connections between your intellectual interests and the financial markets. Whether it's astronomy, physics, math, Magic: The Gathering, or sports gambling.

There are ways to apply and connect your interests to a successful career in trading.

CHAPTER 1

MARKETS ARE THE UNIVERSE, YOU ARE A GRAIN OF SAND

Creativity and perspective in trading

"Even in an industrial civilization, founded on the value of work, the taste for games of chance remains extremely powerful, the exact opposite of what is involved in earning money: The fascination of acquiring a lot of money all at once, and without effort."

Roger Caillois

The most alluring promise made in finance is: "Let me show you exactly how to trade so you can get rich, too!" Unfortunately, that's like saying: "Let me show you how to write books, and you will become a famous author!" That's not how it works. You can learn critical information and save time and energy by learning from others, but there is no simple method that will take you to the promised land. Learning to trade requires that you first abandon Caillois' idea of acquiring money all at once and without effort.

You must absorb the ideas of others and then craft them slowly, through experience and effort, into new and powerful ideas inside your own giant brain. All while remaining solvent, and sane. It's hard.

Once you have a good grasp of the pillars of trading and risk management, you can start to develop your own frameworks and methodologies. You can begin to cross-pollinate your personal knowledge and style of thinking with the well-known frameworks for trading and investing. You can *find your own edge.*

Elite traders cross-pollinate. They bring concepts and knowledge from outside finance into their trading process.

The science of creativity

Think of your brain as two algorithms running simultaneously.

- Algorithm 1: The daydreamer. Your default mode network.[1]
- Algorithm 2: The logician. Your executive control network.

Peak creativity happens when these systems partner up and create novel connections while preserving quality control.

Creativity does not show up on demand. Most breakthroughs happen during incubation periods, when you are not explicitly trying to come up with ideas. That's why it's good to go off the desk once in a while during the trading day. When you go for a quick walk around the trading floor, or step into your backyard and look at the trees for a bit, your brain has time to shut off high-energy active processing and do some random pattern matching.

That's why I often say that I don't really find trade ideas; they find me. I ingest as much useful information as possible and then at some point later—sometimes hours or days later—an idea pops out.

When a poker article I read two days ago has time to converse with the new trading strategy I'm developing, I realize my risk management doesn't bet big enough on the strongest signals. Suddenly, my risk sizing approach is 10% better than it was before because I combined something from trading with an idea from the world of Texas hold 'em.

The weird fast-finger chord pattern you're learning on guitar has a chance to cross-pollinate with your desire to find a faster way to hit the buy and sell buttons—and you realize you should buy a new mini macro keyboard. Suddenly, your news trading is 10% faster.

When you hit the elliptical for 15 minutes with classical music in the earbuds, your brain keeps processing in the background. You can stop actively grinding on various problems and let your brain's automatic creativity software flow in your subconscious.

Many people think creative ability is randomly and unevenly distributed: you either have it, or you don't. That's a limiting belief. And it's wrong. Research shows creativity responds to deliberate practice like any other skill. Divergent thinking exercises, cross-domain exposure, even certain environmental factors can impact creative output. Smart traders build systems to allow for this. They understand the volatility of the creative process and allow time for both focused execution and complementary randomness and relaxation.

Don't let your beliefs about yourself limit your upside.

---

[1] For more on the Default Mode Network (DMN), see *Alpha Trader*, pages 382-384

Just as you can become more conscientious with effort over time, you can work to become more creative. A Danish study of creativity[2] showed that the simple act of learning the neurology of how creativity works increased creativity by 30%. The experiment, called the Alternative Uses Test, asks participants to come up with as many unusual uses as possible for a given common object, excluding unrealistic uses. Each group is given three objects and three minutes to write down the number of uses.

The results show how the simple act of studying creativity made people more creative.

Creativity Test Results Comparison (average object uses reported by test group)

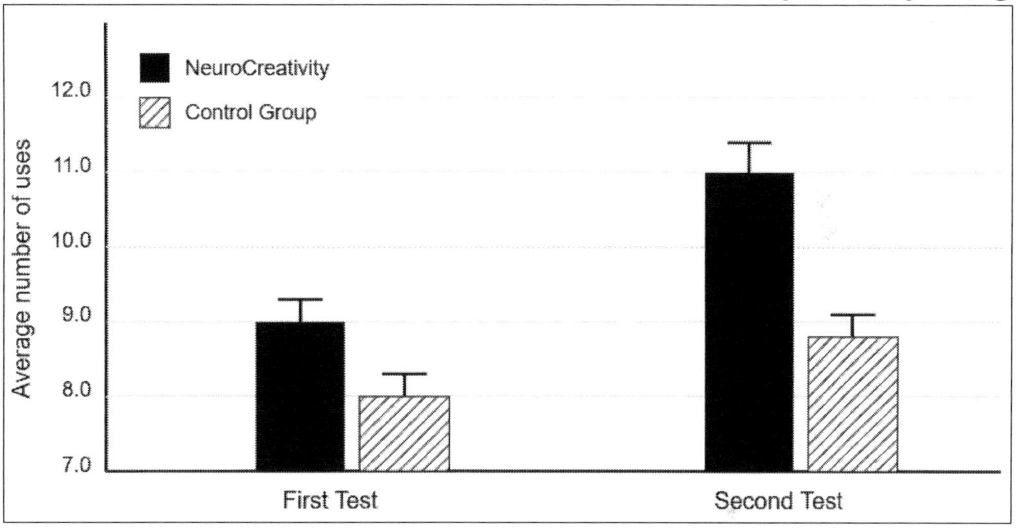

Most of the creativity research covers two main paths to higher creativity.

- **Environment.** The creative environment is the ecosystem that either nurtures or suffocates fresh thinking. If you come into work every day and repeat the same trading process, then go home and read books about trading by yourself, that's not a creative environment. If you lead a well-rounded intellectual life, you will become a better, more creative trader.
- **Training.** This is deliberate practice for the imagination. Like developing any skill, you need to build neural pathways that connect disparate concepts to inspire novel insights. This means you consume varied intellectual inputs, practice divergent thinking, and actively work to become more creative.

As William James put it, way back in 1880:

---

[2] www.frontiersin.org/journals/human-neuroscience/articles/10.3389/fnhum.2013.00656/full

> New conceptions, emotions, and active tendencies which evolve are originally produced in the shape of random images, fancies, accidental out-births of spontaneous variation in the functional activity of the excessively unstable human brain, which the outer environment simply confirms or refutes, adopts or rejects, preserves or destroys—selects, in short, just as it selects morphological and social variations due to molecular accidents of an analogous sort.

In other words: show your brain lots of ideas. It will mostly say "meh, that's stupid" or "uh, that doesn't apply here", but it will store the information and may find relevance down the road. Now and then, it will recall something you considered in the past and connect it to something you are thinking about today.

That's the idea behind this book. I'll throw a bunch of ideas at you. You can accept or reject them. And hopefully (more importantly!) you will see how I take outside ideas and integrate them into how I *think about thinking* about financial markets. Then you can go down your own series of rabbit holes and pop out with a more creative, unique, and profitable approach to trading.

Perspective

A rational approach to markets starts with perspective. You need to understand the enormity of financial markets relative to your own importance therein and embrace the fundamental truths of how they work. You need to understand what you control, and what you do not.

Imagine the market as a superintelligent aggregation of millions of minds, like a form of Artificial General Intelligence (AGI). Each trade is a blip in a circuit inside a massive supercomputer.

There are many ways to compare the size of the market machine to the role of a single trader. You are a drop of water in a massive ocean; you are a grain of sand on a 10-mile beach, etc. You should enter the market each day with tremendous humility, knowing that the market is an aggregate organism formed of millions of minds, billions of lines of code, and centuries of accumulated knowledge. The market does not care what you do, it does not care whether you win or lose, and it is not out to get you. It's just a massive sea, forever smashing against the shore.

If you feel like every time you buy, the market jams it in your face… that's information. Your entry timing is bad. Or you need to upgrade your tactics. It's not the universe laughing at you: it's real-time feedback on your process.

Type A personalities emerging from the best business schools in the world land on Wall Street or in The City and have mostly never experienced failure. They have never been anything but the smartest person in the room. Then they start trading and learn painful and expensive lessons about overconfidence and conventional thinking.

In contrast, veteran traders are humble. This humility is earned the hard way. They know that their best day is often followed by the worst. They know that what the market gives, it takes away. They know that whatever high-Sharpe strategy they employ today, there are 5,000 NVDA GPUs running somewhere in New Jersey looking for strategies just like it and one day soon those computers will find it and arbitrage it down to the bone.

The illusion of control

We do not think clearly about what we control and what we do not. Failure to make this distinction leads to a litany of irrational thoughts and behaviors.

A funny trope that you will see in markets is the trader or strategist who says: "Every time I go on holiday, all hell breaks loose!" They will show charts of the VIX and mark their holidays on all the spikes. They are joking, but some part of them is serious. This is like the retail trader who sells 100 shares of TSLA at $148 and then when it goes $150 bid in 30 seconds they say: "The market is out to get me!" or "Market makers are jamming it in my face."

No. *No*. That is not true. If the stock rallies instantly every time you hit a bid, that means your timing is bad and you are probably chasing momentum. It means you should reevaluate your execution strategy, not shake your fist at God.

The illusion of control is a human bias that makes us think we have more influence over the things that we do *not* control, and less power over those things we *do* realistically control. Many academic studies find people think they control things they do not, for example:

- People pick their own lottery numbers, thinking that will help them win.
- Gamblers blow on dice or roll dice harder when they are desperate for a win.
- Baseball players jump over the chalk lines to avoid bad luck.
- Gamers mash buttons during loading screens in an attempt to speed up a process that has a fixed duration.

How does the illusion of control show up in trading?

- Praying for a market outcome when you have outsized or underwater positions.
- Thinking the market is out to get you, when in fact it's a massive, impersonal machine that knows not and cares not one iota about you.
- Blaming bad trades on luck and attributing winning trades to superior skill.

Illusion of control solutions

Good trading starts with knowing what you control and what you do not:

You control the process, but not the outcome.

Process vs. outcome has been covered in depth in many books, and I suggest you check out Annie Duke's *Thinking in Bets* or *Alpha Trader* (pages 100-103). Or just Google "process vs. outcome" and you will find excellent information.

In life and in trading, your focus should be on elements you control. When I worked at Lehman Brothers as it veered towards the abyss in 2008, I was ranting to a friend of mine about how messed up things were and how my best trading year ever might lead to a zero bonus. I was stressed out and angry. He replied with this email:

> God grant me the serenity to accept the things I cannot change,
> The courage to change the things I can,
> and the wisdom to know the difference.

I didn't know it at the time, but that is the Serenity Prayer. Composed by theologian Reinhold Niebuhr in the early 1930s, the prayer is a core teaching in 12-step programs like Alcoholics Anonymous. It's wise and useful, whether or not you are in recovery. The prayer is predated by many similar sayings from Epictetus (1st-century Greek philosopher), Shantideva (8th-century Indian scholar) and Solomon Gabirol (11th-century Jewish philosopher). Here's Epictetus' spin:

> Make the best use of what is in your power and take the rest as it happens. Some things are up to us, and some things are not up to us. Our opinions are up to us, and our impulses, desires, aversions—in short, whatever is our own doing. Our bodies are not up to us, nor are our possessions, our reputations, or our public offices, or, that is, whatever is not our own doing.

Don't obsess over things you cannot control. Don't worry who is getting promoted ahead of you, or who's making more money than you. There is always someone out there doing better than you, and there is always someone out there doing worse. Play your own game and grow to become the best, most rational, most effective trader and risk manager. That's it. Be great, and things will work out.

Principle 8: Live and trade by the wisdom of the Serenity Prayer.

Here's a nice example, via Billy Oppenheimer[3].

After his second year at Michigan, Tom Brady wanted to transfer.

He wasn't playing in games, and he was so low on the depth chart that he only got 2 reps in practice. Brady met with his coach to express his frustration, "The other quarterbacks get all the reps."

Coach replied: "Brady, I want you to stop worrying about what all the other players on our team are doing. All you do is worry about what the starter is doing, what the second guy is doing, what everyone else is doing. You don't worry about what you're doing."

Coach reminded him, "You came here to be the best. If you're going to be the best, you have to beat out the best."

And then he recommended that Brady start meeting with Greg Harden, a sports psychologist who worked in Michigan's athletic department.

Brady went to Harden's office and whined, "I'm never going to get my chance. They're only giving me 2 reps."

Harden simply replied, "Just go out there and focus on doing the best you can with those 2 reps. Make them as perfect as you possibly can."

"So that's what I did," Brady said. "They'd put me in for those 2 reps, man, I'd sprint out there like it was Super Bowl 39. 'Let's go boys! Here we go! What play we got?'"

"And I started to do really well with those 2 reps. Because I brought enthusiasm, I brought energy."

Soon, it went from getting 2 reps to getting 4 reps. Then from 4 to 10, "and before you knew it," Brady said, with this new mindset that Greg instilled in me – to focus on what you can control, to focus on what you're getting, not what anyone else is getting, to treat every rep like it's the Super Bowl – eventually, I became the starter."

---

[3] www.medium.com/@billyoppenheimer/if-im-going-to-be-here-i-m-going-to-be-great-97db3ea9a27a

Losers obsess over what everyone else is doing. They have no understanding of what they control or what they don't. They try to control the uncontrollable. They abdicate responsibility when things go awry, even when it's clearly their own fault.

They blame failure on bad luck and success on skill.

Winners treat every rep like it's the Super Bowl. They work hard when they don't feel like it. They know what factors and inputs they can control, and they focus relentlessly on them, to the exclusion of exogenous factors they can't influence. They know the difference between luck and skill and understand that both play a role in determining outcomes. They don't get sloppy or lazy, even when they are tired or filled with existential angst.

Work hard and stay disciplined, even when you don't feel like it.

Here's a good tweet on control and agency from Andrej Karpathy:

> **Andrej Karpathy**
> @karpathy
>
> Agency > Intelligence
>
> I had this intuitively wrong for decades, I think due to a pervasive cultural veneration of intelligence, various entertainment/media, obsession with IQ etc. Agency is significantly more powerful and significantly more scarce. Are you hiring for agency? Are we educating for agency? Are you acting as if you had 10X agency?
>
> Grok explanation is ~close:
>
> "Agency, as a personality trait, refers to an individual's capacity to take initiative, make decisions, and exert control over their actions and environment. It's about being proactive rather than reactive—someone with high agency doesn't just let life happen to them; they shape it. Think of it as a blend of self-efficacy, determination, and a sense of ownership over one's path.
>
> People with strong agency tend to set goals and pursue them with confidence, even in the face of obstacles. They're the type to say, "I'll figure it out," and then actually do it. On the flip side, someone low in agency might feel more like a passenger in their own life, waiting for external forces—like luck, other people, or circumstances—to dictate what happens next.
>
> It's not quite the same as assertiveness or ambition, though it can overlap. Agency is quieter, more internal—it's the belief that you *can* act, paired with the will to follow through. Psychologists often tie it to concepts like locus of control: high-agency folks lean toward an internal locus, feeling they steer their fate, while low-agency folks might lean external, seeing life as something that happens *to* them."
>
> **Garry Tan** @garrytan
> Intelligence is on tap now so agency is even more important x.com/hvpandya/statu...
>
> 10:58 AM · February 24, 2025
>
> **2K** Retweets **12.7K** Likes

Don't be a passenger in your own life.

Geo-, ego-, and chronocentrism

Our default as a species and as individuals is to think we're the literal and proverbial center of the universe. We tend to believe there has never been a crazier, more important, more exciting, or more terrifying moment in human history than the one we are experiencing *right now*. We overestimate our own gravitas, we overvalue the present vs. the past and the future, and we don't appreciate that current events often rhyme with the past. Financial markets have a terrible memory. They step on the same rakes and make the same mistakes—over and over and over.

Geocentrism, the *OG* -centrism

Geocentrism is the belief that Earth sits at the center of the universe with everything else revolving around it. This view dominated Western astronomy for 2,000 years.

The ancient Greeks formalized this model, with Aristotle and later Ptolemy developing complex mathematical systems to explain planetary motions. Ptolemy's model, with its epicycles (circles upon circles), successfully predicted celestial movements while maintaining Earth's central position.

A historical geocentric model of the universe, often known as a Ptolemaic cosmological diagram. Concentric circles represent celestial spheres, with Earth at the center, surrounded by the orbits of the Moon (LVNA), Mercury (MERCVRII), Venus (VENERIS), The Sun (SOLIS), Mars (MARTIS), Jupiter (IOVIS), and Saturn (SATVRNI).

This geocentric worldview persisted through Medieval Europe, strongly supported by the Catholic Church as it aligned with theological interpretations placing humans at the center of God's creation. The model wasn't seriously challenged until Copernicus published *On the Revolutions of the Celestial Spheres* in 1543, proposing a heliocentric (sun-centered) system.

Despite mounting evidence from Galileo's telescopic observations and Kepler's laws of planetary motion, geocentrism persisted for 130 more years until Newton's laws of motion and gravitation in the late 17th century made heliocentrism undeniable.

The psychological need to be at the center

Geocentrism reflects a deeper human psychological tendency: We naturally interpret the world from our own perspective. The sun appears to move across our sky, not vice versa. Just like when you sell 100 shares of TSLA and it rips in your face: you think the market is out to get you.

It isn't.

When scientific discoveries challenge this centrality, from heliocentrism to Darwin to modern cosmology, we often resist. Each revelation has pushed humanity further from any "special" position in the universe.

This pattern extends beyond astronomy into how we process information generally. We place ourselves at the center of narratives. The history of geocentrism serves as a potent reminder of how hard it can be to transcend our limited perspective and accept a universe that doesn't revolve around us.

Geocentrism was finally eradicated thanks to reams of irrefutable evidence, but it did not go quietly. It hurts the ego to think we might be just one meaningless planet among billions. It is painful for religious missionaries to admit that their religion is just one of many and their God might not be the *only* god or the most powerful god.

Remember your place in the trading universe. Be humble and accept that the market is bigger than you and will do what it's going to do. With or without you.

Egocentrism

Egocentrism is the inability to differentiate between *self* and *other*. Psychologist Jean Piaget identified it as a developmental stage where children struggle to see perspectives beyond their own. Unlike geocentrism's scientific claims, egocentrism describes a psychological tendency present in all humans. Egocentrism makes it difficult to see markets clearly because we often believe that our view is correct and that other people just "don't get it."

A healthier approach to markets is collecting the thoughts of others, analyzing them, and filtering them rationally with an open mind. You need to understand what others are thinking in order to successfully monitor (for example) the evolution of narrative, sentiment and positioning. If you always think bitcoin is going higher and you cannot hear the competing hypothesis presented by others, you will be trapped in the deterministic echo chamber of your own skull. You must accept that your view is probably not smarter or more sophisticated than the views of others, and you should be open to why you might be wrong.

Egocentrism persists because we have direct access only to our own consciousness, making other perspectives inherently secondary. It takes conscious effort to consider what the rest of the market might be thinking and recalibrate as the thoughts of others change. If you can get inside the mind of others (and the market), you will have an adaptable mindset that understands changes in the market, not a rigid mentality that accepts only confirming evidence of your static, strongly-held beliefs, or forces "square" evidence into a "round hole" through *confirmation bias*.

Second-order thinking, which we will discuss in Chapter 2, requires you to abandon egocentrism and consider what others think. It's an ongoing struggle to balance self-importance and confidence in your views with an open and objective understanding of what others are thinking and doing.

Chronocentrism

> "Children don't heed the life experiences of their parents, and nations ignore history. Bad lessons always have to be learned anew."
>
> Albert Einstein, 1929

Do you feel like you're living in a time of unprecedented technological change? Do you see parallels between the American Empire today and the Fall of the Roman Empire? Do you think a collapse of the U.S. dollar could happen at any moment? Do you feel like the upcoming election in your country is the most important one ever? **You are not alone!** People have felt this way for over 200 years! The following clips show how writers have compared the U.S. to the Roman Empire over the last century or so.

2022

There are ominous signs — politics, culture, national character — that the U.S. might have embarked on the beginning of its end as a great empire, just as insane as Rome in its decline.

2013

It is my firm opinion we are experiencing the decline and fall of the American empire. We are broke; we have no draft; no Army and where has our commander in chief been for the past week?

2007

Avoiding America's decline starts at home

Are we Rome? Is America like the Roman Empire -- you know, declining and falling, and all that ?

No less than the comptroller general of the United States, David Wallace, asserts yes, citing "striking similarities" between American today and Rome then. And while it's tempting, at a time of falling bridges, faltering economics and endless forever wars, to spot ominous parallels without citing the huge differences may be a bit rich.

1987

"The Decline of the American Empire" is not only a dramatic come-dy about the sexes. It takes its title from a premise put forth by one of the professors, that the 'Frenetic desire for individual happiness in our society may well be historically linked to the decline of the American empire that we are beginning to witness." She compares modern-day America to the fall of ancient Rome, and the demise of other once-great civilizations.

1973

Graham: America Declining?

Evangelist Billy Graham says America is beginning to show signs that historians say ancient Rome began to exhibit during its decline. Graham told an estimated 48,000 listeners at the Minnesota State Fairgrounds in St. Paul Friday night: "In many ways, ancient Rome was like America today." "But was a leader in world affairs, but her leadership was threatened because of decadent within." He said that Edward Gibbon in his "The History of the Decline and Fall of the Roman Empire" listed five major reasons for the decline: the rapin increase of slaves, higher taxes, a mad crave for pleasure, the building of gigantic armaments and the decay of religion.

1956

Comparison Made

Fall Of Roman Empire Likened To U.S. Now

UMATILLA—The Rev. McCoy Gibbs, pastor of the Broadway Methodist Church, Orlando, discussed the reasons

[redacted]

for the fall of the Roman Empire in an address to Kiwanians Monday.

He compared the reasons to conditions now existing in the U. S. Points brought out were breaking down of the home, higher and higher taxes, quest for excitement, political pressure for armament without considering the destructive elements that might arise among the peoples of the nation, and the lessening of interest in religion.

1922

BISHOP BURGESS SEES COUNTRY GROW DECADENT

Like Roman Empire in Second Century, He Says—Confirmation at St. Luke's.

1895

Discard Almighty God from your religion, and drive away the schoolmaster from your door, and the United States, like the Roman Empire, is at an end. And as our intelligence far exceeds that of the Roman Empire, so our death would be that much more terrible.

Every election feels like *democracy itself* is at stake.

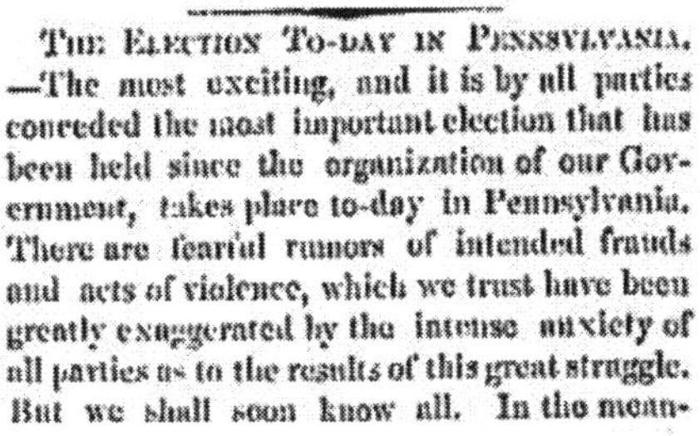

THE ELECTION TO-DAY IN PENNSYLVANIA.—The most exciting, and it is by all parties conceded the most important election that has been held since the organization of our Government, takes place to-day in Pennsylvania. There are fearful rumors of intended frauds and acts of violence, which we trust have been greatly exaggerated by the intense anxiety of all parties as to the results of this great struggle. But we shall soon know all. In the mean-

1856

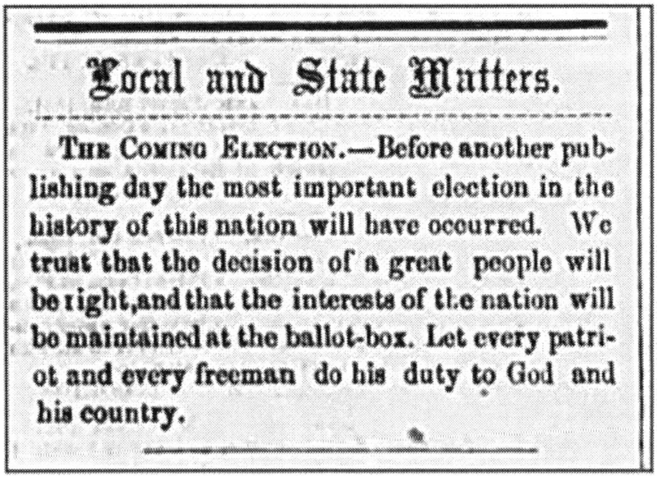

Local and State Matters.

THE COMING ELECTION.—Before another publishing day the most important election in the history of this nation will have occurred. We trust that the decision of a great people will be right, and that the interests of the nation will be maintained at the ballot-box. Let every patriot and every freeman do his duty to God and his country.

1864

"This is the fourth presidential election which Pearl Jam has engaged in as a band, and we feel it's the most important one of our lifetime," Pearl Jam frontman **Eddie Vedder** says in a statement.

2004

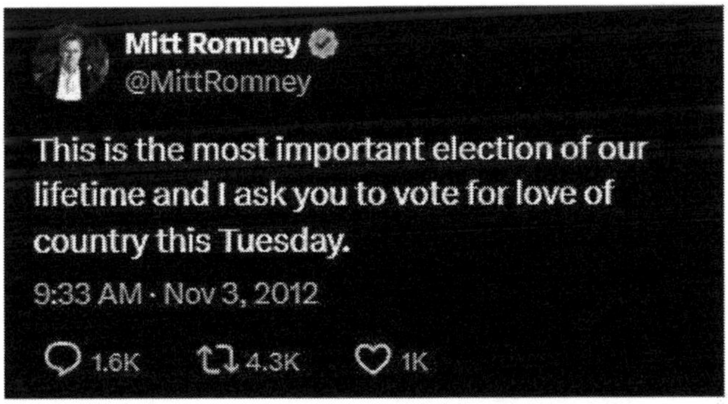

Mitt Romney
@MittRomney

This is the most important election of our lifetime and I ask you to vote for love of country this Tuesday.

9:33 AM · Nov 3, 2012

1.6K 4.3K 1K

2012

2024

Again, we need to consider our place in the universe, and in history. It's almost impossible not to feel like every election, technology or major event we experience is more important, transformative or scary than anything experienced by previous generations.

This phenomenon is called "chronocentrism." Try to rid yourself of this bias and examine current events, technologies, and geopolitics through a more rational lens. Upheaval, disruption and chaos are permanent features of history, not uniquely contemporary phenomena. This millennium features technological disruption, a global pandemic, climate change and global terrorism. So did the last one. And the one before that.

Chronocentrism springs primarily from **recency bias**. The *thing* happening right now is top of mind. We can feel it. We can see it. We always think that the immediate thing is the biggest, baddest or best. This also stems from terminal uniqueness, the belief that we are special as individuals, as an era, or as a society: egocentrism meets chronocentrism. Some examples:

1. The following quote from Hagakure, a Japanese Samurai spiritual guidebook written in 1716, echoes the complaints that every older generation makes, accusing the younger generation of sloth, disrespect, and vanity. You could change a few words, post it on Twitter, and it would be excellent engagement bait.

    > "People have changed in the past 30 years. When young samurai congregate, they engage in vapid talk of money, about profit and loss, their household fiscal problems, taste in fashion, and idle talk of sex. I hear that they see no reason to assemble other than to indulge in such topics of conversation. Warrior customs are deteriorating beyond repair. In the old days, samurai, even in their twenties and thirties, did not harbor such contemptible thoughts and never talked about such things."

2. British statesman Joseph Chamberlain in 1885:

    > "I believe that the British race is the greatest of the governing races that the world has ever seen..."

3. After the Cold War, some Western scholars, like Francis Fukuyama, argued that liberal democracy and capitalism had won and history had "ended" because no further ideological progress was needed. This view underestimated the potential for political upheaval, economic crises, and the rise of populism and alternative governance models. Fukuyama's book was called *The End of History and the Last Man*. It wasn't the end of history, though.

The 2020s culture wars might feel unique, but they are not. We had political correctness and then the blowback to PC in the 1980s. The 1990s featured Affirmative Action and then the blowback to Affirmative Action. Rodney King pre-dated George Floyd. The moral panic over video games and song lyrics repeats, over and over. And so on.

WORLD

A white male backlash

Critics attack affirmative action as reverse discrimination

Cathy Wattendorf is a white 20-year-old student taking a "really cool" engineering course and training to be a U.S. Air Force officer in the southwest Virginia college town of Blacksburg. and lawsuits—that indict the program for producing reverse discrimination and costs to the economy. Critics decry the wide reach of what the Congressional Research Service describes as "a host of federal programs to ate Majority Leader Robert Dole of Kansas, Texas Senator Phil Gramm and former Tennessee governor Lamar Alexander—all stand for an end to race-based law. Only days after the Republican contenders declared their po-

March 1995

POLITICS

Supreme Court of the United States

'Reverse discrimination' case comes to Supreme Court as DEI is under siege

February 2025

Principle 9: There is nothing new under the sun.

In trading and investing, chronocentrism creates the myopic belief that we are living in unprecedented times. *This time is different*, as they sarcastically say.

The COVID shock is a good example. It felt like the end of the world—the market sold off hard and fast—yet a quick review of history showed that massive bull markets quickly followed past pandemics. Same thing in the other direction. Those that believed the technological disruption and fiscal stimulus in 2021 was something new, *unlike ever before*, got sucked into buying ARKK, SPACs, and other toxic securities before they collapsed 90%.

The best way to immunize yourself from this feeling of specialness is to study the history of financial markets. Mind-boggling technological change, asset price bubbles, industry-driven manias and violent stock market crashes happen over and over.

Each cycle echoes prior booms and busts.

The ICO craze that ended in 2018, the NFT madness in 2021, and the memecoin insanity of 2024 all shared many characteristics. The most profitable traders in 2024 were the ones that knew all the behavioral patterns would repeat, not those who believed memecoins were something new or something special. **They're not.**

Chronocentrism in financial markets tends to manifest via statements like:

- This time is different.
- The rules have changed.
- These companies are changing the world.
- The old metrics don't work anymore.
- Valuations don't matter.
- This industry has unlimited growth potential.

History is littered with traders and investors blinded by seemingly new paradigms.

> "Stock prices have reached what looks like a permanently high plateau."
>
> Irving Fisher, months before the Great Crash of 1929
>
> "It is hard for us, without being flippant, to even see a scenario within any kind of realm of reason that would see us losing one dollar in any of these [credit default swap] transactions."
>
> Joseph Cassano, Head of AIG Financial Products, one year before they collapsed in 2008
>
> "Investors beware... Innovation is evolving at such a rapid pace that traditional equity benchmarks are being populated increasingly by so-called value traps, stocks that are 'cheap' for a reason. Critical to investment success will be moving to the right side of change, avoiding industries and companies in the crosshairs of 'creative destruction' and embracing those creating "disruptive innovation"...
>
> Catherine Wood, ARK Invest, December 2020

Below is the performance of Wood's "disruptooors" strategy vs. the NASDAQ. The two lines are normalized to the day Wood made the above statement in 2020. Wood's promise of a new paradigm (along with her questionable stock picking and bad entry and exit timing) incinerated billions of dollars' worth of capital[4].

ARKK ETF (bottom) vs. QQQ NASDAQ ETF (top), 2021 to 2025

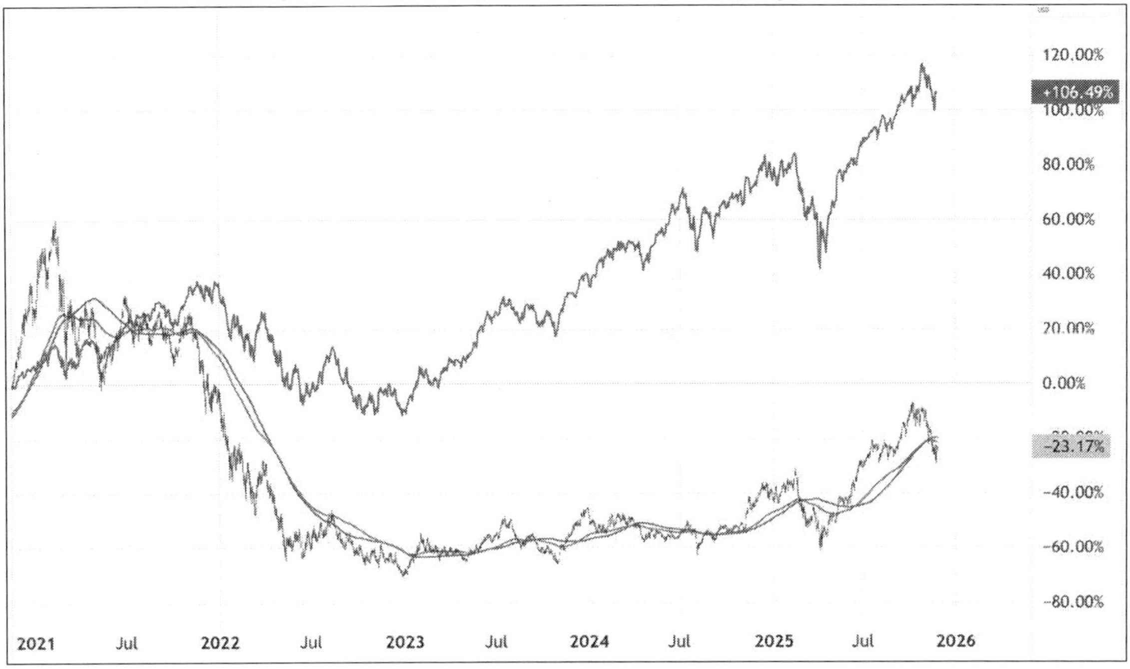

Important note here: The solution *is not* to simply assume that nothing ever changes, and all new trends are meaningless. The solution *is* to understand that good stories eventually get priced in. Exuberance creates a good story. Without a great story, there can be no bubble.

The proclivity towards believing we are the center of the universe is a deeply ingrained way of thinking for most humans and many societies. If everything just repeated exactly the same way, over and over, investing would be easy. But the world does change. Important new technologies emerge. Capitalism and financial markets evolve. Appropriate valuations vary. So, we cannot simply assume that everything now will be just like it was 20, 50 or 100 years ago. History rhymes, but it does not repeat.

The first remedy for chronocentrism is to embrace the fact that human behavior never changes and markets have almost no memory. Therefore, the first thing you need to do is understand the recurring cycles of human psychology that drive markets toward *temporary inefficiency*. This comes from studying history.

---

[4] I don't generally pick on, or trash talk individuals who make bad calls. Everyone, including me, makes bad calls. But when fiduciaries become media celebrities by making outlandish and outrageous forecasts in an effort to attract retail money and media eyeballs, they make themselves fair game.

The most useful books on financial history are the ones that cover human behavior, like Shiller's *Irrational Exuberance* (1999), Kindleberger's *Manias, Panics, and Crashes* (1978), and Charles Mackay's *Extraordinary Delusions and the Madness of Crowds* (1841). The cycles of human behavior change very little over time.

While many believe their high intelligence or hard work alone will lead them to the promised land in financial markets, that's not true.

Principle 10: The most rational trader (not the smartest trader) wins.

Markets have a poor memory and will continue to oscillate from fear to greed and back again. It's their very nature. The more time I spend in markets, the less I believe that anyone makes money studying first-order fundamentals. The money is made by those who can get outside themselves to combine second-order thinking with ultrarational behavior to forecast and exploit the emotional, irrational, and sometimes predictable behavior of the market hivemind.

Now that I've got you feeling small...

Let's move on to Chapter 2: Seeing around corners.

CHAPTER 2

SEEING AROUND CORNERS

Master higher-order thinking and outsmart the herd

Strong players of the financial market game tend to understand both first- and second-order thinking. They are aware of the drivers and nuances of the securities they trade, but they also actively consider and attempt to predict the thoughts, preferences, and impulses that might drive other human beings in the market to act. In markets, you need both external and internal mental models:

- External models help you make sense of capital markets.
- Internal models offer effective ways of thinking—and thinking about thinking.

It's 9:04 a.m. on January 7, 2025. You sit at your desk, fingers twitching, eyes flitting, four coffees deep, scanning headlines. Waiting for something juicy to trade.

A headline pops up on Bloomberg:

***CINTAS PROPOSED TO BUY UNIFIRST FOR $275/SHR IN CASH**

You toggle to the UniFirst trading window (NYSE: UNF) and see it's trading 237.50 / 238.50 and from the look of the 1-minute chart, the news came out about five or six minutes ago. Is your first instinct to buy at $238.50 and capture the free $36.50 as the stock will inevitably rally to $275? Or do you wonder why UNF is not already at $270 or so, like a stock normally would be almost instantly after an announcement like this, as algorithmic robots buy the shares up towards the buyout price, minus a small basis?

Most people's first thought here is to buy the stock. It looks too low. But this is where second derivative thinking is useful and important. You should immediately be curious and radically open-minded when something in the market looks strange. Abnormal behavior in markets is often an indication that something less obvious is occurring.

Markets are very, but not perfectly efficient. You should be humble and first assume that *you* are wrong, not the market. Imagine you are studying a horse race and conclude that a particular horse will be a heavy favorite in next week's race… And then you see the odds posted and your horse is 10-1 and there are three horses favored above it. It is more likely that you are missing something, and the aggregate wisdom of thousands of other bettors has made a different assessment for reasons you've missed or don't understand.

In the case of UniFirst, here's what happened.

UniFirst stock on January 7, 2025 (gray is pre-market trading)

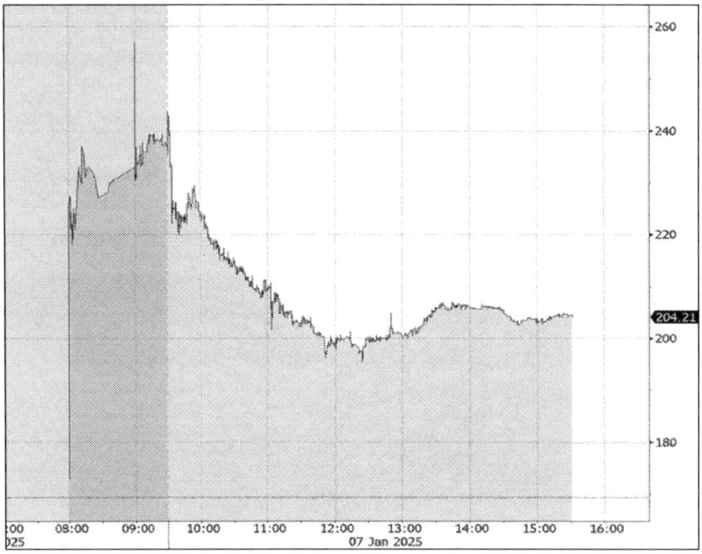

Digging deeper into the story, you learn that this is the third time Cintas has approached UniFirst, and UNF said "no thanks" the other two times. So, the market does not believe the deal has a high probability of closing, thus there is a huge difference between the market price and the supposed buyout price. As people analyze the details, they realize that $237.50 is way too high. The stock goes straight down all morning and finds a base just below $200.

If you bought 500 shares at $237.50 you lost fifteen grand. If you sold 500 shares you had a great day—and the trade was barely ever out of the money. For what it's worth, the market was right to be skeptical here. The deal never happened and in early 2026 the stock was still hovering around $200.

This is not to say you just fade every M&A headline. That doesn't work either. The lesson here is that very often the obvious trade is not correct because many, many people and algorithms have already done the obvious trade and therefore the profitable trade is to do the opposite of what the kneejerk traders did.

This concept also highlights an important point about metacognition: Your first thought is often not going to be your best thought. This is why you don't send an angry e-mail right after someone insults you in a meeting, and it's why you don't blurt out the first response that comes to mind when your spouse says something that makes you uncomfortable.

In his classic 2010 essay, William Deresiewicz (essayist, literary critic, and author of *Excellent Sheep*) puts it this way:

> "I find for myself that my first thought is never my best thought. My first thought is always someone else's; it's always what I've already heard about the subject, always the conventional wisdom. It's only by concentrating, sticking to the question, being patient, letting all the parts of my mind come into play, that I arrive at an original idea. By giving my brain a chance to make associations, draw connections, take me by surprise."

In trading, you don't have a lot of time to sit there *thinking about thinking*, so you need a strong internal filter that always assumes that **the first thought is not the best thought**. Then, you quickly parse and analyze your own kneejerk conclusions without hesitation.

The same day the Cintas headline dropped, there was another counter-intuitive move. Jensen Huang, CEO of NVIDIA, made a series of exciting announcements at the annual Consumer Electronics Show (CES) the night of January 6th and they all looked like super-bullish initiatives for NVDA. The stock crept higher in the pre-market...

NVIDIA stock on January 7, 2025 (including pre- and post-market)

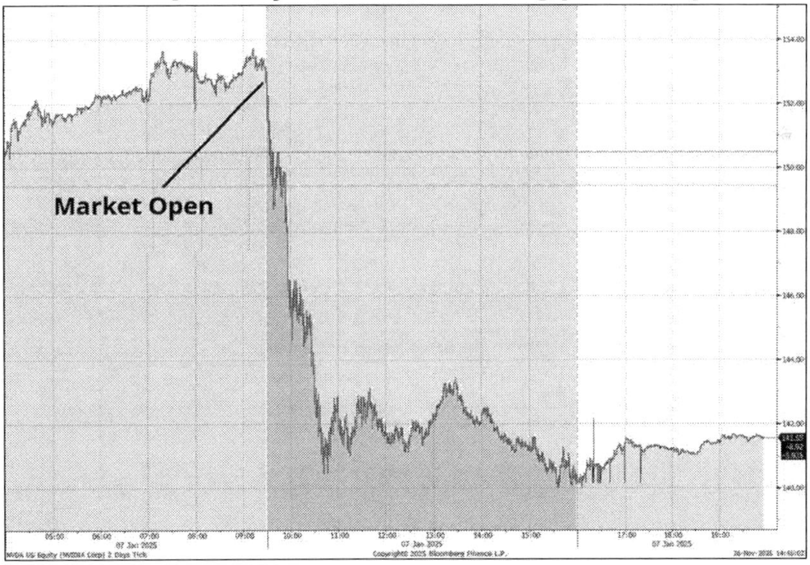

First-derivative thinkers said: "Wow, NVIDIA has a lot of new projects here! This is exciting! I will buy at whatever price and ride it higher all day!"

Second derivative thinkers thought something more like: "Momentum stocks have been struggling lately, Palantir and MicroStrategy both sold off after being added to the NASDAQ, and NVDA already ran up into the CES Conference on the emotional buildup ahead of Huang's speech. A lot is priced in. There is almost no outcome that could be bullish enough now that everyone has had 12 hours to buy the stock before the market open."

Market gaps on the open very often represent fading opportunities because they feature a big news event during a period of low liquidity (after hours). Before the market open, the stock moves higher until it runs into a deep pool of liquidity (supply) that satisfies the final demand after the news. By the time the market opens, **everyone that wanted to buy has already bought**.

This is the same in currency markets. When there is a gap in FX markets between the Friday close and the Sunday open, the opening price action is much more likely to reverse and fill the gap than it is to continue. Instead of running, it turns around and tries to fill the gap.

Gaps inspired by big, exciting news are often turning points, especially when it's hotly anticipated news with an emotional buildup and strong media coverage over multiple days.

To put some numbers on it: A simple strategy that takes the other side of every close-to-open gap in the 20 largest stocks in the S&P 500 delivered steady and stunning returns from 2015 to 2024. While proper risk management is critical when fading gaps, you can see that you make money going the other way, not going with them. If you run a similar study on Sunday gaps in FX, you see a similar result.

A strategy that fades every gap of 2% or more in the 20 largest S&P 500 stocks

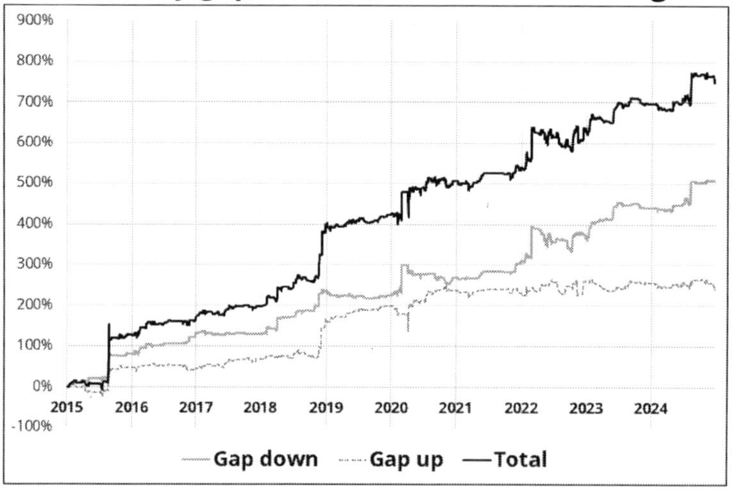

If you were wondering (I was!) what that huge rip higher in the P&L was in August 2015... At that time, there were serious market concerns about China's growth, and markets were particularly worried about Apple's sales there. Chinese stocks crashed Monday, leading to a huge gap lower in Apple. Horrible news out of China! Sell Apple!

Apple then rallied hard on the open, and then after the close Tim Cook announced, "I get updates on our performance in China every day, including this morning, and I can tell you that we have continued to experience strong growth for our business in China through July and August." Great news, right? *Right*?

Apple gapped higher and then sold off hard all throughout the following day. This setup is known to day traders as the "Gap and Trap." Note in the P&L chart that chasing gaps higher loses much less money than chasing gaps lower. This is because stocks trended higher during the period studied, and any event study that involves buying stocks in an uptrend will outperform one that involves shorting stocks. The trend in the data has a dramatic influence on the result of any backtest.

Two gaps and reversals in Apple stock in August 2015

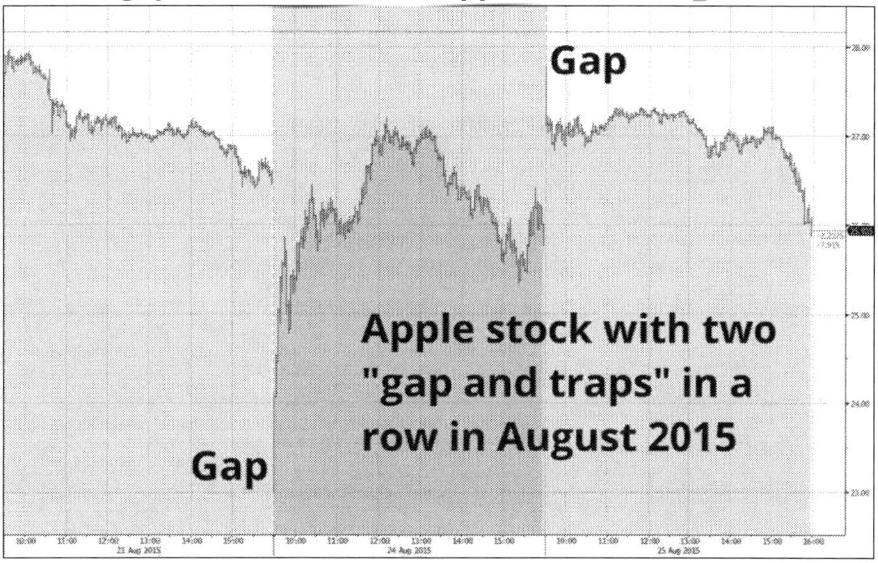

Second-order thinking can apply at all levels of zoom, not just intraday trades like the ones described above. The market is an efficient machine, and it is good at quickly pricing in obvious news. This is not to say that obvious trades cannot work. But if you are entering what seems to be an obvious trade, you should have some reason to think it will continue to run and that participation has been limited so far. Again: If the price looks wrong, be humble and first assume that your assessment is wrong, not the price. Then dig deeper to find out why you might be right.

The point I am making here is nuanced. An all-or-nothing approach won't work either way. You can't always trust your first thought, nor can you automatically rule it out. The concept of going against your first thought every single time is known as The Costanza Trade. This self-deprecating approach was made famous in an episode of Seinfeld called "The Opposite." Here's the key moment in the show.

George : Why did it all turn out like this for me? I had so much promise. I was personable, I was bright. Oh, maybe not academically speaking, but ... I was perceptive. It became very clear to me sitting out there today, that every decision I've ever made, in my entire life, has been wrong. My life is the opposite of everything I want it to be. Every instinct I have, in every part of life, be it something to wear, something to eat ... It's all been wrong.

(A waitress comes up to G)

Waitress : Tuna on toast, coleslaw, cup of coffee.

George : Yeah. No, no, no, wait a minute, I always have tuna on toast. Nothing's ever worked out for me with tuna on toast. I want the complete opposite of tuna on toast. Chicken salad, on rye, untoasted ... and a cup of tea.

Elaine : Well, there's no telling what can happen from this.

Jerry : You know chicken salad is not the opposite of tuna, salmon is the opposite of tuna, 'cos salmon swim against the current, and the tuna swim with it.

(A blonde looks at George)

Elaine : Ah, George, you know, that woman just looked at you.

George : So what? What am I supposed to do?

Elaine : Go talk to her.

George : Elaine, bald men, with no jobs, and no money, who live with their parents, don't approach strange women.

Jerry : Well here's your chance to try the opposite. Instead of tuna salad and being intimidated by women, chicken salad and going right up to them.

George : Yeah, I should do the opposite, I should.

Jerry : If every instinct you have is wrong, then the opposite has to be right.

George : Yes, I will do the opposite. I used to sit here and do nothing, and regret it for the rest of the day, so now I will do the opposite, and I will do something!

(He goes over to the woman)

George : Excuse me, I couldn't help but notice that you were looking in my direction.

Victoria : Oh, yes I was, you just ordered the same exact lunch as me.

(G takes a deep breath)

George : My name is George. I'm unemployed and I live with my parents.

Victoria : I'm Victoria. Hi.

Needless to say, it works out for George. But it won't work out for you. If your instincts are so bad that every thought you have is wrong in markets, you are better off finding a job that better suits your skills. Otherwise, you will soon find yourself thinking the opposite of your original thought was actually your first thought, and then you will be caught in the mental pretzel of whether to do the opposite of the opposite! The Costanza Trade is the funniest strategy—but it's not a real strategy.

When you are confident that the market is wrong and you can explain why, that's a potentially outstanding trading opportunity. When you say the market is wrong, but you can't really explain why or what is going on—it's usually a trap.

High school derivatives refresher

If it has been a while since you took high school calculus, let me provide a quick refresher on derivatives, using a simple example, before we start talking about how this all relates to markets.

Function: Position - Where the car is on the road.

1st derivative: Speed or velocity - The car is traveling 100 miles per hour.

2nd derivative: Acceleration - The car's speed increased from 80 mph one second ago to 100 mph now, meaning its velocity changed by 20 mph (about 29.3 ft/s^2 of acceleration).

3rd derivative: Jerk - The car goes from 80 mph one second to 100 mph the next to 110 mph the next. Its rate of acceleration is declining.

This mental model can be applied to markets. It's the way most momentum indicators such as RSI, MACD, and oscillators function. They measure the speed (rate of change) of the security in relation to past moves.

Here's how the function, first derivative, and second derivative apply to the price of a security. Monster Beverage stock (NASDAQ: MNST) rallies from $100 to $130 in three days.

Function: Price - The stock is trading at $100 on day 1 and $130 on day 3.

1st derivative: Velocity - Momentum

Day 1: Price moves from $100 to $110 ($v$ = 10)
Day 2: Price moves from $110 to $125 ($v$ = 15)
Day 3: Price moves from $125 to $130 ($v$ = 5)
Prices go up three straight days, but at different speeds.

2nd derivative: Acceleration - Change in Momentum

Between Day 1 and Day 2, the price momentum increased by (15 – 10 = 5).
Between Day 2 and Day 3, the price momentum decreased by (5 – 15 = -10).
Negative acceleration may indicate less enthusiasm from buyers.

Humans rarely go beyond the first derivative of price in financial markets, but quantitative systems often do. Here's a chart of gold along with its RSI and MACD. Note that most momentum indicators use similar mathematics and therefore you will not find a major difference between them, and it's not all that important which one you use.

Gold daily chart in late 2024 with RSI and MACD

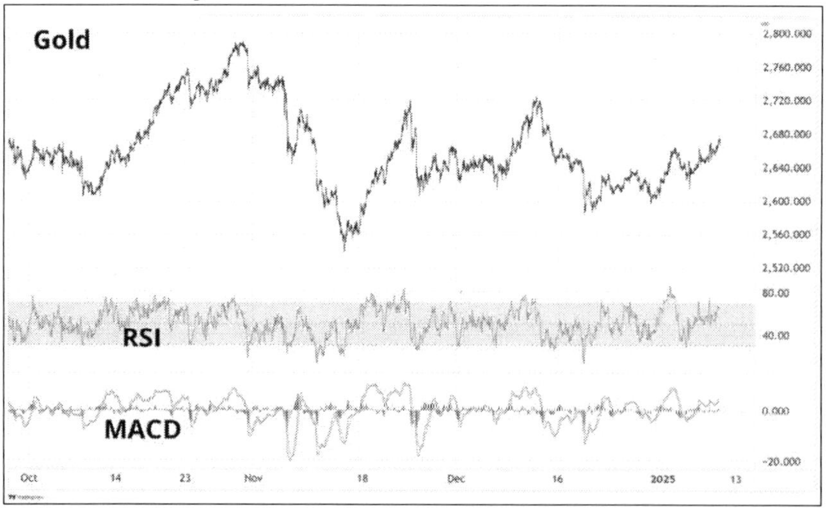

That chart is similar to a position, velocity, and acceleration graph in physics. Markets operate much like natural physical systems, and it can be useful to think in these terms. Some basic elements of physical systems that apply to markets:

- Systems seek equilibrium
- An object's momentum depends on its inertia
- Feedback loops amplify effects
- Extreme momentum usually leads to mean reversion
- Trees do not grow to the sky
- Energy dissipates over time

Going down the ladder of derivatives on Tesla stock, you can see that anything past the second derivative gets super noisy.

2024 TSLA stock price, velocity, acceleration, and jerk

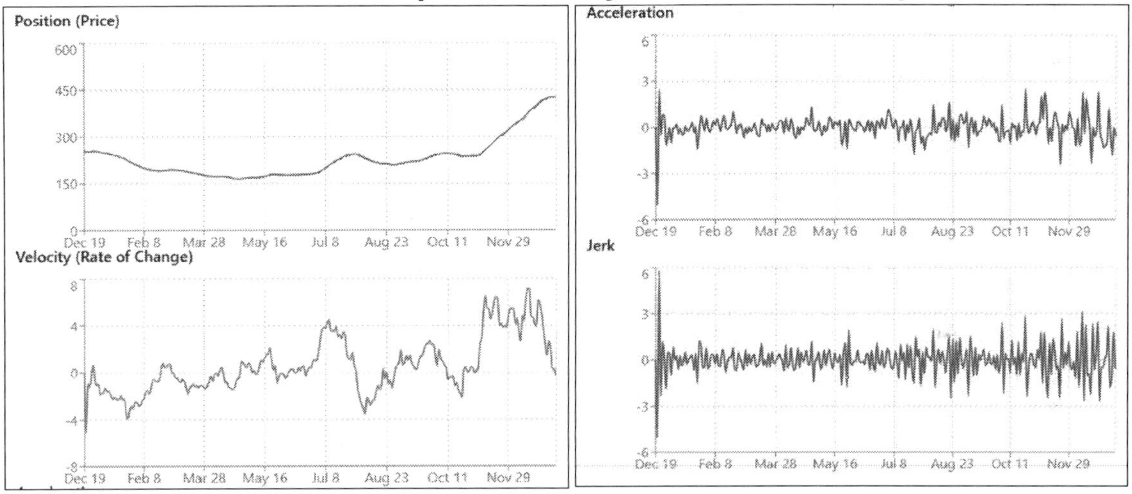

Second-order thinking

The multi-derivative concept can also be applied to thinking. While there can be many levels of thinking, the most important consideration in markets is to employ not just first-order thinking, but also second-order thinking. This means you don't just focus on your own thoughts about the market. You **spend time thinking about what everyone else is thinking.**

Take this example of a second-order thought process: you go to an auction to buy a Paul Newman Daytona (a rare watch). Do you bid what you think the watch is worth? Or do you bid the lowest possible price that you think will win the auction based on your expert assessment of the other bidders? The second order thinker will employ the second strategy—and often pay less at auction.

Third-order thinking would be something like: "What do the other bidders think I am going to bid?" There, you are thinking about what others are thinking you are thinking. When you look at the TSLA chart above, you see that as you attempt to go down the ladder of derivatives, the output gets noisier and noisier.

The same situation applies when we move down the ladder of thinking. There is not much likelihood of useful logic emerging from fourth- or fifth-derivative thinking, just like the bottom panel in the chart that shows the third order of Tesla's price ("jerk") probably doesn't offer any useful insight.

Second derivative thinking in financial markets was first introduced to the mainstream via John Maynard Keynes' Beauty Contest analogy. It is also a feature of contests like "guess 2/3 of the average." These examples offer good insight into what smart second-order thinking looks like.

Keynes' beauty contest

Keynes' beauty contest analogy is from *The General Theory of Employment, Interest and Money* (1936). Keynes asks us to imagine a newspaper which holds a contest where readers are rewarded for choosing which contestant will be chosen by the most other readers. The task is not to choose the most beautiful woman, but instead to choose the woman others will think is most beautiful. Sometimes that's the same woman, but not always!

The excerpt that follows is an amazing look at how Keynes' view of markets is still perfectly relevant today. It is a valid explanation for why you cannot simply calculate discounted cash flows and book value and buy the cheapest stocks.

> "...The professional investor is forced to concern himself with the anticipation of impending changes, in the news or in the atmosphere, of the kind by which experience shows that the mass psychology of the market is most influenced. The social object of skilled investment should be to defeat the dark forces of time and ignorance which envelop our future. The actual, private object of the most skilled investment to-day is 'to beat the gun', as the Americans so well express it, to outwit the crowd, and to pass the bad, or depreciating, half-crown to the other fellow.
>
> This battle of wits to anticipate the basis of conventional valuation a few months hence, rather than the prospective yield of an investment over a long term of years, does not even require gulls amongst the public to feed the maws of the professional;—it can be played by professionals amongst themselves. Nor is it necessary that anyone should keep his simple faith

> in the conventional basis of valuation having any genuine long-term validity. For it is, so to speak, a game of Snap, of Old Maid, of Musical Chairs—a pastime in which he is victor who says Snap neither too soon nor too late, who passed the Old Maid to his neighbor before the game is over, who secures a chair for himself when the music stops. These games can be played with zest and enjoyment, though all the players know that it is the Old Maid which is circulating, or that when the music stops some of the players will find themselves unseated.
>
> Or, to change the metaphor slightly, ...Professional investment may be likened to those newspaper competitions in which the competitors have to pick out the six prettiest faces from a hundred photographs, the prize being awarded to the competitor whose choice most nearly corresponds to the average preferences of the competitors as a whole; so that each competitor has to pick, not those faces which he himself finds prettiest, but those which he thinks likeliest to catch the fancy of the other competitors, all of whom are looking at the problem from the same point of view. It is not a case of choosing those which, to the best of one's judgment, are really the prettiest, nor even those which average opinion genuinely thinks the prettiest. We have reached the third degree where we devote our intelligences to anticipating what average opinion expects the average opinion to be.
>
> And there are some, I believe, who practice the fourth, fifth and higher degrees."
>
> Keynes, *General Theory of Employment, Interest and Money*, 1936

The "prevailing atmosphere" of the market is equally or more important than any objective numerical reality!

Participants in complex, multiplayer games with incomplete information (like trading, poker, and bridge) play best when they understand not just their own strategy and preferences but also the strategy and preferences of the other players. If everyone you talk to is staring at the $420.69 level as major resistance in Tesla stock, you should have that level marked on your charts and you should closely observe how the stock trades around there (even if you think that's a stupid level to care about).

When the market converges on the opinion that a particular level is important, you should pay attention. If that level breaks, the price action afterwards can reveal important information about potential short-term imbalances between supply and demand. A key level that breaks and follows through is indicative of a trending market, while a false break of a level everyone is watching (aka, a Slingshot Reversal[5]) is one of the best indicators for trend reversal.

You should be thinking about what the market is thinking at all times. Much like in poker, you don't just look at your cards and the board, you go through every action that your opponents have taken and attempt to figure out what's going on in their hands (and in their heads).

As a senior manager at various banks, I saw an endless parade of summer interns year after year. Towards the end of each internship, the recruits were inevitably asked to prepare a trade idea and present it to senior management.

95% of these ideas were painfully on-the-nose, first-order ideas involving a long, fancy presentation full of all sorts of fundamentals that were already more than fully priced in. These trade ideas were so blatantly consensus that they made excellent *reverse* indicators and yielded many contrarian trades.

This phenomenon did not occur because the interns were dumb. Wall Street analysts are anything but stupid. It happened because their expensive university education taught them only about the first level of markets. Concepts like valuation, arbitrage, covered call parity, and so on. These mechanical explanations work well in theory and in hindsight, but when it comes to real world markets, you need a thesis that isn't just "the fundamentals here are excellent" but more like:

The fundamentals here are excellent AND not everyone else thinks so. But they will soon.

In the immortal words of Jim Grant:

> "The key to successful investing is to have everyone agree with you—later."

Guess 2/3 of the average

An excellent puzzle to help identify and develop second or third level thinking is the "Guess 2/3 of the average" game. This was first presented in 1981 by Alain Ledoux in the French magazine *jeux & stratégie. There were some amazing magazines back in the 1980s!*

---

[5] For a full explanation of the Slingshot Reversal, please see *The Art of Currency Trading*, pages 155-158

Cover of the first edition of jeux & stratégie

Imagine a contest where 1,000 people are told "Everyone must choose a real number between 0 and 100. If your guess is closest to 2/3 of the average of all the guesses, you win $500." What would you answer?

This contest is common in game theory class. It allows a professor to quickly see a student's depth of reasoning. There is no correct or equilibrium answer to the question because it depends on what everyone else does. Are the people in the group smart? Are they rational? Are they likely to use multi-level reasoning, or just jot down the first thing that comes to mind? These questions matter.

Here are some different, increasingly higher-order levels of how one might approach this problem:

1. I have no idea what people will guess, so I'll just pick a random number.

2. The maximum guess is 100, so no answer above two-thirds of that (66 2/3) is rational. I automatically lose if I guess above 66.666 so I better pick lower than that. In game theory, numbers above 66.66 in this case are said to be "weakly dominated".

3. If everyone goes through step 2 in their mind (and most will), then everyone will rationally pick a number between 0 and 66.66. This now means that the best pick is a number between 0 and 44.44 (2/3 of 66.66). But wait, if everyone is perfectly rational, and everyone assumes that everyone else is rational, then nobody will pick a number above 44.44.

4. So I better pick a number that is less than 2/3 of 44.44.

5. And so on. And so on.

If we continue to believe that everyone is rational, and everyone knows that everyone else is rational, we will eventually iterate all the way down to the assumption that zero is the optimal choice. But is it? If this chain of logic is correct, everyone will pick zero and everyone will tie for the correct answer. So, picking zero can't be rational either because this chain of logic does not lead to a winning answer.

In the end, you must estimate how rational your cohort is and move back up the chain of derivative reasoning. If you think people will stop at the third derivative and guess (on average) something like 33, then you pick 22. But you also know that will be a common guess, so maybe a bit lower? And you don't want to pick a round number because round numbers will be more commonly picked. So how about 21.94? But to make sure nobody picks exactly the same as you, how about 21.943434253?

A Danish newspaper ran this experiment and got 19,000+ respondents, and the New York Times ran it (allowing only whole numbers) and got over 61,000 responses. The winning answers in those two cases were 21.605 and 19 respectively. You could infer that more multi-level thinkers read the New York Times than the Danish newspaper!

Distribution of responses in the NYT "Guess 2/3 of the average" game

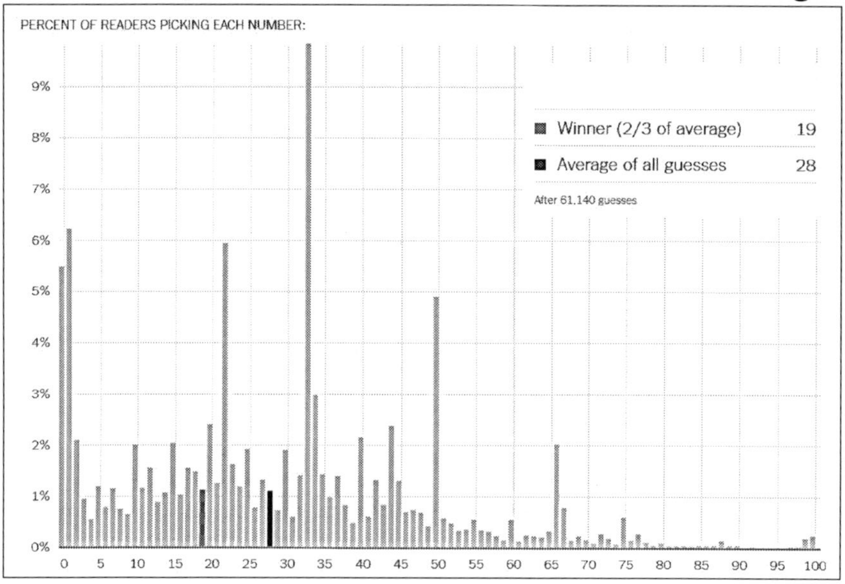

Source: NYT website

What does this have to do with markets?

An extreme example is a speculative memecoin. Everybody knows the terminal value of the memecoin is zero. Everyone knows that everyone knows that. But people also know that other people like to buy things that are going up, even at irrational prices, to sell them higher. If the coin is trading at $0.10 and you think it's worth zero, but you think people think it's going to $2.00 before it goes to zero, do you buy it? You probably should! This is known as the Greater Fool Theory: buy an overpriced asset then profit by selling it at an even higher price to a "greater fool".

The "guess 2/3 of the average" game is an excellent example of the way your brain should work when you think about markets. Consider how others are likely to be thinking about the topic you are thinking about. This will put you one step ahead of most other traders and investors, as they sit hunched over a keyboard, mired in their own spinning thoughts. It's also a great way to get out of your own head and find a different, possibly less biased perspective. Seeing what others see and absorbing some of their viewpoint can offset your bias.

Interesting side note: If you run the "Guess 2/3 of the average" game multiple times in the same group, the average answer will be lower and lower each round as everyone starts to understand the game and iterate more aggressively through the levels of thinking.

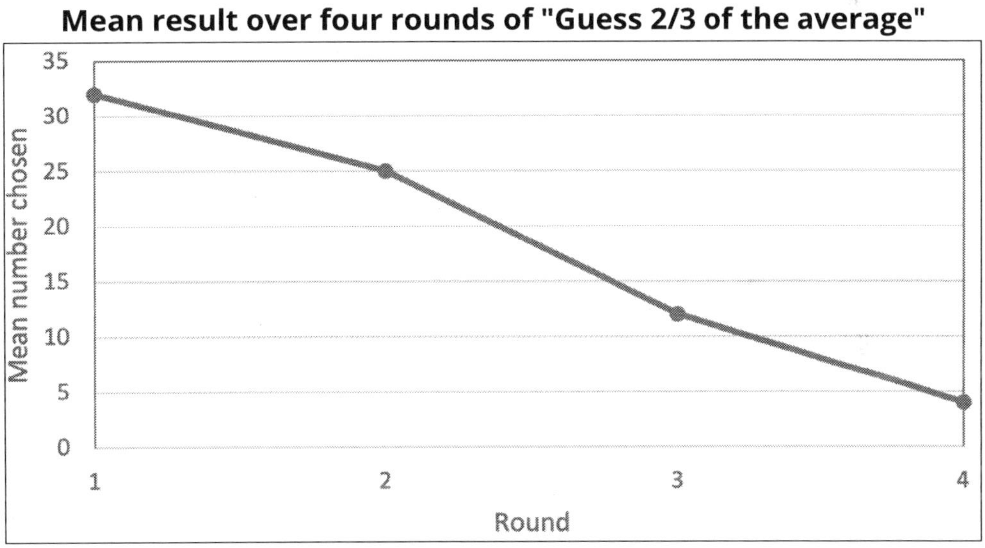

Joey Limm via Wikipedia Creative Commons

Let's look at another second-order method of reasoning.

Smarties or pencils?

Theory of Mind (ToM) is the ability to grasp that other people have their own mental states—beliefs, desires, intentions, emotions, and thoughts—that may not align with your own. It's a core skill for navigating social interactions, as we constantly rely on it to interpret and predict the actions of those around us. It's also a critical skill in financial markets. You cannot sit there studying 10-Qs all day and never take time to think about what others in the market are thinking about as they read those same reports.

Researchers measure Theory of Mind using various tests, most commonly the Sally-Anne Test[6]. My favorite ToM experiment is simple and elegant. It's called the "Unexpected Contents" test or the "Smarties Test" and is discussed in a 1987 paper by Barreau and Morton[7].

A researcher shows a child a smarties tube:

Then they ask the child to guess what's in it. Naturally, every child answers: "Smarties."

The researcher then opens the tube and shows the child that **the tube contains pencils, not Smarties**. Then, the researcher says: "Now, we're going to ask your friend James what's in the tube. What do you think he will answer?"

If the child has developed Theory of Mind, they will answer that James will say "Smarties". Younger children, or those without a fully developed Theory of Mind, will say that James will say: "pencils," because they are unable to separate their own knowledge from someone else's perspective.

Adults in financial markets often operate like the children in the Smarties Test. They think that everyone sees the world the way they do. Or, they insist that everyone *needs* to look at the world the way they do. They will never stop trying to convince you that the tube contains Smarties, even as the pencils stab them in the palm!

You will often hear people telling you that stocks are about to crash, or that rising yields are bad for stocks, or bitcoin is a fraud and it's going to zero, and so on. These groups will never consider an alternative worldview, no matter how much new evidence emerges. This inability to adjust to new information makes it difficult for those people to operate profitably in financial markets.

Principle 11: Good thinkers think about what others are thinking.

---

[6] wikipedia.org/wiki/Sally%E2%80%93Anne_test

[7] www.sciencedirect.com/science/article/abs/pii/S0010027799000463#BIB23

Second-order use of technical analysis

Technical analysis is the study of chart patterns in an attempt to predict future price movements (see *Alpha Trader*, Chapter 10). It is a widely used but still somewhat controversial field that may or may not depend on self-fulfilling prophecy. While there may be some independent value to analyzing chart patterns, a good part of the benefit comes from second derivative analysis. To do this, you don't need to care whether technical analysis works, or whether a particular pattern is valid. You just need to know what levels people care about.

Let's say you are thinking about technical levels on a chart. Do you mostly think about which support and resistance levels matter **to you**? Or do you consider which levels matter **to everyone else**? These are two different approaches. You need to get inside the mind of the market and know what levels matter most to the players you are up against, because their behavior is likely to change as those levels near. They won't care about your favorite levels, but they will care about their own.

For example, in December 2024, bitcoin traced out what is known as a Head and Shoulders pattern. The pattern looked like this:

Bitcoin hourly chart, December 2024

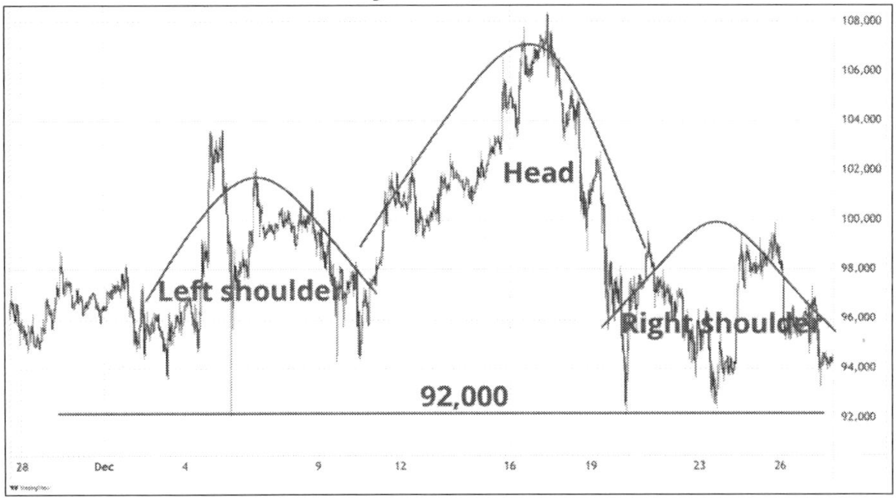

The theory behind a Head and Shoulders pattern is that when the horizontal neckline, in this case 92,000, breaks, a large downward move should follow. A breakdown suggests that the big buyers holding the 92,000 level have been filled, and price needs to go lower to find a new layer of demand.

If you followed bitcoin closely at this time, you probably saw a litany of posts on Twitter and other venues suggesting that a break of 92,000 would be "lights out" for bitcoin or something similar. If you see many, many posts suggesting something is going to happen, your first instinct should be to wonder if maybe the opposite will happen instead. Or, the thing everyone expects will in fact happen, for a moment, then reverse to punish the believers.

In other words, can you predict what the market is going to do based on the crowd behavior that comes out of the common knowledge surrounding the pattern? Most likely, speculators who are long will exit on the break of 92,000 and bears will also go short on the break. This will create a major change in the supply/demand dynamic below 92,000—and could actually create the conditions for a subsequent rally after the initial selloff.

This is not to say you want to live in Opposite World and simply do the opposite of every orthodox, logical technical setup, either. But when the crowd is heavily focused on a particular level, setup or news event, you might sensibly think that the price action around that level could be counterintuitive. Here's what happened.

Bitcoin hourly chart late 2024 / early 2025

When you analyze a market setup, whether it is technical or fundamental, **always take the time to think about what everyone else is thinking**. And if you talk to enough people, you might even figure out what everyone is thinking that everyone else is thinking.

In the past, you could make money in crypto markets by unpacking what the first-order thinkers would do because so many participants in the crypto market were rookies and new traders. This approach is less dependable today as the market is more institutionalized, but for any market you study, you can find what the consensus first-level thinkers think by going through Twitter, LinkedIn, Reddit, r/wallstreetbets, and other social channels.

You can also figure out what the first level thinkers are doing by observing what those outside finance are talking about, and by watching the mainstream (non-financial) media. Magazine covers, for example, are an excellent example of first-level thinking[8]. Journalists outside the world of finance have no concept of what is priced in or what professionals in the market are thinking. They simply write about and broadcast the most obvious themes. These two covers from The Economist capture it nicely.

Two contrarian covers of The Economist Magazine

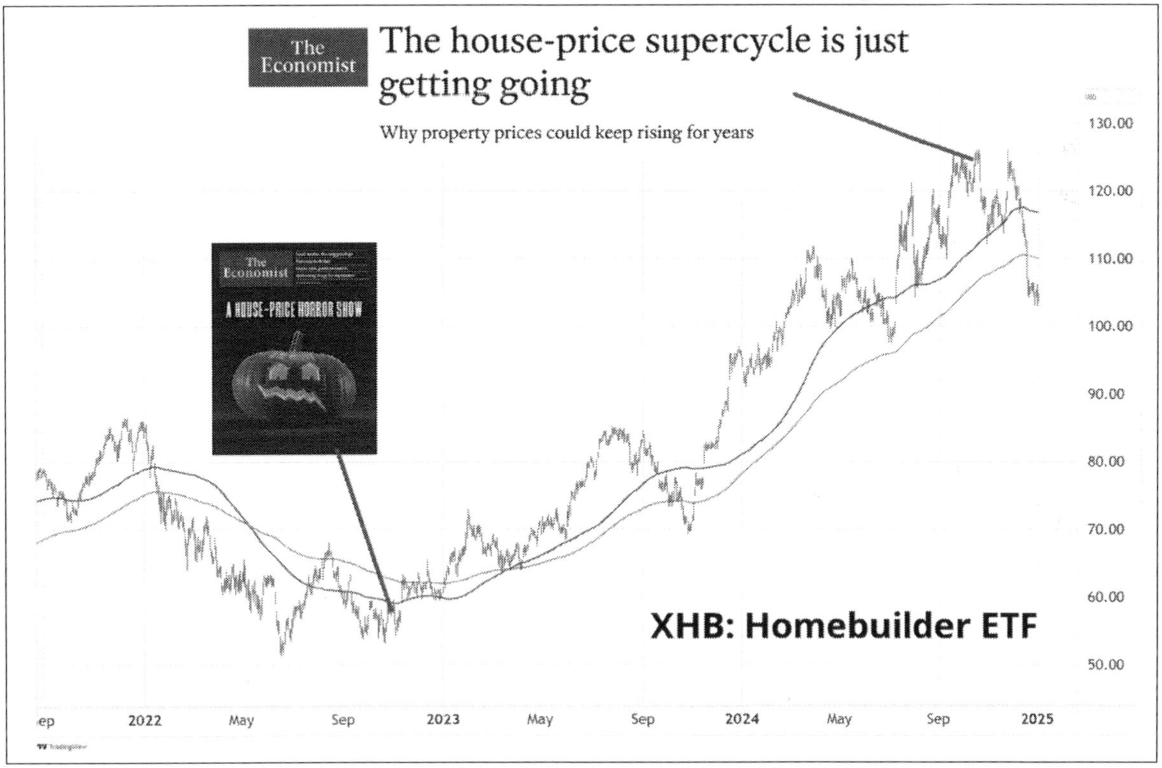

This is similar to the shoe-shine indicator, or the brother-in-law indicator. When someone outside finance starts asking you about a particular asset class, it's a red flag and a reverse indicator.

---

[8] For more on the Magazine Cover Indicator, see www.spectramarkets.com/amfx/the-magazine-cover-indicator/

Second level thinking is the best place to operate. While it feels smart to start thinking on the third or fourth level in markets, this can be dangerous because it leads to decision paralysis. It can yield thought patterns like this:

> "I want to be long, but everyone I talk to is bullish, but also: everyone I talk to is worried about how bullish everyone is, so nobody is long. So, I am going to be long. But what if everyone is thinking what I'm thinking? Maybe I should go short!"

That's too complicated. You need to find the sweet spot between overly simplistic, obvious ideas, and infinitely-regressing overcomplication that turns your brain into a pretzel. Otherwise, you will find yourself thinking Yogi Berra-isms like: "Nobody goes to that restaurant anymore, it's too crowded." Or this sort of thing:

Don't let your brain turn into a pretzel! Generally, your view on a market should emerge from these two steps.

1. **What do you think?** This can be based on fundamental, technical, or any other type of analysis. You come to your own conclusions about the market price and where it might go. Then before putting on a trade, you think…

2. **What does everyone else think?** Is my idea super obvious and most people already have it on? Is everyone waiting for the same catalyst as me and therefore we might see an unorthodox move when the catalyst finally arrives? Are there reasons people might have the same view as me, but they don't yet have the position? Are we early in the narrative, and thus there is room for new participants to join the party? Etc.

Stan Druckenmiller, one of the greatest trader/investors of all time, put it this way:

> "I learned this way back in the 70s from my mentor Speros Drelles. I was a chemical analyst. When should you buy chemical companies? Traditional Wall Street is when earnings are great. Well, you don't want to buy them when earnings are great, because what are they doing when their earnings are

> great? They go out and expand capacity. Three or four years later, there's overcapacity and they're losing money. What about when they're losing money? Well, then they've stopped building capacity. So three or four years later, capacity will have shrunk and their profit margins will be way up. So, you always have to sort of imagine the world the way it's going to be in 18 to 24 months as opposed to now. If you buy it now, you're buying into every single fad every single moment. Whereas if you envision the future, you're trying to imagine how that might be reflected differently in security prices."

Again, you need to be careful about simply *doing the opposite* of what makes sense. Here's a walkthrough of how multi-level thinking might lead to a long position in NVDA, even when it's trading at 30X sales at the all-time highs.

First level NVIDIA is a great company! I see them in the news all the time. My son says their graphics chips are lit, and I hear they are big into this "AI" thing.

Multi-level NVDA is richly valued, but I think they will outperform the most optimistic expectations. I know the stock is high, but I am happy to buy stocks with strong momentum. The market will continue to reward anything with momentum for at least the next few months because everyone thinks the Fed is going to keep hiking rates, but I think the Fed is just about done. Valuations don't matter at this stage of the cycle, and they don't matter for my trading time horizon. Many of the fund managers I talk to have moved to underweight NVDA recently because it is so overbought, and I think they will need to buy back stock to get back to benchmark in the next few months.

Call volumes are high but could still double from here as r/wallstreetbets has been talking more about NVDA and Reddit activity tends to precede increases in call buying by 10 to 15 days. The speed of the break above $100 has left many buyers frozen as we are now trading $120 and they all want to buy the dip down at $100. I don't think that dip is going to happen. I know with all those buyers lined up at $100, if we go below that level, there is something bigger going on and the momentum is burnt out. So I can buy here at $120, exit below $100, and target $195. One major catalyst that I expect is a new Blackwell chip launch. If the new chip isn't launched in the next two months, I will get out of the position.

One person is buying a story, with no knowledge of whether every single human in the world has already loaded up on the same story. The second person is buying the story, but with eyes wide open and a comprehensive understanding of what everyone else in the market is up to.

Here's another, simpler example of multiple levels of thinking around a hot quantum computing IPO, QuantumBitz.ai (QBTZ):

First level QBTZ does quantum computing and quantum computing is the future. And their company name ends with **.ai**! This IPO is gonna be huge!

BUYS THE STOCK.

2nd level This company isn't profitable, and the valuation is a joke. The IPO price was $12 and it's trading at $19 pre-market.

SHORTS THE STOCK.

3rd level This is not a good company, and this valuation is insane, but there is so much hype here. It's way too dangerous to short on the open. I will wait a bit for the dust to settle, go short as volumes contract, and target a move back to the IPO level of $12. I don't need to catch the exact top. I'm better off waiting for lower volatility, peak volumes, and a tradable top. If we get down close to the IPO price, there will probably be a stabilization bid, so I will flip long down there.

SELLS at $26 two days after the IPO.

Rides it down to $14, then flips long.

There are many well-known setups linked to the idea of second-order thinking like:

- "buy the rumor / sell the fact"[9]
- "good news / bad price"[10]
- "Turnaround Tuesday"[11]

I touch on some of them in other books and we will revisit a few.

Here's a fun thing. I wrote this chapter in June 2025 and was editing this section in August 2025. That month, there was a perfect real-life occurrence of the IPO example above. A company called Figma went public, and the market adored the IPO. But the company went public at a stupid valuation[12].

Here's the chart of FIG with the stages of how it played out.

---

[9] 50 Trades in 50 Weeks, page 297

[10] 50 Trades in 50 Weeks, page 169

[11] *Alpha Trader*, pages 222-225

[12] This is not hindsight; I wrote about the overvaluation in am/FX when the stock was still at $135.

FIG common stock, hourly, August 2025

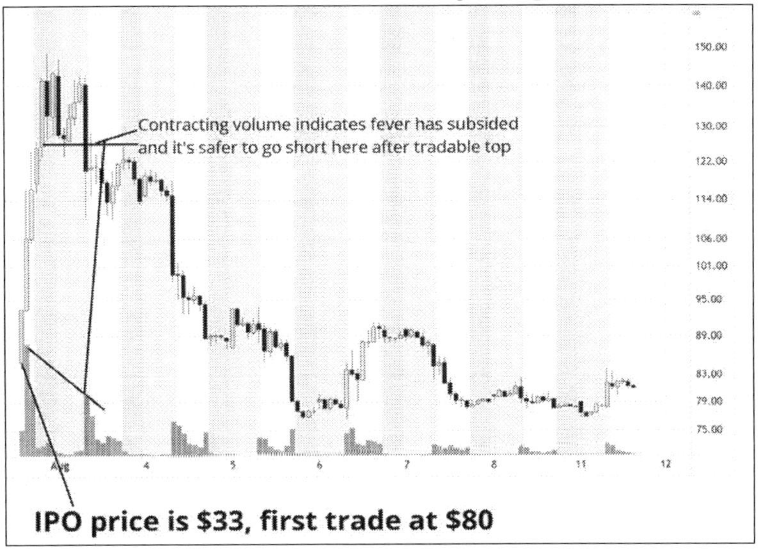

The stock opened at $84, jumped immediately and then was halted, so the first real volume went through at $100. First-order thinkers that bought at $100 lost money. First-order thinkers that sold at $100 lost money. Those who waited for the speculative froth to blow off, and for volatility and volume to contract, got short in the $114-$122 area and did incredibly well.

What multi-level thinking is not

Multi-level thinking is not reflexive contrarianism. It is not someone who says: "Everyone is buying this thing, so I'm gonna sell." That is just a different form of simplistic, first-order thinking. Because markets trend, and the crowd is often correct, you cannot just do the opposite of what everyone else is doing all the time. You need a better thesis than that.

If you want to take the other side of a major trend or narrative, you need to have a reason to do so. Often, expert traders and investors will use positioning data, momentum and reversal indicators, narrative shifts, and other methodologies to time market reversals. One of the worst ways to come up with trading ideas is to look around for what has moved a lot and do the opposite.

Principle 12: "It's come too far, too fast!" is not a good reason to put on a trade.

There is a market aphorism that says: **Early is the same thing as wrong.** If you are too early to a trade, you spend copious mental and real capital on the trade before it comes to fruition. You buy options that expire worthless. You dedicate significant portions of your risk budget to trades that don't do anything, or bleed slowly against you. You get stopped out, over and over. You underperform as you wait for your dream trade to come true and eventually get fired three weeks before it finally works.

Then again, it's important to remember that **late is the same thing as wrong**. A good trading or investing thesis involves a view of the future that is different from the current dominant narrative. That could be a bullish view in a stock that has rallied, because you think it hasn't rallied enough, and you can explain why. Or it could be a bearish view in a stock that is overpriced, and you have a good explanation of why it's the right time to take the other side.

A note on news trading: when news comes out, your first and most orthodox interpretation is often correct. Trading news and events can be more about quick reaction times and rapid, accurate interpretation of the news. If a central bank unexpectedly cuts interest rates, you don't need multi-level thinking because markets don't instantly reprice to the new equilibrium. As such, you can normally sell the currency of a country where the central bank unexpectedly cuts interest rates, even if the currency has already sold off in response.

That said, you should still be thinking about what others think at all times.

If American Eagle Outfitters rallies on a controversial ad featuring Sidney Sweeney, and you think it's stupid that it's rallying, you should also consider that there is an army of 27-year-old male retail traders who will probably buy the stock for the next 48 hours.

If you think it's stupid that Six Flags is rallying because Travis Kelce bought a stake, you should first consider whether 99% of the rest of the world will think he's a cool dude and a great reason to buy the stock. I mean, the ticker symbol for Six Flags is "FUN." You think fading a Travis Kelce headline after three minutes is going to make you money? It won't.

Even on news, you need to have two thoughts at once:

1. Here's what I think the news means.
2. Here's how others are likely to react.

The more time elapses after a surprise news release or event, or the more complicated the situation, the more you need to rely on second-order thinking. A company announcing a surprise earnings warning is not going fully priced after two minutes. On the other hand, a stock that has sold off 20% into its earnings report might rally on a revenue downgrade because experts in that stock understand that the bad news was already in the price.

Conclusion

First-derivative thinkers can do well in specific market regimes. When hype and momentum are driving a strong bull market, most traders and investors will make money. Everyone is a genius in a bull market.

To succeed in the long run and find a real edge in markets, you need to understand not just the facts about the securities you trade, but the common knowledge surrounding those facts. You need to know what everyone else is thinking and adjust your thinking accordingly.

To paraphrase the Keynes quote: professional investors must concern themselves with the anticipation of impending changes in the news, the atmosphere, and the mass psychology of the markets they trade. Start by understanding the top layer of your markets, then dig deeper.

To summarize:

Step 1: Form your own view.
Step 2: Filter out kneejerk, excessively first-order, or biased thinking.
Step 3: Ask "What does the crowd think?"
Step 4: Look for mismatches between your view of reality and consensus.
Step 5: Trade the gap between your view of reality and priced-in consensus with a mind to when that gap will close, and why.

That concludes Chapter 2 and how I think about thinking about thinking.

Let's move to Chapter 3 and talk about how you can use AI, LLMs, and prediction markets to brainstorm, structure your ideas, and better pinpoint what the crowd is thinking.

CHAPTER 3

NEW TOOLS

How to use AI, LLMs, WSB, and prediction markets in trading

Three new trading tools have emerged in recent years, and each has strengths and weaknesses. AI (artificial intelligence) & LLMs (large language models) offer fast—but not always accurate—answers. Wallstreetbets is a good reverse indicator, but you need the right tactics to survive the raid. Prediction markets are an accurate real-time measure of consensus that can help you trade smarter and faster around events. Let's dig in.

AI & LLMs

> "All models are wrong. Some are useful."
>
> George Box, 1976

Artificial intelligence (AI) can give you quick answers to complicated questions. Those answers are not always accurate, but the extra speed can be worth the risk.

It is dangerous to write a chapter about new technologies in trading because things can evolve faster than you can update your manuscript. Computer science and crypto, for example, are evolving so quickly that books written on those topics are often obsolete before publication because technology changes fast and book publishing can be slow.

But I would be remiss if I didn't cover AI and Large Language Models (LLMs) here, at least briefly, because they are increasingly important inputs into my trading process. My general observation is that LLMs make a ton of mistakes and often lack accuracy and precision, but they are excellent tools for idea generation, trade structuring inspiration, summarization, and lightning-fast analysis. They are great idea machines and can be good for data and calculation exercises if you have the patience and diligence to troubleshoot and course correct them as they make many dumb and basic errors.

There are four ways I use AI to trade better:

1. Get a quick and dirty read on confusing headlines
2. Optimize trade structuring
3. Brainstorm backtesting ideas
4. Get unbiased feedback on sentiment

Let's go through them one by one.

1. Using LLMs to rapidly interpret headlines

When a random biotech headline comes out, and I need to understand it quickly, an LLM is my best tool. Here's a quick example from a recent trade I did.

I am at my desk with very little risk on. It's 5:15 p.m. and this headline comes out on Bloomberg:

***CYTOKINETICS: PDUFA EXTENDED TO DEC. 26**

I am not a biotech expert, but I am willing to do the odd hit and run trade on a headline like this. Problem is, I don't know what the headline means! So, I quickly punch it into Claude, along with the detail in the short news story attached. The part in the black box is cut and pasted from Bloomberg, then I type the quick questions below the box to prompt the AI.

Input to Claude after CYTK headline

***CYTOKINETICS: PDUFA EXTENDED TO DEC. 26**

Cytokinetics Announces New PDUFA Date for Aficamten in Obstructive Hypertrophic Cardiomyopathy

Cytokinetics' Phase 1 Trial for CK-4021586 Experiences Decreased Enrollment

are these important headlines? what is the expected stock price impact? give a confidence interval

Claude output

Confidence Interval for Stock Price Impact

Based on analyst reactions and historical precedents for PDUFA delays:

Short-term (1-2 weeks):

- Central estimate: -12% to -8% from pre-announcement price

- 90% confidence interval: -15% to -5%

Is this reliable enough to trade on? It's risky. But when I brought up the stock (CYTK), it had barely moved, and so a 90% confidence interval of -15% to -5% felt like enough of a margin of safety when I could sell the stock down 6% (it was trading $42.80 before the headline, and it was still bid at $40.30, even after I had time to put the info into Claude, read the output, and pull up the Level 2 window). Here's the chart:

CYTK 3-minute chart May 1 to May 5, 2025

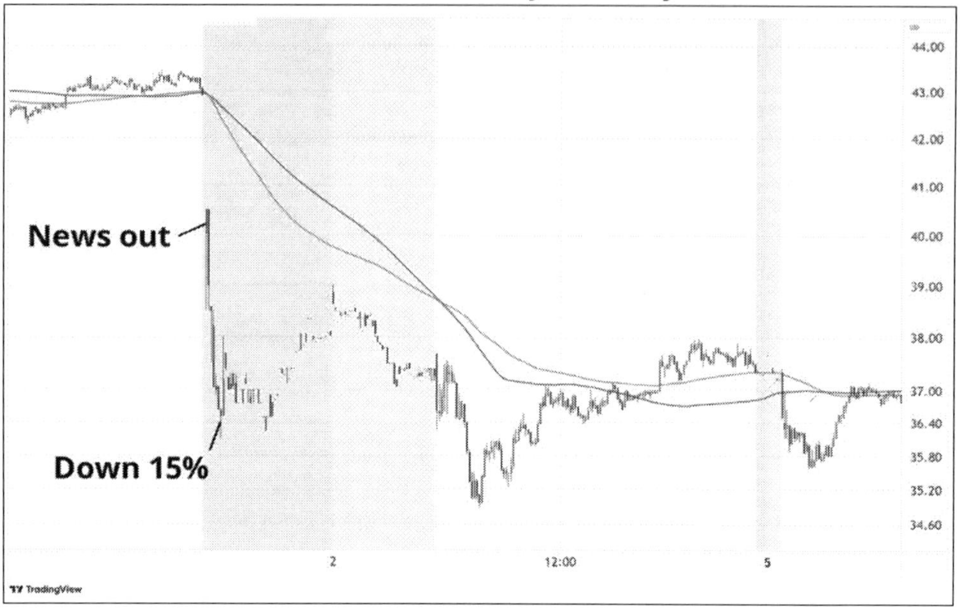

This was pretty much a dream outcome as I had just enough time to sell the stock at $40.30, it quickly went to the bottom of the expected depreciation band (down 15%), then I covered at $36.80. Other times, the AI can be wrong, or the process can be too slow and you miss the trade.

More sophisticated firms now run apps that translate headlines in real time, with estimated security price impact, while others use an API to trade the AI's interpretation instantly and directly in the market. I admit that my approach is manual and unsophisticated, but I am not running an algorithmic trading system here; I'm just looking to use AI to augment my ability to interpret headlines more quickly and accurately.

The huge caveat here is that of course the AI can be wrong. But I would rather trust Gemini, Claude, or ChatGPT when it comes to interpreting a biotech headline like this because my knowledge is so weak there is no chance my interpretation will be better. I am usually only risking 1% of capital on a trade like this—I would never go hard based on an AI interpretation of a headline I do not understand myself.

This trade is an example of the ready, shoot, aim approach I use when trading the news. Here's a quick excerpt from Chapter 4 of *Alpha Trader* that describes this approach. ***Note:*** *System 1 is your lizard brain / first thought while System 2 is your slower, more deliberate thinking.*

> If an important announcement hits the wires, you can't always sit around waiting for System 2 to deliver a verdict. If you don't hit the buttons right away,

someone else will. In other words, some short-term trading requires a "Ready, Shoot, Aim" thinking style. That's OK.

If you are trading headlines, events, and quick reaction time trades, you can overcome the heuristic / fast thinking problem by trading in two steps.

Step 1: When you see a headline or something that makes you want to act... Go ahead and act. Go to market and get set on your position.

Step 2: Once you have the position on, take a step back and analyze your actions using System 2. Is this logical? Or is this a dumb idea? You need to have the force of mind to take a trade off right away, usually at a small loss, if your System 2 analysis says that your System 1 idea was wrong. This is hard because we tend to have trouble selling at a small loss and we tend to overvalue assets (or positions) we already own.

Note that if you enter trades using System 1 (reacting quickly to headlines, for example) then subsequently evaluate them more fully using System 2, you need to overcome both the endowment effect and anchoring bias to get out of bad trades quickly. The endowment effect is our tendency to value something we own more highly than if we did not already own it. Anchoring bias says we will attach importance to the price at which we entered a trade, even though that price is irrelevant once we have the trade on.

If your System 2 says, "this is a bad trade", don't wait for the price to get back to break even. Cut the position and move on. **Good short-term trading involves taking many small losses.**

2. Using LLMs to optimize trade structuring

A second use for LLMs is to brainstorm and optimize trade structuring. There is a vast amount of information available on options trading, so LLMs have a rich and deep corpus to draw from. Let's take a look at a simple example.

Here's a real prompt I fed into ChatGPT in August 2025.

> CRWV is trading at $145, and I think it could go to $110. It's not shortable. I want three option structures that work in my scenario. Don't give me any ideas that are unlimited loss. Limited / defined loss only. Can use calls and/or puts. Show P&L profile of each strategy using an x-axis that goes from 100 to 170 CRWV stock price at expiry 7 days to expiry ... implied vol 95 ... assume I want to risk $20,000 on the trade (maximum loss).

And here is the output. Not too shabby!

Here are three limited-risk strategies for your bearish view on CRWV (currently $145, target $110).

Each one is scaled to max loss ≈ $20k, expiry in 7 days, IV = 95%. The chart shows payoff at expiry.

CRWV Options Strategies as suggested by ChatGPT

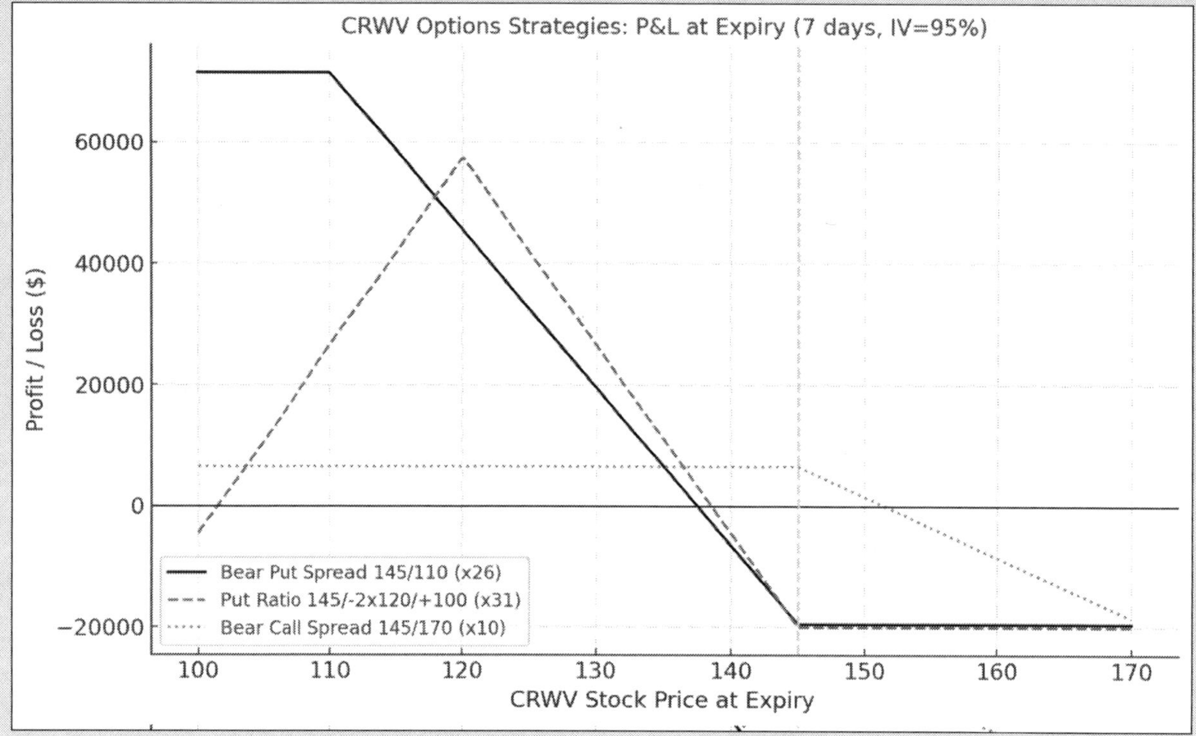

Bear Put Spread (145/110)

Buy 145 put, Sell 110 put

Max profit: ≈ $71.5k if ≤ 110

Breakeven: ≈ $137.50

Use case: straightforward downside play, defined risk, capped upside.

Put Ratio Spread (+145 / −2×120 / +100)

Buy 145 put, Sell 2× 120 puts, Buy 100 put

Max profit: ≈ $57k if CRWV lands around $120

Breakevens: ≈ $138.5 and $101.5

Use case: maximizes profit if stock slides to 120, still defined risk thanks to long 100 put.

Bear Call Spread (short 145 / long 170)

Sell 145 call, Buy 170 call

Max profit: ≈ $6.5k (credit received) if ≤ 145

Breakeven: ≈ $151.5

Use case: Lower reward but works if stock drifts down or stalls under 145.

✅ All three structures are defined-risk, no unlimited loss, and fit a $20k risk cap.

This is a decent rundown of three ideas that make sense. You need to use extreme caution and always **treat LLMs as idea generators, not answer machines**. They will often give answers that are outright wrong. I use them as a starting point and then I look at the real-world pricing to see if the ideas make sense. The more detail you can include in your prompt, the more likely you will get a useful response.

FYI, in this example, the strikes in the third idea provided by ChatGPT are way too far apart (145 vs. 170) and in real life I tend to do very skinny spreads to avoid getting assigned. Ahead of CRWV earnings in August 2025, I sold a $145/$146 call spread and the stock collapsed to $100 in two days. I risked 50 cents to make 50 cents on 200 contracts and it was a decent little trade ($10,000 profit).

Because CRWV collapsed in a straight line, I would have made five times more money if I had simply bought puts. Oh well. My process was good, and the outcome was fine. I try not to fret about *wouldas, couldas,* or *shouldas.*

3. Using LLMs to brainstorm backtesting ideas

Here's another use case for LLMs: using a spreadsheet of MSTR daily Open-High-Low-Close data, I make an open-ended and creative query something like this:

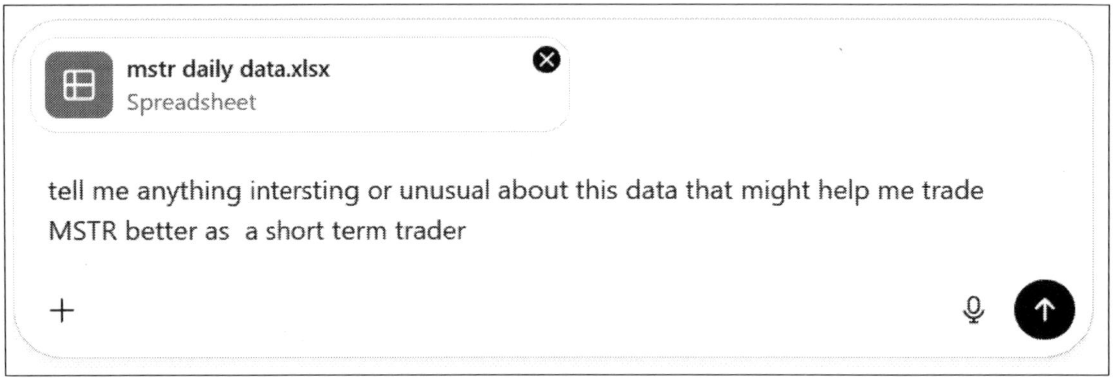

LLMs don't kare about typos

Here is the output.

Here are the clearest tradeable takeaways I found (all stats are from your data only):

- **Next day is slightly mean-reverting.** Today's return vs. tomorrow's return has a -0.096 correlation → fading extremes has an edge.

- **RSI extremes pop**. After **RSI<30**, the **next-day avg return ≈ +5.75%.** After **RSI>70**, the next-day avg is still positive (~ **+1.09%**), but much smaller. This screams "buy the puke, be cautious chasing strength."

- **Big down intraday bounces more than big up continues**. After ≤-5% intraday days, next-day avg ≈ +1.88%; after ≥+5% intraday up days, next-day avg ≈ +0.80%. Fading big green, buying big red looks better.

- **Gap-fill behavior**: **0–1% gaps fill most often**, while **>5% gaps are least likely to fill.** Scale gap-fill attempts with gap size.

- **Volume spikes underperform next day**. When volume z-score ≥2, next-day avg ≈ -0.23% vs +0.73% otherwise → be careful buying the "obvious" high-volume move.

- **Overnight > intraday**. Cumulative **overnight** returns dominate intraday in your sample; holding from close→open has contributed more to total growth than trading just open→ close.

Always carefully double-check the results. These are nice starting points for further investigation, and this sort of open-ended query will often yield some cool ideas that you never would have thought of.

When you go through a list of ideas like this, keep in mind that the LLM has only been trained using brute-force data mined without regard for the accuracy or current relevance of any of that information. What you hope to extract are patterns that make sense and might have some reasonable explanation. You can't just run with every one of these patterns and expect it to work out of sample. That is risky data mining.

Be creative and ask dumb and open-ended questions to your favorite LLM. You will occasionally find gems in the output.

4. Using LLMs to get unbiased feedback on sentiment

I follow the cover of The Economist because it's an excellent reverse indicator[13]. In order to go the other way when The Economist comes out, you need to make a subjective determination of whether a cover is clearly directional, then you need to decide which security to trade based on that cover. This can be tricky.

For example, I might publish a note saying that a cover of The Economist is bearish USA so I am going long dollars. Readers will argue a) the cover isn't clearly bearish or b) I should trade stocks, or some other expression of the view. By putting the covers of The Economist into an LLM, I get an unbiased interpretation and a recommendation for what security to trade. While I won't always agree with the output, at least it's a starting point towards an unbiased interpretation of the information.

Here is the prompt I use (prompt by Adam Donnelly, upgraded with help from Shalenie Devi):

> 🧠 **Magazine Cover Capital — Prompt with Confidence Scores**
>
> 🔍 **IMPORTANT**
> When proceeding to Step 2, it is critical that you use real-time stock data by searching the internet to fetch the current price of the asset. Do NOT return any stock charts in your response. Only textual and numeric information should be included.
>
> 📋 **Step 1: Qualification Criteria (with Confidence Scores)**

[13] See here: www.spectramarkets.com/amfx/the-magazine-cover-indicator/

Evaluate if the magazine cover meets the following four criteria. Provide:
- ✅ or ❌ to indicate if it passes
- A confidence score (1–5)
- A short one-line justification

Criterion	Pass?	Confidence (1-5)	Justification
Asset Focus	✅/❌	#	[Insert 1-line explanation]
Strong Predictive Statement	✅/❌	#	[Insert 1-line explanation]
Obvious to Layperson	✅/❌	#	[Insert 1-line explanation]
Tradability	✅/❌	#	[Insert 1-line explanation]

📝 Confidence Score Guide

- 5: Extremely obvious and direct (e.g., "Bitcoin: The End of Money")
- 4: Clear prediction, but not extreme
- 3: Subtle or debatable
- 2: Only implied or requires interpretation
- 1: Not present at all

✅ Step 2: If ALL 4 criteria are met, return the following trade setup:

```
asset: "[Name or ticker]"
implied_market_sentiment: "[Bullish or Bearish]"
contrarian_trade_direction: "[Long or Short]"
current_price: "$[Real-time price]"
meme_stock: "[Yes or No]"
  entry: "$[Suggested entry point]"
  stop: "$[Suggested stop-loss level]"
  target: "$[Profit target]"
time_horizon: "[e.g., 1M / 6M / 1Y]"
```

📉 Step 3: sample_trade

Write a short paragraph explaining the trade idea, using sentiment, price level context (round numbers, support/resistance), and risk/reward logic. Avoid charts.

❌ If ANY of the 4 criteria are NOT met:

Return:

"Cover does not meet all criteria for a contrarian signal."

I fed ChatGPT the cover image at right, along with the long prompt described above. Always think of this stuff is brainstorming, not searching for exact or correct answers.

Aug 2nd 2025
Greenlash

Output from ChatGPT:

Criterion	Pass?	Confidence (1–5)	Justification
Asset Focus	☑	4	The cover centers on "Greenlash," clearly referencing green energy (wind power), though not naming a single tradable asset directly.
Strong Predictive Statement	☑	4	The bold headline implies a backlash against green energy, suggesting a bearish forward-looking narrative.
Obvious to Layperson	☑	5	The giant wind turbine on a bright green background and the word "Greenlash" make the message immediately clear.
Tradability	☑	4	While it doesn't specify a ticker, the implied trade is in renewable energy stocks/ETFs, which are easily tradable.

```
trade_setup:
  asset: "iShares Global Clean Energy ETF (ICLN)"
  implied_market_sentiment: "Bearish"
  contrarian_trade_direction: "Long"
  current_price: "$13.62"   # real-time price fetched Aug 21, 2025
     entry: "$13.60"
   stop: "$12.40"
   target: "$16.00"
  time_horizon: "6M"
```

sample_trade

> The Economist's "Greenlash" cover implies that green energy is facing headwinds, reinforcing a bearish mainstream view. With ICLN trading near $13.60, close to multi-year support around $13, the contrarian setup favors a long position. The stop is placed slightly below $12.40 to protect against deeper downside, while the target at $16.00 reflects a return to the prior resistance zone. The risk/reward ratio is favorable, and the trade anticipates a sentiment rebound within 6 months as clean energy capital flows return.

Not too shabby! The idea went long at $13.60 on August 2, 2025, and on October 15 the stock was trading 24% higher at $16.88. But again, **be wary**. Think of an LLM as a super smart analyst who loves to microdose psilocybin. Smart, but prone to convincingly realistic hallucinations.

I hope these examples give you a sense of some of the different ways that LLMs can help you trade. The output is only as smart as the questions you ask. Be creative. Mess around. Try different ideas. You will be pleasantly surprised.

BTW, if you come up with any cool tricks, please let me know. I don't check my social media DMs anymore because of spam; so please email me.

r/wallstreetbets

> "Give me tendies or give me death 💎🙌🚀🚀🚀"
>
> riskforbisque69 (r/wallstreetbets)

Social media traders on r/wallstreetbets (WSB) and other forums were briefly a world-changing force of nature. But that only lasted for a few awesome months in 2021. Now, they are mostly a reflection of silly money and the Greater Fool theory. Skim WSB for ideas and to gauge sentiment. Then make money (carefully) going the other way.

The GameStop story was one of the most exciting and well-documented speculative anomalies in the history of financial markets. But now that everybody knows that everybody knows that wallstreetbets triggers only short-term moves and rip-roaring gamma squeezes, the trade is almost always to go the other way.

Nobody has diamond hands anymore. There is no social movement behind wallstreetbets. Every ape is now doing the same thing: Trying to watch all the other apes and get in and get out faster than they do. This is textbook greater fool theory as every trader buying a meme stock or WSB pump knows that every other trader will be looking for the exit from the fire at the disco at roughly the same time—and not everyone will get out alive. So instead of the old skyrocketing moves like we saw with GME, AMC, and a few other stocks in 2021, the moves are shaped like dunce caps.

Recently, we saw this with stocks like Opendoor (OPEN), Krispy Kreme (DNUT), and Kohl's Stores (KSS). These are three businesses of questionable economic strength that saw flurries of speculative interest from the WSB crew in July 2025. Here are the charts:

Three WSB raids (5-minute charts)

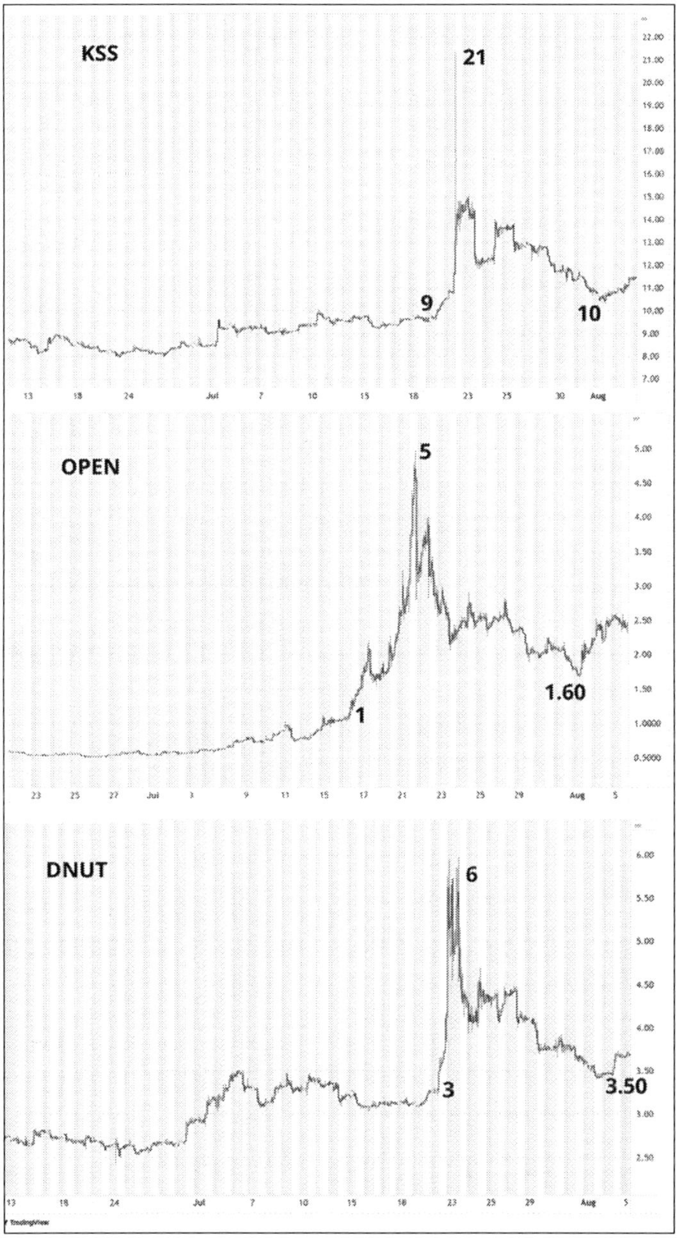

Note: Not every fade works forever. We are playing the odds here, and the time horizon for the fade is one or two weeks. Some of these stocks went on to make new highs, most didn't.

Like interest in fidget spinners, memestock interest is intense. It burns briefly bright, then fizzles fast. The pattern tends to be similar with all these stocks. Interest picks up, the stock rips for a few days, everyone tries to take profit at the same time, momentum fades, and price gives back about 80% of the move.

Here are three ways to play these events:

1. Monitor WSB and StockTwits for sentiment and try to get in early. You need to be extremely well tapped in to do this. Ride it for 2x or 3x and get out.

2. Short around 10:30 a.m. after retail has gone all in and hope for the best. This is insanely risky because the high in moves like this is completely arbitrary and impossible to predict. Your position needs to be small, or your timing needs to be perfect, or you will get rinsed. I don't love this strategy, but I have done it a few times with medium success. To do it, you should watch trading volume and wait for a few hours after a massive volume spike before even *thinking about* thinking about getting involved. Or scale in with small size and an extremely wide stop loss.

3. My preferred method: sell call spreads over the course of one or two days. For example, in Kohl's, I sold a $15/$17 call spread when the stock was trading at $15. You won't get tremendous leverage doing this, but you will have zero risk of ruin, pretty decent returns, and high expected value. I did 1-week options in this case, but you can go further out if you want to try to collect more premium. I prefer a hit and run approach and when these things boot off into gamma squeeze mania, the short-dated options skyrocket in price. That allows you to collect meaningful premium by selling spreads. Your timing doesn't have to be perfect, your strikes don't have to be perfect, and you can't blow up.

Of the three strategies listed here, #3 is my usual approach when WSB raids take place. #1 is too hard and #2 is too risky and annoying. Selling call spreads is a useful template for how to trade any time something goes completely crazy and you want to take the other side.

By definition, implied volatility will become highly correlated with the direction of the move, so selling vol in the direction of the move will do well when things settle down. That's a nice benefit to selling call spreads into a ripper or selling put spreads into a collapse. When the price stabilizes, volatility will normalize, and you have an opportunity to then ride the spread to maturity or take it off at much cheaper levels.

To give you a sense of how the options prices moved around the KSS raid by WSB, take a look at the price of the 19SEP $15 calls.

Kohl's (KSS) 19SEP $15 Calls

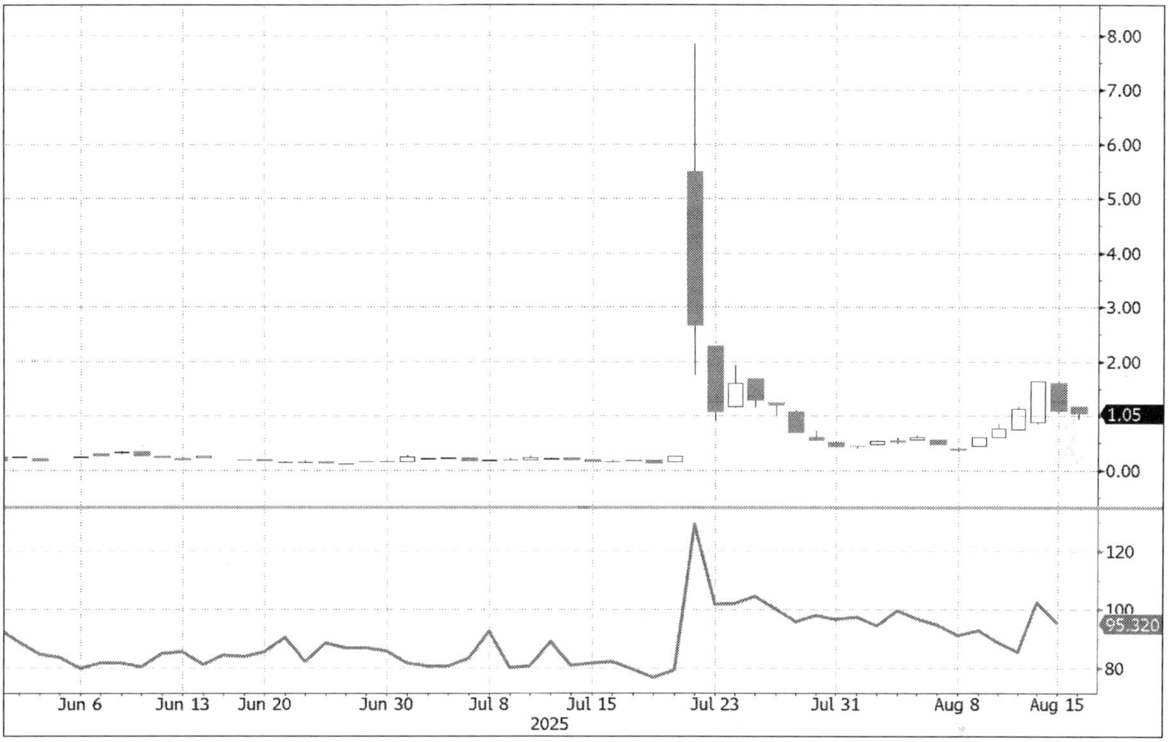

The top panel shows the price of the calls while the bottom panel shows the implied volatility (IV). You can see that IV peaked around 130% on the day the stock spiked, then quickly dropped down below 100% almost immediately. As of mid-August, even though the stock is still trading $14 (the same level it closed on July 22), the 19SEP option lost 80% of its value due to time decay and falling IV. The Beyond Meat ripper was even more extreme, with implied volatility rising above **800%**!

I am relating this strategy to WSB stock raids, but it can also be useful on dislocations in other markets. The blowup in short-term interest rates after the fall of Silvergate Bank in March 2023 is another example where selling call spreads (in SOFR or U.S. 2-year notes) was juicy because once prices settled, vol collapsed. This is not like selling calls outright, because when you do spreads, your loss is capped. If you're wrong, you still get to come to work the next day.

When I suggest trades like this where you are risking $1 to make $1, many of my clients shy away. They want leverage. But good trading is not about seeking maximum leverage. Successful short-term trading is about making many positive Expected Value (EV) bets, over and over and over. You need to think about trades in terms of **expected value, not leverage**. There is no law that says every trade should pay 3:1. Trades that pay 8:1 are often terrible bets: bad trades with good optics.

In fact, the more leverage you get, the lower your EV, *ceteris paribus*, because cheap options tend to be overpriced. Nobody wants to sell you that super cheap lottery ticket; to get someone to do so, you will frequently need to pay a price above EV.

Conversely, there is no law that says that all 8:1 bets are bad. Look at every trade in terms of its EV and make as many positive EV bets as you can in a year. Then the law of large numbers kicks in, variance dissipates, and you become a steady earner. Good traders mix high-leverage and low-leverage bets. They are willing to be long or short carry. They don't have a favorite stock or a favorite asset. They see trading as a never-ending series of small and medium-sized (and occasionally piggish) bets. Some pay off, some don't.

Principle 13: Professional traders maximize expected value, not leverage.

Most people on WSB are not trading to make money. They might say they are, but they are not. They are trading for fun, or for clout. They buy lotto tickets so they can screenshot big gains and they go all in on a single trade knowing worst case they have some juicy loss porn for Reddit karma. A huge loss is just as sexy as a huge gain when your main goal is high fives and upvotes on social media. WSB is the ultimate outpost for traders who look to markets for stimulation, gambling, in-group validation, and LOLs. As a trader who is here for the money, not the memes, you should always be ready to (carefully) take the other side of whatever they are doing.

Yes, there are talented traders on **r/wallstreetbets**. And there are, of course, examples like Roaring Kitty who made cartloads. But then again, there are 19 million people on WSB. Let's imagine 1 million of them are degenerate "traders" and they each flip a coin once a month. Let's ask ChatGPT what that might look like.

A thought experiment for ChatGPT

PROMPT

1 million people start with $10,000 each on day 1. They each flip a coin once per month for one year (12 times). If it's heads, they double their money and if it's tails they lose everything. After one year, how many traders will be left and how much money will they have?

RESPONSE

About 244 traders will still have money, and each of those will have $40,960,000.

Why:

To still have money after 12 months you must get 12 heads in a row, which happens with probability (1/2)^12 = 1/4096

Expected survivors: 1,000,000/4096 = 244.14 = about 244 people (binomial mode is 244).

Each survivor's balance: $10,000 * 2^12 = $10,000 X 4096 = $40,960,000.

Fun logic check: the expected total wealth stays 1,000,000 X $10,000 = $10 billion, just concentrated in a tiny group of big winners while almost everyone else ends with $0.

Roaring Kitty ended up with around $50 million at one point. Real life WSB results are certainly much worse than one million people starting with $10,000 and flipping a coin 12 times for one year. On WSB, a tiny fraction gets rich. Most end with zero. It's ergodicity, baby. Roaring Kitty is probably King of the Coin Flippers.

Flipping coins with limited capital will normally lead to ruin, but sometimes the path will look like this in the interim!

A screenshot from a random dude on WSB

There are smart people on WSB and there are some good ideas. But mostly r/wallstreetbets is a subreddit where people with fun money go to set it on fire and cheer and laugh as they watch it burn. Find opportunities to take the other side of the pumps and do it in a way that eliminates risk of ruin.

Prediction markets

> "All voting is a sort of gaming, like checkers or backgammon, with a slight moral tinge to it, a playing with right and wrong, with moral questions; and betting naturally accompanies it."
>
> Henry David Thoreau, *Civil Disobedience*, 1849

There are many ways to figure out what is priced into markets. For interest rates, we derive policy expectations from forward curves. For economic data releases, we use the median from a survey of economists' forecasts. For earnings, we look at analyst previews. But these sources can be biased, and they don't cover every event you might want to know about. Enter: Prediction Markets.

Heisenberg's uncertainty principle says we cannot simultaneously know both the position and momentum of a particle with perfect accuracy. The more precisely we measure one property, the less accurately we can know the other. This principle is a fundamental concept in quantum mechanics, emphasizing that observation itself alters the reality being observed.

The wisdom of crowds operates on a seemingly opposite principle. When diverse individuals make independent judgments about the same question, their collective answer often proves remarkably accurate. The more we measure, the more accurate the average answer becomes. Francis Galton famously discovered this in 1907 when he observed that the average of 800 people guessing the weight of a particular ox was almost exactly correct, despite the individual guesses varying widely.

In financial markets, the act of observing or analyzing a security can influence its price. Traders and investors react to news and analysis, which in turn affects price movements, and then traders and investors react to movements in price itself, making it difficult to determine whether a market price is in or out of equilibrium. In other words, markets are self-referential. People see the price going up and assume the market knows something, and so they buy. Trend following systems and humans see the price going up, and so they buy.

Behavior drives price and price drives behavior.

The wisdom of crowds is closely tied to the Efficient Market Hypothesis (EMH), which suggests that asset prices reflect all available information because they are determined by the collective judgment of market participants. According to this view, stock prices incorporate all known factors, making it nearly impossible for any individual to consistently outperform the market. Evidence strongly suggests that EMH, while roughly accurate, is not strictly true.

From *Alpha Trader*:

> Most of the time, the errors made by buyers and sellers cancel out and the average of all the transactions is some approximation of a reasonable equilibrium price. This outcome is similar to the jellybean experiment. In that experiment, a crowd of people are asked to guess how many jellybeans are in a jar. The interesting result is that the crowd (the average of all guesses) is always very accurate and often more accurate than ANY individual in the entire crowd. This is astounding and suggests you should be humble when trying to beat the market.
>
> Instead of a bunch of undergrads guessing how many jellybeans are in the jar, imagine 1,000 highly-trained quants who have millions of dollars to invest in jellybean estimation technology. Do you think you can beat them? That's a more apt analogy for the markets.

This collective intelligence underlies the theoretical efficiency of markets. When many participants independently assess value and trade accordingly, prices should converge toward true value. However, market prices frequently deviate from this ideal, rational equilibrium for several key reasons. Let's go through them one by one.

1. Correlation of errors

The wisdom of crowds requires independence of individual guesses. When market participants influence each other through herding behavior, social media, or shared information sources, their errors become correlated, not random. Unlike random errors that cancel out, correlated errors compound, leading to bubbles and crashes. Imagine the jellybean experiment, conducted in a large classroom, but before anyone submits a guess, the smartest kid in the room yells:

> "It's exactly 302 jellybeans! I'm positive!"

Would the wisdom of the crowd still be accurate? Or would it skew away from fair value and towards 302? This is what happens when smart-sounding people talk to less-informed or less confident investors.

2. Information asymmetry

Markets assume all participants have access to the same information. In reality, insiders often possess privileged knowledge. In the jellybean example, imagine a student who came early to class and counted the jellybeans before anyone else arrived.

3. Emotional and psychological biases

Human decision-making deviates systematically from rationality. Confirmation bias leads investors to seek information supporting existing beliefs. Herding makes one trader follow another, or chase price action. Loss aversion causes disproportionate reactions to losses versus gains. FOMO makes people buy high and sell low. Narratives are more powerful than data, so people favor stories over objective information. These, and many other biases drive markets away from rational pricing.

4. Liquidity constraints

Even when individuals correctly identify mispriced assets, they may lack the capital to exploit these opportunities sufficiently to correct prices. Or transaction costs may be too high to make it worthwhile. This creates persistent inefficiencies that would not exist in perfectly liquid markets.

5. Unforeseeable events

In the jellybean experiment, the number of jellybeans in the jar doesn't change. But markets are not static. The right answer is constantly changing. External factors such as geopolitical events, natural disasters, and unpredictable changes in monetary and fiscal policy (for example) mean that even a crowd with perfect wisdom could nail the "correct" value for a security today and be wrong tomorrow. Markets are not a single event with a final outcome. They are an ongoing, never-ending series of auctions.

6. Incentives

Traders and investors are not always trying to find the right answer. Sometimes they are trying to minimize regret, avoid getting fired, keep up with the trader sitting next to them, or stick to a benchmark.

In the jellybean game, imagine the rules are changed. Now, a participant fails the class if they guess a number *below* the true value. **Everyone will guess high**, and the average will be predictably wrong. This is the equivalent of how everyone will own tech stocks, even overvalued tech stocks, during a big rally because they know if they don't, they'll underperform their peers. And thus, tech stock prices remain high until the incentives change.

Markets face their own uncertainty principle. The act of observation (trading) changes the system being observed (prices), especially when participants react to each other's actions rather than independently assessing value. Every time someone expresses an opinion in the market, the price of the asset they express an opinion on can change.

The tension between these concepts reveals that while collective intelligence can produce remarkable insights, it requires specific conditions that markets often violate. Understanding these limitations helps explain why markets periodically fail to harness the wisdom of crowds effectively, and why prices sometimes reflect collective madness, not wisdom.

A critical difference between the jellybean game and markets, one that brings us back to the topic of prediction markets, is that the jellybean game has a correct answer while many markets do not. I say "many markets" because there are markets that will settle at a specific and correct answer.

Overnight Index Swap (OIS) and Fed Funds futures markets are direct bets on the outcome of a central bank meeting. If you bet on a 0.25% Bank of Canada rate cut via OIS, and that's what happens—you win. In contrast, a bet on TSLA stock never resolves to a correct answer. It's a perpetual, never-ending bet, unless the company goes bankrupt and the stock price resolves to zero, or the company is bought out.

Prediction markets are more like the jellybean game. There is one correct answer, and a specific time at which the contract will settle. This makes them interesting and useful both as trading instruments and as accurate, often unbiased sources of collective wisdom about events and outcomes directly related to trading. You can learn a lot about the crowd by studying prediction market prices.

A brief history of prediction markets

Prediction markets can be powerful forecasting tools that outperform experts. They show specific implied probabilities for important events by creating strong monetary incentives for participants to invest significant time and effort in accurate forecasts. The result is that prediction markets yield useful information and forecast accuracy and can be used to enhance your trading and investing process.

Prediction markets are structured betting platforms where participants stake real money on future outcomes, generating prices that can be interpreted as probabilities. When a market says Donald Trump has a 70% chance of winning the election, it is not a polling average or biased pundit speculation. It is the wisdom of the crowds. Much as bettors on a football game converge on stunningly accurate odds, prediction markets offer impressive wisdom.

Before we go through how prediction markets work, and how you can use them to improve your trading, let's look at how we got from back-alley bets on gladiator combat in Ancient Rome to crypto-native blockchain-powered forecasting platforms like Polymarket.

Ancient roots

Humans have always had a thing for predicting the future and betting on those predictions. The Romans bet on chariot races and gladiatorial combat. The Chinese gambled on imperial examination outcomes. These weren't sophisticated markets, but they established the core concept: when money's on the line, predictions sharpen. The first formal prediction markets allowed betting on 18th century British politics.

But the real story, the one that matters for modern markets, starts much later.

Original political betting markets

Before Nate Silver and CNN's Magic Wall, Wall Street brokers ran sophisticated election betting markets. From the 1880s through the 1940s, these weren't shady backroom operations; they were legitimate, well-organized markets with serious volume.

In the 1916 election cycle (Woodrow Wilson vs. Charles Hughes), over $293 million changed hands[14]. Election betting turnover regularly reached 50% of campaign spending and once went as high as two times what was spent on all campaigns combined[15]. Here's a paragraph from a paper by Rhode and Strumpf:

> The extent of activity in the presidential betting markets of this time was astonishingly large. For brief periods, betting on political outcomes at the Curb Exchange in New York would exceed trading in stocks and bonds. Crowds formed in the financial district—on the Curb or in the lobby of the New York Stock Exchange—and brokers would call out bid and ask odds as if trading securities. In presidential races such as 1896, 1900, 1904, 1916 and 1924, the New York Times, Sun and World provided nearly daily price quotations from early October until Election Day.

Election betting markets were highly accurate. The favorite to win the election one month before Election Day lost only once between 1868 and 1940. The next chart, recreated from Rhode and Strumpf, shows compelling accuracy. I think this accuracy is notable given **there**

---

[14] Figure is 2025 dollars, adjusted for inflation.

[15] "Historical Presidential Betting Markets", Rhode and Strumpf (2004)

were no polls conducted in most of these elections[16] and thus the wisdom of the crowd showed an incredible ability to zoom in on a correct answer without outside guidance.

Democrat Odds vs. Popular Vote Margin in Election Betting, 1884 to 1940

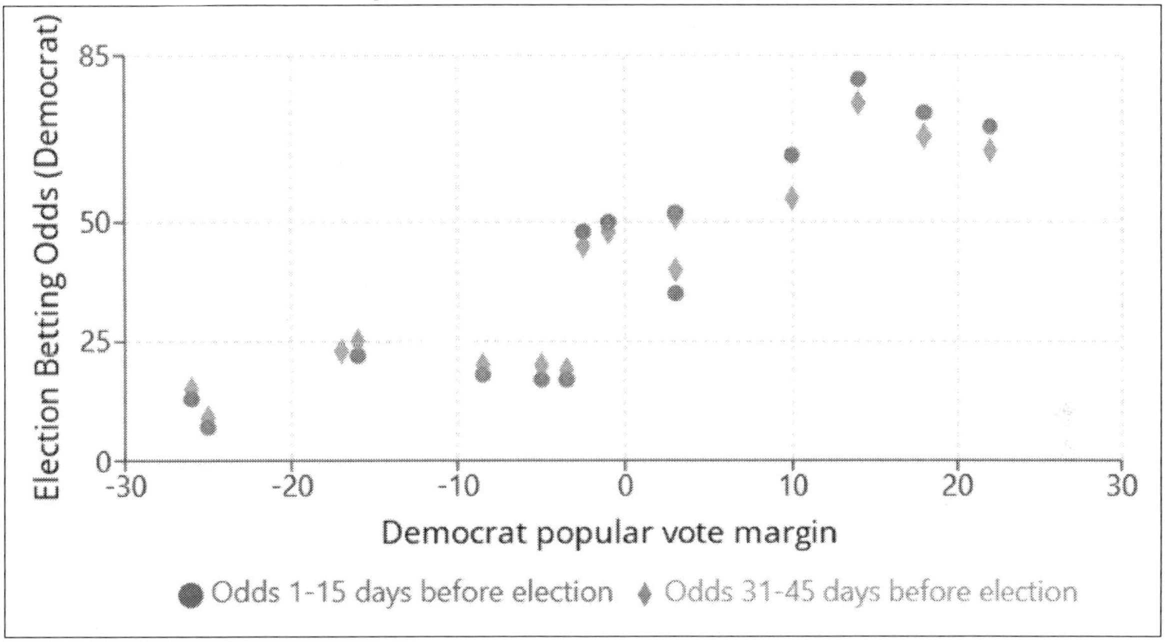

These markets operated simply. Large boards displayed current odds. Brokers matched buyers and sellers. Newspapers reported the odds daily, treating them as the most reliable election forecasts available. The system worked because it aggregated information efficiently, just like prediction markets do today.

Dark ages and renaissance

Increased financial regulations after the Great Depression, combined with a growing moral aversion to wagering, pushed election betting underground after 1930. Election betting withered, and the subsequent rise of scientific polling in the mid-20th century eliminated much of the perceived need for these markets. They slowly disappeared.

Here you can see the frequency of the term: "Election betting" in books published from 1800 to 2022. Note the near disappearance of election betting for almost fifty years and then its rapid resurgence.

---

[16] The first modern U.S. presidential poll was a 1936 Gallup survey.

Google Books word frequency for "election betting" in books 1800 to 2022

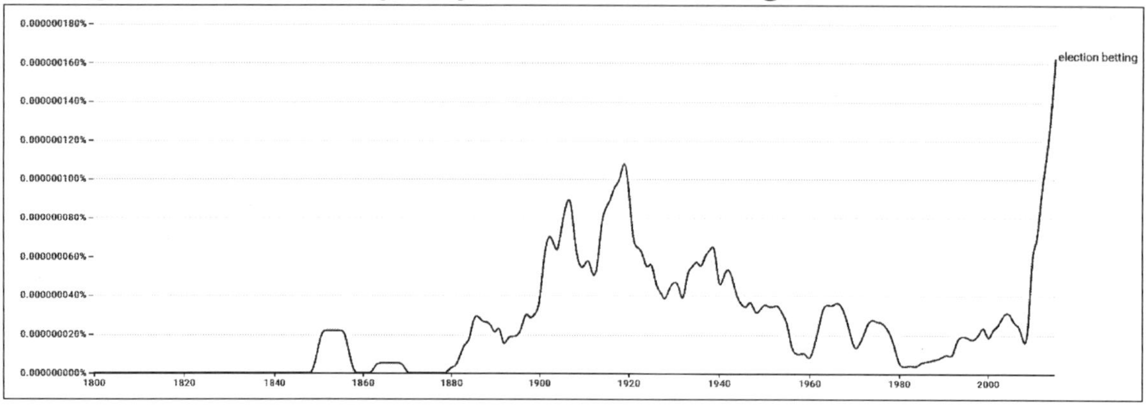

Theoretical underpinnings

The intellectual foundation for prediction markets solidified in the mid-20th century, catalyzed by economic theory. Friedrich Hayek's 1945 essay, *The Use of Knowledge in Society*, offered a seminal insight: markets efficiently aggregate dispersed information through prices and yield superior results to central planning. Hayek's framework, though focused on commodity markets, implied broader applications. Why not harness prices to predict elections or geopolitical shifts? *We will talk more about the Hayek essay in Chapter 10.*

In the U.S., the prediction market concept remained dormant until the 1980s, when the University of Iowa's business school launched "Iowa Electronic Markets" (IEM). Its key innovation was a legal pathway to a prediction market via a no-action letter from the CFTC which allowed the university to run small-scale prediction markets for research purposes.

The IEM showed that even with modest liquidity, prediction markets often outperform professional polling. Skin in the game reveals true beliefs. When people answer polls, they express aspirations or tribal loyalty. And sometimes they lie[17]. But when they place bets, they express their true expectation. This difference has become increasingly important as the rise of populism has led to some grossly erroneous poll results in U.S. and other elections.

As electronic trading revolutionized markets in the 1990s, prediction market technology became cheaper to deploy. Companies like HP, Microsoft, and Google experimented with it internally and found it yielded impressive results. Google's internal markets predicted product launch dates, office openings, and competitor moves with surprising accuracy. The mechanics were simple: create tradable contracts on outcomes, let insiders buy and sell

[17] See, for example: wikipedia.org/wiki/Bradley_effect

based on their private information, and watch the wisdom of crowds emerge through price discovery.

Microsoft ran particularly sophisticated internal markets, finding that predictions aggregated from bets by engineers outperformed official schedules. When engineers could profit from accurately forecasting delays, the truth emerged.

Post-2000 explosion

Three key developments drove prediction markets forward after 2000.

First, academic interest surged. Economists like Robin Hanson, Justin Wolfers, and Eric Zitzewitz documented the efficacy of these markets[18]. Their research showed prediction markets excelled at aggregating dispersed information.

Second, offshore platforms like Intrade created public markets for everything from presidential elections to Saddam Hussein's capture. Intrade's 2008 election betting market famously predicted Obama's 2008 victory within one electoral vote (he won 365-173 over John McCain) while pundits were still calling the race tight until the last minute.

Intrade was the golden child of prediction markets in the early 2000s. Based in Ireland, it allowed traders to bet on global events with real money. But success brought scrutiny. The U.S. Commodity Futures Trading Commission (CFTC) saw Intrade as an unregulated derivatives market rather than a harmless forecasting tool. In 2011, Intrade's CEO died fifty yards short of the peak of Mount Everest and that opened a Pandora's box of legal issues for the company. In 2012, the CFTC cracked down, effectively barring U.S. traders from participating. By 2013, Intrade had collapsed due to financial and legal issues, leaving a void in the market.

The third key development for prediction markets was the rise of blockchain technology. Platforms like Augur, FTX and Polymarket leveraged smart contracts to create prediction markets that operated beyond traditional regulatory boundaries. Smart contracts make for easy and rapid settlement and they're a natural fit for the mechanics of prediction market trading.

One salient feature of the 2020 election was the ability to track market pricing of the outcome in real time via the FTX BIDEN token. At that time, FTX was a new and exciting platform promising to tokenize everything. Sam Bankman-Fried (SBF) was a crypto wunderkind who had found a way to arbitrage global crypto markets and turn $10 million into $10 billion.

---

[18] See "Interpreting Prediction Market Prices as Probabilities", Wolfers and Zitzewitz (2006), for example.

At right is a screenshot I published the day after the 2020 election. Sorry if it's blurry; I can't seem to log in to my FTX account.

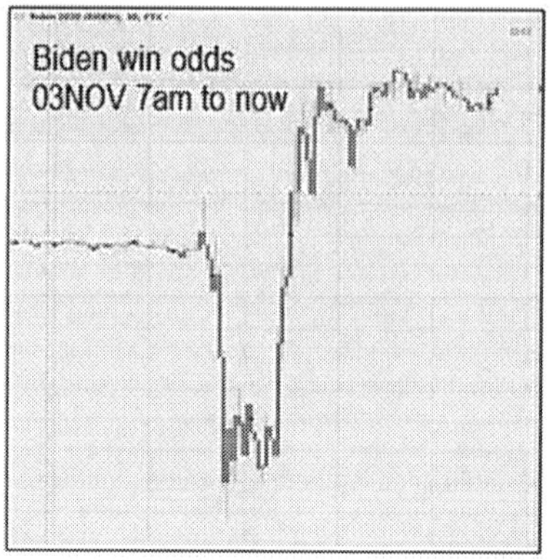

In ye olden days of 2020 we were tracking the BIDEN token on FTX and watching the New York Times needle fly. Now we have more sophisticated methods as U.S. courts have overruled the CFTC and those who do not find U.S. election psychodrama stressful enough can now add risk of personal financial ruin to the potential election outcomes. We now live in the "let's gamble on everything" world and that has unleashed a bunch of great tools for real-time event analysis.

Institutional phase

By the 2020s, prediction markets moved from novelty to mainstream. Kalshi's October 2024 court victory over the CFTC represents a watershed moment, opening the door to fully regulated election prediction markets in the United States. Now Kalshi, Polymarket, and many other platforms offer odds not just on elections, but on a nearly-infinite list of matters both relevant and totally irrelevant to markets. Even Robinhood and Interactive Brokers are in on the game now. As these platforms gain legitimacy, the distinction between gambling, forecasting, trading, and investment becomes increasingly blurred.

As of September 2025, Kalshi is more and more of a sports gambling website as a majority of their volume is not political or other events, it's sports. This shows how the world of prediction markets continues to evolve and the use cases continue to change.

Kalshi Daily Volumes

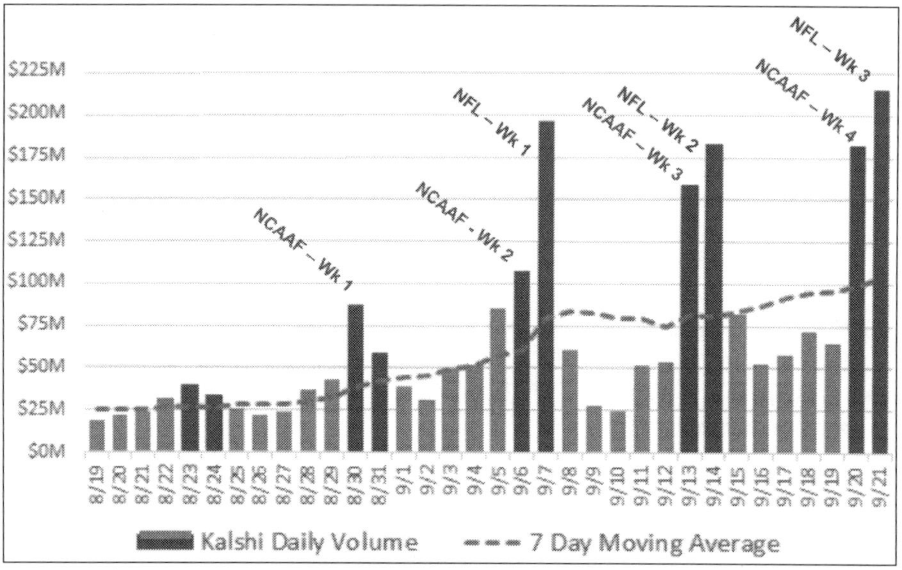

How to use prediction markets

OK, that's the background. But how do we use these things to make money? For professional traders, the significance of prediction markets goes beyond their literal forecasts. They provide:

- Clear information on what is priced in for various events
- Efficient information aggregation when news breaks
- Calibration tools for your own forecasting process
- Early signals of regime shifts or market surprises

Prediction markets aren't perfect. They are not oracles. They are simply an aggregation of human expectations. They can suffer from:

- Thin liquidity
- Credit risk
- Cross-border limitations on arbitrage
- Favorite/longshot bias
- Political bias when traders bet on hopes rather than expectations

Major hedge funds and prop shops now incorporate prediction market data into their models, recognizing that even imperfect aggregation of information provides signal amid noise. Before we look at examples, here's a brief explainer on how they work.

Prediction markets are financial exchanges where participants buy and sell contracts based on the outcome of future events. Unlike traditional markets where you're trading assets, in prediction markets you're betting on probabilities.

The core mechanism is simple: contracts pay out a fixed amount ($1) if a specific event occurs, and zero if it doesn't. The beauty is in the simplicity of pricing; a contract trading at $0.65 means the market collectively believes there's a 65% chance the event happens.

These markets are theoretically zero-sum games. Note, however, that fees are significant on Kalshi! And you are often paying away bid/offer spread.

Let's say a market is trading 48/50 on Kalshi, and you buy $1,000 worth at 50. You're paying $500, which is $10 of bid/offer from mid, plus $17.50 of fees for a total leakage of $27.50 on a $500 notional trade. That's 5.5%! Compared to TradFi markets, that's an enormous fee; it's even more than the standard juice on sports gambling with a bookie[19]. **The high fees are one reason I am not a fan of using these platforms** for anything other than information gathering purposes, and certainly never for trading outcomes on TradFi markets like the

[19] www.sportsbettingdime.com/guides/research/standard-juice-charged/

S&P 500 or crypto. For every buyer expecting a YES outcome, there's a seller expecting NO. The price discovery comes from this constant tug-of-war between opposing views.

Let's walk through a practical example. You see a contract for "Will Bitcoin hit $100,000 by December 31?" currently trading at 40. At this price, the market is saying there's a 40% chance of BTC hitting $100K. But you're bullish - you think the probability is closer to 60%. So you buy 100 contracts at $0.40 each = $40 total investment.

Two possible scenarios follow:

1. Bitcoin hits $100K

Each contract pays $1, giving you $100 total ($60 profit, minus $1.68 in fees), or

2. Bitcoin never reaches $100k

Your contracts are worthless (you lose your $40, plus $1.68 in fees).

Like I said, I prefer to use prediction markets as free information, not as expensive gambling platforms. Let's look at a few examples and go through some of the benefits and pitfalls of using prediction markets in your trading process.

Example 1: Nailing down what's priced in for economic data

But wait! Why would I need prediction markets to know what's priced in for economic data? I already have Bloomberg and Reuters and all that.

There are myriad reasons economist forecasts are predictably wrong. As discussed earlier, the wisdom of crowds suggests forecasting errors should cancel out as some portion of the sample will be too optimistic and another portion will be too pessimistic.

The wisdom of crowds, however, relies on unbiased and properly incentivized forecasters. In the case of economic data forecasting, this condition does not hold and thus there are repeated, predictable errors in consensus economic forecasts. Understanding these errors and using prediction markets to identify them, will help you capitalize on the errors and avoid making them yourself. Let's examine five reasons economist surveys are biased.

1. Herding and clustering
2. Overreliance on models
3. Anchoring bias
4. Stale forecasts
5. Confirmation bias and religiosity

1. Herding and clustering

Economists tend to herd around this central expectation: *actual economic outcomes are much more widely distributed than surveys suggest*. They mostly do this to avoid looking stupid.

Say you are an economist, and you think the number (some economic release) will come in strong. Your model shows the number is going to be SUPER STRONG. Still, there is not much incentive for you to put in an extremely high forecast. If you put a forecast way above everyone else and the number comes in low, you look stupid. If you submit a forecast just a bit higher than everyone else, then no matter how strong the number is, you look smart! And if the number is weak, at least you weren't too far away from the crowd.

This type of gaming is a way they manage career risk, and you will notice over time, and evidence supports, that actual data releases show much more dispersion than the heavily-clustered forecasts would suggest, even though surprises are common.

Herding around the mean is rational if you want to avoid looking stupid or getting fired, but as a market professional you need to be aware that the data is not clustered the way the forecasts imply. Economic numbers, like financial market returns, are not *normally distributed*—they have fat tails. A lack of imagination can catch you by surprise so you should assume that anything can happen, even if nobody is forecasting it!

To illustrate, here is every **estimate** for UK month-over-month CPI from January 2020 to mid-2023 and every **actual** release in a histogram. It's an excellent example of how economists cluster around the median and the dispersion of forecasts is wildly miscalibrated due to risk aversion and herding. The gray bars (the forecasts) are normally distributed around 0% while the actual releases (black bars) are massively skewed higher and generally all over the place.

UK MoM CPI readings, actual vs. estimates, January 2020 to mid-2023

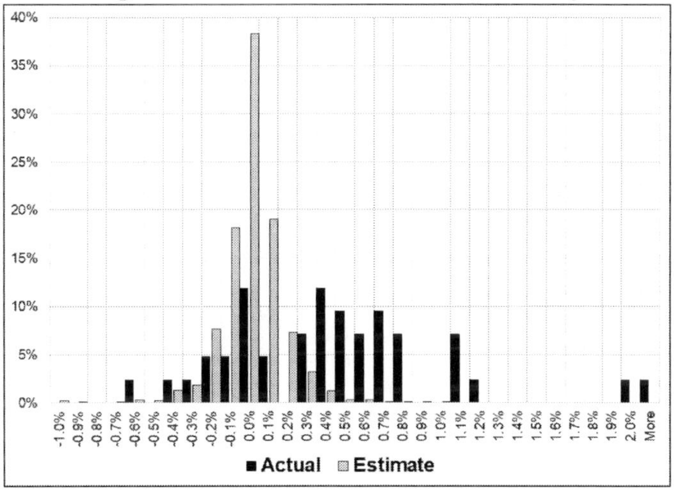

This also reveals that asking economists for point estimates instead of a probabilistic range is not ideal. If you were at the bar the night before UK CPI and you asked your economist:

> "Where do you think UK CPI is going to come in tomorrow?"

He might answer something like:

> "I dunno mate, maybe 0.5% to 1.0% kinda thing? Get me another Tanqueray and Tonic, would you?"

He would likely give a range, but surveys need to use point estimates to calculate a median expectation. This exacerbates a tendency to cluster around the most obvious answer while eliminating less likely, but reasonable answers elsewhere in the distribution.

2. Overreliance on models

Models are great. But they can be wrong. Economists and analysts that rely exclusively on models tend to miss big economic transitions and suffer from an inability to adapt to new regimes. Many models are regime-sensitive: they will work great in one environment but then break down and become useless during a paradigm shift.

The standard model for predicting NFP, for example, estimates demand for workers and then uses this to predict the jobs report. The problem is, after COVID, the dominant constraint on job creation was the *supply* of workers, not the *demand* for workers. Therefore, in 2021 economists **overestimated** job creation because there was a huge shortage of workers. In 2023, economists **underestimated** job creation because many workers who left the job market due to COVID returned to the workforce.

The next chart shows the number of times in a row NFP came in higher than economists' forecasts. Their models completely broke in 2023.

Streak of NFP releases stronger or weaker than expected, 2000 to 2023

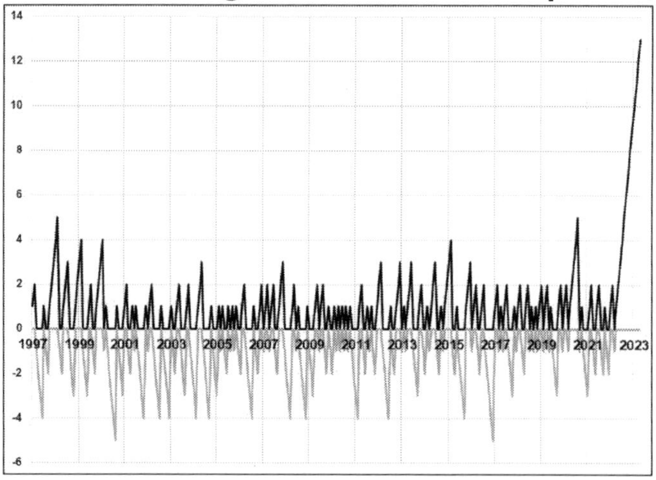

Below is the absolute size of the misses (**actual** nonfarm payrolls vs. median economist **forecast**) from 2021 to 2023.

Nonfarm payrolls (actual release minus economist forecast), 2021 to 2023

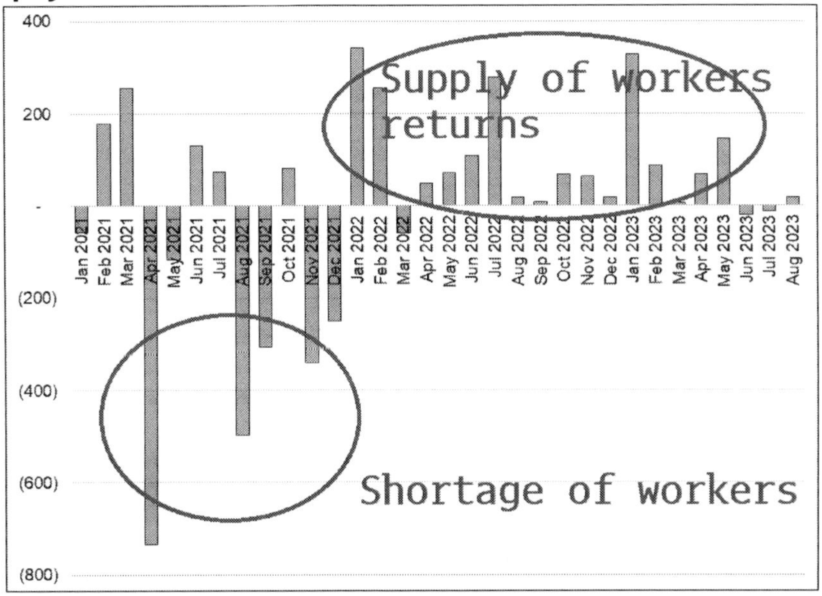

Economists missed NFP in both directions as workers first left the workforce, then returned. Models tend to extrapolate the current regime and perform poorly when regimes shift.

3. Anchoring bias

Analyst and economist forecasts (and human forecasts in general) often rely on *anchoring bias*: when we are asked to predict something, we tend toward the first reference point offered.

Outside of finance, this is commonly seen in negotiations. If we are told the price of a car is $12,000, anything below that feels cheap, while anything above feels expensive. Even if we find out later that the car is only worth $10,000, we still find ourselves anchored on the initial price. Research has proven this.

A simple anchoring experiment: Subjects draw a random number from 1 to 100 out of a bag. Then, they are asked to guess (for example) how many African countries are in the United Nations. Those drawing low numbers offer consistently lower guesses than those who drew higher numbers out of the bag. It makes no sense, but it's true!

Another famous example of anchoring is to ask someone to quickly estimate 1 X 2 X 3 X 4 X 5 X 6 X 7 X 8, you typically get a much lower answer than if you ask them to quickly estimate 8 X 7 X 6 X 5 X 4 X 3 X 2 X 1.

Economists anchor on prior economic data. If the nonfarm payrolls (NFP) number was +325,000 last month and all signs point to a much lower number this month, research shows that economists will tend to anchor on the prior number, and their forecasts (on average) will be too high.

As an economist, if your complex econometric model says that this month NFP should be +38,000, but last month's number was +325,000, your prediction feels kinda low. You will be inclined to submit a number that sounds a bit less extreme or "more rational" like +100,000. In fact, that number is less rational due to anchoring bias.

If you trade the economic data, look for moments when this month's data is expected to be significantly different from last month's. Then, assume the actual outcome will show an EVEN LARGER discrepancy than expected.

4. Stale forecasts

An important hallmark of economists' forecasts is that they are often stale. In other words, economists don't update them every day. Most just submit one forecast a week or two before the economic release and leave it at that.

In the meantime, as the event approaches, new information may come out that would allow a Bayesian forecaster to update their prior prediction. Good forecasters don't just make a single prediction and stick with it. They update their prediction as new information arises.

Analysts with a deep knowledge of leading indicators can find predictable errors in stale forecasts as the event nears. Imagine the following timeline:

25-27 AUG	Most economists submit their forecast for nonfarm payrolls (median +200,000)
28AUG	ADP (the private jobs report) comes in super weak
29AUG	The jobs component of the ISM survey comes in super weak
29AUG	The jobs component of the Consumer Confidence Survey comes in weak
03SEP	Nonfarm payrolls report is released

Looking at the median forecast submitted 25-27AUG, one could easily guess that there is a predictable error in those forecasts. **They are too strong** because they don't incorporate the new information from ADP, ISM, and Consumer Confidence. As such, betting on a weaker-than-expected nonfarms report probably makes sense.

This sort of analysis is always going to be an exercise in probability. There is no guarantee here that nonfarm payrolls will come in weak. The release is noisy. On the other hand, the balance of probabilities suggests that the forecasts are too high. **If you consistently bet on 60/40 outcomes, you will do well over time.** But you must also understand that you could still be wrong. It's OK to be wrong! Betting on an 60/40 outcome is a good decision, regardless of the outcome.

Let's look at a situation where I used anchoring plus newer, fresher data to predict an economic release where economist forecasts were stale. This is an excerpt from am/FX (my global macro daily) on May 30, 2023.

> Germany and France release CPI tomorrow morning. Economists anchor on previous data so when a series is falling fast, they will almost always underestimate the speed of the fall.
>
> My first inclination, then, as inflation is falling fast in Europe, would be to assume tomorrow's German data will be weak. Add to that, though, the important fact that we have already seen Belgian and Spanish CPI (they came out a few hours ago). There is a very high correlation between levels and changes of Belgian and Spanish CPI with Germany's CPI figure.
>
> Here's a simple overlay of German CPI vs. Spain and Belgium. German CPI has been higher than peers and looks set to drop.

A simple model of German CPI vs. actual CPI releases, 2000 to May 2023

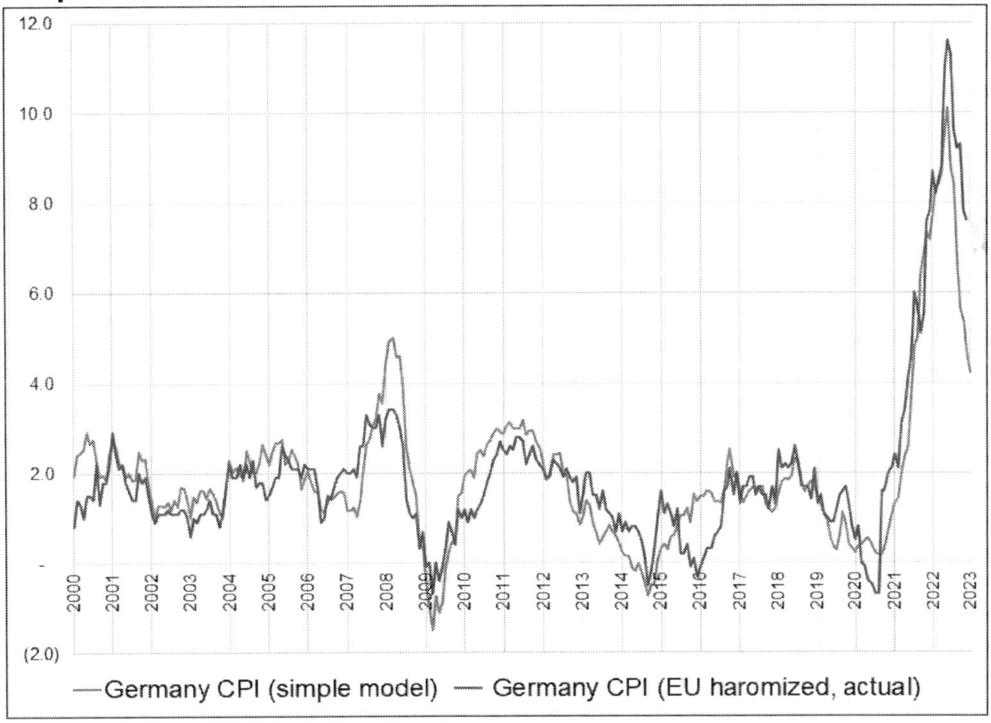

> With German manufacturing in recession, the recent economic data there generally super soft, and China providing zero inflationary impulse... Plus the anchoring effect and the weak Belgium/Spain combo... I would think the odds of a weak German CPI tomorrow are probably 70/30. Short EURGBP is a good expression of this view.

I also posted the analysis on Twitter about 12 hours before the release[20]. Here's how the data came out.

Germany
Economic Releases

	Date Time	A	M	R	Event	Period	Surv(M)	Actual
37)	05/31 08:00				CPI MoM	May P	0.2%	-0.1%
38)	05/31 08:00				CPI YoY	May P	6.5%	6.1%
39)	05/31 08:00				CPI EU Harmonized MoM	May P	0.2%	-0.2%
40)	05/31 08:00				CPI EU Harmonized YoY	May P	6.7%	6.3%

"Surv" is short for "median estimate from the survey of economists". The actual figures came in much weaker than expected and the short EURGBP idea was a big winner.

5. Confirmation bias and religiosity

Economics is often more art than science, but sometimes it's just religion.

If you have read *Alpha Trader*, or any behavioral economics text, you are familiar with confirmation bias. If you don't know about it, give it a Google. It's probably the most important and nefarious behavioral bias.

Nowhere do you see more confirmation bias than in the world of professional economic forecasting. This confirmation bias is bred into economists early, as they tend to subscribe to whatever philosophical school is taught at their alma mater.

As their career progresses, their bias hardens because they become known as the "Freshwater economist" or "Dr. Doom" or "The Passive Investing Boogeyman" or whatever. They become the High Priest(ess) of the particular ideology they preach; they can't allow new information to tarnish it. Economists who are always bullish bonds, for example, will find it economically suboptimal to turn bearish bonds because most of their subscribers are bullish bonds (subscribers also subscribe to feed confirm their own bias!).

If you're the "bitcoin guy", you can't turn bearish bitcoin. If you're the "housing market gonna blow up" girl, you can't turn bullish housing. You will lose too many followers.

---

[20] twitter.com/donnelly_brent/status/1663599879455637650?s=20

These hardened beliefs cause many economists to persistently post forecasts biased towards their worldview. There is so much economic data out there that anyone can always find a bullish or bearish outlook on the U.S. economy by digging through the details, subcomponents, revisions, seasonal adjustments, etc. If you are smart and good with data (which most economists are) you can fudge and cherry-pick your way to either a *recession is imminent* call or an *economic boom* prediction.

A final reason economists have confirmation bias: **Institutional constraints**. If you are head strategist at a major bank, you can't change your view every two months, even if your view in real life has changed! So, you stick with the old view and find evidence to back it up.

Strategists and economists will stick to views they barely believe in because switching costs are high. If you change your mind, you risk looking stupid. You risk looking flip-floppy. And you are less useful as a talking head on TV or in front of corporate clients. Banks want economists and strategists who are 100% confident, all the time. Firms need to have strong views, strongly held, and bang the table on them. They don't want open-minded agnostics who change their mind all the time!

Banks and economists also know who butters their bread. They will be careful not to anger their primary investors and constituents. If I work for a bank that relies on China, I probably won't publish anything bearish on China. If my firm is about to do a secondary for AMZN, I won't publish anything bearish on Amazon. Some views just aren't cool with the powers that be and so economists, analysts, and strategists stay away from them.

Economists rarely have skin in the game. They have no P&L and no stop loss. They can be wrong year after year as long as they remain funny, entertaining, or smart-sounding. Self-preservation and marketing sizzle are often more important than accuracy.

Here's a great quote from Michael Drury, one of the most open-minded and honest economists I know. It's a good behavioral and incentives-based explanation for why there is always so much doom and gloom from mainstream economists.

> We attended the National Association for Business Economics Annual Conference in Philadelphia this week – and our major take away was that despite a generally negative outlook on the macro picture, we did not find many economists who were worried about their particular industry (except housing). This is not unusual, and is part of the reason economics is called the dismal science. As we have often noted, economists are rarely hired to point the way toward growth – that is the job of strategists and CEOs, who more often graduate from business schools. Economists are defense, hired to point out potential pitfalls from changes in government policy, whether monetary, fiscal, or regulatory.

It's hard to find optimistic economists, even in a world where expansion is the norm and recessions are the rare exception. I suppose the assessment, "Things look pretty good—still!—and some stuff is weak but most stuff is fine!" does not sound very smart, even though it's generally the correct view of the U.S. economy.

This is not to say that every economist is biased—**there are many, many excellent, open-minded economists out there**. Some of them are even bullish sometimes! But the biased ones can tilt surveys and expectations if many lean in the same direction.

The beauty of prediction markets is that they overcome the five problems we've discussed:

1. **Herding:** Since betting is anonymous, nobody is afraid of looking stupid by betting very high or very low. People will bet in a way that maximizes profit, not in a way that minimizes fear of looking dumb.

2. **Overreliance on models**: While some bettors will use models to make their bets, others will have a more discretionary approach, so any embedded errors from model bias will be averaged out by the more subjective analysis of other bettors.

3. **Anchoring bias**: Bettors don't care much about what happened last time—all they want to do is make money. So, there will be less anchoring bias.

4. **Stale forecasts:** Unlike economist estimates, which might update weekly (or even less often), prediction markets update in real time. If new information comes out today, you can be sure the new information will be immediately reflected in the new prediction market price.

5. **Confirmation bias and religiosity:** Bettors with confirmation bias will persistently make biased bets and will lose all their money. They will not survive the natural selection process that eliminates irrational, biased risk takers. Skin in the game filters out the pretenders.

Let's say you are interested in this month's nonfarm payrolls (NFP) release. NFP is the main labor market data release in the United States. There are at least three places you can go for predictions. **Always check all three.** First is the Bloomberg survey. It will give you a range of predictions by mainstream economists, and those predictions will cluster close to the median.

NFP forecasts for December 2024 (the data point released on January 10, 2025), show this distribution of economist estimates:

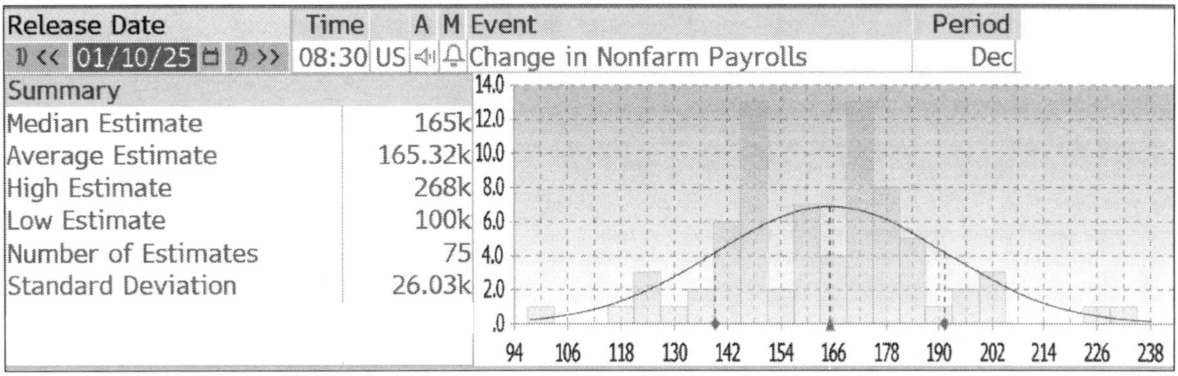

The standard deviation of the estimates is about 26k, while the standard deviation of NFP in 2023/2024 was more like 110k. If you dig into the details, you will see that some of the guesses were as old as December 20, 2024, even though the number came out on January 10, 2025. There was plenty of new and relevant information released in that 21-day period!

If we go to the prediction markets and compare Kalshi to the Bloomberg survey, we see some notable differences. Here's the aggregate expectation of bettors on Kalshi for December 2024 NFP.

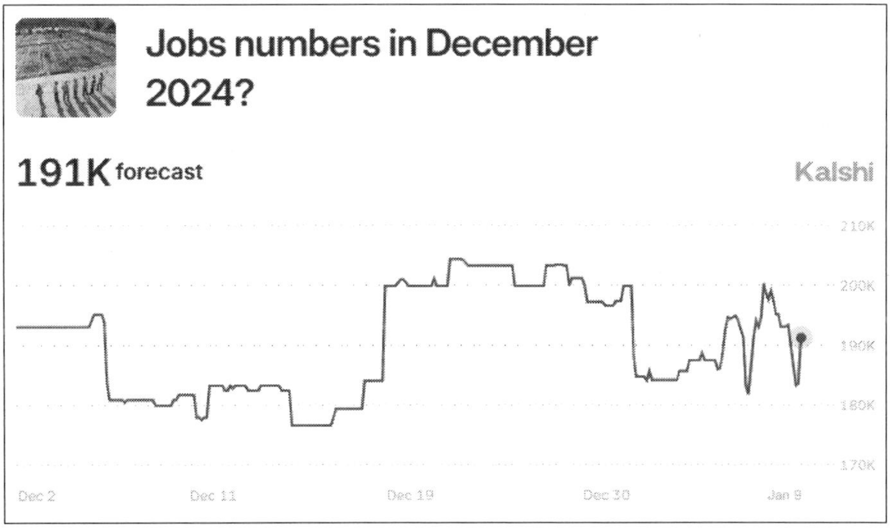

First, you see the evolution of the forecast over time. That can be useful! A rising number probably tells you the market is leaning towards a strong release, and vice versa. You also notice that the Kalshi market is predicting a higher number (191k) than the economists (165k). This is important! The Kalshi number is a much better representation of what the market really expects because it's not plagued by the bias in the Bloomberg survey.

Note that Kalshi creates a weighted average of all the bets to generate the 191k number. In reality, bettors wager on whether NFP will be above or below a certain threshold. Below, for example, are the yes probabilities for each bucket over time.

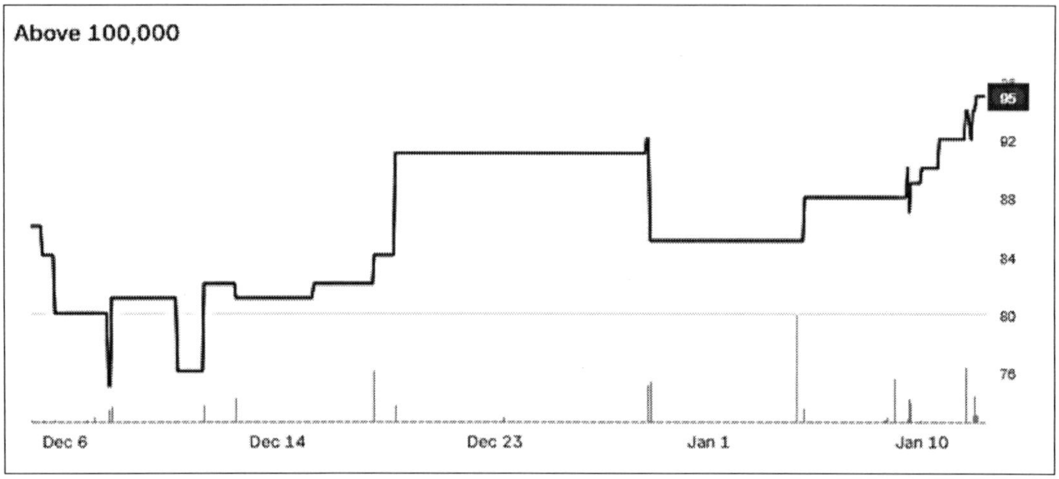

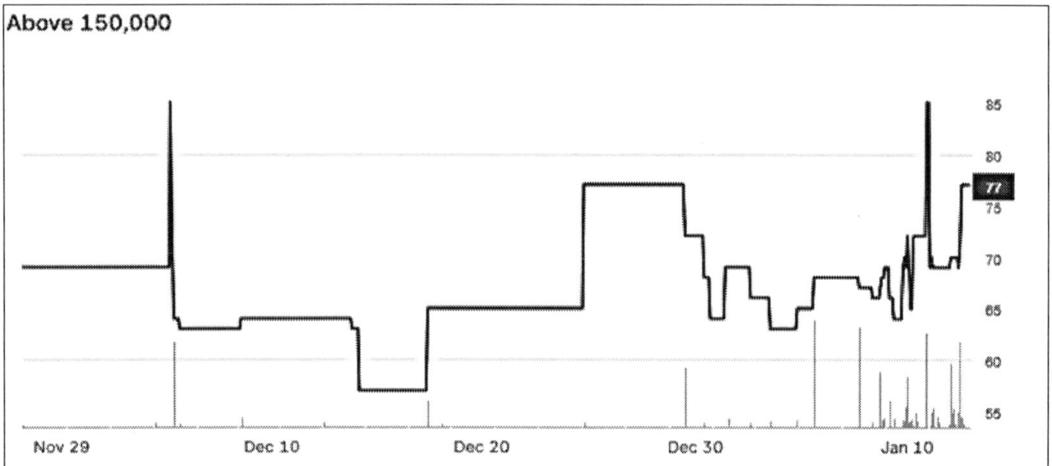

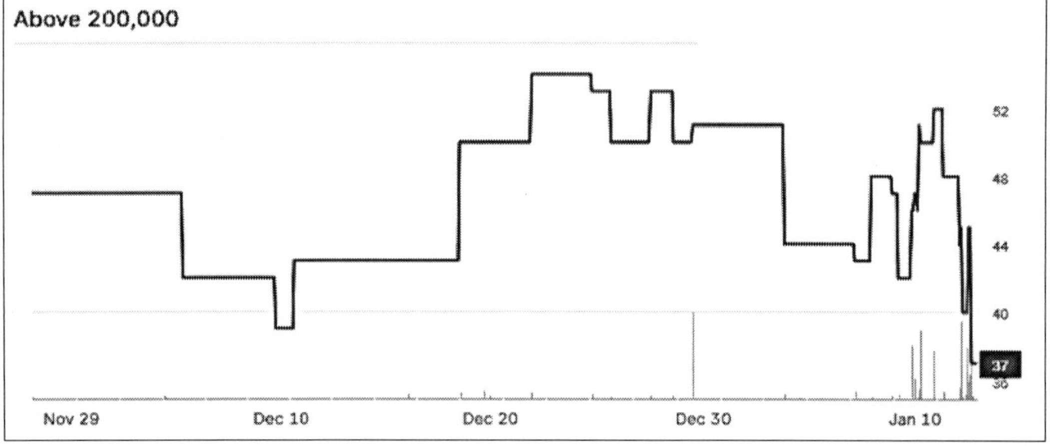

This extra granularity provides insight. In this case, as NFP approached, you could see the market was becoming increasingly confident that the number would be above 100,000 but below 200,000.

The actual release was +256,000 jobs.

Polymarket, a similar betting website that uses crypto instead of USD and caters to non-U.S. clients, offers betting on NFP as well. Here is what their platform looked like for that same NFP release:

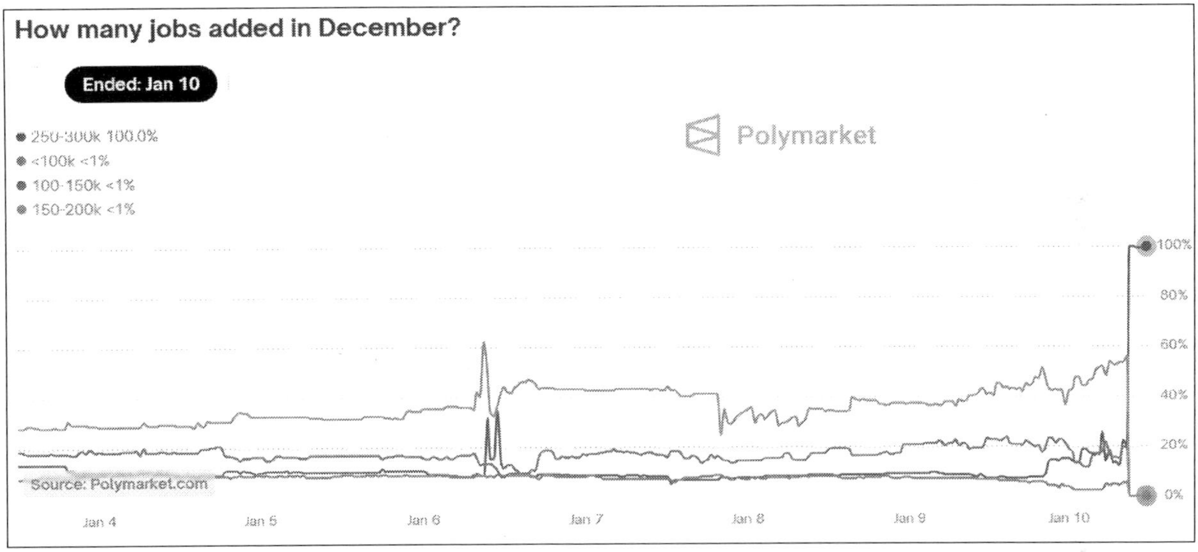

There are some differences:

1. Kalshi halts betting before the event, while Polymarket does not. That is why you see the correct outcome on Polymarket (250k to 300k) shoot higher to 100% right at the end. Going into the event, the 150k to 200k bucket was at 60%, which is roughly consistent with Kalshi's "above 150k" bucket being at 77%. Kalshi has buckets of "x or above" while Polymarket uses discrete 50k groupings.

2. Polymarket does not publish a weighted average, so you see the individual bets, not an aggregate estimate of NFP. You can use the Polymarket data to create a number that matches Kalshi's methodology, but you don't really need to do that. In fact, you can simply use one platform or the other and then do a quick logic check to make sure they match. The two markets should usually mirror fairly closely, even though it is tricky to arbitrage them because one operates onshore in the USA while the other operates only offshore.

As a rule, I look at Kalshi and then cross check with Polymarket to confirm. I will also check the liquidity of any contract I am analyzing because there are occasions when liquidity is so thin that the contract price is meaningless. I also study the evolution of expectations over time, something that you can't get on Bloomberg. *Are expectations heating up or cooling off?*

In this case, the betting markets were more accurate than the Bloomberg consensus and they properly allowed for the possibility of a much stronger headline number. While both Kalshi and Polymarket assigned a realistic probability to an outcome above 250,000, only one economist out of 75 was above 250k. This is common. The distribution of possible outcomes reflected by prediction markets will always be more accurate than tightly clustered economist forecasts.

Note that you cannot simply ignore Bloomberg surveys! Yes, they are just a collection of point estimates from economists and they can be stale, herdlike, and biased. But they are still the gold standard for what the market expects, and most algorithms are tuned to react to the difference between the Bloomberg survey and the actual release. So, you always need to combine the evidence from both economists' expectations and prediction markets.

How I sliced and diced expectations for July CPI on August 12, 2025

The top of the graphic shows the Bloomberg consensus and below that I have used my world-class MS Paint® skills to show the distribution of expectations on Polymarket. You can see that (as usual) the Bloomberg consensus is more tightly wound around consensus, while Polymarket shows less herding and a more realistic distribution. Note that volumes are high for this contract on Polymarket, so the data is reliable. The bid/offer was one or two cents wide for each contract.

Bloomberg and Polymarket expectations, July 2025 CPI released August 12, 2025

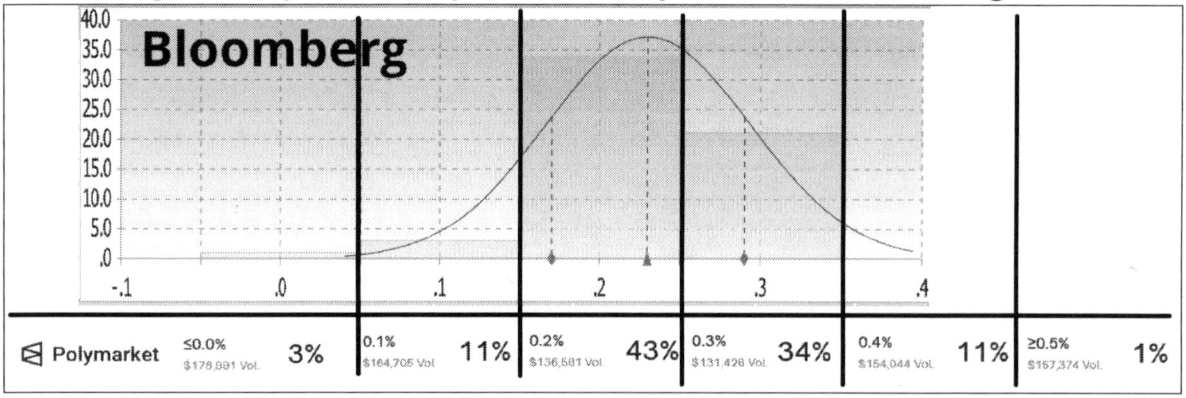

Following prediction markets and carefully studying the probabilities assigned to each bucket provides a much more realistic assessment of the market's expectations for an economic data release.

While prediction markets can be a useful way to fine tune your views going into major economic data, they are not a game changer because you already have the economist consensus as a reasonable (though biased and not fully accurate) guess of what's priced in. In contrast, sometimes betting markets are the only way to measure what's priced in for other discrete events. Let's look at an example.

Example 2: Using prediction markets to trade events in real time

Before prediction markets, traders had to make highly subjective guesses when estimating what was priced in for many events. Now, they can often find precise, objective data. The 2024 Presidential election brought betting markets to the fore, but as outlined earlier, election betting is nothing new. What is new is the ability to see market odds for almost any event under the sun. By providing liquid markets on politics, crypto, and all sorts of wild and woolly outcomes, prediction markets take some of the guesswork out of TradFi as they provide objective probabilities for events that affect mainstream financial markets.

While U.S. election betting is extremely liquid, this is not true for all prediction markets. It's important to assess the liquidity of a prediction market before you incorporate its information into your process. The platforms offer a few ways to analyze liquidity.

First, you can look at the bid/offer spread of a contract. Anything wider than a few cents means liquidity is bad. Let's look at Canadian election betting contracts on each platform in early 2025 to get a sense of liquidity. **First, we'll check Polymarket (at right).**

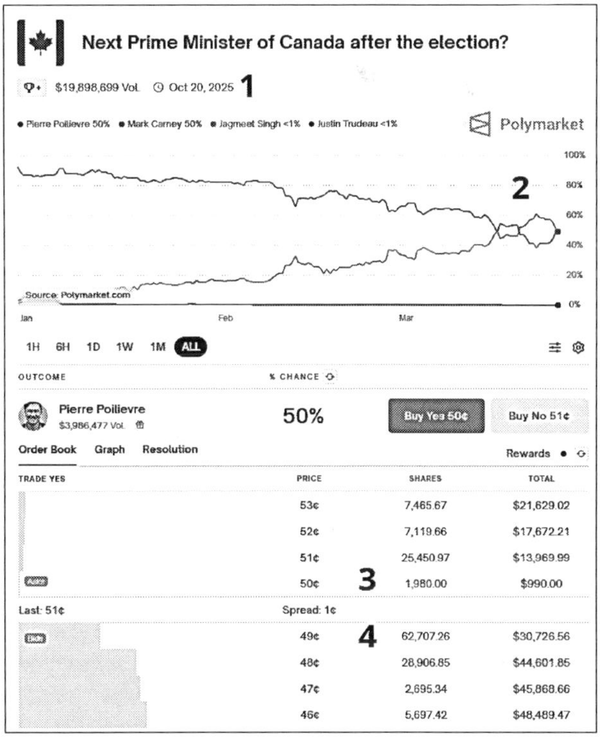

1. The area marked "1" on the graphic shows the total amount wagered, along with the expiry date of the contract. This expiry date can sometimes be important, but in this case the election is set for April 2025 and therefore the result will be known long before expiry.

2. The evolution of the odds over time. The relatively smooth lines indicate excellent liquidity. Similar to traditional markets, smooth price charts are an indicator of orderly markets with good liquidity.

3. The order book, where you can see the size of the individual bids and offers. In this case, you can see there are not many shares on the offer (only $1,000 worth).
4. In contrast, the bid is solid, with 62,707 contracts, representing $30,726 of interest. This is not massive size, by any means, but it's not peanuts.

If the bid and offer are one cent apart and show thousands of dollars of liquidity, that's a decent market. **People tend to overestimate how liquid a market needs to be in order to send a reliable signal.** Going back to the jellybean experiment for a second: Whether there are 250 people guessing, or 25,000, the consensus view on the number of jellybeans is not going to change. In contrast if there are only two people estimating, you have a problem!

Looking at the same contract on **Kalshi** (at right), the odds are slightly different.

Why would Pierre Poilievre be trading at 50 cents on Polymarket and 47 cents on Kalshi? Shouldn't those two prices be arbitraged into equilibrium? No. There are limits to cross-market arbitrage of prediction markets.

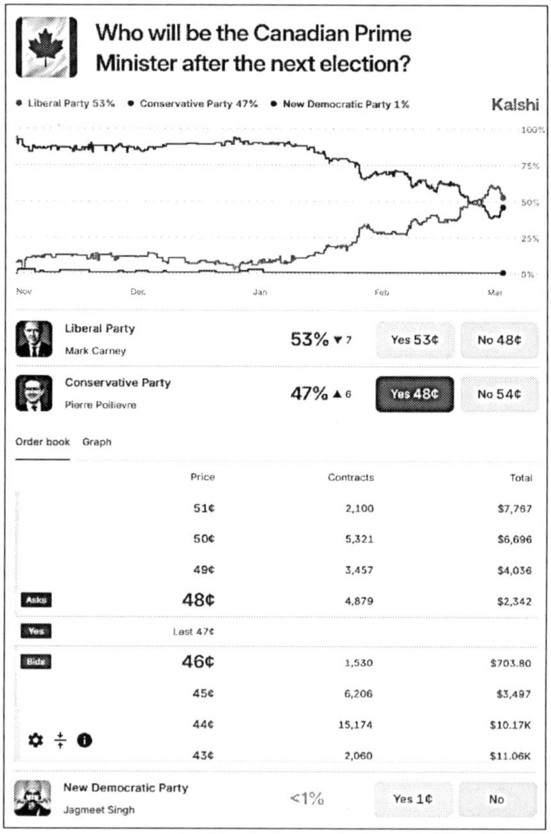

1. Polymarket is an offshore, crypto-based platform. There is theoretical credit risk in USDC and hack and credit risk with the Polymarket platform itself (it's minimal, but this risk is real if you're plopping down 6 or 7 figures). *Note: Polymarket is active in the USA as of early 2026.*
2. Kalshi is a US-based platform and only U.S. residents can trade on it.
3. Even if you can do the arb by opening separate accounts (one onshore, one offshore) your money is tied up for at least a month. Say you bet $1 million on each side of the arb, you are tying up $2m of capital for 4-8 weeks to earn around $55,000. That's not worth it given credit and operational risks are nearly impossible to quantify. Obviously, that is a great annual percentage rate, but it's a one off, not something you can do over and over.

There are too many regulatory, operational, and legal hoops for big money to jump through on both sides to capture what is not that big of an arb. As long as Kalshi and Polymarket are in the same ballpark, they are going to give you all the information you need. Whether the candidate is 47% to win or 50% to win… Close enough! You have a pretty good idea of what is priced in.

In this case, if you think Mark Carney is bullish for the Canadian dollar and you think he's better than a 50/50 shot to win, you might go long CAD. You can use various prediction markets on political events to back out expected values for various financial instruments. In recent years, markets have looked at election odds, tariff odds, legislation odds, and other probabilities as inputs into their investment or trading process.

As you move out the spectrum towards wonkier events, you might see an order book that looks like this:

If you use this contract as an input into your trading of advertising or pharma-related stocks, exercise extreme caution because less than $11,000 of volume has transacted, the bid/offer is 5 cents wide, and there is less than $100 worth of interest on the bid from 22 cents all the way down to 9 cents! This is not a great market. Also note the chart spiked from near-zero odds to 40%, then dropped back to 20%, all within a few days.

As you gain experience watching Kalshi and Polymarket, you will get a feel for what is liquid and what is not, similar to the way you can look at a stock chart and quickly discern whether it's liquid or not. Compare these 5-minute charts of AAPL and DGNX, for example.

A liquid stock and an illiquid stock, 5-minute charts compared

AAPL trades continuously up and down in smooth, controlled fashion while DGNX skips, leaps, zigs and zags. A chart can often give you a clear sense of liquidity because **liquid products trade smoothly and continuously while illiquid products do not**.

At the top of the chapter, I mentioned a few other issues that can pop up and I'd like to quickly run through those now.

1. **Credit risk.** You don't necessarily want to leave huge sums of money on deposit at Kalshi or Polymarket. There is more credit risk and/or hack risk with smaller, less regulated entities than there is if you leave your money at a major bank or brokerage.

2. **Favorite/longshot bias.** Nobody likes risking 99 dollars to win 1. Everybody loves betting 1 to win 99. So you will see that pricing at the extreme ends of the probability spectrum can be off. Gamblers tend to overpay for longshots and steer clear of favorites because of a preference for leverage. This does not matter most of the time but be careful when looking at contracts that trade near 0 or near 100.

3. **Political bias** when traders bet on hopes rather than expectations. There was some argument that Polymarket was distorted by pro-Trump bettors in the runup to the 2024 election. While this is a valid concern, there is a limit to how far a political player can push the odds before big money will simply push back the other way. Yes, prediction markets can be gamed by the megarich, but it's a difficult and risky game to play and requires enormous capital. Keep this bias in the back of your mind when assessing prediction market probabilities, but don't get bogged down by it. A huge majority of the time, prediction market probabilities are close enough to unbiased that they will serve your purposes (assessing what is priced in) perfectly well.

4. **There is a time value of money**. An event that is guaranteed to happen two years from now will not trade at 100% because people don't want to have their money tied up that long. The longer the contract, the further it will trade from 100%, even if it's a sure thing.

Finally, note that traditional finance contracts are also available to trade on some prediction markets. For example, Kalshi will let you bet on the day's close in the S&P 500. In the next chart, you can see the order book for that contract at 3 p.m. on March 24, 2025. The liquidity is super deep (100,000 contracts per side) because algorithms run by funds like Susquehanna simply place orders on both sides at levels where they can successfully arbitrage the real price against TradFi markets.

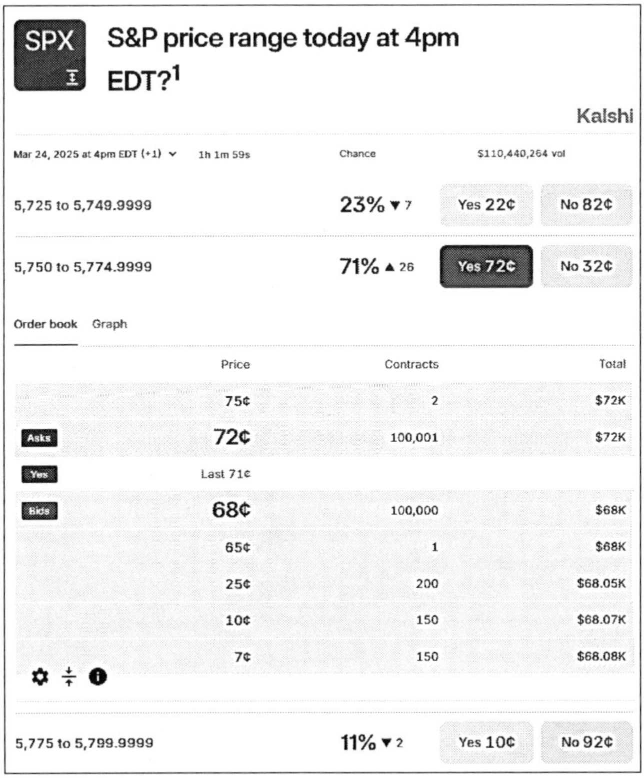

If you trade on that 68 / 72 price, you are trading at a worse level than the equivalent contract in the primary TradFi market. You're giving away money to an algorithmic market maker and paying *ginormous* fees to Kalshi. These might be fun bets for retail traders with small accounts, but TradFi offers cheaper liquidity.

Traders on prediction markets are sophisticated. **Sometimes Polymarket moves before traditional financial markets.** For example, in June 2025, FX traders were trading EURCHF based on moves in this contract on Polymarket:

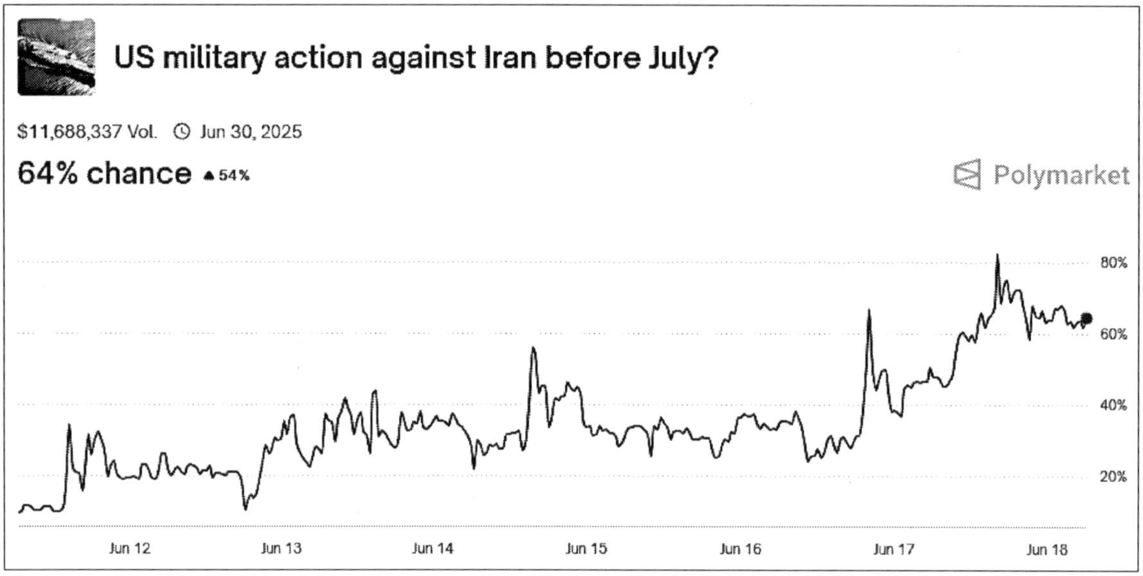

Polymarket was reflecting new information from Israeli and Iranian media sources faster and more clearly than any individual could digest the info, and so it was easier to watch Polymarket than to track a zillion foreign military and local political experts. **Prediction markets can offer a clear one stop shop for consensus and rapid news aggregation.** Bank traders were able to trade EURCHF profitably by simply monitoring changes in the Polymarket Iran attack odds.

Scroll through the active contracts on Polymarket every few days and note anything that might help you get one step ahead of the crowd. During an election or fast-developing story, watch Polymarket or Kalshi odds to get a real-time view of market pricing; you may be able to trade lagging TradFi markets for a profit.

Finally, for an excellent and educational podcast on prediction markets, check out:

riskofruinpod.substack.com/p/new-episode-betting-on-chaos

Conclusion

In this chapter, we discussed the evolution of prediction markets, and how to use them to supplement your TradFi trading process. Prediction markets offer real-time probability estimates for economic, political, and other events and help you continuously evaluate what is priced in. They also give you insight into the direction of travel of pricing so you can not only see what is priced in now, but how pricing has evolved over time.

Before the next economic release, election, or potential market moving event, check the various prediction markets to find unbiased, current and precise probability estimates to inform your trading process.

Further reading

I strongly recommend you check out the February 2026 Federal Reserve paper on prediction markets; it's full of useful and relevant information. The link is below, and here are two main takeaways:

High Accuracy: The study found prediction markets are often just as accurate—and sometimes more accurate—than traditional surveys. Because they are updated 24/7, they provide a "real-time" pulse of the economy that monthly surveys can't match.

A "Distributional" View: Unlike a single "average" forecast, Kalshi shows a range of possibilities. This helps traders see not just what people think will happen, but how much they fear extreme outcomes (like a sudden spike in inflation).

Prediction markets turn the wisdom of the crowd into a hard number. The paper concludes that because these markets use real money and are federally regulated, they provide a reliable, "live" scoreboard for where the economy is headed. You should expect to see more policymakers reference prediction markets in years to come.

Kalshi and the Rise of Macro Markets

www.federalreserve.gov/econres/feds/files/2026010pap.pdf

PART TWO: INSPIRATION FROM OTHER DOMAINS

"Cross-fertilization of ideas is important and necessary. Ideas should be combined with each other to form more and even better ideas. If creative thinking involves forging new links between previously unrelated or weakly related concepts, then creativity will be stimulated by any activity that brings more concepts into juxtaposition with each other in fresh ways."

Richards H. Heuer

Introduction

By this point in your career, you may have read a 10-foot-high stack of books covering fundamentals, technicals, behavioral finance and quantitative approaches to finance. Our goal is to take a few steps out of that box and look at outside domains that may have something to teach us about trading.

Some of the most important trading insights I have gleaned didn't come from books about *trading*, they came from areas like mental health, addiction, poker, initial conditions, and ergodicity. Consider ways you can apply knowledge from seemingly discrete domains to your trading. That's what I will do here in Part Two, where we'll cover psychology, mental health, analogs in other domains, and ancillary and complementary concepts.

This section offers unique perspectives on markets, inspires new ideas and angles for your trading, and dovetails with the four main approaches to finance:

- fundamental
- technical
- behavioral
- quantitative

Digest the information with an open mind. If things pop into your head while you're reading, write them down!

Ideas that occur organically, while you are doing something else, can often be the most creative ones. Rarely will I go more than a few pages through a book without some seemingly random idea popping into my head. Sometimes the idea is related to what I'm reading, but often it does not seem to be. I try to write down these spontaneous thoughts before they disappear, because they are fleeting.

Expose your brain to a wide variety of concepts so that it can mix and match until it comes up with new and fresh ideas. Let's get started with a discussion of the "bible" of psychiatry: The DSM-5.

CHAPTER 4

PSYCHOLOGY AND MENTAL HEALTH

The DSM-5 can help you grow as a trader (and as a human being)

"A stock operator has to fight a lot of expensive enemies within himself."

Jesse Livermore

The market doesn't care about your IQ. It cares whether you can think fast and slow at the same time, execute when your heart is racing, and do the right thing even as your amygdala screams: "Danger!". Your P&L reflects your psychology and your market knowledge equally: mental health and trading success are tightly linked. Knowledge of clinical human psychology helps you identify irrational behaviors like phobia, mania, anxiety, and gambling disorder.

The DSM-5

"We live to survive our paradoxes."

Gord Downie, The Tragically Hip

Psychiatrists use the DSM-5 (Diagnostic and Statistical Manual of Mental Disorders, Fifth Edition) to diagnose mental disorders, and it provides rich insight into harmful trading behaviors. The 947-page beast organizes mental health traits into logical categories, sets specific criteria for diagnosis, and distinguishes between normal variation and actual dysfunction.

The American Psychiatric Association revises this behavioral bible every 15-20 years with new and updated research and criteria. Consider it a psychological playbook: it describes how your thinking breaks down during drawdowns, why you revenge-trade after you crash through your stop loss, and why you risk 5% of capital when your trading rules clearly set your max risk as 2%. The DSM-5 gives specific vocabulary and frameworks to name the many internal enemies that conspire against you like reckless impulsivity, gambling and overtrading, paralyzing anxiety, depression leading to warped risk assessment, and more. We'll examine solutions and strategies to fight these cognitive barriers.

Note: I am not a psychiatrist or a psychologist. I'm just a trader using this psychiatric reference manual to the best of my abilities. Do not confuse a quick reading of the DSM-5 with psychiatric expertise. If you think you have psychological problems that are holding you back in trading, or in regular life, see a therapist or a performance coach. The biggest advances I've made in trading came from collaboration with trading and performance coaches.

In this chapter, we will cover the sections of the DSM-5 that are most relevant to trading:

- Attention-deficit/hyperactivity disorder (ADHD)
    - Side quest: Why stop losses are good, even if they're negative EV
- Anxiety
- Insomnia
- Gambling Disorder

To be clear, this chapter is not about clinical diagnosis of the psychological conditions described in DSM-5. I use them as a launching point to discuss some of the most severe cognitive failings that compromise trading. So, when we talk about anxiety here, we are talking about anxiety in trading, not a clinical diagnosis of Generalized Anxiety Disorder.

Not a doctor.

Let's see how these four topics can level up your trading psychology.

ADHD

> "And right here let me say one thing: After spending many years in Wall Street and after making and losing millions of dollars I want to tell you this: It never was my thinking that made the big money for me. **It was always my sitting.** Got that? My sitting tight!"
>
> Jesse Livermore

Some features of attention-deficit / hyperactivity disorder are:

- Persistent pattern of inattention and/or hyperactivity-impulsivity
- Inattention: making careless mistakes, difficulty sustaining attention, appearing to not listen, failing to follow through on instructions, difficulty organizing tasks
- Hyperactivity/impulsivity: fidgeting, inability to sit still, excessive movement, excessive talking, blurting out answers, difficulty waiting turn, interrupting others

How these behaviors might impact your trading:

Impulsive trading decisions without adequate analysis. Are you pushing buttons for no reason? Do you follow your first thought without a system of checks and balances to account for the fact that *the first thought* is often not *the best thought*?

Difficulty maintaining focus during market analysis or extended trading sessions. Are you toggling in and out of the zone? Or can you stay focused for long periods?

Challenges with detailed record-keeping and trade documentation. Do you promise yourself you'll record your trading data and keep a trading journal, but then never do it because you're too busy trading? Detailed trading data is critical to improvement. If you keep doing the same thing over and over without analysis or course correction, you'll repeat mistakes and suffer from the same leaks, week after week. You can't just do the fun parts of trading and expect to succeed in the long run. **You have to do the boring stuff too.**

Easily distracted by market noise or unrelated information. Can you tell the difference between signal and noise in headlines, or do you trade every headline that comes out and find yourself crossing tons of bid/offer for no reason? Speed is important, but you need to be fast *and* rational at the same time. What percentage of your trades are noise and what percentage actually make sense?

Challenges with patience during trade development. Trading, like hunting ducks, fishing, or watching baseball, is mostly sitting around waiting for something exciting to happen. If you're a day trader running max risk at 1:45 p.m. for no reason every day, you need more patience. Lack of patience can manifest in two ways.

1. Entering too many trades.

2. Bailing at the first contrary price action, random headline or psychic itch. To make real money trading, you need to patiently ride winners, even when they're deep in the money and you're dying to take profit for no reason. Risk averse traders are especially prone to bailing because they don't like to feel uncomfortable.

Far too often, traders will buy, the price will skyrocket, then when it stabilizes, they will say, "I don't like the price action" or "It's stalling out" or "Time to ring the register." If your plan was to buy the thing at 60 and ride it to 80, don't hit a bid just because it went to 66 five minutes after you bought it and you've now got an itchy trigger finger.

You need to sit flat through long periods of inactivity, and you need to sit with huge risk and capture the meaty part of strong directional moves. **You will never succeed as a trader if you cannot sit still. Successful traders spend much of their time sitting uncomfortably, doing nothing, with huge, calculated risk.**

Putting some of these points together, let me share a relevant anecdote from my trading.

Throughout the 2000s, I was an FX market maker, and trading lead/lag correlation was my bread and butter. I was fast and confident. When U.S. 10-year yields went up, I was quick enough to buy USDJPY before everyone else (for example) and make money consistently, especially in fast markets. I would see yields flick higher and my fingers would leap to the buy button, and I would be long 50 million USDJPY and 7 pips in the money before I even knew what happened. My first thought was the right thought, and my video game skills paid dividends.

But over the course of a few years, algorithms and humans caught on to this "free money" trade. It became more difficult to monetize and eventually it disappeared as a source of alpha. Like every good trading strategy, it got arbitraged away. Everyone knew about it, and everyone was doing it. There were finance blogs with AUD vs. copper overlays going viral in Wall Street inboxes in 2012 whereas in 2005, most professional FX traders didn't even have a live copper price feed on Bloomberg.

However... my reflexes never got the memo. So, in 2015 when yields popped, I would blackout and buy 100 million USDJPY, even though my logical brain knew this was no longer a winning strategy. I couldn't stop myself. It wasn't a gambling thing (though we will talk about that later), but simply a persistent pattern of hyperactivity and impulsivity that I could not control. I wasn't trading because I was bored, I was trading because my fingers were operating via intuition without any intervention by my conscious mind.

This went on for ages despite my attempts to control it. My System 1 Lizard Brain was hijacking my P&L by putting on these impulsive trades without checking in with System 2[21]. I was putting on dozens or maybe hundreds of these trades every month. Gold would flicker $5 lower, and I'd sell AUD. S&Ps would rally 8 points and I would buy EURJPY. And on it went. Tiny loss after tiny loss.

Finally, I found a performance coach and made appointments to visit him weekly. The breakthrough came when he asked me to imagine a video of myself doing these unwanted trades. He said:

> "Describe to me the exact process of how it happens."

Through this investigation, I realized that the watchlist of securities on my trading cockpit was stimulating me and causing my hands to go to the buy/sell buttons.

> "Can you turn off the watchlist?"

---

[21] For more on System 1 vs. System 2 thinking, see Alpha Trader, pages 64-70 and Thinking, Fast and Slow by Daniel Kahneman.

Yes, of course I could. But my irrational dumb brain said, "But you won't know where spot gold is trading every picosecond of the day!"

Process upgrade decisions like this have tradeoffs. By deleting my watchlist, I would be less tuned in to the cross-market story. But cross-market trading was my biggest leak at that point. So, it was a difficult, but easy decision. Difficult because it felt extremely uncomfortable to sit there the first few days as my eyes flicked over to see a blank spot where S&Ps futures used to flicker. Easy because the cost was psychological, but the benefits were financial.

I didn't need to know where gold and S&Ps were trading all day every day, tick by tick, because their micro movements were no longer relevant to FX or my trading decisions. I deleted the watchlist from my trading cockpit and the impulsive trading problem went away overnight. Sure, I had no idea where S&Ps were trading intraday anymore, but if I needed to know, I could simply bring them up on Bloomberg.

I felt like I was stumbling in the dark for a while because I had spent so many years staring at that watchlist, but I stopped putting on all those stupid trades and eventually got used to my new process.

Solutions for hyperactive trading disorder

If you have a hyperactive trading behavior that you want to stop, imagine a video of yourself doing it. Observe yourself from the outside. Go frame by frame through that video and determine the steps that lead to bad trades. If you're trading too many headlines, that might mean turning off your headline window. "But I'll miss some amazing headlines!" you might think. You will. But if trading headlines is negative EV, you are going to save yourself money, even if you miss some big winners.

Trading coaches and therapy

I was skeptical of therapy when I was in my 20s and 30s. To me, it was *cringe*. It threatened my worldview and my feeling of absolute self-sufficiency. Let me tell you: self-sufficiency is a great quality to a certain point, but it can become a huge weakness. No human being is without flaws, and no human being is gifted with perfect thinking. A professional who can help you work through some of your defects is enormously valuable.

Also: Through a variety of types of therapy in my trading and personal life, I have learned that the patient-therapist connection is a huge ingredient in therapy success. If you go to a marriage counselor who you don't respect or don't connect with, you are not going to achieve your goals. Don't try one therapist, dislike it and decide: "Meh, therapy is dumb." The therapist, psychologist, or trading coach you work with might not be right for you. Shop around until you find someone you like.

Here are some other considerations when attempting to avoid Trading ADHD.

Structure your trading environment to minimize distractions. This might sound obvious, but I have seen many traders with CNBC blaring in the background for no reason, blinds open to a busy street outside, and babies crying in the other room. It's hard enough to keep your thoughts straight. Irrelevant external stimulus will hurt your trading. Trading crypto on a laptop on a rooftop patio at a hotel in Rio de Janeiro looks super cool on Instagram, but it's not how to structure your environment if you want to make money. Your surroundings are important. Create an optimal work environment for maximum concentration and realization of *the zone*.

Schedule and plan. Maintain a healthy trading environment through proper calendar management. Don't book meetings or appointments in the morning. Prioritize your best times of day for trading and don't let anything or anyone encroach on them.

Get up and walk around. I set a timer on my phone for 10:30 a.m. and 3 p.m. to make sure that I get up and walk around at least three times per day (I always get lunch just before noon). That's a bare minimum for me, and I will try to get up and move around more than that.

Even if you're a market maker at a bank, it's OK to walk around once in a while! Just don't be that guy that randomly disappears off the desk for 90 minutes at a time or during nonfarm payrolls!

You can also use some variation of the Pomodoro technique, which is a time management method that breaks work into 25-minute focused intervals (Pomodoros) followed by short 5-minute breaks. You can use whatever method you like, but take a few minutes to create a thoughtful structure for your day and avoid staring at screens for hours on end.

Maximize your productivity by scheduling unproductive time.

Write down your trading plan. I cover the benefits of writing stuff down in *Alpha Trader* (pp. 98-99) and I created a yearly trading journal (*The Spectra Markets Trader Handbook and Almanac*) for this purpose. It's great to be in the zone trading, but it's better to toggle *in* and *out* of the zone as appropriate.

Staring at *e-minis* when you are limit long is not going to make them go up any faster! A small, pre-printed paper checklist for each trade can also be a useful part of your process. After the close, you can enter these handwritten trades into a spreadsheet for future analysis.

Slow your brain down. My brain is always thinking of a million potential trades, business ideas, sports events I want to bet on, concerts I want to go to, etc. etc. etc. A fast brain is an asset when you're in the zone and trading headlines, but it can be a problem when it is in control all the time.

Meditation is the easiest way to slow down your brain, and you don't need to commit Buddhist amounts of time to it. When you notice your brain is running fast or hot, step away, find somewhere quiet, and meditate for two minutes. I find that's enough of a reset to get me slowed down and back to more "normal" thinking and less frantic. I am not diagnosed with ADHD, but it's a spectrum—and I am on that spectrum!

If you want to go more hardcore on the meditation thing, check out this piece I wrote about a 5-day silent meditation retreat. I continue to feel the benefits of it, months later.

www.spectramarkets.com/amfx/recreational-buddhism/

Automate your stop losses and significant reference points. You don't have to be on high alert all the time[22]. If you manage your intraday stops manually, you're on the edge of your seat nonstop. If you automate them, you can hide in the closet and meditate for five minutes whenever your brain is going too fast, without worrying about a risk management blowup.

> "If I automate my stops, I might get dinged on a flicker!"

That's my dumb brain again, worrying about the few times when price action flickers on something like a bogus news headline and I get stopped out at the lows for no reason. Again, that's a cost of doing business *well*—the benefit of automated stops is ten times greater than the cost. You eat the few times you get knocked out but you gain a steady stream of benefits as your risk management is robotically rigorous. You maintain better focus and you are able to step away from the market as necessary.

Side quest: stop losses

Let's go on a little side quest, because the debate over stop losses never ends. "Aren't stops negative EV? Why would you use stops?" is a good—and common—question.

Yes, stops are negative EV. And yes, I have a stop loss on every single position. The reason is simple.

Stop losses are a risk management tool, not an alpha generation tool.

Fire insurance is negative EV, but it keeps you from going bankrupt if your house burns down. Stop losses are negative EV, yet they keep you from going bankrupt if you are horribly wrong, there is a huge unexpected market move, or you go on a prolonged losing streak.

---

[22] A significant reference point is a key price level or psychological marker that traders use to make decisions or take action. These reference points can include previous highs and lows, round numbers, moving averages, major support and resistance levels, or cross-market triggers. See *Alpha Trader,* pages 325-331.

You have two options:

1. Use stop losses or
2. Don't use leverage.

Traders who use leverage and don't have stops will eventually meet up with the trading gods in a dark alley and be held up at gunpoint.

Even if your positions are too big to use automated stops (rare), you can leave a call level with your execution desk with clear instructions to get out when it hits. One of the greatest traders of all time used call levels to trade with me. When his call level hit, the phone would ring and it would be his execution team covering a billion GBPJPY because he just hit his stop loss. Did he pay a ton in transaction costs when he stopped out like this? *Yes*. Is he still trading after more than 30 years, with zero blowups and amazing returns? *Also yes*.

Let's look at how stop losses can work as downside insurance in a simple strategy for trading S&P futures. If they went down yesterday, you go long at the close, and if they went up yesterday, you go short at the close. This simple UP/DOWN mean reversion strategy is somewhat realistic. You are using 20X leverage in futures. The light gray line shows your P&L from 2015 to 2025 if you do not use a stop loss. The black line shows your P&L if you use a 3% stop loss.

The vertical black bars are all the times you went bankrupt if you didn't use a stop.

P&L of S&P futures up / down strategy with 20X leverage

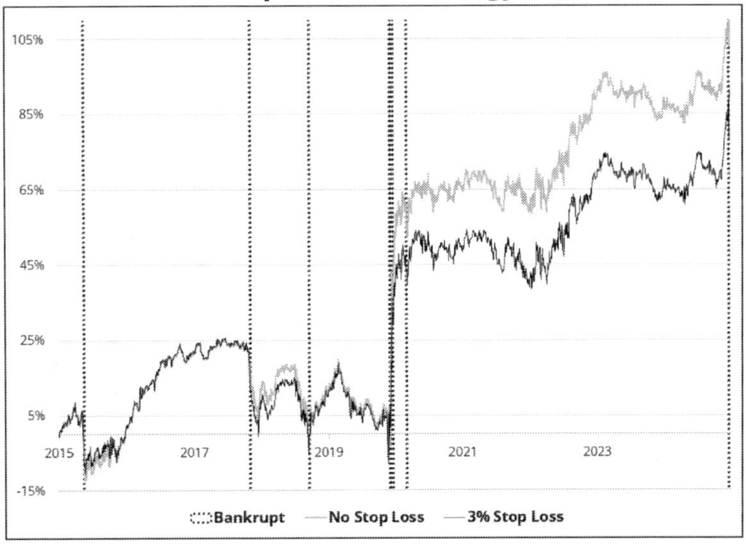

The strategy with no stop loss superficially performs better, but it goes bankrupt *seven times*. So it performs much, *much* worse. There are many good arguments against using stop losses, and it's highly dependent on your trading strategy. Stops change the shape of your return distribution in ways that can be negative EV. They take you out of positions that could be getting more attractive (e.g. "I loved the stock at $7; how can I sell it at $5???")

If you are a directional trader employing leverage, you need stops. If you loved the stock at $7 and now it's at $5, that tells you your idea and/or your timing are wrong; it's not a signal to buy more.

If you don't want to leave stops, you can also use options to hedge the tails, but that is prohibitively expensive, and I hate it. Options should be bought selectively and sold systematically, not the other way around.

I *will* buy an option to protect a position if there is a particular reason to do so. If vol is cheap or underpriced and there is too much whipsaw or event risk to use a simple stop loss, then I'll do an option. But most of the time, I put on my trade and place an automated stop loss in a system right away. Directional traders who don't use stops eventually run full speed into a high-velocity Ford F-150 coming the other way.

Getting stopped out at the highs and lows is a cost of doing business in leveraged trading. Just as food spoilage is a cost of doing business in restaurants. You want to minimize it, but you should also accept it. Don't get emotional about "bad luck" instances where you get dinged at the extremes. Luck is a short-term phenomenon that evens out over time. Good traders get stopped out, and they move on.

Note: If you are often stopped out of trades that would have been winners, that means your stop losses are too tight. You need to employ wider stops and smaller positions.

Principle 14: Avoid risk of ruin first. Maximize returns second.

If you blow up, there will be no returns. For information on where to put your stops, see *Alpha Trader* (pp. 413-414).

A rigorous trading process is the ultimate cure for hyperactive trading. If you know what you are doing, have a solid process and stick to it, you can be as hyperactive as you like because the process is laid out and premeditated by your rational, conscious mind. If you have a repetitive program in your brain that keeps running and won't stop, take action. Employ a more rigorous, rules-based approach to regulate spontaneous overtrading.

Generalized Anxiety Disorder

Disney's "Inside Out" movies explain emotions in a way that kids, tweens, and adults can understand. Human emotions are personified, allowing the viewer to see those emotions in a more detached, abstract, and objective (less emotional!) way. In the second installment of the franchise, Anxiety appears as a new character. Her goal is to protect Riley, the main character, from danger, but she ends up blocking her happiness instead. A key concept in the movie is:

Anxiety hijacks your imagination.

A vivid imagination can be an asset in financial markets. People extrapolate too much. They are married to prevailing narratives and don't spend enough time analyzing alternative scenarios. Crazy stuff happens all the time. When Donald Trump was elected in November 2024, not one person imagined a massive rejection of his policies and the wholesale flight out of U.S. assets that occurred in April 2025. Everyone was long dollars, and the dollar got smacked. By the time the market embraced the *End of U.S. Exceptionalism*, the trade was over, U.S. assets ripped higher, and the dollar rallied.

You need to have enough imagination to see a future that is different from the present. Otherwise, you're always extrapolating and never truly forecasting.

But your imagination can also cook up worst-case scenarios, stress, and anxiety. It can hold you back from pressing buttons, even when your rational mind has a good trade idea. You must trust your process and understand that you are going to be wrong. Often. That's OK.

It is normal to be anxious, especially as a young trader. It can lead to spinning thoughts, difficulty concentrating, irritability, and sleep disturbance. These symptoms then lead to distress and functional impairment causing traders to make suboptimal decisions on entry and exit.

One of the most common ways anxiety impacts trading is that it makes you watch every tick in the price action, looking for clues in the noise.

Most price action is meaningless

A guy got back from lunch and got bored, so he sold 500 e-minis. A woman got a phone call from a friend, decided to leave work early, and bought 200 GC to cover her short. Someone at a pension fund has been working on a thesis for two weeks and finally got board approval to put the trade on so they execute a massive flattener. Don't assume that every flicker in the price is useful information. It's not.

Anxious and risk-averse traders don't like how risk *feels*. They want to relieve themselves of this discomfort and anxiety and thus let their imagination be hijacked by the most trivial of excuses. Many times, I have heard a trader say they don't like the price action, or "it should have gone down by now" or "maybe this isn't a good trade idea, after all." These are codes your irrational brain uses to get you out of risk and into the feeling of peace and comfort that comes from being flat.

Witness your own discomfort. Acknowledge it. Push through it. As George Adair put it: "Everything you've ever wanted is on the other side of fear."

This is true in trading and it's true in life. The good thing is, the longer you trade, the more you will recognize that each individual trade is meaningless in the bigger picture, and you can't white knuckle it every time you put on risk.

Solutions for trading anxiety

Accept that anxiety is part of trading. If you can't handle ongoing anxiety, you should seriously consider doing something other than trading. You will crack under the relentless unease that is an inescapable feature of trading for a living. I don't mean that to sound overly aggressive, but it's OK to take a step back and say: "I'm not built for this. Trading isn't for me." There are plenty of other cool jobs in and outside finance. If you are sure you want to move forward with your trading career, here are some ways to manage anxiety.

First, when I feel anxious, I notice it, I find the precise cause, I extract any useful information, and then I let it go. My four-step process for dealing with anxiety:

1. **Notice it**. This is a simple matter of saying to yourself or a trading partner: "This trade is making me anxious." Or "These market moves are making me anxious." As soon as you name an emotion, you reduce its power and limit its ability to stalk your thoughts.
2. **Identify the precise cause**. "I am feeling super nervous because I am max short TQQQ and there could be a headline or a tweet at any moment that completely rips my face off." This pretty much describes how I felt as I typed this on April 10, 2025, because the last two days of trading looked like this:

Scary chart of TQQQ shows what can happen on a random intraday tweet

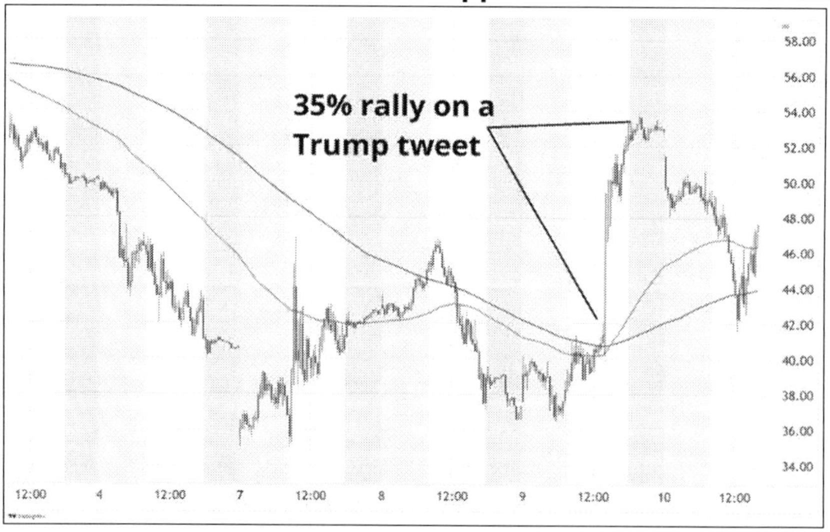

Still, I sat here writing a book while I endured that last little squeeze because a) I have been here a million times and I embrace the feeling of anxiety as positive stress, and b) My stops are all automated, so whatever happens, the machine will get me out at my predetermined level and only lose X amount of money, and c) my strong view is TQQQ will close near the lows today, so I'm short. The P&L amount for X has been predetermined, so whether I stare at the screen and imagine nightmare bullish tweet scenarios, or sit calmly writing a book... The outcome will be the same. So, I may as well write the book.

3. **Extract any useful information.** I was nervous because the convexity was to the topside (bullish tweet) not the downside (closing washout lower). Emotions are almost always a useful source of information. If you are feeling something strong, ask yourself what information is contained there. The information for me was that I was still a bit raw from yesterday's rip (because I was short when the tweet came out) and now that I made almost all the money back, I knew how dispiriting it would be to regurgitate my gains and see my capital end back on yesterday's lows. Maybe my positions were a bit too big. I checked my spreadsheet to see my dollars at risk. This confirmed that my positions were the right size. So, I went back to writing my book.

4. **Let it go.** It's not healthy or useful to ignore or push away emotions. That said, the opposite strategy of letting them rule your mind is not good either. Emotions can be consciously identified, understood and processed. Once that is done, let them go. Easier said than done, but it's the only way.

This four-step process gets easier over time. I have it on a sticky note on my desk.

A Post-it® about emotions, stuck on the bottom of one of my monitors

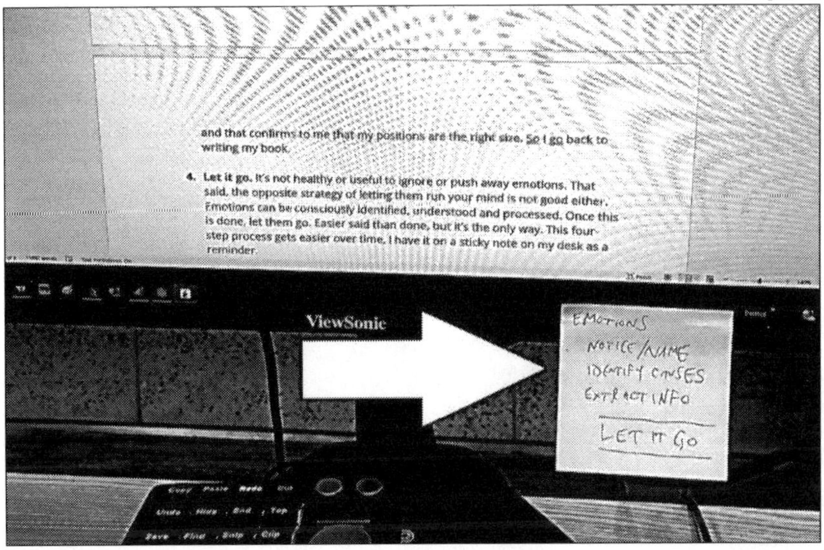

You are reading my book while looking at a picture of me writing my book. Meta.

EMOTIONS – NOTICE/NAME – IDENTIFY CAUSES – EXTRACT INFO – **LET IT GO**.

Beyond this four-step process, here are some other ways to deal with trading anxiety.

- **Trust your trading process.** I outline a rigorous trading process in *Alpha Trader,* and discuss how to audit your trading process in Chapter 10. Without a rigorous, trusted process you are going to be anxious all the time. Markets are hard enough to predict. If you can't even predict what **you** are going to do next, you are going to be anxious. If your brain is asking you questions like: "Will I stop out in time? Will I enter at the right level, or get antsy and buy 1% higher?" … You do not have a clear trading process.
- **Identify the worst case.** If you are sitting on a lot of risk and you feel uncomfortable, write down your worst-case scenario. For example, I'll write: "Worst case I'm down 200k today." I have all my stops automated so I know that I am not going to lose more than that. This moves me towards acceptance. I can lose money on any trade or on any given day but the outcome is not important. Outcomes are out of my control. I accept that I might lose X, and that helps me relax because it removes uncertainty. I don't sit there white knuckling every market jiggle, worrying. That's too exhausting.
- **Breathe.** Learn about 4-7-8 breathing. Google it and give it a try. You can't just try it once and say it's stupid, though. Try it for a few days and see how it goes. Whenever something makes you anxious, do some 4-7-8 breathing.
- **Identify.** In your trading journal, write about anxious moments you had during the day and how you dealt with them. Over time, you will become more familiar with your triggers, you will see them, name them and they will have less power over you.
- **Challenge negative thought patterns**. Notice when your mind jumps to worst-case scenarios. Ask yourself: "What's the evidence for this thought?". "Is there another way to look at this situation?", or "What would I tell a friend who had this worry?" Cognitive restructuring helps break the cycle of anxious thinking.
- **Automate** your execution and stops or outsource them to someone you trust. You know who is good at doing the right thing? *Computers.*
- **Create a checklist** for your process and carefully track your orders. There are few things more anxiety-provoking than lying in bed at 2 a.m. wondering if you left a stale order with a bank or in a system. Use a checklist at the start and end of the day to avoid missing any important operational aspects of your process. Random losses from operational errors are extremely discouraging.
- **Take a break.** If price action is making you nauseous, recognize it and step away from the computer. Staring at prices all day is stressful and can create vertigo and anxiety. Give your brain a cooldown when you feel it heating up. Physical activity releases endorphins and other neurochemicals, reduces stress, and improves mood. A 5-minute walkabout can provide immediate relief. And regular exercise builds resilience against future anxiety by regulating stress hormones and improving sleep quality.

Position sizing anxiety

A final, specific source of anxiety in trading is related to position sizing. Very often, traders get anchored on a position size because it feels comfortable and they are not able to vary, even if they understand that position sizes should vary depending on volatility. Someone who is used to trading 500 shares of various stocks might feel weird buying 5,000 of something, even if it's proportionally less volatile.

Or they might trade 500 shares of a stock like META (currently $564) while also trading 500 shares of DJT (currently $20). That makes no sense. Similarly, I often had juniors working for me who would be comfortable trading 10 or 20 million USD positions in FX, but once they were promoted to a more senior role, they got super anxious when I told them to start trading 50s. I cover the art of position sizing in both my other books, so I won't repeat it.

I will just review how to manage the emotions around position sizing.

Don't get anchored on one position size. Your position size should be an output from a rigorous risk management framework and should not be influenced by your mood or bias. It also should not be shaped by silly premises like "it's too scary to have 10,000 shares on".

Your position size should vary, based on expected volatility of the product you are trading, your chosen stop loss, and the amount of capital you manage. If you're trading a $4 stock that moves 10 cents per day, you might be trading 15,000 shares of it while you are trading 60 shares of META. If you are a bank trader comfortable with $50 million position sizes, you might go to a hedge fund and start trading positions of $3 million—or $200 million!

If you're lucky enough to play the long game and trade your whole life, you will have wildly different capital at your disposal at various times. If a trade size generated by your risk process feels stupidly small or frighteningly large, but you are sure the outputs are correct... Listen to the process, not your emotions.

Scaling bets without emotion is an important skill.

If you have $100,000 in your account in year 1 and are managing $2 million in year 3 ... Your position size should be bigger in year 3 than it was before! This might sound obvious, but people get psychologically anchored on specific position sizes.

Use basis points (bps) for risk units, not dollars. Develop a system where you think in units of P&L, not in number of shares or absolute position sizes. Basis points (bps) are a good unit of P&L because they help you move away from dollars at risk and add a level of abstraction. Much as I don't think of the balance on my Starbucks card as real money (and thus I spend more, exactly as the folks at SBUX would hope!), thinking of your P&L in basis points can make it easier to scale.

Say you have $100,000 in your retail trading account and you decide that 3% per day is the right amount of risk. So you set your daily stop at 300 bps. You also decide that you will never risk more than 100 bps on a single trade or idea. So today, you're risking 100 bps (1% or $1,000) per trade. But if you kick ass for two years and now you've got $1,000,000 in your account—you still risk 100 bps on each trade so it feels like nothing has changed. Your spreadsheet spits out new trade sizes, but you're just risking 100 bps like you always have, even if your positions are 10X larger.

Anchoring on basis points of P&L and risk units measured in bps helps the psychology of linear and infinite scaling of risk, both up and down. It avoids the situation where a trader moves from a bank to a tiny hedge fund, feels like all his positions are ridiculously small, then trades too big and blows up. It eliminates the problem of the portfolio manager who gets her capital 4X'd but only doubles her position sizes and never hits her vol target.

Note that even if you're a robot who can scale up and down perfectly, every strategy has a capacity limit due to liquidity. If your spreadsheet tells you to get long 40,000 shares of a stock that trades 8,000 shares per day, that's obviously not possible.

Be methodical and unemotional about position sizes. If you are improvising, you are doing it wrong.

Note your emotions when your position is too big, or your stop loss is unrealistically close. You will often know what mistakes you're making while you're making them. You will feel that dizzying discomfort like when a roller coaster drops. Again, your emotions often convey information. *But not always*. Your discomfort could be the normal feeling that everyone gets when they take risk, and you just have to deal with it. Or, it could signal that your position is way too big and your intuition is telling you that you're going to get stopped out no matter what, because your stop is 0.1% of a day's range away.

Feelings are not facts. Sometimes they tell the truth and sometimes they lie. Analyze them and unpack them.

One last thing: In hindsight, every position you take is always the wrong size. If you made money, it should have been bigger! If you lose money, it should have been smaller. This is a transparently stupid way to think and yet everyone thinks this way sometimes. "Oh man, I knew this move was coming! I should have been 10X the size!"

Well, I mean, you "knew" it was coming now. But you didn't then.

Trading is about acting rationally in the face of uncertainty. Size your positions rationally and systematically. Persistent position sizing errors will eventually blow you up. If you don't have a clear system based on basis points of risk per trade, per day, week, month, or whatever, create one. It will make you a better trader and reduce a good portion of the anxiety that comes from finger-in-the-air position sizing.

A rigorous process reduces anxiety. Nothing creates more anxiety than the feeling that you don't know what you are doing, or that you can't trust yourself to do the next right thing.

Anxiety plagues everyone to various degrees, inside and outside the world of trading. We've covered tactics for dealing with trading anxiety, but these are just starting points.

Many factors can trigger and fuel your anxiety. Many books are directly or tangentially useful in dealing with anxiety and other psychological issues around trading[23]. But if you want to properly dig into your mental flaws or weaknesses, you need to do more than read a few books.

Get help from a therapist or coach. I waited until I was in my 40s before ever asking for help from anyone about anything, and I will tell you: Asking for help is a sign of strength, not weakness. Self-reliance is a strength, too, but in excess it can be crippling.

Self-reliance is great, *most of the time*. **Ask for help when you need it.**

Insomnia

I am writing this section in mid-April 2025, and I have been suffering from insomnia over the last two weeks. Since April 2, known as "Liberation Day", the markets have been flying all over the place and any position I have when I go to bed at 10:30 p.m. could be deep in the money or severely loss-making by the time I wake up.

In these markets, I tend to fall asleep easily at night, but wake up at 3 a.m., brain racing, anxious about where the markets are trading. **The worst thing to do in this situation is check your phone.** Trading decisions made in the blur of partial sleep are negative EV. This is why if you're a bank trader or hedge fund portfolio manager, it's not generally a great idea to leave call levels. When you are woken up at 2:40 a.m. by a phone call, you will not make clear and rational decisions, and you won't have the mosaic of market information of someone who is watching the market. It's like waking up in front of a chess board, it's your turn, and you have 15 seconds. Your opponent is strong, and you are weak.

Insomnia plagues me whenever the market is extremely volatile. I went through months of this during the 2008 Global Financial Crisis, again in the Eurozone Crisis in 2011, the China

[23] Some favorites: *The Body Keeps the Score* by Bessel van der Kolk, *The Power of Now* by Eckhart Tolle, How to Stop Worrying and Start Living by Dale Carnegie, Why Buddhism is True by Robert Wright. ... And if you want to increase your anxiety... check out *The Reset*, a financial thriller by Jack Moore. ;)

deval in 2015, and COVID. While I have never fully solved the problem, here are some things that have helped:

- **Turn off your phone** when you go to bed and put it far, far away from you. I leave mine turned off, downstairs, in the bathroom.
- **Never get out of bed** before a specific time. I found I used to wake up at 3:30 a.m., then lie there for 20 minutes, curiosity burning as I desperately wondered where the market had moved while I slept. Finally, around 4:00 a.m., I'd say "screw it" and get up. Then, there was no turning back because once I got out of bed, it was game on. Now, I don't allow myself to get out of bed until 5 a.m., no matter how curious or bored I am lying there. I find that knowing I'm not allowed to get out of bed removes the option of going to check the market, and I tend to get bored and fall back to sleep. As a commitment device, I told my wife that I am never getting out of bed before 5 a.m., no matter what. That way if I do, she will call me on it.
- **Read a paper book** before bed, don't watch USDJPY or NASDAQ futures or whatever. And don't play Clash Royale.
- **All the usual stuff** you can find on Google: avoid coffee after 12 noon, take melatonin supplements, exercise every day, even if you don't feel like it, and so on. I try to lift weights or do yoga at least 15 minutes a day. You don't need to spend 90 minutes in the gym to get benefits.

Insomnia is a huge drain on your mental health. If you can't get it under control, talk to a doctor or therapist and ask them for strategies.

Gambling Disorder

> "Get your dopamine somewhere else."
>
> Trading coach, 2024

Trading is a lot like gambling. Both involve uncertain outcomes, incomplete information, risk of loss, probability, dreams of free money, risk of ruin, and so on. Bad trading, without knowledge and discipline, is gambling. Good trading is not. It's that simple.

Trading is the ultimate siren, calling punters toward infinite riches and then killing them on the rocks.

Those who treat trading as a way to acquire money without effort are gambling and have negative expected value. Excellent traders expend tremendous psychological effort and have an edge. An excellent trader running a rigorous process over many years will demonstrate skill in generating somewhat consistent returns. A gambler will lose all their money, eventually, because their process does not create a positive expectation. It can be hard to tell gambling from trading because measuring skill vs. luck is famously difficult.

A questionnaire later in this section will help you determine whether your trading is more like a solid, positive EV endeavor, or straight up gambling.

While my plan with this book was to avoid touching on topics already covered in *Alpha Trader*, I wanted to go deeper into gambling because it's such a critical topic. From the first-time retail trader who blows up his account trading for fun, to Jesse Livermore, perhaps the greatest pure trader who ever lived, who went from richest man in America to bankruptcy and death by suicide in less than 10 years... Gambling disorder plagues many, many traders.

The lines between investing, trading, and gambling are wafer thin. To be honest, my trading oscillates between positive EV when I am trading well and something that looks more like gambling when I'm not.

Here's a comparison of investing, trading, and gambling:

Aspect	Investing	Trading	Gambling
Time horizon	Long-term (years/decades)	Short to medium-term (seconds to months)	Very short-term (minutes to hours)
Risk level	Moderate, can be managed	High, especially with leverage	Varies
Skill vs luck	Very few investors outperform the index	Can show persistent skill, most do not	Mostly luck-based (some skill in poker/sports)
Expected value	Positive over time (bullish drift)	Most fail, a few succeed massively	Usually negative (house edge or vig)
Goal	Wealth accumulation, retirement, income	Short-term profit, fun, status	Entertainment, thrill, quick profit
Emotional control	Important, but lower urgency	Crucial due to rapid decisions	Often emotional, can lead to addiction

There is plenty of academic work comparing trading and gambling, summarized in the January 2017 issue of the academic journal "Addictive Behaviors" in an article called: "Excessive trading, a gambling disorder in its own right?"[24] An excerpt:

> The systematic review showed that some traders were comparable to pathological gamblers in terms of clinical personality profiles and the severity of the loss of control. Like many pathological gamblers, they experienced a

---

[24] Marie Grall-Bronnec et al, doi.org/10.1016/j.addbeh.2015.12.006

> number of small early wins, chased their losses, lost control over the money they invested and had similar cognitive distortions including selective memory, gambler's fallacy or rationalization. However, they seemed to be better socially adapted than pathological gamblers, with less personal and family damage linked to their activity. They had a higher educational level and were more cooperative.

Here are some of the symptoms of gambling disorder from the DSM-5 and what they mean for traders.

1. **Need to gamble with increasing amounts in order to achieve the desired excitement.**

This is common in all areas of trading: Bank traders, retail traders, and hedge fund PMs can all fall victim to the excitement that comes from trading max position size. If you love the feeling of excitement you get from trading, be honest about it and self-aware. Ask yourself regularly:

Am I trading for fun, or to make money?

A significant percentage of retail traders are trading for fun, whether they admit it or not. Your position size should be the result of a mathematical calculation. If you find yourself putting on the "correct" position size and then 15 minutes later doubling it because you're bored... You're trading for excitement, not to make money.

2. **Restless or irritable when attempting to cut down or stop gambling.**

Do you always have a position? Like, even when you know you should probably get flat (going into a weekend or a vacation), you still keep a few positions just so you have something to watch? The trader that can't bring himself to square up before a vacation is usually someone that has the gambling bug.

I find it incredibly difficult to get completely flat because I like how risk feels. I like checking the market to see how things are moving. I like the dopamine I get from watching the market. I have to force myself to get flat now and then because my rationality knows that flat is an incredibly powerful position. It's the only time you are totally unbiased.

Sometimes, after trading one side for ages, I feel a massive weight lift when I finally square up. As I write this, I have been mostly short stocks for the past two weeks and finally got completely flat on Friday. Today, I am unbiased and ready to go long or short—whatever makes sense—whereas Friday I was still locked into a bearish view and was fixated on selling rallies. Positions cloud your judgment and give you strong confirmation bias.

Try to get flat once in a while. It feels good. It lets you rest. It reduces confirmation bias. If you cannot go on vacation flat, you are doing a huge disservice to your career because you will burn out. The concept of burnout sounds ridiculous if you're in your 20s or 30s. You feel invincible, like you can trade hardcore every day, forever. You can't. People get tired. You need to conserve energy and defrag your mental hard drive now and then.

Flat is the strongest position.

3. **Repeated unsuccessful efforts to control, cut down, or stop gambling.**

This one is pretty self-explanatory. If you can't follow your own rules, you will blow up. Even if you're the best trader in the world, gambling leads to ruin. That is the most important lesson from *Reminiscences of a Stock Operator*. Jesse Livermore was perhaps the greatest pure trader in history. But he failed because he couldn't stop gambling.

Willpower is a mighty thing, but it's not infinite. I have had more success admitting that my willpower sucks than I have had trying to bolster it. When you admit you are fallible and have weak willpower, you develop processes that will help you cope. Instead of saying "I'll stick to my stops, tomorrow, for sure!" - you automate your stops. Instead of being a PM who says: "I will stop shorting e-minis every day for no reason!" - you tell your execution desk to remove e-minis from your list of tradable products.

Which is more likely to work? Promising yourself you won't look at your phone while you are out on a nature walk with your 5-year-old son during market hours? Or turning your phone off and leaving it in the car before you go? If you have compulsive trading behaviors, building up more willpower might not be the answer.

Admit your weaknesses and find systems that protect you from them.

4. **Pre-occupation with gambling**

Traders pre-occupied with effortless upside are at risk of economic annihilation. Success is not achieved without effort. It requires enormous mental sacrifice, infinite patience, incredible self-knowledge, rigorous rationality, and many other rare traits and skills. If you dream of big wins, home run trades and upside convexity more than you dream about risk management and market and macro outcomes, you are on the wrong psychological track.

Every good trader is pre-occupied with the market. The obsession with markets is what makes great traders great. As with most human characteristics, an abundance of a particular trait can be an asset, and an overabundance can be a defect. If all you think about is markets, you will find that they never give you what you really need from life. They will give you money, and maybe fun, but in the long run it's family, friends, and community that lead to real happiness.

Don't forget this.

Go hard when the markets are humming but give yourself permission to take time off and chill when volatility is low. Volatility isn't always predictable, but often you can tell in mid-July that it's likely going to be quiet. Take a week off. Plan a three-day trip away with just you and your daughter. And when you take time away, *stop checking the market.*

Finally, take note of how often you check your phone. Those futures are going to go up and down whether you are watching or not. Your stop loss in USDJPY is either going to get done or not get done.

Staring at your phone for 90 minutes before bed monitoring the BOJ isn't going to have any positive impact on your P&L or your mental health.I don't bring my phone with me if I'm doing something with my wife (watching TV, playing a game, etc.) and I stay off Twitter, Bloomberg, and anything finance-related on Saturday.

Sunday at 1 p.m., I'll take an hour or two to read emails, get caught up on news, and think about trades I want to do on the market open. Then I try not to check my phone more than four more times. I check once when FX opens (1 p.m. or 3 p.m. NY time), once when futures open (6 p.m. NY), once when single names open (8 p.m. NY), and once before I turn my phone off.

Sitting there staring at futures for four hours Sunday night is a complete waste of time, but it's also an easy thing to get sucked into if you're a market junkie like me.

Are you obsessively checking the market, even when you're not at your trading desk? *Stop.*

5. **Gambling when feeling distressed or betting after large losses in an attempt to make the money back.**

If life at home is hard, you might find relief when you get to work. You might find even more relief from the excitement and "in the zone" feeling of trading.

You might find so much relief that this becomes your true motivation for trading.

If you are down, tired, depressed, or struggling with relationships, be extra vigilant about your risk management. It's easy to fall into a trap where you want trading to save you from malaise elsewhere.

It's also important to be aware when you are distressed about your trading losses.

r/Forex
elpersonaa

Help me I'm can't stop revenge trading

I am so pissed at myself I can't stop revenge trading and I don't stop. Every time I say I won't I will it's like an itch in me. I will not quit but I just need some help controlling my feelings after losing trades. I just put myself in a deeper hole after revenge trading☹

This leads to a situation known as "tilt", where you chase losses by increasing risk. If you ever feel yourself tilting, you need to physically remove yourself from the trading environment. Turn off your computer and walk away. If your account was $100,000 and now you've burned 40% of it and you're angry and your mind is telling you to double down so you can get from $60,000 back to $120,000... You are about to blow up. Walk away.

Trading while distressed about outside issues, or while distressed about trading itself is a near guarantee of failure. Be aware of strong emotions and when you feel distress, anger, disappointment or a lump in your throat: Take a timeout. Go for a walk. Take a day or two off and reboot. Whatever you do, make sure you have the correct position sizes or risk units in writing on a piece of paper in front of you *before* you start trading again. **Catching yourself right before you are about to do something stupid can save your account and your career.**

6. **Lying to conceal the extent of involvement with gambling.**

For some of the craziest stories of traders turned desperate loss-chasing gamblers, we can look at Nick Leeson, Jérôme Kerviel, John Rusnak, and Toshihide Iguchi.

Nick Leeson was a British trader who single-handedly caused the collapse of Barings Bank, Britain's oldest merchant bank, in 1995. This was a huge story the year I started trading, along with the Bre-X fraud and the Quebec Separation vote in Canada. Leeson, who worked as a derivatives trader in Barings' Singapore office, engaged in unauthorized speculative trading, and hid his mounting losses in a secret account known as "88888" while falsely reporting profits to his superiors.

When the Kobe earthquake caused Asian markets to plummet in January 1995, Leeson's already huge losses grew to approximately $1.3 billion, exceeding Barings' trading capital[25]. He fled Singapore and was eventually arrested, convicted of fraud, and sentenced to seven years in prison. Leeson's case became one of the most notorious examples of rogue trading in financial history.

---

[25] $1.3 billion used to be a lot of money.

John Rusnak was an American currency trader who perpetrated one of the largest bank frauds in U.S. history while working at Allfirst Bank in Baltimore. Funny enough, he was one of the biggest trading customers at the bank I worked at in 1997/1998. At the time, we had no idea he was committing fraud, he just seemed like a heavily-engaged, fun guy, and an active trader.

He was hired to evolve Allfirst's FX business away from simply hedging and towards profitable risk-taking. Between 1997 and 2002, Rusnak lost approximately $691 million through risky foreign exchange trading, then systematically concealed the losses by creating fake hedging transactions and forging documents showing his positions were protected.

He attempted to recover his mounting losses through increasingly desperate trading strategies. When his scheme collapsed in 2002, he pleaded guilty to bank fraud and was sentenced to eight years in federal prison. The scandal forced Allied Irish Banks to sell Allfirst to M&T Bank and led to sweeping reforms in financial oversight and risk management protocols across the banking industry.

Jérôme Kerviel and **Toshihide Iguchi** chased their losses in similar fashion, leading to similar results.

If you make a trading mistake, admit it, own it and cover it right away. Trading errors happen all the time. If you lie about a trading loss, you will destroy your reputation. Every manager understands that mistakes happen. It's not the mistake that matters; it's how you handle it.

Solutions for traders who gamble

Which side of the fine line between gambling and trading are you on? Do you oscillate back and forth, or are you always making rational, positive EV decisions that are never motivated by dopamine, frustration, or revenge? If you show signs of gambling, here are some fixes.

1. Admit that you gamble

Fixing any behavioral issue or mental weakness that affects your trading almost always starts with self-awareness. If you don't acknowledge that you are gambling, you will never take the necessary steps to stop.

Take 30 seconds to fill in the following chart: put an X in the relevant frequency for each row. Count the X's in each column, write in the total and multiply by the number shown. Add up your score to get an idea of whether you are trading or gambling. Anywhere you answered "Often" or "Frequently", think about what it might mean for your future, and what you can do about it now, before an unfortunate future transpires.

	Never	Rarely	Sometimes	Often	Frequently	
My positions are too big						
I put on low or negative EV trades when I am bored						
I have trouble getting flat or squaring up, even when I know it's the right thing to do						
I have tried to trade less or trade smaller positions but have been unsuccessful						
I am constantly thinking about trading, reliving past trades, or planning future trades, even during non-trading hours						
I deviate from my risk management rules and my trading plan						
I check trading apps or websites compulsively throughout the day, even at inappropriate times (social events, work meetings, family time).						
Trading helps me escape and forget about problems in my outside life						
After losing money in the market, I take bigger positions so I can make back losses						
Emotional highs and lows I experience from trading significantly impact my daily mood and functioning						
I have lied to family members, friends, or others to conceal my trading activity						
Count						
Multiply by	x	x	x	x	x	
Multiplier	0	1	2	3	5	
TOTAL SCORE						

This is a screening tool and not a diagnostic instrument. If you are concerned about your trading behavior, consider seeking professional advice.

Almost 2,000 traders completed this survey for me in 2024 and the results are below. My objective was to establish a baseline for context when a trader rates their own behaviors, but there are some other useful takeaways as well.

An exercise of this sort requires us to get honest about suboptimal behaviors. The raw data from the survey isn't shocking to me, but the breakdowns by trading experience and retail vs. institutional did kick out some unexpected results. First, here's the synthesis of all 1,930 responses.

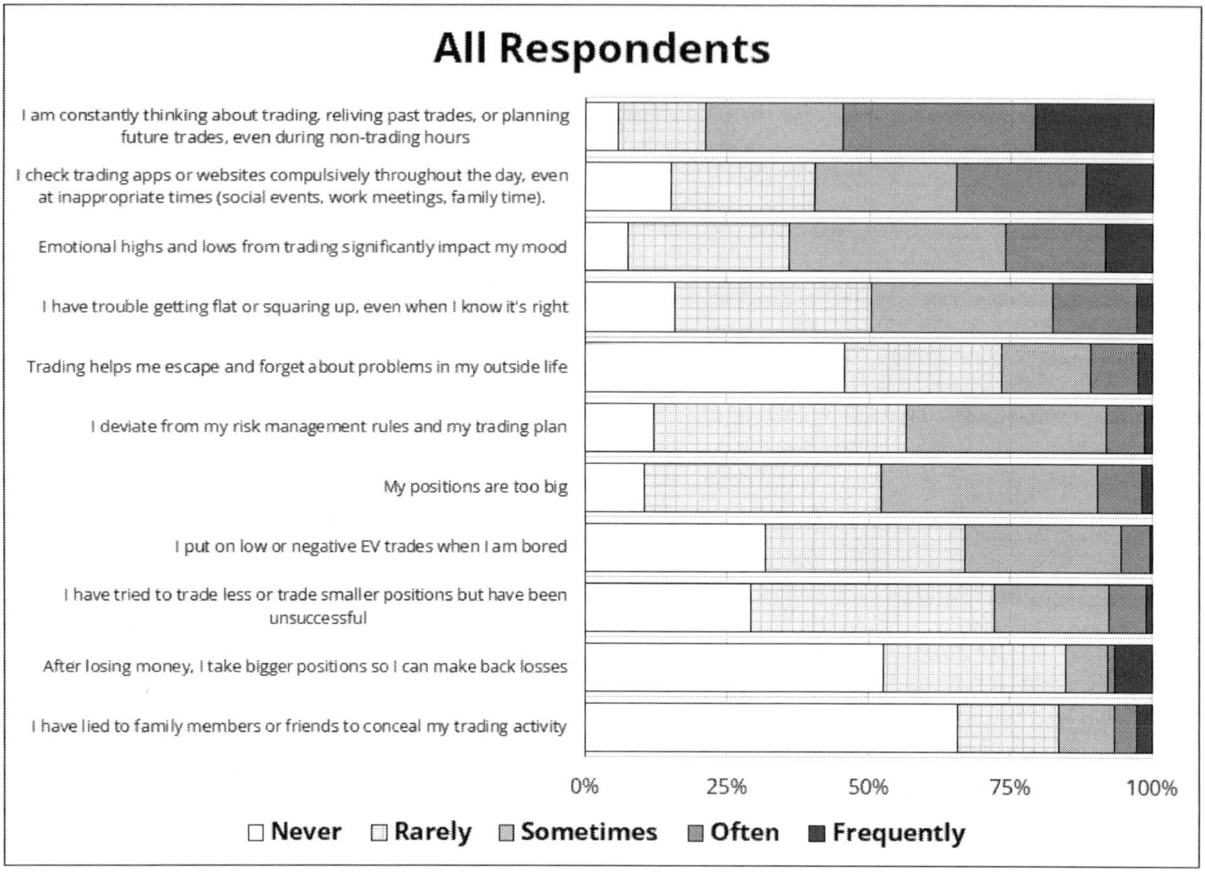

Key takeaways from a few of the questions:

- **Time spent thinking about trading:** The obsession with trading is real. My best guess is that very low levels of "Frequently" for those first two questions could actually be a bad sign because excellent trading requires some amount of constant preoccupation. When competing against other obsessives, it is good to be somewhat obsessive yourself. The golfer who never thinks about golf when she's off the golf course probably isn't going to be on the leaderboard at many LPGA events. But it's a question of balance. Where is the right point on the scale? I aim for "Often" but usually end up living with "Frequently".
- **Checking apps and websites:** The frequent checking of market prices is probably a less useful trait and "Rarely" is probably the optimal response here. Those who responded "Frequently" may have some work/life balance issues but then again, you need to make hay while the sun is shining so one could argue that "frequently" is OK a few times per year when things are booting off. There are no right answers here, only questions. The right answers are personal to the individual, and the idea here is to simply think about your own right answers.

- **Trading as an escape:** I was pleased to see that not many people use trading to escape from real life. It's definitely a red flag for me. If I am struggling with something at home, and then get to work and think trading is going to make it all better… It won't.
- **Lying to friends or family:** Lying about gambling or trading behaviors is the biggest red flag of them all. There are big, Nick Leeson level lies. And there are smaller ones like when you go to the bathroom four times during Thanksgiving Dinner to check whether your ETH stop loss triggered and then when your wife asks you what's up you say: "Huh? Oh, just drank too much water today, you know how it is."

There is a substantial difference in unwanted, gambling-adjacent behavior between new and experienced traders.

Here is the differential between how often noobs (1-3 years of experience) reported an issue "often" or "frequently" as compared to veteran traders (10+ years trading experience).

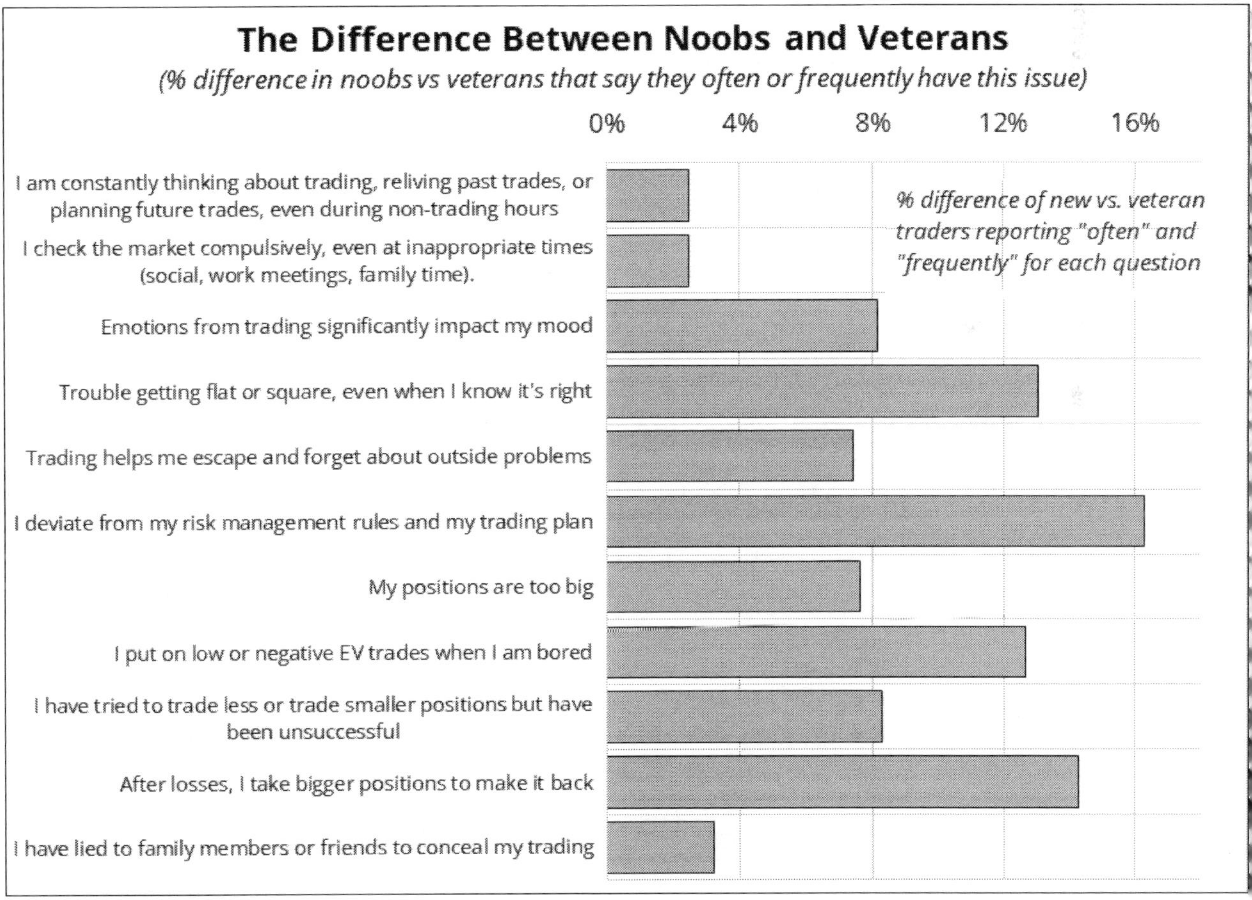

Experienced traders stick to their plan and don't chase losses.

I was also curious about differences between retail and institutional traders, regardless of experience. I think market makers and institutional traders tend to look down on retail and refer to it as "dumb money" but there is a huge cohort of extremely successful top-tier retail traders who are as good as, or better than any hedge fund trader. Here are the results:

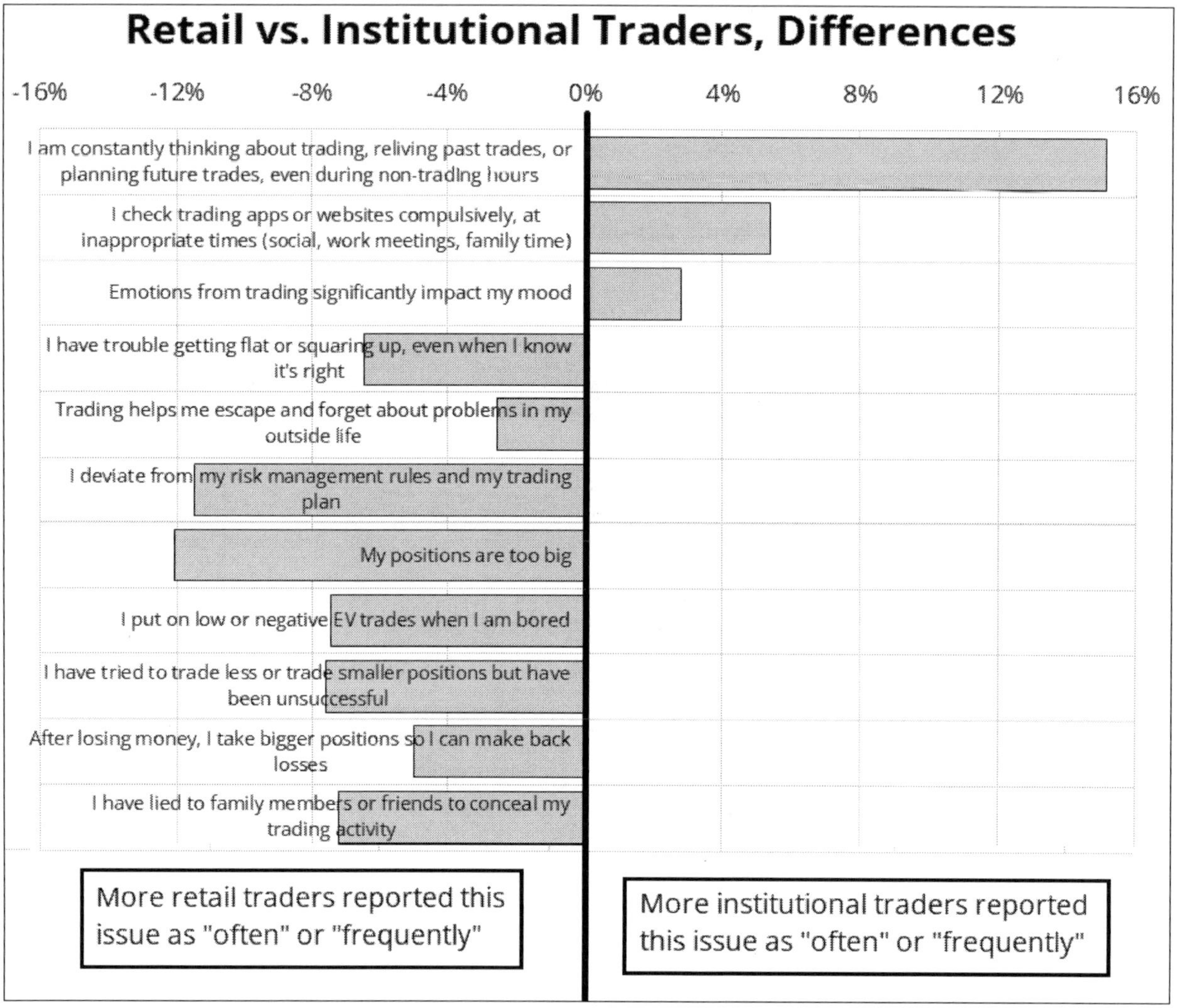

I found this logical but still surprising. Institutional traders are far more obsessed with the market and are constantly thinking about trades and trading.

Finally, the trading vs. gambling issues are highly correlated across respondents. That is, if you've got an issue with one of these behaviors, you probably have an issue with many of them. I selected all respondents who answered "frequently" to: *My positions are too big*, then looked at their responses to the other questions. Here's what that looks like. For context, compare this to the chart of all respondents.

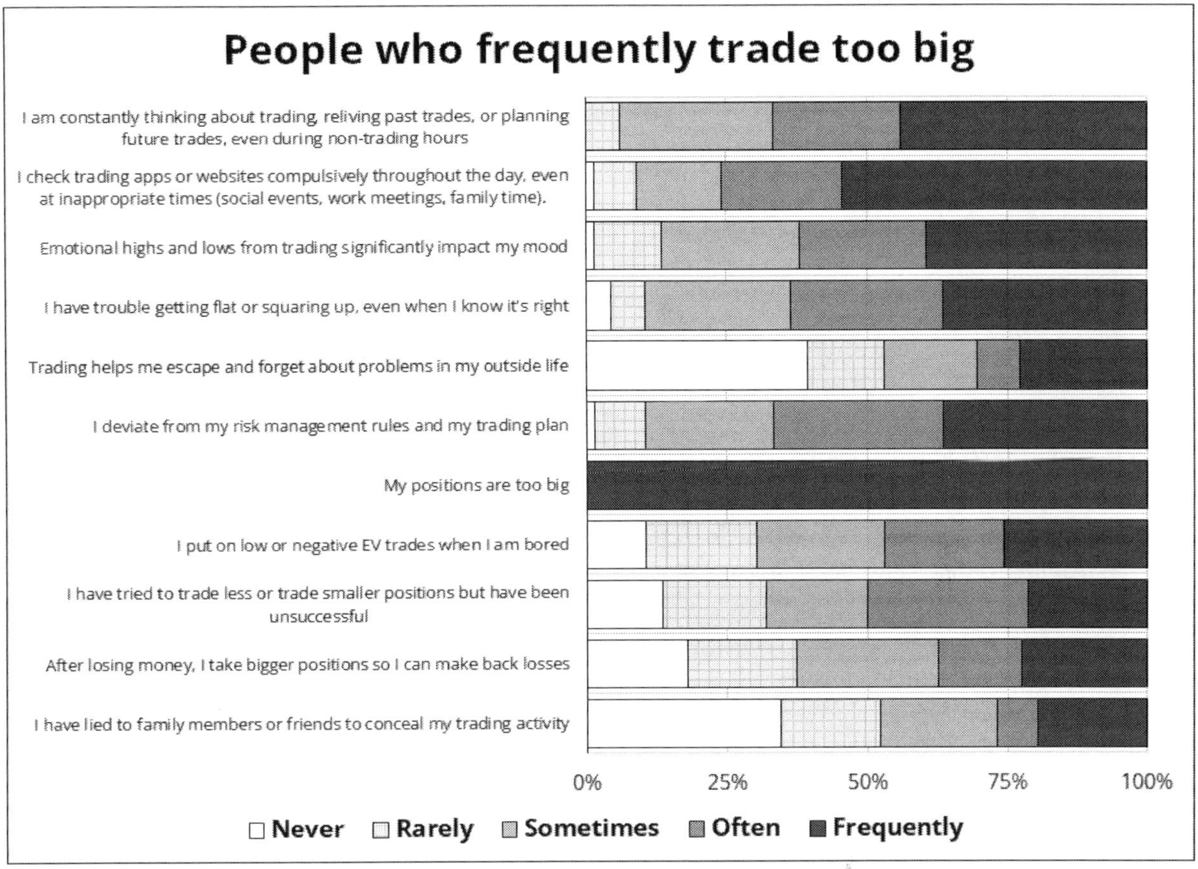

Trading in The Zone can be good and bad!

Trading in the Zone by Mark Douglas is one of my favorite trading books. It identifies The Zone as a positive force that channels your attention and energy towards strong focus and excellent decision making. This is usually how we think about The Zone, in academics, sports, trading, poker, creative writing, or any other task that requires concentration. Trading in the zone is characterized by:

- **Detached confidence.** You're confident but not overconfident. You trust your edge and don't second-guess yourself, because you're not emotionally attached to the outcome of any single trade.
- **Lack of fear.** You're not worried about being wrong, losing money, or missing out. Fearlessness allows you to follow your plan with precision.
- **Effortless execution.** Actions feel smooth and natural. You see setups clearly, and you pull the trigger without hesitation. You're not battling your thoughts.
- **Presence and focus.** You're in the moment, engaged in what is happening, not what might happen. You're not dwelling on the past or anxious about the future.

- **Acceptance of risk.** You've fully embraced the inherent uncertainty of trading. Losses don't disturb you, because you've accounted for them as a part of the process.
- **Lack of ego.** You're not trying to prove anything. Wins and losses aren't personal victories or defeats, they're feedback on your system and discipline.

Trading in the zone is a position of strength where you disappear and become one with the market for a while and then pop out and stare at a huge P&L number.

But there is another type of zone that is less *extreme focus* and more *addiction*. **The Dark Zone.** This state is often associated with machine gambling, the most addictive form of casino gambling. It shows up in trading, too. Here's how Kruger et al. explain it in their paper: *Contrasting Mind-Wandering, Dark Flow, and Affect During Slot Machine Play*[26]:

> Some slot machine players describe entering a trance-like state while playing the slot machine, a feeling which they call the "slot machine zone". Gamblers report a strong desire to be alone in order to enter this "zone" and once in this state, problem gamblers become so absorbed with the machine that they experience an extreme narrowing of attention and feelings of positive affect. This extreme narrowing of attention and trance-like state that gamblers describe is somewhat reminiscent of flow states referred to in positive psychology: total engagement with the current environment to the point where attending to task-relevant stimuli is effortless.
>
> Although flow is typically viewed as something favorable, Dixon and colleagues refer to the slot machine zone as a state of "dark flow" because of the potentially negative consequences this state engenders for the player (e.g., spending more time or money than initially planned at the slot machine).
>
> Dark flow may also help alleviate symptomology attributable to mood disorders such as anxiety and/or depression. In fact, researchers have shown a reliable association between mood disorders and problem gambling status. Underlying this relation, it appears that a subset of problem gamblers may use gambling as a way to self-medicate depressive symptomology.

Below is a quick explanation of the gambling addiction process from Howard Shaffer et al. in the *Harvard Journal of Psychiatry*[27].

---

[26] pmc.ncbi.nlm.nih.gov/articles/PMC8866259/

[27] www.researchgate.net/publication/7970947_Toward_a_Syndrome_Model_of_Addiction_Multiple_Expressions_Common_Etiology

> The potential for addiction emerges when repeated interaction with a specific object or array of objects (a drug, a game of chance, a computer) reliably produces a desirable subjective shift.
>
> When individuals engage in repeated interactions with a specific object or objects of addiction, and the neurobiological or social consequences of these interactions produce a desirable (i.e., sought-after) subjective shift that is reliable and robust, the premorbid stage of the addiction syndrome emerges. This sought-after shift in subjective state is requisite for the development of the addiction syndrome. During this stage of the syndrome, people teeter on a delicate balance that can shift them toward either more or less healthy behavior.

I sometimes find myself in this dark zone after trading a fast market for a while, even when the market has slowed, the opportunity set is gone and we are back to random drift. Instead of taking the money, I remain stuck in the zone, staring at my headline feed, hoping for another hit and run opportunity (and another shot of dopamine). I start trading random headlines to remain in this pleasant zone of non-self, where time is slowed and the outside world disappears. I am chasing the zone instead of chasing profits.

A slot machine gambler's experience is not just about their predisposition towards gambling disorder. It's a complex interaction between their brain and the machine itself. A slot machine that looks like a video game and is programmed to detect and monetize a player's weaknesses will exert a more powerful pull than one with a mechanical arm. The interaction between human and object creates the addiction, not the individual or the object alone.

Think about this if you overtrade. What aspects of the machine (your trading platform, media consumption, research process, etc.) trigger your overtrading or gambling instincts? Can you prune some of them away? As mentioned, imagine a video of yourself gambling in markets and break it down frame by frame. What part of the market "slot machine" is stimulating your behavior? What sights and sounds are the direct precursors to pushing the buy and sell buttons?

Break down suboptimal trading activities frame by frame to find important insights that support behavioral change.

This excerpt from Scientific American[28] explains the different types of gambling and why one can be more addictive than another.

---

[28] www.scientificamerican.com/article/how-sports-betting-apps-use-psychology-to-keep-users-gambling/

> Not all forms of gambling carry the same levels of risk. Engaging in a game of poker with friends, for example, is less dangerous than playing a slot machine. Slots have long been casinos' greatest moneymaker because of their addictive potential. Jamie Torrance, a psychologist studying gambling at Swansea University in Wales, chalks this up to the machines' incredible pace—unlike in a game of poker or blackjack, only seconds pass between placing a bet and winning or losing. This makes the experience more immersive, leading some slot players to enter a trancelike state called "dark flow" in which they become completely absorbed by the game, Torrance says. The fast turnarounds can closely link the act of pressing the button with the rush of dopamine of a potential win, conditioning a person to keep pulling the lever.

The implication is that if you are prone to overtrading or gambling, you should structure your environment and your machine interactions to minimize the risk.

- Do not use gamified apps like Robinhood.
- Do not trade on your phone at night.
- Don't check the market when you are out with friends.
- Take breaks from trading so that you are not so fully immersed in trading that you enter the Dark Zone.

Just like deleting the Twitter app from your phone will help you reduce your intake of social media, deleting the trading app off your phone will reduce your overtrading. Will you miss a few cool trades? Yep. Will your life and your P&L improve dramatically?

Also yep.

A simple way to ensure that "In the zone" doesn't become a darker version where you lose control is to create endpoints or break times. Get up and move away from your computer at least once per hour, even on busy days. A simple seventh-inning stretch will do the trick. In *Addiction by Design,* Natasha Schüll explains why the zone you enter while playing slot machines is so much more immersive than most other forms of gambling. The day trader who is so in the zone that they never come up for air may find 40% of their capital is gone when they finally resurface.

> Unlike chess, ritual trance, or the execution of a surgical operation, all of which have natural endpoints, machine gambling is a potentially inexhaustible activity whose only sure end is the depletion of gambler funds. The operational logic of the machine is programmed in such a way as to keep the gambler seated until the point of "extinction" is reached.

2. Don't count on willpower

Create process and rule-based barriers to overtrading and gambling. This excerpt from *Addiction by Design* will probably ring true for many traders.

> Julie breathlessly recounts the recalibrations that transpire over the course of a typical play session:
>
> "I got four aces four times, 800 credits each time. That means I could have cashed out 800 dollars total. But each time I hit, I'd play it down to 200 credits from 800 credits and I'd say, "well, I'll just hit the aces again and then I'll leave." Then I'd get four of a kind and have like 437 credits and I'd say "I'll just go to 400 and leave" and then at 400 I'd just push the button again and drop below 400, and I'd say, "Well now I'm down past 400 I'll just get back up to 400 and then I'll cash out." And then I'd find myself closer to 300 and I'd say "Once I get down to 300 I'll go," and then when I got below that I'd say "Well, I might as well keep going, I've already blown what I was gonna blow–I might as well try to get the aces again."

How many times have you thought: "If I just get back to flat, I'll square up." Then you get back to flat and the cartoon dollar signs spin in your eyes, and you add to your positions, instead of squaring up. Or something similar.

If you recognize this pattern in your P&L management, either you do not have a rigorous process, or you are not sticking to your own rules. Is there a way you can enforce the rules better? Can you share your rules with someone who has visibility of your trading and can therefore serve as a commitment device?

Enforcement, automation, and commitment devices work better than willpower. If I am up $1,000,000 on the day and decide I will square up if I get back to $500,000... I know I will struggle to keep that promise to myself, so I send an email to my boss, like:

> "I'm up $1m ... Will cut everything if I drop to +500k. Have a good day."

It's easier to let yourself down than it is to let down others.

You are being prodded and manipulated by corporations that rely on flow.

If you are a retail trader using Robinhood, Coinbase, e-Trade, or a similar platform, identify and understand if and how you are being manipulated into trading more. Most businesses that profit from addiction prey on addicts either intentionally or unintentionally because the addict is the best possible customer. This targeting can be subtle. Most companies that benefit from addictive behaviors will urge customers to drink or bet responsibly while simultaneously hunting you down and monetizing degenerate whales. Naturally, many whale-like consumers of addictive products are addicts. Pareto's Law applies.

When you receive communications from investment or trading firms, whether it's direct email, ads on the internet, clickbait articles from Forbes or Zerohedge, push notifications on your phone, or sound effects on the trading app you use... Dissect the intent of these communications and be mindful about whether they are encouraging you to overtrade.

For example, **Wall Street pretty much only hands out buy and hold, not sell recommendations.** The innocent explanation is that stocks mostly go up in the long run, so it makes sense to mostly buy or hold. The cynical explanation is that Wall Street firms rely on companies for lending and underwriting and therefore avoid the potentially dangerous idea of telling their clients to sell a company's stock. It's generally just not very good for business.

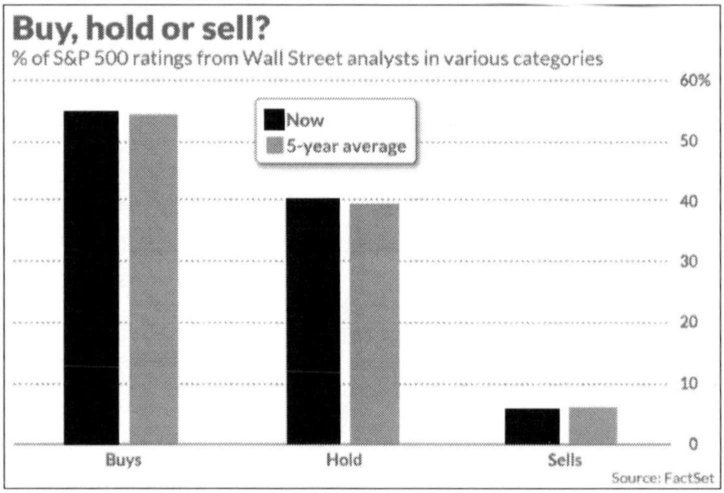

Also, since a huge majority of investors are long-only, buy recommendations generate more flow and more money for the firm. Sell recommendations can only generate flow from existing holders; buy recommendations generate flow from everyone.

A takeaway from this bullish bias is that you should pay more attention to sell recommendations than buy recs. The bar to put out a sell recommendation is extremely high and thus probably reflects a higher confidence level than a buy or a hold recommendation.

Wall Street continues to create products with shorter time horizons and more leverage because these products prey on overtrading and gambling (and that's what the people want!). The shorter the time frame and the more leverage a product offers, the more it triggers the dopamine release that gamblers crave. Are you trading a high-leverage product because it's fun, or because it's the correct expression of your view?

Share of S&P index options expiring the same day

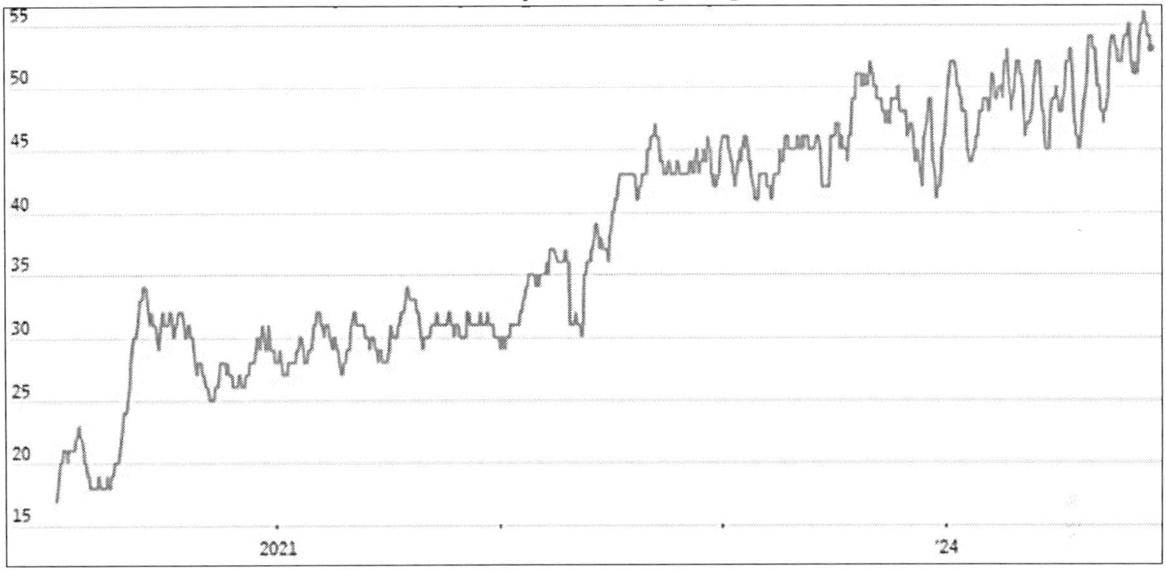

Source: SpotGamma

Gunjan Banerji of the Wall Street Journal writes, for example[29]:

> I was sitting in the back of a Gamblers Anonymous meeting in a Murray Hill church basement earlier this year and I couldn't believe what I was hearing.
>
> One man called stock options the "crack cocaine" of the market. Another said he faced hundreds of thousands of dollars in trading losses after borrowing from a loan shark to double down on the market. A fourth brought his mom and girlfriend to celebrate one year since his last bet, which had included risky options trades.
>
> They were among several men that night sharing stories of compulsive gambling, not on sports or lotteries, but in financial markets like crypto, options or stocks. I found that more and more American men are getting hooked on trading in financial markets. Men told me they had lost millions of dollars and ended up in debt from trading. Yet they couldn't stop.
>
> The financial consequences were bad, but the emotional consequences were even more harrowing. Some had marriages that ended in divorce because of

[29] www.wsj.com/finance/stocks/stock-market-trading-apps-addiction-afecb07a

> trading addictions. One man told me he couldn't stop until his wife threatened to leave him.
>
> "She gave me an ultimatum," Cachia said. "'You need to stop this, or I'm done."
>
> Treatment centers around the country told me they expect the problem to get worse, with the speculative boom in markets reaching new heights this year.

Avoid clickbait articles and tweets with crazy price targets. These are rarely issued by serious market participants. Wild and crazy price targets are a marketing tool. They are specifically designed to trigger FOMO and lottery ticket reflex and attract media attention. The easiest way to get media coverage in finance is to issue a crazy price target.

If you see headlines like these, look away immediately. You are being manipulated.

NEWS

Why Cathie Wood Sees Bitcoin Price Soaring To $3.8 Million

Nobel Laureate Thinks Bitcoin Is Going to Zero

"It's only digital gold if it has a use. If it doesn't have a use, it's just paper. Not paper, it's air, not even air," the economist said.

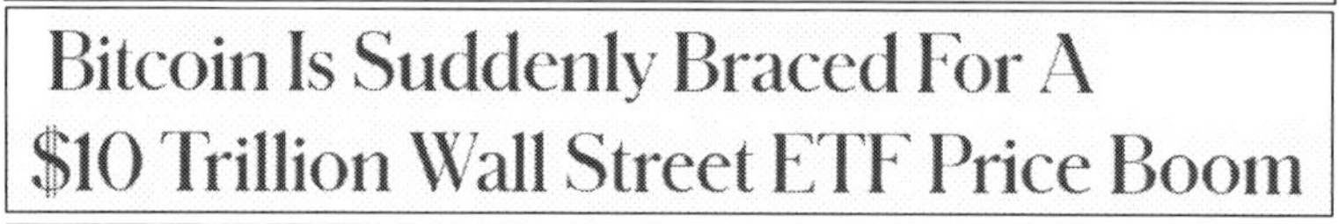
Bitcoin Is Suddenly Braced For A $10 Trillion Wall Street ETF Price Boom

Why Tom Lee thinks Ethereum will rally to $16k in 2025

Ads for stock recommendation websites lure gamblers with backward-looking statements like: "If you bought $1,000 in XYZ five years ago, you'd have $189,270 today. Click here for the stock that could be the next XYZ!" Hindsight is one hell of a drug.

Crypto is where gamblers go looking for lottery-like payoffs, particularly in alt- and memecoins. The problem is that the industry is more and more dominated by insiders and opportunists, so the memecoin casino offers much worse odds than Las Vegas. There is a reason it's called "pumpdotfun" not "pumpdotprofit"[30].

Most meme and altcoin traders are looking for fun and lottery-style returns, not sustainable profits or edge. Platforms cash in through gamification, email marketing, and other methods that prey on gamblers' worst instincts. When you get an email from Coinbase that says: "Bitcoin is up 10%! Will it go higher???" What do you think they're trying to do? They are trying to get you to trade. So they can collect fees.

While these manipulations are hard to prove in court, Robinhood recently paid $7.5 million to settle a dispute with the State of Massachusetts after it was charged with gamifying its trading platform and encouraging novice investors to make trades that were not financially prudent. Robinhood frequently faces scrutiny as its user base is particularly young and vulnerable, but most of the stimulation offered by Robinhood can be found on CNBC, IBKR, e-trade, or anywhere else. All these companies rely on trading volume for profit. The more people overtrade, the more money they make.

10% of Americans consume more than 60% of all the alcohol sold in the USA. 4% of Brits consume 30% of all the alcohol sold in the UK. Without alcoholics, the alcohol industry would be bankrupt. The economics of most industries selling addictive products rely on super-users.

Similarly, various lawsuits and complaints accuse sports gambling websites of targeting gambling addicts. From NBC Sports[31]:

> Baltimore has sued DraftKings and FanDuel for exploiting problem gamblers.
>
> "These companies are engaging in shady practices, and the people of our city are literally paying the price," Baltimore mayor Brandon Scott said in a press release. "DraftKings and FanDuel have specifically targeted our most vulnerable residents — including those struggling with gambling disorders — and have caused significant harm as a result. This lawsuit is a critical step to hold them accountable and protect all Baltimoreans."
>
> The lawsuit alleges that the companies hope to lure bettors to bet, until they're addicted to betting. Neither company provided comment to ESPN.com in response to the lawsuit.

---

[30] pump.fun/board -- Note how their website looks like a video slot machine. Not a coincidence.

[31] www.nbcsports.com/nfl/profootballtalk/rumor-mill/news/baltimore-sues-draftkings-fanduel-for-allegedly-exploiting-problem-gamblers

> "Defendants are not interested in people merely dipping their toes in the water," the complaint alleges. "They want bettors to bet, in significant amounts, over and over. Some get hooked, and that's the point."

Some of their (alleged) predatory tactics are:

- sending emails to large bettors when they go quiet (luring back addicts who are trying to quit)
- advertising bets with the highest profit margin and worst expected value (multi-leg parlays, etc.) to prey on bettors' longshot bias
- using consumer profiling combined with push notifications to maximize gamblers' activity and motivate them to return from hiatus

Imagine an alcoholic trying to get sober and two weeks after his last drink he looks at his phone and sees a notification on his phone from the local bar: it's a coupon encouraging him to stop by for a free beer. *Not good.*

Risk and the duty to manage that risk are increasingly being downloaded onto individuals as regulatory bodies like the SEC step back from oversight, regulatory frameworks fail to provide protection, and the retail market is dominated by speculative vehicles like memecoins, get-rich-quick trading videos, leveraged ETFs, and other questionable products.

This evolution of financial markets requires individual traders to see that the water they swim in is toxic. Every communication you receive from a financial firm should be considered suspect. Find reliable sources of information and exclude all others. There are reputable firms in finance, but you need to be careful that you know who is trustworthy. We are in the golden age of fraud, and nobody will protect you from exploitation.

Companies may be trying to manipulate you directly or they may end up encouraging you to overtrade by accident. Either way, the result is the same. Recognize the manipulation and absurdity of many financial products and headlines, especially from organizations that prioritize clicks and online ad revenue. Many formerly respectable media outlets have devolved into engagement-focused organizations (as opposed to truth- or information-focused) or have been taken over by private equity and turned into clickbait machines.

Insulate yourself from communications that stimulate your overtrading or your urge to gamble.

A substantial portion of investor underperformance can be explained simply by the fact that investors are active when they should be doing nothing. This is proven again and again by the consistent and sizeable outperformance of index funds vs. active managers and by the poor returns in retail accounts. Most of the time you should be doing nothing!

3. Get professional help

As discussed in previous sections, a therapist, psychiatrist, performance coach or trading coach is often the best way to deal with psychological issues around trading. You may find out some things you could not admit before. Maybe you're self-destructing on purpose after large gains because you don't feel you deserve money made without physical effort. This is a common subconscious leak, especially for traders whose parents worked in less abstract fields like construction, teaching, or emergency services.

To stop unwanted gambling in markets, you need to take a few simple steps:

- See the behavior and acknowledge that it is unhealthy.
- Admit that willpower alone will not fix everything.
- Develop systems and a process that directly pushes back on your gambling and overtrading instincts.
- Use a trading or performance coach (or a therapist) to help you work through your gambling and overtrading issues. This doesn't have to be a huge commitment; three or four sessions with a professional can do wonders for your trading psychology.

Removing the urge and proclivity to gamble can be the most important step you ever take in trading. Gambling and overtrading are common, massive leaks, especially for short-term traders. Take this issue seriously because it is the one that takes down even the greatest traders.

Principle 15: Elite traders don't gamble.

Conclusion

In this chapter, I have covered some of the major types of clinical psychology that impact trading. There are other conditions, like depression, obsessive compulsive disorder, and substance abuse, that can also impact how you trade. These are diseases that are not always curable by simply pulling up your socks and trying harder. If you have any sort of mental difficulties that you persistently find unfixable on your own, get help.

Many people, especially men, are not strong enough to admit they need help. Asking for help is not a sign of weakness. Try it and see.

CHAPTER 5

BETTER TRADING THROUGH POKER

What Hold 'Em can teach you about trading

"In the long run there's no luck in poker, but the short run is longer than most people know."

Rick Bennet

Trading is a high-intensity pursuit with a low success rate and immense financial rewards for the few that come out on top. This makes it a lot like poker. Due to the many overlaps between the two domains, poker offers useful lessons for professional trading. Studying and playing good poker can make you a better trader.

Financial markets and poker both demand self-awareness, discipline, and risk management in games where outcomes are probabilistic and participants have incomplete information. Both pit skilled players against each other in a battle where edge is measured in fractions and mental fortitude is as important as technical knowledge. Both are adversarial and adaptive problems, not physics problems.

As someone who has spent time in both worlds, I've found the parallels interesting and useful, and the skills transferrable. Talents that make world-class poker players—emotional control, bankroll management, reading opponents, and handling variance—also separate consistently winning traders from the losing majority. Let's examine how studying poker can improve your trading.

The psychology of the game

Trading and poker are both psychological battlegrounds. The market doesn't care about your Ivy League degree or your sophisticated models any more than your opponents in poker care about your time spent on solvers or your knowledge of game theory. Both arenas reward those who can maintain emotional equilibrium under extreme pressure and uncertainty. Let's go through some commonalities between the two games and see how knowledge of poker can make you a better trader.

Emotional torture

To me, the most salient similarity between poker and trading is that they both feel the same when you play. The ups and downs. The euphoria. The in-the-zone runs and tilty drawdowns. The eventual realization, as you mature, that you cannot let every win and loss affect you emotionally or you will implode under the stress of constant cortisol production, high blood pressure, and clenched fists. Over time, good traders and good poker players find emotional balance as they understand that swings due to variance are part of the game.

Tilt

In poker, "tilt" describes the emotional state where a player abandons rational play and makes increasingly poor decisions, often after a bad beat[32]. It's fascinating how predictable this behavior is and how eerily similar it is to traders after a significant loss. The word "tilt" is borrowed from pinball. It is a built-in failsafe to prevent players from lifting or turning the machine to make the ball go wherever they want. When a pinball machine is lifted, pushed, slammed, tilted, or pushed too hard, it shuts down. Flippers stop working, the sound turns off, and the machine goes dark.

This is your brain on poker

[32] A hand in which a player loses despite having far superior hole cards.

When you take a heavy loss, especially one that feels unfair ("A pair of sevens beat my pair of kings?! Cmon, man!"), your limbic system often overrides the prefrontal cortex and your mind starts to shut down. You go numb with rage and frustration. You go on tilt.

Tilt is a huge problem for poker players. Many times, I have shoved chips in the pot with negative EV because my brain went numb after the previous hand and I see nothing but red. This problem is particularly intense for poker players who have been drinking alcohol. Poker and drinking don't mix[33].

In trading, tilt is similar. The cognitive part of your brain blacks out and your lizard brain starts pressing buttons. You revenge trade. You double down on losing positions. You watch the market go through your stop loss level and you remain frozen. Afterwards, you sit there under the weight of crushing demoralization, wondering what you've done.

Tilt can lead to nearly instant ruin.

I have seen this in real-time as a trader adds to a short in a skyrocketing microcap simply because he cannot see straight as the huge, flashing red P&L number gets bigger and he is on full tilt. His rational brain is flooded.

You need to recognize tilt before, or as it happens, and immediately step away from the game.

The polyvagal system, a concept originally developed by American psychologist Dr. Stephen Porges (founding director of the Traumatic Stress Research Consortium), explains how our nervous system reacts to stress and safety through three main states:

- **Ventral vagal**: Calm and connected
- **Sympathetic**: Anxious, fight, or flight; and
- **Dorsal vagal**: Shut down or numb.

The adjective "vagal" refers to the vagus nerve, which is the longest cranial nerve in the body. It runs from the brainstem all the way down to the abdomen and affects key parts of your body like the heart, lungs, and digestive system. It plays a big role in keeping our body running smoothly, and helps control heartbeat, breathing, speech, and digestion.

As a key part of the parasympathetic nervous system (which helps the body relax after stress), the vagus nerve helps us calm down after something intense or scary. Polyvagal Theory explains that the vagus nerve has two sides to it: the ventral vagal branch which

---

[33] Source: My personal experience.

helps us feel safe, connected, and relaxed, and the dorsal vagal branch which can make us shut down or freeze when we're overwhelmed[34].

These states help us respond to the world around us, depending on whether we feel safe or threatened. The idea of tilt is closely related. When we go on tilt, we're shifting out of the calm, ventral vagal state into fight or flight and then ultimately into dorsal vagal state.

When the body perceives a massive threat, the dorsal vagal state is activated, and the mind reflexively hits the "freeze" or "shutdown" button. It's like the Microsoft Windows blue screen of death—inside your mind. This state is often triggered by shock or trauma, and features immobilization and dissociation. The following diagram outlines the polyvagal view of the three primary states of the nervous system.

The Polyvagal Defense Hierarchy

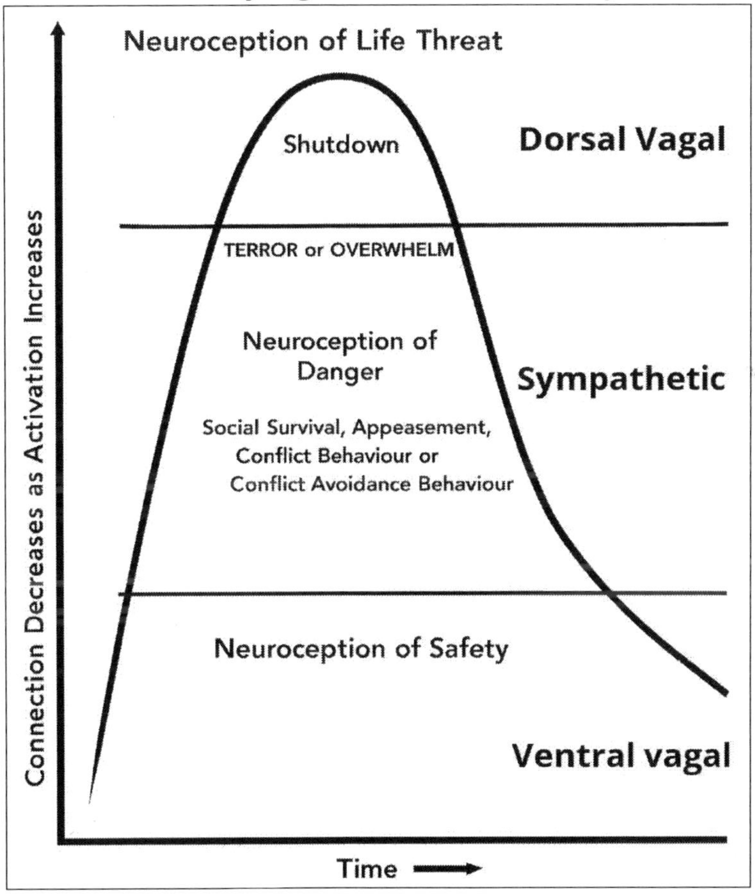

[34] You can read more about polyvagal theory and dorsal vagal shutdown (including strategies to soothe a dorsal vagal shutdown) here: neurodivergentinsights.com/dorsal-vagal-shutdown/

Once you get into the dorsal vagal (tilt/shutdown) zone, you dissociate from the real world and may have difficulty coming back. Make sure you don't get there in the first place.

Poker pros (and traders) avoid or deal with tilt through rigorous self-awareness. They know their emotional triggers and have systems in place to catch themselves before the dissociative spiral begins. Many top poker players leave the table when they notice an approaching wave of tilt. Self-aware traders and poker players have the ability to go out of body and see themselves entering mental breakdown. Then they get up and take a walk.

Create a personal "tilt protocol." This might include:

- **Square up.** Take the L. If you just lost 20% of your capital and your mind is on fire, get out. Survive to trade another day. You can't attain a rational state until you square up the positions that tilted you.
- **Step away.** Institute a mandatory 30-minute break after any loss exceeding a predetermined threshold.
- **Get help.** Give a trusted colleague permission to call you out when you're tilting.
- **Know when you are DFD.** Set daily and monthly downside P&L limits that, once hit, mean you're done—no exceptions. I call this daily limit "DFD" (done for day) and as a market maker I had a firm rule that once I hit DFD, I sent an email to my manager with the subject line: "DFD" and a short explanation of what happened.

This form of automatic journaling helped me immediately admit I hit my limit and helped me process the causes behind the loss. Sometimes, it was simply bad luck, or a good decision that led to a bad outcome. Other times, it was the result of a specific negative behavior. By calling myself out, I made it black and white and forced myself to honestly self-evaluate.

One trader I know keeps a small mirror propped on his desk. After any significant loss, he forces himself to look in the mirror and verbally state his next trade and rationale. This small pattern interrupt helps him identify when he's trading from emotion and helps him get outside of his own head.

Tilt is generally associated with losses, but there is a related concept called Winner's Tilt. In my personal trading, I find Winner's Tilt to be the more common type. Winner's Tilt is when you are winning big and you start betting bigger, taking risky shots with house money. It can lead to huge drawdowns from high water as you start to feel invincible after big wins.

If you experience any of the following, you are probably on Winner's Tilt and you should reduce your risk:

- You are euphoric about your P&L and/or feel invincible.
- You take a screenshot of a winning position or your account P&L.
- You are high fiving, yelling "LFG!" or singing songs on the trading floor.

I find it hard to reduce risk when I'm winning because I don't want the good times to end. But they will. I can allow them to end the easy way, or the hard way. I use conditional formatting in my P&L spreadsheet to tell me when I am earning way above trend. When cells start to light up yellow and orange, I plug my nose and reach for the buttons to pare down my risk. I hate it, and I really, really don't want to do it, but I am always glad I did.

You can also stay on the lookout for Winner's Tilt in the wild and use it as a potential reversal indicator. You will see it on Twitter, wallstreetbets, and on the trading floor. When other traders are euphoric en masse, traders are posting screenshots of big wins in a particular stock, or traders you work with are high fiving or pumping their fists in the air, the market is probably about to turn.

Reading the table vs. Reading the market

Poker players don't just play the cards; they play their opponents. They develop an intuitive ability to detect variations in behavior that reveal information their opponents are trying to conceal. In poker, these are called "tells".

Poker tells are subtle physical or behavioral cues that cause a poker player to unconsciously reveal information about his hand. These nonverbal signals include micro-expressions, timing variations, body language, and betting patterns that experienced players can detect and interpret.

Common poker tells include:

- hand tremors when holding strong cards
- prolonged staring at good hands
- glancing briefly at chips when planning to make a big bet
- unnecessary conversation to mask nervousness
- changes in breathing patterns under stress

The ability to read these subtle cues won't help an elite poker player win every single hand. Instead, they occasionally offer home run opportunities where the astute player gains a huge probabilistic advantage at a critical moment.

When the market eats an Oreo

In *Rounders* (one of the best poker movies ever) the famous "Oreo scene" illustrates the concept. During a high-stakes game, protagonist Mike McDermott (Matt Damon) notices that his opponent, Teddy KGB (John Malkovich), handles Oreos differently depending on the strength of his hand. When Teddy KGB has a strong hand, he splits an Oreo and eats it, rewarding himself. But when he is bluffing or weak, he only breaks open the cookie—he doesn't eat it.

Mike's recognition of this pattern allows him to avoid a costly mistake at a key moment, and he folds a strong hand when he realizes KGB has an even stronger one. Thanks to a clever observation, Matt Damon's character avoids going broke. Then, with momentum on his side (spoiler alert!) he eventually roars back and takes all of Teddy's chips.

The most lucrative tells in poker and in markets are not obvious. They require careful observation, pattern recognition, and the ability to connect opponent or market behaviors to underlying psychological states.

Identify the moments when the market is eating an Oreo.

Unusual price patterns, high volume price rejection at key levels, multi-sigma order flow imbalances, and divergences between related assets all provide information about the market's strength, weakness, and emotional state. As a poker player might see that his opponent's betting line makes no sense, a trader sees that the market is doing something odd. **When a poker opponent, or a market you trade, does something strange... Sit up and take notice.** It probably reveals something about what will happen next.

When you are dialed in, you may notice the market action is odd. *Something weird is going on.* Listen to your Spidey Sense. Here are five tells I watch for in markets.

Market tell #1: Good news/bad price

How did your market react to news today? One of the best tells in markets is a market that fails to react to good or bad news. This setup, called good news/bad price or bad news/good price, tells you that stronger hands are getting busy in the market and using the news as exit liquidity. More often than not, **a market that doesn't respond to clearly good or bad news is going to trend in the opposite direction for the next 24 to 48 hours.**

When positive news (like strong earnings or favorable economic data) is met with a price decline instead of a rally, it's a signal that an uptrend may be exhausted, or smart money is going the other way.

We saw a powerful example of this phenomenon in 2025 after Donald Trump's tariffs on Canada were announced. The market expected a large tariff on Canada would trigger massive selling of CAD (and thus a bullish move higher in USDCAD). And each time tariff news landed, it was worse than expected... And yet **USDCAD could not rally**.

The most egregious example of this was when Trump put a 25% tariff on all Canadian goods over the weekend of February 3, 2025.

USDCAD Hourly price action, Late January to mid-February 2025

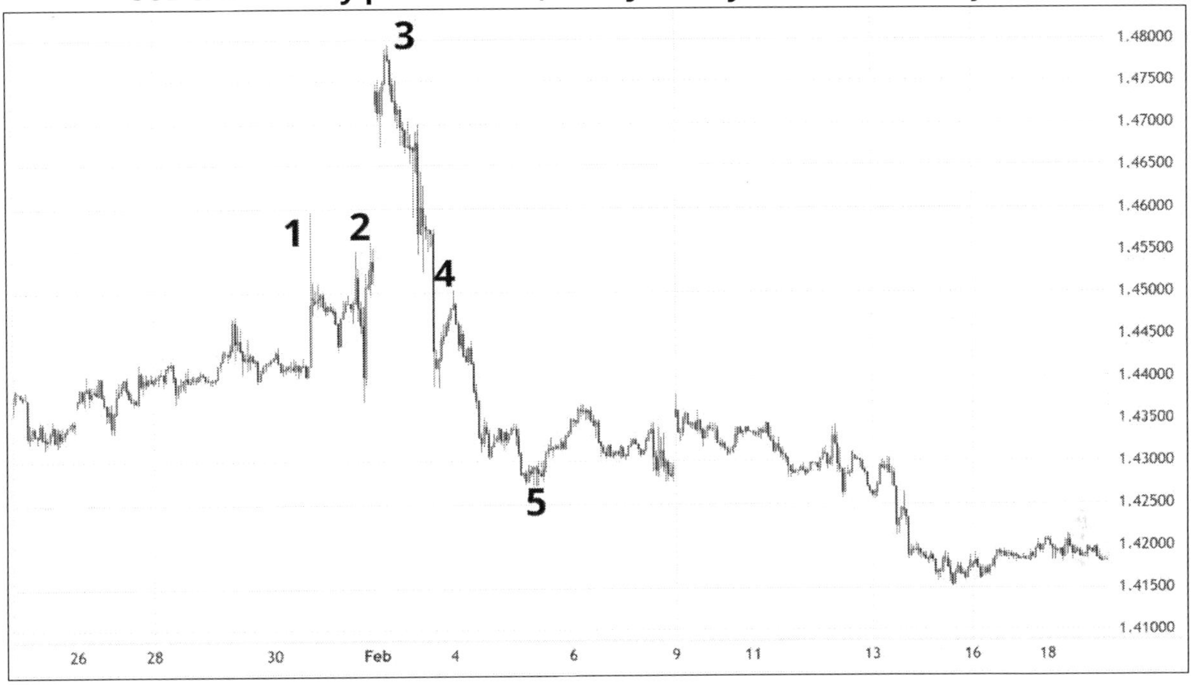

Point 1 on the chart is the moment Trump threatened to put 25% tariffs on imports from Canada and Mexico. The market initially bought USDCAD, but the move was rejected as the prevailing view was still: "Meh, Trump's not serious. It's a bluff."

Then, as the Friday close approached (point 2 on the chart), Trump again said the tariffs were coming soon. USDCAD rallied a bit, but market participants were shocked at how small the move was. The popular rule of thumb was that every 1% of tariffs should move USDCAD 0.5% higher. In other words, a 25% tariff should have triggered a 12.5% rally in USDCAD (roughly).

That weekend, the tariffs were officially announced. You can see at point 3 that the market gapped higher on the Sunday open. But a few hours later (point 4) the Sunday gap was filled, and USDCAD was trading unchanged vs. the Friday close.

At this point savvy traders started to short USDCAD around 1.4400 because it was clearly a good news/bad price setup for USDCAD[35]. These good news/bad price setups tend to be a

[35] You could also call this a bad news/good price setup for CAD, but FX traders always talk in terms of the base currency conventions. In the case of CAD, the quoting convention is USDCAD and therefore we always talk about USDCAD going up or down. USDCAD up = weaker CAD and stronger USD.

great tell for direction over the next 24 to 48 hours, and you can see that almost exactly 48 hours later, USDCAD was trading 150 pips lower at 1.4250 (point 5 on the chart).

The market erroneously believed that higher tariffs were bullish for the USD and the Pavlovian desire to buy USD on tariff announcements cost many traders a fortune in Q1 2025. Even as the tariff news got worse and worse, the USD continued to sell off right into May 2025. So, the good news/bad price setup actually showed the way for the next 700 points in USDCAD as you can see in the next chart.

Note that the market AGAIN bought USDCAD when the tariffs finally went into effect because it was 100% clear at that point that the tariffs were not a bluff. The market will often make the same mistake over and over, and if you can read the tells and ignore the herd, you can profit.

USDCAD Hourly, September 2024 to May 2025

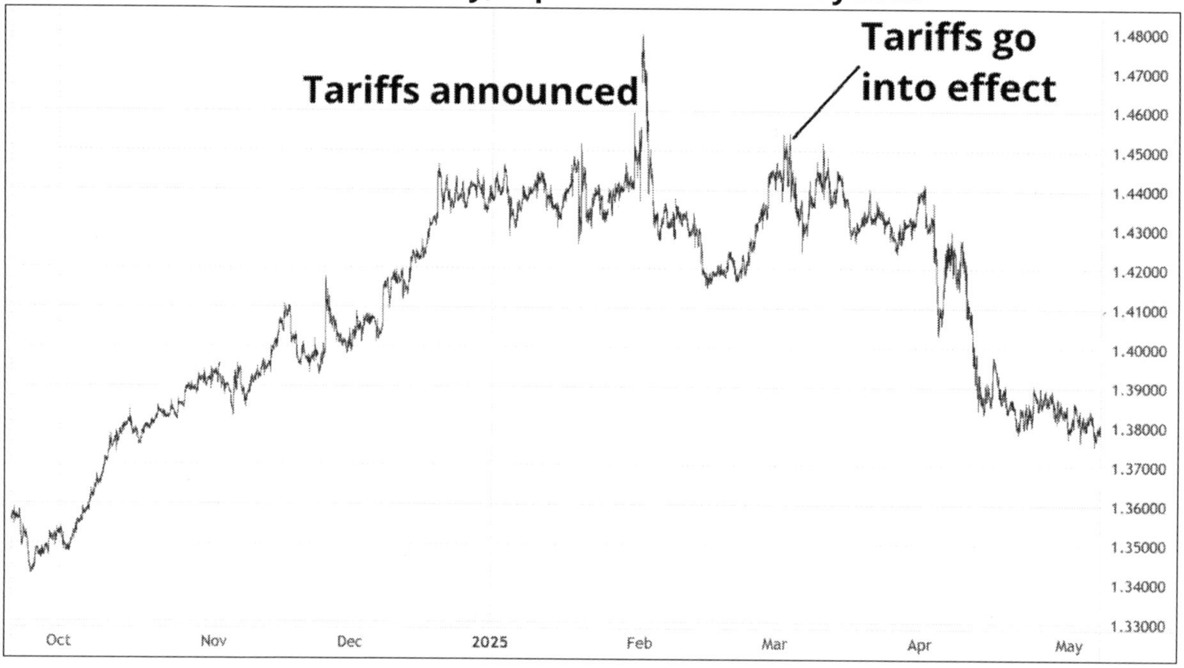

To make money on good news/bad price setups, you need to rid yourself of the idea that things always have to make sense. Remember: Stocks can go up on bad news. Currencies can drop on good news. When the market does something bizarre, it's often shouting information from the rooftops. You need to listen.

Market tell #2: Everybody's tilting

Earlier, we talked about what it feels like when *you* go on tilt. You see red. You trade emotionally. You press buttons out of fear, not because there is a rational trade to be done.

Or you double your long position at the highs because you feel invincible as you stare at a giant green P&L figure.

In poker, the dream scenario is you run into a player on tilt. They are easy to read, they play loose, and they repeatedly put their chips in with the second or third-best hand. When you run into someone on tilt at the poker table, you can extract a ton of money from them in a short period.

The same applies to markets. Can you identify when the market is on tilt? It's often pretty easy to see, especially if you talk to many traders. A market on tilt is characterized by:

- High conviction in the direction of a trend with significant momentum.
- Strong emotions and heavy leverage.
- Multi standard deviation low or high in the Relative Strength Index (RSI).
- Inability to see the other side of the trade. When I have a view and I know that if I say it out loud, people are going to laugh at me; that's a sign the market is on tilt. If it feels stupid to say "I'm bullish", the market is probably way too bearish.
- Much higher-than-normal volatility.
- Media and FinTwit freaking out. Ever notice that whenever Bill Ackman freaks out on Twitter or CNBC runs a "Markets in Turmoil" special it marks a near-term bottom in stocks? This is not a coincidence.

Emotional meltdowns and fear-based headlines are classic signs of a market on tilt. Here are the forward returns of the S&P after every CNBC "Markets in Turmoil" special[36].

[36] Dates extracted from a Charlie Bilello tweet. Note that these specials started in 2010, and we have mostly been in a bull market since then. Any backtest of any strategy where you look at a strong bull market will show almost only bullish 1-year returns. The trend in the price of the security in a backtest is often the number one driver of the average return of the condition you are backtesting.

S&P 500 returns after CNBC features a "Markets in Turmoil" special

	1m	2m	3m	6m	12m
6-May-10	**-6.9%**	**-5.1%**	2.7%	12.9%	20.0%
4-Aug-11	**-2.2%**	**-8.4%**	4.8%	17.4%	20.0%
4-Jun-12	7.0%	9.1%	10.9%	17.0%	33.6%
24-Aug-15	2.4%	9.6%	0.7%	10.5%	13.1%
19-Jan-16	1.9%	9.1%	10.7%	13.7%	26.2%
5-Feb-18	2.9%	**-1.7%**	4.2%	8.9%	9.2%
11-Oct-18	**-0.1%**	**-2.8%**	3.0%	5.6%	15.1%
27-Dec-18	6.2%	12.2%	11.8%	16.0%	25.2%
5-Aug-19	3.3%	3.8%	13.7%	**-12.5%**	17.7%
24-Feb-20	**-23.3%**	**-12.1%**	**-0.3%**	7.4%	29.6%
5-May-22	-0.6%	**-7.3%**	-8.8%	-7.1%	7.2%

Average return	**After a markets in turmoil special**	**-0.8%**	0.6%	4.9%	8.2%	19.7%
	All days 2010-2025	0.9%	1.7%	2.5%	6.3%	10.2%

The average return 3 months, 6 months, and 12 months after a "Markets in Turmoil" special on CNBC are significantly higher than average because the market is on tilt when these specials air, and panic selling dominates. It's important to note, however, that buying these selloffs is not free money. There is considerable volatility, and further short-term losses are common.

- Extreme sentiment readings. When I say extreme, I mean *mega* extreme. Positioning and sentiment follow price, so you cannot reflexively go against them, or you will reflexively fade every trend. Look for occasions when sentiment or positioning are at least 2.5 to 3.0 standard deviations away from the norm. Look for readings so extreme that they happen once or twice per year. Everything in between is not a market on tilt, it's a market that is trending.
- Extreme contango/backwardation shifts. When futures curves show extreme stress, that can be a sign of forced liquidation and tilt. For example, when the VIX futures curve inverts from contango (upward sloping) to extreme backwardation (downward sloping), it often signals tilt. When the crude oil curve inverts

dramatically, it can be a sign of short-term tightness in the physical market. These inversions are usually short-lived and signal a market that is either being forced to trade due to margin calls and risk limits, or is trading on extreme fear, tilt, or FOMO.

When you see a market on tilt, adjust your strategy and prep for a reversal. Are you on tilt with the rest of the herd? Or are you calmly planning your tactics to take the other side using rigorous risk control?

An important difference between poker and trading is that in poker, a player usually tilts alone. In trading, the scary news or euphoric narrative are very likely to cause everyone to tilt at the same time. As Rudyard Kipling says in this poem: "If".

> If you can keep your head when all about you
>   Are losing theirs
> Yours is the Earth and everything that's in it,
>   And—which is more—you'll be a Man, my son!

Or a woman, if you're female. Take note of your emotions and those of other traders, media, and colleagues. Is the market on tilt?

Market tell #3: Correlation breakdown and regime change

When correlated assets suddenly decouple, that's a tell. For example, gold and silver typically move together; if gold starts to rally while silver lags (or falls), this divergence can signal a change in market dynamics. **Correlation breakdowns are often an important signal of regime change.** The weirder the correlation break, the more important it is.

Detecting regime change is a critical skill and one of the biggest advantages humans have over algorithmic and systematic trading opponents. There are three types of correlation break, each with a different meaning.

1. Temporary correlation break caused by flows or noise.
2. Temporary correlation break caused by micro- or macroeconomic news flow.
3. Persistent correlation break due to regime change.

There is a huge difference between a temporary correlation break and a regime change. Let's look at each type.

1. Temporary correlation break caused by flows or noise

These temporary breaks caused by ebbs and flows in two correlated assets are bread and butter trades for lead/lag traders. Lead/lag is a form of short-term trading where you look for signals from directional moves in one asset to predict movements in another.

For example, when a major U.S. bank stock rallies, one would expect that other bank stocks will be more likely to rally in the short term (all other things being equal). For example, here's JPM (J.P. Morgan) and C (Citigroup) over three weeks in Q1 2025:

JPM and Citigroup stock, 5-minute chart, February 17 to March 8, 2025

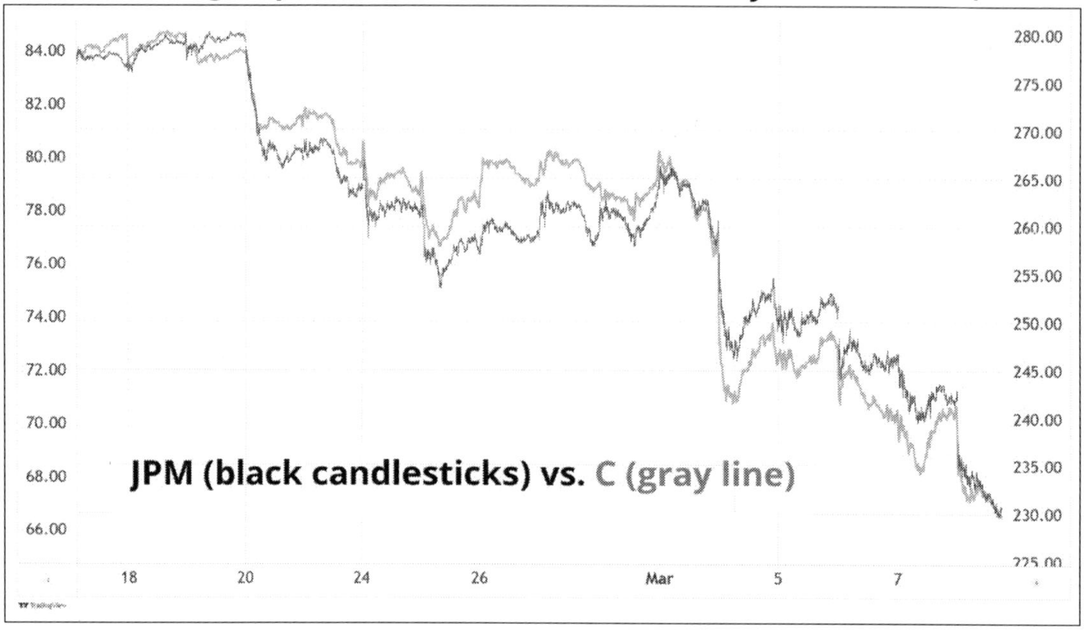

Imagine J.P. Morgan (JPM) and a bunch of other U.S. bank stocks all shoot higher by 2% at around the same time while there is a pension fund trying to offload one million shares of Citigroup.

C might languish unchanged for a while, even as the other bank stocks rally. Lead/lag traders will buy C, because the asset with momentum (JPM) tends to be the directional tell, and the lagging asset catches up later. As discretionary traders and algorithms buy C, the one million share sell order gets chipped away. Finally, when the sell order is filled, Citigroup stock rips 1.5% to catch up to where it "should" be relative to its peers. This style of lead/lag trading is discussed in detail in *The Art of Currency Trading*.

Stocks in the same industry tend to trade in sympathy. If a chip maker like Broadcom (AVGO) runs into trouble and its stock falls, a direct competitor like NVIDIA (NVDA) will likely sell off in sympathy. You see this clearly around earnings releases. If GOOG (a big advertising company) reports good earnings, META (which is also reliant on ad revenue) will probably jump.

Here are GOOG and META after Google released strong results in 2025.

Google and Meta stock, 1-minute chart on April 24, 2025

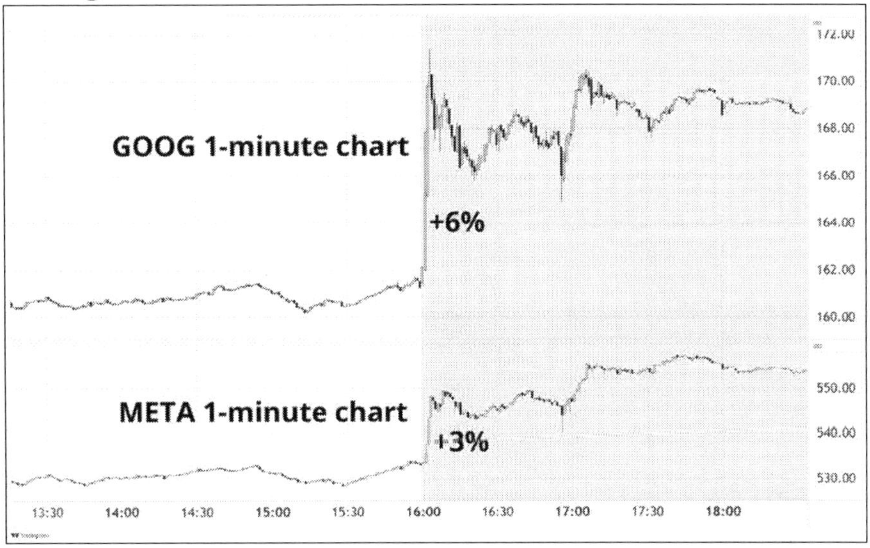

Note the moves up and down are just about tick for tick. META moves in the same direction as GOOG, but with less magnitude. Algorithms are perfectly tuned for this sort of trading because they use history to calculate the META reaction function for a move of X% in GOOG.

Computers are watching every single relationship in the entire trading universe, scanning for disconnects, correlations and sympathy plays, and jumping on them in microseconds or nanoseconds. A nanosecond is one billionth of a second. It takes you 200,000,000 nanoseconds to blink. You are never going to be faster than a computer when it comes to basic correlation trading in a stable regime. In the 1990s, humans could win in the short-term lead/lag arena. Now, they cannot.

Let's move to the next type of correlation break.

2. Temporary correlation break caused by micro- or macroeconomic news flow

What if U.S. airline Jet Blue (JBLU) announces it is shutting down and going bankrupt? The stock drops from $4 to $1 in a flash and algorithms detect this instantaneously and sell its nearest competitors such as Southwest Airlines (LUV), another budget U.S. airline. Human traders who understand that JBLU's bankruptcy reduces competition and will open up new, highly profitable routes for Southwest can buy the dip in LUV as they understand that there is likely to be a correlation break here. In this case, what is bad for JBLU is good for LUV.

As correlation and lead/lag algorithms sell LUV on the JBLU news, smart discretionary traders see an opportunity because the standard correlation does not make sense here. It's likely to break temporarily.

You see little deviations like this all the time and can profit from them if you are fast. What we have here is still a correlation break, not a regime change. For one moment, the normal regime (airline stocks positively correlated to each other with a predictable beta) breaks as the news is bearish JBLU and bullish LUV. This does not mean that future drops in one airline stock are bullish for other airline stocks. It's a one off.

Sometimes, however, a correlation break *does* signal a regime change. So, the first thing to ask when you see a breakdown in correlation is whether it's a one-off, or a possible indication of something bigger.

3. Persistent correlation break due to regime change

There was an epic correlation breakdown in April 2025 after the U.S. government imposed massive tariffs on most trading partners. Let's walk through it and see what it meant and how it can help you spot regime change in the future.

I started trading in 1995 and throughout my career, the most reliable correlation in currency markets has always been the relationship between yields and FX. In developed markets (also known as G10 FX), when a country's interest rates go up, it usually means that growth is solid, inflation is steady or rising, and the country's central bank is in rate hike or restrictive mode. In other words, high yields are good news for a currency.

All other things being equal, a bond investor would rather invest in the USA and earn a 4% yield than invest in Swiss bonds and earn barely zero. Marginal changes in interest rates tend to track with changes in currency values. Here's a chart of how USDJPY usually trades vs. the US/Japan interest rate differential.

USDJPY vs. US/Japan 10-year rate spread, hourly, August 2024 to February 2025

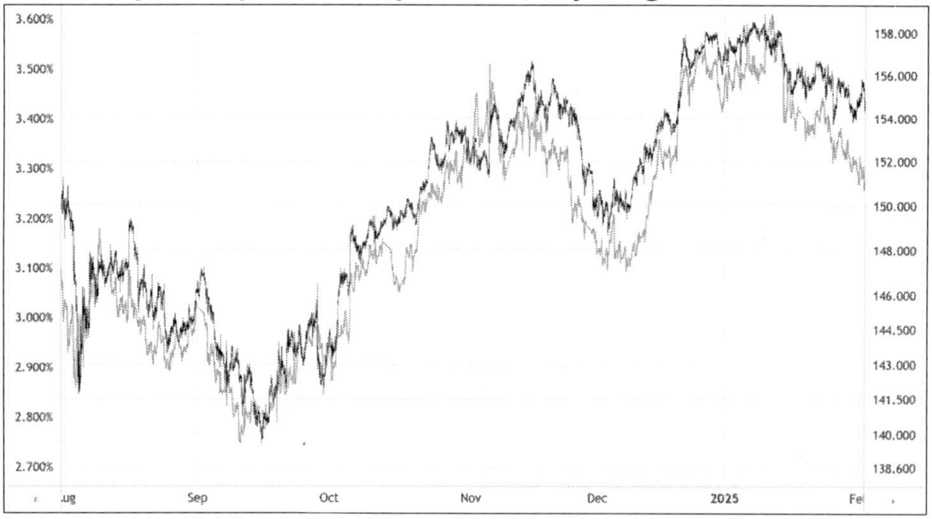

Most other currency pairs look similar, even non-USD pairs like AUDNZD or NOKSEK.

In emerging markets (EM) the relationship is often the opposite. When interest rates go up in South Africa, it is often a sign that investors are fleeing the country and selling its bonds because they are worried about government policies, runaway inflation, or the country's ability to pay back its bonds. When an emerging market is in trouble, their yields go up and their currency goes down as money flees the country.

In rare circumstances, you will see this happen temporarily in a more developed market. For example, when Liz Truss introduced a mini-budget that markets viewed as worrisome for the UK fiscal position in 2022, there was a freakout where UK bonds and currency sold off aggressively and in tandem. Here's a chart.

GBPUSD (bars) vs. UK 10-year yields (line), February 2022 to September 2023

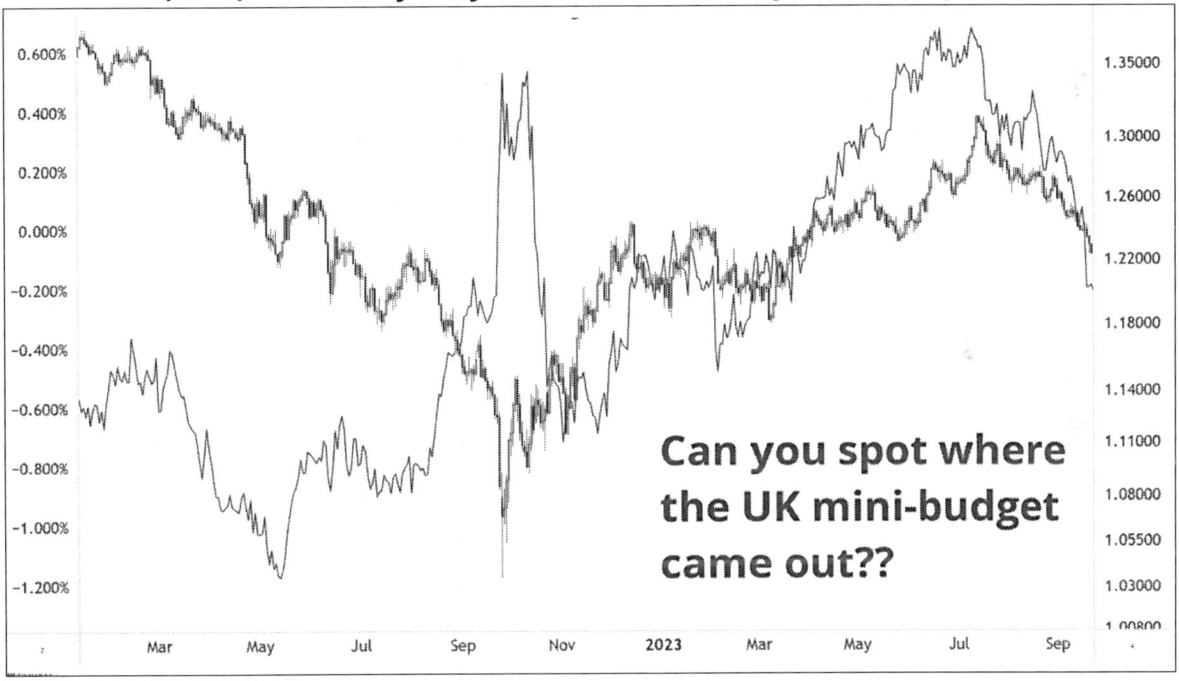

In September and October 2022, GBPUSD went down, while yields skyrocketed. Then the UK government and central bank intervened aggressively and order was restored. The currency and yields went back to normal and traded, once again, with a positive correlation.

When the U.S. government announced massive tariffs on April 2, 2025, you saw a similar reaction as the U.S. dollar was trounced, and U.S. bonds sold off at the same time. This had not happened to this degree since before 1990. Here is how USDJPY traded compared to yields in the months leading up to April 2025.

USDJPY (bars) vs. US/Japan 10-year rate spread (line), July 2024 to March 2025

Below is how they traded after. Note the correlation flip. The USD went down as yields went up and the market treated the U.S., with the largest capital markets in the world by far, like an EM country.

USDJPY (bars) vs. US/Japan 10-year rate spread (line), March-April 2025

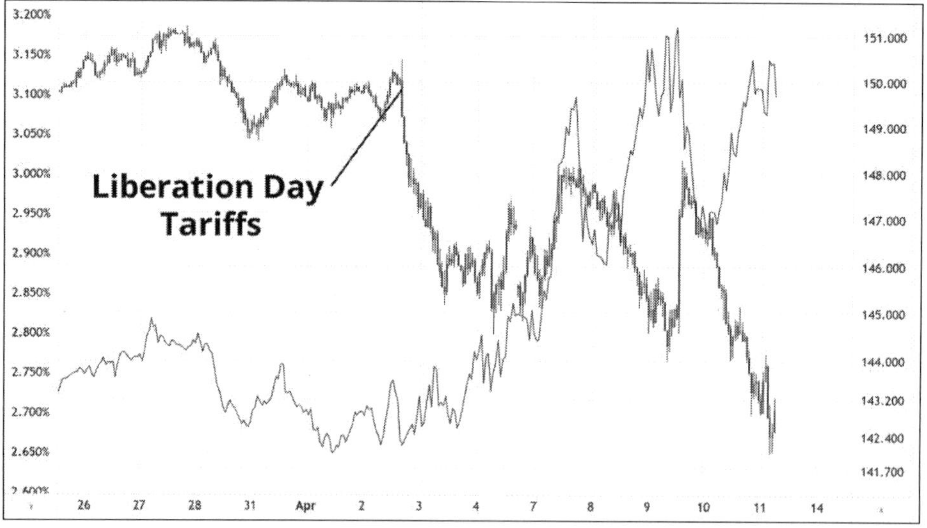

In May 2025, we didn't know how the story would play out, but many believed that we were in the early stages of a regime shift where money would flow out of the United States as isolationist policies left investors cold. This was wrong. In fact, money flowed out of the U.S. for a few weeks, then we went back to the old regime where yields and the USD moved up and down together.

The biggest decision every trader and investor must make is whether a change in market behavior is truly a regime shift, or simply a one-off reaction to news or flow. The bar for regime shift is high, and you should assume that the current regime will remain in force unless you have very strong macro or economic evidence for a change.

There have been a number of important regime shifts over the years, and they have all had important impacts on investment portfolios, medium-term correlations, and intraday price action. Let's review a few important examples.

Regime shift #1: USD and oil

The USD is no longer inversely correlated to oil: the U.S. used to be a massive net importer of oil but is a net *exporter* today. Before 2019, there was a strong, reliable relationship between oil and the dollar. If oil went up, you could be almost certain that the USD would fall. More broadly, this has meant that the group of currencies formerly known as the "commodity currencies" has much less of a correlation to commodity prices. AUD, CAD, and NZD still respond to changes in commodity prices, but much less than they did in the past.

Regime shift #2: Gold and other shiny metals

Gold decoupled somewhat from other precious metals for a good part of the last 20 years. It used to be almost certain that gold, platinum, and silver would move in the same direction over time. But in recent years, gold went to the moon while the other precious metals remain parked on the launch pad. Here is a chart of gold, platinum, and silver. You can see silver start to play catch up with gold somewhat, while platinum flatlined near $1,000.

Gold, silver, and platinum, daily, 2001 to April 2025

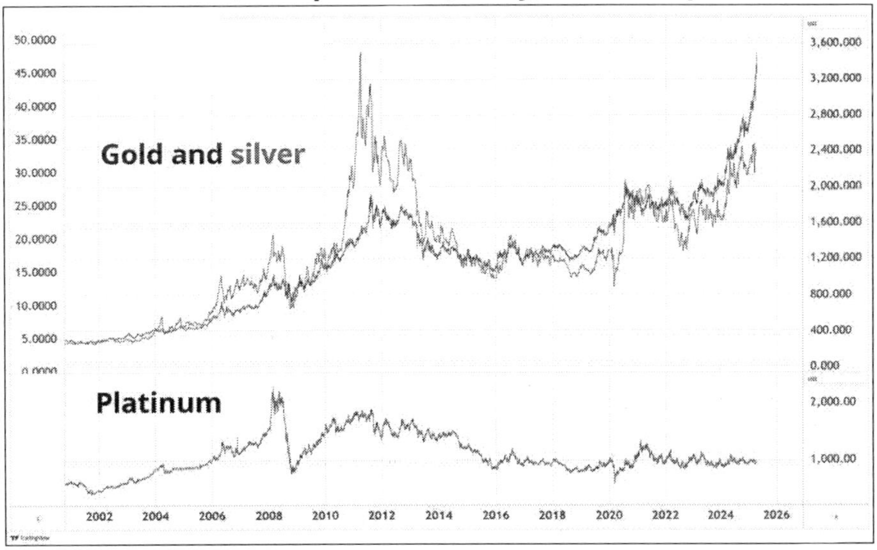

Silver peaked at $50 in 2011 (left y-axis), while gold peaked around $1,900 that same year. In mid-2025, silver was still well below its 2011 peak, while gold almost doubled!

Meanwhile, platinum used to ebb and flow with the price of gold, and it traded above $2,000 in 2009. By mid-2025, platinum was still around $1,000 despite the massive rally in gold. For years, the market tried to buy silver and platinum for the "catch up" trade. But they never caught up. There was a regime shift as gold became its own, separate asset class after 2011. This was an important shift as central banks accumulated gold as a reserve asset, but not other metals. Those who recognized the regime shift (instead of continually arguing that silver and platinum were too low and bound to catch up) were the winners.

Note that in the second half of 2025, as gold breached $3,400, we started to move back towards the catch-up trade regime as some buyers of gold found the price too expensive and demand for substitutes picked up. Silver and platinum gave chase as Asian buyers rotated out of gold into other, cheaper shiny metals.

Regime shift #3: Stocks and bonds

Stocks and bonds oscillate between regimes. They are positively correlated during times of low inflation and central bank accommodation, and are inversely correlated in times of high or rising inflation and tight central bank policy. The reason is simple: When inflation is hot, central banks need to hike interest rates aggressively, and that tends to be bad for both stocks and bonds. The two assets go up and down in tandem when inflation heats up and then cools. Here is a simple look at stock vs. bond correlation regimes:

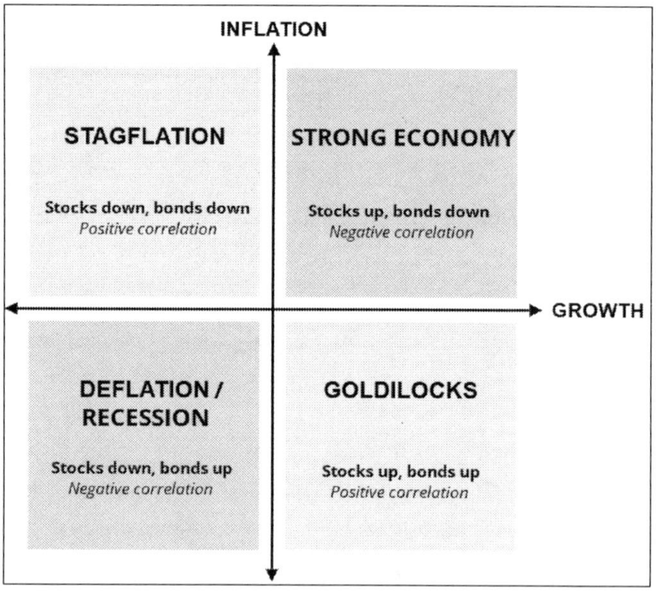

Investors and traders must know the stock vs. bond regime that they are in. The regime will determine whether bonds are a hedge for stocks, whether different economic data is good or bad for stocks, and more. The challenge is that the stock/bond correlation regime is not stable. Turning points from one regime to another are critical moments where traders and investors prosper or get wrecked.

Watch for correlation breaks and assess whether they are more likely temporary or permanent. When you see a correlation break, examine why it's happening. Is there a macroeconomic argument? Has government policy or the macroeconomic world changed?

Are geopolitics exerting an influence, for example, on the correlation between oil and the stock market[37]? Or is the correlation break simply tradable noise?

Advanced thoughts on correlation: Finding good explanations

I have written extensively over the years about how to trade market correlations and my thinking has evolved over time. My first observation, in the 2003-2006 period was simply: *Hey! When this happens, this other thing tends to happen after!* For example, when the price of gold went up, the Australian dollar went up against the U.S. dollar (AUDUSD higher).

That was fine for a while, and when I tried to put some rigor behind it I found most mathematical approaches did not add value over and above simple observation and graphical overlays. If anything, regression created false precision and implied a static or forward-looking mathematical relationship when the relationships between assets are anything but static, consistent, or scientific.

Still, simply observing relationships doesn't give you enough insight to predict future correlations. If all you know is that when oil goes up, the USD goes down (as was the case for much of my career), you are not going to be in a strong position when that regime changes and the relationship breaks down, disappears, or even reverses.

So, I try to think more deeply and uncover the logic and transmission mechanisms behind correlations I observe. Some of this was inspired by a philosophy that has gained momentum as my career progressed: **If you can't explain what's going on, you're going to struggle to predict what happens next.** And the less you can explain a phenomenon in markets, the more likely it's random. That's why I spend so much time trying to explain why seasonality is real (or not), and why correlations make sense (or don't). Good explanations are a necessary input to good forecasts.

What causes cross-market correlation? Are there mediators?

My thinking has been influenced by *The Book of Why* by Judea Pearl and Dana Mackenzie. As a non-statistics person interested in correlation and causation, I really enjoyed that book. It's niche and a bit wonky but understandable enough.

Chapter 8 of the book is titled "Mediation: The Search for a Mechanism" and begins as follows:

> In ordinary language, the question "Why?" has at least two versions. The first is straightforward: you see an effect, and you want to know the cause. Your

---

[37] For example: Oil rising because of war: Bad for global stock markets. Oil rising because of synchronized global GDP growth: Good for global stock markets.

> grandfather is lying in the hospital, and you ask, "Why? How could he have had a heart attack when he seemed so healthy?" But there is a second version of the "Why?" question, which we ask when we want to better understand the connection between a known cause and a known effect. For instance, we observe that Drug B prevents heart attacks. Or, like James Lind, we observe that citrus fruits prevent scurvy. The human mind is restless and always wants to know more. Before long we start asking the second version of the question: "Why? What is the mechanism by which citrus fruits prevent scurvy?" This chapter focuses on this second version of "why."
>
> The search for mechanisms is critical to science and everyday life, because different mechanisms call for different actions when circumstances change. Suppose we run out of oranges. Knowing the mechanism by which oranges work, we can still prevent scurvy. We simply need another source of vitamin C. If we didn't know the mechanism, we might be tempted to try bananas.
>
> The word that scientists use for the second type of "Why?" question is "mediation." You might read a statement like this: "The effect of Drug B on heart attacks is mediated by its effect on blood pressure." This statement encodes a simple causal model: Drug A → Blood Pressure → Heart Attack.
>
> In this case, the drug reduces high blood pressure, which in turn reduces the risk of heart attack. Likewise, we can summarize the effect of citrus fruits on scurvy by the causal model Citrus Fruits → Vitamin C → Scurvy. We want to ask certain typical questions about a mediator: Does it account for the entire effect? Does Drug B work exclusively through blood pressure or perhaps through other mechanisms as well? Mediation is also an important concept in the law. If we ask whether a company discriminated against women when it paid them lower salaries, we are asking a mediation question. The answer depends on whether the observed salary disparity is produced directly in response to the applicant's sex or indirectly, through a mediator such as qualification, over which the employer has no control.

I thought this was an interesting excerpt as it pertains to the now-solved AUD currency vs. Terms of Trade puzzle. For several years, market participants relentlessly banged their heads on keyboards, going long AUD in response to massive improvements in the country's terms of trade. But AUD never cooperated.

The mediator in this case was RBA policy.

If a booming Australian terms of trade transmits to the jobs market, capex, and eventually interest rate policy (as it did during the commodity supercycle 2010-2013), it matters for the AUD. If it doesn't transmit (like in 2018 and 2021), it matters much less. Or not at all.

Here's an excerpt from a piece I wrote in 2023:

> **am/FX: Oswald's Boots**
>
> About once every six months, I feel like I need to write a piece going through my thoughts on why AUD is so weak. It has persistently underperformed terms of trade for the past few years and there are numerous explanations including:
>
> - Commodity strength in this cycle does not generate capex or jobs like it did 2011-2014.
> - Strength in commodities generates dividends, not capex in this cycle, so the profits from mining in Australia have no transmission to the real economy. They make investors rich, but don't impact growth much.
> - Strength in Australian terms of trade has no transmission to monetary policy for the reasons stated above. If commodity strength does not impact monetary policy, it's not necessarily relevant for the currency.
>
> While I often post AUD vs. copper and similar correlation overlays, now and then I have to zoom out and remember the following chart.

AUDUSD vs. Terms of Trade and 2-year yield differential

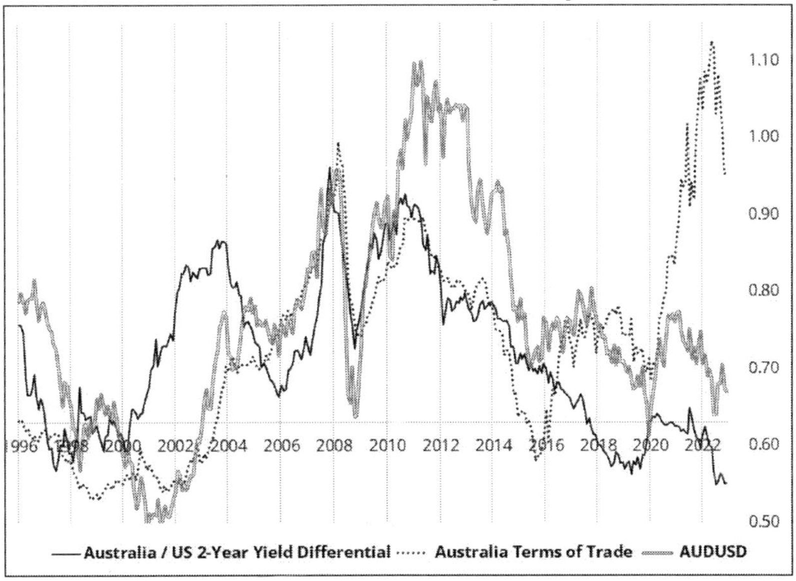

> In short: The terms of trade explosion doesn't mean much if there is no transmission to monetary policy. If commodity prices go up, but the Australian economy is mostly unaffected because high commodity prices lead to large dividends but not more capex and jobs, then the commodity rally doesn't mean much for AUD. I have to keep reminding myself of this.

Think about the process by which a correlation operates. What are the direct and indirect causes, and what are the mediators? In *The Book of Why*, they use simple cause / effect diagrams, and I think those can be useful. These diagrams force the analyst to think about logic before constructing models or calculating r-squareds.

Does AUDUSD listen to copper, for example? That makes sense given Australia's reliance on copper exports. Does copper listen to AUDUSD?

That's harder for me to get my head around and therefore if I were drawing a causality diagram, I would put the arrow from copper to AUD, not the other way around. This exercise is subjective, but going through a logical thought process and coming to a conclusion is more likely to work compared to brute force data mining that reveals a relationship with no macroeconomic logic.

Or maybe because I'm not a quant, that's just how I think. I strongly prefer cause/effect statements that I can explain with underlying logic. As a thought experiment, I created the causality diagram below for copper and AUD, to help understand correlation better. I used "higher copper" and "higher AUDUSD" to make it easier to understand, but everything would work in reverse, too.

Many relationships between two variables in markets can be explained simply and effectively by this: **A third variable drives them both.** Here I've listed global growth, Chinese growth, the direction of the U.S. dollar, and global risk appetite as four important confounders of the copper/AUD relationship because all those things drive both copper and AUD.

I added one new dimension to those used in *The Book of Why*. Time is measured on a logarithmic scale where time passes quickly at first and then more slowly as you move left to right.

This diagram is not meant to be a complete list of everything that happens when copper and AUD tango; it's meant to tickle the idea generation and explanation machines in your brain.

A causality diagram for copper and AUDUSD

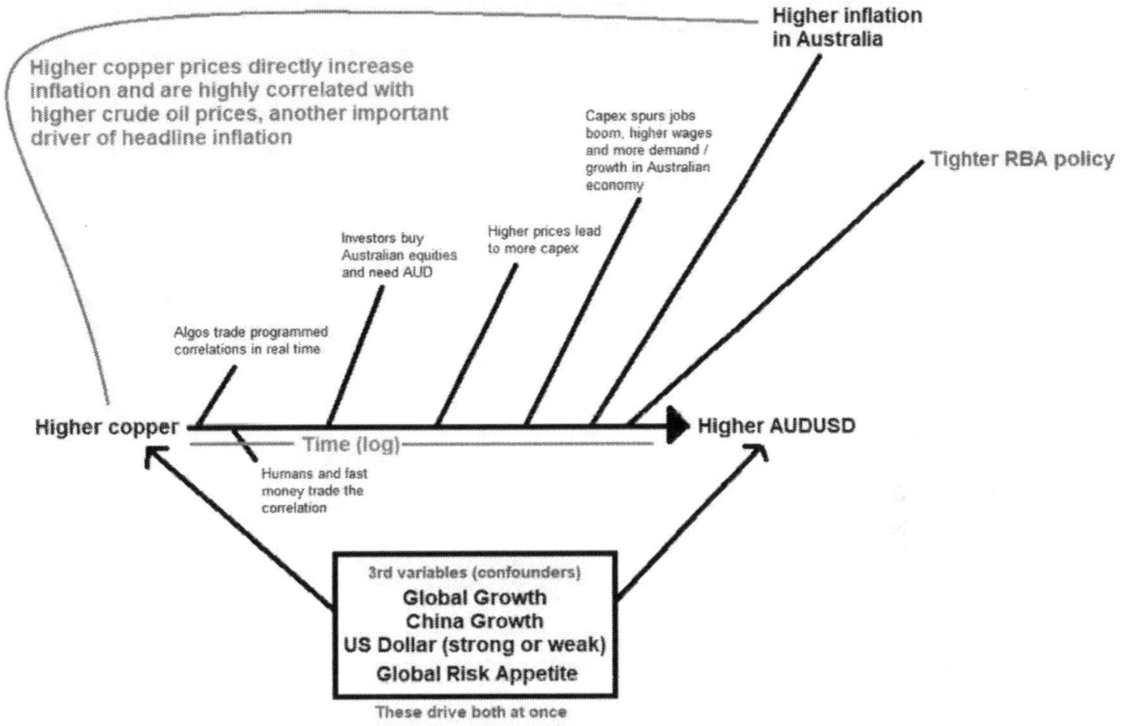

Constructing accurate diagrams of this type can help predict when correlations will change in the future. They help me think through the mechanisms of correlation and possible causation. Over time, I can compare my cause-effect diagrams to empirical evidence and evaluate their ongoing validity.

Think of global markets as a massive, interconnected, infinitely complex system where movement in one area can signal potential future movements in another. Much as flamingos abandoning low-lying areas can warn of a coming tsunami, movements in one market can often give us information about future movements in another.

Market tell #4: Volume spike with price reversal

When a market approaches a significant support or resistance level and volume suddenly increases dramatically, that is a tell. It says the market cares about the level, and many participants of various time frames are getting involved, in size. Small volume bars indicate that noise traders and algorithms are active. Huge volume bars indicate institutional and medium-term big money players are involved.

The combination of aggressive price rejection and abnormally high volume frequently precedes a major reversal.

Make sure you understand the intraday volume pattern of the products you trade so that you can understand what is and what is not a meaningful volume spike. Huge volume in a single stock at 9:30 a.m. is standard. A huge spike at 2:10 p.m. is not. Let me walk you through an example of a volume spike tell that helped me take profit on a long Hertz (HTZ) trade, then flip short for another spicy profit.

Hertz is a large U.S. rental car company. I was long HTZ following the momentum and short squeeze triggered by the announcement that Bill Ackman had invested in the company and was advocating for a partnership with UBER.

In Q2 2025, I was long HTZ around $7 and looking to the $9 level as potential resistance and my take profit area. Short squeezes can go higher and faster than you expect, though, so I was ready to be greedy. If $9 was cleanly broken, the stock could easily go to $11 that same day. Here's the chart:

Hertz (HTZ) stock, 4-hour chart, late 2023 to April 2025

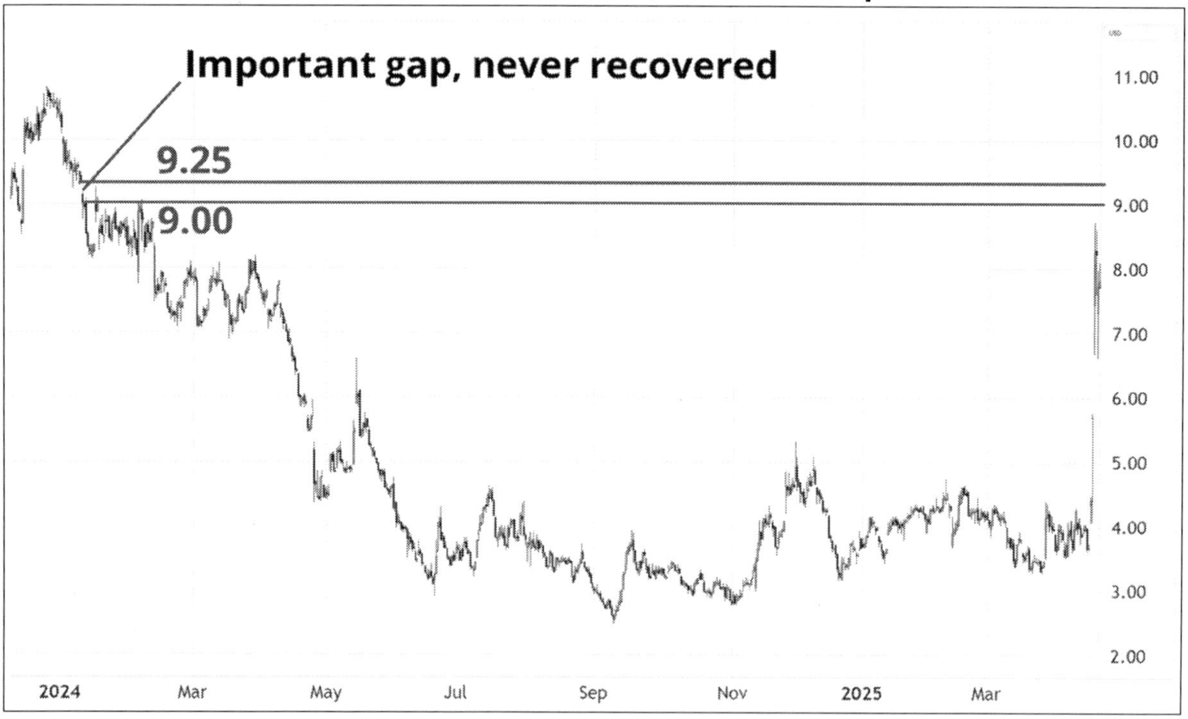

In early 2024, HTZ gapped down through $9.00/$9.25, tested the gap, then ran lower from $9 all the way down to sub-$3. This left an important (and tight) resistance zone at $9.00/$9.25. Let's zoom in and look at a 5-minute chart of the price action in April 2025.

HTZ 5-minute chart, April 3 to April 23, 2025

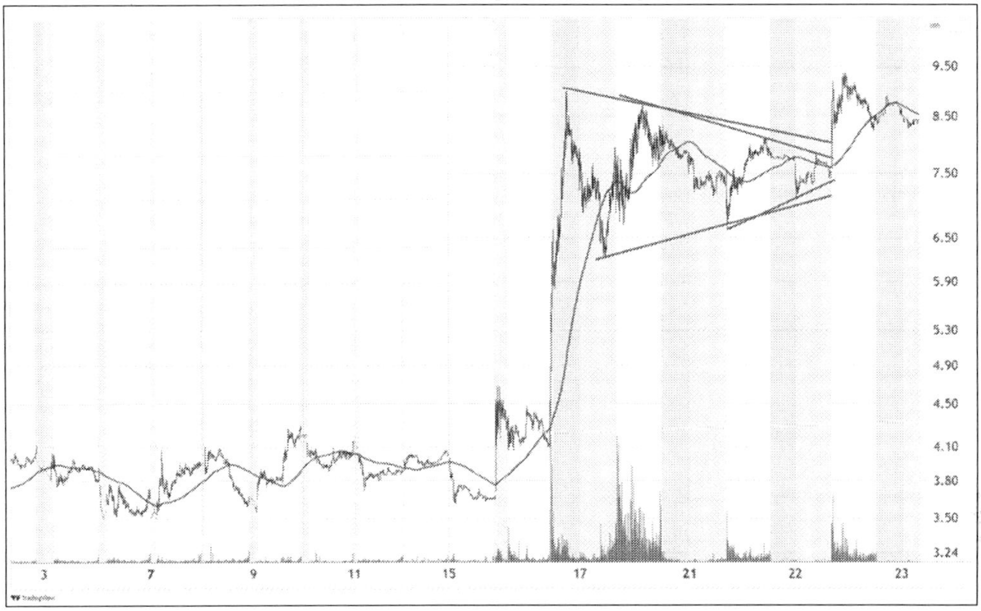

There is a beautiful bull flag formed by the rally from $4.00 to $8.60, and when the flag's triangle broke, we had a nice push up towards that $9 level. Note that in the volume bars at the bottom there is always a volume spike at the open (as with all stocks). So, we ignore the 9:30 a.m. spikes and focus on surges at other times of the day. Let's zoom in even more.

HTZ 5-minute chart, April 22 and April 23, 2025

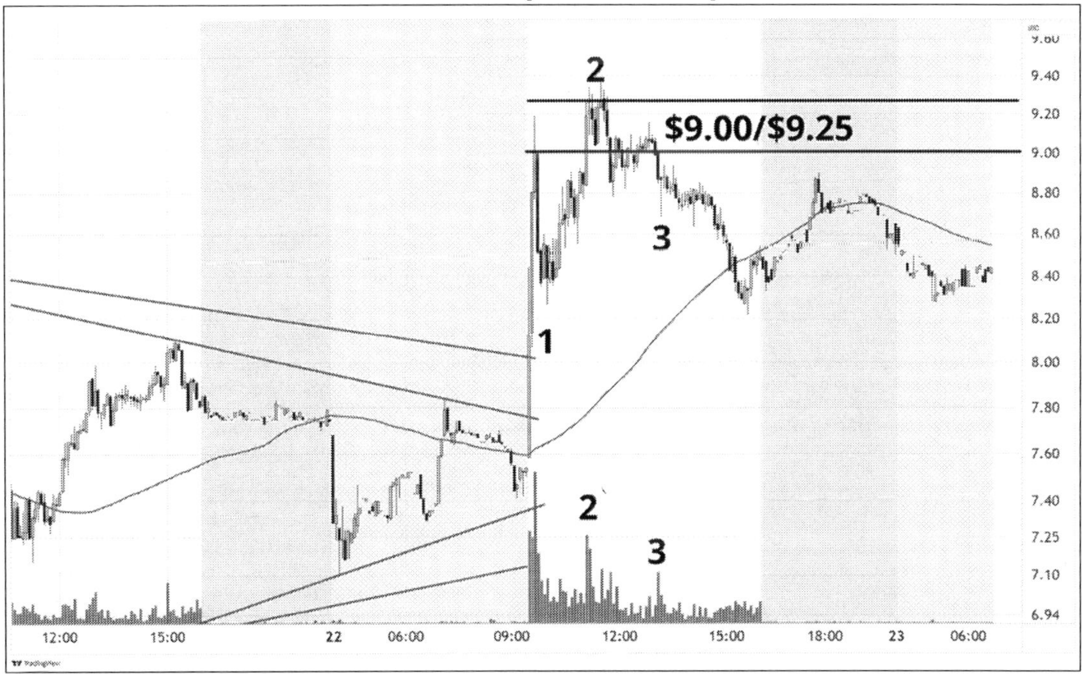

At point 1 you have a massive price surge on the open, and standard (huge) opening volumes. At point 2 HTZ breaks up into the critical resistance zone. Note the volume spike, along with the price move into resistance. At point 3 there is another volume spike as the market clearly rejects the thrust higher and drops back below resistance. **This is bearish.**

The market spent a ton of energy pushing up into the band of resistance, and clearly some big players rejected the move. This activity might reflect new medium-term short sellers, or gigantic longs exiting.

Either way, the market shows an aggressive rejection of a high-volume attempt to break important resistance. This is Teddy KGB eating an Oreo. An obvious tell.

This move is the equivalent of a poker player shoving all their chips into the pot preflop and then sending a clear tell that he's nervous. That doesn't mean he is going to lose the hand necessarily, but you know he is weak, and you know it's time to push back twice as hard. Remember, everything in markets is probabilistic.

Even if the market shows itself to have a pair of 3's against your pair of aces, you are not guaranteed to win. Crazy stuff happens. There are bad beats in markets just like in poker.

With HTZ trading $8.85, I decided the bull trade was over and I exited my longs. The market dumped to $8.20 shortly after. Even better, I got short at $8.85 on that next and last push up on low volumes in the pre-market because I believed that earlier price action reinforced the importance of the $9.00/$9.25 level and so I knew I could get short risking around $0.71 to make $1.10. I put my stop loss at $9.56 and my take profit was the bottom of the old bull flag ($7.70).

Why did I pick $9.56 as my stop? The stop loss needs to be above the $9.25 level, and I always leave a buffer to be safe. I would rather have a slightly smaller position with a slightly wider stop; that gives me significantly increased odds of survival.

When I shorted HTZ, the rally was in its third day, the weak shorts most certainly would have had plenty of time to cover, and the **sellers showed complete control above $9**. The bullish trade was exhausted, and I was able to flip short on a random, meaningless, low volume pre-market rally.

Here's how the short trade played out:

HTZ 5-minute chart, April 22 to April 30

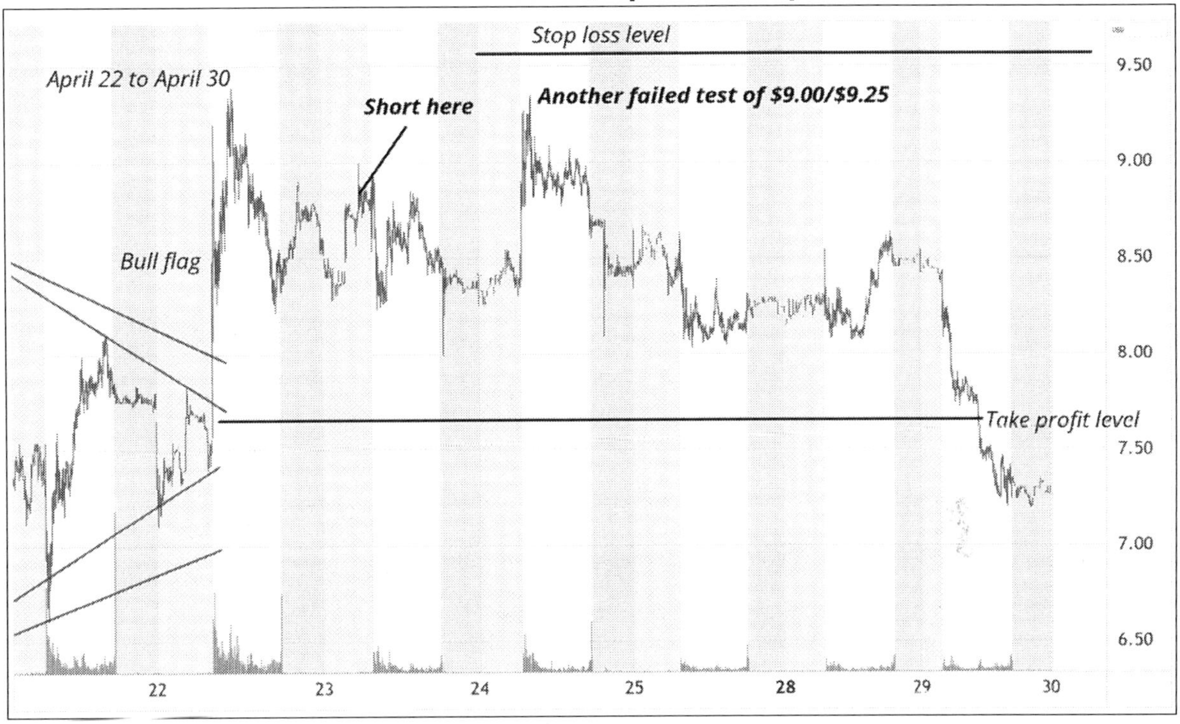

There was another strong push higher right at the open on April 24, key resistance held again, and I managed enough patience to sit short and cover at my target four trading days later. To be honest, 8 times out of 10 I would have been bored by the two-day consolidation between 8.00 and 8.50, but because I was writing about the trade for this book, I was more tuned into my process and I stayed disciplined. That helped me grind nearly $15,000 profit out of the short. This trade shows great flexibility as I was bullish HTZ on April 21 and 22 but had an open mind and saw the massive rejection on high volume and so I flipped short. Liquidity in HTZ in this period was incredibly deep and you could flip 10,000 shares within a few cents.

Note that a week later, the stock was trading below $6.00, but I don't generally care what happens to a trade after I am out. Don't waste your time watching where a security goes after you exit. Your job isn't to catch every single penny or every single move. Your job is to catch the juicy parts, get out, and move on to the next trade.

Market tell #5: Gaps

Another important market tell is when markets open with a significant gap higher or lower than the previous close. This tells you there is a major order imbalance, and the market is desperately searching for liquidity. Gaps tell you price was out of equilibrium, and they send important information about the trading activity of strong hands.

Gaps often occur at extremes because (in the case of a gap higher) desperate buyers will continue to raise their bids into the liquidity vacuum until they finally find a seller. Weak hands will stay away, waiting for price discovery to take place, and only strong hands will be sellers. When those sell orders finally appear, the buyers get filled, the panic subsides, and the strong hands (the sellers) gain control.

Both sides of a gap are automatically important support or resistance for me because gaps clearly identify areas of disequilibrium where traders and investors are trapped. When price moves back into a gap, those who are trapped will use the Get Out of Jail Free card to reduce their risk.

Treat both sides of a gap as significant reference points for price. You can then use those points (and the gap area itself) as pivots for high leverage trades going forward. As price returns towards a gap, start to get involved, and put your stop loss on the other side of the gap. Here is an example.

After the election of Donald Trump in November 2024, the market viewed TSLA as a big winner due to Elon Musk's campaign financing role, which helped crown the new administration. Tesla stock traded to $363 immediately after the election, then corrected back to touch a low of $303 on November 13 before closing that day at $321.

The following Monday (see bottom left of chart), TSLA gapped higher to open at $335. That gap showed that weak holders were done selling and new, stronger buyers had emerged.

Tesla (TSLA) Hourly, November 13 to December 16, 2024

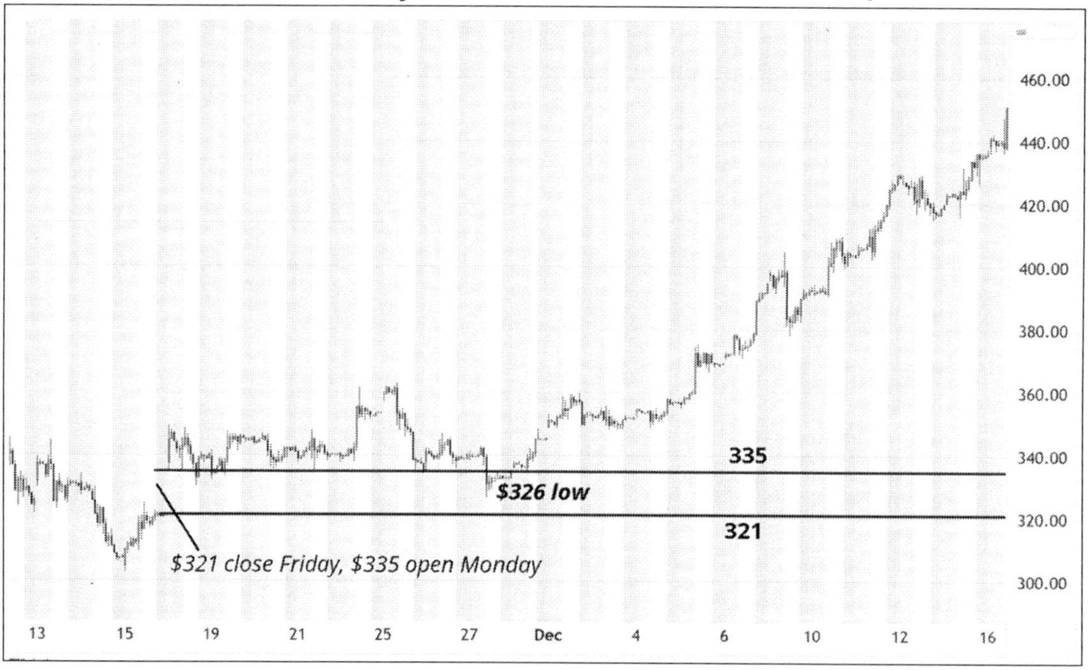

If you were looking to get long the stock, you had a clear buy zone: The gap from $321 to $335. You had three separate opportunities to buy at $335 with a stop loss below $321 before the stock went on a rampage to $480 by year end.

While buying a gap like this does not always work (of course), it offers a high leverage situation because you can risk $15 to make $100 or more and you know exactly where you are wrong.

My best trades tend to look like this: Buying or selling with a tight stop loss using technicals to tell me exactly where I am wrong. I would never do a trade like this solely because of the chart—the chart provides the tactics for a good idea and gives you leverage so you can take a big position and monetize a trade with excellent risk/reward.

Market tell #6: Falling volatility

The final market tell we'll discuss is falling volatility. When a market enters a tight trading range after a significant move and volatility begins to contract sharply, it tells you that the order imbalance in the market has been rectified, and a more stable short-term equilibrium has been found. Even if the security continues to rally, this falling volatility is often a sign of imminent trend exhaustion and can offer clues as to the right time to fade a large move.

Tony Crabel captures the ebb and flow of markets nicely in his 1990 book *Day Trading With Short Term Price Patterns and Opening Range Breakout*:

> The principle of Contraction/Expansion is defined as the market phenomenon of change from a period of rest to a period of movement back to a period of rest. This interaction between the phases of motion and rest are constantly taking place, with one phase directly responsible for the others' existence. This principle is applicable to any time frame.

In other words, things go wild for a bit, then they calm down. You need to observe what part of the process your market is in and understand the relationship between volatility and future price action. Strong market moves are angry and impulsive and leave those on the wrong side of the trend gasping for air. Slow, grinding moves imply that there are strong countertrend participants and supply and demand are nearly in balance. Look at crude oil for example.

Crude Oil futures (top panel) and rolling 10-day volatility (bottom panel)

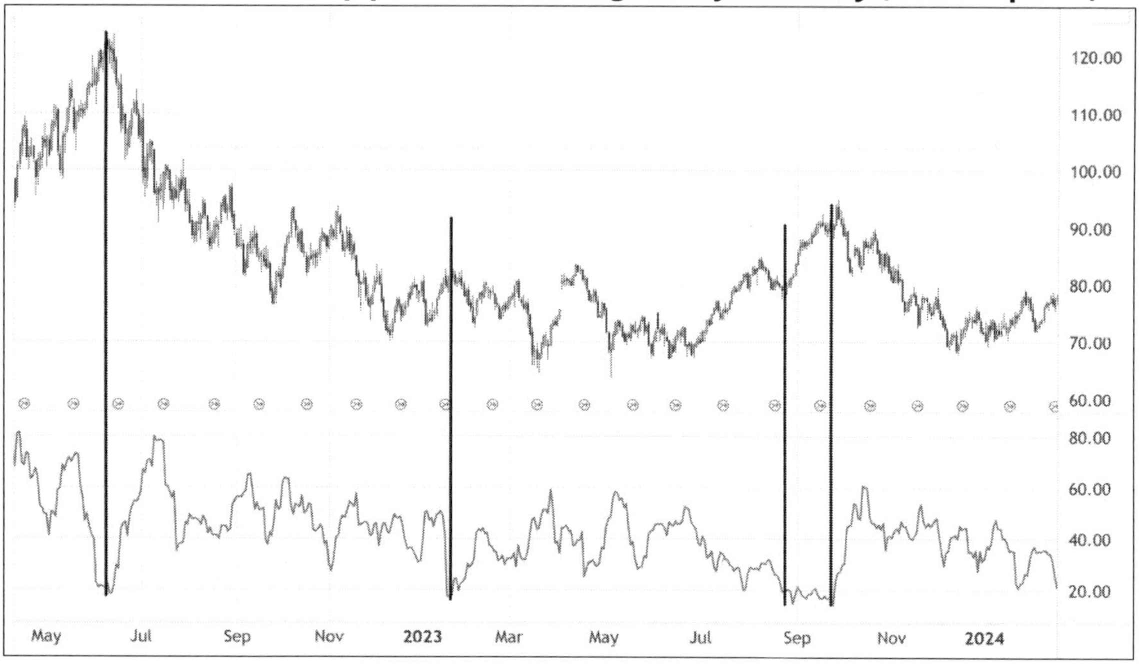

I marked the four times realized volatility fell below 20%. Each time, it was a sign that the current direction was exhausted. Many days of low volatility create great setups for fading an uptrend because you know that if you get short with a fairly tight stop (say, two average day's ranges away), you have a chance to risk a little to make a lot.

In poker, a tell is a change in a player's behavior. Similarly, as traders **we are looking for changes in a market's behavior**. This can be falling volatility, large gaps away from equilibrium, volume spikes, correlation breaks, good news/bad price, or anything else that looks weird. Think of market data and price action as a collection of all the thoughts and actions of every market participant. Then look for tells.

Look for moments when the market eats an Oreo. Then pounce.

Mental stamina

> "Enthusiasm is common. Endurance is rare."
>
> Angela Duckworth

Trading and poker represent ongoing cognitive challenges characterized by persistent uncertainty and psychological exertion. Both activate heightened neurological responses and outcomes trigger neurochemical fluctuations: of cortisol in periods of high risk, and of dopamine when you win.

Both domains constantly test your mental fortitude through uncertainty and pressure. You make constant decisions with consequences, many triggering a stress response. The pressure accumulates throughout the trading or poker session, and accumulates over days, weeks, months, and years.

You're rarely truly settled. After you close a profitable position or win a huge pot, your mind shifts to evaluating the next opportunity or threat. This perpetual state of vigilance taxes your mental resources. Decision quality can deteriorate as the day progresses. By afternoon, your trading judgment can be compromised by the sheer volume of choices you've already made. Costly mistakes can occur.

The psychological parallels of long trading and poker sessions include:

- Persistent fight-or-flight activation
- Anticipatory stress about potential outcomes
- Constant conflict between desire for certainty and inherently uncertain activities

This environment can break you down, or it can build exceptional mental resilience. Your brain naturally seeks stability, so learning to function effectively without that stability can give you a competitive advantage. Be aware of when you are emotionally or mentally taxed and take a break. Meditate, recharge, go for a walk, whatever. **You do not possess infinite mental resources or energy**. Whether you're at a poker table all night, or you're trading all day… Be thoughtful about mental stamina and take timeouts to destress and recharge.

Probability and expected value (EV)

Poker and trading are games of incomplete information where decisions are made based on unknown probabilities rather than certainty. This differentiates them from chess, checkers, or even blackjack or roulette, where the odds are known ex-ante.

Understanding expected value (EV) is fundamental to both disciplines. You need to think about probabilities, not outcomes, since markets are always probabilistic, not deterministic. When someone says "such and such stock is going to zero, it's just a matter of time" or "such and such cryptocurrency is going to a million, it's just math" they are acting as if the outcome is predetermined. It's not. Assigning probabilities to outcomes and then betting on the payoff of those outcomes, relative to the probabilities, is the way you make money trading. Not by going all in on one idea and hoping for the best.

When you think probabilistically, you leave room for the idea that you may be wrong. Ideally, each trade you put on should be accompanied by a statement in the form:

> "I will know that I am wrong if X happens."

X could be a level breaking, an event occurring, an amount of time passing, or hitting a specific loss threshold. It's important to attach these circuit breakers to your ideas because unlike poker, which is a series of discrete events, trading tends to be an endless river of price changes and information flow. Good traders say: "If TSLA breaks 304, I'm wrong." Bad traders buy TSLA at 350 and when it hits 300, they say: "Wow, I like it even more now!"

Create falsifiable hypotheses and discrete endings by setting exit parameters for your trades.

An amateur poker player will celebrate when their pair of 4's beats a pair of aces in an all-in showdown, whereas a professional poker player will be more likely to cringe if they win after making the wrong decision to get all their chips in with the second-best hand. Professionals self-evaluate based on whether they repeatedly maximized expected value over many sessions, not on the outcome of any single hand. The same applies to trading. A trade that loses money can still be a good decision if it had positive expected value when it was initiated.

Assess your trades based on the information you had when you entered, not on the outcome:

- Was your position size appropriate given your edge and the risk?
- Did you have a clear thesis supported by evidence?
- Were your entry and exit points logical based on your strategy?
- Did you follow your plan for entry and exit?

Over time, focus on improving your decision quality rather than obsessing over results (i.e., P&L from individual trades). The process vs. outcome distinction is extremely important. It's easy to understand, but hard to internalize. You can learn more about it in:

- Thinking in Bets, by Annie Duke
- Alpha Trader, pages 240-241
- The Art of Currency Trading, pages 345-347

Variance

Before we start this section, the following is a fantastic piece on variance by poker professional (and nice guy) Phil Galfond, shared this with his permission.

Variance: Beyond the Surface

Variance is one of those words people throw around as if they fully understand it and its implications. In actuality, it's a confusing and abstract concept.

Today, I want to share the three most common misunderstandings relating to variance among poker players (who understand it much better than the rest of the world!).

Unintuitive Results

The human mind isn't built to handle variance well. We evolved to learn from our actions. A caveman only needs to put his hand in a fire one time to learn never to do it again. That's a fast education! We take an action, we get a result, and we calibrate our actions based on that.

Imagine if that caveman had two options:

- Put his hand in a fire.
- Put his hand in cool water.

But instead of things working the way they would in the real world, the fire burns him 70% of the time, and the cool water burns him 30% of the time.

It's going to be a lot harder to learn which is the better option.

Definition

In poker, people tend to equate variance with bad luck and downswings:

"I've been dealing with some variance lately."

That's not what it really means. Variance is a statistical measure that represents the degree of spread in a set of data points. It quantifies how much the numbers in a dataset vary or differ from the average (mean) value of the dataset. In simpler terms, it addresses the question:

How much might my results differ from the average result?

You don't need to understand how to calculate variance, or that the standard deviation in a data set is the square root of the variance. But you do need to understand its impact on results. In poker, you have your expected result (expected value, expected winrate), and variance.

The higher the variance, the more likely it is that your actual results will differ from your expected results. Let's get into the misunderstandings, starting with the least misunderstood.

#3: It Can Really Get That Bad (and Worse!)

Most everyone underestimates variance. When I was just starting in poker, I remember reading the words of a successful player that really stuck with me:

"If you play poker long enough, you'll eventually run worse than you ever thought possible."

I've seen it happen to myself, and to countless other players. The losses somehow keep piling up in spite of it seeming astronomically unlikely. In your local $1/$3 NL cash game, with a winrate of 5 big blinds per 100 hands, what do you think the odds are that you'd win over one year of playing? Well, at 30 hands/hour, and 16 hours of play per week, you'd play about 25,000 hands in a year.

The chances of losing over that year are something in the neighborhood of 13%. Play better than your opponents for an entire year, and you still have a thirteen percent chance of losing! What if you play for three years? Surely by that time, the long run will have hit, right?

Well, sort of.

Now it's only 2.5% likely that you'll be losing after that three-year stretch.

That's still one out of forty players! And what's worse is that in a sense, every time you play, you're starting the clock over. Over the course of 10 years, there are countless opportunities to start a 3-year downswing. You might fade the first 2.5% by winning a lot in year one, only to lose over years two through four.

I know what some of you are thinking:

"OMG. That's what happened to me!"

This brings me to the next misunderstanding...

#2: Variance Works in Both Directions

If bad runs can go on longer than we think... Guess what?

Good runs can too. How many of you thought, "OMG. I've been winning for three years without studying. I must be running hot!"? How often have you felt like you were running above expectation for a long time?

Many people don't ever feel this, because they think they deserve to win. It's easy for your mind and ego to construct a story around you winning:

"I'm playing great."

"I knew I was a genius."

"I studied preflop charts for 30 minutes."

And it's just as easy to construct a story around losing:

"I've been so unlucky."

"My opponents always hit their stupid draws when I have a big hand."

"If I didn't get my aces cracked three times, I'd be winning this month."

Even for more advanced players who know otherwise, it's easy to think that variance only happens in one direction. This leads players of all skill levels to overestimate their winrates and abilities. It makes them play in games they shouldn't and experience even more "variance".

So, what can you do about it? How can you reduce variance? This brings me to the most common misconception of all:

#1: Variance Reduction

"I know I should 3-bet 10% of hands here, but I feel better 3-betting just my premiums to reduce variance."

"I could bluff here, but I don't know if it'll work. Giving up is lower variance."

"I'm probably ahead, but many rivers will be tough to play, so I'll just fold to reduce variance."

Let's go back to our example – a 5bb/100 winrate over one year of play – and see what impact reducing our variance would have. If we play a variance reduction style, we might take the standard deviation from 70bb to 50bb/100. Now, instead of losing 13% of the time, we lose only 5.7% of the time. Cut it in half! Not bad, right?

Here's the problem: When you take alternate betting lines instead of the "right" ones in order to reduce variance, you are, by definition, playing worse. You're passing up on spots where you could win money on average because they are riskier. You become much easier to play against, which, if players notice, is going to hurt your winrate even more.

What happens in practice is that your 5bb winrate may get reduced to 2bb/100. And now, with a 2bb/100 winrate and the "lower variance" of 50bb/100 standard deviation, you'll lose after one year 26.4% of the time.

You doubled the chances of losing!

What Does This Mean?

Does playing a tighter, more passive, nitty style reduce variance? Yes.

But reducing variance doesn't mean reducing the chance of downswings. Usually, it means increasing it! You see, if you play around with a variance calculator for thirty minutes, you'll figure out that "swings" depend on exactly one thing:

The ratio of your winrate to your standard deviation.

Let's say instead, we keep the standard deviation at 70bb and we double our winrate to 10bb/100.

Now, after one year, we lose only 1.2% of the time. From 13% to 1.2%!

If your goal is to reduce your swings, you don't need to reduce your variance. You need to get better at poker. And your winrate has importance that goes far beyond your swings... Even if we took the standard deviation down far enough to make you only lose 1.2% of the time with a 2bb/100 winrate (which isn't realistically possible), your average outcome on the year would be +$3,000.

With the 10bb/100 winrate, your average outcome would be +$15,000.

The Bottom Line

Are there scenarios where changing your strategy to reduce variance makes sense? In theory, probably some. Should you ever do it? I'd argue, no.

Your winrate is everything. A sacrifice of your winrate to the gods of variance is unlikely to be worth the cost.

If this post scared you, good. Take that fear and do something positive with it. Don't leave your fate up to luck. Study, hire a coach, run variance simulations, work on your game.

Don't be one of the many people reading this right now who give in to their delusions. Delusions that they're unlucky. That they know "enough" about the game. That they've won for a few months because they've figured it out.

Not one great poker player has ever learned enough that they couldn't still improve. Variance is scary.

And fear is a terrible thing to waste.

Phil Galfond

I love this piece because it fits so well with trading. You don't become a better trader via risk aversion or smaller trades, but rather by increasing your win rate and betting big when you have high leverage. Size your positions appropriately relative to your free capital, i.e. how much you can lose... At a bank or hedge fund, that's your stop loss, as a retail trader, that's your account size.

No matter how good you are at poker, if you have $200 in your pocket, and you step up to a table where the blinds are $5 and $10, you're going to lose all your money. This is because variance will dominate, and a bad streak of luck will wipe you out.

I feel like people have a better understanding of variance in poker than in trading, because it's more mathematical and intuitive. In trading, it's harder to know your odds.

Good traders collect data on individual trades, or daily or monthly P&L, and over time will get a strong sense of their win rate and profitability statistics. With this information, you can build a simple simulator and estimate your variance. I strongly recommend this. You can do it in Excel, a Google Sheet, code it in Python, or get an LLM to help you.

This process will help you understand your variance, and it will also allow you to gauge whether you have sufficient capital. Let's say a retail trader has $50,000 in an account. They risk $2,000 per trade (4% of free capital), they have a 51% win rate, and their winners are 1.2X their losers. Here's how they will do over the course of 100 simulations of a single trading year (252 trading days per year).

100 P&L simulations of the same strategy

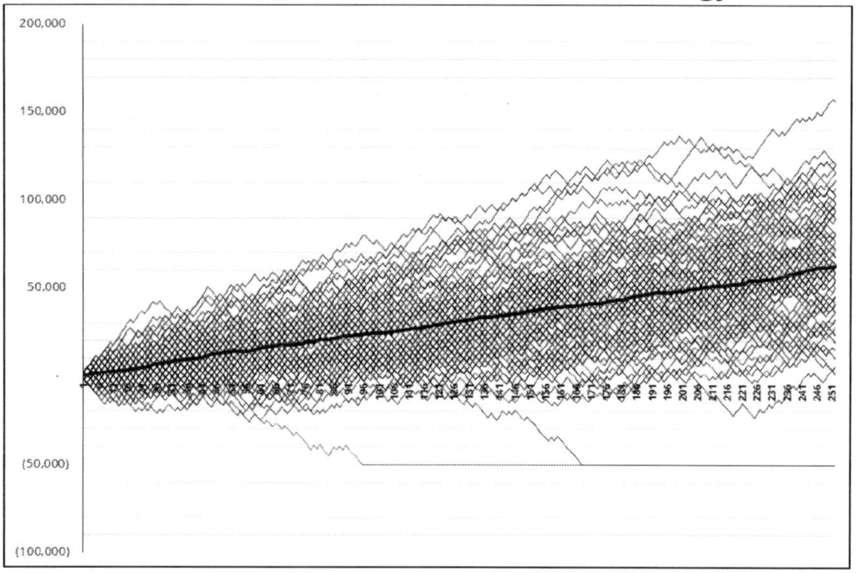

You can see that:

- Only 2 out of 100 simulations result in ruin
- Average P&L is around $50,000
- Most outcomes are in the +$10,000 to +$110,000 range.

If you are confident that your win rate and win$/loss$ ratio estimates are somewhat accurate, you end up with a good idea of your variance. You can find the spreadsheet for this simulator at www.spectramarkets.com/simulateprofitandloss.

As you tweak the variables in your simulation you can visualize the effects and learn:

- What is a reasonable budget/expectation for your yearly P&L?
- What % of free capital is reasonable to put at risk per day or per trade?
- How much variance should you expect?

When you understand the variance of your strategy, you are less likely to freak out about drawdowns and losing streaks. A strong professional poker player knows they will experience bad sessions.

Variance is painful. It's one thing to internalize the concept and it's another thing to live through it. Excellent traders know the difference between routine variance and process breakdown or psychological tilt. When you are having the worst week of the year, remember: There are 52 weeks every year, and one of them is going to be the worst. That's just how it works. It doesn't mean you have lost your edge, or you suck, or you have forgotten how to trade. There is a good chance it's just variance.

For more on variance and position sizing, please see Chapter 11 of *Alpha Trader*.

Before we move on to the next bit, I want to talk about an important aspect of position sizing that often comes up.

> Should I vary position size based on my conviction level?

Before we dive in, let me be clear on one thing. Everyone should vary their position size based on their available free capital and the volatility of the product(s) they trade. These are absolute musts. But varying position size based on conviction is controversial because we don't know our odds or our edge ex-ante. We might think we know, *but do we*?

Side quest: Do good traders vary bet size?

Alpha Trader and *The Art of Currency Trading* have detailed discussions of how to vary bet size according to market volatility and conviction level. Varying bet size according to volatility is not controversial. If the S&P is carving out 5% ranges every day, you need to trade smaller than when it's trading 1% per day. It also stands to reason that if you are extremely confident in a trade, you should invest more than you would in a trade where your confidence level is 60%.

But maybe that's wrong!

Betting based on confidence could be flawed because it's only sensible if there is a known, positive relationship between confidence and accuracy. If your highest conviction trades have the same hit rate as your "I'm not totally sure on this one!" trades… There is no reason to correlate your bet size with your convictions.

Bet sizing problem

Bet sizing is one of the most important topics in trading because it relates to risk management and allows you to leverage your best ideas, but there is no single correct answer or best methodology.

One thing is clear: Bet sizing is critical to both successful trading and good poker. You don't put your life savings at risk on one hand, even pocket aces, because 15% of the time you're bankrupt. The same applies to trading.

If you've read any trading books or spent time around experienced traders, you've probably heard somebody say: "Good traders vary bet size." "Vary bet size" means "bet bigger on better ideas, and smaller on lower-quality ideas." This is timeless wisdom in many trading circles, like "take small losses" and "let your winners run."

This makes sense, especially for veteran traders who are good with probabilities and know their edge. However, there are reasons that this advice just doesn't click with other traders. Let's take a look at some arguments for and against varying bet size according to confidence level.

Are confidence and accuracy correlated?

Unfortunately, there is no simple answer to this question. Some think the answer is obvious. "Of course, higher confidence leads to higher accuracy!" But if you study the literature, it's not clear. At all. Various accuracy/confidence scatter plots offer wildly different conclusions.

One study asked participants to monitor their heart rate in reaction to various stimuli and report on changes over time. They were also asked how confident they were in their assessment. Here is the scatter plot of confidence vs. accuracy:

Study 1 result: Confidence vs. accuracy

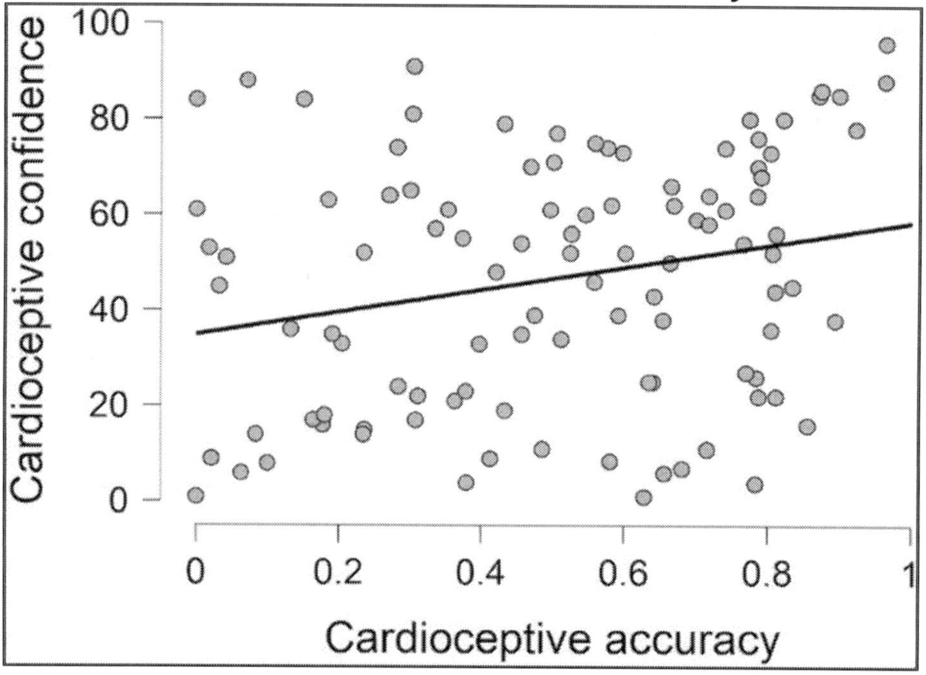

Noisy! Here's a second chart, this time from a study of confidence vs. accuracy in the realm of avalanche prediction:

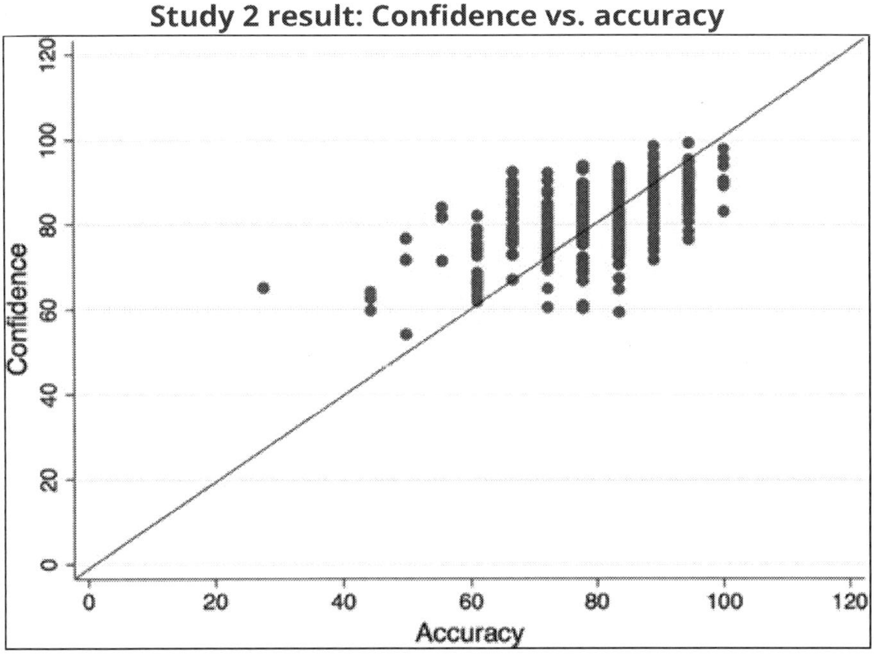

Again, there's a weak positive relationship there, but if it wasn't for that 45-degree line on the chart, it would be hard to see!

Confidence and overconfidence

There is an enormous body of literature on biases and failures in human decision-making. Essential books in the genres of decision theory and behavioral finance include *Thinking, Fast and Slow* by Daniel Kahneman and *Psychology of Intelligence Analysis* by Richards J. Heuer.

As these books and countless studies detail, people are overconfident in most measurable aspects of human behavior. People think they're better at forecasting than they actually are; clinicians think they're better at diagnosis than they actually are; celebrity economists are often wrong, but rarely in doubt.

Therefore, the average trader might look at an opportunity and think they have a 70% chance of being right. But most actually show closer to a 50-55% win rate, so it sounds like this trader is possibly overly optimistic. The only way to know is to gather data.

Gather as much data as possible, at as granular a level as possible. I am sad to say that I have not collected data on my conviction level on trades or trading days over the years. While I know my daily win rate is close to 50% most years back to 2006, I have no idea if that win rate correlates with ex-ante confidence.

The lesson is: **Record your conviction level on each trade.** This will allow you to create a database that shows the relationship between your confidence and your accuracy and systematically answer the question: "Should I vary bet size based on conviction?" If you don't have data, you are guessing.

Kelly is key

A critical concept in any optimal bet size discussion is the Kelly criterion, a formula in probability theory that maximizes gambling returns over time. It takes your edge, your payoff, and your available capital, and prescribes the mathematically optimal bet size in any situation, offering the best tradeoff between maximum return and minimal risk of ruin.

If you are not familiar with the Kelly criterion concept, it's worth taking some time to read about it. *Fortune's Formula* by William Poundstone is a fun read that explains the history and application of Kelly .

Here is a graphic from the Wikipedia page for Kelly criterion:

Kelly criterion output

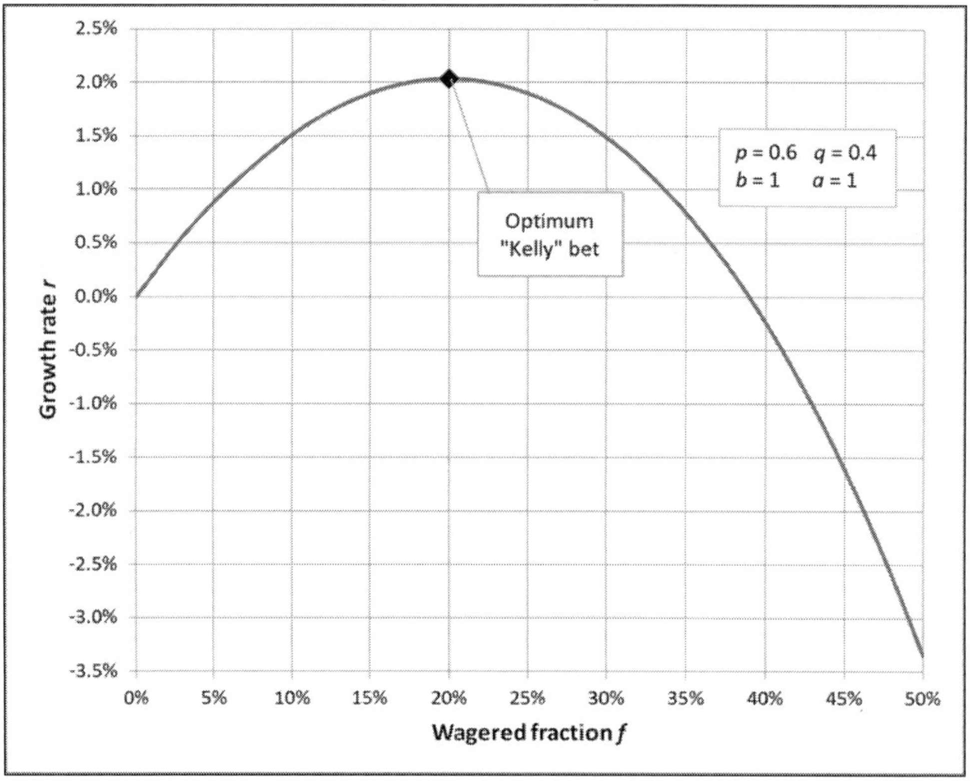

Here's a less mathy way of looking at it:

Stylized view of Kelly Criterion

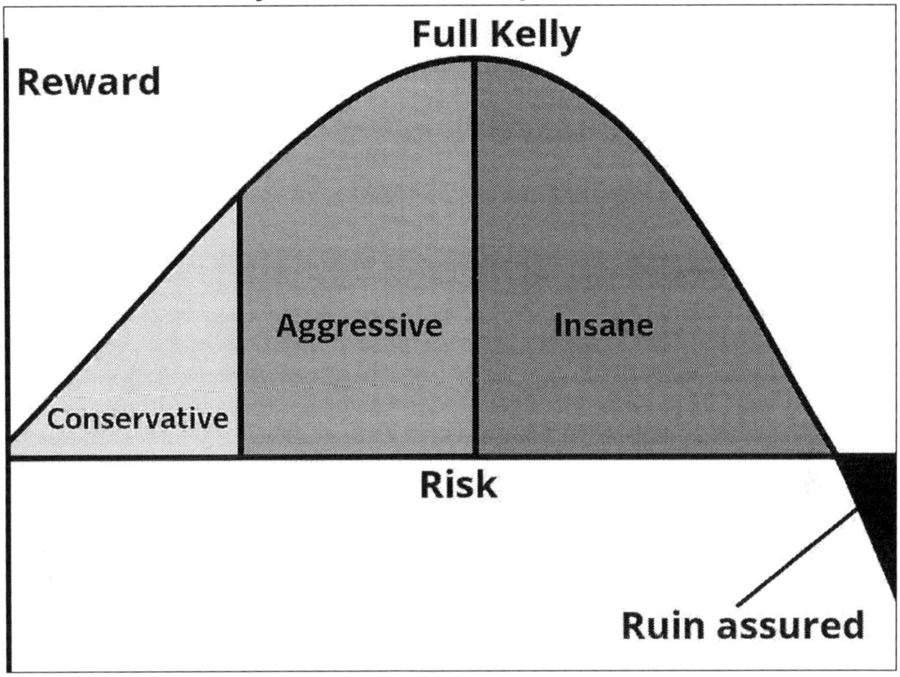

An important caveat: the Kelly criterion maximizes returns when the **probability of the outcome is known**. It works for coin tosses, where you know with certainty that you have a 50% probability of winning; it works for card games, where despite the immense difficulty of calculating the odds, there are defined odds. Poker players can use the Kelly criterion. In sports gambling, Kelly is also useful because there is a huge database of historical information that can be used to objectively and accurately estimate future odds before an event.

Can *traders* use the Kelly criterion? The answer is not obvious. The market isn't static—**it doesn't offer us repeating opportunities,** strictly speaking. Every single tick, every second, every regime, is different from every one that preceded it. A 55% hit rate last month does not mean a 55% hit rate this month.

Can traders realistically assess the ex-ante win probability of a trade? Maybe not new traders. What about experienced traders with years of experience? Good traders get better at thinking probabilistically over time, and the skill associated with any endeavor goes up and to the right over time as a rule. Also, those who know more are at least slightly better at knowing what they *don't* know.

When it comes to the specifics of assessing probabilities in trading, the question must be answered with data, on a trader-by-trader basis. The only way to assess the outcomes of your probabilistic predictions over time is to **document every trade, before you trade.**

Once you have a good idea of your win rate based on probability, you plug it into Kelly, adjust to a determined percentage of Kelly, and place your bet. This is the most sophisticated and difficult but high-leverage way to size your trades based on conviction.

A second, simpler option

Until you have data that tells you whether your win rate and confidence level on trades correlate, you can use your historical win/loss statistics to figure out the ideal $ at risk for each trade and stick to that. Assume your conviction is not correlated with success and bet the same amount every time. This makes life easier, with one less variable to juggle and one less question to ask yourself every time.

For example, if you have a 57% win rate and your winning trades make 1.5X the average loss of your losing trades over the past three years, use those stats with a modified Kelly calculation to determine your sizing. There is something to be said for this level of simplicity. It doesn't allow you to increase leverage on higher confidence ideas, but it preserves mental capital by reducing complexity.

If you think you know your trading stats pretty well (either trade-by-trade or daily stats), you can plug them into this formula:

% of Capital to Risk = Win% - ((1-Win%) / (AverageWin / AverageLoss))

So let's say it's the first trading day of the year and you have $4,000,000 of free capital. You know from your historical P&L data that you made money on 50% of your trades in the past 3 years, your average winning trade was $370,000 and average losing trade was $300,000. These figures approximate real data for someone without much flow who generates around $10 million dollars per year of P&L at a commercial bank.

Plugging these numbers into the Kelly formula we get:

% of Capital to Risk = 0.50 - ((1 - 0.50) / (370,000 / 300,000))

= 9.4%

So 9.4% times $4,000,000 free capital suggests that this trader should risk $378,400 on their first trade of the year. **The Kelly number tends to be surprisingly high** because it represents the most aggressive allocation possible to maximize upside. Most traders should use **half-**Kelly or **quarter-**Kelly sizing because full-Kelly sizing is very aggressive for trading.

The Kelly Criterion is better suited to gambling games than to trading. It was developed for gambling scenarios where you know the exact odds beforehand, and every bet is made in a series. Kelly is a good conceptual starting point for position sizing exercises but should not be used to get the final answer: it also assumes you are making bets sequentially whereas in trading you might have multiple concurrent bets.

A third, simplest option

The simplest approach to bet sizing is assuming a) conviction doesn't correlate with accuracy, and b) historical trading stats may not predict future outcomes. So you simply bet a fixed percentage of your capital on each trade.

Betting 2% or 3% of free capital is conservative and will keep you out of trouble.

Simple Kelly, or Kelly adjusted for conviction level, is more aggressive and offers greater and more asymmetric upside than conservative, fixed bet sizing... But it's riskier and more complicated. There are always tradeoffs.

Systematic, automatic

Alpha Trader Chapter 11 presents a tiered sizing system where confidence is the input and bet size is the output. In that system, a run-of-the-mill mean reversion trade merits a smaller bet than a once-a-year "perfect" macro setup with a tight stop loss. The latter gets the bigger bet size.

The math says that if you're aggressive on your "best bets," and your confidence is correlated to your accuracy, your winners will vastly outweigh your losers over time. Your P&L will grow dramatically as you increasingly capitalize on your best ideas. This is why veteran traders are telling you to vary bet size: because you want to leverage your best ideas.

In *The Art of Currency Trading*, I describe 5 levels of confidence. In *Alpha Trader*, there are 3. Now, we are debating whether there should be any variation in bet sizing by confidence. This is a hard question and that's why it's worth debating.

Whether you use five, three or just one level of conviction for trade sizing, always consider the possibility that one day there could be an outlier that deserves a bigger bet. If you're good, you will know it when you see it. And you'll record the results so that over time you learn what you know, what you think you know, and what you don't know.

So, what's the right answer?

There is no right answer to the varied bet size question. It depends on the trader. It depends on your experience, confidence, calibration and risk tolerance. As is often the case with questions of trading styles and methodologies, the answer varies by individual. Decide what kind of bet sizing protocol is right for you.

If you're the kind of person who is good at snap judgments and probabilities, and you already have an extended history of trade journaling that shows a strong confidence/accuracy connection… Vary your bet sizes. If you're up 12 million dollars on the year and you keep finding outstanding opportunities, then bigger bets might be for you. If you are confident, your confidence is well-calibrated to reality, and you can afford to take some extra risk, you will benefit from varied bet sizing when you play your cards right.

But if you're not the kind of person who wants extra risk, higher variance, increased stress, or extra mental load, **that's okay too.** When added complexity does not yield tangible, measurable benefits, take the simpler route. Maybe you are self-aware enough to know that you don't have a clear sense of which opportunities are better or worse. You simply have a binary way of looking at trades: they're good enough to put on, or they're not. That's fine.

Your goal should be to use data to establish whether there is a correlation between your confidence and your accuracy. To summarize, choose one of three sizing methods:

1. **Easy.** Use a fixed percentage of free capital as your bet size on all trades.
2. **Medium.** Use historical win rates and trading stats and a modified Kelly criterion percentage to pick a bet size and stick to that every time.
3. **Hard.** Vary bet size according to conviction. Use rigorously collected data on win/loss percentage, size of average win and loss, and modified Kelly to determine the appropriate risk on each trade.

Position sizing is one of the trickiest and most important aspects of trading. Be thoughtful about your position sizing process and revisit it once per year. As you gain experience, adapt and improve your position sizing and extract more juice from your best ideas.

End of side quest.

Game selection

Elite poker players understand that edge comes not just from playing well, but from playing against the right opponents. Similarly, successful traders know that trading the right markets at the right times dramatically impacts their profitability. We will go into game selection in detail in Chapter 7, but for now I just want to say:

Good traders and good poker players pick a game they can win. They avoid games where they have negative expectation.

Are you playing a game you can win?

Exploiting market inefficiencies

Poker players seek opportunities to exploit opponents who make predictable errors. A player might notice that an opponent always check-raises with strong hands and always check-calls with medium-strength hands, creating an exploitable pattern.

Markets have similar inefficiencies, often created by structural factors like quarter-end rebalancing, option expiration dynamics, time of day effects, and other distortions caused by flow. Any trading strategy that exploits market inefficiency with an understanding of why that inefficiency exists is likely to be robust. If you understand why an inefficiency exists, you will also be able to predict when it might disappear. By identifying structural inefficiencies, you can develop strategies that exploit predictable market behaviors rather than trying to outguess the broader market.

Tight/aggressive

One of the most well-known successful approaches to good poker is called "tight/ aggressive". The concept is that you don't want to be involved in too many pots, but when you are involved, be as aggressive as possible. In other words, wait until you have great cards in good position and then go for it. While you never want to literally go all in when trading, the tight/aggressive strategy from poker is a great analogy.

Wait, wait, wait… And then when everything lines up: POUNCE!

Metagame and continuous improvement

The best poker players and traders are relentless in their pursuit of improvement. The winning style of poker in 1998 is not the style that wins today. Trading strategies are the same. Adapt or die.

Database analysis and review

Elite poker players use tracking software to analyze thousands of hands, identifying patterns and leaks in their play. They review difficult decisions with peers and coaches, constantly refining their strategy. Excellent traders implement a similar rigorous review process with a detailed journal of entry/exit points, thesis, and outcome. They conduct weekly or monthly reviews of their trades and categorize performance by strategy, market and result.

Identify the patterns in your trading. Find the strengths to leverage and weaknesses to address. **Poker can be an excellent laboratory for you to practice the skills required for good trading.** You get more reps in poker than in trading because there is no down time other than scheduled breaks.

Play a few hundred hands of poker and think about it as a mirror held up to your trading. Do you fold mediocre hands? Can you avoid tilt? Can you concentrate for eight straight hours while integrating appropriate periods of rest and mental reset? Can you maintain a state of boredom and concentration at the same time? Can you slow down your mind, act rationally, and avoid negative EV traps?

Playing poker in a purposeful way can help you practice emotional balance and rational thinking. Do the right thing at the table and you will develop and reinforce mental patterns that help you on the trading floor, helping you become a stronger trader.

Conclusion

The parallels between poker and trading run deep, but perhaps the most important one is that both are ultimately tests of self-mastery. The market, like the poker room, will repeatedly present situations designed to trigger your worst instincts—fear, overconfidence, tilt, greed, and revenge.

Your success depends not just on your technical knowledge but on your ability to recognize the psychological traps and avoid them. The best traders, like the best poker players, aren't just experts in market dynamics or probability, they're experts at managing their worst selves.

Applying these lessons from poker can help develop a more disciplined, process-oriented trading approach that focuses on optimal decision-making, not chasing outcomes. Over time, this approach will improve your results and reduce the emotional toll of trading.

Remember: the goal isn't to win every poker hand or make money on every trade. The goal is to make many, many decisions with positive expected value. Over, and over, and over. Then let the law of large numbers take care of the rest.

CHAPTER 6

CONCEPTS I WISH I'D LEARNED EARLIER

On open minds and ancillary notions

"Anyone who isn't embarrassed of who they were last year probably isn't learning enough."

Alain de Botton

This chapter digs into seven less mainstream financial concepts that I came upon later in my career. Each has helped me level up my understanding of markets. Ergodicity and quantum mechanics, for example, have practical applications in trading. Initial conditions and narrative contagion are important concepts in economic forecasting. Adverse selection is a key concept for market makers and anyone that uses limit orders.

For each topic, I'll do my best to provide a layman's introduction, then explain how the concept applies to trading and markets.

Ergodicity

Ergodicity is a critical but confusing concept that carries important implications in finance. The simple definition of an ergodic system is one where the expected value of an activity performed by a group is the same for an individual carrying out the same activity over time. Rolling dice is ergodic. If 200 people roll a six-sided die, the expected value is the same as if you alone roll a six-sided die 200 times.

In contrast, a non-ergodic system would have different outcomes for the group and the individual. Imagine a game where there is a gun with one bullet in the chamber (1-in-6 chance of dying) and 100 people play the game (they aim the gun at their own head and pull the trigger), one at a time. Those who survive win $10,000,000. If 100 people each play this game once, *as a group* the average member survives and gets $8,333,333 (5/6 of $10,000,000). But individually, some players don't make it.

Some might consider playing this game once.

Nobody would choose to play this game 100 times in a row because the expected outcome is almost certain death. In a non-ergodic system like Russian Roulette, the individual experience may differ greatly from the average group result.

To bring it closer to home, imagine this trading strategy: A coin flip (50/50) where you bet all your money; it pays 50% if you win and costs you 40% if you lose. Positive expected value for any individual trial, so it seems like a pretty good proposition, right? Let's have one person start with $1 and flip the coin 150 times in a row and see what happens. In almost every instance, the player ends up effectively bankrupt. They will experience some huge rides higher in their P&L, but the end result will be sadness because the system is non-ergodic.

10 simulations of a game where you flip a coin to win 50% or lose 40%

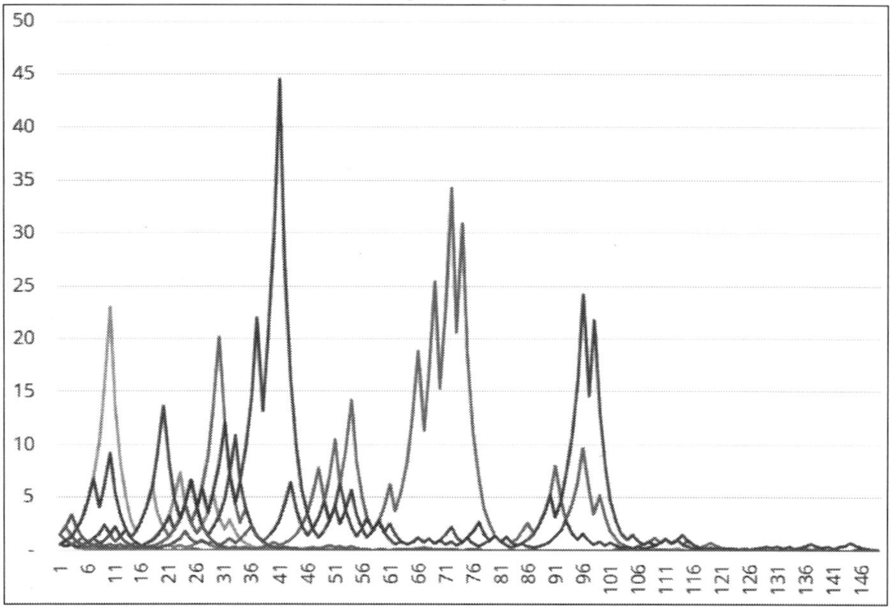

Why do you lose money, even though each flip has a positive expected value? What makes this confusing is the difference between:

- Arithmetic mean (ensemble average) = +5% expected return per bet.
- Geometric mean (time average) = What actually happens to your money over time.

Even with a positive expected value, a high-variance strategy can lose money over time if the geometric mean is negative. This is the essence of non-ergodicity; the time average can differ dramatically from the ensemble average. With full bankroll or leveraged betting, over many trials, your portfolio will eventually hit a sequence of losses that drive your capital toward zero. This happens because:

- **Multiplicative Process**. Your bankroll after N flips is the initial amount multiplied by either 1.5 or 0.6 each time.
- **Law of Large Numbers**. With enough flips, you'll eventually hit a streak of losses that overwhelms previous gains.

In practice, random sequences won't be perfectly balanced and so the Absorption Property creeps in. The Absorption Property says that if (when!) your bankroll gets extremely small (e.g., after several consecutive losses), it becomes nearly impossible to recover because you're betting smaller and smaller amounts.

To clarify the ergodic vs. non-ergodic distinction we can ask: If 1,000 traders each take one trade simultaneously, and one trader takes 1,000 trades sequentially... Will their outcomes look the same?

Yes → the system is ergodic.

No → it's non-ergodic, and the path matters.

Think about it: If you can play a coin tossing game that pays 3:1… How many times do you play if you must bet your entire stake every time? It has positive expected value every time, but negative expected value on any reasonable timeframe beyond one or two flips.

Now let's make things even more realistic. You are looking for a systematic trader to work at your huge hedge fund, and you plan to interview Jimmy Sharpe, one of the best traders on the street. He has a 60% win rate and his winning trades average $250,000 while his average loss is $200,000. He does 100 trades per year and shows you his running P&L over the past two years (200 trades).

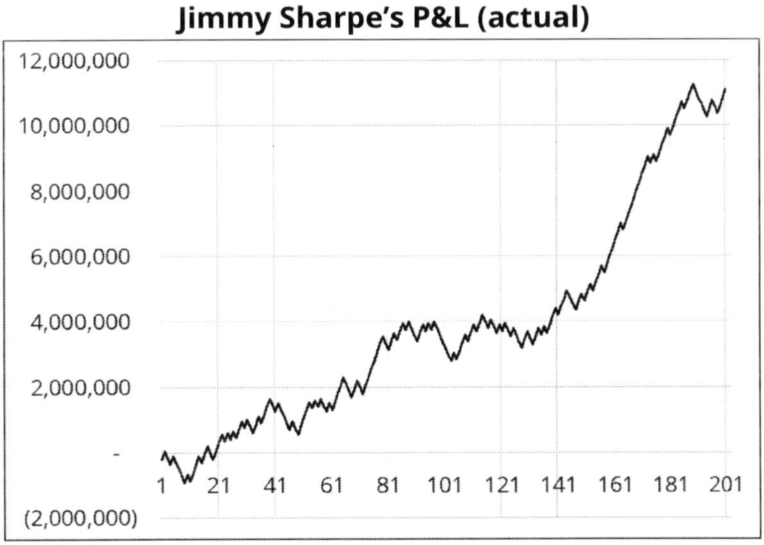

He had a stop loss of $2,000,000 and made $4,000,000 in Year 1 and $6,000,000 in Year 2. Looks pretty good! You are afraid to ask what his strategy is, but you do ask and he says he combines some rolldown in interest rate futures with option selling with a directional macro bias in equities and currency markets. Sounds reasonable.

You run a few simulations using his statistics with a sample size of 200 trades and you feel pretty good about the future. Here are four simulations using the same data (60% win rate, $250k winners, $200k losers).

Jimmy Sharpe's P&L across four simulations

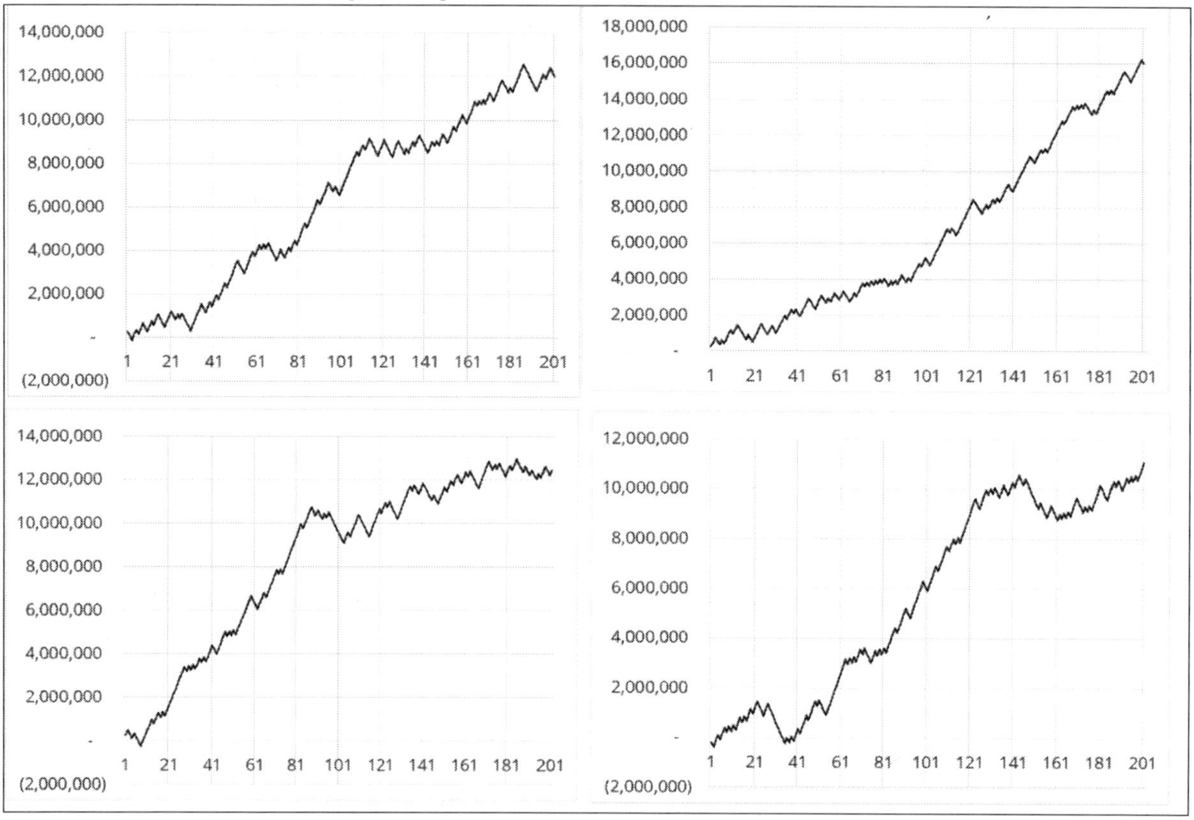

You have a pretty good idea of what to expect and it looks good. You hire him.

Little did you know, the real distribution of his P&L was: 60% win rate, 39.9% loss rate, 0.1% of the time he blows up and loses $50,000,000. Bad luck for you, the one-in-one-thousand event happens 55 days after he starts at your firm and his P&L ends up looking like this:

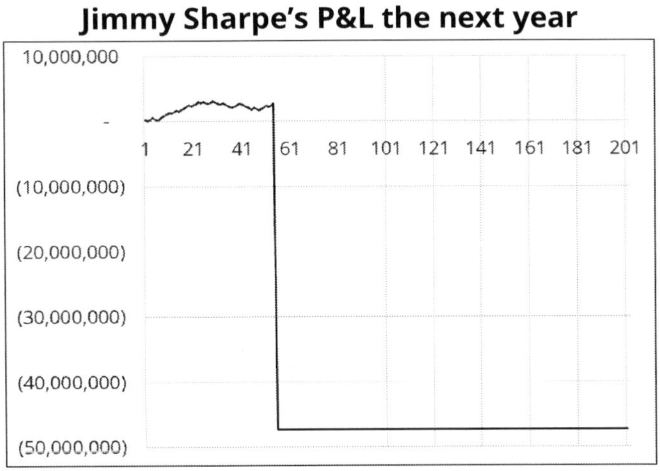

If that seems like an exaggeration, it is not. There are countless traders who make $Y for three or four years and then lose 25*Y in year 5. Victor Niederhoffer was famous for this, but many others have gone down the same road. I worked next to a trader who sold wings in natural gas futures (low-delta options). He was well known as a big boy in that market and had made big money over the prior five years. He blew up six weeks after he sat down next to me: Hurricane Katrina hit.

Non-ergodic trading systems make money on many timelines, but if you run them enough times in a row, they blow up. The textbook example of this is the seller of low-premium options. She collects pennies year after year, then gives back $100 bills when an unexpected event hits.

This non-ergodic process is covered in detail by Nassim Taleb in several of his works and it's a critical concept for you to understand as a trader, risk manager or hedge fund allocator. If you don't understand how you are making money or how the person you invested in is making money, you expose yourself to high Sharpe strategies with huge downside. High Sharpe Ratios can camouflage convexity for a long time, but not forever.

A strategy does not have to have fat tails to be non-ergodic. To take an extreme example, a Martingale Betting Strategy in Binary Options is also non-ergodic, even though the returns do not have fat tails. Imagine a trader uses a Martingale strategy: doubling their position size after each losing trade, aiming to recoup all previous losses plus a small profit when they finally win. The trader is operating in a market or instrument with bounded, binary outcomes. For example, a fixed 1:1 payout binary option. Each individual trade has a predictable and capped outcome:

Win: +1 unit
Loss: -1 unit

No single trade can cause a "fat tail" event like a 30% drawdown. The outcomes are not extreme, they're small and symmetrical. Despite the lack of fat tails, this strategy is non-ergodic because over time, the inevitable losing streak leads to ruin, even though the strategy often wins in the short term. The bet sizing brings the ergodicity, not the distribution of returns of the instrument. If you simulate 1,000 traders doing this for a while, most will win. But if one trader does this for long enough, they will lose everything.

The mathematical structure of compounding losses leads to infinite risk over time. Even with a 50% win rate and no volatility shocks, the system is non-survivable in the long run. That's non-ergodicity without fat tails. If you keep doubling down, or keep going all-in on single bets, you will lose everything.

Below is what the mathematical distribution of Martingale returns looks like betting $1 on a coin toss and doubling your bet every time you lose, until you win. You have $1,000 and there is no betting limit. Here are six simulations of the P&L of 1,000 trades.

Simulating Martingale Betting Six Times ($1,000 bankroll, $1 bets)

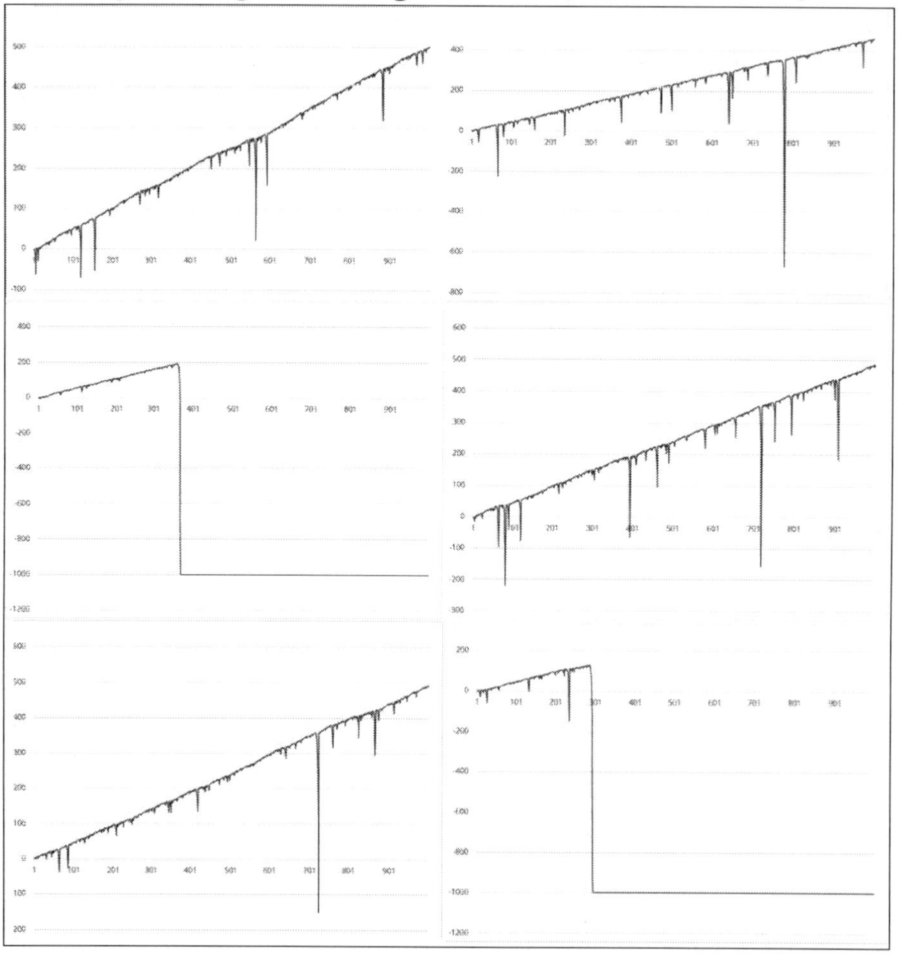

In non-ergodic systems, you can have long and profitable runs, but eventually you blow up. Whether that non-ergodicity comes from your risk management system, or fat tails in the distribution does not matter.

Ergodic systems in real life

When each trade is risk managed properly with specified downside, you have an ergodic trading strategy. Market making tends to be ergodic, as does any strategy that employs many discrete trades, each with a start and an end, along with a rigorous stop loss system. Solid traders who want to succeed in the long-term run ergodic strategies. Hot shot traders run all gas and no brakes. That is, they run non-ergodic strategies.

Imagine a day trader running a high-frequency strategy that captures tiny inefficiencies in liquid markets. They risk 2% of free capital per trade, cut losers quickly, and take hundreds of trades over time. Each trade has a slight edge, say a 55% win rate with a 1.2-to-1.0 reward-to-risk ratio. No single bad trade or bad day or bad run can blow up the account.

The trader compounds slowly and survives natural variance. Risk is tightly controlled, and outcomes are smoothed across many trials, so their results over time reflect the long-term statistical edge. This is ergodic behavior: **the trader can expect to realize the average outcome across time because they survive long enough for the probabilities to play out.**

Now consider a trader with a massive edge who takes infrequent, high-conviction trades with 20-to-1 leverage. Maybe they only trade a few times a year, risking 50% of their account on a macro idea or earnings bet. The expected return on paper could be impressive. In backtests, the average return looks great across all periods where the trader didn't get wiped out.

But in real life, the approach exposes the trader to path dependency: one or two bad trades in a row can end the game. This is non-ergodic behavior: although the strategy is amazing "on average" across many simulated paths, it's unrealistic for a single trader following a single path to consistently survive and achieve that aggregate outcome. Most end up ruined before reaching the average.

Here's a real-life example:

Any system that sells tail options and any system that uses leverage but does not use stop losses will tend to be highly non-ergodic. A trading strategy that earns carry but occasionally takes massive drawdowns can be non-ergodic. There are countless real-life examples of non-ergodic strategies whose P&Ls looked excellent, until they didn't.

Jesse Livermore (1877 – 1940)

Widely regarded as one of the greatest traders of all-time, Livermore went from rags to riches to rags to riches and back to rags by the time of his death. His natural talent, intuitive pattern recognition, and connections allowed him to capitalize on some of the biggest stock market moves in history, including the Crash of 1929. He was the richest man in the world in 1930, but by 1940 he was bankrupt and died by suicide.

Livermore's repeated risk management failures meant he lived and died inside a non-ergodic system. Livermore had strategies that, over multiple iterations, could produce massive gains. But each iteration also carried the possibility of catastrophic loss. His actual life path—one individual over time—was non-ergodic. Unlike a Monte Carlo simulation with infinite lives, he had only one.

He frequently used leverage, borrowing to amplify returns. This increased his exposure to ruin. In a non-ergodic system, ruin resets the game to zero permanently and leverage increases the risk of ruin. While his trades had a positive expected value, they carried a high risk of ruin, and they were bad bets for a single-life path.

Long-Term Capital Management (LTCM) (1998)

The fund was profitable for a while, but their models assumed historical market behavior was a reliable predictor of future outcomes and that correlations between asset classes were predictable. These assumptions proved incorrect and the fund blew up. LTCM employed a variety of carry strategies and carry tends to be non-ergodic compared to directional macro.

Amaranth Advisors (2006)

This hedge fund invested in natural gas futures, assuming predictable seasonality. Hurricane Katrina delivered huge returns in 2005, but in 2006 the sudden drop in natural gas prices drove the fund out of business. Its huge bet sizes and bad assumptions triggered the fund's collapse.

Archegos Capital (2021)

This family office used total return swaps to generate huge leverage, betting on a few media and tech stocks. The fund generated strong returns for a while, and assets grew to $20 billion… then went sub-zero in a few days when volatility exploded in 2021. And... It was gone.

Archegos Capital Management, Net Asset Value, $bn (2012 – 2021)

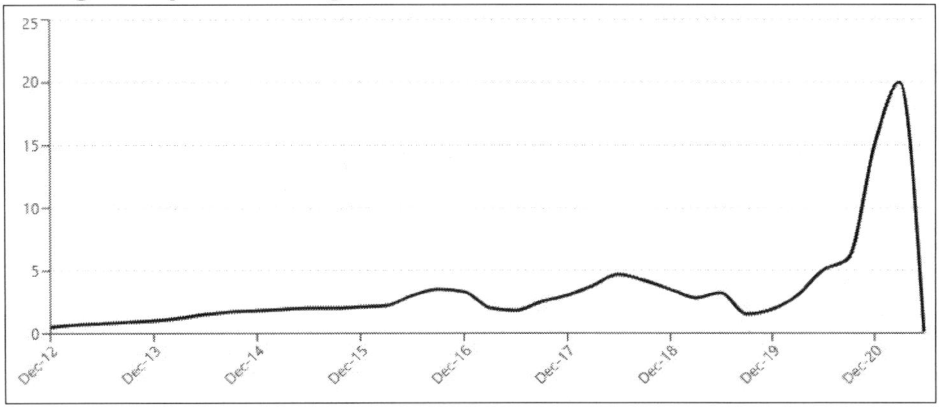

Data source: Credit Suisse Report on Archegos Capital Management

Note that technically, ergodicity is a binary property. A system is either ergodic, or it isn't. But in practice, especially in finance and trading, we can talk meaningfully about systems being *more* or *less* ergodic as a spectrum or degree of fragility and path dependence. In strict terms, a process is ergodic if time averages equal ensemble averages, a true or false condition. However, a non-ergodic process can vary in terms of *how* non-ergodic it is, i.e. how divergent the outcomes can become over time. The more non-ergodic the process, the more sensitive the path is to compounding, volatility, and/or ruin.

This does not mean that non-ergodic systems should be avoided—it simply means that you need to understand the systems you trade or invest in and can manage the challenges and higher risk they present:

- Design strategies given that **extreme events happen**.
- Avoid systems where long-term survival is jeopardized by **tails.**
- Use position sizing and risk management to **make your personal experience more ergodic**—so you can survive the path to positive expected value.

Retail day traders sometimes run into problems trading stocks after hours because the features of regular trading during primary market hours (automated stop losses, quick exits, continuous price action, no gaps, etc.) are not present after hours. Many excellent day traders make money during the day but find they perform poorly pre-market and after hours. The intraday market is much more ergodic than pre-market or after-hours trading.

Understand the nature of any trading system you employ or put money into. Is it ergodic, or non-ergodic? Backtesting and modeling will not always tell you the answer. **You need to use common sense and judgment** to fully understand the path and returns of a trader, hedge fund, or strategy you employ.

Finally, it's worth noting that non-ergodicity is one of the weaknesses of Bayesian thinking[38]. You can update your prior view as new information comes in, but if you don't understand the distribution of the data, you might be gaining increasing confidence about the future as more and more data rolls in... And setting yourself up for ruin.

If you develop a strategy with a high Sharpe ratio and keep adding more capital to it over time as it continues to perform, and that strategy has a non-ergodic distribution, you will blow up. This is because you are increasing non-ergodicity via your risk management while you are already in a non-ergodic distribution. Not good!

Nassim Taleb covers this nicely in his book *The Black Swan*. His "turkey problem" is as follows:

> A friendly farmer comes to the barn and feeds Tom the Turkey every day. Tom the Turkey is a good Bayesian and therefore each day that the farmer feeds him increases the turkey's belief that the farmer will feed him again tomorrow. The day before Thanksgiving, the farmer walks into the barn, carrying an axe. Tom the Turkey thinks nothing of it because he has been updating his priors all this time and knows the farmer is his friend. The farmer grabs Tom by the neck. Minutes later, Tom the Turkey is dead.

120 Days in the Life of a Bayesian Turkey

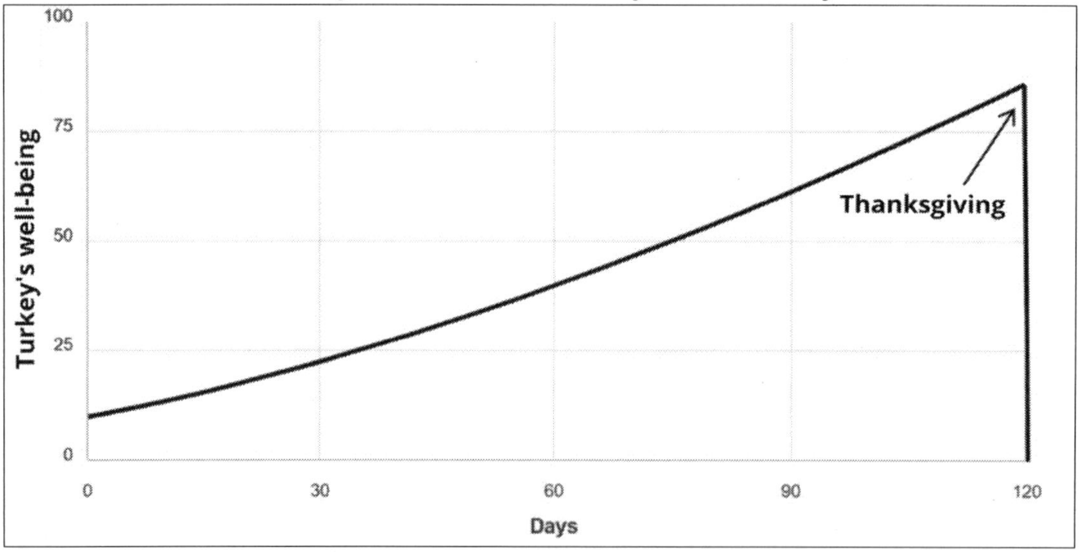

[38] Bayesian thinking is the practice of updating your beliefs based on new evidence, where you start with a prior probability, incorporate new data, and arrive at a more refined posterior probability that better reflects reality. See pages 80-81 in *Alpha Trader*.

This illustrates how inductive reasoning can fail catastrophically, especially in non-ergodic and fat-tailed environments where rare, high-impact events ("Black Swans") dominate.

Bayesian thinking: You update your beliefs as new evidence comes in. If the turkey is a Bayesian, its posterior probability that the farmer is his friend increases with each feeding. Taleb's critique: The turkey is being "rational" in a Bayesian sense. And yet it dies. Taleb is not criticizing Bayesian reasoning per se but highlighting its limitations in certain types of systems. **Did you notice the Turkey chart and the Archegos chart are identical?**

In a non-ergodic system, the future is not like the past, so you can't assume the past will repeat. One extreme event (slaughter) can override all previous data. The turkey faces epistemic uncertainty due to its limited model of the world. It doesn't even know Thanksgiving exists.

So, Taleb argues against naive or overconfident Bayesian reasoning in domains with incomplete models, hidden risks, structural breaks (regime shifts), and fat tails (rare but devastating outcomes). Bayesian reasoning is only as good as your priors and model structure. In non-ergodic systems, where the structure itself can change or is unknown, Bayesian thinking can give you false confidence.

Think about what sort of system you are operating in, and work to make it more ergodic.

Skew

Most professional traders have a solid understanding of fat tails and an intuitive feel for skew and convexity. In options markets, skew is the difference in the cost of options in each direction. For example, equity puts will usually cost more than equity calls because the distribution of returns tends to work that way (stocks grind up and crash down) and because the supply and demand for puts and calls is not balanced. There are always natural sellers of calls and fewer natural sellers of puts.

Whatever market you trade, you should know the skew in the options market because that (usually) reflects the skew in the distribution of returns. USDJPY goes down faster than it goes up. EURNOK goes up faster than it goes down. And so on. This is important, even if you don't trade options, because it helps you understand how your market behaves.

Options market skew can also be a good sentiment indicator. Changes in skew reflect changes in supply and demand for puts and calls. If the market is bidding for calls, it's usually a sign of bullish sentiment. At the extremes, it can be a reverse indicator. Look at this USDJPY risk reversal from 2021 to 2025.

USDJPY 25-delta risk reversal, 2021 to 2025

The risk reversal is the premium for calls vs. puts, expressed in percent. -2.00 on the y-axis means that the implied volatility of puts is 2% higher than calls. If the number is positive, it means calls are more expensive than puts. You see in USDJPY, puts almost always cost more than calls (that is, the number rarely goes above zero).

The two huge downward spikes came as USDJPY cratered, in August 2024 on a super weak U.S. jobs report and April 2025 during the great Liberation Day panic. USDJPY skew mostly hovers in a range, but occasionally goes to an extreme. The next chart marks USDJPY with the times that risk reversal went -2% or lower (bid for puts). I overlaid USDJPY so that you can see how options skew was a good reverse indicator for the currency.

USDJPY with times risk reversal was -2% or lower (bid for puts)

The timing wasn't perfect but extreme skew was a signal that the market was panicking. You find put/call relationships in any market where options are traded and use those relationships to ferret out the extremes when buyers and sellers of options are losing their minds. Then consider going the other way.

It is also critical to understand skew when you use overbought and oversold indicators like RSI. Here's a quick blurb I wrote about this in am/FX:

> A client asked me yesterday about EURSEK and the currently low RSI reading. I took a look and found that when the RSI goes below 30, it tends to precede more losses for EURSEK, not a rebound. There are 15 instances of RSI below 30 in EURSEK since 2010. Here is how EURSEK traded after the signals.

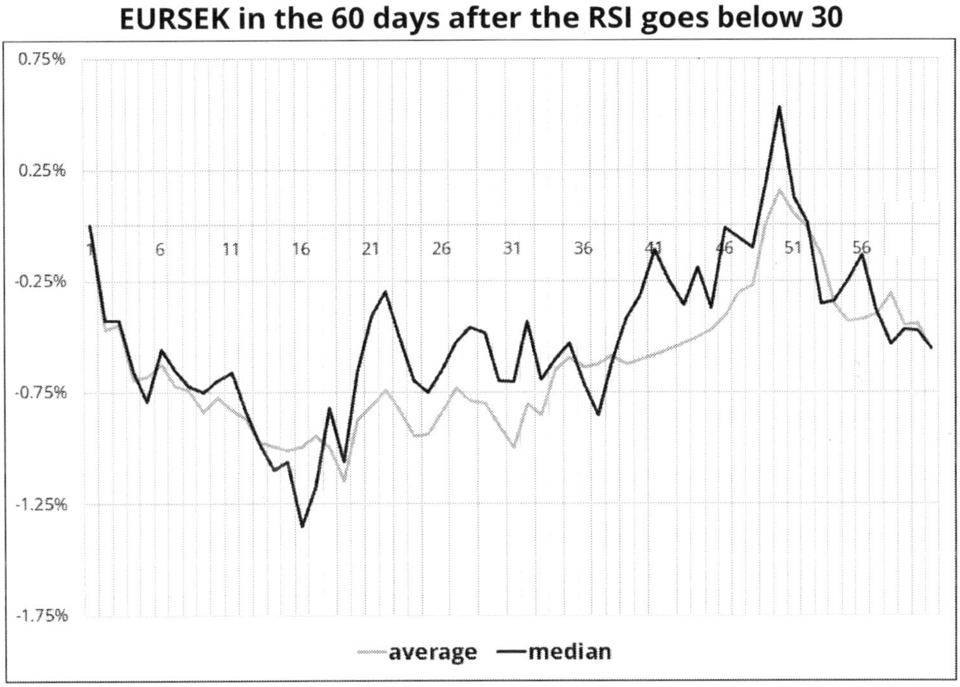

> This is consistent with what I have seen in other products: RSI can be either a trend indicator or a reversal indicator, depending on the skew of the market. Interestingly, if you look at the times when RSI went above 70, it DID work as a reversal indicator. This makes sense because EURSEK is convex. It grinds lower and spikes higher so **a low RSI means it's in grinding, trending mode, while a high RSI means it's ripping higher into a blowoff**. Just some food for thought when you're looking at RSIs.

Low and high RSIs are more relevant in a product that tends to blow off in that particular direction. Another example: USDJPY RSI below 25 is super **bullish**, while USDJPY RSI above 75 is modestly **bullish**. If you are watching RSI, the skew or convexity of the product you trade matters. A lot. USDJPY grinds up slowly, sells off fast and recovers fast.

There is a broader lesson here for when you are backtesting. If you only look at things in linear terms, you will miss some important aspects. Another example is that AUDJPY is highly correlated with stocks if you look only at days where SPX moves more than 1.5 standard deviations, but you will barely see a relationship if you backtest using all the data. Again, the convexity matters for correlations, too. Keep this in mind when you're backtesting.

When you watch a market, be sure to keep the skew or convexity of the distribution in mind. Study past returns and look at option market skew. If you don't know whether your market goes up fast and down slow, or the opposite, or neither or both, your trading, understanding, backtesting and forecasting will be suboptimal.

Initial conditions

From macroeconomics down to short-term trading, initial conditions are a critical and often overlooked factor. They represent the foundational state of an economic system or market environment before a particular shock, policy change or catalyst occurs. While traders chase headlines and economists debate the latest data points, underlying structural conditions often determine the impact of news, events, economic data, and other external market shocks, large and small.

It matters when it matters, and whether it matters or not often depends on initial conditions.

The concept of initial conditions draws from chaos theory, where small differences at the beginning can lead to vastly different outcomes over time. In financial markets, initial conditions encompass everything from balance sheet strength and employment levels to investor positioning and market microstructure. They act as the invisible foundation upon which all market reactions are built, yet they remain hidden in plain sight while participants fixate almost exclusively on the shock itself.

A common example comes from the world of monetary policy. People look at the economy and say: "It's worsening! It's getting weaker as we speak!" and conclude that a central bank will be dovish and cut rates.

They fail to properly weigh the importance of initial conditions.

Initial conditions in this case could mean:

1. **The state of the economy**: Is it starting from a point of strength, or weakness? Analysts sometimes focus too much on rates of change and not enough on starting levels. They scream that M2 growth has turned negative, but they don't look at whether it's above or below trend. They fret over weak sentiment data when consumers have trillions in excess savings. Or they expect new Chinese stimulus to trigger a zippy economic rebound while China is mired in an epic balance sheet recession or real estate collapse. The impact of exogenous shocks on an economy depends not just on the size of the shock, but also very much on initial conditions.

2. **The central bank's policy rate level relative to neutral**: If the policy rate is below neutral (accommodative), there may be no need for a rate cut, even if the economy is weak. A policy rate below neutral is already stimulative. If the central bank's policy rate is above neutral (restrictive), they might be justified in cutting rates, even if inflation is above target, because they feel that they need to be *less* restrictive. Starting points matter.

Analysts spend copious time looking at the economy and reading the tea leaves but don't always appreciate how much initial conditions matter.

Nassim Taleb's concept of antifragility helps us understand initial conditions. In his book *Antifragile,* Taleb distinguishes between systems that are:

- **fragile** (harmed by volatility)
- **robust** (unaffected by volatility)
- **antifragile** (benefit from volatility and stress)

A system's initial condition of fragility or antifragility often determines whether an external shock will strengthen or weaken it.

2023 and impending collapse

A striking and recent example of economists failing to account for initial conditions occurred throughout 2023. As U.S. consumer sentiment indices plummeted to recessionary levels, financial media buzzed with warnings of impending economic collapse. The University of Michigan Consumer Sentiment Index dropped to levels typically associated with severe recessions, while business confidence surveys reflected increasing pessimism about future conditions.

The immediate market reaction was predictable:

- traders positioned defensively
- recession calls proliferated
- many investment strategies centered around an anticipated economic contraction

However, this analysis fundamentally misread the initial conditions underlying the American economy.

The United States entered 2023 with historically tight labor markets, unemployment near all-time lows (3.5%) and job openings vastly exceeding available workers. Consumer balance sheets had been fortified by pandemic-era savings accumulation, with debt service ratios low and household net worth at record highs. Corporate balance sheets were similarly robust, with many companies maintaining substantial cash reserves built during the uncertainty of 2020-2022.

These initial conditions meant that deteriorating sentiment represented a healthy normalization from previously euphoric levels rather than a harbinger of collapse. Another word for "initial conditions" is simply ***context***.

In Taleb's framework, the American economy exhibited robust or maybe even antifragile characteristics in 2023. Interest rate hikes increased the disposable income of those on fixed incomes. The stress of negative sentiment actually revealed the underlying strength of the economy rather than exposing weakness. The tight labor market provided a crucial buffer against economic slowdown, while strong consumer finances meant reduced confidence did not immediately translate to lower spending. The disconnect between sentiment and fundamentals created opportunities for those who recognized the structural strength beneath the surface pessimism.

Taleb's analysis of the restaurant industry in *Antifragile* provides a perfect illustration of how initial conditions determine survival during stress. He observed that small, family-owned restaurants with low fixed costs, flexible operations, and strong local relationships often survive economic downturns better than large chain restaurants with high overhead and rigid systems.

2022 tech selloff vs. 2000 dotcom crash

Consider the technology sector during the 2000 dotcom crash versus the 2022 tech selloff. In both cases, high-growth technology companies experienced significant earnings disappointments.

However, the initial conditions were vastly different. In 2000, many technology companies had no earnings at all and were burning cash rapidly, with business models that were largely theoretical. In contrast, in 2022, major technology companies were profitable businesses with strong balance sheets and monopoly-style moats, despite facing growth headwinds.

This difference in initial conditions helps explain why the 2022 technology selloff was severe but didn't approach the devastation of 2000-2002. Companies with strong initial conditions weathered temporary growth slowdowns, while those with weak foundations did not. The stress test of rising rates and slowing growth in 2022 separated antifragile technology companies with profitable business models and strong cash flows, like MSFT, NVDA, and AMZN, from fragile ones (those dependent on continuous capital infusion and revenue growth, like PTON, ZM, and just about every single IPO and SPAC of the post-COVID era).

GameStop 2021

The GameStop short squeeze of 2021 showed how initial conditions in the form of high short interest could turn routine buying pressure into an explosive price move. The underlying fundamentals of GameStop hadn't dramatically improved, but the initial condition of excessive short positioning, infinite YOLO retail money from government stimmy checks and no sports to bet on created a feedback loop that drove prices far beyond levels any sane person would have expected.

Develop a systematic approach to assess not just the changes going on in the systems you study, but also the initial conditions. You can do this when analyzing economies, companies, or individual securities.

The building is only as solid as its foundation. In the complex interplay of economic forces and market dynamics, initial conditions serve as the foundation upon which all other events are built. Starting points determine whether shocks become crises or opportunities, whether policy changes achieve their intended effects, and whether market reactions prove sustained or temporary.

Master this analytical approach and look beyond the immediate signal to understand the foundational context. Find profitable opportunities in the gap between perception and reality.

In a world increasingly focused on immediate reactions and breaking news, the patient analysis of initial conditions provides a sustainable competitive advantage. The more you know about a building's foundation, the better you can predict how the building will hold up in an earthquake.

COVID-19 pandemic (2019/2020)

This principle was dramatically illustrated during the COVID-19 pandemic. Restaurants with antifragile initial conditions: low rent, ability to pivot to takeout, loyal local customer bases, and minimal debt not only survived lockdowns but often emerged stronger with less competition. Meanwhile, many well-capitalized chain restaurants with seemingly stronger balance sheets failed because their business models were fundamentally fragile. They were dependent on high volumes, they had inflexible lease structures, and they sagged under complex supply chains[39].

Investors who understood these initial conditions could identify which restaurant stocks would thrive versus which would struggle, regardless of their apparent financial strength on paper.

European sovereign debt (2011)

During the European sovereign debt crisis, bond markets initially treated all peripheral European countries similarly, with yields rising across Spain, Italy, Portugal, and Greece. The assumption was that eurozone membership created uniform risk exposure.

This analysis ignored crucial differences in initial conditions.

- Germany entered the crisis with strong export competitiveness, low government debt, and a robust banking sector
- Italy, despite high government debt levels, had relatively low private sector debt and substantial household savings
- Spain, in contrast, had experienced a massive property bubble with high private sector leverage
- Greece faced structural fiscal imbalances and competitiveness problems

The market's failure to differentiate these initial conditions created opportunities for discerning investors. German Bunds became dramatically undervalued relative to their fundamentals, while Spanish assets were oversold given the country's underlying strengths once banking sector recapitalization occurred.

2025 once again revealed these issues as U.S. and U.K. assets got punished when those countries increased spending while German assets rallied when the Germans increased fiscal spending. The U.S. started with 130% debt/GDP, the UK was at 100%, and Germany was closer to 60%. We saw opposite market reactions to identical policy announcements because the market viewed the U.S. and U.K. starting points as fragile, and Germany's initial conditions as robust.

Earnings surprises provide another arena where initial conditions matter. A 10% earnings miss means something very different for a company trading at three times sales than it does for one trading at 40 times sales, yet algorithmic trading often treats all misses similarly on the kneejerk reaction.

---

[39] For example, restaurant chains that went bankrupt in 2020: Sizzler USA, Ruby Tuesday, Chuck E. Cheese, California Pizza Kitchen, Pain Quotidien USA, and NPC International (huge Pizza Hut/Wendy's franchisee).

Inflation

Finally, inflation provides perhaps the clearest example of how initial conditions shape economic outcomes. A 4% inflation reading means something entirely different in an economy where inflation expectations are well-anchored versus one where expectations are becoming unmoored. The 2021-2022 inflation surge in the United States is a case study.

Many analysts, noting rapid price increases in the USA, predicted a 1970s-style wage-price spiral would develop. However, the initial conditions were fundamentally different from the 1970s. Inflation expectations, while elevated in the short term, remained anchored in longer-term surveys. After initial hesitation, the Federal Reserve somehow maintained credibility via a series of meaty rate hikes. Labor unions, which had amplified wage-price spirals in the 1970s, represented a much smaller portion of the workforce.

These initial conditions meant that aggressive monetary policy broke the worst part of the inflation cycle without triggering a severe recession. Understanding this context allowed investors to position for a "soft landing" scenario rather than the severe economic contraction that history might have suggested. While the Fed never got inflation back to target following the 2021 spike, they tamed it enough to calm markets and consumers.

Finally, initial conditions also operate at the micro level through market positioning and microstructure. The same news event can trigger vastly different price reactions depending on how market participants are positioned beforehand.

Good forecasts

> "The most common market take can be described as: person who didn't see this coming is now 100% confident about what happens next."
>
> Morgan Housel

The quote above is glorious. Most financial forecasts on TV or the internet are guesses that will be continually revised as the market moves.

For example, you can guess the average Wall Street 1-year forward S&P 500 forecast by simply taking the current level of the S&P 500 and multiplying by 1.08. But if the market rallies, the "forecasters" will raise their "forecasts".

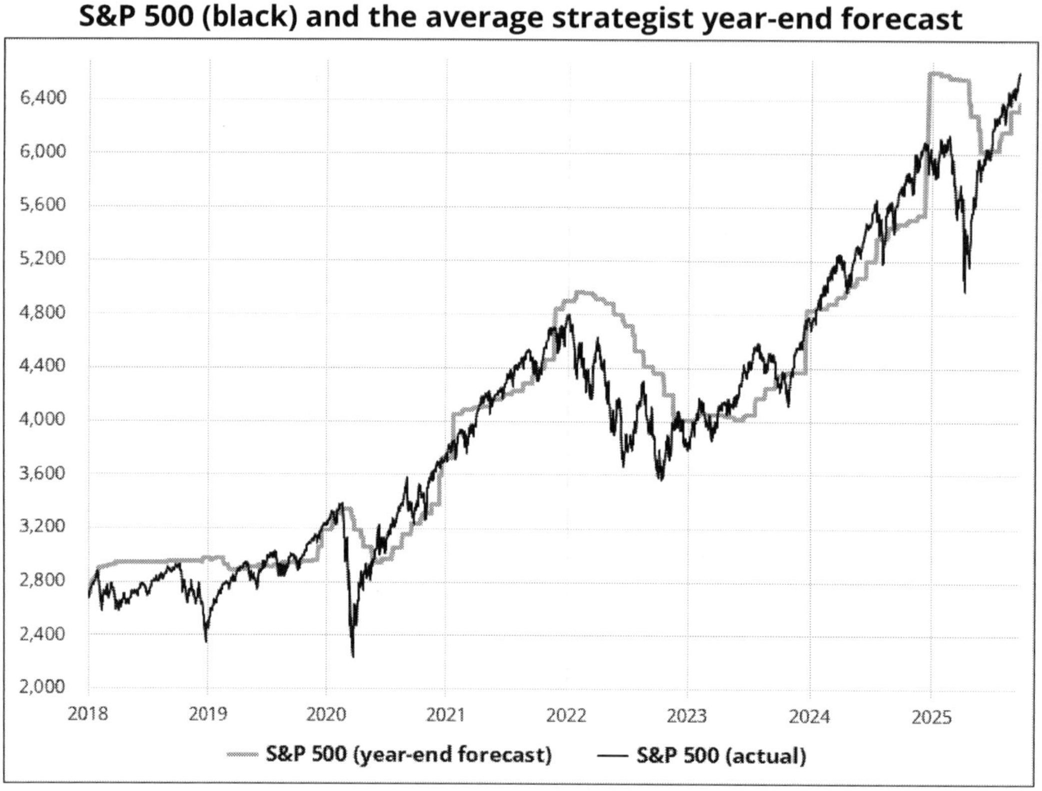

Note how the black line (actual) leads, and the gray line (forecast) follows. Your first reaction when you hear an analyst forecast should be to shut it out. Ignore it. If you want to find the research report and read the analyst's logic, that's fine. But Wall Street S&P 500 forecasts on their own are just a reflection of a) where SPX is trading and b) the fact that Wall Street is always bullish. Forecasts in commodities, single names, FX, and everywhere else have the same issue. Strategists make forecasts, then upgrade and downgrade them as the market moves.

In contrast, ***good*** market and economic forecasts have the following characteristics:

Specific and measurable. "Amazon is going to the moon" or "The U.S. dollar is screwed" are not useful forecasts. There is no way to measure whether the forecaster was right or wrong.

Explanatory logic. "Amazon is going to $1,000!" or "ETH is going to $10,000!" are the kind of useless forecasts you will often see on Twitter. A useful forecast includes explanatory logic which can be evaluated. Often the analysis is the useful bit, not the point estimate or specific forecast. Many forecasts are issued exclusively with the aim of getting eyeballs or clicks and are deliberately insane.

Time condition. In 2010, a group of economists published a letter warning that quantitative easing (QE) would trigger massive inflation or hyperinflation in the United States. In 2017, when inflation still hadn't arrived, those economists were criticized. "Just wait," they responded. "*Eventually*, QE is going to cause inflation." A forecast made in 2010 that hasn't come true by 2017 and remains open with no time limit is completely useless.

"When the yield curve inverts, a recession always follows" is another example that is dangerous because it omits a time frame. This forecast has a perfect track record. Every time the yield curve has inverted (that is, 3-month T-bill rates go above the 10-year bond yield in the USA) there has been a recession in the US. *But here's the rub:* The lag between the inversion and the recession has been anywhere from **6** to **39** months. If you sit waiting for a recession throughout that purgatory period; you get smoked.

Conditions for cancellation or reassessment. Excellent forecasts describe specific conditions where the forecast will be invalidated or reassessed, e.g. "If X happens, I'm wrong." In trading, this comes in the form of a stop loss. For example, "I expect AMZN stock to rally from $95 to $200, but if it trades to $70, I am wrong and I will get out." Or: "I think the U.S. labor market is going to weaken but if the next two payroll reports are strong, that invalidates my view and I will reassess." Most forecasters will just keep revising their forecast higher or lower as the market moves; they will never stop out or change their minds. That's bad.

Dynamic and Bayesian. Excellent forecasts are not static. They update when new information arrives. This is not the same thing as: "The stock price went up, so I will raise my forecast for the stock price." That's extrapolation, not forecasting. And it's extremely common. And dumb.

Smart updating of forecasts means, for example, if an airline's main competitor goes bankrupt, you upgrade the stock because you think it can absorb the competitors' customers with its excess capacity. This goes to the Bayesian and probabilistic approach. New information matters, whether it confirms or contradicts your prior view. The key nuance here is good forecasts update because of **new information that affects the security**, not because the price of the security moved.

Finally, and this will sound funny, but it's completely serious:

- **Good forecasts are not wrong over and over and over.** You might be surprised at how many forecasters (including many finance celebrities) simply forecast the same thing over and over, all the time. If someone forecasts a crash in 2002, 2003, 2004, 2005, 2006, 2007 and 2008... And there is a crash in 2008... Was that person correct? There is a huge cohort of forecasters who simply forecast the same thing, all the time. Some popular examples:

- Higher gold prices
- Lower stock prices
- Stocks are going to crash
- U.S. recession is imminent
- The USD is going to crash
- ETH to the moon
- BTC to $1,000,000
- The USD is going to lose its reserve status
- Hyperinflation is coming

Etc., etc., ad infinitum. Forecasters who always predict the same thing, and sound extremely intelligent while consistently wrong... Are worse than useless; they are actively harmful. Be wary of those predicting the same thing year after year. They are almost certainly locked into that one view forever; it is costly and virtually impossible for them to abandon it.

Permabears are the worst offenders, but you will find economists, strategists and forecasters of all types locked into inflexible and dogmatic market and economic forecasts. These are not really forecasts; they are just manifestations of the person's worldview and the result of endless efforts to rationalize that view no matter how much contradictory evidence refutes it. If someone is continually wrong, their framework is broken and they are not adapting to new information and new regimes. Sure, they might be right one day, but a stopped clock is right twice a day too.

Be aware of the bias of the forecasters you follow and more importantly: Maintain flexibility in your own views. It's OK to be wrong. In fact, **admitting you are wrong is a superpower.** Here's how one of the greatest thinkers in human history put it.

> "I have approximate answers, and possible beliefs, and different degrees of uncertainty about different things. But I am not absolutely sure of anything and there are many things I don't know anything about. I don't feel frightened not knowing things."
>
> Professor Richard Feynman

Bad forecasters with no skin in the game broadcast their calls and hope for the best. When the prediction finally, randomly comes true, the forecaster can declare: "See! I was right!" But their forecast was completely useless.

The chances that this forecast made anyone any money, besides the person selling it, are comically low. That's the thing about bad forecasts—they are products in themselves. They aren't produced to help you make money; they're created to make money for the *author*.

Professional market forecasts that feature good thinking and intellectual honesty sound something like: "I expect market X to move to level Y by time Z. My confidence level is X out of 10. If A or B happens, I will revise my forecast or conclude I was wrong." More detailed forecast logic will also include a cone of uncertainty around the forecast. This helps users of the forecast understand the logic of the forecast and make their own judgments about its accuracy as new information rolls in.

Be both a thoughtful *consumer* and *producer* of forecasts.

Narrative contagion

> "A man is always a teller of tales, he lives surrounded by his stories and the stories of others, he sees everything that happens to him through them."
>
> Jean-Paul Sartre

Market decisions are made by human beings, and by computers programmed and operated by human beings. Human beings are wild-eyed dreamers and fearmongering haters. Human beings buy high and sell low. Some are risk averse and some love to gamble. And they all love (love!) a good story. They are nothing like the robotic and rational "homo economicus" imagined by John Stuart Mill.

Who is homo economicus? Homo economicus is an imaginary character who plays a leading role in many economic models. He is the dominant species in the Land of Theory. Homo economicus is a person with infinite capacity to make rational decisions, who has perfect access to information, and who is exclusively motivated by self-interest. Does that sound like anyone you know? Infinite capacity to make rational decisions. LOL. Many economic theories are rooted in the idea that humans, in aggregate, behave like homo economicus.

In aggregate, human beings have an incredible capacity to be effective and efficient. Therefore, as a whole, markets *are* very efficient. And as individuals, humans have *some* capacity to make rational and consistent decisions. If we could neatly model human beings and they were consistently rational creatures, there would be no cycles of fear and greed.

Human beings as a species have always placed huge importance on storytelling. Stories weave information and emotion in a way that sticks with us more durably than information alone. This is why so much teaching and communication involves storytelling, and why stories have been our primary communication medium since the beginning of humanity.

Note that when you hear the word "story," you might think: fiction—stories of make believe. When your teacher says you had quite the "story" for why you didn't complete your history assignment, her implication is that you are lying. But stories and narratives are often true!

Usually the risk is not that market narratives are false, but that markets overcommit and exaggerate the importance of stories or focus on story too much and forget about the limitations imposed by the real world. Stories go viral in a way that data and facts do not.

Market narratives can be fun, exciting, interesting, and easy to understand. They can also be scary, provocative, and titillating. They will lead you over a cliff if you don't stay rational.

By understanding narrative, you position yourself as an observer of the herd and avoid getting sucked in by viral, emotional stories. As a story goes viral, watch dispassionately while the crowd goes mad. You should think:

"Oh, interesting, look what they're doing. That doesn't look very rational."

Markets are social systems, not machines that take in fundamental information and spit out logical prices. Most stories in the market are based on some objective truth but they morph, expand, and become caricatures disconnected from reality through *narrative contagion.*

Narrative contagion is the process whereby a story shared by one person or organization prompts others to share their own stories, spreading narrative themes organically through a community. Unlike direct persuasion or simple diffusion of the same story, narrative contagion emphasizes the tendency for more people to engage in storytelling, which motivates group behavior, collective sentiment, risk appetite and ultimately, price action.

Some examples:

- **Meme stocks**: The GameStop saga started with a few posts on Reddit, which prompted thousands to share their own experiences and reasons for buying, spawning a self-reinforcing narrative that drove prices far beyond fundamentals.
- **Market crashes**: Stories of panic or impending doom ("*Recession coming!*") can prompt others to share their own fears, amplifying selling pressure. Once the market starts thinking about recession, for example, you will notice social media is full of anecdotes that seem to portend imminent recession. As more people join in, it feels safer for others to share their own thoughts, creating a feedback loop.
- **Bull markets**: Narratives about new technologies (AI, crypto, EVs) can spread, with each participant adding their own twist, fueling optimism and investment.

Research on narrative contagion shows it tends to have six specific features[40]:

- **Emotional arousal**. Posts with higher emotional content prompt more engagement and storytelling. Fear, greed and hope spread faster than facts, leading to herd behavior and volatility.
- **Simplicity**. Easy-to-understand, relatable stories spread better than complex ones. A simple investment thesis ("This stock will 10x because of AI") will be more contagious than nuanced, complex analysis.
- **Familiarity**. A story that has a close analog in the past is more likely to grab someone's imagination versus a scenario that has never happened before. People will compare every new technology to the internet, or every bearish setup in the stock market to 1929, 1987, or 2008. Connecting a current narrative to a past event makes a story more viral.
- **Exaggeration**. "Fed money printing will lead to a replay of the Weimar Hyperinflation!" is a more captivating narrative than "Fed money printing could lead to a 0.8% increase in Core CPI." Even if someone believes the latter, they are more likely to tout the former if they are looking to monetize their socials or book more hedge fund meetings. *Never let the facts get in the way of a good story.*
- **Moral or social meaning**. Market narratives with a moral angle will spread more easily. "QE steals from the poor and gives to the rich!" is a story that can easily go viral because it is packed with social relevance.
- **Repetition and reinforcement**. Many finance gurus pick a story and pound it foir their whole career. Stories like "The U.S. empire is just like the Roman Empire" and "Bitcoin is money" are repeated frequently and repetition creates reinforcement.

Watch for these distinguishing features to differentiate between stories that are probably true and those that are simply popular due to their viral nature. Avoid getting sucked into stories that trigger strong emotions and bypass the rational part of the brain. Stay rational when everyone else is losing their minds.

Here is how Nitin Agarwal and Inna Gurung describe narrative contagion in social media[41]:

> We live in a hyper-connected world where narratives travel at lightning speed, transforming individuals into groups and groups into mobs. Recent events illustrate how narratives on social media can be weaponized and spread

---

[40] See, for example, "Analyzing narrative contagion through digital storytelling", Zhao, Ma, and Ma (2024)

[41] "Are Narratives Contagious? Modeling Narrative Diffusion Using Epidemiological Theories", Gurung and Agarwal (2025)

> rapidly to sow discord. These insidious threats, aimed at influencing beliefs and behaviors, must be viewed as modern weapons of cognitive warfare.

Account for narrative contagion when a new narrative arrives on the scene, so you can evaluate whether it might become an important story for markets. Note just how fast narratives can spread once they hit critical mass.

The emotional reaction and feeling of wonder you get the first time you use an LLM or a text-to-image AI platform told you right away that AI had the potential to become an important story for markets. In contrast, a story like banking deregulation, which is complex, devoid of emotional energy, and unfamiliar ground for most market participants, is less likely to be a narrative worth trading.

Good traders and investors have their ear to the ground and see new narratives coming before those narratives become fully contagious. Buy a theme early and get out when it hits the mainstream.

Identifying narrative contagion

The best way to identify new narratives and track current stories in equity land is to monitor social media. Platforms like X (Twitter), Reddit (particularly r/wallstreetbets), and Bloomberg chats are breeding grounds for narrative contagion. Watch for rapid increases in storytelling around a ticker or sector.

Each morning, I scroll through r/wallstreetbets to see what the mainstream is thinking and to see which stocks might be in play. Then, I read all my Bloomberg chats to see what is in the macro zeitgeist. Over time, you will start to get a good sense of what is going on with retail investors and which stocks they like and dislike. You will detect new narrative patterns in the macro conversation. If nobody was talking about credit spreads last week, and today you have three people mentioning them, that's meaningful.

Often, I will see a new narrative on X or r/wallstreetbets before I hear about it on Bloomberg or Reuters. The challenge, of course, is to separate the nonsense from the useful bits because there is plenty of nonsense on social media!

For bigger picture narratives on the economy, macro, and markets other than single name stocks, you can read Twitter, Substack, and bank research to get an idea of current and upcoming narratives. Alternative data like Ben Hunt's Perscient, trends.google.com, and the NT function on Bloomberg can also help you sniff out new narratives before they hit the mainstream. Finally, reading publications like am/FX and following analysts who you believe are ahead of the curve can also help. Narrative hunting is a profitable sport when you know what you're looking for.

Catching a new narrative a little before everyone else can be a huge edge. When you see a new story on the horizon, test it against the six features of narrative contagion and assess if it's likely to go viral. At this stage of my career, I feel like my ability to sense new narratives before they have fully formed is a big edge.

Mastering markets is not just about numbers. It's not just about solving equations or analyzing fundamentals or tossing number salad. Take the time to appreciate how stories and narratives drive capital markets. Understand the facts, the numbers… And the stories.

This is true at every fractal. Whether you are an analyst covering microcap technology companies, or a hedge fund portfolio manager trading global macro, you need to know the current state and path of the narratives driving both your markets and the world economy.

When you understand the narrative cycle, you will get in early. And you will get out when the narrative has become too widespread and emotional, signaling a crowded trade and a potential reversal.

Narrative is always relevant. Every day. On every time horizon. Here's a good explanation of the tension between long-term valuation and short-term price movements via the OG, John Maynard Keynes:

> It might have been supposed that competition between expert professionals, possessing judgment and knowledge beyond that of the average private investor, would correct the vagaries of the ignorant individual left to himself. It happens, however, that the energies and skill of the professional investor and speculator are mainly occupied otherwise. For most of these persons are, in fact, largely concerned, not with making superior long-term forecasts of the probable yield of an investment over its whole life, but with foreseeing

changes in the conventional basis of valuation a short time ahead of the general public.

They are concerned, not with what an investment is really worth to a man who buys it "for keeps", but with what the market will value it at, under the influence of mass psychology, three months or a year hence. For it is not sensible to pay 25 for an investment of which you believe the prospective yield to justify a value of 30, if you also believe that the market will value it at 20 three months hence.

Thus, the professional investor is forced to concern himself with the anticipation of impending changes, in the news or in the atmosphere, of the kind by which experience shows that the mass psychology of the market is most influenced.

You should always have a sense of the following in the economies and markets you follow:

- What stories have been driving my markets recently?
- Are we early, middle or late in those narrative cycles?
- What narratives could emerge in the future and therefore should be on my radar going forward?

When done well, narrative analysis is a coherent and fluid combination of ever-changing micro/macroeconomic fundamentals and behavioral inquiry. It is often about nailing down the one, most important story the market wants to trade right now and seeing when that story nears its expiry date.

It doesn't really matter what *you* think about a theme or a narrative: it matters what *the market* will think about it. Sure, you might think that 3D printing is a fad. But if it's just coming onto the market radar and it's a cool narrative that has short-term virality, go with it! Second order thinking demands you think about what the market will think, not what you think yourself. If you want to fade a narrative, wait until it has gone viral and is on the cover of a mainstream magazine. Early is wrong.

To recap, narratives are more likely to go viral when they have the following features:

- Appeal to emotion
- Simplicity
- Familiarity
- Exaggeration
- Moral angle
- Repetition and reinforcement

Keep these ideas of narrative contagion in mind as you scroll through Twitter, Reddit, sell-side research, and Bloomberg. Think about where your markets are in the narrative cycle and what new narratives lurk over the horizon. And manage your risk accordingly.

I find it useful to occasionally whip out this map of the narrative cycle (from *Alpha Trader*) and plot where we are in narratives I am following. This helps me level set and stay thoughtful about the current state of the zeitgeist.

The standard narrative cycle

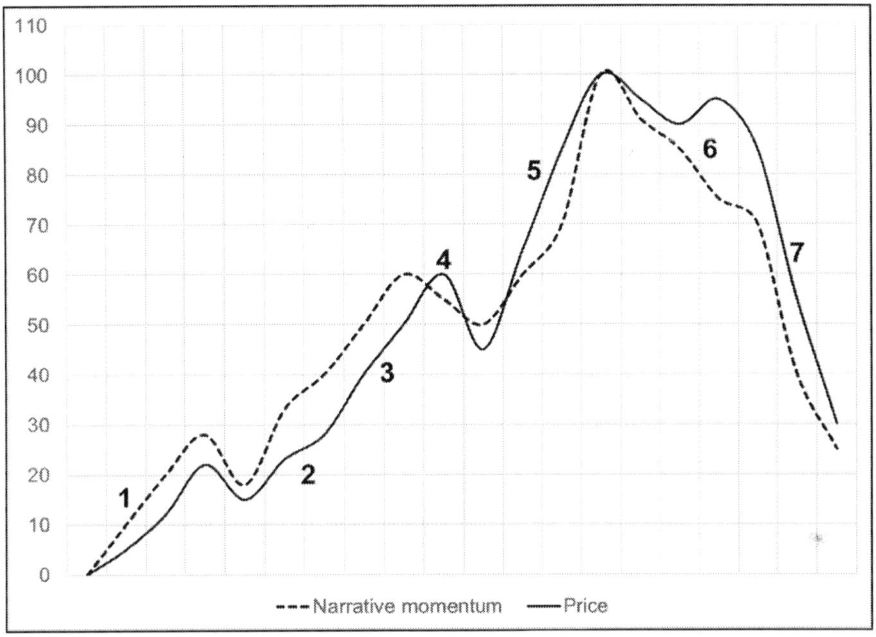

The stages of the narrative cycle are:

1. Under the radar
2. Momentum builds
3. Primary trend
4. First cracks
5. Final wave
6. Peak
7. Turn

By mapping the narrative, I solidify my understanding of its progress and what things might look like if I am right. Or if I'm wrong. Much as you can stop out of a trade because of a change in price, you can also use price to stop out of a narrative.

Adverse selection

George Akerlof (Janet Yellen's husband) wrote the seminal paper on adverse selection in August 1970. This excerpt from the essay "The Market for Lemons"[42] explains adverse selection in the used car market.

> The example of used cars captures the essence of the problem. From time to time one hears either mention of or surprise at the large price difference between new cars and those which have just left the showroom. The usual lunch table justification for this phenomenon is the pure joy of owning a "new" car. We offer a different explanation. Suppose (for the sake of clarity rather than reality) that there are just four kinds of cars. There are new cars and used cars. There are good cars and bad cars (which in America are known as "lemons"). A new car may be a good car or a lemon, and of course the same is true of used cars.
>
> The individuals in this market buy a new car without knowing whether the car they buy will be good or a lemon. But they do know that with probability q it is a good car and with probability (1-q) it is a lemon; by assumption, q is the proportion of good cars produced and (1-q) is the proportion of lemons.
>
> After owning a specific car, however, for a length of time, the car owner can form a good idea of the quality of this machine; i.e., the owner assigns a new probability to the event that his car is a lemon. This estimate is more accurate than the original estimate. An asymmetry in available information has developed: for the sellers now have more knowledge about the quality of a car than the buyers. But good cars and bad cars must still sell at the same price - since it is impossible for a buyer to tell the difference between a good car and a bad car. It is apparent that a used car cannot have the same valuation as a new car—if it did have the same valuation, it would clearly be advantageous to trade a lemon at the price of new car, and buy another new car, at a higher probability q of being good and a lower probability of being bad. Thus the owner of a good machine must be locked in. Not only is it true that he cannot receive the true value of his car, but he cannot even obtain the expected value of a new car.

---

[42] www.sfu.ca/~wainwrig/Econ400/akerlof.pdf

This is the problem of asymmetric information. Not everyone in a market has the same information and one can logically assume that if someone is willing to sell to you, you probably don't want to buy. The only cars for sale will be lemons.

In markets, this manifests as adverse selection for price makers. If you put a bid in the market, it's a reasonable assumption that anyone who sells to you has better information than you do and whenever you get filled, you will wish you did not get filled!

It's a reasonable assumption, but it's **often wrong**. If adverse selection dominated, nobody would ever trade because everyone would be afraid that everyone else has better information than they do. In reality, a substantial proportion of the trades going through in any market are noise trades by uninformed buyers and sellers. In FX markets for example, many trades are related to corporate cash flow hedging, cross-border mergers, equity hedging, and so on. Rarely would someone trading EURUSD have asymmetric information compared to their counterparty.

On the other hand, in a thinly traded stock or bond, it is much more likely that you are trading against someone who knows more than you. Unless you are an expert in that stock, you probably do not know the flows, orders, or even the fundamentals of the company as exhaustively as the human and electronic market makers do. Same goes for a thinly-traded currency like the Colombian Peso. Furthermore, if you do get adversely selected in a liquid product, it's cheap to get out. In a South African bond, it's not. This is not to say you should not trade these products, but if you don't have an edge, you are more likely to suffer from adverse selection.

Here's an excellent description of adverse selection from Agustin Lebron's book *The Laws of Trading*.

> You are a market maker in South African mining companies. Through years of effort and continual improvement, you have built a trading model for the company Veldt Resources. You walk into work, ready to set up your trading for the day. It's a stock that doesn't trade much, and usually there are only two market makers: you and another (we'll call her Jo). She's sharp, and she competes well to trade against customer orders that come in.
>
> Your model has Veldt valued at 54.35 ZAR (South African rand). You're going to start quoting the stock, so you're about to turn on your machine making a market 54.25 - 54.45 (1,000x). Before you turn on, you check the current market and notice that Jo has already turned on and she's making her market 53.50 - 54.00 (2,000x). If you were to turn on your machine, your market would cross her market, and you would buy 1,000 shares from her for 54.00.

You now need to make a decision. Whose model do you believe more, yours or Jo's? If you believe yours, you should turn on your machine, trade at 54.00, and expect to make money. If you believe Jo's model, you should adjust your own model parameters to match her market and turn on, making a similar market to hers.

What to do? As with many dichotomies, this is a false one. And as with many decision processes, Bayesian reasoning lights the way...

...Jo presumably believes Veldt is worth around 53.75 (the average of her bid and offer). But how confident is she in her belief? The width of her market can give you a clue. It's 0.50 ZAR, whereas yours was going to be 0.20 ZAR wide. All other things equal, you should think that Jo only has 40% (0.20/0.50) of the confidence in her fair value as you do in yours.

On some absolute scale of confidence, you can say you had a belief-strength of 100 in your fair value of 54.35 (before seeing Jo's market), and Jo has a belief-strength of 40 in her fair value of 53.75 (before seeing yours). And it turns out the weighted average of these two beliefs is quite a reasonable way to combine them: 100/140 * 54.35 + 40/140 * 53.75 = 54.18. Your updated fair value, having seen Jo's market, is thus 54.18 ZAR.

This procedure is a quick, heuristic, and reduced version of Bayesian belief-updating, and a good reference on the subject is A.L. Barker's 1995 paper.

After updating, you now believe that the stock is worth 54.18. Assuming your trading costs, risk limits, and return requirements are satisfied, buying 1,000 shares for 54.00 is a good trade. Naively, you might just put out a 54.00 bid for 1,000 shares, trade with half the 2,000 share offer, and hope to collect your expected-value ZAR.

In practice, however, you might be able to make even more. If Jo is making a 0.50 wide market, maybe she'd be willing to sell lower than 54.00. It's conceivable that if you put out a 53.90 bid for 1,000 shares, Jo will sell at that price, and you collect an extra 100 ZAR!

Of course, Jo could react differently. She could see your bid and use that information to change her market, in much the same way you did before turning on. These are difficult decisions, ones where experience with the

> product and the market make a big difference in being able to eke out a little extra edge. Let's play it safe however and pay 54.00 for 1,000 shares.
>
> You trade, and Jo reacts by immediately canceling her market. This is not an uncommon occurrence in illiquid stocks, especially in emerging markets, so you're not too surprised. You wait a couple of minutes, mentally visualizing Jo in front of her six monitors, evaluating her trade and her model.
>
> Finally, she turns back on. Her new market is 53.50 - 54.05 (10,000x)! You reason that Jo has seen that someone (you) disagrees with her valuation of the stock. Jo is a good Bayesian like you, and so she has incorporated that information into her model and updated her beliefs about the fair value of the stock. Her updated belief is that she now wants to sell even more stock, at a marginally higher price. Clearly, she almost entirely discounts the information you've communicated to her with your trade.
>
> How should you react? It seems fairly clear that, assuming Jo is not a crazy or incompetent market maker (usually a fair assumption), your trade was a bad one. You bought 1,000 shares, when in retrospect, you would have wanted to buy much less, probably zero.
>
> Imagine instead that Jo had turned back on with a market of 54.00 - 54.50 (1000x). Her reaction now clearly indicates the information you gave her with your trade is valuable, and she has adjusted her beliefs accordingly. Your trade was probably a good one. Don't you wish you had bought all 2,000 shares on offer?
>
> No matter what Jo's reaction is, you will be unhappy with your trade. Note that Jo will be unhappy too, since retrospectively she should have either made her initial market bigger or smaller. Welcome to the joyous world of trading!

Adverse selection is not just a problem for humans. Electronic market makers constantly struggle with the adverse selection problem. If you are streaming a bid and an offer in a security, and 15 other banks are streaming the same security at approximately the same width, there is a high probability that when someone trades with you, it's because your price was wrong.

While adverse selection is a real issue in markets, it can also lead traders to adopt a loser's mentality. They will say things like:

- "Somebody knows something!" when the market moves
- "He picked me off!" when they are filled and the market moves against them
- "The market's rigged!"
- "The second I buy, the market makers push it lower to stop me out."
- "The bots are screwing up this market!"
- "I knew it was a trap!"

That last one is a post-trade rationalization that frames any loss as exogenous rather than take responsibility for a calculated risk gone wrong. The idea that you are always at a disadvantage and every time you trade you have are adversely selected is a like the comic at right.

If you assume adverse selection and efficient markets all the time, you will never trade, or you will drown in a losing "woe is me" attitude.

If you are a good trader who knows what you're doing, you will be the one adversely selecting others. You will have confidence in your trading strategy and your edge, and you will own it when you lose money. Don't blame the bots, a sneaky cabal of market makers, or the government.

Avoiding adverse selection

It is well known that limit orders can be a cheaper way to transact than market orders. Some traders refuse to leave limit orders or are reluctant to do so because of adverse selection. They feel like they are giving away a free option to the market makers. This is not wrong, but there are tradeoffs.

Every time you buy or sell a security, you need to make the important decision about how to transact. You can:

- leave a limit order at or just ahead of the best bid or offer
- bid or offer at mid
- set a limit outside the current price
- use a market order

If you trade frequently, the aggregate of those decisions over time will be a massive determinant of your P&L.

Note: I never use true market orders in anything I trade. There is always the risk of a wonky fill with a market order. If a stock is trading $25.50/$26.00 and I want to buy 2,000 aggressively, I might bid $26.10 or $26.50 (bidding through the offer), but I would not send a market order (especially in a fast market) because if the seller pulls a fraction of a second before I hit enter, I might buy at $28.50 by accident. It's unlikely, but always possible. Better to set a limit outside the current bid/offer and create what is essentially a market order with a tolerance filter. This won't make a difference most of the time, but once in a blue moon it will save you a ton of money and angst.

Transaction costs

Traders generally underestimate transaction costs. I emphasize this in my other books. **Estimate your transaction costs judiciously** so that you clearly appreciate how much money leaks out of your account every day. "Commission-free" trading has created the false impression that retail equity traders don't pay transaction costs. Super-tight spreads in FX make it feel like hedge funds are barely paying anything to transact. But imagine paying a tiny road toll every time you turn onto a new street. It adds up!

Here's an example of why there is a time and place to use limit orders. I sometimes do more than 100 trades in a day and each time, I am paying a tiny tax to Citadel, SIG, or some other high-frequency market maker out there. This tiny tax is hard to measure, but we can easily measure the cost of crossing the bid/offer. Let's say I do just five trades in a day, all in CoreWeave (CRWV), and the Level 2 for CRWV looks like this:

CRWV 103.89 +13.65 (+14.98%)

Bid				Ask			
MM Name	Price	Size	Mn Trd Sz	MM Name	Price	Size	Mn Trd Sz
DRCTEDGE	103.70	900		DRCTEDGE	104.00	300	
IEX	103.60	100		NSDQ	104.00	700	
NSDQ	103.60	400		BATS	104.20	400	
NSDQ	103.51	100		NSDQ	104.20	100	
ARCA	103.50	100		NSDQ	104.24	300	
BATS	103.50	100		NSDQ	104.25	300	
MEMX	103.50	400		NSDQ	104.30	200	
NSDQ	103.50	2,200		NYSE	104.33	200	
PEARL	103.50	100		NSDQ	104.40	300	
NSDQ	103.49	100		ARCA	104.45	200	
NSDQ	103.46	200		IEX	104.45	100	
NYSE	103.46	200		ARCA	104.46	100	
NSDQ	103.44	500		NSDQ	104.46	100	
NSDQ	103.42	100		NSDQ	104.49	100	
ARCA	103.36	200		NSDQ	104.50	200	
NSDQ	103.35	200		ARCA	104.51	100	
ARCA	103.30	100		NSDQ	104.51	100	

30 cents wide doesn't seem too bad. If I want to buy 1,000 shares here, I can do a few things:

- buy at 104.00 right away
- if nothing is really going on and it's not urgent, leave a bid at mid (103.85) or just above the current best bid e.g. 103.72

This might seem like an inconsequential decision, but it's not. Here's the P&L at the end of the day for the two strategies, assuming that we are filled at mid, or we cross the full spread. This simulates a trader with $100,000 risking up to $4,000/day (4% of free capital), only trading CRWV.

	Market Price		Trade	Position
Buy 1000 to get long	103.65	104.00	Buy 1,000	1,000
Flip short at high	105.75	106.00	Sell 2,000	(1,000)
Cover and get long	104.60	105.00	Buy 2,000	1,000
Buy more to get longer	103.50	103.85	Buy 1,000	2,000
Exit at end of day	102.55	103.10	Sell 2,000	Flat

P&L if I trade at mid	P&L if I cross the spread
$ 300	$ (1,250)

This trader does the same series of trades and makes $300 in one scenario and loses more than 1% of her account in the other. The obvious issue with these assumptions is that the one time you leave a limit order and do not get filled, it can be a killer. The market runs away from you and your attempt to save fifteen cents costs you two dollars. My baseline is always to use limit orders near mid unless I have a reason not to. If I think there's a good chance I can get filled on the bid (instead of mid) because there's tons of two-way, I'll do that. If I think it's more urgent, I will cross the full spread or more to get in.

In most cases, leaving limit orders very close to the market allows you to reduce transaction costs and benefit from bid/offer bounce and noise trading. Occasionally, you will be adversely selected as news comes out or a massive flow comes down the pipe, and you are instantly out of the money. But this would have been the case anyway had you entered via a market order.

Obviously, the big risk with limit orders is that you don't get filled. As I was typing this section, I was short TSLR (the leveraged TSLA ETF). I wanted to cover the trade, and the market was 25.85/25.91. That's pretty wide for TSLR, so I left my bid for 2,000 shares at 25.88 (iceberged to show 100 shares). Here's what happened.

Intraday TSLR, May 28, 2025

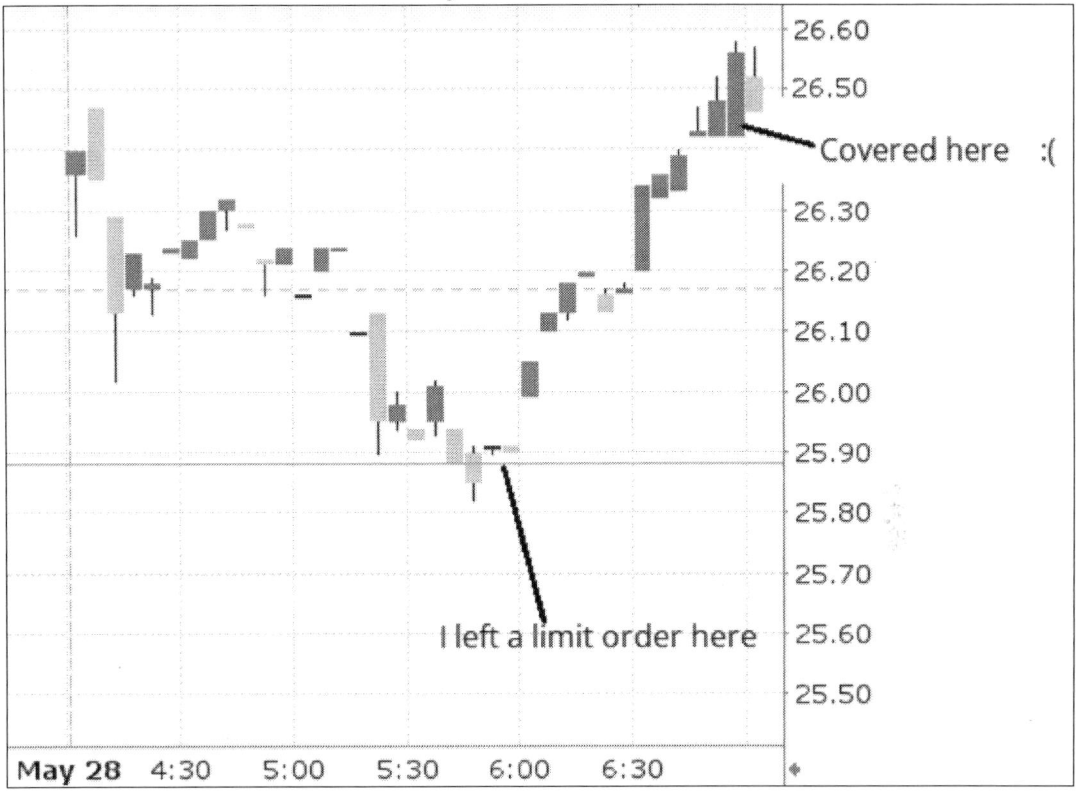

The line at 25.88 shows where my order was, and you can see what happened. Instead of ripping the ask at 25.91, I put in a bid, and the stock went up. I covered at 26.44, for a differential P&L of negative 53 cents on 2,000 shares. So my attempt to save 3 cents cost me 53 cents. Boo.

That's the negative asymmetry you must accept when you leave limit orders. Over the course of many, many transactions, one needs to assess whether all those 3-cent savings offset the occasional, much larger loss. I feel that my decision-making between limit and market orders is good enough to justify this asymmetry. But it hurts when it doesn't work!

Stale or far away orders

If a stock is trading $20.50 / $20.60 and you bid $20.51, there is a solid chance that your bid will get filled by bid/offer bounce, or noise trading. If you bid $20.10 in that same stock, the odds your bid will get filled by noise trading are almost zero. Instead, you will more likely get filled via adverse selection. Here's an example that recently cost me a few grand.

GameStop announced that they were adding crypto to their treasury. At the time, the crypto treasury idea was a fad and I was skeptical of any short-term positive impact on the stock.

GME was very late to the party on crypto and while a higher BTC price would obviously help GME, it wasn't clearly bullish to me that they were buying. There are plenty of listed ways to buy bitcoin now, so I didn't think this would attract many new buyers to GME, other than retail specs looking to catch a quick flip higher.

The news came out at $25; I sold at $28 and $29 with a stop loss at $30.56. The stock traded in a 27/30 range for just about exactly 24 hours, and I decided to cut 1/3 of the position before going home. GME was trading 27.80/28.00 and I lazily left a bid at $27.10, which was the breakout and old resistance right after the news had come out.

Here's how it played out.

GME Hourly Chart, March 25 to March 31, 2025

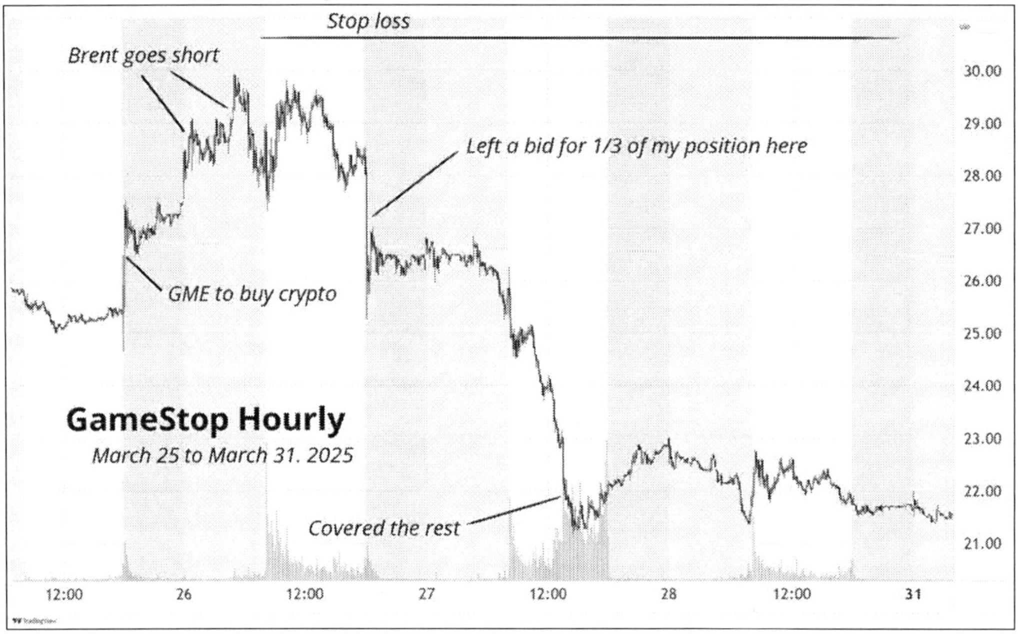

GameStop announced a secondary stock offering at 4 p.m. the next day. This is pretty silly behavior by management because sending out positive corporate news the day before you do a secondary offering is a bit pump-and-dumpy. But obviously it was great news for my short! Unfortunately, the market sliced straight through to 25.00 and my 27.10 bid was adversely selected by another trader or an algorithm. There was absolutely no reason for me to have that bid sitting there and it cost me $6,000 or so. Dumb.

Headline risks

Any time you have a position, you should know the potential headline risks. For example, if you are short a biotech, or a small cap that's a takeover candidate, you are exposed to enormous topside headline risk. If you are trading a semiconductor stock and today is

NVDA's earnings release, you are exposed to after-hours gap risk as your stock may move in sympathy with NVDA. If you are long a meme stock that's ripping higher, you are exposed to secondary issuance risk as the company might want to capitalize on the high stock price.

You can get even more granular. Because secondaries are usually announced after the market close, the 4:00-5:30 p.m. New York window is a particularly dangerous time to own skyrocketing stocks. Biotechs that have soared on good news are particularly hazardous to hold in this time window because they often do secondaries and get pummeled when the headline comes out.

When you have a meaningful position, think through the headline risks, regardless of whether your stop loss strategy will mitigate those risks. Consider whether you have unintentionally left any limit orders that could be adversely selected on headlines. Wargame all reasonable headline risks ahead of time to avoid getting caught off guard, and so you can react quickly and rationally if news does come out.

It is also useful to think through potential headlines that might affect securities you are not currently trading, so you are ready and able to pull the trigger right away when news comes out.

The two main reasons professionals leave limit orders away from top of book are:

1. they are going to bed and want to stick to the plan while sleeping
2. they believe the market is more likely to touch the limit order level and then mean revert, not gap through it

The second option is particularly relevant around economic data. Let me explain.

Say you are short e-minis, and you think U.S. CPI is going to come in strong. If it does, stocks will get hit. You look at the historical data and see that a 0.2 beat on CPI triggers a maximum drop of ~1.5% in stocks. If e-minis are trading at 6000, you then leave a limit order at 5910 knowing that the initial market reaction to data is an overshoot and the extremes of the day are touched in the seconds or minutes after the data release.

Leaving limit orders through events where you expect mean reversion from a specific level is an excellent strategy. It's a way to take advantage of panicky market orders and reckless momentum chasers.

While it might feel like limit orders leave you vulnerable to adverse selection, they also allow you to take advantage of poor decisions by others. If a stock is trading at $321 and you want to sell at $324, you might think it's better to just wait for it to get to $324, then see what's happening and sell if it's not skyrocketing. But you will often miss the move by doing this.

On this move in TSLA, for example, anyone that left a limit order at $324 got a great result, and those who worried about adverse selection probably missed it.

TSLA 5-minute chart July 30, 2025

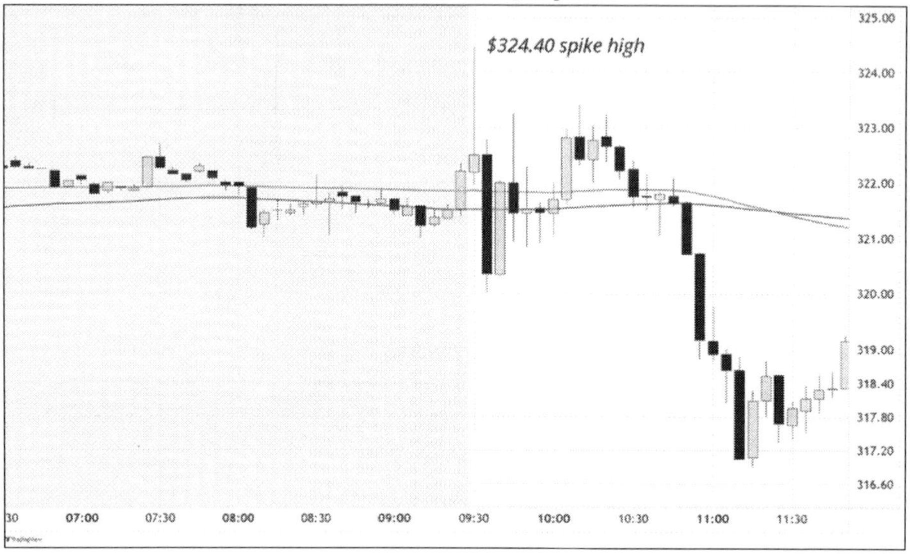

The psychology of adverse selection

Sometimes after news comes out, there is a surprisingly deep pocket of liquidity, and you start to think that maybe the person you are trading with knows something you don't. When bullish news comes out about a company, and you are easily able to buy 2,000 shares in the after-hours market, and the price hasn't moved… You can either think "Hmm, maybe this seller knows more than me" or you can think "This is definitely positive news, and I am confident in my interpretation of it. I'm going to rip another 2,000 shares from this guy."

It comes down to your skill, knowledge, and confidence. Over time, traders with expert ability to trade the news gain confidence and can hold two separate ideas in their heads at the same time:

1. I am confident that I know more than the average market participant. I will trust my judgment and trade the news aggressively. When there is a large pocket of liquidity, it's more likely a gamma pocket, a resting order from a participant with a different time frame, or an uninformed speculator - not a market maker with superior knowledge or information. Good post-news liquidity can be a gift.

2. Sometimes I will be wrong. Sometimes markets don't make sense. I will always manage my risk with the knowledge that no matter how confident I am in my interpretation of the news, the market doesn't always do what is logical. My interpretation of the news is not *always* correct. The market is often wrong. But so am I.

Here's an example where I chickened out because I was afraid of adverse selection. Before I explain this situation, some background: when I see a company beat earnings, beat on revenue, and guide significantly higher for the future, I feel the stock rarely prices in the new information fully and completely right away. You can buy the stock wherever it's trading, even knowing that algorithms have beaten you to the punch. A double beat with bullish guidance is somewhat rare, and one of the biggest ones I've seen was PEGA on April 22, 2025.

Here are the headlines that day:

```
*PEGASYSTEMS 1Q ADJ EPS $1.53, EST. 49C
*PEGASYSTEMS 1Q REV. $475.6M, EST. $356.5M
**Pega GenAI Powers Accelerated Q1 2025 Results
```

AI was super-hot at that time, so those two beats in combination with a GenAI shout out looked like powerful stuff. Those are egregious beats. 476M vs. 357M on revenue is huge!

The stock closed at $67.50 and was immediately trading $73/$74. This seemed like a fairly small move to me given the raging bullish headlines, and I was a bit surprised I was able to buy 1,000 shares at $74. I bought another 1,000 at $74 and the seller was still there. Dozens of prints were flying by on the time and sales window, and it was still offered hard at $74. Tens of thousands of shares were printing. I bought another 500 shares. All this was happening very quickly, and the seller was only there for about four minutes. But those four minutes felt like an hour.

I contemplated buying more, but started to think:

> "Hmm, maybe I'm missing something. Maybe there is some kind of fly in the ointment, or I missed a headline. Did they announce a secondary offering? Does this guy know more than I do???"

I scrambled through all the headlines, looking frantically for anything I might have missed. I checked Bloomberg, Dow Jones, and Reuters. *Nothing*. By the time I got through this process and returned to the Level 2 window, PEGA was $76/$78. Lifted at $78. And… $80 bid.

I took profit, scaling out from $82 up to $87 and the stock opened at $89 the next day. I made a ton on the trade, but I could easily have bought another 3,000 shares at $74 if I'd had a bit more confidence. Instead of making $50,000, I made under $25,000. An excellent trade, but this was the type of opportunity that only comes around a few times per year. A clear double beat and raise with enormous liquidity on the offer side is super rare. And I chickened out after 2,500 shares.

The message here isn't to go all in, throw risk management to the wind, and buy willy nilly. But I could easily have managed 5,000 shares of PEGA in this instance. I just had an amateur moment, thinking that someone else must know more than me. I got scared and backed off.

1-minute chart of PEGA on April 22, 2025

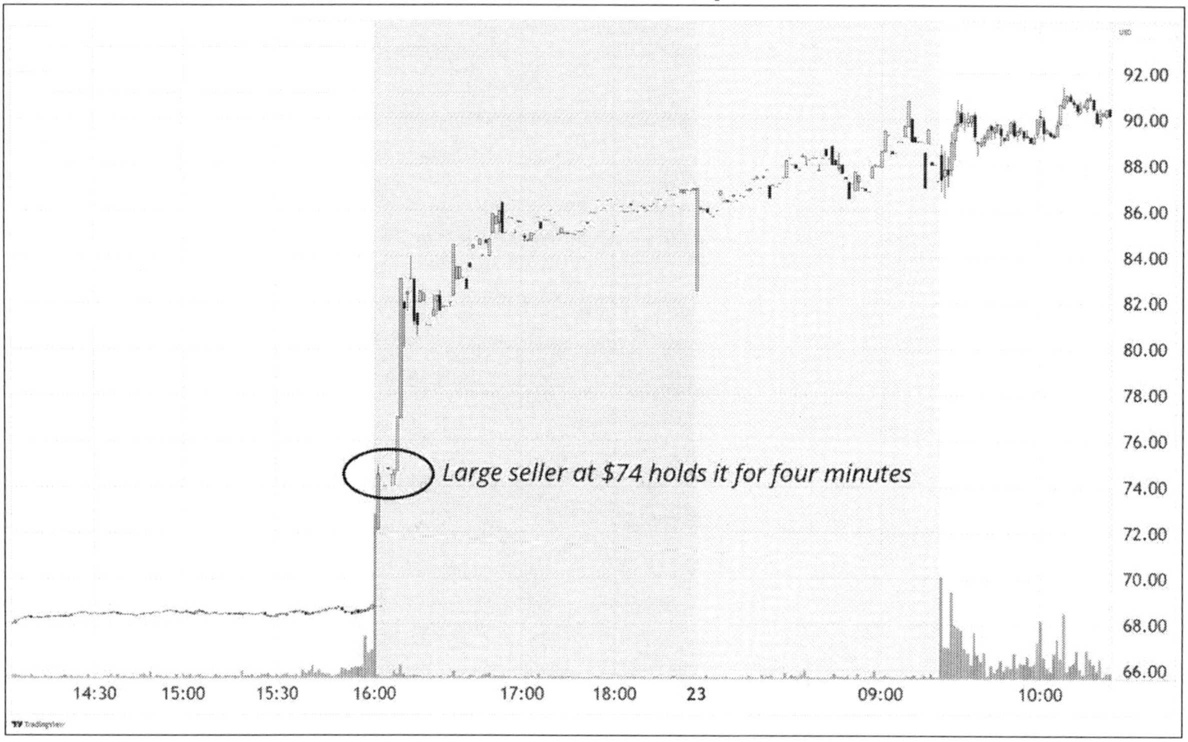

This situation differs from one where super bullish news comes out and three hours later, the stock is lower. That's good news / bad price. But in the seconds and minutes after news comes out, there can be a huge battle as the invisible hand attempts to determine what the new, correct price should be. Don't say things like "it should have gone higher by now!" when only a few minutes have elapsed. I often hear people saying this in FX after an economic number.

You can't judge what USDJPY has done on nonfarm payrolls by looking at the price three minutes after the release. The new equilibrium takes time and some of the biggest edge in markets is available to those who can confidently and aggressively take the view that the short-term price is wrong, and the final equilibrium will be substantially different. Many of these successful event traders are featured in *Unknown Market Wizards,* Jack Schwager's excellent 2020 release.

It's reasonable to wonder why this fella might have been offloading so much PEGA at $74, but the idea that you need to know why the other side is transacting before you can put on a trade is not reasonable. The seller could be offering shares at $74 for all sorts of reasons, many of which are irrelevant to you. For example:

1. It's a market maker with a huge limit order to sell 100,000 shares at $72 or better for a client. The market maker is happy to sell to you at $74 and fill their customer at $72.50. Everybody wins.

   I have experienced this phenomenon many times as a market maker. Say my normal position size is $100 million and my max position size is $200 million. I have an order to buy 1 billion euros for China at 1.1000. The market is 1.1014/16.

   News comes out that is clearly bearish EURUSD. The price drops and I start to get filled on my 1.1000 bid. Sure, I could pull the bid, but if I do, and the market trades below 1.1000, I am short 1 billion euros. So, I will buy at least 500 or 600 million euros before pulling the bid, to avoid massive, unwanted risk. Everyone selling to me at 1.1000 could be thinking that I know something, but really I just have a client with a medium-term time preference, and my risk limits do not allow me to be short 1 billion euros. So, I buy hundreds of millions of euros at 1.1000 and as soon as my bid is filled, EURUSD goes whoosh… It's trading 1.0970 and all the sellers are like: "WTF was that guy doing at 1.1000!" Different time and risk preferences, that's what!

2. The seller went long 50,000 shares at $67 before earnings, expecting a strong release, and plans to sell in clips of 10,000 from $74 to $84.

3. He left a GTC sell order at $74 and forgot that earnings were out today. He's at the bar with friends, and tomorrow morning he will see that he sold at atrocious levels.

4. He is long gamma and simply needs to sell 10,000 shares for every $5 move in the stock. He doesn't fine tune it or try to pick the top, he just sells according to a price ladder.

5. They bought the stock four years ago at $6 and their take profit target was $74. They're happy to sell to you and you're happy to buy from them.

6. They are one of those people that just loves to fade every move and say "Meh, this stock is up 10% on earnings, imma sell it."

7. They misread the headlines.

8. Etc.

If you believe in the strong version of adverse selection and/or efficient markets, you will think that every buyer and seller is operating with superior information and identical economic incentives. There are many, many traders in the market who are less informed than you or have completely different incentives and time horizons.

- Corporations buy dollars because they have cross-border transactions, not because they have secret information that the dollar is about to rally.
- Corporations buy their own stock methodically in the market, regardless of whether the macro news is bullish or bearish.
- Insiders sell stock to buy a new mansion, fund an unrelated investment, or to diversify their wealth.

Sure, sometimes counterparties are more informed than you, but usually their motivations are random, and irrelevant to your analysis and strategy.

Adverse selection is an important concept, but don't let it paralyze you. If you know what you are doing, you will be adversely selecting others much more often than you are adversely selected yourself. Be open to the possibility that you are wrong, but do not fear that everyone else is always right.

A quick summary of this section:

- Adverse selection stems from information asymmetry. When one party in a transaction has better information, it gives them an advantage.
- It's more pronounced in illiquid markets. Adverse selection exists across all markets, but poses the greatest risk in thinly-traded securities where informed participants are more likely to have superior knowledge and exit costs are higher.
- Limit orders can mitigate transaction costs. Despite the risk of adverse selection, strategic limit orders near the market can significantly reduce trading costs over time, as the benefits from bid/offer bounce and noise trading outweigh adverse selection.
- Avoid "loser's mentality" where you constantly attribute losses to adverse selection ("somebody knows something," "I got picked off"). Whatever happens, own it.
- Distance and timing matter. Stale or far-away limit orders are much more likely to be filled through adverse selection rather than market noise. If you are leaving a limit order far away from top of book, you should have a clear reason.

Understand adverse selection, when it applies, and when it does not. Don't freak out about it. Buyers and sellers come to market for many reasons, not just because they have super-double-secret information.

The multiverse

The many-worlds interpretation of quantum mechanics suggests that every time a decision is made, or an event with multiple possible outcomes occurs, the universe splits into parallel branches, with each possible outcome realized in a separate, non-communicating world. This means that for every action you take, there are versions of you in other universes experiencing outcomes that are not happening in your universe.

You can imagine that every time you make a decision, the world splits into a new set of parallel worlds where different outcomes unfold probabilistically. While this might seem unrelated to trading, I found that once I got a core understanding of the many-worlds idea[43], it helped me understand expected value, process vs. outcome, hindsight bias, and other concepts that have made me a more rational risk taker.

The intersection of multiverse thinking and expected value theory in trading addresses one of the most persistent psychological barriers to successful trading: the human tendency to judge decisions based on outcomes rather than process.

Every trade entry represents a branching point where the present splits into multiple possible futures. When a trader buys EURUSD ahead of a Federal Reserve announcement, they're not simply making a binary bet on whether the currency will rise or fall. Instead, they're positioning themselves at the nexus of two outcomes (profit or loss) that could be influenced by many possibilities: surprise rate cuts, hawkish commentary, dovish surprises, technical failures, geopolitical interventions, or flash crashes triggered by algorithmic errors.

In our observable universe, only one of these branches unfolds. The trader will experience either profit or loss, success or failure. But in the multiverse framework, all possibilities exist simultaneously until the moment of observation. When the trader closes their position, they collapse the wave function into a single, realized outcome in their universe.

This perspective can influence how you evaluate trading decisions. Outcome-based analysis looks at the single timeline you just experienced and judges accordingly. Multiverse thinking acknowledges that we lived through just one branch of an infinite tree of possibilities, and our job as traders is not to predict which branch we'll experience, but to ensure we're consistently betting on decisions that lean in our favor.

Expected value serves as the mathematical compass for navigating the multiverse of trading possibilities. It's the weighted average of all possible outcomes, considering their probabilities and magnitudes. When calculated correctly, expected value represents the theoretical long-term average result of repeating the same decision infinite times across infinite parallel universes.

Consider a trader analyzing a potential breakout trade on a major currency pair. In the multiverse framework, they might envision several scenarios: a 30% chance of a major breakout yielding 200 pips, a 40% chance of a false breakout resulting in a 50-pip loss, a 20% chance of sideways consolidation with minimal impact, and a 10% chance of an unexpected fundamental catalyst causing a 300-pip move in their favor.

---

[43] *The Beginning of Infinity* by David Deutsch influenced my thinking on this topic. HT Suvadeeep.

The expected value calculation:

$$\begin{aligned} EV = & (0.30 \times 200) \\ & + (0.40 \times -50) \\ & + (0.20 \times 0) \\ & + (0.10 \times 300) \quad \mathbf{= +70\ pips} \end{aligned}$$

The trader knows they'll only experience one outcome, but the decision to enter the trade is easily justified by the positive expected value across all possible timelines. When the actual timeline reveals itself, it should feel nearly irrelevant because it's out of the trader's control. The chips will fall wherever they fall. The decision was made. It was a good (positive EV) decision.

One of the most profound benefits of multiverse thinking in trading is the psychological liberation it provides. Traditional trading psychology focuses heavily on managing emotions around wins and losses—the outcomes experienced in our single timeline. But multiverse thinking shifts the focus from results to process, from outcomes to decision architecture.

When you embrace the multiverse framework, a losing trade isn't necessarily a bad trade. Instead, it becomes one data point from one possible timeline. This gives us a stronger appreciation for the traditional process vs. outcome grid[44].

	GOOD OUTCOME	BAD OUTCOME
GOOD DECISION	**Win.** Will probably lead to more good process and more good decisions.	**Disappointing.** **Nothing to worry about.** Do not respond emotionally to these outcomes or revisit them with the benefit of hindsight.
BAD DECISION	**Lucky.** Will probably lead to more bad process and more bad decisions. Good thinkers know when they get lucky despite doing the wrong thing and are willing to admit it.	**Disappointing.** **Change is required.** Learn from bad outcomes. Are you making the same mistakes over and over? Keep a list of your errors and see what patterns emerge.

[44] For a full discussion of Process vs. Outcome, see *The Art of Currency* Trading (Donnelly), pages 345-350.

Unfortunately, the real-world version of the chart often looks more like this:

	GOOD OUTCOME	BAD OUTCOME
GOOD DECISION	**I'm a jenius!** Nailed it! My analysis was spot on. Time to triple my position sizing.	**The market screwed me.** I was right, aCtuALly, but the algos, trading gods, market makers, and Illuminati conspired against me.
BAD DECISION	**I knew it would work!** Gut feeling paid off. Who needs analysis, amirite?	**Bad luck, again!** Everything that can go wrong, does go wrong. Why do bad things always happen to me!??!

The more you see each trade as a branch of a tree where you're on the winning side of probability, the less emotional volatility you experience from short-term results. You will stop riding the destructive roller coasters of overconfidence after wins and self-doubt after losses.

The multiverse framework can also influence risk management as it encourages you to think about position sizing across all possible timelines. Consider outcomes other than your base case or dream scenario. A trade with a 98% chance of a small win and a 2% chance of a catastrophic loss might have positive expected value, but it's too non-ergodic. Proper multiverse-informed position sizing would reduce the bet size to ensure survival across a full range of possible outcomes, even if it means sacrificing absolute returns in the timelines where the trade works.

If you know there's a 1-in-100 chance of blowing up on a high-EV trade and then you do the trade and you blow up… Was that bad luck? Or a bad decision? There is only one right answer here.

One of the most elegant solutions that multiverse thinking provides is resolving the apparent contradiction between maintaining strong conviction and acknowledging uncertainty. How can a trader be confident in their analysis while simultaneously accepting that they might be wrong? This conviction vs. uncertainty paradox is the root of aphorisms like "strong opinions, weakly held."

The answer lies in understanding what conviction actually means in a probabilistic universe. Strong conviction isn't about certainty of outcome—it's about confidence in the decision-making process and the expected value calculation. A trader who has high conviction on a 60/40 trade is not certain of winning; **they are confident that their analysis correctly identifies the probability distribution and that the trade has positive expected value.**

This distinction allows traders to maintain the psychological strength necessary for decisive action while retaining the intellectual humility required for effective risk management. They can enter trades with conviction while simultaneously preparing for timelines where they're wrong.

Post-trade analysis becomes less about whether the trade won or lost and more about whether the original analysis was sound. Ask yourself:

- Did the actual outcome fall within the anticipated range of possibilities?
- Were the probability estimates reasonable given the available information?
- Was the position sizing appropriate for the level of uncertainty?
- Can you hone your probability estimates over time using historical trading data?

Work towards the ability to think in terms of distributions, not just direction or point estimates. Consider all possible paths and destinations to best position yourself to properly structure your trades. For example, deciding between cash and options is all about the direction, variability, and probability of the possible paths.

The marriage of multiverse thinking and expected value theory transforms trading from a series of discrete win/loss events into an infinite game of probability optimization. Consider all possible timelines, hone your decision-making, and embrace high conviction with inevitable uncertainty. I have found that multiverse thinking is a practical framework that helps me better understand and embrace probabilistic thinking. Give it a shot.

Conclusion

I hope that coming out of this chapter, you have a better understanding of ergodicity, skew, initial conditions, good forecasting, narrative contagion, and adverse selection. And I hope you can keep an open mind about the relationship between expected value and the multiverse. Build more ways of thinking about markets on top of your primary frameworks, and you will see new things and come up with novel ideas.

You will avoid common traps, reduce your risk of ruin, and make more rational decisions.

CHAPTER 7

CHOOSING THE RIGHT GAME

The Metagame, Part One

"A game without a metagame is like an idealized object in physics. It may be a useful construct, but it doesn't really exist."

Richard Garfield, inventor of Magic: The Gathering

Traders and investors spend countless hours on trade ideas, technical analysis, risk management, spreadsheet building, and so on, but often neglect one of the most important aspects of a career in finance: **The metagame**.

Before we talk about markets, tactics, strategies and frameworks, you need to think about the many games that can be played in financial markets. You need to choose which games to play and which to avoid, and know the metagame specific to your role.

In this chapter, we'll cover the metagame concept and specifics of the *game within the game* of finance, including how the game changes in different contexts and at different times, knowing which games you can win and when you should quit, and thinking about why you are playing at all.

Let's go.

What does "metagame" mean?

"Meta" comes from the Greek prefix and preposition *meta-*, meaning after or beyond. As an adjective it means "demonstrating or indicating an explicit awareness of oneself" or more simply, "self-referential". Here's a 2009 usage of "meta" in TV Guide:

> A new comedy about fantasy football, which follows a group of armchair quarterbacks as they try to tackle life. How meta would it be if people started betting on what was going to happen on the show?

Very meta fence graffiti:

Meta was first attached to "game" by British game-theorist Nigel Howard in his 1971 book *Paradoxes of Rationality: Theory of Metagames and Political Behavior*. His work broadened the concept of game theory: considering not just the defined rules of the game, but the context in which decisions are made, including the preferences, goals, and perceptions of the other players. It was immediately viewed as a useful lens on decision-making in political and social contexts where rigid rules do not always fully define the game.

Some of the key takeaways from Nigel Howard's work:

- Game theory assumes everyone acts rationally. Metagame theory does not.
- Analysis and strategy in complex games should consider the goals, motivations, and emotions of the players, not just the formal rules of the game.
- Must one always follow the rules?
- What less obvious strategies might others use?

The parallels to markets are obvious. Many humans do not act rationally in markets. The goals, motivations, and emotions of market participants are critical for forecasting. And less obvious strategies often have more edge than obvious ones.

Howard also examines paradoxes of rationality, where individuals acting purely "rational" can lead to worse outcomes for the group overall. One example of the paradox of rationality is "The Tragedy of the Commons", where individual farmers with shared pasture each have a rational incentive to graze more cattle there to maximize their personal profit. When all farmers follow this individually rational strategy, it leads to overgrazing that destroys the pasture, harming everyone.

This is akin to the paradox of thrift, popularized by John Maynard Keynes, which states that while saving money is beneficial for an individual, if everyone increases their savings simultaneously it harms the overall economy. As incomes fall, people are forced to save even more, further reducing spending and deepening recession. Thus, saving can be harmful when practiced collectively, because the economy relies on spending to generate income and growth.

Another example is driving route selection. When commuters individually choose the fastest route during rush hour, they select the main highway, because it's theoretically quickest. However, this collective behavior creates congestion, making everyone's commute slower than if some drivers had rationally chosen alternate routes. The individually rational choice creates collective gridlock. Like the famous quote:

> "Nobody goes to that restaurant anymore. It's too crowded."
>
> Yogi Berra

This sort of strange logic is often seen in markets. In the 1980s, there was a saying: "No one ever got fired for buying IBM," which implied portfolio or mutual fund managers were individually rational for buying IBM at any price because it protected them from criticism, even if it led to poor returns for investors. The optimal metagame was to follow the herd, even if the herd was headed for a cliff, to minimize career risk (discussed later in the chapter).

Metagame is often used in realms like chess, professional sports, and video games.

In chess, metagame means you study opponents' known preferences, predict opponents' strategic variations in response to their study of your own shown preferences, exploit known weaknesses (for example, playing slowly on purpose to rattle an anxious or impatient player) and so on. Everything that happens outside of the formal rules of chess can be considered the metagame.

In sports (and finance), the metagame involves substantial and never-ending iteration as teams innovate and counter-innovate. For example, in basketball, a few innovators realized that maximizing 3-point attempts delivered higher expected scoring than the traditional approach that mixed 2-point and 3-point attempts. Those teams started shooting 3-pointers at a much higher rate.

Heatmap of NBA shots 1997-1998 vs. 2017-2018

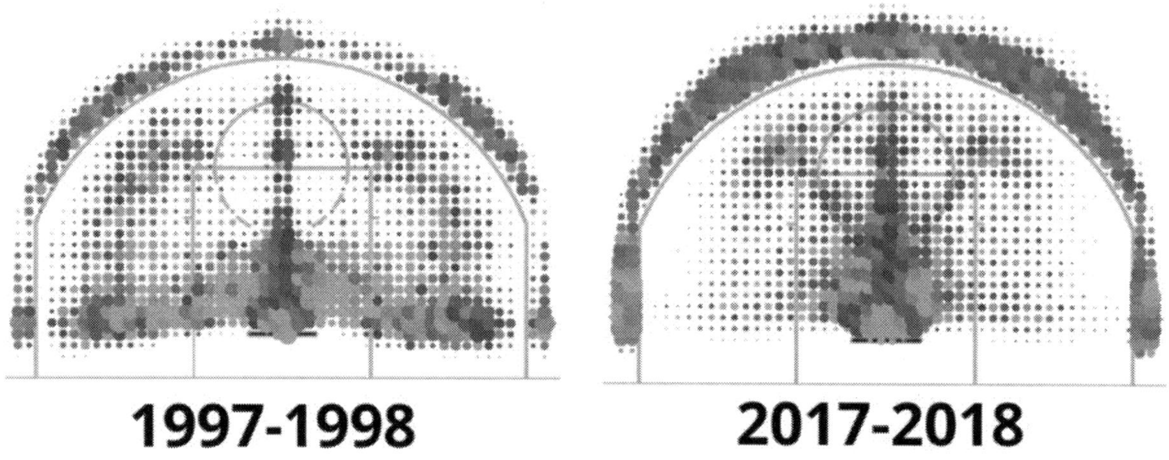

Over time, other teams saw the success of the 3-point approach and adopted it themselves, so the advantage disappeared. Favoring 3-pointers was a winning strategy for a while, but it slowly became just a way to avoid losing. The rules stayed the same from 1998 to 2018, but the metagame changed.

These shifts in the metagame can also lead to changes in the formal rules of the game, because they can create boring or predictable outcomes. For example, after the analytics revolution in baseball, teams realized they could move ***all*** their defensive players to the side of the field where the hitter was strongest, known as "The Shift". Hitters were stymied unless they hit the ball high and far, so they adapted by simply swinging hard for either a strike out or a home run. This became boring for fans and Major League Baseball eventually changed the rules to prohibit these extreme defensive alignments.

If players take advantage of a rule in financial markets, regulators will step in and change it. Then, players will look for ways to get around or exploit the new rule. If a trader finds an edge in a market, other traders will sniff it out and eventually extinguish it. Either way, the metagame has changed and the players must adapt.

The emergence of YOLO call buyers in equity markets in 2021 is a good example of a change of metagame. Retail traders learned that if they all moved into the options market in the same security at the same time, they could create outsized moves as market makers could not adequately hedge the options exposure. So this happened:

Trading Volume of Equity Calls on all U.S. Exchanges, 2001 to 2025

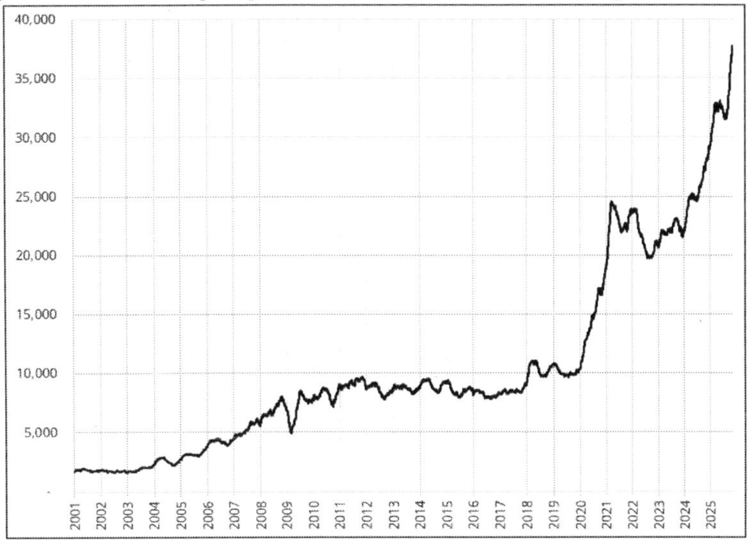

90-day average of total share volume

Call volumes were steady from 2010 to 2020 but more than tripled post-COVID as the metagame now involves much more retail buying of calls. There have been many other changes to the financial metagame over the years and understanding these changes can be the difference between successful adaptation, long-term success and profitability… Or a rigidity which leads you flame out, go bankrupt, or get fired.

Your personal metagame

Changes in the markets metagame described above are external change to how the broader game is played. But first, let's talk about your **internal** metagame.

- Are you playing a game you can win?
- Do you actually know and understand the rules of the game you are playing?
- Are you playing the game to win? Or not to lose?
- Is the game even winnable?

The first order of business when thinking about the metagame is selecting a game that you can win. Much like an amateur poker player should not sit down at a high stakes table full of pros, a new investor or trader should look at the world with realism and humility. They should look for a game they might be able to win.

The statistics on active investing and trading are distressing, to say the least. Five percent of day traders make a sustainable living. There is a reason I called Chapter 2 of *Alpha Trader* "If it was easy, it wouldn't pay so well". Games with massive financial rewards are difficult to win because they are dominated by a tiny slice of elite players. Only a very tiny percentage of high school golfers will get to the PGA Tour, and only a tiny percentage of day traders will find ongoing success.

Many people think of trading and investing as zero-sum games and that feels like cause for optimism. Like Garrison Keillor's fictional Lake Wobegon where "all the children are above average", almost everyone believes they are better than average at almost everything. "Since trading is a zero-sum game, we just have to be better than the next guy to win, right?" Wrong.

Trading and investing are *negative-sum* games.

Transaction costs and slippage are a significant drag for traders, and fees are a major drag for investors. Therefore, you need a significant edge to not only make money, but also to make enough money to exceed execution, technology, operational, and other fees. And in trading, grinding out tiny profits isn't enough. There is so much risk and uncertainty involved that for it to make any sense, you need to significantly exceed the income you could make in a lower risk profession. The bar for success in trading is *Olympic pole vault* levels of high.

In investing, the debate between active and passive approaches has raged for years, but the evidence strongly supports that the longer the time horizon, the more active fund managers' luck disappears, trading costs add up, and passive investors outperform.

U.S. Domestic Funds Outperforming Benchmarks, 2002 to 2023

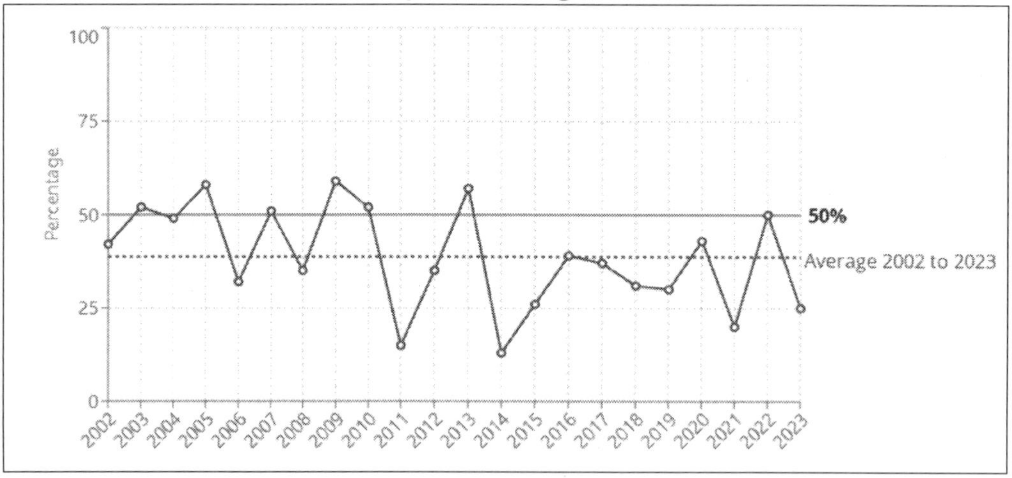

The chart shows that most years, fewer than 50% of the mutual funds operating in the U.S. outperform their benchmark. In other words, you're better off owning index funds, not actively managed funds most of the time. And in the long run, because of management fees, transaction fees, bad timing, overtrading, herding, and narrative chasing, **active managers (in aggregate) always produce worse returns than passive indexes**.

So, your starting point should always be: *This is a tough game… How can I win?* The answers to this question are numerous and complicated. It comes down to understanding whether or not you have an edge. If you can't clearly define exactly what your edge is—you probably don't have an edge.

Your starting point should be that you are playing *not to lose*. Then, as you develop an edge, you can aim for a more aggressive, offense-based strategy where you play to win.

Knowing what you're good at, and what you can be good at, is how you deliberately choose a game you can win. Punting around in stocks with no edge is not a good game to play. It's gambling. It's too hard. Selling options without understanding tail risk is not a good game to play. It'll blow you up. It's too hard.

Those who gamble in the markets always lose. **If you want to gamble, go to a casino.** If you *insist* on gambling in markets, admit it honestly, open a small account for that purpose, and go nuts in there while leaving the rest of your money in passive, low-fee strategies.

In the hedge fund business, you often see the contrast between playing to win and playing not to lose. Many managers work to maximize returns *when they have small assets under management*. This is the right game because they need strong returns to attract more capital. They are playing to win.

On the other hand, *very large funds tend to play not to lose*. They take less risk, target lower returns and volatility, and focus more on retaining investors. There's already a huge fee base when you have a ton of assets under management. Do you want to risk all that by taking enormous risks? Or maybe just hug the benchmark and be happy with the management fees?

Either one is fine but make sure you understand the game you are playing and whether it's the right or wrong game for your place of work. If you get a job at a big firm, you have to understand the goals of your managers and directors and know what game *they're* playing, so that you can use your seat the way they need you to use it. In other words, being a great trader or analyst is essential—but you also have to know how your seat fits into the larger direction of the firm.

For most non-professionals, buy and hold or index fund investing is the optimal solution. They should play not to lose. Playing to win involves higher transaction costs, verifiable bad odds, and a host of behavioral biases. Better to just stick your money in an index fund and avoid wasting your time and mental capital on a pursuit where you have no edge.

Too many individual investors play to win and end up losing big. Here, for example, are the actual returns for a bunch of asset classes and way over there on the right is the actual return individual investors achieved in thousands of Charles Schwab accounts. Through overtrading and bad market timing, most investors throw away a huge part of what would have been easier gains if they had just played not to lose, instead of playing to win.

20-year annualized returns by asset class, 1996 to 2015

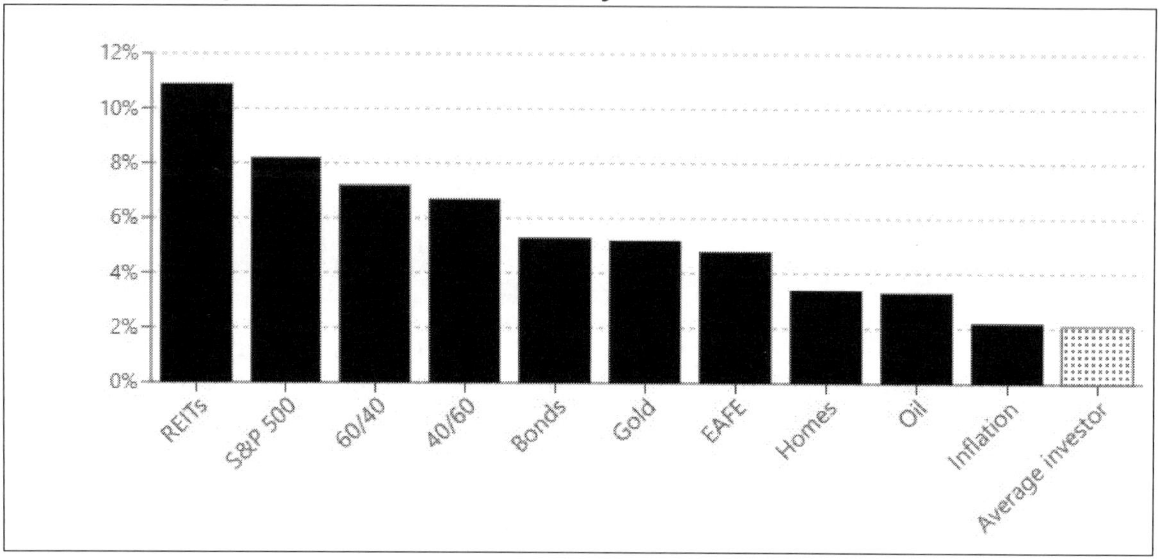

The classic essay on this topic is "The Loser's Game" by Charles Ellis[45]. Here's a quick excerpt:

> Dr. Simon Ramo, an eminent scientist at TRW Inc., identified the crucial difference between a winner's game and a loser's game in his excellent book on playing strategy, Extraordinary Tennis for the Ordinary Tennis Player.
>
> Over many years, Dr. Ramo observed that tennis was not one game, but two–one played by professionals and a very few gifted amateurs; the other played by all the rest of us. Although players in both games use the same equipment, dress, rules, and scoring, and conform to the same etiquette and customs, they play two very different games.
>
> After extensive scientific and statistical analysis, Dr. Ramo summed it up this way: Professionals win points; amateurs lose points.
>
> In expert tennis, the ultimate outcome is determined by the actions of the winner. Professional tennis players stroke the ball hard, with laser-like precision, through long and often exciting rallies, until one player is able to

---

[45] www.empirical.net/wp-content/uploads/2012/06/the_losers_game.pdf

drive the ball just out of reach or force the other player to make an error. These splendid players seldom make mistakes.

Amateur tennis, Dr. Ramo found, is almost entirely different. Brilliant shots, long and exciting rallies, and seemingly miraculous recoveries are few and far between. Instead, the ball is often hit into the net or out of bounds, and double faults at service are not uncommon. The amateur seldom beats his opponent, but he beats himself all the time. The victor in this game of tennis gets a higher score because his opponent is losing even more points.

As a scientist and statistician, Dr. Ramo gathered data to test his hypothesis in a clever way. Instead of keeping conventional game scores – love, 15 all, 30-15, and so forth – Ramo simply counted points won versus points lost. He found that in expert tennis about 80 percent of the points are won, but in amateur tennis about 80 percent of the points are lost. The two games are fundamental opposites.

Professional tennis is a winner's game: the outcome is determined by the actions of the winner. Amateur tennis is a loser's game: the outcome is determined by the actions of the loser—who defeats himself.

Whether you are forecasting, investing, trading, or running a hedge fund, you need to decide whether you are playing not to lose, or playing to win. **Or just not playing at all.** The guy responding to my tweet below gets it.

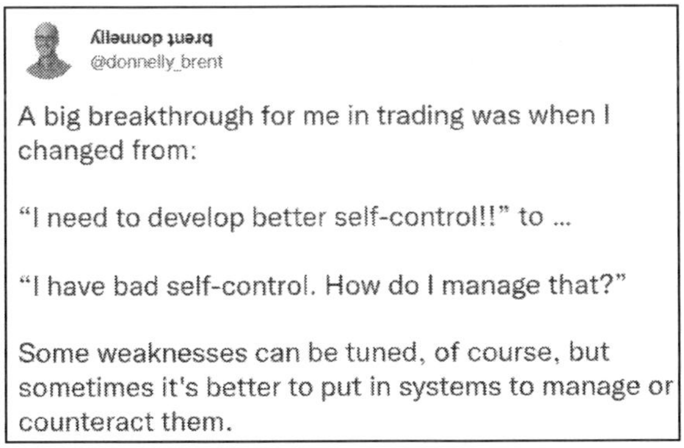

ʎllǝuuop ʇuǝɹq
@donnelly_brent

A big breakthrough for me in trading was when I changed from:

"I need to develop better self-control!!" to ...

"I have bad self-control. How do I manage that?"

Some weaknesses can be tuned, of course, but sometimes it's better to put in systems to manage or counteract them.

Akrasiabros
@akrasiabros

Replying to @donnelly_brent

A big breakthrough for me in trading was when I changed from:

Trading to...

Not trading.

Generating alpha in trading and investing is difficult, but not impossible. Choose a game you have a realistic chance of winning and always consider ways in which the rules of the game are changing.

If, despite all the evidence, you insist on playing to win, you still need to have a strong defense. That is, you must still be acutely aware of liquidity risk, gap risk, and risk of ruin.

Do you understand the risks you are taking? Are they measurable?

Imagine a game where you flip a coin and if it's heads you get $1 and if it's tails you pay $0.50. Sounds like an awesome game; let's go! You play the game 100 times and you're up $33 and then the coin is flipped for the 101st time, and it hits the table, bounces, spins and then comes to a stop on its side. The gamemaster says: "Oh! Side-lander! You owe me $500."

You thought you were playing a game of heads or tails, but the coin had a third outcome that was not even in your frame of reference. This can happen in financial markets when people don't fully understand tail risk. You go short NFLX into earnings, risking $20 to make $50. The stock gaps $250 higher on a huge earnings beat and then your computer crashes. And when you log in 10 minutes later, your password is rejected.

Finally, after talking to tech support, you log back in 2 hours later and you lost $400 per share, or 20X what you thought you were risking. You are forced to sell all your assets— a 1993 Suzuki GS400 and 2 bitcoin—to cover the loss.

Not good.

These unexpected, hard-to-measure, or even unknowable risks show up all the time in financial markets. Very often, they involve some sort of options selling or synthetic options selling strategy that has a Sharpe ratio of 3. Until it blows up. Then it has a Sharpe ratio of negative infinity. If you cannot precisely measure the risk you are taking on a given trade or investment, you should not engage. This is the lesson of Jesse Livermore, Victor Niederhoffer, Bill Hwang, Gabe Plotkin, and every other trader that ended up on the wrong side of a nuclear convexity moment.

For much more on risk management, see *Alpha Trader*, Chapter 11.

The too-hard pile

Once you have chosen a game to play, you can still choose what levels to play, and which levels are too difficult.

For example, starting out as a currency trader, I found the nitty gritty details of interest rate trading to be relevant. But whenever I would go in and start to learn about basis, forward curves, OIS, and other topics related to short-term interest rate trading (STIRT), I would see a huge mountain in front of me. And I would ask myself: Is it worth the effort to climb that mountain?

My answer was no. I learned enough to understand how central bank policy influences interest rates and how to use market pricing to decipher future expectations for central bank meetings. And I placed just about all of the rest of short-term interest rate trading in the "too hard" pile. Importantly, one of the big reasons I didn't become an expert in STIRT is because I do not find it interesting. I don't shy away from hard topics, but if the answer to the following three questions is yes, I put the topic in the too hard pile.

1. Not particularly interesting.
2. Not critical to developing an edge in my business.
3. Complex and time consuming to learn.

I decided it would take years to reach expert level in cross-currency swaps, forwards, OIS, repo, and all the other complex intricacies of STIRT and those years could be better spent learning more useful things. The incremental value that I might get from a near-mastery of short-term interest rate trading would barely move the needle on my global macro career.

You can't get into billiards and then three weeks later decide you also want to be an expert at darts and poker. Better to level up your billiards game for at least five years before venturing into those other games.

Taking the time to achieve expert status with regard to the stock market has clearly been worthwhile for me. Unlike the nitty gritty of short-term rates markets, the stock market is integral to all things global macro. The ability to converse intelligently about the stock market and identify its inflection points has tons of value. You can't really trade global macro (or write about it every day, like I do) if you don't have a detailed knowledge of the primary drivers and internal dynamics of stocks.

Same goes with monetary policy. Anyone working in capital markets needs at least a solid working knowledge, if not expert knowledge, of monetary policy because it is a macro input to almost every trading and investing decision. Whether you're trading stocks, commodities, currencies, rates, or even crypto, you need to understand monetary policy; it's universal.

And when it comes to options, I just find them extremely interesting, so I was willing to spend the years necessary to learn about them. My curiosity drove me to investigate options and derivatives even though they are complex and not critical to understanding global macro.

The *too-hard* pile is about making thoughtful decisions with regard to how you want to spend your limited time.

The *too-hard* concept was popularized by Warren Buffett, who sidestepped the two technology bubbles of the 2000s by simply admitting: "These companies are too hard to evaluate using my frameworks." He didn't participate in the runups, and he didn't get killed when the bubbles collapsed. He just sat on the sidelines and ate popcorn, watching the herd go mad in both directions.

Principle 16: Admit what you don't know.

An actual thing on Warren Buffett's desk

Be judicious with your energy and don't be ashamed or feel lazy if you decide to label some stuff as: **Too hard**.

Choose a game you can win.

The institutional metagame

The rules of the game in financial markets change every day. Sometimes, Fed policy is the big driver, then it's geopolitics, or a speculative bubble in AI, or a short squeeze in meme stocks accelerated by a rogue trader illegally using leverage at a hedge fund.

Methodologies and frameworks that work today are unlikely to work forever. Efficient markets arbitrage away profitable strategies. Probabilities are subjective, not objective. You are playing an incredibly complex, opaque game with wildly varying, hard-to-define rules.

But that's only part of it! On top of all those confusing parameters, you also need to understand the limitations, constraints, rules, politics, and emotional preferences of your manager, his manager, and her manager, along with the fickle institutional preferences of your firm. You need to understand the internal rules, incentives, politics, and risk management framework where you work and incorporate these into your risk management decisions. And often, you also need to consider your personal financial needs, your family situation, and so on.

The internal rules of the game are different for hedge fund managers, bank traders, and retail. I have sat in all three seats, so here is some advice for how best to handle each one. I present this advice with the utmost humility; I have had plenty of good trading years and plenty of disappointing ones!

The hedge fund metagame

Here's how to think about your job as a PM at a hedge fund.

Know the real rules. Your contract probably has a stop loss in it, but be 100% certain of your *real* stop loss. The two numbers are probably not the same! What kind of intraday, daily and weekly volatility will your boss find mildly, or very disturbing?

There are the printed rules of the game and then the actual rules. Make sure you know both. Stay away from management pain points.

Your approach needs to be different if you work at Rokos, where returns look like this:

Rokos Macro Hedge Fund Returns

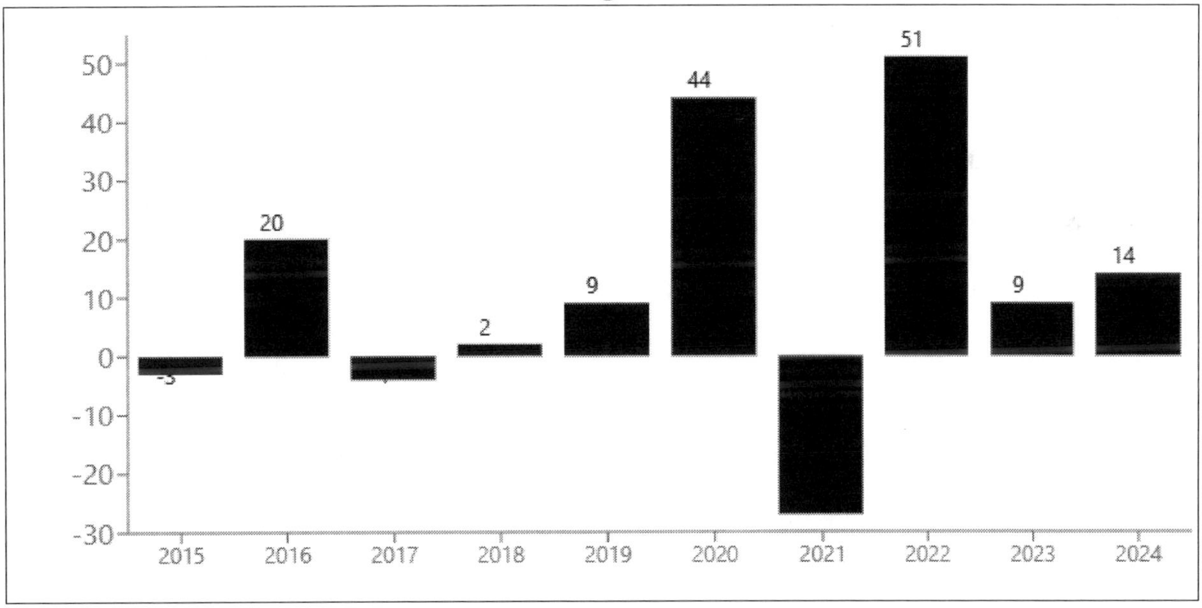

Data from Bloomberg

Or Millennium, where returns look like this:

Millennium Hedge Fund Returns

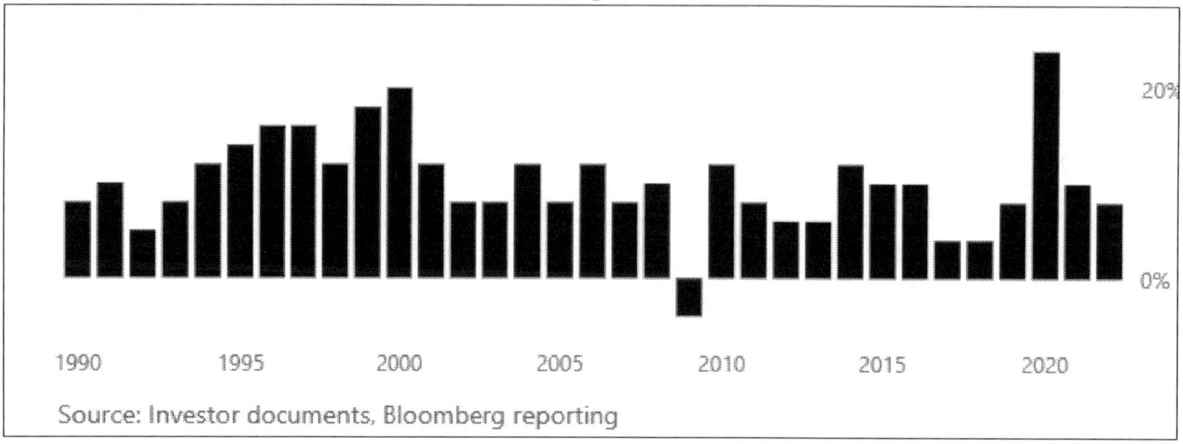

Your priority is to prove yourself as a good risk manager. Self-policing is important. Nobody wants a phone call from management, ever… but especially not in Year One. Understand the real risk framework of your firm, plus any political or emotional aspects of management. If your manager leaves and a new, *nervous Nellie* arrives on the scene, reconsider your risk appetite for a bit.

Start slow. You may want to show the firm what a good hire you are by putting up a 3% return in Month One. If anything, though, that will probably set off alarm bells for high volatility, not elicit high fives for stellar returns. If you succeed at a hedge fund, success will be measured in years, not months. Play the long game and settle in before you get aggressive.

Sprinting out of the gates is a bad strategy!

No matter how strong your view is when you sit down on Day One, there is too much path dependence in a hedge fund seat to be max aggressive. Even if you are placing what you think is an 80/20 bet, if the 20% comes up, you are hobbled, your confidence is impaired and that can threaten your liftoff. It's not worth the risk.

Build your base and be like a call option with limited downside and unlimited upside. You cannot have the same risk appetite on Day One with zero P&L in the coffers as you can have on Day 274 when you are up 15 million dollars. In an *ideal* world, you should always vary your risk appetite based on conviction and market opportunity. But in the *real* world, start slow and build risk over time.

Also, there is something special and scary about the zero bound in P&L. Say you want to make $10 million this year and your stop loss is $4 million. You will find that going from +$2 million to +$1 million feels significantly less bad than going from +$500k to -$500k, even though both are P&L declines of $1 million. Any red number next to your name feels bad.

Loss aversion theory says that if a gain gives us X pleasure, a loss of the same magnitude gives us 2X pain.

This is not all just psychological, though. As your P&L falls below zero, your ability to take risk (your leverage) decreases. There is a non-linear real-world impact of losses as you move below zero and closer to your stop loss. When you are below zero P&L, you wear a slowly-tightening straitjacket.

Even if your stop loss is $4 million, you are in big trouble trading-wise way before then, because you will need to reduce your position size to avoid getting the shoulder tap. Also, if you start with a big loss, you run into the Problem of Percentages: if you lose 1%, you need to make more than 1% to get back to flat. *That's annoying.* Here is a chart for your enjoyment:

Starting account size: $100 million
Trader alternating losing 1% then gaining 1% daily for 252 days

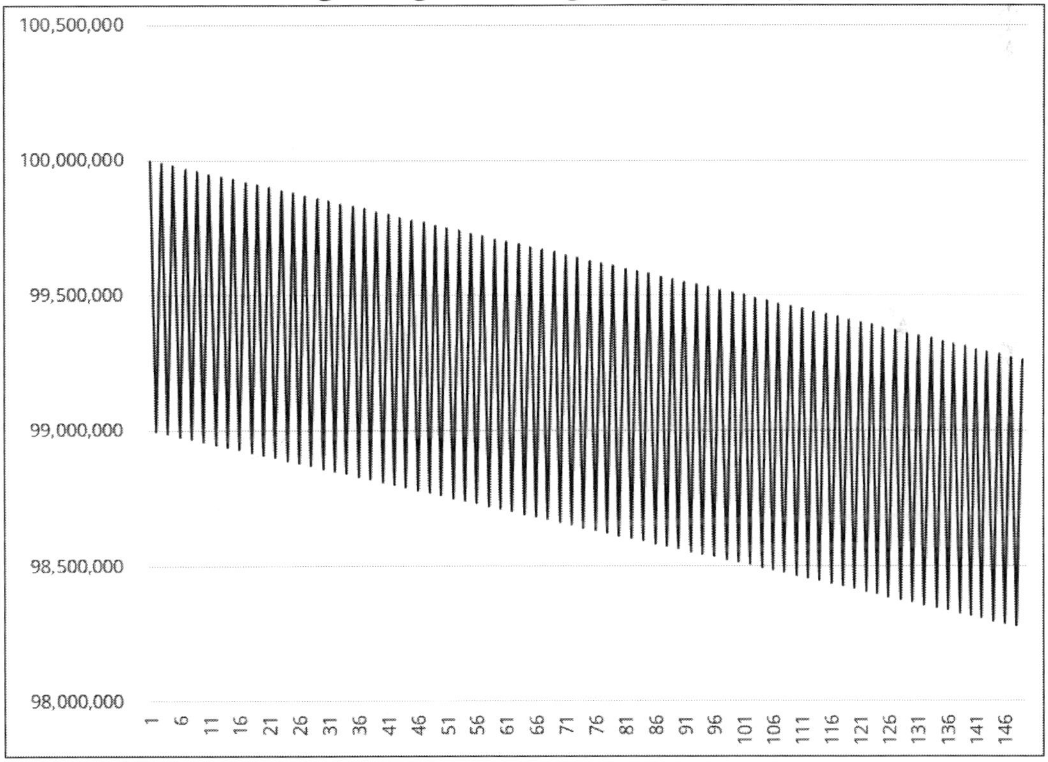

This volatility drag is painful and important.

Get safely away from the zero bound and when a mega-opportunity arrives and you have a cushion … go for it. If you are +$1.5 million on February 25 and there is a fantastic opportunity, you're in position to risk a bigger chunk of cash on the idea without worrying about sinking.

Path dependence is an important concept for every professional trader: future steps of a process depend on its history. A series of coin flips is not path dependent. If you flip 10 tails, the coin has no memory, and the 11th flip is fair and 50/50.

In contrast, each month in a trading year is path dependent. Your performance in January will determine your free capital and your state of mind for February. It's essential to avoid actions in one period that could be overly detrimental to future periods.

For example: you work at a bank where the P&L resets every January 1. There is a perfect, 5-star set up in S&P futures and you have never been so confident that they are about to (finally!) crash. Your approach to this trade, the sizing you choose and the amount of capital you will risk should be different in January than in August.

While this is illogical from a purely rational or mathematical point of view, in reality there is too much path dependence in January for you to go all-in; act more conservatively since your performance in January will influence the following 11 months. On the other hand, if your annual target was $5 million and you are up $7 million in September, you could lose $2 million on a trade without much negative impact on your final three months of the year.

I know this might not seem rational, but believe me, it is.

Playing the multi-period metagame correctly is just as important as maximizing P&L for a given period.

Another way path dependence matters is when you start a new job in trading. If you make money for eight straight years, you don't attract much attention if you lose money in Year Nine. A new hire that loses money in his first four months of trading might make a manager question their hiring decision.

Even the most sophisticated financial firms and investors are generally not good at separating luck from skill or at comparing market regimes to trader performance. The absolute number next to your name matters much more than any context surrounding it. So when you start a new trading job, understand how much runway you have.

As ridiculous as it sounds, your ultimate success or failure at a hedge fund is usually determined within the first 12 to 18 months. Your entire career (or lack thereof) at the fund will be anchored by that initial performance. The trader that comes out hot and shoots the lights out will be given plenty of slack going forward and can probably draw down in future without too much hassle.

The equally-skilled trader who comes in and loses money for the first five months will be under heightened scrutiny, even if those five months were the lowest volatility period in the history of his asset class and he is known to be a trader that performs well in high-vol markets.

Protect against this path dependence when switching firms by ensuring you have at least one (and hopefully two or three) strong supporters in the new organization. And make sure that the strong supporter who brought you in is planning to stay! Once your sponsor leaves, your life or death in that firm becomes even more path dependent. Try to avoid relying on luck by ensuring that you have sufficient runway when you go to a new firm.

Play your own game. Nobody watches you as intensely as you watch yourself. Don't avoid a trade because it "seems dumb" or is too micro, etc. Your job is to make money and generally the only thing your boss cares about is your vol and your P&L. Do you want to be smart, or make money?

Avoid style drift. If you have been a spot FX trader your whole life, and you go to a hedge fund, your brain is going say: "Whoa look at all these flashing numbers, this looks fun!" like a kid in a candy store. Don't start piling into a short wheat position just because you can. Many people I have seen rapidly and unceremoniously booted from hedge funds have been a victim of style drift. They were hired because they had an edge in their product(s). Yes, there is a lot to learn by touring other assets and markets but spend most of your time focused on markets where you are an expert.

Be careful when they increase your capital! When you perform well, you will probably get an increase in capital. Remember that you are trading and getting paid in dollars, not basis points. If you make 10% on your initial allocation of $100 million, then they up you to $200 million and you lose 5%, you're back to flat. That's not good! If your allocation doubles, don't just double all your position sizes right away. Scale into your new capital.

The moment your capital increases is the moment you are most likely to be overconfident.

A. You have been crushing it, or the increase would not have happened, and
B. The increase itself is strong validation for your ego.

Don't be overconfident! The day you get an increase in capital, turtle a bit and get defensive until the overconfidence risk passes. Time is the best cure for every extreme emotion.

Identify where the world is in the macro cycle. Are you joining as a commodity PM in 2012? As an FX carry trader in 2006? As an oil trader in 2016? The fact that you have been hired to the role you were hired for might have information content. Hiring and firing is procyclical. Also, unless you are a very short term trader, the stage of the cycle should impact your trading bias. In early 2009, after the Fed, Treasury, Europe and China changed all the rules, a famous investor put a Post-It note on his monitor that read "Long or flat". I don't like locking into a particular side of the market, but depending on what product you trade, a similar Post-It might be appropriate.

Find other ways to add value. Sure a PM's main value is the P&L, but people that add value in other ways have more runway. Be an information hub, volunteer to meet investors, overcommunicate with your risk manager, walk around the floor and get to know people. If you are more than just a number, your implicit stop loss is wider, and you have a greater probability of success. Furthermore, you absorb information when you talk to people. If 19 out of 20 PMs at your firm are bearish stonks, it's time to add to your longs.

Relax and have fun. It's hard to have perspective when you sit down at a hedge fund for the first time. On the one hand, the stakes seem higher than ever. That is scary. On the other hand… You made it! You're living the dream. Look around and see how far you have come. You are probably there for a reason.

Believe in yourself, relax and get to work.

The market maker metagame

Market making usually involves some directional risk-taking, but it also forces you to be a salesperson, researcher, and team player. And you need to understand your franchise and how to monetize it. Here are some tips for market makers.

Study as many other traders as possible, but don't copy them. Adopt a personal trading style that matches your personality, interests, strengths, and weaknesses. I have never seen a new analyst come in and copy a senior trader and become successful. Good traders develop their own style by amalgamating tidbits and setups and tactics from studying other traders, reading books, and thinking of their own ideas. Find a trader you respect and spend an hour asking them about their process.

As Bruce Lee said:

> Research your own experience.
> Absorb what is useful, reject what is useless...
> ... and add what is essentially your own.

Find traders with different styles and pay attention to what they are doing. Incorporate only the methods and tactics that make sense to you. If you see traders making tons of money trading news headlines, but you always sucked at video games and you like to ruminate before taking action… Don't trade headlines.

Nobody has a trading style when they start. Try one on. If it fits, keep it, but try some others as well. Experiment. List all the ways you see that people make money. This will also serve you well in the future when the awesome trading style you adopted and made money for seven straight months suddenly stops working.

Good market makers can make money on client flow and spread, market direction, news, techs, sentiment extremes, flow patterns, time of day patterns, cross market correlation, lead-lag trading, bid/offer bounce, etc. Don't pick one style and be like "I'm a breakout trader". That will work in some regimes and not in others. Specializing in a market is good but specializing in a trading style is not. Different market regimes reward different trading styles.

Work to be the go-to expert in the market you trade. You can become expert in a specific market in as little as two years. Get to know every aspect of your market as deeply as possible. You should know the following about any market you trade.

Macro drivers

- What are the cyclical and structural global variables that drive your market?
- What is the narrative in global macro and how does that feed into to your product?

Idiosyncratic drivers

- What are the endogenous drivers of your market?
- What flows, stories, and intermarket variables drive your particular product?

Microstructure

- Current and historical volatility and vol of vol. What does a quiet market look like? What does a crazy market look like? Where are we right now on that continuum?
- Liquidity and volatility by time zone and time of day
- Time zone bias. Does Asia tend to sell, and NY tends to buy (for example)? Or is it random?
- Upcoming economic events and catalysts
- Important clients trading in each time zone

Execution

- What footprint/slippage can a client expect for x, y, and z size?
- What execution strategies are most appropriate in different regimes? In fast markets, your execution strategy should be different than how you execute in quiet markets. At 9 a.m. you might use a different strategy than you do at 3 p.m.
- How to best manage client expectations? (overcommunicate)

The players

- Who else trades this product, or correlated products, at my bank? How can I get to know them? Travel to foreign branches to meet your colleagues in other centers: it's an excellent use of the bank's money.

- What other banks are good in my market? Who are my main competitors? Why are they good? What makes them good? Can I emulate that?
- Which clients are most important? Hedge funds, real money, corporates, and central banks all play varying roles in different markets. Which ones matter in your market?

Excellent bank traders are world-class experts in the markets they trade and become reliable sources of information for clients.

Understand and embrace the fact that your number one edge is the seat. With some notable exceptions, bank seats have positive embedded franchise value. One of the big advantages of being a risk taker at a bank, and not a prop shop or hedge fund, is the franchise annuity that pads your risk taking, buffers the downside, and makes you valuable even when you are not making money. Before you rush to take a lot of directional risk, make sure you have done everything you can to master the basics of professional execution, client service, and flow monetization.

Execution is a skill. Try different approaches. Watch how others execute. Experiment with limit orders, market orders, TWAPs, VWAPs, and so on. When you place a level one order, do algos front-run you immediately? How can you manage that? Risk taking is sexy but servicing the franchise pays the bills and keeps you employed. Bank trading jobs have a lower ceiling than pure trading jobs, but they also have a higher floor. If you are a good market maker who keeps the clients happy, you have a lot of runway and time to learn how to trade. Master everything related to client service first. That's the most important part of most market making roles. Once you're solid on the basics of market making and keeping clients happy, you can work towards becoming a real risk taker.

Be proud of your seat and your franchise. Act like a business owner. Your seat and your franchise are your business, and you are there to build it. Sure, sometimes a juicy trade from sales is just free money dropping into your book and you might feel like you don't deserve that P&L or it's "funny money." You deserve that money because you earned the seat.

Something to remember for the future: Don't trade down to a smaller seat because you think you will get paid for alpha generation. Banks generally do a poor job of normalizing P&L vs. franchise value. You always want the best franchise and the best seat. You will get paid more by making $10 million in a seat that is worth $20 million than you will by making $5 million in a seat that's worth $1 million.

Trade your own view. If you trade someone else's idea, you will inevitably do something wrong. You may stop out at the wrong level because your conviction will not be high when the trade goes against you. If you are trading someone else's view, you might not know when their view changes. Frequently you will hear someone moaning about following someone else's idea then having insult added to injury when they find out that the original trader exited long ago or even flipped their position. Successful traders do their own work and come to their own conclusions.

I remember a particular moment when I was in my 20s and my boss was a loud, legendary fellow who was much-loved by everyone in trading and sales (Hi, Ed!). He always had a strong view, and his view was constantly broadcast at full volume. It was very hard to be short when he was a raging bull because you would look stupid if you were wrong. He never got on people for trading a view opposite to his, but it was intimidating to do so. I remember the day I had a big short USDCAD and he was bullish, and I realized that I didn't really care about his view anymore.

You will know you have moved to the next level of trading when you are perfectly happy to be short when your boss is mega long.

By the way, if your manager doesn't like you trading a different view than the "house view," that is unfortunate. A healthy risk-taking environment respects individual traders' risk-taking and if management wants to have a view, they should put that view on themselves. The worst type of management is the managing director that sends an email saying something like "Given the events transpiring in Europe, it behooves us to be short EUR. Interpret that as you see fit." If a good manager is bullish and he sees everyone on the desk is short, he'll go long in the management book and let the traders trade.

If you make a mistake, own it. As a manager, the one thing that made me instantly turn on a junior was any sort of sketchy, dishonest, or questionable behavior. If you make a mistake, don't hide it. Cover the risk or market exposure at a loss and move on. If you were supposed to sell 50 and you bought 50… Sell 100 right away. Don't sit there saying "well… I'm bullish anyway, I'll just slip these out slowly over the next coupla hours and the bossman is at lunch anyway so prolly no one will even know…"

A young trader doing even the most slightly gray area stuff is a massive red flag. *Don't.*

Learn the systems and pay attention to the details. This is a weak spot for me because I don't like boring stuff. Operational errors, out trades, fat fingers, dupes, and other general sloppiness are unprofessional. In every organization, there is "the person that knows all the stuff". Figure out who that person is at your bank and learn from them.

Go into the menus in your trading systems and check out all the features and functions. You might be surprised to learn there is a function in there that not one person on the desk has ever used or even knows about. Most bank systems have little documentation or training, so don't just assume what you have been shown is all there is to know. Institutional knowledge and memory are weaker than you would think.

If you're new, **find the right balance between keen/curious and annoying.** It's great for a junior analyst to ask questions and show ambition, but don't be the person that won't leave senior people alone. Don't ask for 20-minute Zoom catchups just so you can say *Hi* to or "check in" with someone you respect. Have a purpose, and keep queries focused and short. Don't follow up the follow up to your follow up emails with another eight questions saying "now that I have you..." People do not have unlimited time or patience. Be keen, but respectful.

The junior analyst spectrum

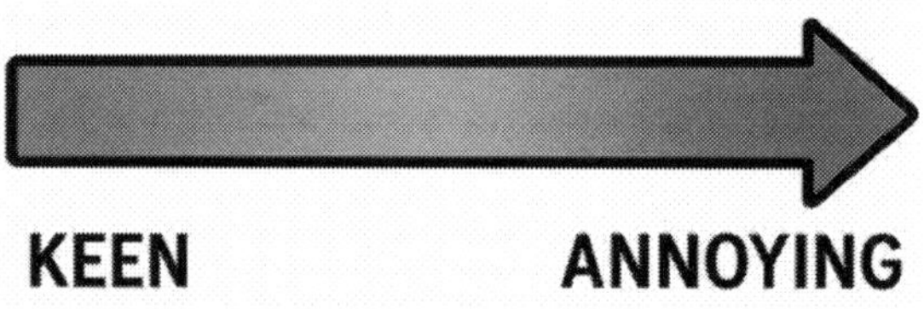

Gradually figure out your edge. Developing a defined edge is a key to success in trading. Edge in trading is too long of a topic for this book; it's covered in detail in *Alpha Trader*. But there is another type of edge to think about: What is your edge in the world of finance? What makes you different from everyone else? Every one of your peers is super smart and probably top 2% of their high school and college class. How will you outperform them?

Over the past 20 years, Wall Street hiring has narrowed to focus almost exclusively on elite schools and quantitative factors like GPA. As such, quantitative skill and book smarts on their own are not differentiators, they are the bare minimum.

Creativity, street smarts, communication skills, writing ability, sophisticated Python skill, and EQ are a few examples of characteristics that may give you an edge. One of the traders I talked to while brainstorming this piece said: "U just need to find ur edge ... whether its big picture macro or being epic on flow and spreads ... or drinking with sales..."

😊 It's funny cuz it's true.

Be humble. No matter how well you are doing, markets are fluid and the second you become overconfident, you will get punched in the mouth. To succeed as a sell side trader, you must have an unshakable belief in yourself, but not be arrogant or overconfident... That is a tricky line to walk.

Learn the internal rules. What does your bank care about most? What does your boss care about most? If your boss is a long-time trader trying to 4X the risk profile of the desk, that is a completely different metagame than reporting to an ex-salesperson who runs both sales and trading and only cares about building the client franchise. Match your priorities to the priorities of management and the firm.

What gets people paid in your bank? Is it just P&L? Or is it more about client interaction, content creation, and other facets of the role? Sell-side trader roles are about much more than just P&L. If you focus on P&L and management prioritizes quality of market commentary and trader/client interaction… At bonus time there will be a big disconnect and your expectations will be crushed.

Does your compensation flatline once your P&L hits a certain threshold? If so, remember that if you hit that threshold, losses will cost you more in compensation than gains will help. Adjust your risk accordingly.

Collect data. The more detailed information you capture on your trading and P&L, the faster you learn. Track P&L by client, by time of day, flows vs. views (alpha vs. beta), and so on.

If you don't want to be a manager, don't accept the promotion. It's hard to say no to a promotion but many careers have been interrupted or ruined by a promotion to management. You often make less money and have less fun as a manager than you do as a high-producing trader. It's OK to say "no thanks" when offered a promotion to run the desk or to run a business! It feels bad at the time, but it's often the right call. One of my few career regrets was saying "yes" to too many promotions in the 2010s and ending up in many HR and IT meetings, when all I wanted to do was trade and write.

Don't hold onto flow just because it's out of the money. When a client trades with you and the market goes immediately against you, you will tend to anchor on the rate you got hit. If you got filled in at 55, you think "Man, if I can just get out of these at 55, I'll be happy." The market does not care what rate you traded at! Use market logic, not anchoring bias, to determine how and when to hedge the flow. If you're bullish and short… That's bad. Don't convince yourself it's fine and sit there bullish and short all day. Make rational trading and hedging decisions based on your best unbiased forecast of where the market is going, not where a client transacted.

Pick a single time horizon. Trading is difficult enough and if you mix up your time horizons, it becomes impossible. Your time horizon should match the product you are trading and its liquidity and volatility profile. Spot FX traders generally should not be putting on 6-month views because there is 0% probability that a spot FX trader has an edge on that time horizon. In contrast, with a good understanding of narrative, flows, positioning, and so on, a spot FX trader can easily have an edge on a 1-day or 3-day time horizon.

Pull the trigger. Good trading takes courage. When you have a strong view, have the courage to take meaningful risk within well-defined, rule-based risk parameters.

Be nice and be a team player. One thing that blows my mind as years go by is the number of random connections and actions from long ago that echo through my life. People remember how you treated them and how you behaved, even 10 or 20 years later. All your actions accumulate in the long run. Be nice to the person that cleans the floors in your office. Treat the PAs, salespeople and brokers the same way you treat the trading MDs. If nobody wants to work on the holiday, put your hand up.

Principle 17:
An excellent reputation accrues enormous value over time.

One trader I talked to boiled market making down to five words: **Know your market. Know yourself.** That's a great summary!

Retail day trader metagame

As a retail trader, your metagame is completely different from that of an institutional trader. You are free from the politics, risk aversion, and arbitrary rule changes of a bank or hedge fund, but you have a host of other considerations and challenges. Here are a few aspects of the retail trading metagame for you to consider.

You are often underfunded and it's easier to blow up

Retail traders, even those who are highly skilled, are much more likely to blow up because they have access to more leverage. A hedge fund with $20 billion under management isn't going to be able to take enough risk to crater their entire fund in a single day. A retail trader often can. One bad trade at 2:1 leverage can wipe out a retail trader in an hour. Even properly-funded retail traders can blow up.

Simple example: You have $50,000 in your margin account and you buy $100,000 worth of some random insurance stock. Before the open, they announce a massive accounting fraud and the stock gaps down 70%. You are not only ruined, you owe more than you started with. Does this sound unrealistic? It's not. Extreme concentration and access to leverage are the biggest risk in retail.

When I was day trading at a small firm in 2000, a popular day trading football stock was Emulex (NASDAQ: EMLX). One afternoon when the stock was trading around $50, a press release came out saying their earnings were going to miss by a huge margin. Many of the guys around me sold the stock on the news. They went max short at $30 or so and it was soon trading at $25.

Two guys were fully margined short (they had $100,000 in their account and were short $200,000 worth of stock). Then, disaster. The stock was halted. Nobody knew why for about 2 hours, then NASDAQ announced that the press release *was fake*[46]. The stock reopened at $62, and both traders got margin called by the office and lost their entire accounts. Careful with leverage, especially leveraged shorts.

Emulex stock, daily, August to October 2000

You have a shorter runway

Retail traders must have a good sense of how long they can survive, and create the right conditions for success. No retail trader can succeed with a $1,000 trading account because the income generated from the most successful strategy will be too small to move the needle. Even a 300% return will not be enough to make a difference so the trader is likely to employ too much leverage and blow up the account by gambling.

A tiny trading account is OK for learning the markets and it's much better than paper trading. It can give you a sense of the emotional and psychological hurdles that come with live trading, but it will never give you a chance to really know what kind of trader you are.

---

[46] wikipedia.org/wiki/Emulex_hoax

There are thresholds below which you cannot hope to succeed. For a young retail trader with no family to support and low expenses, this amount could be as low as $25,000. For a dentist with three kids in private school looking to quit his job and trade full time, this number would be significantly higher. If your runway is too short, you are not giving yourself a fair chance at success. Wait until the metagame is better. Don't play a game you can't win.

The short runway problem relates to both capital and time. Retail trading has an opportunity cost: The income you could have been earning doing something else. If you don't earn a certain amount of money in your first two years, will your spouse get antsy and ask you to get a "real" job? If that is the case, you should calculate whether your process can possibly achieve that goal.

You need your family on board, or you will find life difficult. Trading is incredibly hard. It will test your belief in yourself. If those around you (especially your family and/or the person who provided your trading capital) don't believe in you, it will be impossible.

For people trading their own money, a healthy environment means enough runway to learn, make mistakes, bounce back and eventually prosper. Capital is crucial, but so is support from family, financial flexibility, and the ability to focus and get in the zone all day.

You own your life, so if you want to be a trader, do it. But pick the right circumstances to give yourself a proper shot at success. There is nothing worse than wondering what could have been. Quite often, you can work full time and find ways to trade on the side (and more importantly, study trading) so that as you gain experience and confidence in trading you are still earning a steady income. Then, once you have a decent amount of money in the bank, you have a bit of runway to try trading full time and see if you have what it takes.

Retail traders don't have to worry about intraday liquidity

Many strategies that work for retail traders are out of reach for large institutional traders because they are too small to move the needle—they have too little capacity. A simple example might be a strategy in currency markets that makes $2,000/day but cannot be scaled any more than that because transaction costs eat up the alpha. This is common. There are zillions of tiny positive expected value strategies out there that are not worth doing if you are managing a $2B hedge fund.

It is rare that retail traders will struggle to get their size on or off, with the exception of the largest retail traders or the tiniest microcap stocks or memecoins. This can be a big advantage. Try to use it. If you can find small inefficiencies in the market, and scoop up a few grand per day, you can make a nice living. Like a pilot fish orbiting a shark, a retail trader can collect the delicious crumbs that the big sharks are too big or lazy to eat.

Retail traders rarely have to worry about liquidity and this is a huge advantage. They can trade anything, whenever it's open, and never have to worry about liquidity. Yes, they need to worry about transaction costs, but they don't have to worry about being able to buy or sell when they want (or need) to. I have heard retail traders complain that if they only had a bigger account, they could succeed in trading. That is almost always false. It's like saying: **"I can't win this race on a jet ski... If only I had an aircraft carrier!"**

A larger account is more difficult to trade, especially now that almost every asset class has minis, fractional shares, or unlimited divisibility (crypto). The only time a small account is a handicap is if you need to make X amount of money and your account size is too small to do that. Generally, smaller accounts have more leverage, pay lower transaction costs, have more assets to choose from, and achieve higher percentage returns.

In contrast, when hedge funds grow larger than about $1 billion, the list of products they can trade slowly shrinks. Small caps and thinly-traded credits or many short-dated options (for example) become impossible to trade when you are a behemoth. As a retail trader, you can trade whatever you want.

Compare the liquidity of EWZ, the popular Brazil ETF (which is heavily traded by many institutions) and a ridiculously thin stock like DGNX.

EWZ 27.81 -0.24 (-0.86%)

Bid				Ask			
MM Name	Price	Size	Mn Trd Sz	MM Name	Price	Size	M
AMEX	27.80	200		AMEX	27.81	200	
ARCA	27.80	68,500		ARCA	27.81	74,400	
BATS	27.80	19,100		BATS	27.81	39,700	
BYX	27.80	2,000		BYX	27.81	500	
DRCTEDGE	27.80	4,500		DRCTEDGE	27.81	5,300	
EDGEA	27.80	700		EDGEA	27.81	6,300	
IEX	27.80	13,700		IEX	27.81	20,900	
MEMX	27.80	3,700		MEMX	27.81	15,400	
NSDQ	27.80	28,100		NSDQ	27.81	30,800	
NYSE	27.80	10,600		NYSE	27.81	15,400	
PEARL	27.80	12,400		NYSENAT	27.81	3,800	

DGNX 44.00 -2.50 (-5.38%)

Bid				Ask			
MM Name	Price	Size	Mn Trd Sz	MM Name	Price	Size	M
NSDQ	44.00	800		NSDQ	46.10	100	
BATS	43.83	100		BATS	46.28	100	
ARCA	43.25	100		ARCA	46.85	100	
EDGEA	43.12	100		EDGEA	47.03	100	
ETMM	43.12	100		ETMM	47.03	100	
DRCTEDGE	43.00	100		ETMM	48.41	100	
ARCA	42.50	100		NSDQ	48.55	100	
NSDQ	42.02	100		ARCA	49.16	100	
NSDQ	42.00	100		WBPX	49.22	100	
ETMM	41.80	100		ARCA	49.32	100	
NSDQ	41.50	300		WBPX	49.54	100	

EWZ is deep enough for 100 hedge funds to punt around at will, but no institutional trader could ever touch DGNX. Neither should you, but you get the point. As you move left to right on the spectrum towards greater account size, you move right to left on the spectrum of number of assets that you can trade.

Retail traders (usually) don't have a boss

This is a double-edged sword. One of the biggest advantages to working at a bank or a hedge fund is mentorship. As a retail trader, you don't have access to as much professional training or thoughtful leadership. You are on your own. You don't need to cater to the whims of fickle and often risk-averse managers, but you need to create your own strict set of rules and a rigorous risk management process: It's easier to do dumb stuff when you don't have a boss!

Successful retail traders think and trade like professionals

The institutional environment fosters growth, learning, and a more rules-based risk management and trading process. If you are trading on your own you need to find ways to emulate this. Think of trading as a serious profession, don't half-ass it and work three hours a day thinking you have it all figured out. If you think that, you are about to get smoked.

For retail traders, I believe there is a huge benefit to working in a trading office, not at home. You have people to learn from, share ideas with and share the pain with when things go wrong. A robust network of peers allows you to talk about specific trades, risk management and emotional highs and lows.

Build a strong network of trading peers, online or IRL. Learning takes longer if you have to figure everything out yourself.

Event trading

In the book *Unknown Market Wizards,* many of the interviewed traders specialize in event trading. The market is a fairly rational and efficient machine most of the time, but the most notable exceptions often coincide with the release of new information.

If markets were perfectly efficient and could instantaneously process new information, then when the U.S. jobs report came out, USDJPY would look like this:

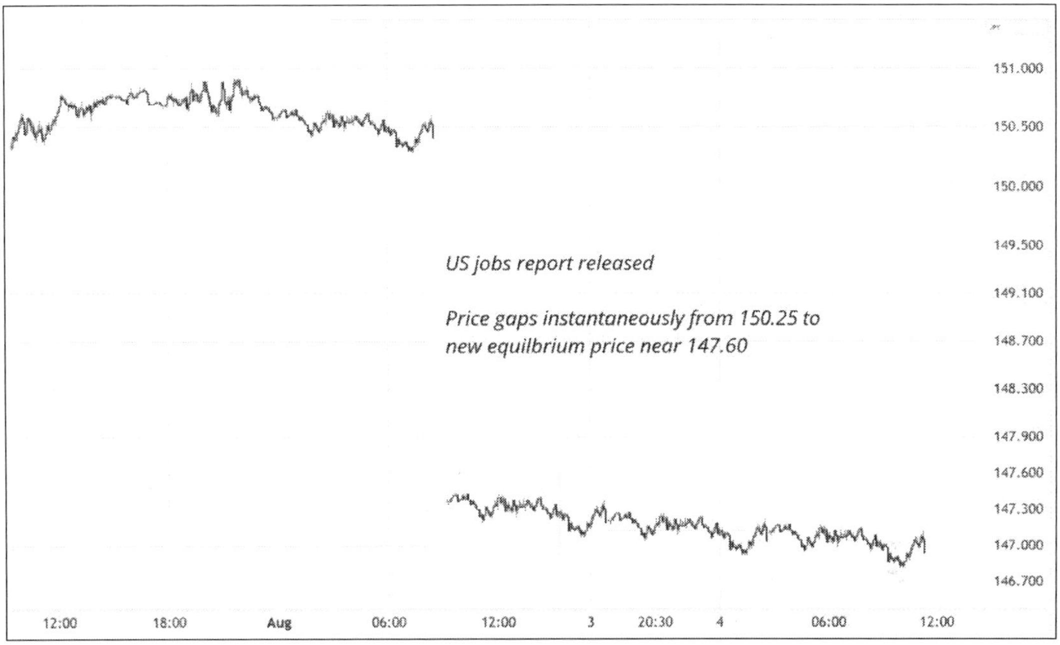

In real life it looks like this:

USDJPY 5-minute chart after nonfarm payrolls, August 2025

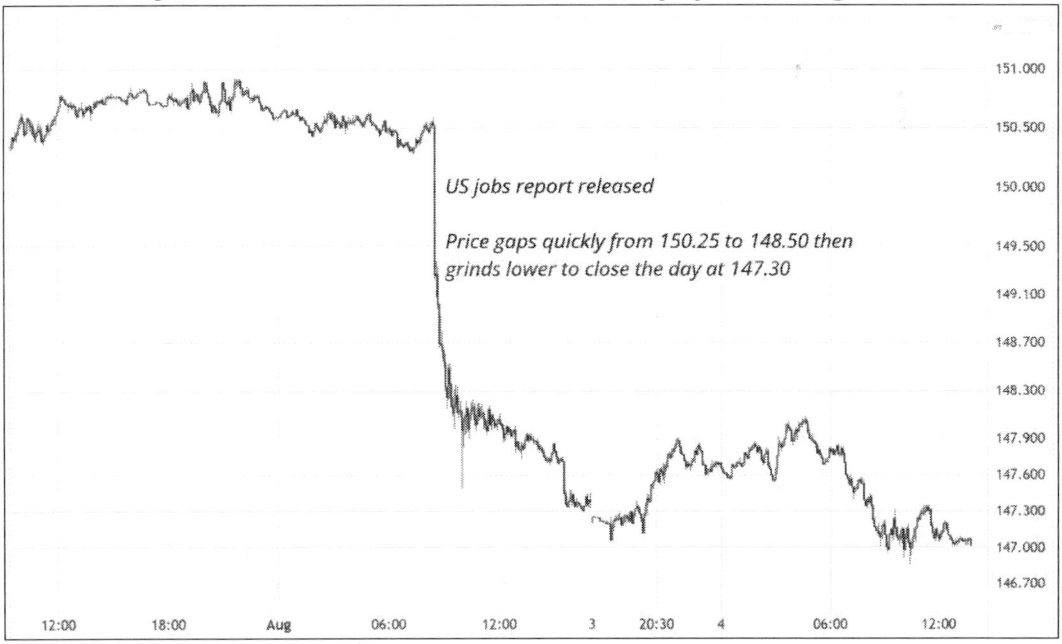

I am using USDJPY as my example here, because it's one of the most liquid and efficient markets in the world. Many stocks are much less efficient when they seek a new equilibrium after news.

Here's another example. The day the Liberation Day tariffs were announced, it was universally viewed as aggressively bearish USD and bearish for U.S. stocks. Here's how USDJPY traded in the hour after the announcement:

USDJPY 5-minute chart, April 2 and 3, 2025

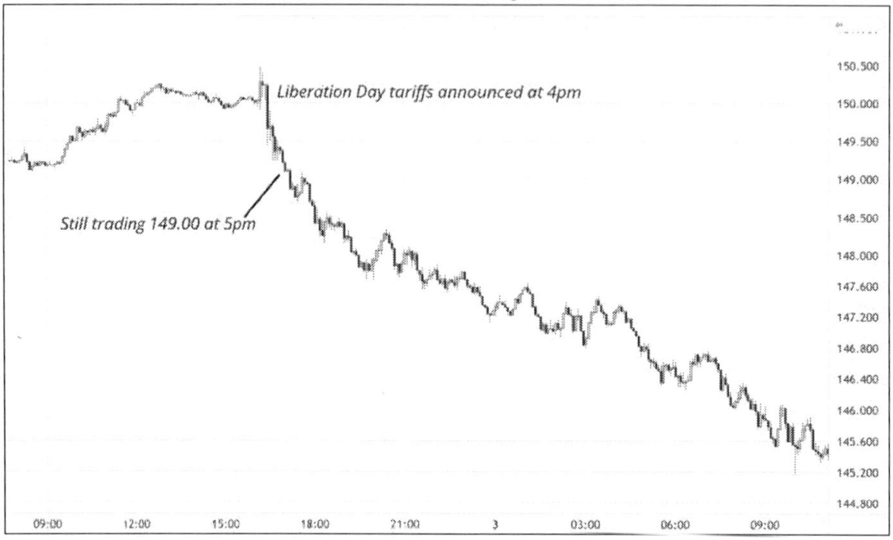

The interesting thing about this was that many of my clients pinged me around 5 p.m., with USDJPY still trading at 149.00, saying something like:

- "Wow, USDJPY trades well! I guess it's not going down!"
- "I guess it's too late to sell USDJPY, right? It's already down so much."
- "I can't believe I missed selling USDJPY!"

Then, USDJPY went another 400 points lower in a straight line. There are many reasons that markets don't instantaneously reprice to a new equilibrium including:

- Resting orders in the market that provide liquidity all the way up and down
- Differing opinions on the importance of the news
- Reluctance of speculators to buy high or sell low
- Time of day issues (Liberation Day tariffs were announced at 4 p.m., a time when many traders were not at the desk)
- Non-price-sensitive buyers and sellers that are using the news as liquidity to exit large positions
- Gamma, exotic options hedging, etc.

Prices don't adjust instantaneously! If something hasn't instantly sold off on bad news that doesn't mean you should go the other way or avoid selling it. There is all sorts of friction around price discovery and this makes event trading very profitable for those who know what they are doing.

To make serious money short-term trading around events, especially if you're trading a small or medium-sized pool of capital, you must check **all six** of these boxes:

- ☐ I understand the major variables responsible for the current equilibrium and what news might move price away from that equilibrium
- ☐ I can quickly read and interpret news and understand likely price impact
- ☐ I can act quickly and with high confidence
- ☐ I can judge whether liquidity will be sufficient to get out of the chosen position size if the view is wrong
- ☐ I have the courage to take meaningful risk in fast markets (periods of high volatility and high uncertainty)
- ☐ I can admit quickly when I'm wrong and exit losing positions without hesitation

If any one of these is a "no", then event trading is probably not for you. Also note that due to capacity and liquidity constraints, event trading is much easier and relatively more profitable for traders with smaller accounts. You can't trade 500 million USDJPY back and forth on news very easily, but you can trade 500 shares of SRPT back and forth on every headline as many times as you like.

How to trade events is a topic that could fill an entire book, but here are a few tips:

Study past events

Determine how securities reacted to beats, misses in earnings and other announcements. You will learn this from experience, but you can also look at history for guidance. For example, if you trade a lot of NVDA, spend an afternoon looking at how much the stock moved on various news days, and how fast. Get a sense of what logic the price follows as it moves towards equilibrium. Get a sense of when you might want to fade an earnings-day move. The better you understand the reaction function of your security to past news, the better you will have a good feel when you're trading in the zone after the next headline.

Know the catalysts in advance and be prepared to act

If you trade USDJPY, for example, and don't know the historical and probable price impact of a two-standard-deviation miss in nonfarm payrolls, you are not ready to trade that event. Look at historical data to calculate how much your security normally moves on economic data, earnings, etc.

Maintain a list of possible headlines and plan your reaction to them

Once you have researched past events and analyzed how a security reacts to them, keep a list of future headlines and a plan for each.

In August 2025, for example, I knew that if Bolsonaro endorsed Tarcísio de Freitas for President of Brazil, that would be a massively bullish event for Brazil and for EWZ (the Brazil ETF). This news could have come out any day at any time, or never. But whether it did or not, I was ready.

My plan was to immediately buy 50,000 EWZ on the headline, risking 70 cents or $35,000. My plan was flexible. If the headline came out, I would be a strong and fast buyer of EWZ because I already knew exactly what I was going to do and didn't have to think about position sizing, whether to go nuts or be conservative, or anything else. I would just execute my plan as fast as possible.

Preparing for low-probability (but possible) events can be the difference between success and failure. When China devalued the yuan in 2015, traders who were ready for it reacted quickly with confidence. Those who hadn't really considered the scenario of a Chinese deval were caught flat-footed.

Make a list of headlines that might be major market movers and know exactly what you plan to do if they come out.

Understand the three ways to make money trading market events

Your plan for a headline event might include some, all or none of these:

1. **Trade the runup.** Known events often make a predictable runup as the event approaches. *The runup trade* is explained in *Alpha Trader*. I find the runup trade to be a profitable approach as you analyze positioning and other factors ahead of an event and predict how people will trade as the event nears. For example, if the market is heavily short bonds and the chatter for an upcoming jobs report is biased to the weak side, you will often see short covering and aggressive bond buying in the days leading up to the report. Predicting what human beings will do in the runup to an event is often easier than predicting the outcome of the event itself.

2. **Predict the result of the event.** As mentioned, this can be extremely difficult because events like earnings and economic data are sliced and diced 1,000 ways by 10,000 professionals before they are released. Still, there can be predictable biases such as anchoring in market forecasts and I have a suite of models I use to try to *outpredict the predictors* of economic events.

3. **Trade the aftermath.** Going into an event flat with no bias and trading the outcome is often a profitable approach. Price does not instantly move to its new equilibrium, so you

can often make money buying a stock on an earnings beat and guidance raise, for example, if you're quick and confident in your analysis. There is also money to be made fading overreactions to events, especially when you have a good handle on historical reaction functions and positioning going in.

Create automated trading systems

This requires more technical sophistication but can be enormously profitable over time and can deliver very high returns with an exceptional Sharpe ratio.

Make sure your sizing is appropriate!

Trade size must adapt to volatility, so be sure you are not trading too big around events. If you are used to using finger-in-the-air sizing and you trade 1,000 shares of AAPL on a regular day, you are going to get *rekt* trading 1,000 shares of AAPL fifteen seconds after earnings. This is especially true because after-hours trading is thin and does not allow for automated stop losses.

Know the technical levels

Be aware of the technical levels that matter. Even if you're trading a random tech stock after hours, that stock will often respect major technical levels post-event. Knowing where the big levels are can let you leave limit orders nearby that will allow you to exit into the panicky overshoot.

Write down your stop loss

Immediately after you get into a position post-news, write your stop loss as a note to yourself. In fast markets, it can be incredibly useful to have a Post-It Note staring at you with an established stop loss level. It will help you avoid falling into the trap where you go long a stock, the price evaporates, and you have no exit plan so you sit there frozen watching the huge red P&L number on your screen grow and grow. If I enter a trade on a random headline, I always write my stop loss down on my pad immediately. This forces me to pick a stop loss level and forces my conscious mind to acknowledge the stop level I have chosen as it nears (while my subconscious mind is probably telling me to double down!)

Risk management is critical when trading events because news and catalysts lead to fast markets with high volatility and spotty liquidity. You need to know exactly when and how you are going to get out if you are wrong. You will be wrong quite often!

The process whereby the invisible hand takes price from a starting point to a new price level after a news event can be choppy, iterative, and exciting. Professionals with quick minds and quick fingers can make a career just trading events.

Career risk, rationality and EMH

One of the primary assumptions that drive market theories like the Efficient Markets Hypothesis (EMH) is that human beings behave rationally, in aggregate. Do they? Most of the time, but not *all* the time.

One major reason you often see herding and overshoots in markets is that an unwritten rule of the game is that a huge percentage of market professionals are not actually optimizing for the highest absolute returns. They are optimizing for the lowest amount of career risk or "looking stupid" risk. This can create opportunities for those that act more rationally.

Imagine a well-known technology fund manager who is on TV all the time preaching the upside of the latest technological revolution. She is known as a bull and has ridden the innovation and disruptor wave higher and higher, generating large returns for her investors. Now, imagine she thinks everything has overshot. All the stocks she owns are overvalued. Does she exit everything and get short? Or does she stick to the bull view, keep going on TV, and hope for the best?

It might feel much riskier for her to pivot, even if she believes it's rational, because even if she's somewhat confident of a coming bear market, she obviously doesn't know for sure. She has to make the determination:

> If I am wrong about being bearish? What is the cost to my career?
>
> What if I stay bullish and I'm wrong? My whole brand is built around my bullish view on disruption. My whole identity is built around my bullish view on technology.

She might correctly surmise that the optimal choice is to stay bullish and hope for the best because her chops as a bearish stock picker are not in demand, whereas her position as a tech boom permabull is well established and could remain unscathed by a bear market.

Similarly, a long-time bond bull might realize that if he turns bearish bonds, or bullish on the economy, he is going to lose more subscribers than he'll gain. While it's intellectually dishonest, it might be the best strategy for him to just stay bullish bonds and keep looking for that recession the way true believers look for Bigfoot. This can manifest consciously or subconsciously. People that are well known for a particular view have considerable trouble changing that view. Their switching costs are extremely high. They are literally getting paid to have a particular view through appearance fees, social media subscribers and views, and podcast listens. It's a branding issue more than an intellectual flexibility issue. Make sure you know the bias of the "gurus" you follow.

This applies to managers more generally too, because many are focused on how to remain employed and avoid looking stupid. This is human nature. If you can be wrong in one direction and keep your job, but if you're wrong in the other direction, you'll be fired—your incentives warp your views.

The **need to avoid looking stupid** forces many into trades that they don't really love. If technology is hot and you're a long-only manager who benchmarks against the S&P, a huge percentage of your portfolio needs to be in tech, or you will underperform. If you are a Danish pension fund manager and the MSCI World Index is 72% USA, you will look stupid if you GDP-weight your equity portfolio and underperform for 10 years straight.

During the Eurozone crisis, career risk was a huge, obvious driver of widening bond spreads and the lower euro. Let's say you are a European bond trader at a large investment fund and it's 2011. There is blood in the streets and Italian yields have gone from 3% to 6%. You own a ton of Italian bonds.

Thing is, you think things are about to turn. You think the ECB is about to intervene and buy up all the bonds and send yields back down to 3.5%. Then again, you know if Italy leaves the euro, it's going to look bad. Most of your friends that trade Italian bonds are getting out or are already out. Your investors will ask why you ignored such an obvious risk.

> "It was literally on the front page of every newspaper! How could you not see this coming?"

Your wife just delivered your third child, your oldest kid goes to a private school that costs $50,000/year, and you just upsized to a 5,400 square foot, 3-acre Modern Farmhouse style mansion in Westport, Connecticut. Maybe it would be better to just plug your nose and sell the stinking Italian bonds? If the bonds rally, that will suck. But you'll still have a job. If Italy defaults, you will get fired. Once framed this way, the decision becomes pretty easy for most people. They will do the "rational" thing, *not* the rational thing.

Herding is often caused by fear related to career risk. Going against the herd often feels riskier than following along. Doing the opposite of what everyone else is doing is hard! It goes directly against human nature.

Most people also react strongly to incentives, especially those involving self-preservation, so instead of solving for: "How can I make my investors the most money?" they solve for: "What will give me the best chance of keeping my job?" Even if they are not doing this consciously, there is a good chance their subconscious is influencing them.

Focusing too much on career risk makes you a worse investor and trader, and it's a source of herding and negative edge. Focusing on markets and making rational decisions in the context of the primary game (maximizing profit) not the metagame (minimizing the risk of getting fired) is a positive edge.

The calendar metagame

Finally, the metagame around calendar year end is strange, complex and often irrational. Hedge fund managers who have made a ton of cash want to book their gains. Those who are behind benchmark don't want to make things worse. Many traders and investors are on vacation so markets often experience lower liquidity and less volatility. Speculators who are fully engaged have an edge in December simply because so many of their competitors are risk averse or asleep at the wheel.

Average VIX Level by Month, 2010 to 2025

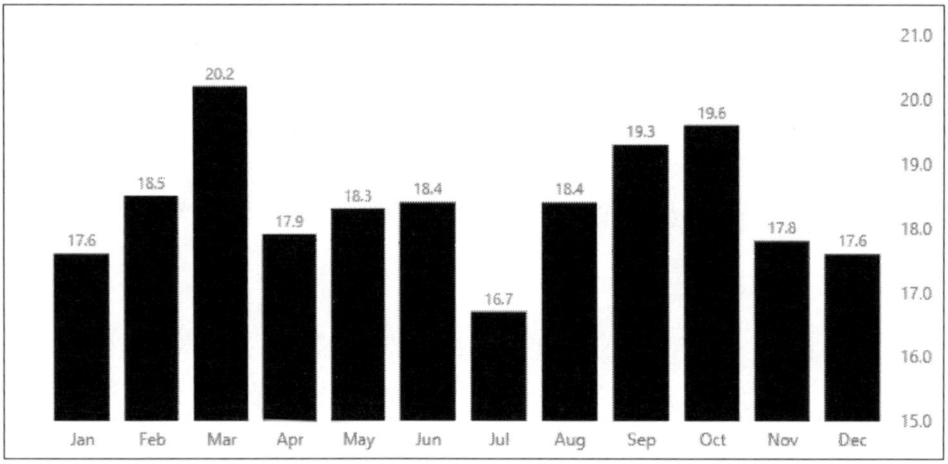

I once worked at a bank where fiscal year-end was October, and this was a competitive advantage. Our risk appetite was strong in December when the opportunity set and dislocations were plentiful.

Stay engaged in December and look for anomalies caused by non-price-sensitive flows. There are often incredible opportunities in beaten-down small caps and currency markets as year-end hedging dominates and markets overshoot because they are too illiquid to absorb large flows in one direction. I have caught some amazing moves in EURCHF, EURSEK and USDJPY around the turn of the year by simply watching for wacky disconnects and taking the other side once the dust settled by midday on December 31.

Conclusion

Trade ideas, risk management, a good process, creative thinking, and rational behavior will get you far, but not all the way to trading and investing success. The often-overlooked aspects of the game within the game will get you over the finish line.

CHAPTER 8

SHORT SELLING, THE HARDEST GAME OF ALL

The Metagame, Part Two

"Short sellers are the market's real-time financial detectives."

Jim Chanos

"You can't sell houses you don't own. You can't sell cars you don't own. But you can sell stock you don't own!? This is BS – shorting is a scam."

Elon Musk

Short selling is the hardest game to play, and many careers have been wasted or extinguished going for glory on the short side. Every aspect of the short selling game is rigged against you. Math, convexity, risk management, politics, and long-term trend all argue against short selling. Yet I still do it all the time. If you are going to short stocks, go in with eyes wide open.

Short selling is ludicrously difficult.

When it's time to choose what game you want to play in financial markets, think very long and hard before you decide to be a short seller.

The math of short selling

Shorting stocks is by definition more difficult than trading from the long side. While the stock market is not the economy, they both tend to grow over time. Positive nominal GDP growth most often leads to positive stock market appreciation in developed economies. Because economic growth and prices tend to gradually go up and to the right over time, stock markets do too.

Here are a log and a linear chart of the S&P 500 from 1928 to now. Note that this is just the index price and does not include dividends!

S&P 500, linear and log, 1928 to 2025

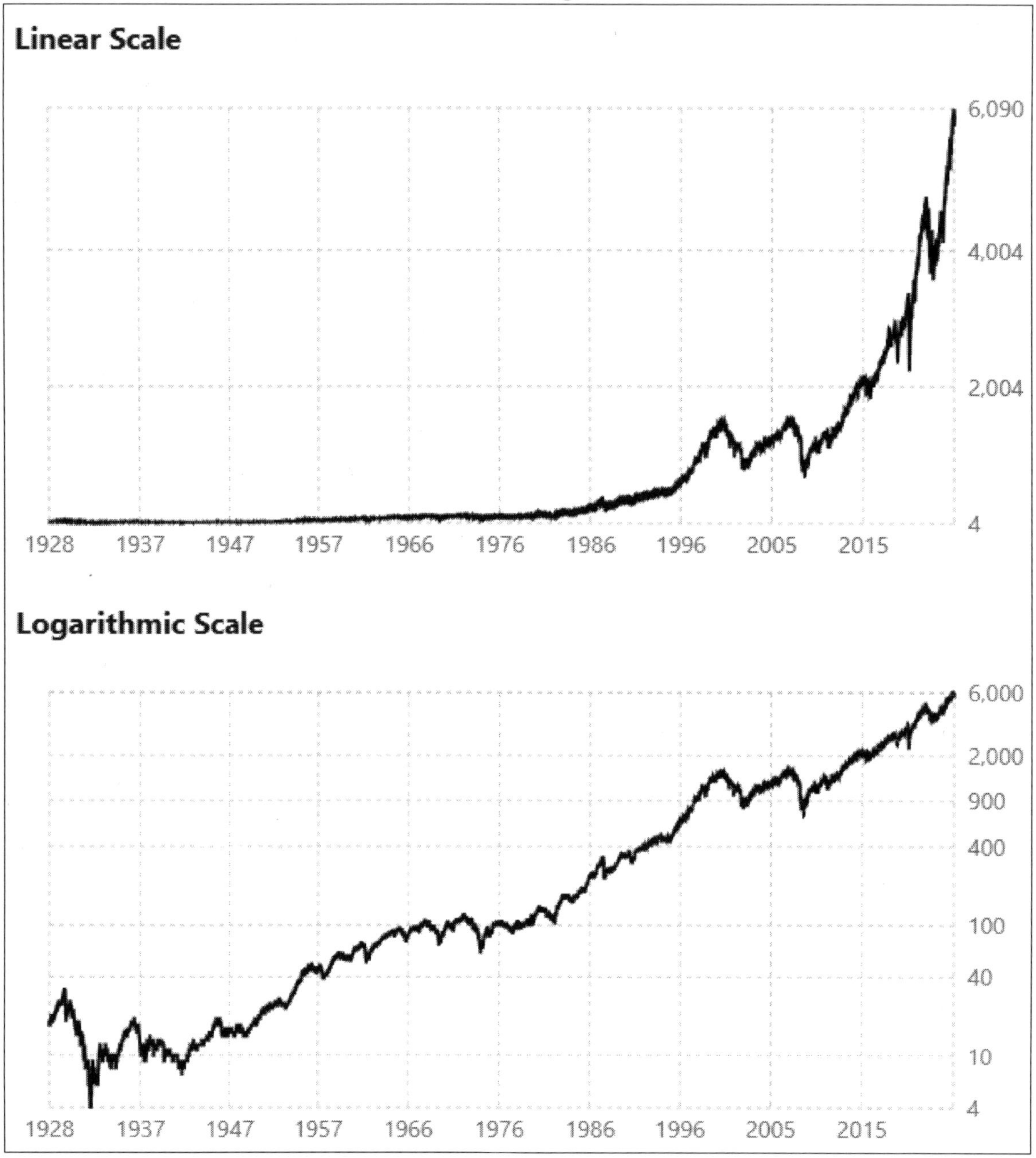

If we compare this to nominal GDP growth, they obviously both trend in the same direction.

U.S. GDP, linear and log, 1928 to 2023

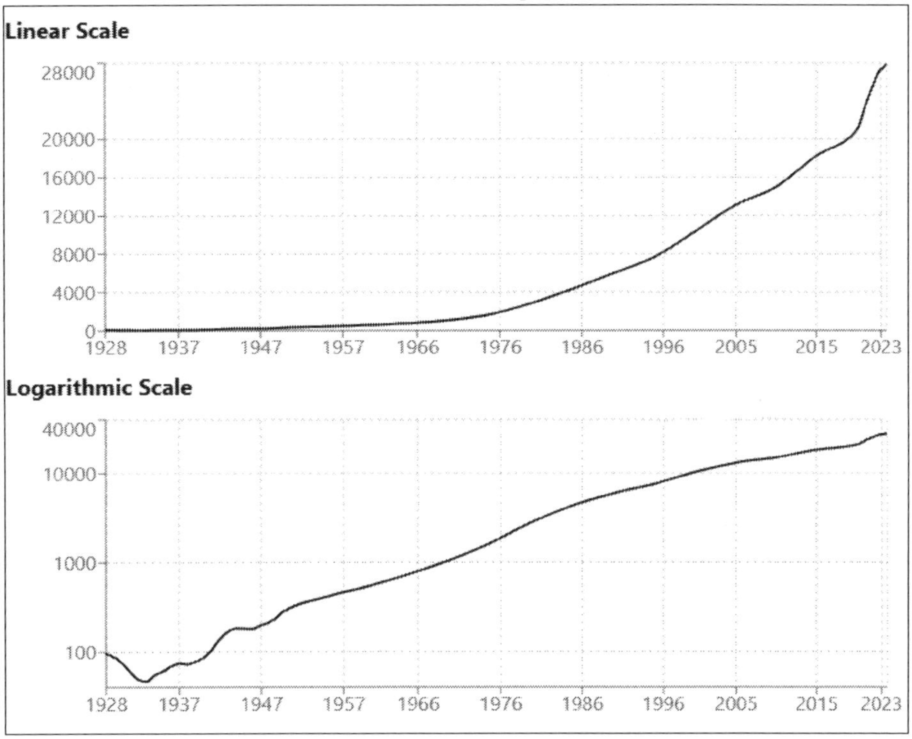

The stock market does not track the economy perfectly, but if you are betting against the stock market, you are **betting against the primary long-term trend**. **That's strike one.**

Strike two comes from the asymmetric and convex mathematical nature of equity returns, especially in single names[47]. Stocks can go up an infinite percentage, but they can only go down 100%. If you're short, you can **make 100% or lose infinity**. If you're *long* you can **lose 100% or make infinity**. If you repeat this process enough, you will find that losing infinity is an extremely unattractive proposition. 😊

What's worse, if you short a stock and it rises, your position gets bigger. For example, if you employ $1,000 of capital and go short 200 shares of a stock at $5 and it goes to $20, you now have a loss of $3,000 and $4,000 of gross exposure. *Yuck*. From there, further percentage gains become exponentially more devastating as the stock rises.

In contrast, if you do the opposite, and buy 50 shares of a stock at $20 (again employing $1,000 of capital) and the stock falls to $5, you have lost $750 and you now have gross exposure of just $250. Your exposure *disappears* as you lose money, in contrast to the short where the more you lose, the bigger your exposure gets.

[47] "Single names" refers to trading the stock of one company. MSTR and AAPL are single names.

Change in position size and P&L on longs and shorts (200 shares at $5)

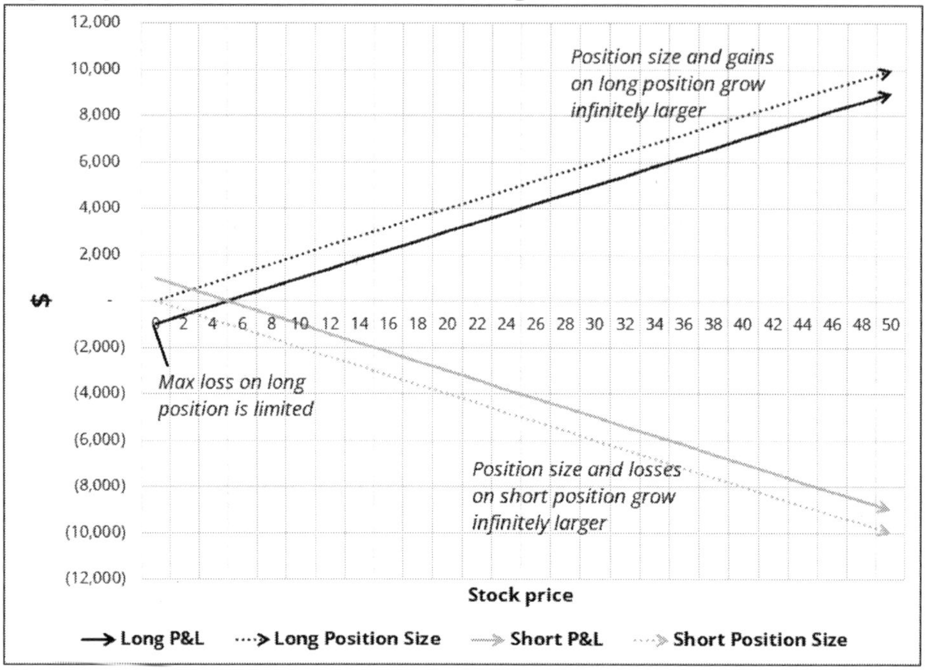

The loss on the short position can grow much, much larger than the maximum loss on the long. Longs naturally disappear as they lose money and shorts naturally balloon. Shorts are more difficult to risk manage and are more likely to blow you up than longs.

In an extreme case like GameStop, which went $5 to $480 in 2021, your chart looks like this:

GME short position size (dotted line) and P&L (solid line)

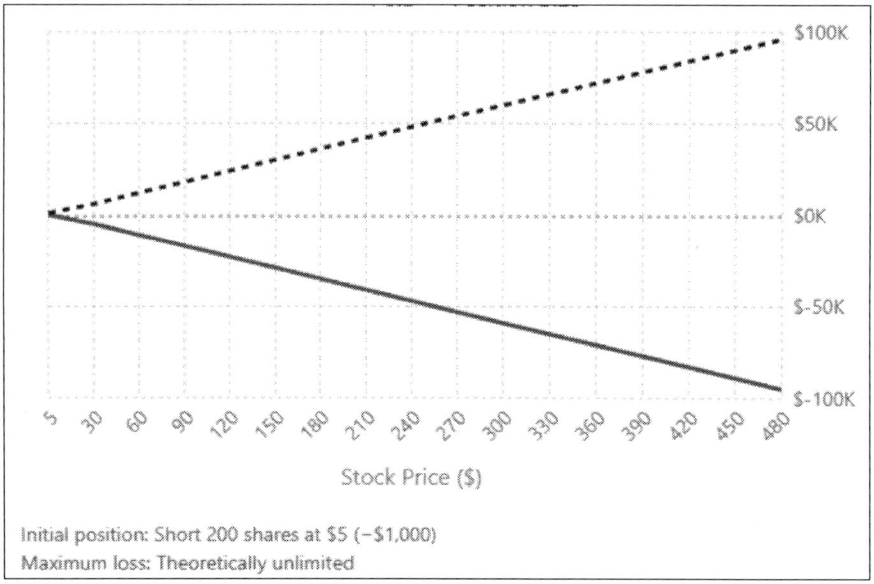

You had $1,000 of capital and lost almost $100,000. Horrible. While naturally traders will try to cut their losses before such an extreme move, it's not always possible to exit during a short squeeze because of bad liquidity, mental tilt, and/or emotional devastation.

As the bitcoin maxis say: **it's just math**. But in this case, it *actually is* just math. For real. Stocks tend to go up, and when they squeeze, you're dead.

To look at a realistic situation in the recent past, imagine two traders. One goes long Beyond Meat (BYND) on October 8th, 2025, and one goes short. A few weeks later, there was an epic r/wallstreetbets raid as the market squeezed BYND from penny stock land up to nearly $8. Here's the chart.

BYND Hourly, October 5 to November 22

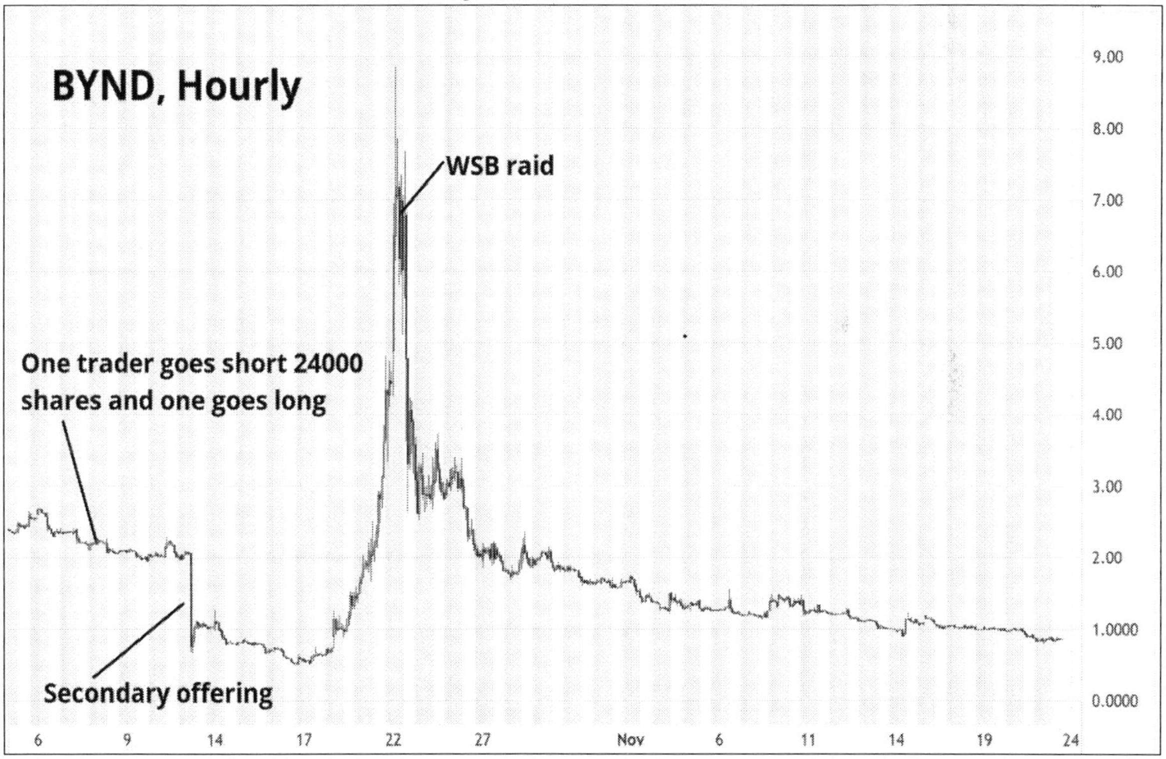

The two traders have similar account sizes. One shorted $50,000 worth of the stock at $2.08 and the other went long the same amount at the same price. Here are the two P&Ls.

P&L of long or short 24,000 shares of BYND October/November 2025

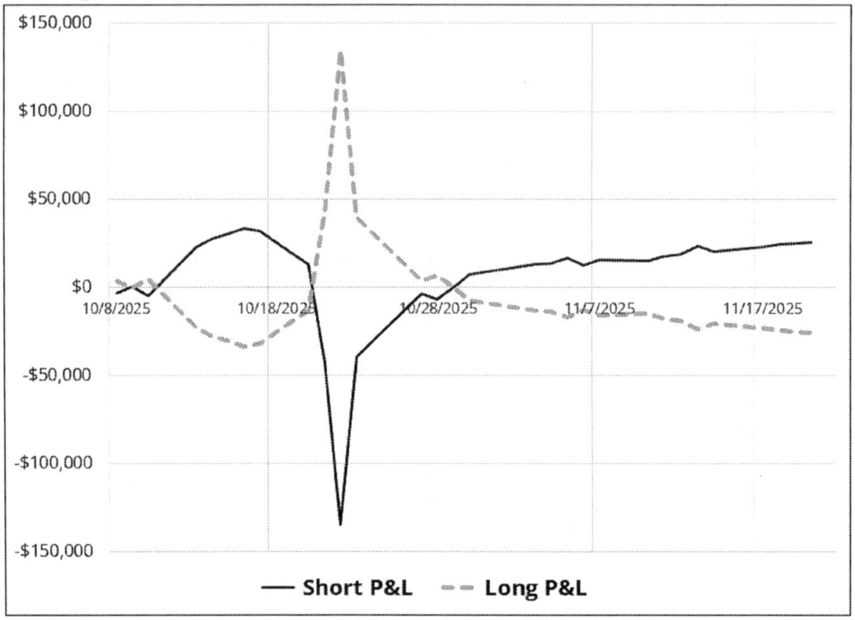

Note when the secondary offering happened and the stock collapsed, the long trader was down $40,000 or so. Bad, but not catastrophic. The dude who went short is wearing a loss of more than $130,000 about two weeks in. In the end, the short wins, and collects $25,000—in theory. But he had to survive a monster drawdown and avoid a margin call, or a panic buy as the thing was skyrocketing to who knows where. That's strike two against shorting: **horrendous convexity**.

And here's **strike three**. Shorting is costly and difficult because:

- You can't always borrow the shares you want to sell. There can be some adverse selection here because the juiciest shorts are the hardest to borrow.
- You are charged any dividends distributed by the company while you are short.
- You pay a fee to borrow and short a stock. These fees can be low, or they can be exorbitant. For example, if you short $10,000 worth of Exxon Mobil (XOM) for a year and it goes nowhere, you pay a tiny 0.25% borrow fee plus $360 of dividends and end with around $9,638. If you are long and it goes nowhere, you end the year with $10,360. This differential adds up. And XOM is an easy and cheap-to-borrow stock. There are stocks that cost >100% per year to borrow!
- Many adverse events can blow up shorts, including takeovers, buybacks, regulatory approvals for biotechs, and so on. While there are events that can help you too, those events are going to make you 100% at most (e.g., a surprise bankruptcy announcement) while adverse events can cost you much more.

Shorting indexes is tough because they have positive drift. Shorting individual stocks is tough because they have negative convexity. And you pay a fee to be short stocks, while you earn dividends when you're long. It all adds up to a fiendishly difficult enterprise for the short seller.

On top of all this, the politics and history of short selling also conspire against you.

The politics and history of short selling

Short sellers are sometimes viewed as predatory and cynical: a destabilizing cadre of pessimists who prey on misfortune. While this is mostly untrue, it doesn't matter. If you are a short seller, the authorities are going to make your life difficult. For example, during panics, governments will often ban short selling to help stock prices stabilize.

Authorities use regulatory and legal action to go after short sellers. Running a high-profile short selling business is fraught with legal and public relations issues and over the last 10 years most famous short sellers have shut down either because of bad returns or regulatory and criminal indictment risks. Short sellers are often viewed as anti-patriotic and opportunistic in a way that equity longs never are. I think this is grossly unfair, but it doesn't really matter what I think because it's not going to change.

Meanwhile, the track record of most short sellers is not good. This should be evident when you examine the frequency and scale of stock market downturns. For every ten shorts that caught the crashes of 1929, or 1987, or 2001, or 2008, or 2020, there are probably eight or nine who were destroyed on the subsequent rebounds. Crashes, bear markets, and recessions are the exception over the last 100 years. It is possible to profit from them, but your timing on entry and exit need to be superhuman.

When you see an expert introduced as "the man who predicted the 2008 crash" or something similar, ask the question: Did he also predict a crash in 2009, 2010, 2011, 2012, and so on? Most of them did.

Even Jesse Livermore, who caught the Crash of 1929 from the short side and became one of the world's richest men because of it, was bankrupt ten years later. Not many shorts get long-term rich, even if they make great names for themselves after periodic violent downturns. Don't be a permabull, but don't get sucked into the mainstream media or social media doom and gloom stories. They will cost you a fortune.

Shorting is a useful, opportunistic, and tactical trading and hedging approach. It should be hit and run most of the time. Shorting is seldom a good long-term strategy. The negative convexity and high cost of shorting eventually catches up with the best of the bears, often even when their thesis is right!

For every Enron, there are five Carvanas:

Enron stock, 1985 to 2002

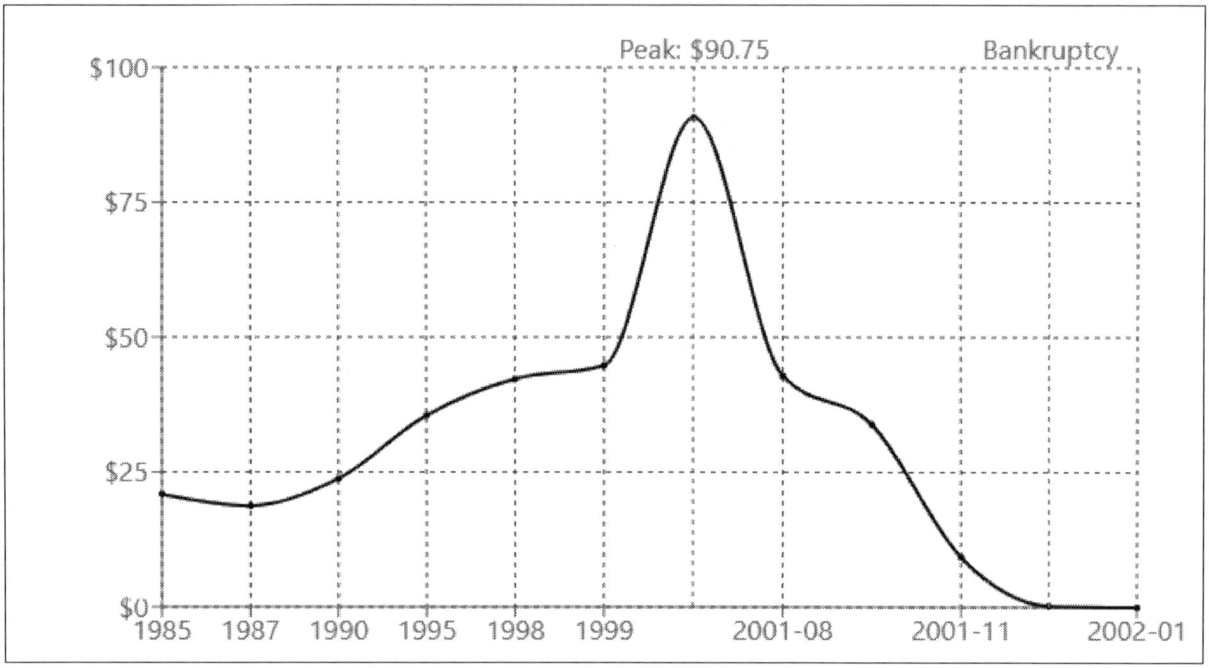

Carvana stock, 2020 to 2025

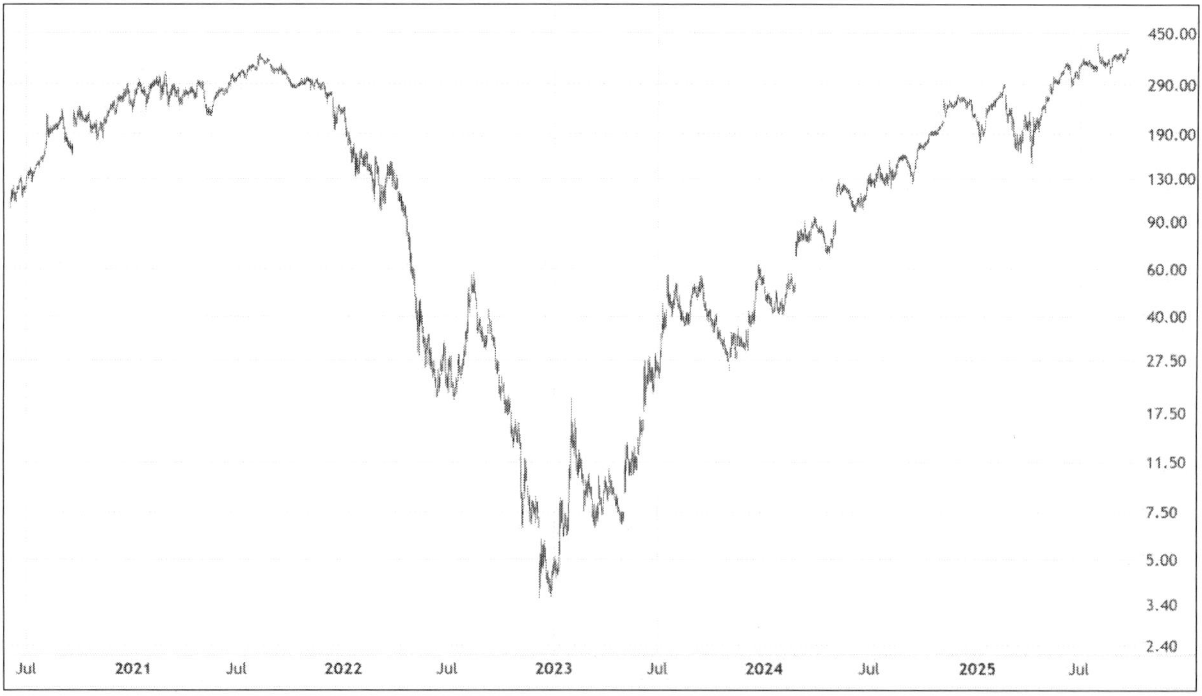

The problem is: short selling is hard and expensive, and buying puts is easy—and even more expensive. There are always natural sellers of calls, but there are fewer natural sellers of puts and therefore puts tend to be extremely expensive. There is no easy way to be short. Whether you short outright, or via options, you have to be right; and you have to be right quick.

To be clear, I am not against shorting—I short stocks all the time. But I am careful and selective and tactical about it. Besides outright shorting and buying puts, there are other good bearish strategies you can employ, as we will discuss in Chapter 10.

Conclusion

Short selling is hard. Many short sellers who are smarter than you or me have come and gone over the years. While the few successful short sellers acquire folk hero status, most burn out or fade away. Short selling is a legitimate trading strategy when it's tactical and properly risk managed, but a horrible state of mind to adopt full time.

PART THREE: FRAMEWORKS

Introduction

If you are comparing Tesla's market cap to Ford's, or stock market valuation to GDP, you are playing the game wrong or you are playing the wrong game. One of the biggest leaks in trading and investing is the use of frameworks that are useless, irrelevant or obsolete.

Before you can make money trading or investing, you need thorough knowledge of what makes your market move. In Part Three, we look at both faulty and solid frameworks for trading and investing and why some frameworks are useful and others are not.

Analysts in ivory towers poring over theoretical frameworks often come down to the real world and get wiped out slowly, or immediately. Most theoretical finance literature offers fun, clean, mathematically-satisfying explanations of how markets work. But most of those explanations don't help predict where markets are going.

Street smart traders and investors who use practical frameworks and adapt as markets evolve will outperform high-IQ booksmart peeps who rely on faulty or purely academic tools. The most intelligent, erudite, and intellectually satisfying explanations for why markets *should* move a particular direction are often the most dangerous.

In Part Three we'll discuss both faulty and useful trading frameworks, decision-making, self-auditing and historical record-keeping, moving averages, seasonality and other practical trading topics, then we'll delve into the fuzzier side with subjects like ethics, courage, reputation and self-awareness.

Let's get into it.

CHAPTER 9

NINE WAYS TO SOUND SMART AND LOSE MONEY

Discounted cash flow analysis will not help you trade memecoins

"Beware of geeks bearing formulas."

Warren Buffett

Fundamental analysis is difficult because there are so many different ways to analyze so many different data sets, and there are thousands of competitors out there all doing the same thing. You can have the smartest people in the world, and the best data sets, and still lose money because your theoretical frameworks do not explain what's happening in the real world. Wrong frameworks give you wrong answers.

Imagine a devoted Wall Street analyst employs a team of assistants who diligently take detailed photographs of the left elbow of every cashier at every Walmart (WMT) location in the United States. He uses proprietary satellite data to track the number of garbage pickups at Walmart over the course of three years. And he has accurate data on the average age of every customer that goes in and out of the store. He uses these variables in a complex three-factor model to predict the direction of WMT stock price. Surprisingly, his predictions are not good.

Maybe he is looking at the wrong variables?

While this example sounds stupid (because it is), it's not so different from less-blatant examples like:

- using Tesla car deliveries to predict the path of Tesla stock
- using Bank of Japan policy to predict the 6-month outlook for USDJPY
- a currency strategist who uses purchasing power parity to predict the future path of the Swiss franc.

These sound more logical than the silly Walmart example, and that's what makes them even more dangerous!

Smart-sounding but useless frameworks are common on Wall Street and if you want to trade or invest successfully, you need to recognize them. Then, you need to plug your ears and close your eyes before they infect your mind. Let's focus on some of the *wrong* ways people analyze markets, then we will take a more positive tack and look at useful / practical frameworks in Chapter 10.

Here are nine commonly used, mostly unprofitable ways to analyze and forecast markets.

1. Time horizon mismatch and valuation
2. Overreliance on models
3. One trick pony
4. Disregard for mental capital
5. Single variable analysis
6. Bad breadth is bearish
7. Underestimating or ignoring gap risk
8. Don't fight the Fed
9. Fading Jim Cramer

Faulty Framework #1: Time horizon mismatch

In the mid-2000s, when I was still newish to writing about markets, I would often send out a writeup full of interesting, coherent analysis along with a trade idea that featured a badly mismatched time horizon. I would write a big piece about Australian Terms of Trade and the employment situation in Australia and so on... And then go long AUDUSD with a stop loss 1% away. My analysis was suitable for a 1-month or 1-year trade, but my trade idea was mega short-term and my stop loss was barely more than one day's range away.

When trading (and investing), **your time horizon must match your analysis**. Don't analyze the demographics of India, decide you are bullish the Indian stock market, then buy 1-month calls! That's a time horizon mismatch. Don't buy two week puts on PLTR because its price/sales ratio is too high. Both are time horizon mismatches.

People spend way too much time on analysis that is borderline irrelevant or dangerously distracting. Know your trading or investing time horizon and construct hypotheses that will play out within that time horizon. Then structure your trades to match.

Have you seen a graphic like this one?

Market Cap vs. Revenue for the Major Automakers, June 2025

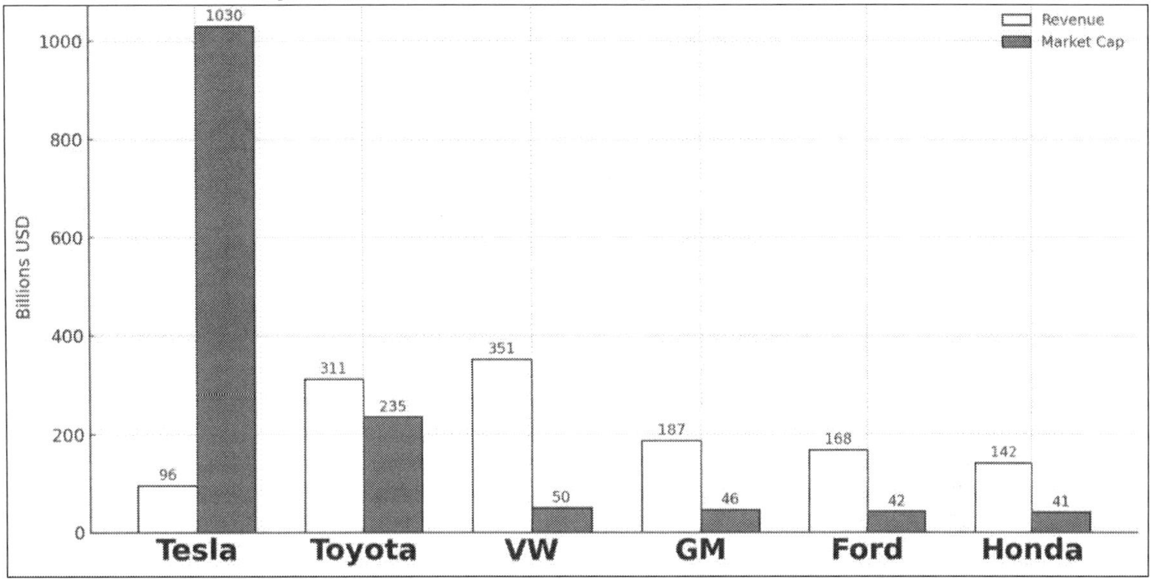

The implication is that Tesla is grossly overvalued because the stock trades at an insane revenue multiple compared to its peers. This next chart plots Bloomberg stories containing both "Tesla" and "overvalued" (vertical bars) along with Tesla's stock price (wavy line).

Bloomberg stories about TSLA overvaluation (black bars) vs. TSLA stock price (gray line, left y-axis)

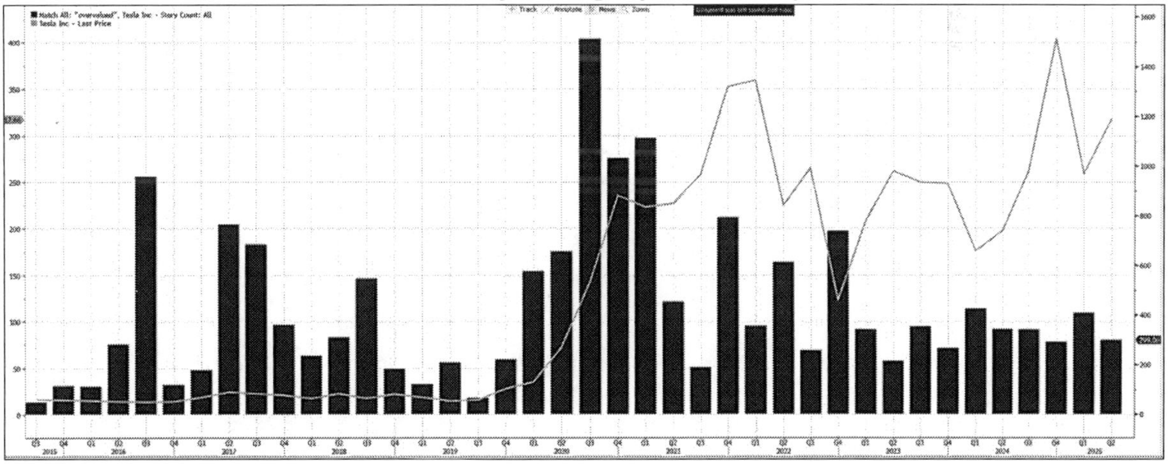

A basic discounted cash flow (DCF) valuation, price/sales ratio or any other metric would have told you that Tesla stock was consistently overvalued from 2016 to 2025. And people have been trying to short it the whole time!

There were feverish outcries about TSLA valuation in 2016 at $15, in 2017 at $30, and in 2020 at $140. And yet the stock kept powering higher and has spent the past few years averaging $300 or so. People could be excused for arguing it was overvalued based on traditional metrics in 2016, but those saying it's overvalued based on the same metrics ten years later are showing a distinct inability to adjust their framework.

This doesn't mean you should never be short TSLA, and it definitely does not mean you should always be long. One can argue that in the long run, valuation will matter for TSLA, but this logic would have kept you short the stock from 2016 to 2025, and you'd still be short today. By the time your framework is correct, you're bankrupt.

Even if you have a 50-year time horizon, there is no world where you can make money staying short a stock that goes up 20x in 2 years and then stays up there for 5+ years. Abandon intellectual arguments and make predictions and forecasts that match a realistic time frame for your trading or investing.

Principle 18: Match your analysis to your trading time frame.

To be clear: It is pointless to say that Tesla is always a buy, no matter what the valuation. We need to find an explanation for why the stock goes up and down. If you don't understand why it moves, you can't forecast its future movements. This should be obvious, yet it's a common mistake.

We discussed this in Chapter 6: Good forecasts require sound foundations. Some will argue that Tesla is more than a car company; it's a technology company and its potential is predicated on self-driving cars, autonomous robots, and maybe a merger with SpaceX and xAI. This is a better framework, but the first one is always too bearish, and this framework will always be max bullish. You want a framework that is pragmatic, probabilistic, and agnostic, not rigid, dogmatic, theoretical, or deterministic.

Principle 19:
Elite traders are pragmatic, probabilistic, and agnostic.

If your framework always points the same way for an asset or security, it's not flexible or adaptive enough. It might work if you have an unlimited time horizon and no stop loss, but that's not trading or investing the way I think of those things—that's just buy and hold (or short and pray).

So, what is a better way to understand and attempt to forecast the price of Tesla?

I think of Tesla stock as a retail sentiment barometer/liquidity sponge. There is a huge constituency of retail traders and investors who love to put excess cash into Tesla stock. This is similar to the way crypto is a retail sentiment barometer. In fact, if you overlay Ethereum and TSLA, you get a good fit. And that makes sense.

TSLA and ETH, late 2024 to mid-2025

The ups and downs of TSLA and ETH matched throughout late 2024 and all of 2025, despite the many, many company-specific things going on at TSLA. Their CEO was crowned as the President's right hand man (bullish), there was a massive backlash against Musk and the company's global car deliveries collapsed (bearish), there was a strong push by the U.S. government to help Tesla shares rebound (bullish) and finally Elon Musk and Donald Trump angrily parted ways (bearish). None of those events had anything to do with Ethereum, and yet the cryptocurrency showed the way for TSLA throughout that 9-month period.

This is not a coincidence or overfitting; it's a reflection of the fact that waves of retail money flow into and out of meme stocks and cryptocurrencies at the same time. Whether TSLA earnings and deliveries are up, down, or sideways doesn't matter much to those with a HODL mindset. They buy when they have extra money and sell when they lose confidence in bullish markets or need to raise cash.

There are other ways to look at TSLA stock, but none of them involves comparisons with other car companies.

Tesla is one of many examples where you will see traders operate with a framework that is clearly disconnected from reality. In the world of FX, you will often be treated to 20-page write-ups on currency valuation, current account balances, NIIP, REER, terms of trade, and any number of variables that are sometimes applicable and sometimes totally irrelevant to why currencies go up and down.

Whether you are focused on PLTR's price/sales ratio, or the valuation of the Swiss franc, you are doing something akin to adding up the shoe sizes of every player on a rugby team and then trying to use that number to predict the outcome of the next match.

Before you can predict a market, you need to understand how it works. What drives the price in real life? What variables matter some of the time, but not all the time? In other words: What makes your market go up and down? This is an absurdly simple question and one that you can clearly see hasn't been given much thought by some traders, investors, and strategists.

Knowing which variables matter (and which variables don't) is one of the most important and overlooked skills in finance.

Forecasting the price of TSLA by using a DCF model is a bit like forecasting a recession by watching for yield curve inversions. You need an infinite time horizon and no stop loss, and you are still not guaranteed to ever be correct. Let's talk a bit about the yield curve inversion recession signal. It's another great example of smart-sounding analysis that does not match any useful trading or investing time horizon.

As of November 2025, the U.S. yield curve inverted 37 months ago. People started calling for a U.S. recession because of the inverted yield curve in October 2022. Imagine sitting there long bonds or short stocks all that time.

This is the longest inversion without a recession since 1966, and it's a nice reminder that yield curve inversion works very well in hindsight but is not a useful tool in real life. In fact, the "inverted yield curve predicts recession" meme has been one of the costliest truths in finance in three of the last four cycles. The only one where it nailed the recession was COVID, and we have to put an asterisk by that one.

Yield curve inversion is only a useful predictor of recession in hindsight

Inversion date (3m/10y)	Recession start date	Months elapsed
10/27/2022		37
3/22/2019	2/29/2020	11
1/18/2006	12/31/2007	24
9/18/1998	3/31/2001	31
3/28/1989	7/31/1990	16
10/27/1980	7/31/1981	9
11/1/1978	1/31/1980	15
6/1/1973	11/30/1973	6
9/8/1966	12/1/1969	39

Indicators like DCF and yield curve inversion take too long to play out and have no relevance to almost any trading or investing time horizon. They are worse than useless because if you pay attention to them, you are forever waiting for Godot.

The idea that long-term valuations matter is one of the most pervasive, dangerous, and costly frameworks in finance. Not because valuation doesn't matter, but because it will usually *not matter* for so long that it doesn't really matter if it ever eventually matters (!) because you will be bankrupt before it matters.

You can't mix one analysis time horizon with a different trading or investing time horizon. You can't invest in Indian stocks because of demographics and then get out two years later because the trade isn't working. Demographics are slow, generational shifts that take decades to develop. Similarly, you can't trade or invest on most meaningful time horizons using long-term valuation metrics. **If you want to make money in markets, stay away from long-term valuation models**.

As discussed, stocks like TSLA can stay overvalued relative to peers or discounted cash flow estimates for 10+ years. Or forever. There are currencies like CHF that have been "overvalued" for 20 years.

The Swiss franc is always overvalued!

In that chart, you can see that by 2019, most equilibrium models were still telling us the franc was massively overvalued. Then it rallied another 15% from there.

% Deviation of Swiss franc Effective Exchange Rate from its Equilibrium Value

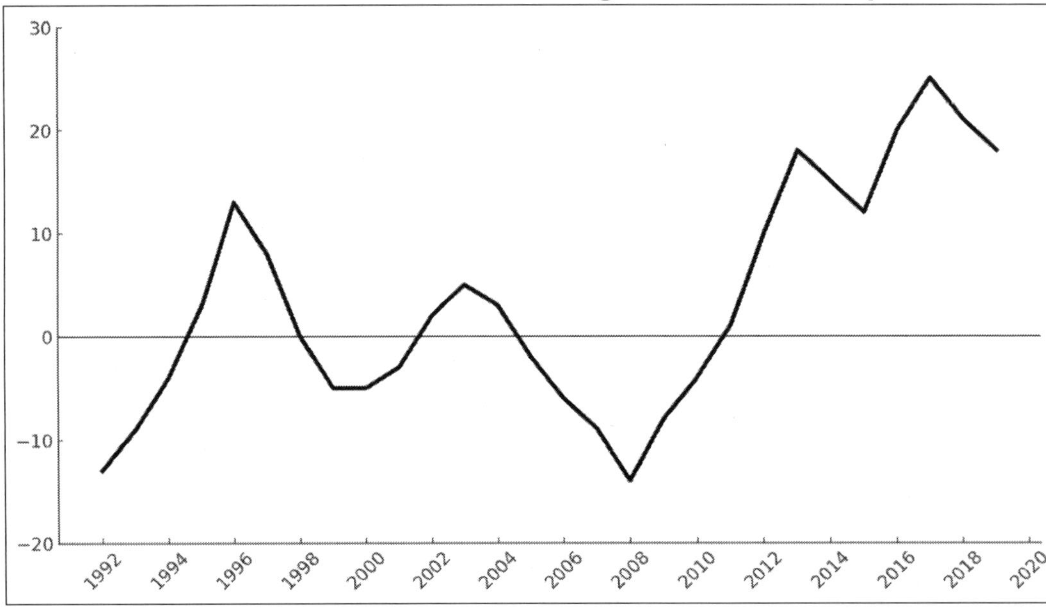

Data from OECD

The biggest issue with long-term valuation models is that their output barely changes over time and therefore they can keep you anchored on a losing view for years and years. Valuation measures are only useful for very long-term investors who have high confidence in the accuracy of their valuation models. That's probably not you.

Another popular long-term valuation method that has been a terrible framework for forecasting stocks is called "The Buffett Indicator." While Warren Buffett tried to disassociate himself from the indicator because of its obvious oversimplification of a complex system, as of 2025 many still point to it as a reason to be bearish stocks.

The Buffett Indicator divides the total value of U.S. equity market capitalization by GDP. The theory is that the stock market roughly constitutes the present value of all future U.S. economic activity, while GDP represents the current value of economic activity and therefore there should be some kind of relationship between the two. So, you will see headlines like these, all the way up during a bull market:

The Buffett Indicator: Often popular, never useful

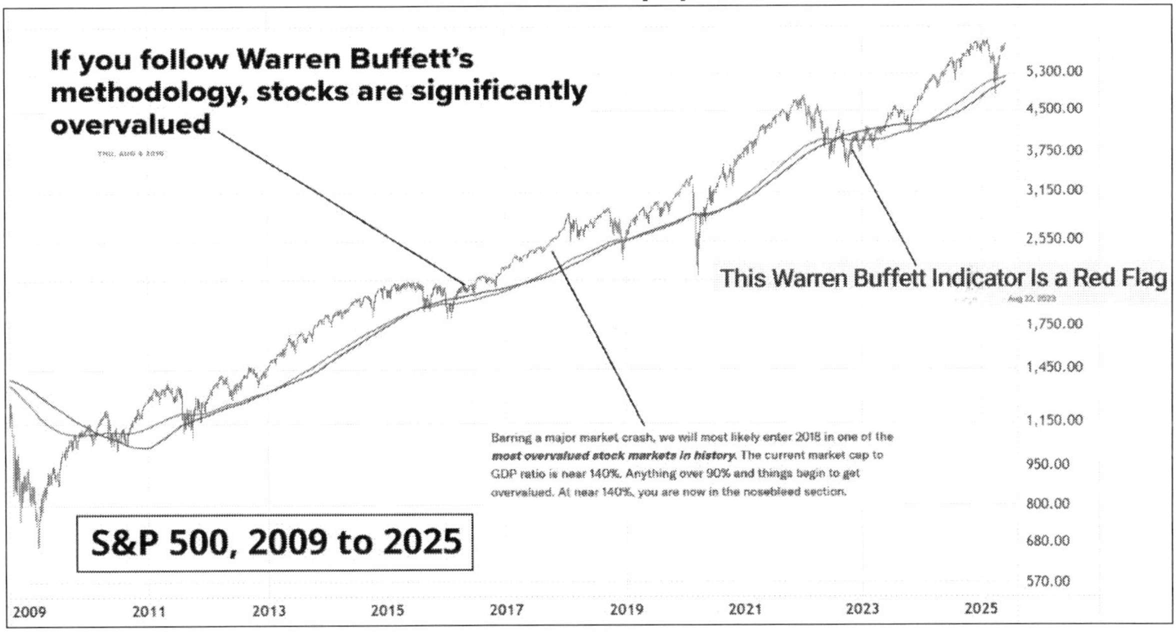

This is an excellent example of a long-term valuation indicator repeatedly leading people astray. It's amazing to me that even in 2025, after more than 10 years of touting the indicator as a bearish red flag, some analysts and journalists still see it as a concern. At some point, you have to throw out the garbage indicators.

There is a reason this indicator is useless: It fails to capture profit margins. Imagine if GDP was steady, but U.S. companies became much, much more efficient at generating profit per unit of GDP? Presumably, stock market valuations would go up, even with GDP unchanged.

That is: If profitability rises, the ratio of the stock market to GDP should rise. Stocks are not necessarily overvalued, they simply reflect increased profit margins (a better ability to extract more profit from a given unit of GDP).

If you look at corporate profitability over time, you will see that it mostly goes up and down with the Buffett Indicator.

The Buffett Indicator ebbs and flows with U.S. corporate profit margins

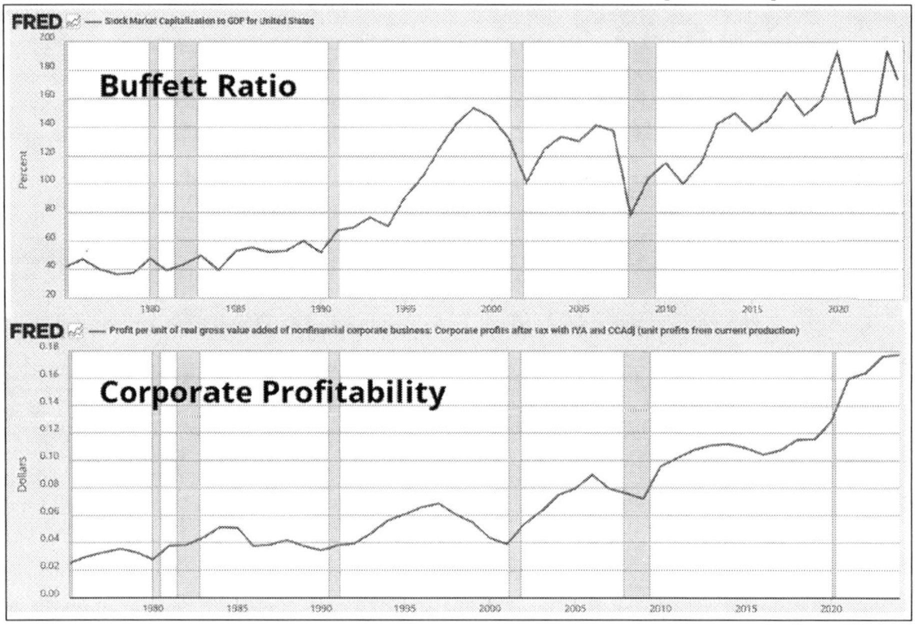

Even if we had a perfect model for valuing stocks or whatever asset we trade, remember that real markets don't move tick-for-tick with fair value. They are driven by fear, greed, flows, and random noise that can all push a market away from its "logical" level. The real world looks more like this:

Theoretical look at how an asset price and fair value might change over time

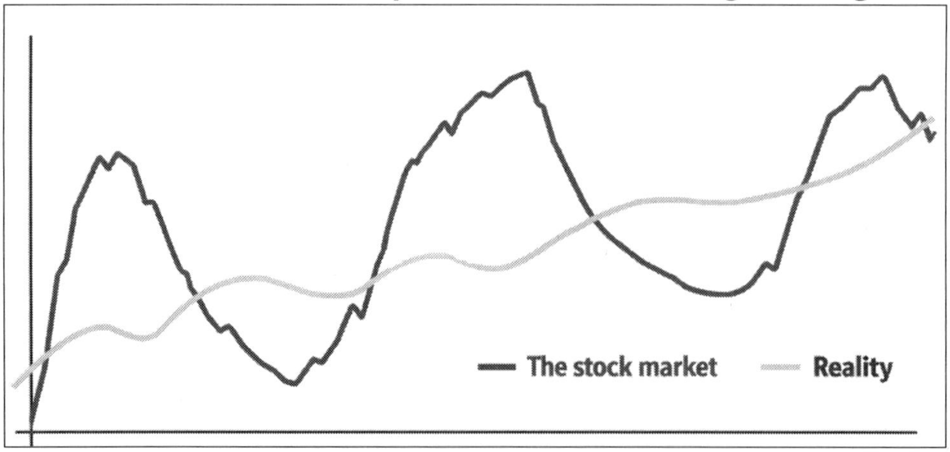

That graphic is an optimistic view of how things play out because sometimes fair value (reality) goes one way, and the price of the asset goes the opposite way. There is no law of finance that says price has to revert to your favorite measure of fair value. Maybe your measure is wrong. Maybe your framework is wrong.

> "In the short run the market is a voting machine. In the long run, it is a weighing machine."

This quote, attributed to Ben Graham by Warren Buffett, is useful. It means that the market oscillates above and below long-run equilibrium (fair value) because speculators and their emotional trading decisions drive short-term price action. In the long run, fundamentals matter. But then again:

> "The long run is a misleading guide to current affairs. In the long run we are all dead."
>
> John Maynard Keynes, 1923

This concept of market time or behavioral time should not be underestimated. It is one of the greatest gaps between theory and practice in finance. This excerpt from Cory Hoffstein's *15 Ideas, Frameworks, and Lessons from 15 Years*[48] explains it nicely.

> **Behavioral Time is decades longer than Statistical Time**
>
> I recently stole this one from Cliff Asness. This point has less to do with any practical portfolio construction thoughts or useful mental models. It's just simply acknowledging that managing money in real life is very, very, very different than managing money in a research environment.
>
> It is easy, in a backtest, to look at the multi-year drawdown of a low-Sharpe strategy and say, "I could live through that." When it's a multi-decade simulation, a few years looks like a small blip—just a statistical eventuality on the path. You live that multi-year drawdown in just a few seconds in your head as your eye wanders the equity curve from the bottom left to the upper right.
>
> In the real world, however, a multi-year drawdown feels like a multi-decade drawdown. Saying, "this performance is within standard confidence bands for a strategy given our expected Sharpe ratio and we cannot find any evidence that our process is broken," is little comfort to those who have

[48] blog.thinknewfound.com/2023/08/15-ideas-frameworks-and-lessons-from-15-years/

allocated to you. Clients will ask you for attribution. Clients will ask you whether you've considered X explanation or Y. Sales will come screeching to a halt. Clients will redeem.

For anyone considering a career in managing money, it is important to get comfortable living in behavioral time.

Returning to the subject of fair value and fundamentals. This next chart shows the Shiller Cyclically Adjusted Price-Earnings ratio over the last 145 years. Stocks oscillate loosely around a fair value of approximately 17.5 times earnings.

Shiller CAPE, 1872 to 2025

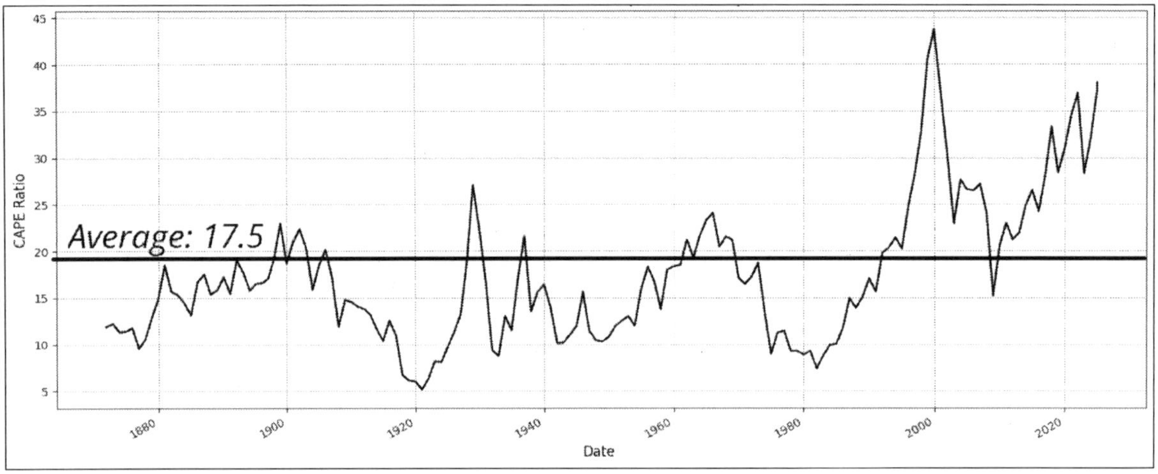

The *weighing machine* tries to keep stocks anchored to earnings, but the voting machine can keep stocks beaten down and cheap (e.g., 1970 to 1985) or ebullient and overpriced (e.g., 1929, 2000, 2021).

If you are a big valuation guy (or gal), and you only to go long stocks when the market P/E is below its historical average; you have been out of the market since, umm… 1993 or so? The S&P 500 is up 1,000% since then. You missed quite a rally.

It's worth mentioning here: While long-term valuation is a red herring, **there are short-term valuation methods that are useful**.

A simple long/short equity model, for example, might tell you that if American Airlines moves 5% lower today, JetBlue is more likely to go lower than higher over the next 10 days. A more sophisticated short-term fair value model for an airline stock might include the price of competing airlines, the price of crude oil and jet fuel, and the overall demand for tourism over the last six months. That's a valuation model that would align more closely with a trading or investment strategy. Discounted cash flow models, on the other hand, require a nearly infinite horizon.

Again, to be clear: A huge chunk of the successful systematic trading community uses short-term fair value models. I am not saying fair value models are bad. I am saying your model (and analysis) needs to match your trading time horizon.

We will discuss useful short-term models and many other strong frameworks in the next chapter. For now, just know that you are better off thinking about stocks as tokens reflecting the current narrative and popularity of the company, not accurate representations of fair value as determined by discounted cash flows.

Faulty framework #2: Overreliance on models

In Chapter 3, we talked about how economists rely too much on models, creating predictable forecast errors. When you see persistent errors like the ones made by economists forecasting the U.S. jobs market in 2021/2022, it suggests they are using the wrong framework. If you have a better-adapted approach, you may be able to predict where forecasts will be wrong and profit from it.

Models and other applications of big data are, by their nature, reliant on history. They take reams of historical data and use it to make predictions. This can lead to huge failures in predictions and risk management when there is a regime change because old data doesn't fit an unprecedented regime.

You saw this in 1998 and again in 2008 as risk models relied on assumptions that proved false when the world started to blow up. You saw it again in 2023 to a lesser extent, as many hedge funds made assumptions about how much U.S. interest rates could move—and rates moved much more than they ever had before. In all three cases, there was a flurry of hedge fund blowups as risk management systems with false premises allowed portfolio managers to take way too much risk.

Combining models with human judgment has repeatedly been shown to offer better predictions and superior risk management than models alone. Human beings should use data-driven models, but we should also use experience, intuition, and subjective information—and data not accessible to the models. Combining models and judgment was important in the past but has become even more vital with the advent of artificial intelligence (AI). AI generates output that cannot be explained or understood by the user. AI is a black box. Black boxes are trained on past data and the future does not always conform to the same patterns.

Some of the best opportunities in event forecasting come when you have a strong view that the standard models used by market practitioners are likely to be wrong. During regime shifts, this is often the case and the direction in which the models will err is predictable.

Rely on data, but do not defer exclusively to numbers. Use common sense, experience, stories, and logic to look for gaps in the models and to assess why past performance may not predict future results. Models work well in stable regimes, and less well across a regime shift.

Human judgment and pattern recognition is often very good at boiling down a problem to its essence. A nice paper by Brighton and Gigerenzer[49] captures the idea of why less is often more and pure rationality does not require infinite complexity. Here's the abstract:

> Heuristics are efficient cognitive processes that ignore information. In contrast to the widely held view that less processing reduces accuracy, the study of heuristics shows that less information, computation, and time can in fact improve accuracy. We discuss some of the major progress made so far, focusing on the discovery of less-is-more effects and the study of the ecological rationality of heuristics which examines in which environments a given strategy succeeds or fails, and why. Homo heuristicus has a biased mind and ignores part of the available information, yet a biased mind can handle uncertainty more efficiently and robustly than an unbiased mind relying on more resource intensive and general-purpose processing strategies.

They offer a great example:

> Consider how a baseball outfielder catches a ball. The view of cognition favoring omniscience and omnipotence suggests that complex problems are solved with complex mental algorithms. Richard Dawkins[50], for example, argues that "He behaves as if he had solved a set of differential equations in predicting the trajectory of the ball. At some subconscious level, something functionally equivalent to the mathematical calculations is going on". Dawkins carefully inserts "as if" to indicate that he is not quite sure whether brains actually perform these computations. And there is indeed no evidence that brains do.

[49] "Homo Heuristicus: Less-is-More Effects in Adaptive Cognition", Brighton and Gigerenzer (2012)

[50] Side note: Dawkins coined the word "meme" and was first to discuss the concept

> Instead, experiments have shown that players rely on several heuristics. The gaze heuristic is the simplest one and works if the ball is already high up in the air: Fix your gaze on the ball, start running, and adjust your running speed so that the angle of gaze remains constant. A player who relies on the gaze heuristic can ignore all causal variables necessary to compute the trajectory of the ball–the initial distance, velocity, angle, air resistance, speed and direction of wind, and spin, among others. By paying attention to only one variable, the player will end up where the ball comes down without computing the exact spot. The same heuristic is also used by animal species for catching prey and for intercepting potential mates. In pursuit and predation, bats, birds, and dragonflies maintain a constant optical angle between themselves and their prey, as do dogs when catching a Frisbee.

Finding a simple way to explain a phenomenon, whether it's why a market is moving, or how a baseball outfielder is moving, can allow you to ignore many more complicated details. The gaze heuristic is used in conjunction with one or two other simple rules (e.g. walls are solid, another player may be closer), allowing the outfielder to track down the ball without any complex physics calculations.

The point here is that you need to find the sweet spot. One variable is rarely enough. But too much information will expose you to too much noise and lead to overfitting, wasted time, confusion, and analysis paralysis.

Faulty framework #3: The one trick pony

If you have been in finance for a while, you may have noticed that there is an industry of economists and content providers whose exclusive mission is to go through the millions of economic data points in the U.S. and point out *only* the ones that predict recession. Yes, it can be profitable for them to predict a recession every single year. But it's not profitable for you to follow them. Yes, recessions happen. But if someone is perennially predicting a recession, they are an intellectual one trick pony.

Many traders fall into a similar trap by specializing in one style of trading. While it's great to be an expert in a particular market, it's not as useful to be an expert in a particular trading style. Trading styles do not work across all market regimes. Breakout trading works in some vol environments and not in others. Short-term correlation lead/lag trading worked for years then stopped working. Selling vol works; until it doesn't.

Here's a good example of this one trick pony problem from my career, and how I solved it. When I was running the spot desk at a commercial bank in the 2010s, my manager criticized us for always buying options.

"Your business is implicitly long vol, so why are you always *buying* options?"

In other words, when volatility is high, market making desks tend to be profitable because the franchise is busy, clients are active, and flows are plentiful. When volatility is low and markets are quiet, the franchise dies down and the business struggles. So when we bought options, we were adding to the long volatility risk of the franchise without truly understanding what we were doing.

At this point, the idea of *selling* options had never even entered my mind. I thought it was just the domain of professional options desks and suckers who are inevitably gonna blow up.

After some study and brainstorming, I started to sell volatility using structures with limited downside. This was a good idea. This way, when the market was dead, I was earning money on my short vol trades and when things got busy, my short vol trades might lose, but our franchise was rolling. When there was a great opportunity to buy options for leverage, we did so with eyes wide open, knowing we were doubling down on our desk's implicit long vol bias.

Similarly, traders that work at hedge funds are often biased to buy volatility when they should do the opposite if their P&L is positively correlated to vol. A good directional macro trader with a long carry book on the side will often realize a better Sharpe ratio than the one without the carry book because carry is implicitly short volatility while directional macro is implicitly long.

Expertise in one asset class with diversified strategies in that area of expertise is less regime dependent. If you need VIX above 30 to make money because most of your trading involves breakouts and fast moves, you are going to go through epic periods of pain when the VIX bobs around 14. Have some other strategy running in the background. For example, a systematic strategy, a discretionary short vol or long carry strategy, trend following strategy, etc.

Don't be amazing in a specific regime but barely able to survive all others. Markets change. A stationary time series has a constant mean and variance over time. But most market data and economic data are nonstationary. They evolve. Regimes can shift overnight. This is why models that worked for an extended period often fail suddenly without warning. Volatility rises. Correlations flip. Behavior mutates.

Be more of a Swiss army knife and less of a one trick pony.

This holds true for those who love to sell volatility, too! Unless your mandate is specifically to be short vol all the time, keep a flexible mindset. If you tend to lean long emerging markets carry or long stocks, for example, develop a suite of signals or a personal edge in determining when to reduce, eliminate, or reverse the position. Some of the best traders I have worked with run long carry and short vol ten months of the year but flip long vol and short risky assets for two months as they either have a quantitative early warning system or a good Spidey sense for when things are turning.

Great traders don't pigeonhole themselves and say, "I'm a great trader in a crisis," or "I do best when stocks are going up." Great traders adapt to shifting regimes and understand how to make money in different conditions.

Ask yourself:

1. Is my trading style correlated to volatility? If so, can I find systematic or discretionary strategies to add to my main style that might diversify my returns when my preferred volatility regime is not in force?
2. Is my edge concentrated in one regime-specific approach? If I am good at buying 0DTE options, will this strategy still work when the VIX is at 40 and implied volatility triples?
3. Do I complain about the regime or how "the market sucks"? If so, I need to find a more adaptable overall strategy. Just because I can make money trading breakouts in a crisis or positioning short gamma / long vol in FX does not mean I will make money in the long run. How does my strategy perform in various regimes? Collect data and compare it to market measures of volatility, dispersion, and trend.
4. Am I constantly thinking about new tactics and strategies that I can layer onto my existing approach? The thing I am doing today will be discovered by the invisible hand and arbitraged away over time. Trading headlines used to be a high-Sharpe, high returns approach, but then the algos took most of that over; trading commodity prices vs. FX correlation used to be a high-Sharpe, high returns approach but then terms of trade lost its relationship to FX. The more profitable my strategy, the more likely someone else will discover it. Keep stacking new ideas on top of old ones. When the old ones stop working, the new ones will pay the bills.

Faulty framework #4: Disregard for mental capital

Mental capital is an important, underappreciated and finite resource. Much as you only have so much financial capital or time in a day, you also have a limited supply of mental capital. You can only devote mental energy to so many ideas and trades in one day, and if a trade sucks up too much mental capital, it can exert a negative influence on you, even if it makes money.

A trade that consumes tremendous mental capital is one that:

- goes on for a long time
- requires significant attention day-to-day, and/or
- creates stress due to difficult risk management

A large short position in a small cap biotech stock with poor liquidity could do nothing for two weeks and still consume enormous mental capital because you are on edge, worried that their flagship drug will get surprise approval and the stock could 5X in one day. This sort of trade could be mathematically positive EV but be so mentally taxing that even when it works, it has cost you more than you earned. Trades like this are also often mismanaged because the moment the trade starts to work (or not work) you are tempted to square up prematurely to relieve yourself of the mental anguish it's causing.

Another mentally draining approach is having a strong bias in a particular market that you can't overcome. If you are bearish Palantir stock because of its high valuation, and you short it a few times, then stop out, then it sells off 10%, you will feel sad. If it rallies another 30%, you think that it's *even more overvalued* and you want to short it again. This can lead to situations where **you feel like you are at war with a market or security.** When that happens, take a step back. Notice how you feel.

Can you just let it go? Can you put Palantir in the "too hard" bucket for a while? When I am battling with a security like this and getting frustrated, I will first square up any position I have in that security and then I will write down a clear plan. *On a piece of paper.* The plan could be simple, like: *I will not trade PLTR for the next three months. Look again on August 15.* Or it could be more complicated, something like:

> I am getting frustrated with PLTR, and I don't want it to sap all my energy. But! I really think it's going lower soon because it's so overvalued and other meme stocks and cryptocurrencies are all 10% lower in the past two weeks. PLTR looks vulnerable. I don't want to spend every day for the next two weeks white knuckling this stupid stock, so I will take a smaller position than usual with a wide stop and I will spend 2% of my capital on a 1-month 25-delta put spread. Once I put these trades on, **I will not touch PLTR again until my put spread expires.**

I print that, cut it out, and put that piece of paper on my desk, under my monitor. If you do all this and *still* can't stop trading Palantir, you need to work on your discipline with a coach or therapist. *For real.*

Most stocks, bonds, currencies and commodities have lifespans measured in years or decades or centuries. It is vanishingly rare that you will short a stock at $12, it declares bankruptcy two days later and the stock is cancelled, and you pocket the twelve bucks. Mostly, markets are a never-ending sea of waves, and you are just trying ride some of those waves to the promised land.

If you can create ways to make your trades finite instead of infinite, that can help preserve mental capital. For example, a trade like this is good for your mental capital.

> Nonfarm payrolls come out next Friday and I think the bond market is going to run higher into the release because labor market momentum is weak, bond traders are short, and therefore there will be significant buying over the next few days. I will buy TMF (the leveraged bond ETF in the USA) at $37.10 with a stop loss at $35.89 and take profit at $39.99. If neither the stop or the take profit hit, I'll cover Friday morning at 7:30 a.m., one hour before payrolls.

I love this sort of trade. You know exactly what you are doing, and when. The trade has a clear beginning and end: that's powerful. If you are an experienced trader, this sort of trade should require very little mental capital because you are comfortable with being uncomfortable, you have specifically defined your risk, and you know that markets are probabilistic. Many of your past trades were losers and many of your future trades will be losers. This one might be a loser. That's okay.

You put on the trade, sit back, and do some research knowing that whatever happens is going to happen and you don't need to stare at the TMF level 2 screen all day trying to coax the thing higher.

Consider the difference between watching a 30-minute TV episode, and scrolling Twitter. Watching TV, you know when the thing is going to end. There is a defined moment when the loop will close and the show will be over. With Twitter, you can keep on scrolling forever, and there is no point at which it tells you stop. In fact, through algorithms and social engineering, it is subtly telling you *not* to stop, hijacking the brain's reward system and causing addiction-like behavior. Twitter drains your mental energy in a way that no 30-minute TV show ever could.

A trade like this can be a similar vise, slowly squeezing your brain:

> I have been bullish EURUSD for two months because I have a strong view that the USD will weaken this year due to structural factors. There has been good news on the European side, but the USD has stayed strong overall because U.S. stocks are doing fine and the U.S. economy continues to defy gravity. I have been expecting a U.S. recession for the past 18 months because the yield curve inverted, and I know the big USD down and U.S. recession trades are coming soon. I bought EURUSD at 1.18 and stopped out at 1.16 and then bought some 1-month EURUSD calls that expired worthless and now EURUSD is 1.1450 and this looks like a great point to add to the longs that I put on at 1.1505. If I am honest with myself, the chart shows the perfect entry point is 1.1150 now, but I don't want to miss it and there's a good chance we could bounce from here. If I can catch one big move to 1.22 this year, I will clean up.

This structural view with no time condition and the continued desire to add to an idea that has been losing money is the kind of setup where you spend all your mental capital on EURUSD and can't think of anything else. If EURUSD does rally but you only have half your size on, you make money but you're still angry and full of *woulda coulda shouldas*.

Create time and level parameters that allow you to reevaluate your trades so they don't become infinite time horizon, no stop loss trades marked by FOMO, doubling down, and loss after loss. Your whole year should never depend on getting one call right.

Understand the difference between perpetual markets with infinite duration (like stocks) and markets that resolve to a final destination on a manageable time frame (like interest rate futures and options). You can say the price of TSLA is "wrong", but it might never come back to your version of reality and be "right". In contrast, when you bet on a short-term interest rate future or make a wager on Polymarket or Kalshi, there is a correct and final answer coming. Same thing with options.

This is important because you can look at interest rate futures or a specific option and decide that the price offers positive expected value and take the other side knowing that you will be vindicated—or proven wrong—by a specific date. If you risk manage the trade properly, you can think in terms of right or wrong answers and a fixed time horizon.

Bets that resolve on a specified time frame have a big advantage in that they use finite mental capital.

Jimmy the TSLA Permabear is tormented by the stock for years. He takes shot after shot from the short side but gets no satisfaction. By Jimmy's 80th birthday, every U.S. soldier has been replaced by a TSLA humanoid robot, TSLA's global self-driving car network has bankrupted Uber and Waymo, and an xAI Agent was recently elected President of the United States of America. TSLA stock is trading at $420,690,000,000 per share. Jimmy the Permabear is rocking back and forth in his tiny room at the retirement home, CNBC blaring in the background as he mumbles incoherently about auto delivery numbers. Not a good use of mental capital.

Here's an excerpt from one of my favorite trading notes of all time, "Riffing on Risk" by Horselover Fat (reprinted with the permission of Traderade).

> In poker, you start with a stack of chips (i.e. your trading capital), and good poker players wait for hands where they know they have a statistical edge based on the strength of the cards. When they receive a "strong" hand they bet accordingly (i.e. heavily). During tournament poker, a key part of any winning strategy is the ability to fold hands that are unlikely to win. To me, it's

the same in trading. You have to be willing to cut losers and/or wait patiently for a setup that has demonstrated a high likelihood of success in the past.

If I'm entering a trade in the middle of nowhere, with no key support/resistance, no clear order flow information, etc., well that trade is essentially a coin toss. The market is just as likely to move against me as it is to move in my favor. To stay with the poker analogy, that's a hand I would fold.

But let's say the market is at a key area of confluence, and there's a VERY good chance it'll change direction, and I'm seeing order flow to support that thesis. Well now I have a slight edge, so technically my position size should increase from whatever my minimum size currently is. We can represent this thinking with a basic graph:

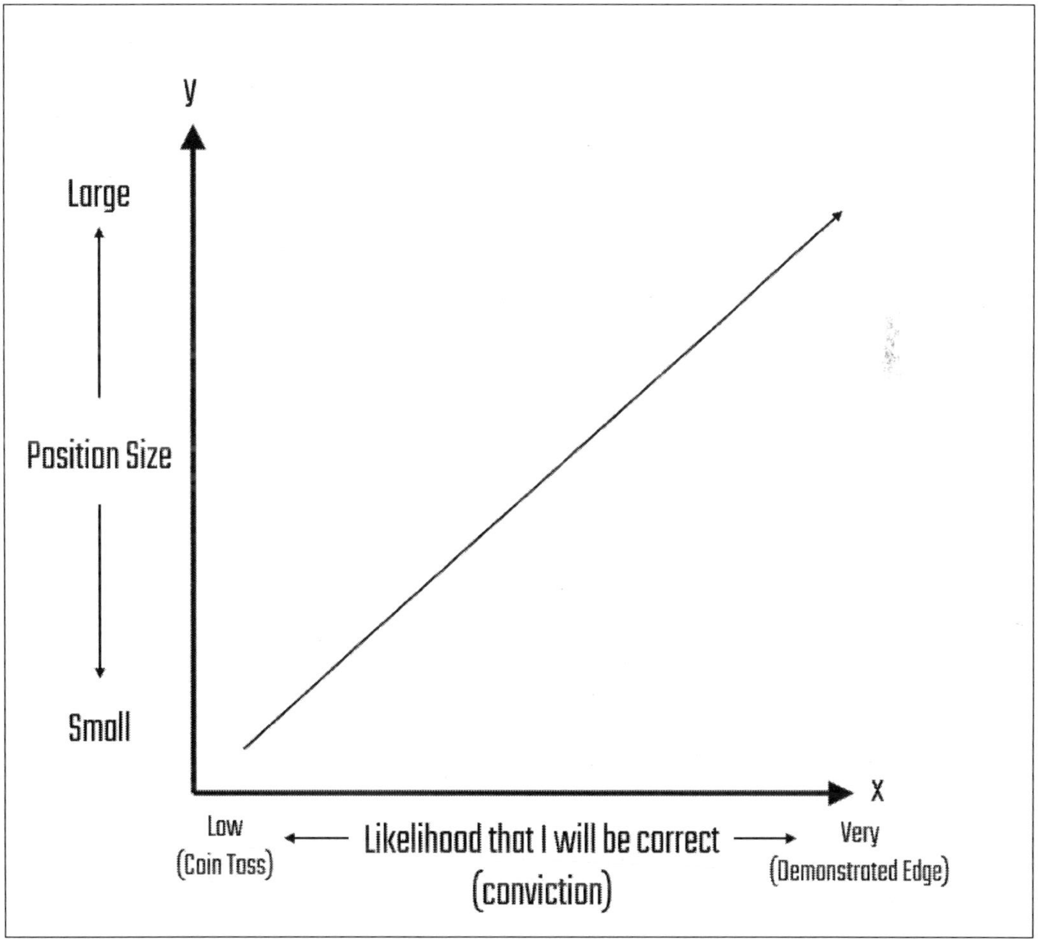

Wouldn't it be nice if risk management was this simple? It's not. Now we have to introduce a third factor on our Z axis: **Time.**

Specifically, the time it will take me to know if I am right or wrong in my thesis.

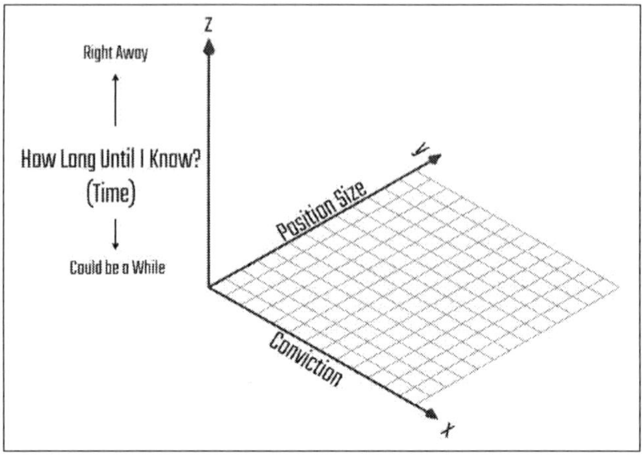

You might be thinking, "Horse what the hell does time have to do with risk management?"

That's a valid question. It has to do with opportunity cost.

Again, referencing our poker analogy, I have a limited stack of chips. I cannot place unlimited large bets with high conviction. I have to "manage" my chip stack, my capital. Therefore, I can't have too much tied up for an indeterminate amount of time hoping my thesis is correct. For me, it's sort of a "shit or get off the pot" scenario. The longer I have to wait to know if I'm correct absolutely impacts my likelihood of being correct AND my position size. In my opinion, this is why macro investing is so difficult. You could enter a position with a very sound thesis, but over time things change and you end up being dead-ass wrong... Through no fault of your own. The more time that elapses, the more opportunity for things to change that impact your initial thesis. I'm a trader in this for the long haul, I need to adjust position sizes and stop losses based on new information and time.

Here are two examples:

DWAC: One of my best equity trades this year was the DWAC SPAC (Note: Unintentional yet hilarious rhyme). Here's how it went down and how I thought about it in my weird "mental risk model" that we're discussing:

I developed a thesis for the trade after the markets were closed for the day. I heard the news about Trump possibly getting involved with a SPAC deal. I checked the price of DWAC after-hours, and it was sitting almost at NAV (~$10), which had me scratching my head... Why hadn't this thing run? Well, the answer was simple: The news JUST broke and it wasn't priced in yet. So, I decided that I'd take a very large position size pre-market the next day because I figured my likelihood of being correct (e.g. that it would pump on the news) was very high. I also factored in the time for our thesis to play out (our z-axis) and determined that I'd know RIGHT away if I was right or not. The likelihood of it falling below NAV was extremely low, so it was "all systems go" for me and time to make an aggressive trade. The rest, as they say, is history.

[Note from Brent: Here's the chart of DWAC at the time Horse did the trade:]

DWAC stock after the Trump October 20, 2021

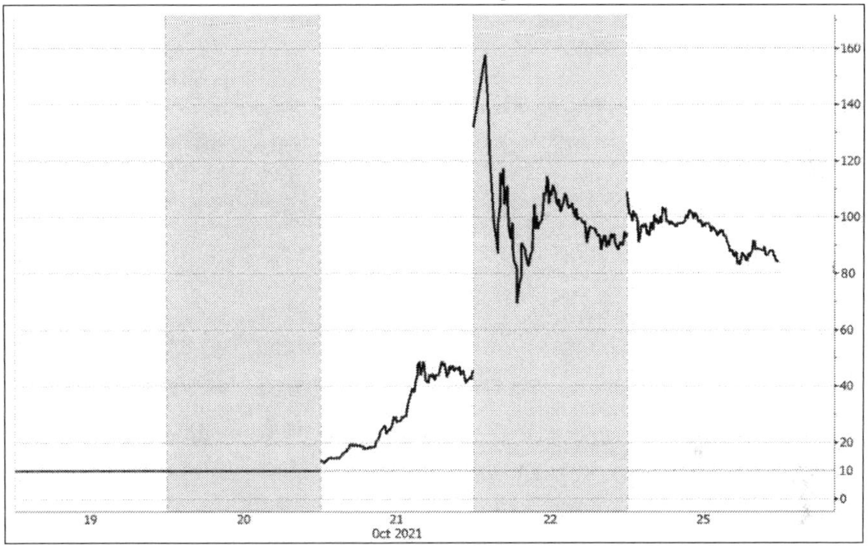

GOLD: Another example that better showcases adjusting my risk management approach using the 3 factors we've discussed is a recent gold swing trade I took. In the final days of September, I started a large swing trade in gold micro futures. The inflation narrative was picking back up, and even though gold is a bona fide piece of shit for an inflation hedge, my thesis was that the general public is too dumb to know that, plus gold had recently been beaten to a pulp and I figured it was oversold and there was an opportunity to BTFD. I also figured portfolios would be getting rebalanced Sept 30-Oct 1 and IF gold was to run it would likely happen FAST due to EOM rebalancing. Additionally, the technicals looked good to me as well. So all of the factors I was looking for were there: A reasonable bull thesis based on the incompetence of Average Joe investors, likely bounce area from a technical perspective, and I'd know quickly if I was right or wrong due to end of month (plus some key Fed talk and inflation data drops on the horizon).

Some of you may remember from my obnoxious Twitter bragging, but I practically bottom ticked it and gold took off on a nice 7.5% bull run.

But I'd be lying if I said I held that position full size for the entire run. **I didn't.**

I trimmed it and I'll tell you why: My mental model for long-term risk management changed. In early November gold started to slip again, so I naturally questioned two of my key factors: Likelihood of being correct and time.

At this point, I had been in the position for over a month and truthfully, I thought it would run harder than it did given the intensity of the inflation narrative. The index futures were looking more and more attractive in early November, as I was anticipating seasonal bullishness and continuation of recent momentum. So, things began to shift on my mental risk model.

Did I really want that many of my "chips" tied up in that one "hand" anymore, or would they be better deployed somewhere else? I determined it was time to trim the position considerably. Of course gold ended up ripping right after that. But hopefully you get the point of this example: If I deem the likelihood of continuing to be correct has decreased AND the time it will take me to know is longer than anticipated, then I will actively manage my exposure (risk) and make changes.

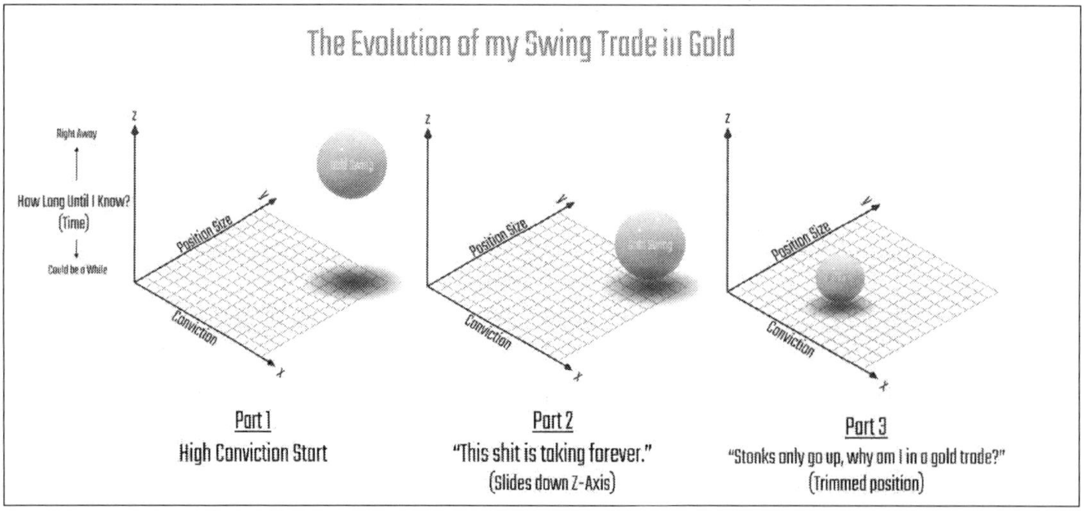

These are ever-changing factors. As soon as you enter a trade they begin to change. This is the main reason I prefer to trade futures intraday: I am better at it than equities/options (therefore I typically have a higher likelihood of being correct) and I know IMMEDIATELY if I am right or wrong. Since futures are a leveraged product, I am able to quickly size accordingly, and size large if the thesis is strong.

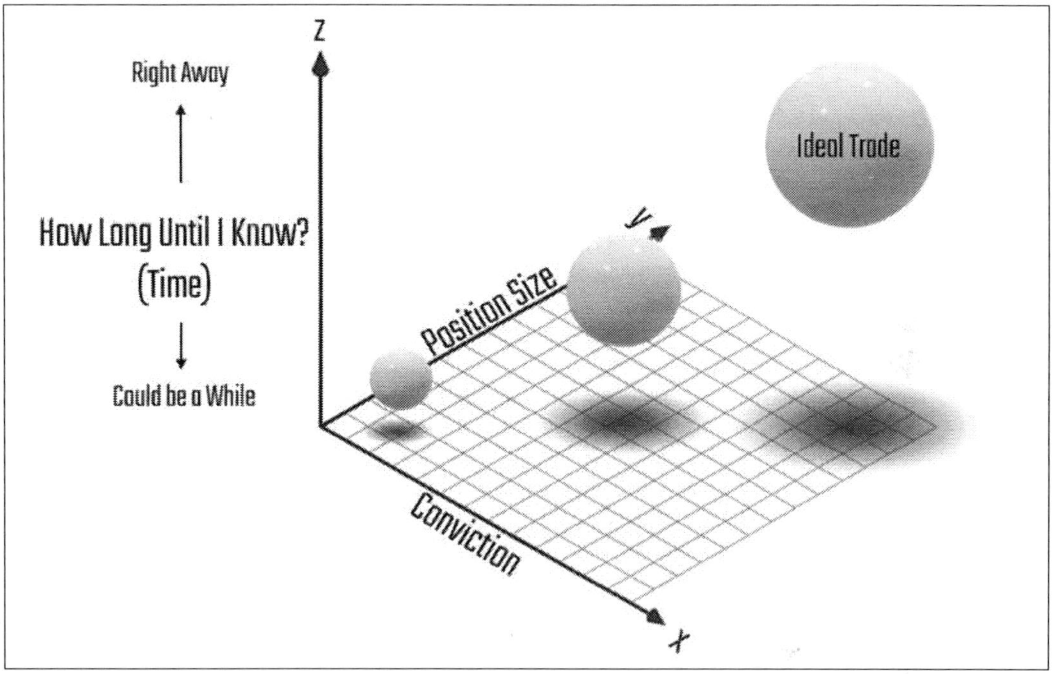

I love seeing a great equity swing trade pan out over time. Absolutely love it. **But I'm also very realistic about my strengths**, so my risk management approach needs to align with that awareness. When I see large orders on the Limit Order Book tipping their hand at a key level of confluence, I am usually VERY certain what is about to happen in the next 5 to 10 minutes. I can't say the same for swing trading stocks, therefore I can't size the same.

I'm a firm believer that to be a sustainable trader, risk needs to be viewed on a "macro" scale. For example, I mentioned in the "How I Day Trade" videos that my sizing for short trades is ALWAYS smaller than my sizing for long trades. Why? Because markets are inherently bullish due to the incredible amount of passive investing flows. Seems like a small detail, right? Maybe. But not if you plan to sustainably trade for years to come.

Thanks for reading and thanks for being here. *Horselover Fat / Traderade*

I love that post because it is a perfect explanation of how a time condition in a trade allows you to manage your mental capital. In his examples, Horse knows the trade should work by X time, or the risk/reward starts to decay.

While I think options tend to be overused, their underappreciated benefit is conservation of mental capital. You don't have to worry about getting stopped out of your short when you're long a put. But you pay a meaningful price for this improved ability to sleep at night.

The other side of the coin

On the other hand, successful trading pretty much requires mental pain and struggle, by definition. Nobody gets to put a trade on and watch it rip instantly in the money and go to the moon every time. That's not how this works. Good trading requires courage, pain tolerance, and the ability to sit there uncomfortable with huge risk on the books. Here is an excerpt of a recent email from my friend LL (quoting with his permission).

> Hey Brent –
>
> I've been thinking about my own trading psychology and would like to share some thoughts. A lot of this will be familiar to you because it recycles concepts and ideas that I've picked up from various sources like Stoicism, Buddhism, other trading books and of course, your own writing.
>
> What I've noticed is that people have similar trade ideas but not everyone makes money. People who do really well (at least in macro discretionary) are able to size up when opportunities are asymmetric. What makes them able to do this? Why is this hard? How do I do the same?
>
> **Why is trading so hard – managing the amygdala?**
>
> I think trading is hard because humans naturally crave pleasure and avoid pain. I think this craving interacts with our cognitive biases which are well documented. Morgan Housel said that the price of investment outperformance in the stock market is fear, uncertainty, doubt, and anxiety. I have found the same in my trading. A lot of times, the right trade is the trade that feels uncomfortable, both in terms of entry timing and sizing. I think most people have similar ideas and experience similar emotions in response to the market. Being able to understand and work with our emotions is incredibly important, because in a head-to-head fight between the rational part of our brain and the amygdala, the amygdala will eventually win.

Ideally when trading, the rational part of our mind should be in the driver's seat and our emotions are simply one of many inputs to our thought process and I think there is a lot of signal value in our emotions. But keeping our emotions at bay takes a lot of mental capital because the big, powerful emotions are produced by the amygdala which can take over your thinking at any moment. Once we exhaust our mental capital, the amygdala takes over and we trade emotionally, usually with bad results. In this framework, the trading process is a tool that helps you conserve mental capital by systematizing some of the decisions.

That's not to say that overriding our fear will always lead to positive outcomes. That has to be paired with a sensible risk management framework so you don't blow up ("market can stay irrational for longer than you can stay solvent") and/or exhaust your mental capital. However, understanding that 1) emotions can be an important source of information and 2) managing your emotions costs finite mental capital, has helped me trade better. Everyone has a different reserve of mental capital, and some can maintain equanimity better than others in the face of a drawdown. You have to understand where your limits are and work to budget your own mental capital if you are to avoid amygdala-hijack. For me, stop losses are also important because a losing trade consumes a lot of mental capital. The real cost of a losing trade is not just its P&L, but the opportunities that your mind is unable to see because the emotions make you blind to them.

As an aside, negative self-talk, perfectionism, and "woulda-coulda-shoulda" thinking all activate the amygdala and are therefore harmful to your P&L.

Craving pleasure and avoiding pain

Buddhism says the craving for pleasure and avoidance of pain is the source of all suffering. Our craving for pleasure and avoidance of pain show up in different ways in our trading. Here are some pleasure-seeking behaviors : It feels safe and comfortable to go with the herd (consensus trades). If something has been going up with low volatility, perceived uncertainty is low (carry trades). Adding when prices confirm your thesis feels safe, but it also weakens your position if there is a pullback.

And here are some pain/uncertainty-avoiding behaviors: Stopping out is painful because it threatens your narrative about yourself as a smart person.

Going against the herd is painful because it feels risky. Stepping in to buy in a big selloff is scary. Putting on a large size when prices have not yet confirmed the thesis feels uncertain.

However sometimes, perceived uncertainty may be just the opposite of the true probabilities of the trade being profitable. When perceived uncertainty is high, prices are probably low and buying is likely to be profitable. When perceived uncertainty is low, prices may be at their most stretched levels. Nothing that I'm saying here is new, but I found that it helps to frame it as craving of pleasure and avoidance of pain.

Cost of outperformance is discomfort

This leads me to my final point that I think the price of outperformance is mental discomfort. Either you pay the price upfront by taking a larger position size than you feel comfortable with (and accept the risk of losing money), or you pay it later when your entry isn't as good and you have to suffer.

Here is a stylized example to make my point:

Trader A and B both have the idea that EURUSD is going higher. Let's say EURUSD is at 1.0500.

Trader A avoids pain and craves pleasure.

1. It "feels" uncertain, so Trader A puts on a small position to watch how it goes (avoiding uncertainty).
2. Once EURUSD goes up, it feels more certain, more people are talking about it, so the trader increases his position (pleasure seeking).
3. When EURUSD has a pullback, he cannot hold and stops out of it, ultimately making no money (avoids discomfort of losing money).

Trader B leans into discomfort:

1. It "feels" uncertain, but trader B thinks the price is good, so despite his discomfort, takes a large position (leans into discomfort).
2. Once EURUSD goes up and as more people talk about it, it feels uncomfortable to reduce the position, but he does so.
3. He is now in a stronger position to add on a pullback.

My thanks to LL for sharing his thoughts in such detail. One cool thing about covering so many clients after writing a book is that you get to interact with a lot of smart traders and learn from them just like they (hopefully) learned from you.

Managing your mental capital

1. Put on trades with clear parameters and then mentally let them go. Many of your trades are going lose money. Accept it. You can control the process and put on a smart trade with clear entry, exit, time, and other reassessment triggers. Then you can choose to let it go—or you can let it drag you across the gravel for hours, days, or weeks. Let go of the outcome and take the attitude: "whatever happens now, happens,", freeing up mental capital that can be spent looking for new ideas and strategies. Put on the trade, then let it go.

2. Create a trading process where your post-entry mental load is minimized. Structure trades properly and automate your stop losses. Good, well structured trade ideas don't require you to stare at the screen 24/7 with your fists clenched. Outsource or automate as much of your risk management as possible

3. Listen to your emotions and figure out what information they are trying to send you. Emotions contain information, but you can only extract the information if you listen. When you feel a strong emotion, ask yourself why: is your position too big? Is the option you bought super high leverage, but way too short of an expiry to match the time horizon of your view? Or is this just the normal discomfort everyone feels when they put on meaningful risk?

A ski jumper can be nervous because ski jumping is nerve-racking, or they can be nervous because they know they shouldn't be competing today given their knee injury hasn't fully healed. These are two different issues and need to be handled differently. If a trade is getting on your nerves, or draining you, or you feel like you are at war with the market… There is information in that. Figure out the problem and take appropriate action.

1. Journal your emotional state once per day for five minutes. Everyone knows that journaling is great for self-awareness—but barely anyone does it. Put a recurring pop up in your calendar daily at 11:15 a.m. that says "Journal for five minutes." Observing yourself and documenting your thoughts and emotions gives you many of the benefits of seeing a therapist. And it's free.

2. Maintain perspective. Trading is not life or death, even when it feels like it. Each trade is a brief moment in a successful career that will span decades. Nobody looks back on a trade from 25 years ago and says "Man, my life would be so different if I had not stopped out of that JDSU short in 1999." The longer you trade, the more you learn that even an excellent, repeatable trading process runs into massive losing streaks, stupid ideas, runs

of bad luck, and perfect bullish ideas that are stopped out at the lows before skyrocketing to all-time highs. As LL said earlier: The cost of outperformance is discomfort. Note your discomfort, acknowledge it, and move on.

As a quick follow up to point three above: I am a proponent of the idea of emotions as information. We can choose to listen to them or ignore them. Here is how I would catalog various emotions and their possible information content, specifically for traders.

Emotion	What it might mean	
Fear	Position size too big	Danger imminent
Frustration	Fighting the market	Failure to follow process
Joy / Euphoria	Overearning relative to normal	Peak P&L
Hope	Hanging onto losers	Unrealistic expectations
Regret	Living in the past	Hindsight bias
Anxiety	Living in the future	Don't trust yourself to stick to process
Impatience	Struggling to stick to the plan	Trading style mismatch with personality
Guilt	Actions and values do not align	
Panic	Position size too big	Unprepared

Faulty framework #5: Single variable frameworks

A common error traders make is to believe that they can explain markets using a single variable. This gives rise to statements like:

- "Fed Balance Sheet up, stocks up!"
- "Money printing equals inflation!"
- "Higher interest rates are bad for stocks!"

In the real world, the Fed's balance sheet has completely decoupled from the stock market[51], money printing did not lead to inflation until fiscal policy went bonkers, and the impact of interest rates on stocks is highly conditional on the regime.

The stock market reaction to the bond market depends on why yields are rising, and how fast. As a general heuristic, rapidly rising yields due to inflation **do** cause the stock market to fall. In contrast, rising yields on stronger growth often come right along with stock market

---

[51] So nobody talks about the Fed's balance sheet anymore!

strength. Any framework that relies on bond yields to predict stock market movements needs to incorporate much more detail such as: why are bond yields going up or down? Is it growth, inflation, fiscal fears, or??? What stage of the cycle are we at? What is bond market volatility doing? And so on.

Why and *how fast* bond yields are rising are good starting points in a useful framework for predicting the stock market. Yields on their own will lead to many erroneous conclusions. Furthermore, many of the people using the "yields up = bad for stocks" framework will also tell you that falling yields are bad for stocks because "the bond market knows something" or "bonds don't lie".

Be cautious of any framework that explains markets using a single variable. Financial markets are fiendishly complex, adaptive systems. It's unlikely that such a simplistic description of why a market moves will be useful[52]. Here's a comparison of a useless yields vs. equities framework, and a more realistic one.

How do rising bond yields impact the stock market?

	Faulty Framework	Solid Framework
Core Assumption	Rising bond yields are bearish for stocks	It depends: Context matters
Key Variable	Bond yield direction (up or down)	Yield direction, cause, speed, macro context
Cause of Yield Movement	Not considered	Growth, inflation, fiscal risk, Fed policy
Speed of Movement	Ignored	Rapid vs. gradual changes in yields have different impacts
Bond/equity relationship	One-way causality (yields up = stocks down)	Dynamic relationship
Resulting Insight	Overly simplistic, often wrong	Nuanced, probabilistic, and more accurate over time

Note that a 100-variable framework is not useful either. One of the most compelling and attractive (but useless) ways to look at markets is to create huge multi-variable regressions that attempt to unpack how many factors impact a security's price all at once. These are (by

[52] The one single-variable explanation that sometimes feels useful is *liquidity*. When central bank liquidity goes from minimal to plentiful, it can be the only thing that matters for a while. In these periods, you can focus exclusively on liquidity and do quite well.

definition) backward looking and tend to look good in the backtest and perform poorly out of sample.

Good frameworks can usually explain market movements by pointing at a few important variables, but not just one. While this approach sounds simple, it's not, because the variables that matter are hard to identify at any given moment, and they change over time.

Faulty framework #6: Bad breadth is bearish

Are narrow stock market breadth or extreme market concentration bearish? No, not really. People were worried about narrow leadership in the NASDAQ starting in 2013 with the index at 4,000 and still worried about it in 2024 as the NASDAQ broke through 20,000.

When someone says: "Without the top seven stocks, the stock market's performance would barely be above average!" it's as if they are saying: "Without Michael Jordan, the 1995 Chicago Bulls would have been just an average team!" Strong index performance is sometimes evenly distributed and sometimes dominated by a sector or group of companies. Bad stock market breadth doesn't have much predictive power.

Michael Mauboussin, one of the most respected minds in quantitative finance, wrote a solid piece in 2024 and came to a conclusion similar to most research I have read on this topic. **Concentration is a coincident indicator, not a predictive one.** Here's a quote from the Mauboussin piece:

> The S&P 500 has delivered returns above the average when concentration was rising and below the average when concentration was falling. The results were pronounced for the concentration changes associated with the inflating and deflating of the dot-com bubble, with compound annual returns of 23.5 percent from 1994 through 1999 and just 3.6 percent from 2000 to 2013.

Analysts often point to 1999/2000 concentration levels as a warning, but that was an unusual time because valuations and concentration were rising, but earnings were not. In contrast, throughout the 2010 to 2025 rally in the NASDAQ, earnings have been rising rapidly among big tech and very slowly elsewhere. Again, from Mauboussin:

> Fundamental results can justify rising concentration. From 2014 to 2023, the top 10 stocks were 19 percent of the market capitalization, on average, while the companies made up 47 percent of the total economic profit. In 2023, the top 10 equities were 27 percent of the market capitalization and the firms contributed 69 percent to the total economic profit. The relative market capitalizations of the stocks of these companies is not without a fundamental foundation.

If you spend half an hour on Google, you can find warnings of bad breadth almost every year going back to 1990. Here are a few examples, but there are many more:

Fear of bad breadth is evergreen

Again, if you're a long-term investor or a long/short investor, breadth may have some useful information in terms of sector allocation or portfolio construction. But it's not useful if you are trying to forecast the direction of the stock market.

The reality is that **aggregate breadth throughout U.S. stock market history is bad.** A minority of stocks make up the majority of gains in every index over the past 100 years. Part of this is just math. A stock can go up 5000%, but it can't go down 5000%, so the biggest upside outliers are always going to deliver an outsized portion of returns.

In a well-known 2020 paper, Hendrik Bessembinder looked at lifetime returns of every stock traded on major U.S. exchanges back to 1926[53]. He found that the top-performing **2.4% of stocks account for <u>all</u> of the $75.7 trillion in global stock market creation** from 1991 to 2020. Furthermore, over the same period 55.2% of U.S. stocks and 57.4% of non-U.S. stocks performed worse than risk-free 1-month U.S. T-bills.

In the U.S., just 86 stocks account for half of the $16 trillion in wealth created by the stock market over the past 90 years. That's 86 out of 26,000. How's that for bad breadth?! Bad

[53] "Wealth Creation in the U.S. Public Stock Markets 1926 to 2019," Bessembinder, Hendrik (Hank), (2020).

breadth is a fundamental characteristic of the stock market. It gets better and gets worse, but it won't help you predict anything.

Faulty framework #7: Underestimating gap risk

Gap risk is one of the most important and often neglected risks in financial markets. To survive and thrive as a trader over the long run, **you must avoid risk of ruin**. To avoid risk of ruin you need to understand gap risk. Here are a few need-to-know points.

There are four types of gap risk. I will save the most dangerous for last.

1. **Gap between market close and open.** A stock closes at $50 on Friday and then over the weekend their CFO quits, and the company announces they fired their auditor. That doesn't sound good! The stock opens at $25 on Monday morning. Yikes. If you have a $50,000 account and you went home long with 2X margin, you're done. Ruined. That's gap risk number one.

Here is an example of that sort of gap risk, as I contrast the normal, continuous price action in oil with a big Sunday gap after a weekend OPEC announcement.

Continuous and discontinuous price action in NYMEX crude futures

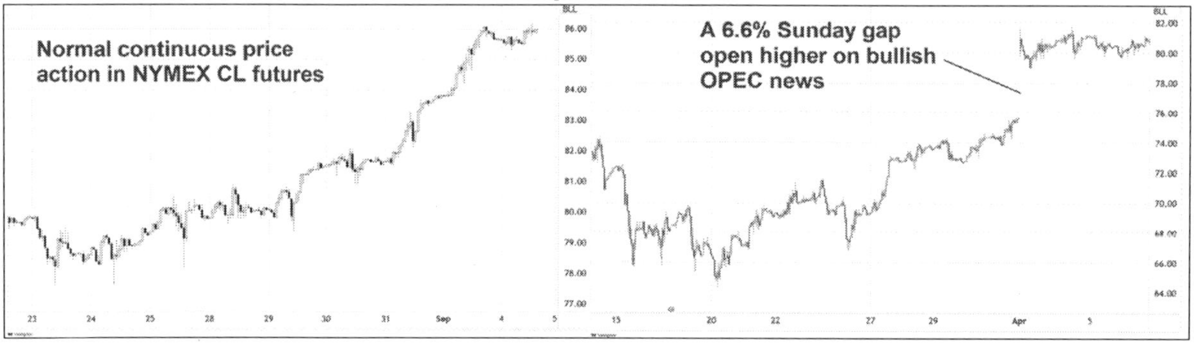

2. **Gap around events.** When the U.S. jobs report comes out the first Friday of each month at 8:30 a.m., S&P futures and USDJPY (and other markets) often jump to a new level without trading continuously from A to B. For example, USDJPY might be **112.10** at 8:29:29 and then the jobs number comes in strong and the first trade after 8:30 could be **112.68**. If you go into the number short USDJPY and don't have a good understanding of gap risk, you might get wrecked.

3. **Markets that are pegged, capped or floored by central banks or other entities.** One famous example of this is the EURCHF floor at 1.2000. The Swiss National Bank tried to enforce an exchange rate and eventually, when they gave up, the largest one day move in the history of foreign exchange happened. In about two hours. EURCHF traded from

1.2000 to 0.8500 in a matter of minutes. There were almost no trades from 1.20 to 1.01, a scenario that was totally unheard of until that fateful day.

4. **The most dangerous gap risk comes from liquidity.** The assumption of somewhat continuous liquidity is dangerously naive and has blown up many a speculator. Hedge funds sell short-term interest rate contracts or sell calls in those markets and assume that they can get out if things go pear shaped. Then the market goes offerless and gaps more than any white label interest rate model could have possibly predicted.

Or they sell a stock at $5 and assume they can get out at $10 and find it impossible to buy back their position as the market explodes up through $50.

Or a retail trader goes short 2,000 shares at $10 on a Bear Report recommendation. They try to cover at $20 and whiff. It's $30 bid. $40 bid. They try to cover at $50 and whiff. They finally exit at $66.50 and their account is gone.

Liquidity is unpredictable and negatively correlated to volatility. If you blow up due to gap risk, you are not unlucky: you did something wrong. You were too slow to see the regime shift and its impact on liquidity and vol. You had too big of a position. Or maybe you just didn't have a big enough imagination. The first goal of every trading strategy and every trader must be to eliminate risk of ruin. **Once-in-a-billion-years events happen once every few years.**

Be thoughtful about major gap risk. This does not mean you shake in terror at night, worrying about a simultaneous 19-sigma move in every one of your positions. It does not mean you can never carry a position through economic data or over the weekend. **Gaps around economic data and over weekends can be reasonably estimated.**

It *does* mean that you should not massively short a tech bubble stock into earnings. You should not go short USDHKD at the top of the band, and you should seriously consider your weekend positions and whether or not they are worth the risk. Oil can gap 10% over a weekend. USDJPY can gap 100 to 150 pips.

If you cannot measure the risk, you should not have the position. Avoiding risk of ruin is more important than maximizing returns.

Faulty framework #8: Don't fight the Fed

"Don't Fight the Fed" is one of the few clichés that is often wrong. Sometimes the Fed wins right away, and stocks make an instant bottom like they did in 2020. But not always. The Fed's impact on the stock market is nuanced. If they cut into okay economic growth, it's bullish. If they are cutting due to oncoming recession, it's bearish. Again, you can't just look at one variable (Fed policy) and predict what markets are going to do. *If only it were that easy.*

Federal Funds Rate and S&P 500, 1998 to 2025

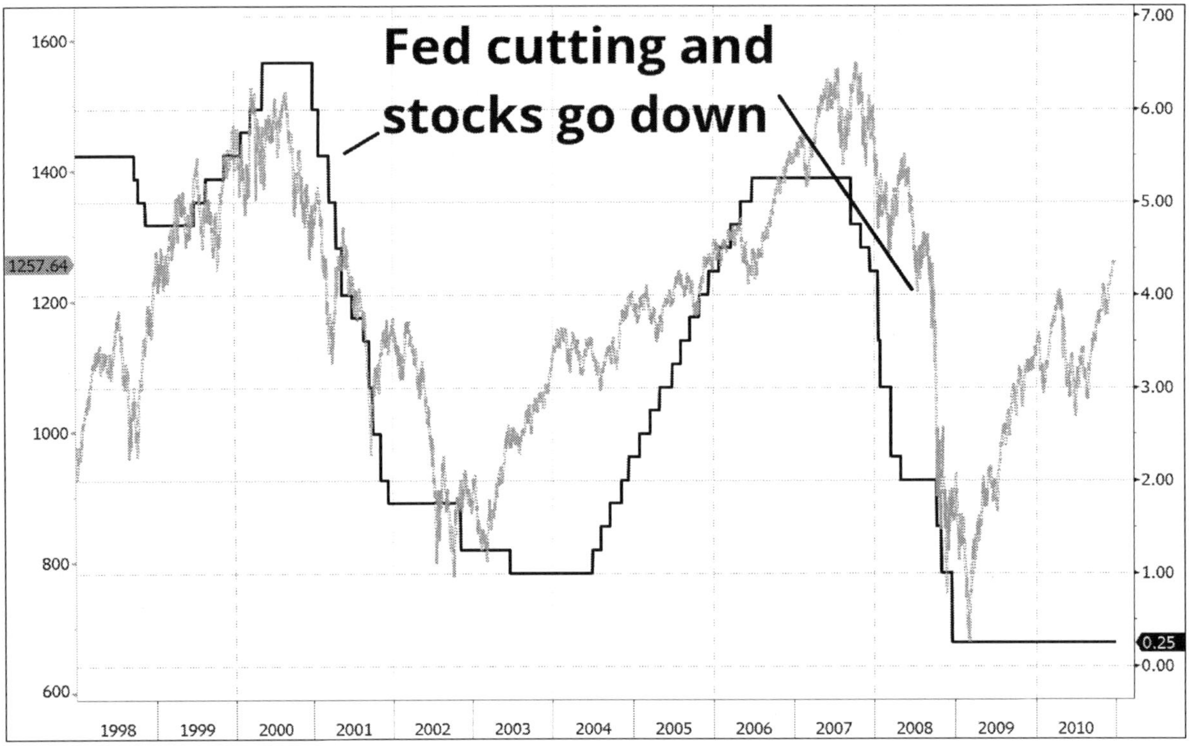

Faulty framework #9: Fade Jim Cramer

I threw this one in for fun, but there are some useful takeaways from the never-ending war against Jim Cramer. People love to point out Jim Cramer's bad calls because:

- Many find his personality, style, arrogance, and bravado annoying.
- Dissing him is a funny meme and a way to farm engagement on social media.
- Schadenfreude.
- It helps them feel better about their own inadequacies and bad calls.

The problem with fading Jim Cramer is that it doesn't work. He makes literally 1,000s of calls, so if you see someone ripping him for being bullish Coinbase at $425 right before it crashed to $32, they are cherry-picking his worst call without acknowledging that he makes 700 to 800 stock price calls per year and another 4,000 or so directional mentions of stocks. He is going to be wrong a lot!

When you are looking at funny anecdotes like this, ask whether the anecdote is representative or not. If everyone says "Oooh, look, Barron's cover is bullish, I guess we gotta be bearish!" ask yourself if that's true. Are Barron's covers contrarian? I did a comprehensive study to answer this question and the answer is: No.

First up, let's look at the P&L of simply doing whatever is on the cover of Barron's. If the cover is bullish, you buy. If it's bearish, you go short. After 30, 60, 120, 252, and 504 trading days, here's the P&L.

P&L of going with Barron's covers, 1997 to 2025

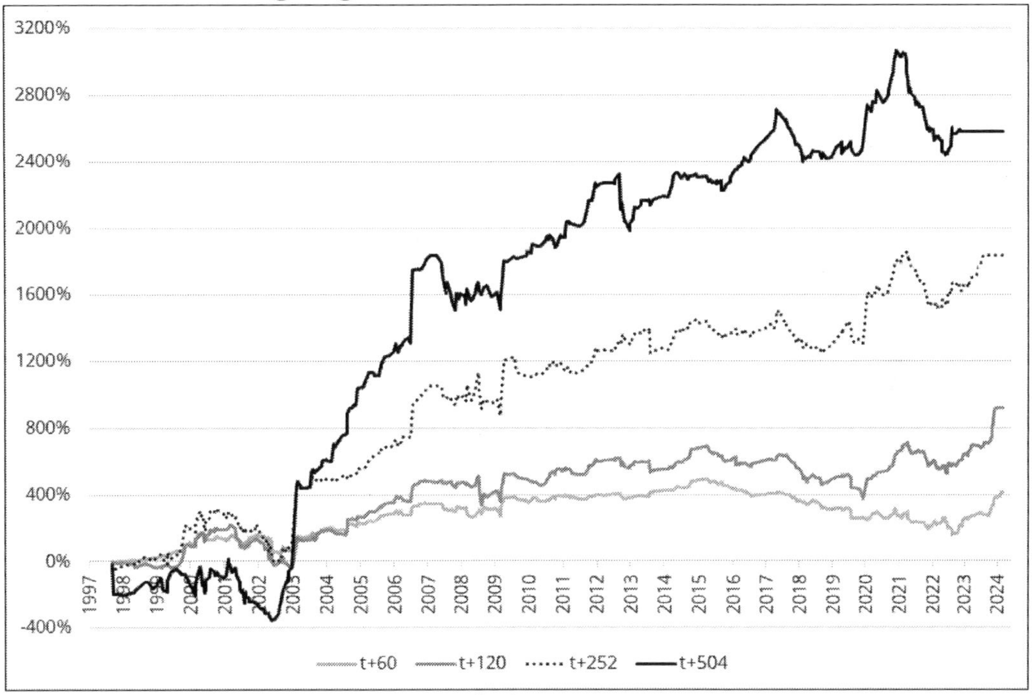

There is a simple explanation for this: Barron's skews bullish and it skews toward covers about individual stocks. 1997 to now has mostly been a raging bull market. Therefore, there was a much greater probability of a bullish cover leading to a long trade and positive returns. A salient example of this is when Barron's recommended long XM Satellite in February 2003. See this screenshot.

BARRON'S COVER · MAIN

A Sound Idea

Satellite radio is here, and XM looks like a winner

Feb 17, 2003, 12:01 am EST

ON A TYPICAL DAY, America's 200 million adults listen to the radio for at least two hours, mostly in their cars. But many spend much of that time fiddling with the tuner, struggling to dodge a ceaseless barrage of commercials or simply seeking an airwave favorite, be it Howard Stern, J.Lo, Sinatra, Ja Rule, Streisand, Dolly Parton, Eminem, All News All the Time or Wolfgang Amadeus.

This article was outright bullish on XM Radio at $4, and the stock soon went to $40.

There were, of course, many terrible calls, but the bullish bias of Barron's and the rising tide lifting all boats from 1997 to now means that fading Barron's covers was a disastrous strategy overall. To get a less biased sample, we can look only at covers where Barron's was bearish a security and thus the contrarian strategy would have been to go long. Here are the stats in each direction.

Barron's cover bearish so we go long					
	t+30	**t+60**	**t+120**	**t+252**	**t+504**
average	0.3%	-0.6%	-0.2%	-1.9%	2.5%
median	-0.2%	0.1%	-1.0%	-2.1%	1.3%
win%	**47%**	**51%**	**47%**	**47%**	**55%**
Trades	105	105	103	99	97
Wins	49	54	48	47	53
Losses	56	51	55	52	44
average win	7.2%	8.6%	13.6%	22.5%	31.4%
average loss	-5.7%	-10.3%	-12.2%	-24.0%	-32.5%

Barron's cover bullish so we go short					
	t+30	t+60	t+120	t+252	t+504
average	-0.5%	-1.1%	-2.9%	-5.6%	-9.8%
median	-0.7%	-1.2%	-3.2%	-4.8%	-5.4%
win%	**43%**	**41%**	**40%**	**42%**	**39%**
Trades	324	322	321	314	300
Wins	139	132	127	133	118
Losses	183	189	194	181	182
average win	6.3%	9.3%	14.4%	19.9%	25.8%
average loss	-5.8%	-8.3%	-14.2%	-24.3%	-32.9%

The longs are a coin toss, and the shorts are horrendous. Here's a fun example of a contrarian trade that *did* work:

Fannie Mae stock (FNM), 2012 to 2017

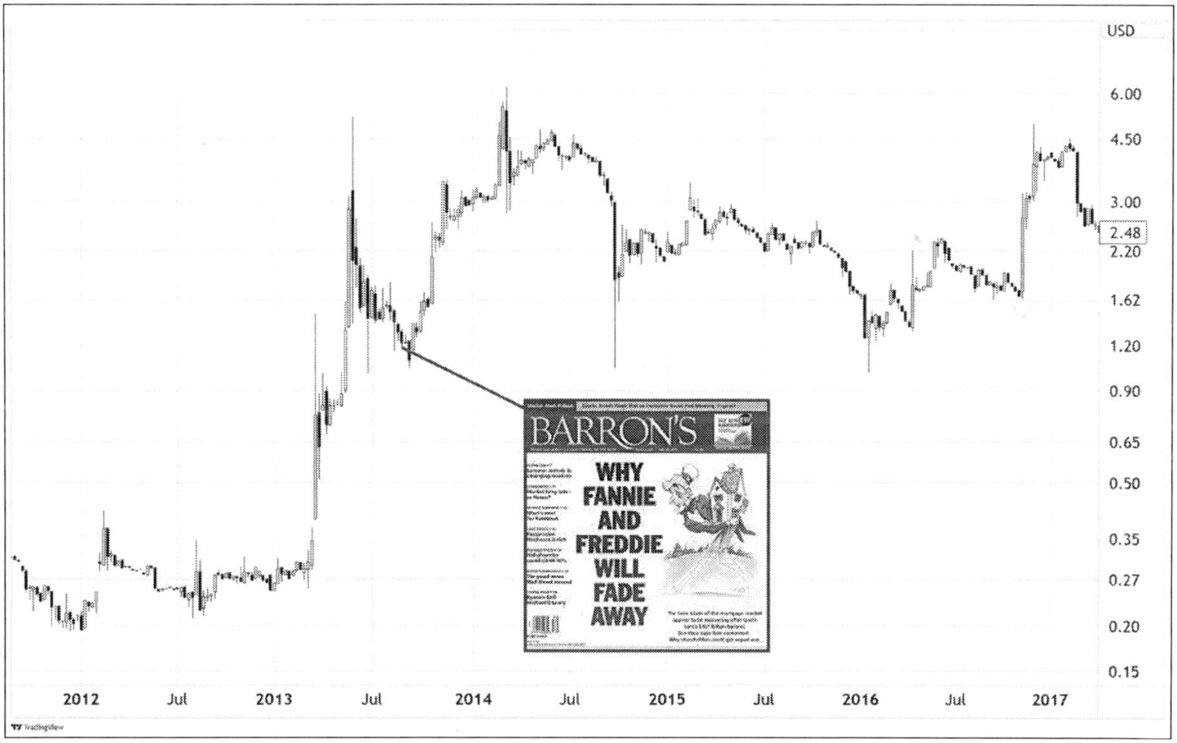

Look at the y-axis. *Oh dear.* They put the "It's going to zero" idea out with the stock at 95 cents and it went straight to six bucks. I suppose an optimist would say "at least they didn't put the article out when the stock was at 25 cents!".

For good order, I also reviewed Barron's covers relating to macro, FX, bonds, etc. and the conclusions are all the same. **Fading Barron's is a coin toss.** So, next time someone sends you a Barron's cover and tells you that asset class or security XYZ is going the other way, just shrug. Barron's is a real-time, coincident indicator with a bullish skew. Their ideas will outperform in bull markets and underperform in bear markets.

Same for Jim Cramer, folks. A snarky ETF distributor tried to create an ETF to fade Jim Cramer's picks. Thankfully, it attracted very little attention or assets under management. Here is how it did before it was put out of its misery in early 2024.

SJIM: The Inverse Jim Cramer ETF

And if that wasn't enough evidence, there is a remarkable body of research on this niche topic! For example, Matthew Dakken of Minnesota State University concluded that Jim Cramer's picks have a large market impact on Day One and no lasting influence after that[54].

Retail buyers who follow Cramer's advice generate what is known as the "Cramer Bounce". This is not because Jim Cramer has skill, it's because people blindly follow his Mad Money picks and the stocks mentioned move higher due to this temporary increase in marginal

---

[54] www.minneapolisfed.org/-/media/files/mea/contest/2017papers/dakkenmatthew.pdf

demand. Similar effects can be seen when Barron's speaks positively about a stock: It gaps higher the next day then reverts to a random walk immediately thereafter.

This next chart shows the returns of Jim Cramer's Mad Money calls over time, along with the performance of the S&P 500. You can see that there is momentum before the call (Cramer tends to favor buying things that are already going up) and there is a spike on the Cramer recommendation and then the stock reverts to the mean performance of the broader market.

Jim Cramer Mad Money recommendations vs. the S&P 500

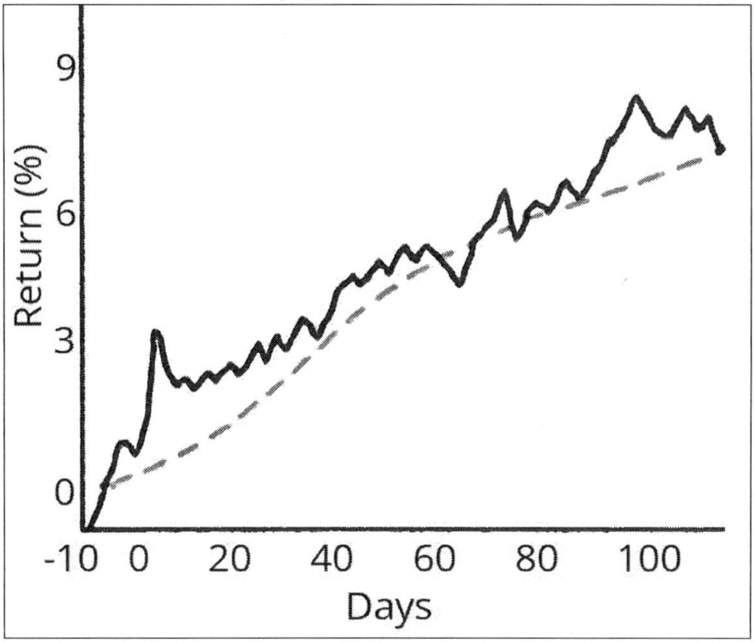

Jim Cramer triggers a bump and then mean reversion. That's it. He's not contrarian. There are piles and piles of evidence.

While it's fun to post cherry-picked examples of how "Jim Cramer is always wrong" on the social media platform formerly known as Twitter, don't mistake random anecdotes for useful forecasting. If you are going short something because Jim Cramer said to go long, you will perform about as well as the SJIM ETF performed. Badly.

One of the few anecdotal signals like this that works well when you backtest it, and has worked well out of sample since being backtested in 2016 and again in 2021 is the Economist Magazine Cover Indicator. I have written about this at length, and you can watch as I update the calls in real time on X/Twitter (@donnelly_brent).

Conclusion

Many frameworks don't work. Take a step back once a month or so and make a list of your primary views, trading styles, and frameworks. Isolate anything that is not working for you and determine whether you are seeing things through a faulty framework.

Adapt your approach to match the current market regime and be aware not just of what you think is important, but what everybody else knows that everybody knows is important. Your approach should adapt as market regimes change. Just because valuation is irrelevant to the stock market today, does not mean it will be irrelevant tomorrow. There could be a regime switch where the market spent five years ignoring valuation, then spends the next five years relentlessly crushing any stock that is the slightest bit overvalued.

Next we'll pivot to positive changes and the solid frameworks that successful traders use to make money and stay out of trouble.

As with all my writing, I don't expect you to adopt and embrace everything. When you're reading the next chapter, pick one or two ideas you could successfully incorporate into your process. Find a new concept, approach, or attitude that can be transformative and give it a shot.

Let's go.

CHAPTER 10

CHOOSE YOUR WEAPON

Practical frameworks for profitable trading

"Amateurs think about how much money they can make. Professionals think about how much money they could lose."

Jack Schwager, *Market Wizards*

You might be smarter than everyone else, beam with confidence, exude risk appetite, and execute faster than anyone. And yet you might still fail. Chapter 9 covered faulty frameworks and common pitfalls to avoid. This chapter will explain some of the many ways to look at markets, going beyond the fundamental, technical, behavioral and quantitative approaches in *Alpha Trader*.

Decision-making and good thinking

The first three frameworks emphasize the importance of sound decision-making processes and objective evaluation of data and statistics.

Practical framework #1: Probabilistic vs. Deterministic

When someone tells you with high confidence: "The U.S. dollar is doomed!" or "Bitcoin is going to $1 million!" or "There's going to be a recession next year, for sure, dude."

The most appropriate response is always: *Maybe*.

We don't know. The future hasn't happened yet. If we think we know the future with certainty—we're wrong. Nobody has perfect foresight and in a complex system like financial markets, good thinkers don't see the future as a single pre-determined outcome. Overconfident, religious and/or deterministic thinkers do. Reality unfolds as a series of probabilistic outcomes in the multiverse, not a single, predetermined, or preordained result. Yes, TSLA stock is going to be either higher or lower tomorrow, next week, and next year, but even the most gifted analyst in the world equipped with perfect information cannot predict where it's going with high certainty.

Anyone predicting a market outcome with 100% certainty is wildly overconfident—or their true passion is marketing, not trading.

A nuanced point of view can sound wishy-washy to naïve observers who just want the "right" answer. Plus, crazy forecasts are fun and stimulating! Many consumers of financial media want clear, confident forecasts, not a boring grid full of possible and probable scenarios. But traders understand that anything can happen, new information sometimes matters, and admitting you're wrong is a sign of strength, not weakness.

Think in probabilistic terms about the path of market prices, future economic data, and any market-moving event that has not happened yet. Avoid overconfidence and **consider alternative scenarios**.

Most economist and analyst estimates are deterministic point estimates, not probabilistic distributions. This is not the optimal way to think about the future as a market professional. Good traders have properly-calibrated confidence and a sense of approximate uncertainty around their analysis and predictions.

When you have a strong market view, think about:

- Your confidence level with regard to that particular outcome
- Other outcomes that are possible and your estimates of their likelihood
- Specific signposts or new information that would increase or reduce your confidence in your original forecast

Say the European Central Bank (ECB) is meeting tomorrow, and you can feel in your gutthat they are going to hike rates by 50bps[55]. The market expects a hike of 25bps, but you are almost certain it'll be 50. And you think the press conference after the hike will be super hawkish as the ECB will telegraph more rate hikes to come. A bad trader thinks: "50bp hike incoming, buy euros, let's get rich."

You think like this:

[55] Or, maybe that's just those three hot dogs you had last night?

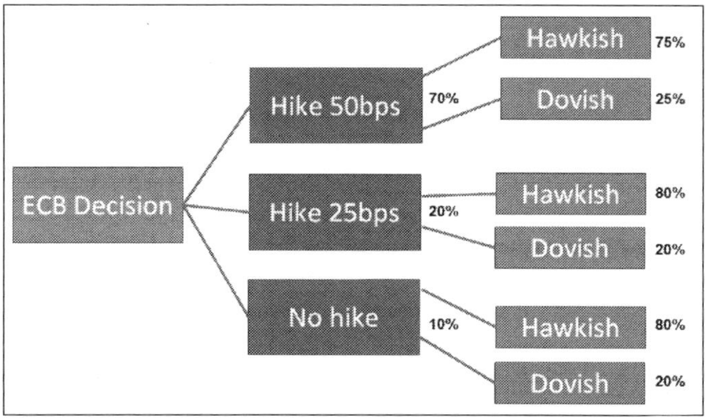

Much as you would like to assign 100% probability to the 50bp hike, you know that's unrealistic. There is always a chance the ECB does the less exciting thing.

As you build out the decision tree, a possibility you hadn't even considered—no rate hike—appears. The odds of a *no rate hike* outcome are also not zero. The decision tree forced you to focus not just on the base case you're excited about, but on outcomes that are less probable—*but still possible*. This is good, probabilistic, rather than deterministic thinking. You may have identified a risk of ruin scenario depending on how you were going to structure the trade.

Excellent traders think through and prepare for scenarios that are unlikely *but not impossible.*

Calculating Expected Value (EV)

Your estimates of probability and EURUSD close on each outcome can be used to estimate the expected value of EURUSD after the event. Take the EURUSD start (1.10) and where it will end up in each scenario, times the probability of each scenario, and add it all up.

EURUSD : Expected Value calculation based on ECB scenario analysis

EURUSD before the meeting: 1.1000

		A	B	C	D	E	
		A	B	C	A X B	D X A	
		Estimated EURUSD close today	Probability 1	Probability 2	Probability of both	Probability X expected EURUSD in this scenario	
Hike 50bps	Hawkish	1.1250	70%	75%	53%	0.5906	
	Dovish	1.1200	70%	25%	18%	0.1960	
Hike 25bps	Hawkish	1.1100	20%	80%	16%	0.1776	
	Dovish	1.0950	20%	20%	4%	0.0438	
No hike	Hawkish	1.0900	10%	80%	8%	0.0872	
	Dovish	1.0800	10%	20%	2%	0.0216	
				Total	100%	**1.1168**	Expected value of EURUSD at the end of the day

If your probability estimates are correct, the average value of EURUSD after the ECB meeting if you ran this scenario a million times is 1.1168.

That's a huge positive EV and a big move higher from 1.1000, reinforcing your bullish view. Since you took the time to think probabilistically, you have a nuanced look at the event, including an estimate of the worst-case scenario: the 2% chance that EURUSD goes to 1.0800. You're prepared for all scenarios, and you have defined the **cone of uncertainty** in a way that will allow for superior risk management.

Don't include *every* possibility in your decision tree. Something like "Extraplanetary invaders abduct all ECB members" does not deserve a branch on the tree. There is skill to determining what is a plausible outlier, and what is not.

The more confident you feel about a view or a market narrative or market direction, the more you should chill out and think probabilistically. If you are super excited about a view, and ready to go all in, make a decision tree to ensure that you are not becoming overly emotional or deterministic.

If you don't know how to calculate expected value, you need to learn! Just give it a Google; there are many good explainers online (YouTube, Wikipedia, StackExchange, etc.)

Practical Framework #2: Cyclical vs. Structural

Traders and investors often get enamored with structural narratives that might sound important, but have marginal impact on markets in the short term. Focus on cyclical variables and narratives most of the time but keep one eye on the horizon for major changes in the structural story.

Cyclical views are much more useful and profitable for trading than structural views, most of the time. If you are a buy and hold "bitcoin and/or gold and/or stocks to the moon" person, that's awesome, but that's not trading and thus not what this book is about. That is a deterministic, structural view. It might be correct, or it might be incorrect, but it's irrelevant here.

As explained earlier, structural trends and repricings take years to play out and are mostly irrelevant for traders. The notable exception to this is the beginning or end of a structural story. I spend most of my time analyzing cyclical factors and stories when I look at currency markets. The cyclical narrative is almost always the marginal driver of FX rates for anyone trading a sub-three-month time horizon.

A 14-year shift in reserve manager preference for the Chinese yuan as it goes from 1% of global central bank reserves to 7% is a slow burn story, as structural stories tend to be. It's a good one for the FT and for the de-dollarization people on FinTwit, but it's not actionable and has no visible impact on the price of the yuan or the dollar.

On the other hand, if Europe has had structurally tight fiscal policy for 15 years, and they suddenly make announcements that suggest they are going to loosen the purse strings: That's tradable! If the U.S. announces a radical policy change and foreign money panic hedges their U.S. dollar holdings, that's actionable. Those are structural stories at inflection points that will have a huge impact on the market.

But eight months after the EU announced that it decided to spend more on defense, that structural tailwind for the euro should be priced in and it will only be a tiny marginal positive going forward. Cyclical forces will re-exert themselves once again.

It's usually changes in fundamentals, not levels, that matter for markets. Structural changes are the glacier moving over the landscape and cyclical news is the daily weather. Structural factors move slowly, are hard to track, and rarely have much relevance to trading.

For most traders, cyclical factors are the dominant market driver on their time horizon, most of the time. Structural stuff can be huge at inflection points but the rest of the time it's just a distraction.

Practical Framework #3: Missing data and survivor bias

Imagine there are just five hedge funds operating in the world; performance in the table.

Now, I ask you: What is the average return of investing in a hedge fund over the past five years? "10%! Obviously!" But that's not necessarily true. Were there hedge funds that closed down in the past five years? Probably. Were their returns worse than average? Almost certainly, that's probably why they failed. When you look at returns like this, you are looking only at the *survivors*. This is called **survivor bias** or a biased sample.

	Average return over the last five years
A	10%
B	8%
C	-5%
D	14%
E	23%
Average	10%

Another example of this is when someone comes to me with a back-tested strategy where the returns look like this:

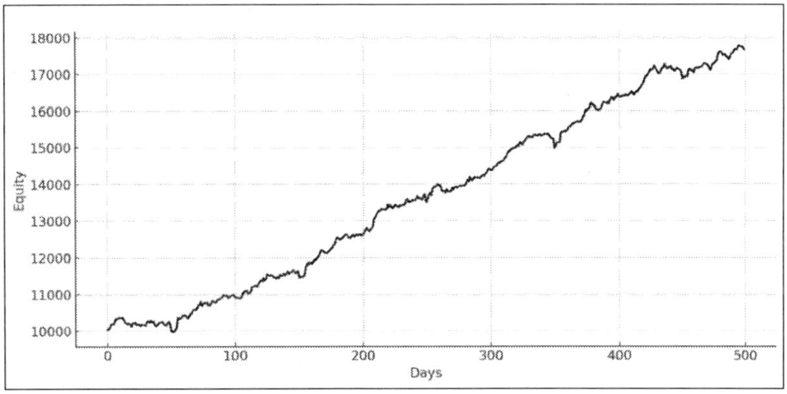

Wow! A Sharpe ratio of 4.08. Super cool. But instead of, "How much can I invest!?" my first question is, "How many other strategies did you test before you found this one?" The person is showing you a sample size of one. They might have tested fifty other strategies using a similar logic and methodology before they found this one. If your first instinct is: "The Sharpe is too damn high!" You are probably right.

When you look at only the surviving subset of a sample, your thinking will be overly optimistic. This is similar to the MBA program advertisement with its glossy images of all those successful CEOs who graduated from the school. They leave out the failures and convicted felons, natch.

When you look at a dataset, ask yourself what is missing. This is tricky because the missing data, by its nature, is invisible. This requires a smart, engaged thinker. It also goes to the broader question of looking at data with healthy skepticism. Don't just take charts and tables and information for granted. Think about what's missing.

Execution and tactics

The next three frameworks focus on specifics that can help improve your trade identification and execution approaches and methodology.

Practical Framework #4: Something weird is going on

As a trader, your intuition sharpens over time and you become a pattern recognition machine. When there is a violation of a normal pattern in markets, that should cause you to sit up in your seat and ask: "What's going on here?"

When you drop a golf ball from a height of six feet, you expect it to bounce about four feet back up off a concrete surface. You don't need a physics degree to know this; you have watched enough golf balls bounce off hard surfaces to have a pretty good idea of how it works. If you drop a golf ball onto concrete and it barely bounces, you instantly have a ton of information about the ball. Specifically, it does not conform to normal standards and is probably made of some other material. Or it's broken. Or something. An experienced professional looks at markets and sees cause and effect: when X happens, I expect Y. If Y is not the result, there is something unusual happening. Unusual stimulus/response patterns are an important way to find trade ideas, or for them to find you. **Weirdness is information.** It's a signal that perhaps unusual supply and demand dynamics are in force and these dynamics are impacting prices in ways one would not usually expect. Let me provide two different examples that were useful in real time as they were clear indicators that the normal cause and effect pattern in markets was broken.

People frequently ask me how I come up with trade ideas, but the reality is that often I don't so much find trade ideas—they find me. As I scan a huge universe of market-related information, I see patterns emerge and those patterns speak to me and suggest possible actions. Much as creativity comes from feeding your brain a ton of information and letting it mix and match… Trade ideas do too.

A critical skill for every trader is the ability to detect market anomalies. Scan your markets constantly and when you detect an anomaly, understand its meaning. Let me provide two examples of this type of indicator.

In February 2025, we saw the unusual combination of a huge rally in commodities, plus a fall in oil. The price of oil is a major input into the production of many commodities and there are many drivers of any commodity prices that should drive them all in the same direction at once (e.g., global growth, China infrastructure spending, inflationary psychology, etc.) It is uncommon for most commodity prices to rip higher while oil goes down.

One way to look at the relative prices of two securities over time, when they have dramatically different volatility profiles, is to calculate the historical rank of the current prices. For example, if we're looking at a one-year history, and BCOM (the Bloomberg Commodity Index) is trading at its highest price in a year, the rank would be 1. If it's trading at the low of the year, the rank would be 252 because there are 252 trading days in a year.

This next chart compares the rolling rank of BCOM to the rank of crude oil, looking back one year.

Rank of BCOM price minus rank of CL1 price (1-year lookback)

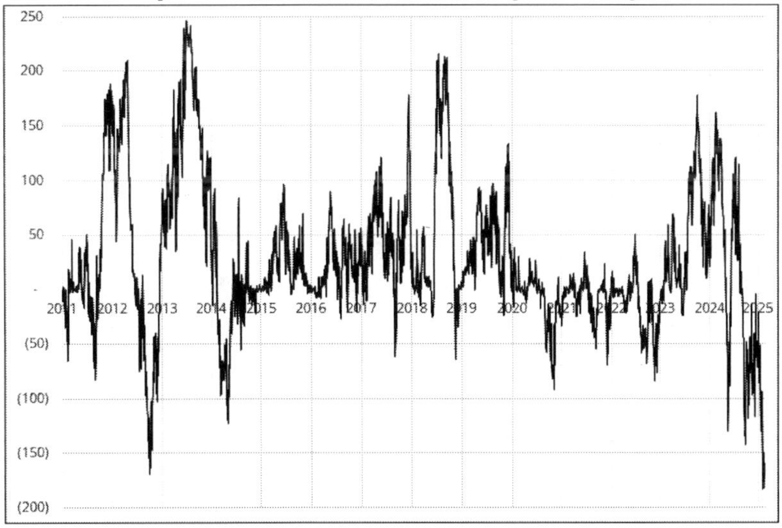

This is noteworthy, and the extreme nature of the output makes me keenly interested. An RSI of 27 isn't too exciting, for example. It happens quite often. But an RSI of 9, which might happen less than once per year, is worthy of more serious investigation.

With this chart in hand, I backtested to see what happens when you have such a crazy divergence. I filtered for the 2% most extreme data points and came up with this chart.

You have a sample size of just three regimes, so caution is warranted. That said, BCOM dropped hard after all three occurrences so this looked like a possible signal to get short commodities. At the time, I had some other reasons to think commodity prices might be too high, so I sold DBA, the Deutsche Commodity Price ETF. I chose that one because it features agricultural commodities, not oil.

Here's what DBA did after February 20, 2025, the date I came up with the idea:

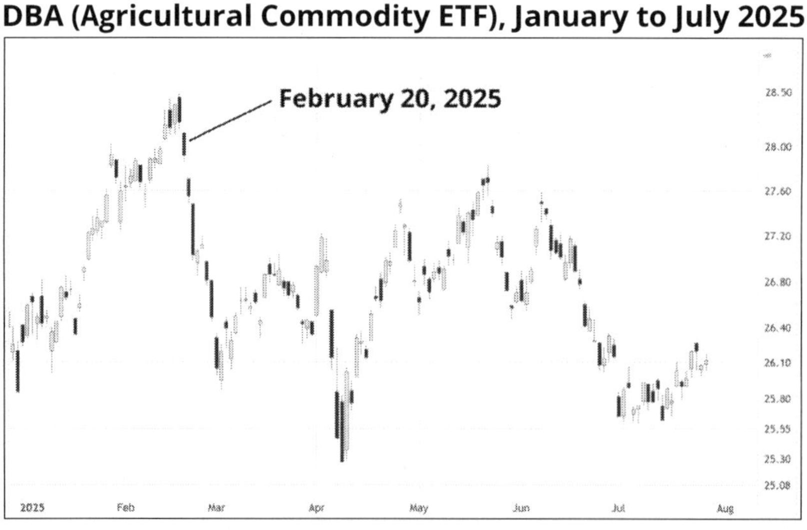

As with most of my trades, a single factor or backtest was not enough of a reason to buy DBA puts in late February 2025. But the "something weird is going on" approach put non-oil commodity prices on my radar at a time when I was already considering a short. And while the sample size of the backtest was too small to use in isolation, the setup added to other factors and was the difference that led me to pull the trigger.

One more example, using microstructure: June 13, 2025, I was short GME because I believed (and still believe) that unprofitable companies buying bitcoin are not worth owning at 3x book value. If anything, they should trade below book value because they are slowly setting cash on fire losing money in their core business and accumulating transaction costs in an asset that anyone can buy for near-zero fees. And, they pay out massive management compensation.

I don't just sit there short GME all the time, but I went short because the stock had rallied from $35 to $37 on a meaningless announcement about GameStop purchasing bitcoin. We already knew they were going to buy bitcoin, so the announcement meant nothing, and yet the stock rallied from $35 to $37 on the news. I sold at $35 on the way back down. The stock had already rallied from $28 to $35 in anticipation of GME's annual meeting and it was a textbook buy rumor / sell fact trade.

I got lucky as I held onto that GME short and ten days later they announced a secondary offering, which dilutes existing holders and usually hurts the stock price.

GME Hourly May/June 2025

I exited a good portion of my short at $28.50 (before the secondary announcement) but had about 30% of a position left when the secondary hit, so I was still watching. My plan was to take profit on the rest of the short at $20.07, but the stock didn't quite get that low.

Then something weird happened. Stocks normally have steady liquidity and volatility profiles so if you look at a 1-minute chart of GME today, it should look like a 1-minute chart of GME yesterday or the day before. The prices and trend will be different, but the price patterns, sizes of the 1-minute candles, and size of an average move over an hour or two should remain similar. Below are two 1-minute charts of GME from two normal random days. I don't recommend using 1-minute charts very often, but at times when you are in the weeds on microstructure, they can be helpful.

Two 1-minute GME charts from two random days in 2025

Now look at the 1-minute chart on June 13, 2025.

GME 1-minute chart on June 13, 2025

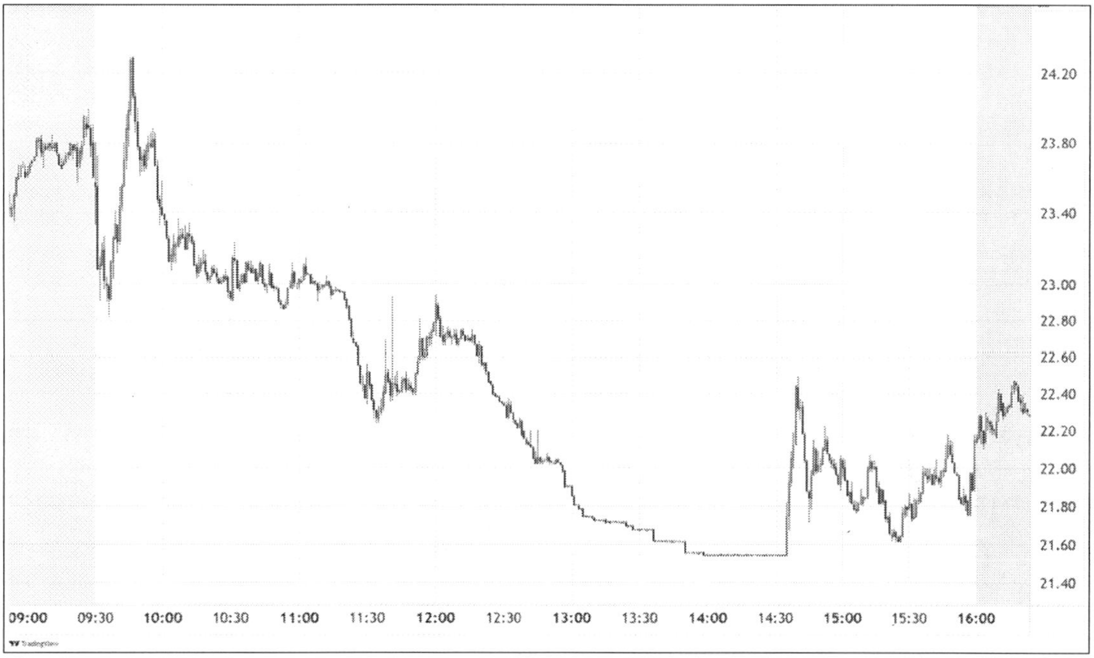

It's pretty clear that something strange was happening, starting around 13:30.

At 14:00, there was massive sell pressure and **there was a bid that looked to be absorbing infinite shares**. I watched and watched, and it was clear that whoever was on the bid was incredibly motivated. I could see on the Level 2 screen that the bid was refreshing over and over and over. The buyer absorbed all and any supply for almost half an hour so it was clear to me that staying short GME at that point was not smart. I covered, and about 20 minutes later, the price spiked as the selling pressure finally ran out.

When you see an extreme contraction in volatility and a flatline in price at a particular level, it tells you there is a huge order there. It doesn't always pay to respond to such an order, but in this case, I had ridden the trade for $10 lower and was trying to extract the final $1.40. The risk/reward on staying short was horrendous given the new information.

Don't front run every big order that you see, but take note when there is a bizarre price pattern or microstructure setup and try to figure out what it means to you.

Another place you sometimes see odd behavior is in your P&L. If you are long five different stocks, the index drops half a percent, and your P&L doesn't change, there is probably information there. Your basket of stocks (and your P&L) has outperformed what you would expect given the drop in the index and is probably set to rally from here.

Another behavior I often see in my P&L is that it peaks around the same level intraday, over and over. This is a function of the amount of risk I take times the volatility of the products I trade. If you tend to trade about 100 million USD notional in FX, and currency markets often mean revert after a 1% intraday move, you will notice that your P&L tends to peak around $1 million intraday and often mean reverts from there. That's information! If you are a short-term trader, be sure to collect daily open, high, low, and close data for your P&L. You might see some patterns.

As you become intimately familiar with the markets you trade, your P&L, and the patterns they normally obey, you will learn what is normal and what is not. When price action, volume, market maker behavior, price response to news, cross-market correlation, or some other feature of the market looks off, use some first- or second-order thinking and try to figure out what it might mean.

And speaking of trying to figure out what it means, let's look at one last example. As I write this section of the book, I have come to the realization that "something weird is going on" is pretty much my number one source of trade ideas these days!

July 7, 2025, CoreWeave (CRWV), an AI hardware hyperscaler, announced it was buying Core Scientific (CORZ). This is a straightforward deal where Core Scientific shareholders receive 0.1235 newly-issued shares of CoreWeave for each share of CORZ. Just before the announcement, CRWV was trading at $165, and as is typical after a deal announcement like this, the stock sold off. The dilution effect of paying for a company with shares normally drives the stock of the acquirer down, so this was not unusual. You see in the chart that CRWV dropped to $155, then bounced and traded $156/$162 all day.

CRWV common stock, 5-minute chart around July 7, 2025

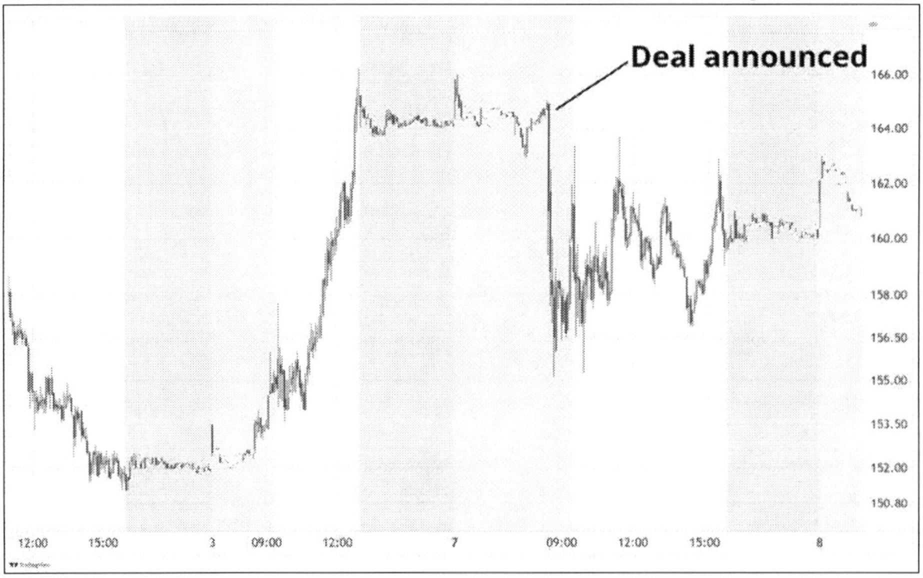

A reasonable investor would look at this and simply multiply something like $156 X 0.1235 and see that CORZ (the company being bought) should trade around $19.25. Here are the approximate values of CORZ at different levels of CRWV:

CRWV price	Implied CORZ price
165	20.38
160	19.76
155	19.14
150	18.53
145	17.91
140	17.29

In a normal world, these prices would hold because if CORZ traded significantly below the implied conversion price, you could simply short CRWV and go long CORZ and capture risk free money when the deal closes. There would be a small discount or basis in there because the deal might fall through, but in this case that discount should be small because there is no antitrust concern. Here's what CORZ did:

CORZ 5-minute chart around July 7, 2025

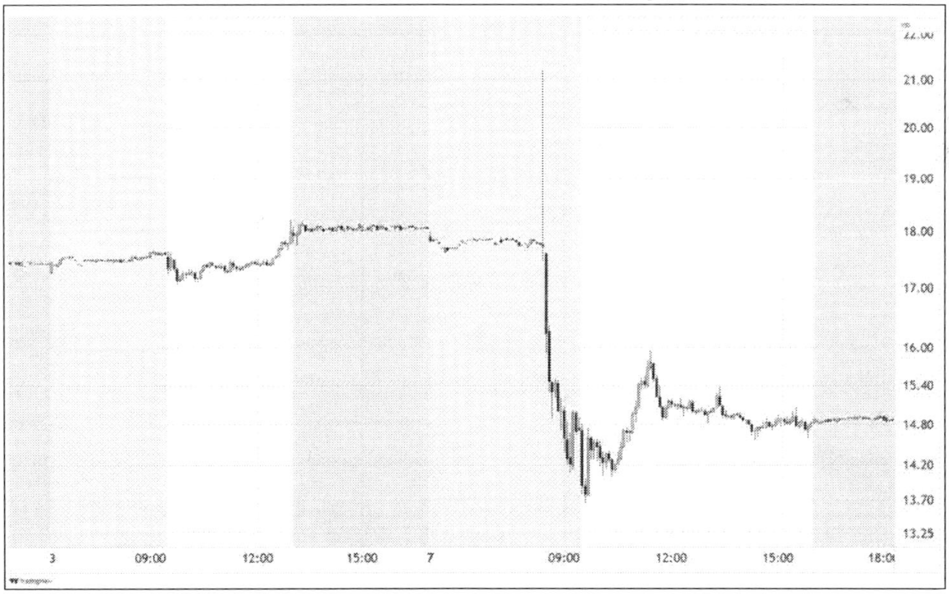

Oops. It spiked to the "logical" level at first, then cratered and immediately traded at a massive discount. It should have been trading around $19 or so, and by the time the market opened at 9:30 a.m., CORZ was trading at $13.80. I lost a lot of money buying CORZ at $17 and $16 and shorting CRWV at $157 after doing the conversion calculation quickly after the deal was announced. Ouch.

I realized I must be missing something and got out. It turns out that borrowing CRWV shares for six months was a) difficult because the stock was hard to borrow and b) insanely expensive (143% per year). There was no way to make money doing the apparent arbitrage, so there was no arbitrage. In my rush to do the trades, I forgot to check the CRWV cost to borrow.

A similar situation happened in September 2025 with the ASST / SMLR buyout. When the borrow on the acquirer is expensive or impossible, the merger arb trade isn't there.

This CRWV/CORZ thing was a bad trade for me, but it opened my eyes to a whole universe of research on expensive-to-borrow stocks and taught me the perils of M&A arb. It is nearly impossible to make money shorting stocks that have a borrow over 100% because you need a nearly-instant move in the stock price or the borrowing fees will greatly outpace the profits on the short position.

Instead of getting angry about bad trades, I try to learn something from them so that the loss feels more like tuition and less like a pure waste of money. After the losing CORZ trade, I went into the rabbit hole on hard-to-borrow stocks and learned some interesting and useful tidbits. Let me share them with you.

Side quest: Hard-to-borrow stocks underperform

Check out these two charts from Lionel Smoler-Schatz at Verdad.

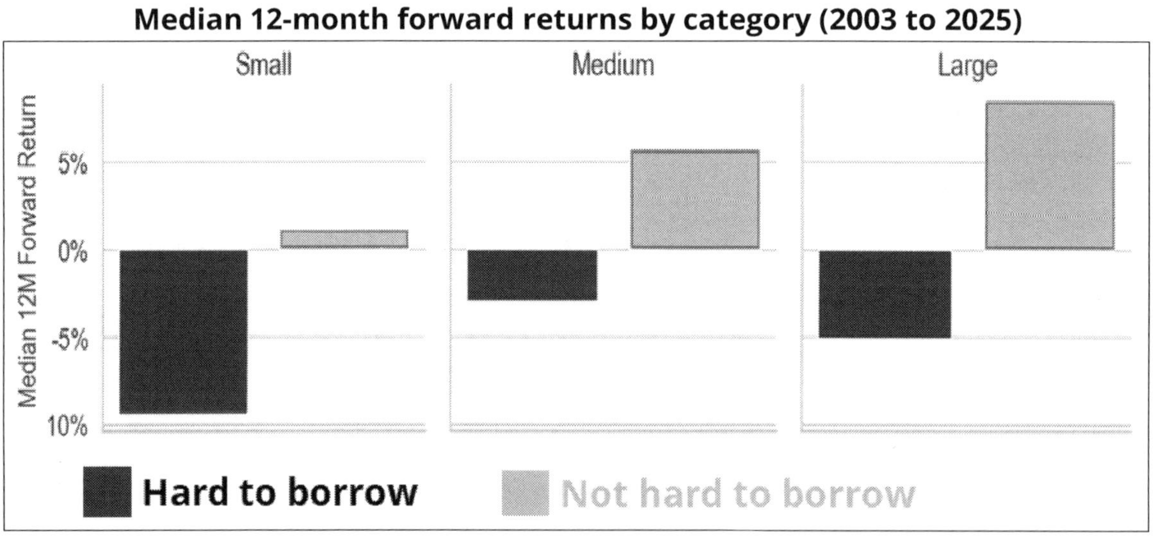

Verdad's study covers more than 30,000 stocks over 18 years, so it's an excellent sample. Here's the money chart:

Average 3-month forward return by borrow cost decile

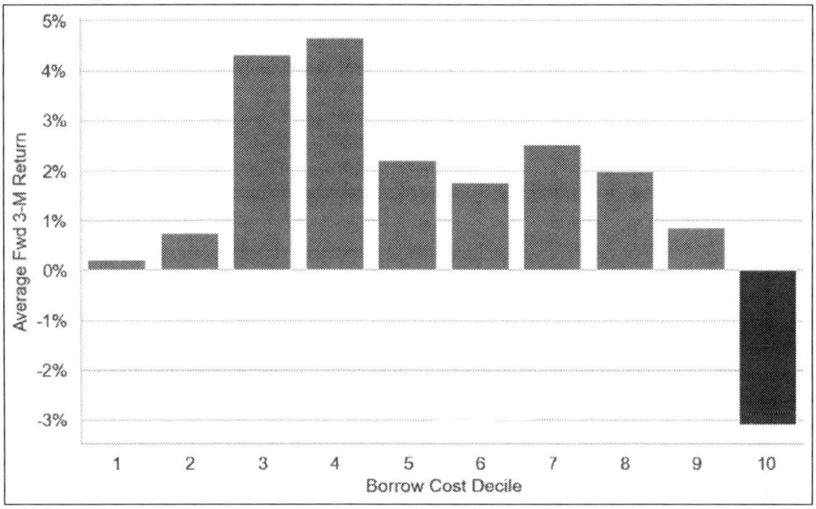

Mamma Mia! This is spicy, and almost certainly not random. The most heavily shorted stocks are heavily shorted for a reason, but markets are efficient and there is no free lunch. The stocks go down a lot, but they are expensive to borrow and thus the borrow cost wipes out the positive expected value of the short.

This is confirmed in other research, such as a 2020 piece by Hendrix and Crabb[56].

> Borrowing fees set in the securities lending market contain reliable information about the cross section of short-term expected stock returns. Using securities lending data for 14 developed and emerging markets from 2011 to 2018, we find that stocks with high borrowing fees tend to underperform their peers over the short term. Moreover, stocks that remain expensive to borrow continue to underperform, but persistence of high borrowing fees is not systematically predictable. While the information in borrowing fees is fast decaying, it can still be efficiently incorporated into real-world equity portfolios.

If the borrow fees wipe out the gains on the short, how can this be "efficiently incorporated into real-world equity portfolios" you might ask? **Exclude expensive-to-borrow stocks from your portfolio.** Here's how they put it:

> ...an efficient approach may be to temporarily refrain from purchasing the most expensive-to-borrow small cap stocks. Implementing this approach in

[56] Hendrix, Kaitlin and Crabb, Gavin, "Borrowing Fees and Expected Stock Returns" (2020)

> a daily investment process can efficiently incorporate the short-term information in the latest securities lending fees and enhance investment outcomes in a low opportunity cost manner.

Quantrocket comes to a similar conclusion and shows that a long-only portfolio that excludes expensive-to-borrow stocks outperforms one that does not.

Know the cost to borrow of all the stocks you trade and invest in. Not because you necessarily want to go short, but because the cost to borrow contains important forward-looking information. And don't fall into the trap of thinking that because a stock is heavily-shorted, it's a good long. It might be a good short squeeze candidate, but only if your timing is perfect. Generally, heavily-shorted stocks are heavily-shorted for good reason. In aggregate, they underperform.

Stocks with top decile borrowing costs are extremely bad longs and can sometimes be candidates for hit-and-run shorts. If you know the cost to borrow a stock, you have useful information about the market's perception of the company.

One last thing. A simple and often effective way to avoid expensive borrowing costs if you are bearish a stock is to simply sell at the open and cover before the close every day. You are risking that the thing will gap lower overnight, of course, but you avoid a certainty: massive bleed due to fees. I did this while bearish CRWV in July 2025, and it worked out well as the entirety of the move lower came in regular trading hours.

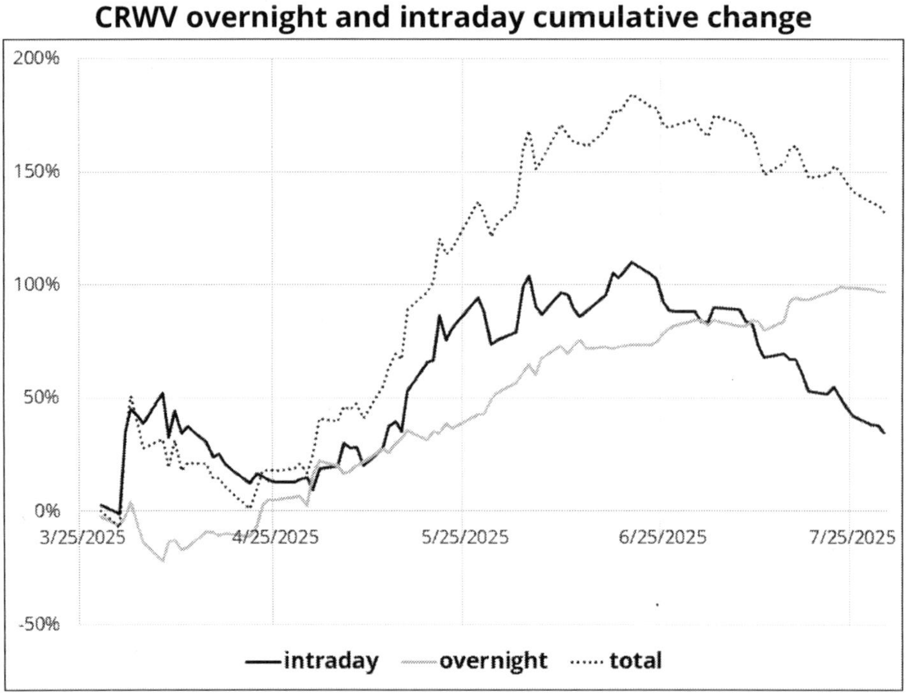

You can see that the intraday price action captured *more than* 100% of the move lower because there was a modest drift higher to the stock in overnight action. This method can generate transaction fees, but if you know what you are doing, it's extremely cheap to transact at the open and close of regular trading. Much cheaper than paying a borrow fee above 100%.

Practical Framework #5: Monthly trading audit

In *Alpha Trader* I boiled the formula for successful trading down to:

Alpha Trader = rational + intelligent + skilled + conscientious + calibrated confidence

Many traders are skilled and intelligent, but most are not rational. In fact, no one is completely rational. But **a process can be 100% rational**. That's why just about every trading book you will ever read hammers home the concept of process.

Rigorous process is the critical determinant of trading success because a good process pushes you toward rationality and away from emotional trading.

Most traders are also not conscientious enough. They want to make money and have fun trading, but they don't want to do the boring prep work that successful trading requires. If you are truly conscientious, you will take the time to do a monthly trading audit that examines your process and looks for flaws, laziness, and leaks. This audit process is described in the pages that follow.

Completing tasks like this takes you away from what *feels like* more productive time in front of the screens, but you cannot improve if you keep repeating the same mistakes. Much like a golfer who goes out on the course and smashes his driver off every tee without considering in real-time or after the fact whether or not his driver is the right club to hit… Traders who keep trading day after day and week after week without any time for self-reflection and proper auditing will continue to perform poorly.

Take one hour at the end of each month to go through this three-step audit. In this section, we study performance in one-month chunks. First you orient and observe, then you decide, then finally, once you've done the audit, you act. The self-reflection gained will make your actions more rational and your trading more profitable.

This iterative process, known as an OODA loop, was developed by Air Force Colonel John Boyd, known as "Forty Second Boyd" for his standing bet that he could defeat any opposing pilot in less than 40 seconds, and the architect of the strategy to invade Iraq in the Gulf War of 1991. Originally developed for air combat, his OODA loop concept has been adopted in litigation, war strategy, and business management.

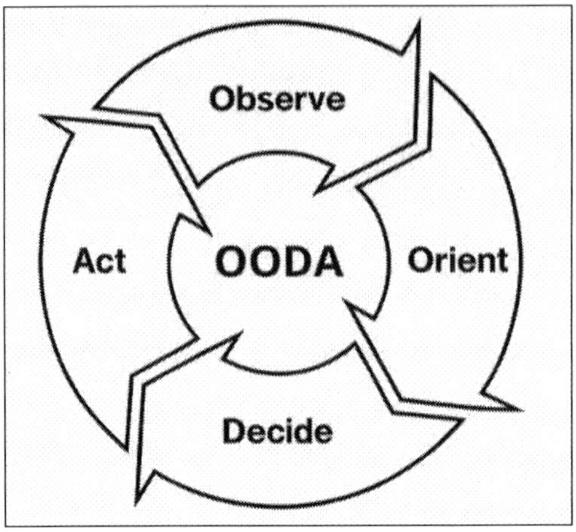

The following forms will help you complete your monthly trading audit. You can find larger versions in Excel and PDF format at:

www.spectramarkets.com/TOTBaudit

Monthly Trading Audit

1. **Observe** by taking stock of the current state of your markets. Keep it simple and high level. Record thoughts on any market you regularly trade.

Monthly Trading Audit Page 1 - State of the Markets			
	Quick description of current regime (keep it simple, only mention salient points)	Is this regime likely to persist next month?	What might change this regime? Data, events, price level breaks, etc.
Narrative			
Economics			
Correlation			
Sentiment			
Positioning			
Volatility			
Liquidity			
Range or Trend			

2. **Orient** yourself by taking stock of your performance last month. Again, you don't need to go into incredible depth here. The idea is to get you to think about what you are doing and step outside yourself to view your trading in the third person. **If you were an unbiased trading coach evaluating your trading performance over the past 30 days, what would you say to yourself?** Be honest. Specific questions for this step are in the TOTBaudit pdf link on the previous page.

3. **Decide** what to do next month. You set risk limits and goals and then print them out and keep them on your desk for constant reference.

<table>
<tr><th colspan="3">Monthly Trading Audit Page 3 - Plan for next month</th></tr>
<tr><td rowspan="4">Limits for next month
(where applicable)</td><td>Risk per trade or day (% of free capital)</td><td></td></tr>
<tr><td>Daily stop loss</td><td></td></tr>
<tr><td>Monthly stop loss</td><td></td></tr>
<tr><td>Yearly stop loss</td><td></td></tr>
<tr><th colspan="3">Process Tracker</th></tr>
<tr><td colspan="2"></td><td>1 to 5</td></tr>
<tr><td rowspan="9">1: never
2: sometimes
3: often
4: most of the time
5: always</td><td>Position size determined by math</td><td></td></tr>
<tr><td>Stop loss set with technical analysis or math</td><td></td></tr>
<tr><td>Risk units clearly defined (% of capital)</td><td></td></tr>
<tr><td>SL, TP and reassessment triggers on all trades</td><td></td></tr>
<tr><td>Emotional check-ins in calendar</td><td></td></tr>
<tr><td>Consistent time frame</td><td></td></tr>
<tr><td>Pre-trade or morning checklist?</td><td></td></tr>
<tr><td>Asymmetry for trades known
(price convexity, headline risk)</td><td></td></tr>
<tr><td>Wrote in trading or personal journay</td><td></td></tr>
<tr><th colspan="3">One Goal for next month</th></tr>
<tr><td colspan="3"></td></tr>
</table>

4. Finally, you're ready for next month, and you **act**. This loop should continue indefinitely. In case you don't remember every word of *Alpha Trader*, here's why I believe you should only set one goal per month and then evaluate that goal at the end of the month.

> I am a big believer in working on just one or two measurable and achievable goals at a time. Let me explain.
>
> When I was a senior manager at a bank, we used a formal corporate goal-setting system and usually it allowed for somewhere between five and fifteen goals to be entered. I found that was just way too many goals for me to supervise or coach as a leader and way too many goals for an employee to manage as an individual.
>
> I eventually instituted my own "One Goal" system. I told the people that worked for me that all those goals in the corporate system were great, but all I cared about was their one most important goal. I asked them to e-mail me that goal and explain why it was important and how they planned to achieve it. This was effective. I saw much more impact from this One Goal system than I ever saw from more formalized, multi-goal systems.
>
> So... After reviewing your trading journal, come up with a short-term goal for the next month or two.
>
> A goal like "I will not drink any soda for the next month" is more realistic than "I'm never going to drink soda again." Achievable short-term goals develop habits and processes that will lead to achievement of bigger-picture, longer-term goals.
>
> Here are a few hypothetical examples that might emerge after auditing your prior month's trading:
>
> - No S&P futures trades for 30 days. All the money I make in other assets, I give back with my irresistible urge to go short S&Ps!
> - My trading journal entries are much more emotional than usual. Tighten daily stop loss to $15,000. My normal stop is $30,000 but I have been trading badly and I know I'm in a weird state of mind because my Dad is really sick.
> - No trades between noon and 3 p.m. Those trades hit 35% of the time vs. 57% of all trades initiated outside that time frame.

Practical Framework #6: Red line-items

In the late 1990s, I was a day trader at Swift Trade, one of many day trading firms popular during the dotcom bubble. My seat was free, and I paid a few pennies per share in commission to the firm. The commissions added up, but it was a fair deal.

My methodology at the time was simple. I had the S&P 500 futures pit squawk on headphones and six high-value, wide-bid/offer stocks like JDSU and QCOM on my screen. When the futures ticked higher in the pit or a huge buy order came in, I would get on the bid in the stocks I watched, especially if there was good bid-side liquidity to back into. Then, as soon as I got filled, I would offer the shares out one or two spreads higher. In most cases, these stocks traded fifty cents to one dollar wide, so two spreads might be $1.50 total. On 300 shares, that's $450.

I would also trade whatever random headlines and nonsense I could. Joe Kernan would tease his Stock of the Week, for example: "This $3-billion medical device company based in Austin, Texas could be set to soar. Stay tuned for our Stock of the Week, after the break."

CNBC would go to commercial and I would frantically search for the company on Yahoo! (this was before Google was a thing). If I found it, I'd buy 500 shares, then flip them for a $3 profit when Kernan came back and revealed the name of the stock.

At Swift Trade, one trader who was persistently unprofitable and had to keep reloading his account over and over asked: "Hey, how is it possible that every single time I walk past, every position you have is in the green?"

I honestly didn't know, so I just shrugged and said something self-deprecating. But as he walked away, I realized the answer: I didn't have any red line items because I always cut them. I was almost exclusively doing trades that were either *correct right away*, or *wrong right away*. And I was disciplined about cutting losers.

Not everyone can trade in such a clean way and instacut their losses, but this echoes something we discussed in Chapter 8: Trades that go right or wrong immediately use far less mental capital than trades that last days or weeks. If you are impatient and twitchy, it's good to have a trading strategy like this.

Multi-day and even multi-week traders can learn here, too. Go through the line items in your P&L on a regular basis, and find the positions that are in the red. Ask yourself:

- Why do I still have this position?
- Do I still believe in the view, or is it stale?
- Is this position draining my mental capital?
- Would it be useful to cut this trade and move on?
- Where is my stop loss?

Sometimes after I have been fighting with a stock or currency position all day, or even for a week or more, I will make the determination to surrender. The trade is positive EV on paper—if it's bugging you, and it's in the red, consider cutting it. The longer you fight a particular market or security, the more difficult it becomes to walk away.

There are instances where I am trying to catch a major top or bottom and I am willing to fight. But often when I'm fighting the market, it's just not worth it. There are so many other trades and ideas I could be working on. Staring at a big red number beside a trade I don't love is a sign that it's time to let go. The mental relief you feel when you cut one of these trades is immense.

Finally, if you are a short-term trader, review your red line items around 3 p.m. each day and decide which ones are worth keeping overnight. Often, the answer is: none. Each of those red lines has emotions attached, sometimes strong ones. Don't carry negative emotions over from one day to the next. If you lost 3x your normal daily loss today because of bad discipline, you are not doing yourself any favors by leaving the losing trades in your blotter overnight, hoping to get out at a smaller loss tomorrow. That trade that took all your mental capital today will be sitting there ready to drain you again the moment you turn on your computer tomorrow.

Trade structuring

Practical Framework #7: Skillful structures

While investing generally involves a one-dimensional decision of "what to buy?" ... Trading sits at the other end of the decision-making complexity spectrum. The trader's decision process has many dimensions:

- Long or short?
- What asset?
- At what price?
- How long do I hold?
- How to structure it: cash, futures, or options?
- Where to put the stop loss and take profit?
- What are the other reassessment triggers?

Trade structuring is an underappreciated, under-studied topic. People spend all day figuring out which way a stock is likely to go, then they press buy or sell without considering the speed of the possible move, headline risks, gap risk, convexity, or transaction costs. They think about the destination, and forget to consider the path.

Some traders always place directional trades. Others only buy volatility. Some only sell volatility. This is too rigid. Accurately estimating the path of the security on the way to its destination can be more important than accurately determining direction itself.

For example, let's look at EURUSD in 2025. Everybody was bullish EUR and bearish USD. Some people cleaned up. Others lost money being bullish, even as the view came true in spades.

EURUSD daily with 50-day moving averages (SMA and EMA)

EURUSD broke higher through the moving averages in March 2025 as the market ricocheted from bearish to bullish. European defense spending announcements and wildly unpredictable U.S. economic policy broke the USD bulls and by April 2025, pretty much everyone was bullish EURUSD.

Those that bought spot or sold puts in March did well, no matter where they put their stop loss. Those that bought options did great if they took profit early enough and didn't buy anything too long dated. Many who bought exotic options lost their entire bet because EURUSD went up too fast.

On the other hand, those who bought spot in April mostly got stopped out. Those who bought options made a small profit, but not much, because EURUSD was unchanged from mid-April to mid-June (1.1300). And those who bought exotic options did well as their calls paid off but their knockouts never triggered.

Speed, timing and direction of a move are equally important, and you should always be thinking about all three.

While the specifics of what option to buy in different circumstances is too big of a topic for this book, the structuring decision should start with the question: Cash or options? If you are shorting a stock, for example, the two big questions are:

1. How much do you expect the stock to fall?
2. Do you have a specific time frame or catalyst in mind?

In short: **How far and how fast?**

There is an appropriate strategy for each speed and size of an expected move. The most extreme example: if you expect a stock to drop to zero tomorrow, options will give you much more leverage and you don't have to worry much about timing or time decay (theta). And you want the farthest possible strike because that will give you the most leverage.

In contrast, if you expect a stock to do nothing for a while and eventually drop 20 percent or so at some unknown time... Options are not going to look as good and low-delta strikes are certainly no bueno.

Why options can be better

Options help you accomplish specific goals in a trade. Here are situations where options can work better than cash:

- **Avoid getting stopped out.** Once you buy an option, you are in the position until the option expires. In a cash trade, you might get stopped right before the trade idea goes your way. In choppy, headline-driven markets, options keep you in the trade.
- **Maximize leverage.** If you buy an option and there is a gigantic move right away... Your option will make more money than a cash position would have.
- **Maximize positions more easily**. If you want to be short 500 million AUDUSD, it's tough to run a cash position with a stop loss. But you can (fairly) easily strap on a billion AUD of puts that give you a delta of 500 million. Options are good for putting on huge trades.
- **Avoid gap risk and limit risk.** If you went short ZM stock into earnings in 2021, you are probably reading this on your phone while on break from your job at Krusty Burger because you blew up your account. In contrast, if you bought ZM puts, they went to zero and your risk was finite. When you buy options, you decide how much to spend and then you either lose that much, or less. When you go long or short in cash markets, you expose yourself to gap risk on news, weekends, or after hours.
- **Achieve custom payout profiles.** If you think a stock is going to go up but not to the moon, you could trade a spread that gives you high leverage for your view while substantially reducing your premium outlay.

You have no choice but to do options when a stock is prohibitively expensive or impossible to borrow, as was often the case in 2025 with CoreWeave (CRWV), an AI stock that many viewed as an excellent short when or if the Artificial Intelligence (AI) bubble ever burst.

The problem with hard-to-borrow stocks is that the put options reflect this. There is unusual demand for puts in these stocks because people that would normally sell the stock short are unable to. And the cost of a put includes the stock's cost to borrow. Therefore, even if you think it's a great short, puts will be way too expensive. In this situation, the best play is very often to sell call spreads. You could also sell naked calls, in theory, but usually this is much too dangerous for anyone who is not a well-trained options professional. Even options professionals go bust selling outright vol. Better to take lower absolute returns while eliminating risk of ruin.

I was able to make good money selling CRWV call spreads by picking a strike very close to the current price of the stock, selling it, and buying the closest strike right above that.

A stock is trading at $150. You sell a $150 call and buy a $151 call, earning 50 cents. That is, you risk X to make X. If your normal risk amount is $2,500 per trade, then you would do 50 contracts, earning $2,500 if the idea works, and losing $2,500 if it does not.

By doing a spread with two nearby strikes, you reduce the risk of getting exercised. If you sell a $150/$155 call spread and the stock closes anywhere in that $5 window, you will get exercised on the short call. This is bad news for anyone using most of their margin most of the time (like me!)

Maximize the premium pickup while minimizing the chances you will get exercised.

You cannot get huge leverage using this strategy, but you rarely get huge leverage buying puts on a stock like CRWV either because the cost of the puts is so high. You have to buy options that are way out of the money to get any leverage, and you will usually find they expire worthless. In contrast, when you sell a skinny, nearby call spread, you're hoping for the stock to go down—or do nothing. You don't need perfect timing, and you don't need an epic move in the stock.

Why options can be worse

- Timing is critical, especially on short-dated options.
- If the market goes nowhere, you lose money. This is called time decay, or theta. Each day you wait, you bleed. Cash positions do not generally have this feature.
- You can be right and lose money. If the asset moves your way, but not enough to cover the option premium, you lose money. The price you pay and the strike are key.
- Bid/offer is wider in options.
- **Events and obvious catalysts tend to be overpriced.** Events and catalysts are the two setups where you most want to use options, and they are the most expensive. The dream scenario for option buyers is when you have a view on an event or catalyst but that view is not priced into the options market.

There is a big speech from the Deputy Governor of the RBNZ tonight. People know about it, but nobody cares. You believe the central bank could be about to pivot and there is a decent chance the Deputy Governor may say something important: you have a divergent view on volatility. The market thinks the speech is a nothingburger and you think it's important. This is a good setup for buying options.

Those are the main points on options vs. cash. To understand which one provides a better expression of a trade you like, build a spreadsheet. It's easy and it forces you to analyze what you're getting into.

Pros and cons of shorting and options strategies

	Pros			Cons		
Short the stock	No upfront cost	Timing not as critical	Profit increases as stock falls all the way to zero	Stop loss adds new risks	Gap risk	Negative carry
Near or at-the-money put	No stop loss required	Don't need a huge move lower to get to your strike	Liquid with volume and reasonable bid/ask (usually)	Expensive	A straight cash position is often better for most outcomes	Not much leverage
Low delta put		Big leverage gives it home run potential	High % returns when you are correct	Easy to be correct (the stock falls) but lose money (it didn't fall enough)	Longer dates can still be expensive	Timing has to be good
Put spread		Cheaper than vanilla and nice compromise between low delta and ATM strategies	Less premium and more precision if you have a high-confidence downside target	P&L is capped by the far strike	Wide bid/offer--If you change your mind it's expensive to square up	Can be tricky to manage short strike at expiry

Not every catalyst is well-understood and priced in. When you have a differential opinion on an event, that can be an incredibly juicy setup. For example:

Say NVIDIA is hosting a quantum computing conference on June 15th and you know the CEO of Rigetti (a quantum computing firm) will be there. You think there is a decent chance that he'll announce a new partnership with NVDA, but the conference hasn't been publicized much yet. Buying options that expire on June 16 or June 17 could offer significant leverage if the market has not adjusted the level of implied vol.

To take another example: You think that if 125.00 breaks in USDJPY, it will lead to a huge stop loss run and breakout. Buying 125.00 or 125.50 USD calls could offer outsized leverage because technical breaks are almost never priced into the options market. In contrast, buying an option for a corporate earnings release or nonfarm payrolls is always going to offer much less leverage because the market easily and efficiently prices in events like this.

The decision on how to structure a trade comes down to three factors:

1. Where do you think the market is going?
2. What path do you think it will take to get there?
3. How much do options cost?

Trade structuring ideas

You don't have to put all your eggs in one structure. Consider layering your trades with a few different strikes and expiries. This avoids the bad luck risk of putting all your money on a single options trade and then pinning the strike at expiry. For example, If you are bullish MSTR on a 2-week time horizon, and it's trading at $400 you can buy 1-week $420 calls, and also go long some stock with a stop loss at $374.

Treat your trading as a business. How might particular trade structures help or hurt you in the bigger picture? How does trade structuring fit into the overall business?

For example, as mentioned in the section on one-trick ponies: In my first 10 years as a market maker and desk manager, I always bought options and never sold them. Over time, I realized this was wrong-way risk because higher volatility is always good for a market making franchise and therefore if vol went into the toilet, the market making business would suffer and all those options I bought would expire worthless at the same time.

On the other hand, if you are a retail trader, your plan needs to minimize risk of ruin. An option trade can help, even if it has lower expected value than a cash trade, if it eliminates risk of ruin. If you want to short a $12 biotech stock but an FDA approval might cause a $40 gap overnight, puts are less risky than shorting the stock, even if they're expensive.

Structuring influences future flexibility. Call spreads are cheaper than outright calls, but they significantly reduce your flexibility. If you buy a $40 call and the stock rips from $35 to $40, you have many choices: you can trade delta against the strike, you can sell the option, or you can sell a higher strike to turn it into a call spread and lock in a ton of profit. In contrast, if you own a $40/$45 call spread in this situation, you are pretty much locked in: it's very hard to delta hedge spreads or exotic options. More complex structures also usually involve higher transaction costs.

However: If you overtrade, reduced flexibility can sometimes be a good thing because it stops you from trading your way out of good positions. Know thyself.

When you trade options, make a plan. As soon as you put on an options trade, know what you're going to do if it starts to work. Otherwise, you will find yourself trading out of winners and giving away the leverage you had by using options in the first place.

I have been guilty of buying an option and then when the trade worked right away, delta hedging too much of it, thinking: "I can trade around the strike a few times, and pay for my premium!" Then, the security keeps ripping and I have traded out of an amazing position.

I now have a firm rule that **I never trade more than 1/3 of my notional at the strike**. This helps avoid the trap where leverage from options creates a larger than normal position and the P&L volatility is too much, or the temptation to trade around the position too inviting.

Each day is cheaper than the last. Matt Gittins gave me this tip: If you're buying short-dated options, always buy at least one more day than you were thinking. The price of extra days is tiny compared to the first one or two days.

For example, below is the cost (in bps) of short duration 150.00 USDJPY call options, priced on July 15, 2025. Currency options are priced in 1/100ths of a percent, or basis points.

Cost and marginal cost increase of short-dated options in USDJPY

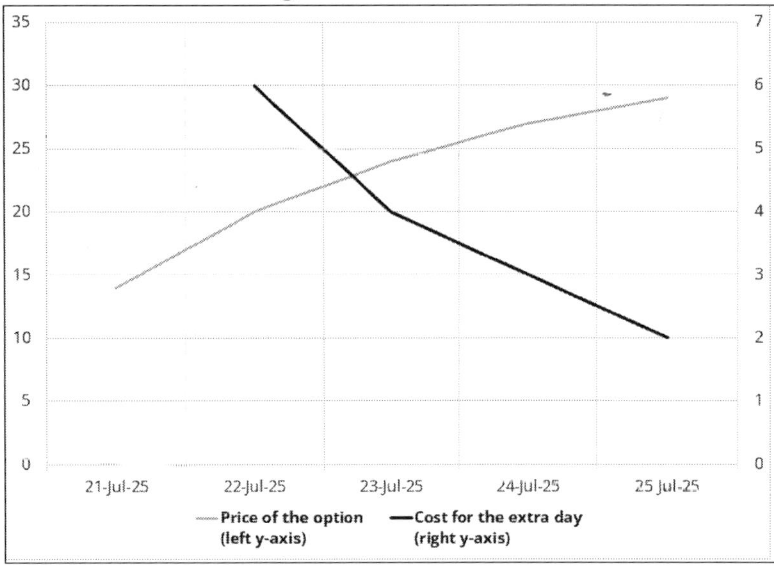

Expiry	Price of the option (left y-axis)	Cost for the extra day (right y-axis)
21-Jul-25	14	
22-Jul-25	20	6
23-Jul-25	24	4
24-Jul-25	27	3
25-Jul-25	29	2

You can see that as you buy more days, the option gets more expensive but the incremental cost for each day goes down. There is always a tradeoff between leverage (the cheapest option with the largest notional) and positive expected value (an option that won't expire worthless right before whatever you predicted actually happens).

An example from the world of equity options:

I am typing this on July 23, 2025, and Google earnings come out tonight. If I want to capture the earnings release and nothing else, it would make sense to buy the shortest possible date to maximize leverage. But say I think GOOG earnings are going to miss, the stock is going to run lower for a while afterwards because equity seasonality is poor this time of year, and a big earnings miss could lead to a series of downgrades as analysts start to worry that

Google is losing search share to ChatGPT and others. In that case, I may want to own an option that lasts a few more days. Let's compare.

The stock is trading at $190 right now, and I think a large move is coming, so I am interested in $180 strikes. Here is how the cost evolves as we go out the curve.

Cost and marginal cost increase of short-dated options in GOOG

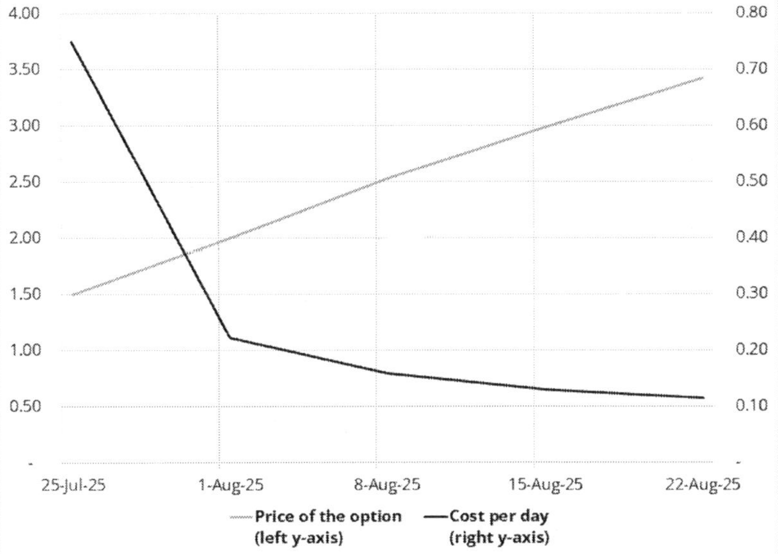

Expiry	Option cost	Days to expiry	Cost per day
25-Jul-25	1.50	2	0.75
1-Aug-25	2.00	9	0.22
8-Aug-25	2.53	16	0.16
15-Aug-25	2.98	23	0.13
22-Aug-25	3.42	30	0.11

Options pros understand the non-linear increase in short-dated options prices: **price goes up by the square root of time, not by time.** This is especially true over events, but I did not always have a good handle on this! The second day relative to the first day is particularly attractive in FX options because overnight options generally expire in less than 24 hours.

Similarly, when the front date is an event, the subsequent dates will be relatively cheaper to add because much of the cost in the option (such as in this example over Google earnings) is the event premium.

There is no one-size-fits-all structure that is best for trading. Every time you have a view and a trade idea, think about the path, speed, destination, and risk management nuances of the trade and then thoughtfully structure your trade around these parameters. Different ideas require different structures. Sometimes cash is best. Sometimes options.

Principle 20: Different views require different structures. Be flexible.

Practical Framework #8: Moving averages

A simple and beautiful framework is filtering all your ideas using MAs (moving averages). Trading around moving averages can lead to chop during rangebound regimes, but if you are confident in your ability to call direction and trend in your market, you should be comfortable using a moving average to signal yes or no. You will never find yourself in prolonged losing trades that eat up huge chunks of mental capital if you employ this sort of framework.

You are bullish bonds, bullish stocks, and bearish USD. You believe the signals from the 20-day moving average best capture the trend on your time horizon. Simply set a rule that you are never long below the moving average and you are never short above it. **The moving average becomes an on/off switch** that automatically keeps you from fighting the market.

The other nice feature of using MAs as a filter is that you have a built-in trailing stop when you make a correct call. As the price rises, the MAs rise, and your exit parameters slowly lock in profits automatically.

People often ask me what moving average(s) to use. There is no correct answer. Find moving averages that approximately fit the slope of the primary trends in the time horizon and product you are trading.

Here's how I test a few MAs in GBPUSD.

Finding an MA that roughly fits the trend in GBPUSD by trial and error

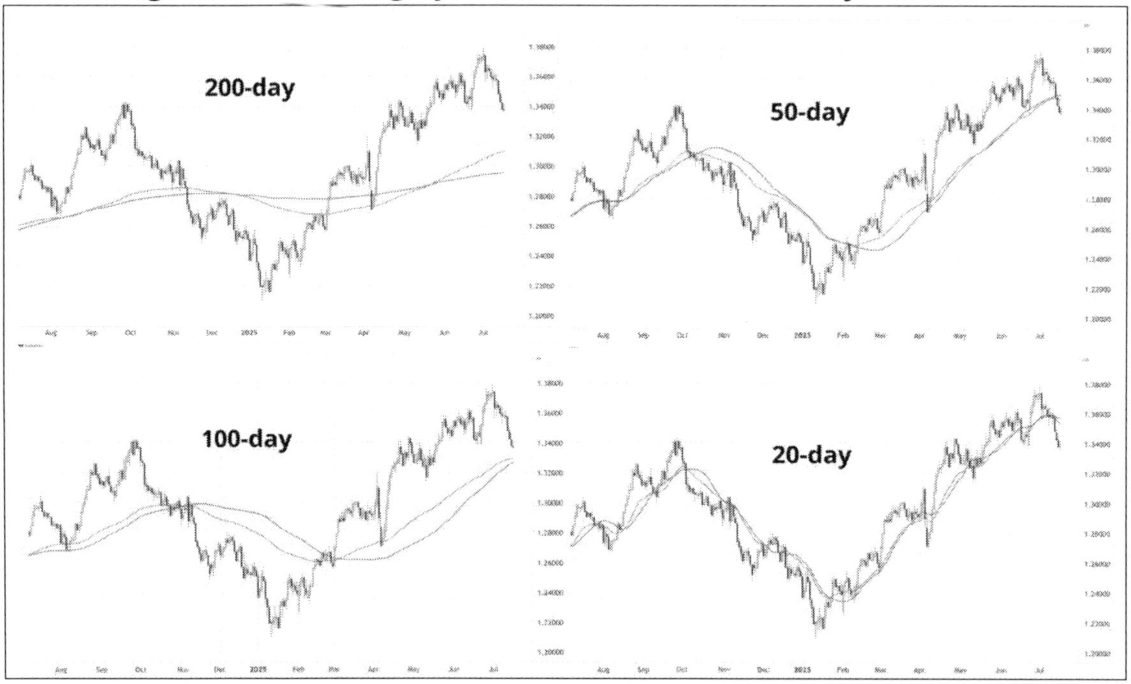

Eyeballing those, the 200-day clearly does not define the trend, at all. The 100-day is OK... Getting better. The 50-day has clearly defined the trend in both directions - this is good. The 20-day is too fast, it's getting chopped to bits. So I use the 50-day moving averages as my trend indicator.

"Aren't you just backfitting here?" Yes! I am making an implicit assumption that the trend and volatility characteristics of GBPUSD will remain somewhat stable going forward. If we were about to enter a crazy regime shift in the UK, I would not make that assumption. But in this case, I think that the current regime in GBP trend and vol will continue. Trend and vol regimes by currency pair in FX are fairly stable over time.

I like using the simple and exponential moving averages in tandem because they provide a clean trend definition. When they cross, they signal a likely trend change. If you use (for example) a 50-day and a 100-day moving average on a chart, you have separate signals that cross over one another very slowly, but if you use the 50-day EMA and SMA, you have a clear trend and a quick crossover.

Practical Framework #9: Seasonality

"Seasonality is bullsh*t." "Seasonality is just your imagination." "Apophenia, dude." "There is no statistical significance to your observations. Your sample size is too small."

Those are rebuttals when I write about seasonal patterns in market data. There *is* reason to be skeptical of seasonality: if you torture a big enough set of daily, weekly, and monthly data in enough currencies or asset classes, some of it is going to imply seasonality, even if there is no rhyme or reason.

As such, I'm not a huge fan of data mining or intentionally *looking* for seasonality. If you look hard enough... You will DEFINITELY find some seasonality in your data simply because seemingly meaningful patterns will always emerge from random data if your data set is large enough.

On the other hand, I have observed the flows that drive seasonality firsthand from my market making seat and they are anything but random or bullsh*t.

If you can observe or measure the seasonality of the flow, and that seasonal flow pattern matches the seasonal pattern of the price, you're onto something. If you can observe such patterns, say, 10 years ago, and they continue to work to this day, out of sample... Even better.

Seasonality in FX

A glaring example in FX is the tendency for large U.S. corporations to buy USD to hedge global revenues on the third last business day of each month, "Corporate Month-End", "t minus 2" or "t-2". "t" represents the last business day of the month and "minus 2" means: minus two business days.

Spot currency trades are settled after two days so if you want a trade to settle on the last day of the month, the simplest way to do that is to trade t-2. Many U.S. corporations are natural USD buyers and for simplicity, they hedge each month or each quarter on t-2. This might sound unsophisticated, but these companies are in the pharmaceutical, smartphone, software or *whatever* business, not in FX speculation. They hedge programmatically as revenue comes in. It would be expensive and time-consuming to hedge every day, so they either do it once per month or quarter.

Here is the performance of long USDJPY and GBPUSD on t-2, back to when people first started talking about the effect and I started noticing corporate activity spiking.

USDJPY cumulative performance on t-2 (2014 to 2024)

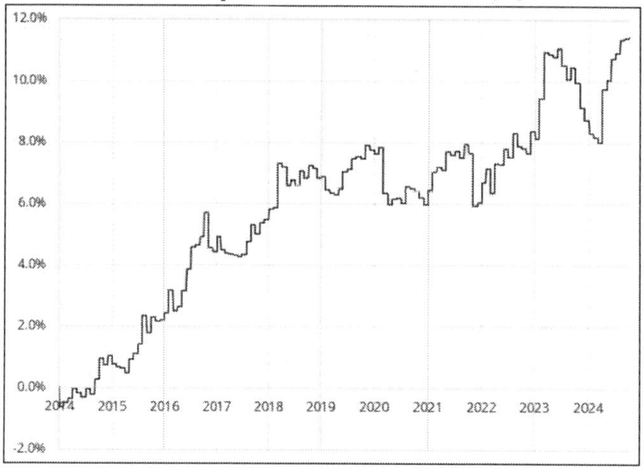

GBPUSD cumulative performance on t-2 (2014 to 2024)

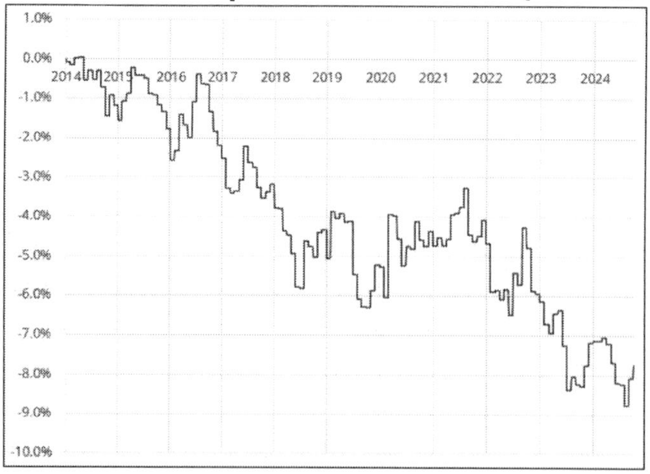

The odds of GBPUSD going up or down on any random day are close to 50/50. On t-2, GBPUSD's up/down odds are 37%/63%! USDJPY's up/down ratio is 54%/46% on t-2 and 51%/49% on all other days. The USD buying effect is persistent and does not have anything to do with the trend in the currency pair. And like I said: as a market maker I have seen the flows. They're huge.

This is a good example of logical, observable seasonality of price that reflects seasonality of flow. Note that seasonality doesn't work every time! There could be economic data, large moves in risky assets, or other events and circumstances impacting currency markets on t-2. Seasonality is a probabilistic framework that tells you an asset is more likely to move one way or the other. No guarantees!

Another seasonal pattern in FX is USDJPY around Japanese fiscal year end, March 31. This pattern has been known for years, yet it continues to work out of sample. Again, I have seen these flows while working at a Japanese bank and at banks that serviced Japanese customers. The big funds in Japan buy foreign assets and sell JPY around fiscal year end and do large portfolio window dressing right at the turn of the fiscal year.

If you pick any 8-day period at random in USDJPY, the odds of USDJPY going higher are 50/50. If you look only at the window around fiscal year end, USDJPY went up 15 out of the last 20 years (75%). If you randomly noticed this effect, it would sound like fitted parameter selection or datamining, but if you see something happening in real life, then verify it with the data, that (to me) is a completely different result. A sample size of 20 is small, but the data supports the observation and thus I believe the bar for statistical significance is lower.

Here is the P&L of long USDJPY only from March 27 to April 5 every year.

Cumulative P&L of USDJPY long from March 27 to April 5 every year

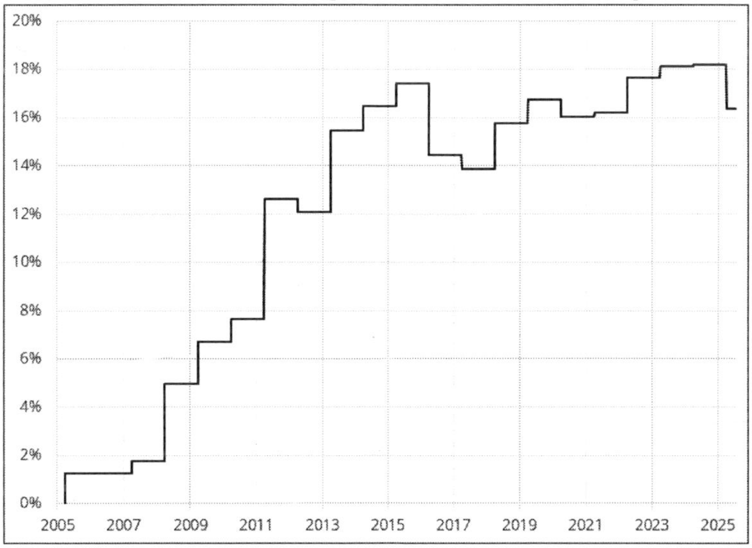

Again, it doesn't work every time obviously. This is like seeing a data set that shows a tennis player hit 15 of 20 good first serves for a 75% first serve success rate. That data on its own probably doesn't tell you much. But if you are watching the player and she shows evidence of excellent form and identical, repeatable mechanics, you probably trust the data more. Since I saw the flows that created that seasonality from 2009 to 2021, I am close to certain it's not the product of complete randomness.

Will these observed behaviors and patterns continue forever? No. Are they more than the product of snooping around in the data? Yes. The seasonality I am describing here is like a scientist making observations, coming up with a rational hypothesis, then using data to confirm or disprove the hypothesis. The more data, the better, of course.

Seasonality in stocks

I have never been a market maker in stocks, so I have to take a different approach here. Academic literature supports persistent seasonal effects in equities, such as the Halloween Effect (aka *Sell in May and Go Away*) noticed in the 1970s and which has worked well out of sample since then.

But if I can't find an explanation for it, I can't strongly believe that it will persist, and I'm not a fan of waving around academic studies because many can't be replicated or don't work out of sample, even if they're methodologically sound.

Fortunately, in equities, there is plenty of flow data available, and it's fairly easy to estimate the timing of major equity flows. Other than wages and salaries, here are the major cash flows (in and out) that impact households during the year.

January/mid-February

Incomes dip as seasonal work ends and overtime falls off. Retail and hospitality businesses cut worker hours drastically as consumer spending drops after Christmas.

Mid-Feb to mid-March

Not much.

Mid-March to early May

Tax refunds (total $250B+)

May to August

Peak home buying season (money out of stocks to make down payments)

August/September

Tuition and tax payments ($600B+) trigger withdrawals from the stock market and income falls as summer jobs end and seasonal summer industries (tourism, landscaping, agriculture) wind down. Summer vacations also lead to a hiring lull as companies transition from summer to the Q4 holiday push.

October/November

Tax payments.

December

Seasonal employment rises, more overtime, plus Christmas gifts and bonuses.

I'm not just trying to find cash flows to match the seasonality of the stock market! This is just how money flows through households, generally. This chart from JP Morgan shows median monthly income in the U.S. over the course of the year.

Median monthly income in the United States, estimated

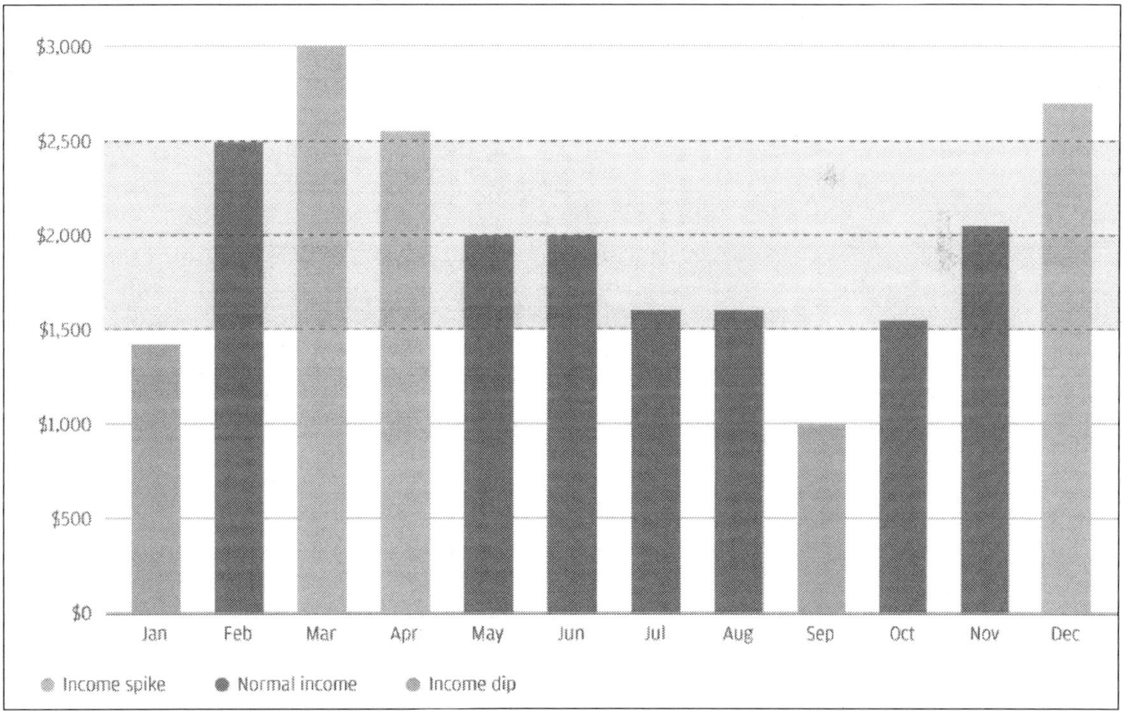

www.jpmorganchase.com/institute/all-topics/financial-health-wealth-creation/tax-refunds-and-household-spending

Cash flows into and out of households match equity seasonality quite closely.

Average monthly performance of S&P 500, 1990 to 2025

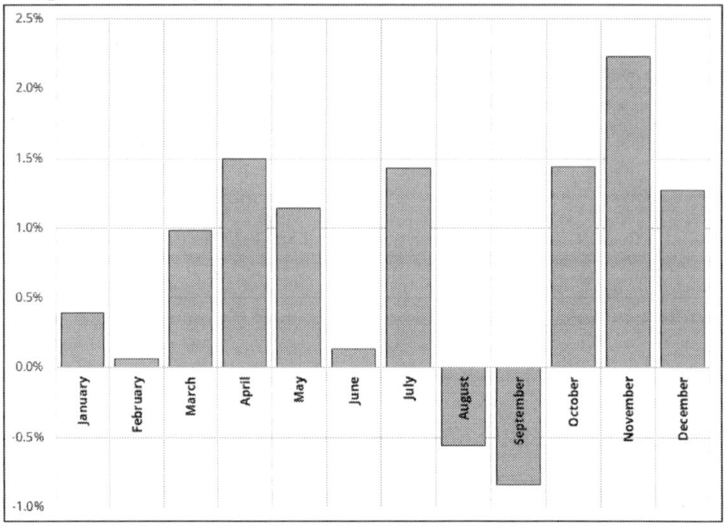

Do the flows match the price perfectly? No. We should not expect them to. Do they match enough that maybe you've got a logical explanation for equity seasonality? I think so.

If the flows matter on a month-to-month basis, they should matter even more on any given day. There is so much that goes on in any month: economic data, political news, etc. But on any given day, huge flows, if they appear, are more likely to dominate price.

In the USA, people get paid on the first, fifteenth, or the end of each month. Some portion of that money is automatically invested into 401Ks (U.S. retirement accounts). As such, if flows matter, you would expect stocks would do better around the start, middle and end of the month. Here is the data:

Cumulative performance of the S&P 500 by day of month, 2000 to 2025

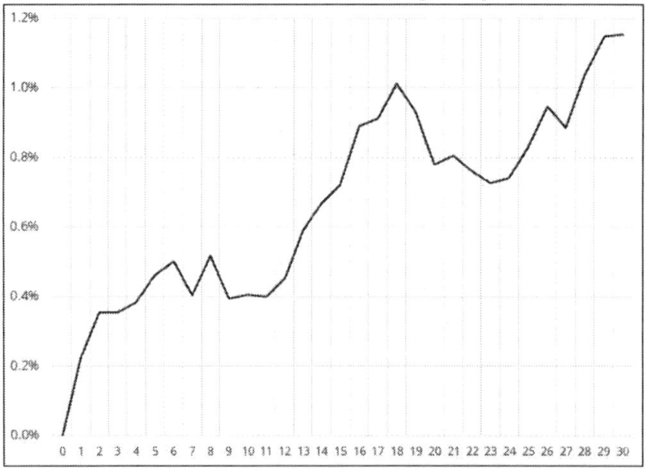

The data matches the hypothesis. Flows matter! Here is the win rate (% positive days) for the S&P 500, by day of the month.

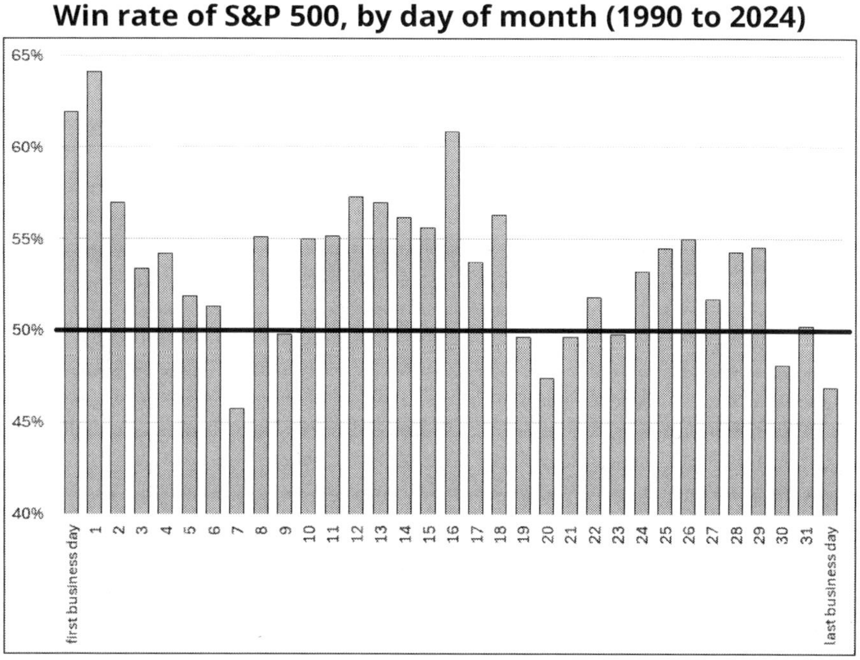

The intriguing aspect of equity seasonality is: it was well known by the late 1970s, but it remained in force long after (i.e., the effect continued out of sample):

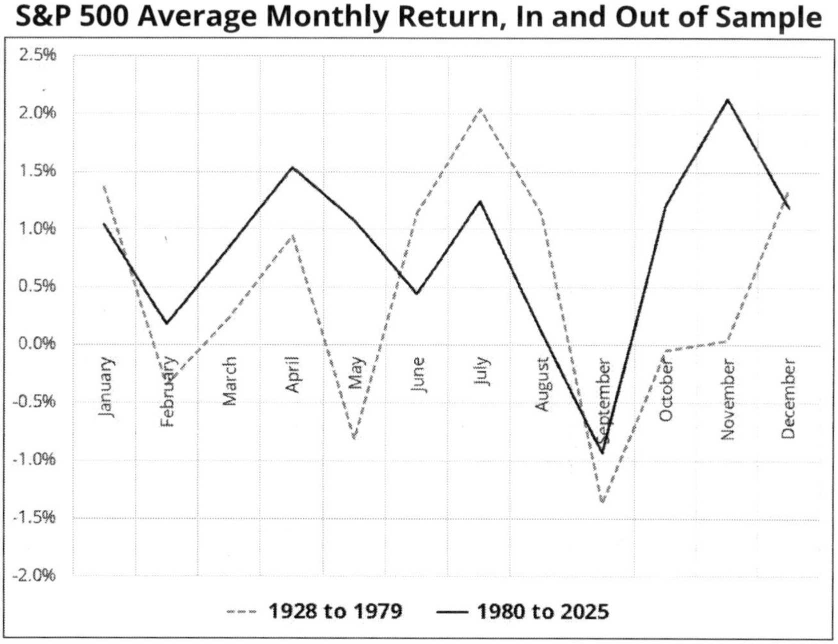

Do markets have memory?

A time series has memory if past values help predict future values, meaning the series exhibits non-zero autocorrelation. By contrast, a random walk has independent increments, so past changes do not predict future changes.

I like to compare the market to various natural and mechanical systems because that's what it is: a huge machine driven by the aggregate behavior of millions of people and computers. It is sort of a collective consciousness or hivemind. Some natural and mechanical systems have memory and some do not.

Rabbit, wolf, and fish populations have memory. As the rabbit or wolf populations increase, resources are crowded out. Food becomes scarce, and the population dwindles. Similarly, overfishing leads to smaller fish populations, fishermen leave, and the population can come back. Most animal systems have population series with memory. Here, for example, is a typical rabbit/fox population graph.

Predator-Prey Population Dynamics

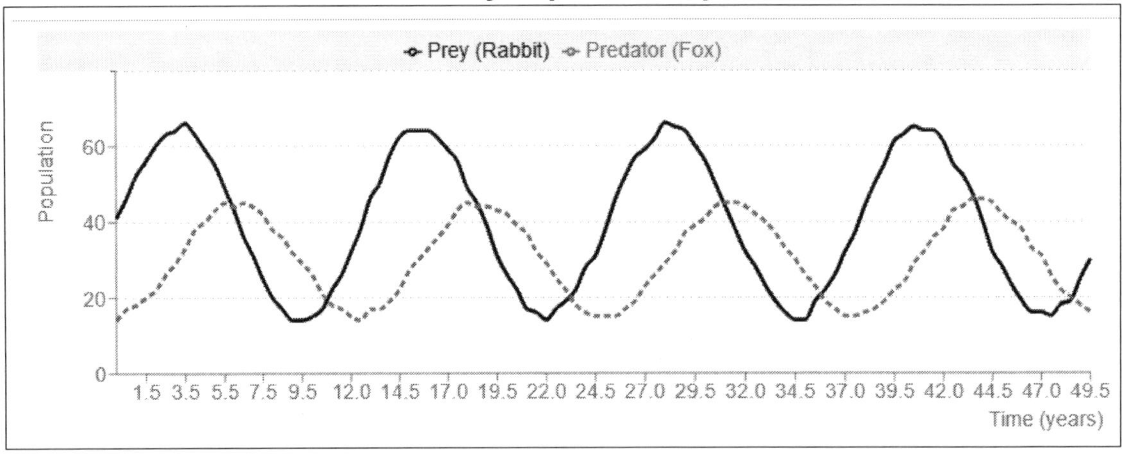

Human sleep data has memory. If you sleep one hour per night for four straight nights, I could make a good bet that you will sleep more than one hour on night five. If you sleep one hour again on night five, I will still take the bet you will sleep more than one hour on night six. Sleep deprivation will eventually lead to sleep. That's how it works.

Sprinting speed data has memory. If I do 10 sprints of 100 meters with a 30-second break in between each sprint, each succeeding sprint will almost surely put up a slower time.

Epidemic data has memory. The faster a disease spreads, the faster the spread will decline as the disease runs out of suitable victims. Epidemics are mean reverting, by definition.

These are all mean reverting time series, but of course there are also time series with memory that show drift or trend such as home and television prices, computer microchip speeds, urban populations, video game graphics quality, etc.

The question is: **Do markets have memory?** There is a ton of evidence to support the idea that markets do have some limited memory. That's why I thought this was a fascinating tweet and response. Funny enough, I think both people involved are off base.

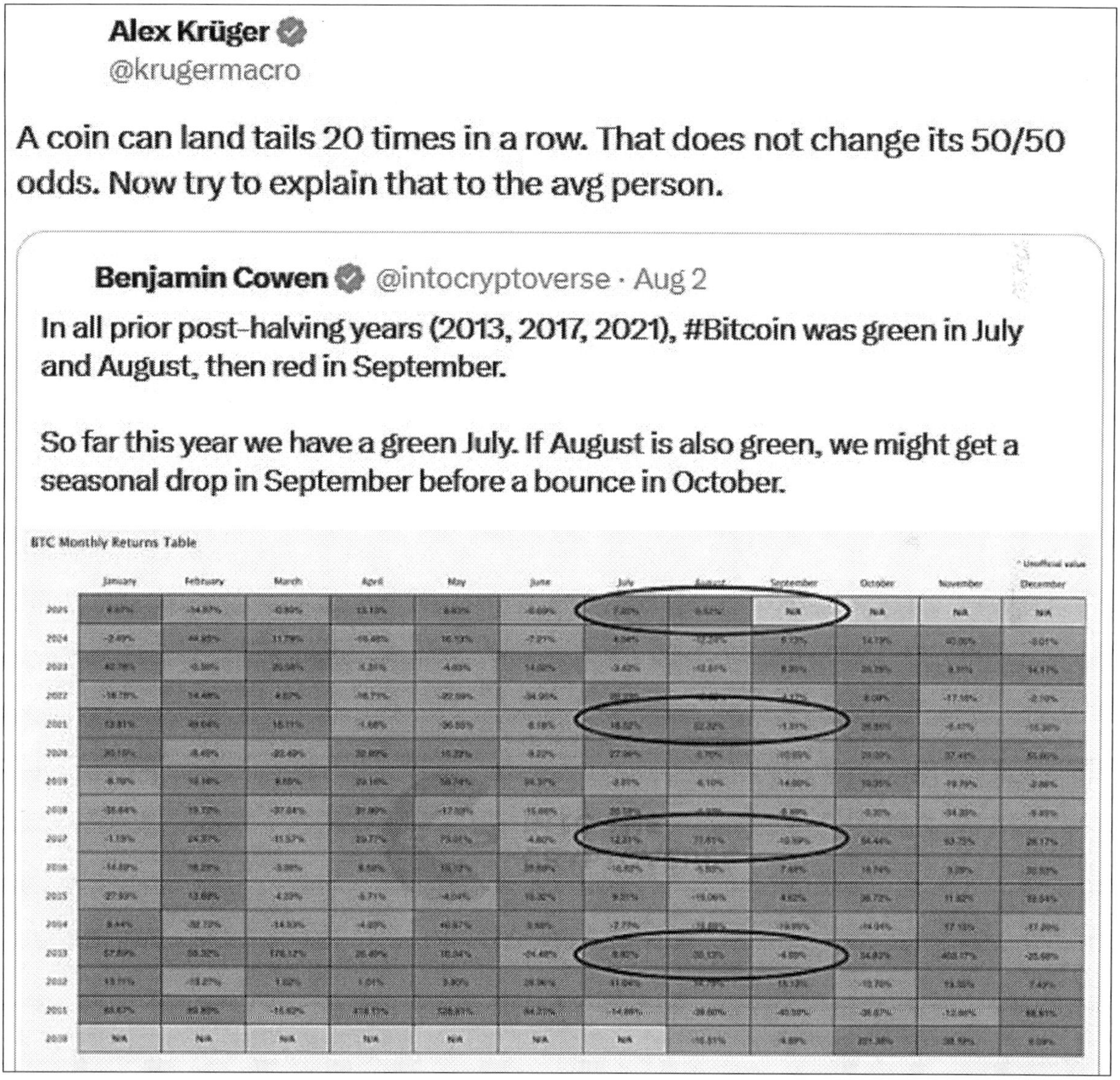

Cowen looks to be falling victim to apophenia and small sample size issues (maybe staring a bit too hard, looking for patterns that are not there), while Kruger tries to wreck the guy by saying that each month of the year is like a coin toss that is 50/50.

I will leave the patternicity issue in the original tweet to your discretion, but Kruger's assertion is more interesting. Are each day, week, and month of the year a 50/50 coin toss with no relationship to prior history? I argue strongly that the answer to that is no.

> Markets have weak, but not zero, memory

Examples of this abound.

- Volatility clusters (low volatility today makes low vol tomorrow more likely, not mutually exclusive)
- Trend following and momentum strategies make money (autocorrelation between periods, not mutually exclusive)
- Seasonality trading is profitable for many hedge funds (recurring patterns of behavior, not mutually exclusive)
- Mean reversion strategies work in particular markets and on particular time frames, especially longer periods. For example, high oil prices lead to more exploration and greater supply which eventually leads to lower prices. High corn prices when soybean prices are low will lead to substitution effects where people stop buying corn and buy soybeans instead. This will lead to price convergence/mean reversion.

"The cure for high prices is high prices" is a cliché for a reason. Clichés are nearly always true—otherwise they would never have achieved cliché status!

Today's price does not exist in a vacuum, it affects supply and demand in an ongoing feedback process. Humans make the same mistakes over and over across generations. Corporations and individuals have funding and investing needs that are predictable and often time-contingent more than price contingent. These effects are not arbitraged away instantaneously.

To say that markets have no memory is to strongly embrace the Efficient Markets Hypothesis (EMH). While EMH holds in the super big picture, it does not hold on all time frames. There are inefficiencies in markets all over the place, all the time. Discovering and monetizing these inefficiencies is what trading is all about. If you believe in EMH, you should stop trading now. Each day is not mutually exclusive. The walk is random *most* of the time, but some stutter steps within that walk can be predicted in advance by dedicated professionals.

Apophenia

Remember! As discussed in *Alpha Trader*... Humans are designed to see patterns. It's how our biology works! It allows us to simplify and process a complex world. It is called apophenia: The human tendency to perceive "meaningful" patterns within random data. See this random image of a portion of the surface of Mars, for example.

A hill with a V-shaped collapse structure on Mars

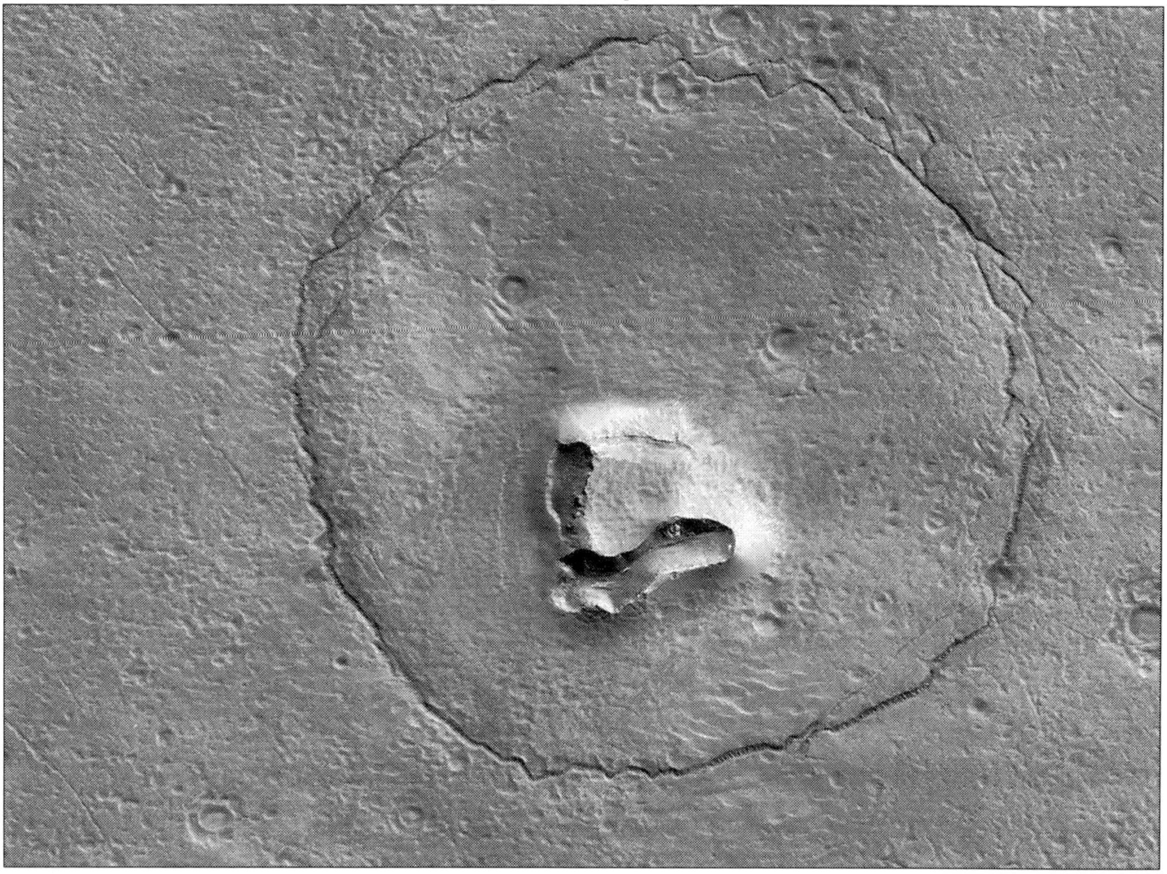

Looks bearish!

So, we always need to be extremely careful when we think we see a pattern. It might be real, or it might be our dumb, creative human brain at work.

Critics of seasonality make valid points. Seasonality is subject to confirmation bias, can be the product of biased sampling and overfitting, and can be the product of data mining or apophenia. Sample sizes are often too small to have statistical validity.

On the other hand, a logical, well-selected hypothesis supported by data can reveal underlying flows in a market, and those flows may exhibit persistent seasonality.

Seasonality appears in market data on various fractals and there is money to be made by incorporating seasonality into your process. If you can explain seasonal price irregularities using logic, or you can explain them with flows you are seeing as a market maker, there is a strong possibility that the seasonality is not random. If you data mine like a banshee and come up with all sorts of hard-to-explain seasonals, you are probably gonna be fooled by randomness.

Think of seasonality as a single input into a probabilistic process. Seasonality will rarely take you all the way to shore, but it will help you assess the prevailing winds and get you tacking in the right direction. Don't overestimate the importance of seasonality, but don't ignore it either.

Conclusion

We've covered nine practical frameworks that have helped me make money over the years. See if you can find a way to incorporate new ways of thinking into your trading.

To sum it up:

1. Think probabilistically.
2. Focus on cyclical factors and the variables that actually move your markets.
3. Look for missing data.
4. If something weird is going on in your market, stop to think what it might mean.
5. Audit your trading at least once per month.
6. Be ruthless with losing trades. Don't let them suck up mental capital.
7. Find more creative and intelligent ways to structure your trades.
8. If you fight the market too much, use a moving average filter to stay out of trouble.
9. Understand any persistent seasonality in your market.

Continually upgrade your thinking. Throw out frameworks that are not working and find new ones that will.

CHAPTER 11

WHAT ARE WE DOING HERE?

Money, ethics, greed, and success

"If you don't know who you are, the stock market is an expensive place to find out."

George Goodman, 1967

Throughout my life as a trader, I have thought about how well I get paid relative to the value that I add to the real world. It's hard to justify or rationalize why someone can watch numbers go up and down on a computer screen and push buttons at precise moments as the numbers wiggle and then get paid millions of dollars for doing so. A baseball or football player may be overpaid, but at least they provide entertainment.

Successful trading can be disorienting. It can feel like you are the best shape sorter in the world, and you get paid millions of dollars to sort shapes every day without understanding why any of it makes sense.

"Am I just a highly-paid shape sorter?"

First of all, I am here to tell you that the feeling never completely goes away. You can justify your existence by saying how well you support your family, and donate to people in need, and fund a wholesome existence on the planet, and all that. But many people in finance, especially thoughtful, good-spirited people, will have existential questions like, "If I wasn't on Wall Street, would I be doing something more useful and productive?"

The first step is to accept your role—or change it. If you do not believe you are worthy of the sums you are earning, there is a good chance it will lead to subconscious self-sabotage. If participating in a potentially rent-seeking industry sits poorly with your conscience, that guilt is telling you that your values and your actions don't align. If you feel guilty about working in finance, work through it, or get out.

As discussed throughout this book, you can trade for fun, or to look smart, or to feed a gambling impulse. Or you can trade to make money. This excerpt from *Man, Play, and Games* (Roger Caillois, 1958) captures the difference nicely.

> It is certainly much more difficult to establish the cultural functions of games of chance than of competitive games. However, the influence of games of chance is no less considerable, even if deemed unfortunate, and not to consider them leads to a definition of play which affirms or implies the absence of economic interest. Therefore a distinction must be made.
>
> In certain of its manifestations, play is designed to be extremely lucrative or ruinous. This does not preclude the fact that playing for money remains completely unproductive. The sum of the winnings at best would only equal the losses of the other players. Nearly always the winnings are less, because of large overhead, taxes, and the profits of the entrepreneur. He alone does not play, or if he plays he is protected against loss by the law of averages. In effect, he is the only one who cannot take pleasure in gambling.
>
> *Property is exchanged, but no goods are produced.* What is more, this exchange affects only the players, and only to the degree that they accept, through a free decision remade at each game, the probability of such transfer. A characteristic of play, in fact, is that it creates no wealth or goods, thus differing from work or art. At the end of the game, all can and must start over again at the same point. Nothing has been harvested or manufactured, no masterpiece has been created, no capital has accrued. Play is an occasion of pure waste: waste of time, energy, ingenuity, skill, and often of money for the purchase of gambling equipment or eventually to pay for the establishment. As for the professionals— the boxers, cyclists, jockeys, or actors who earn their

> living in the ring, track, or hippodrome or on the stage, and who must think in terms of prize, salary, or title— it is clear that they are not players but workers. When they play, it is at some other game.

You could argue that the statement: "Property is exchanged, but no goods are produced" is an apt criticism of trading. Then again, one could cynically argue that the oil in your engine doesn't produce anything, even as it lubricates the gears and allows the entire car to run. But the Caillois excerpt is important because of how it ends.

> "As for the professionals... When they play, it is at some other game."

This, of course, ties into Chapter 7, where I asked: "What game are you playing?" You are not here to save the world, or to gamble, or to rescue baby turtles. You are here to make money.

If you want justification for why finance is ethically permissible and maybe even useful, let's review one line of reasoning. Putting aside criticisms of capitalism itself (a topic too huge for this book), think about the important role played by prices in society. How would economic transactions happen without prices? How would companies plan production? How would farmers know what crops to plant or how many? Prices are the way global intelligence passes around the world in a highly-decentralized manner to optimize production and the use of resources in the most efficient way possible. **Trading and speculation allow for the price discovery that a functioning capitalist system requires.**

This is explained beautifully in "The Use of Knowledge in Society," a 1945 Friedrich Hayek essay[57]. Hayek explains that an efficient economic system operates not through central planning, but through the decentralized actions of individuals. Hayek's essay is a philosophical defense of economic freedom and the spontaneous order brought about by the price mechanism.

Hayek begins with a simple question: what is the real economic problem society must solve? He argues that classical economics often approaches this as a problem of optimization, as if all the data about resources, preferences, and production were available to a single mind. If that were the case, allocation would be a purely logical process, one of mathematical precision and efficiency. Hayek asserts that this is not the real economic problem that society faces. The world we live in is not static, and all knowledge is never possessed by any single person or institution. Instead, knowledge is dispersed into bits held by countless individuals, each with limited, often local, and sometimes contradictory information.

---

[57] www.kysq.org/docs/Hayek_45.pdf

Hayek emphasizes the *practical knowledge of time and place*. Scientific or theoretical knowledge can be taught and centralized, whereas practical knowledge is context-bound. It includes knowing which local supplier has excess inventory, which roads are under construction, or which employee has a specific skill. These are facts that no planner, regardless of expertise, can fully access or process in real-time. Yet, these minute decisions form the backbone of a functioning market-based economy.

To illustrate how such dispersed knowledge can be put to use without centralized control, Hayek offers an example about tin. Imagine that a new use for tin has emerged, or perhaps that a major source of tin has been disrupted. In either case, tin becomes more scarce. Importantly, most users of tin do not know *why* this scarcity has occurred, but what they do notice is that the price of tin has risen.

This price change acts as a signal. In response, users of tin begin to economize. Some may switch to alternative materials or redesign their products to use less tin. Producers may redirect their existing stock of tin to more profitable uses. These individual decisions, based solely on localized information and a single price signal, rebalance the use of tin across the economy. None of these actors need to know the cause of the scarcity; they simply respond to the price.

As tin is conserved, substitutes become more in demand, causing their prices to shift, triggering further adaptations. These changes cascade through the economy, coordinating countless individuals, moving them in "the right direction" as Hayek puts it.

> The marvel is that in a case like that of a scarcity of one raw material, without an order being issued, without more than perhaps a handful of people knowing the cause, tens of thousands of people whose identity could not be ascertained by months of investigation, are made to use the material or its products more sparingly; i.e., they move in the right direction.

This, for Hayek, is the miracle of the price system. **Prices are compressed knowledge signals.** They communicate to each individual what others know and what is happening elsewhere in the global economy. In this sense, the price system functions as a decentralized information network, enabling individuals to make decisions that are aligned with broader economic realities, even if they don't understand those realities in full. Hayek again:

> We must look at the price system as such a mechanism for communicating information if we want to understand its real function—a function which, of course, it fulfils less perfectly as prices grow more rigid. In abbreviated form, by a kind of symbol, only the most essential information is passed on and passed on only to those concerned.

> It is more than a metaphor to describe the price system as a kind of machinery for registering change, or a system of telecommunications which enables individual producers to watch merely the movement of a few pointers, as an engineer might watch the hands of a few dials.

Hayek contrasts this organic, adaptive process with rigid central planning. As planners work with statistical aggregates and forecasts, they inevitably abstract away from critical differences in time, place, and quality. No statistic can tell a planner that a small factory in a remote town is about to run out of bolts unless someone intervenes. And even if such data were obtainable, the process of collecting, analyzing, and responding would be too slow. By the time a central authority reacts, an opportunity or crisis may have already passed.

Hayek insists that the marvel of the market is not that it achieves perfect outcomes, but that it achieves any rational coordination at all under conditions of imperfect knowledge. And you, my trader friend, are a tiny little piece of this decentralized pricing process that ultimately greases the engine of the most successful economic experiment in history: capitalism. The essay is only thirteen pages. I highly recommend it.

Another great essay on capitalism and the significance of decentralization comes from Leonard E. Read. It's called: "I, Pencil". It's short. Give it a read[58].

To wrap it up: A functioning capitalist economy needs prices and there are no prices without markets—and there are no markets without you. Sure, we're not saving sea turtles or teaching life skills to troubled teens, but maybe we are necessary the same way plumbers and electricians and truck drivers are necessary.

Speculators provide liquidity, price discovery, hedging capability, and risk absorption. Without speculators, many prices would not be efficient, and the gears of the big global economic machine would grind to a halt. There would be inefficiencies galore.

If you don't find these justifications comforting, you can always resort to the absurd:

> A guy walks into a psychiatrist's office and says, hey doc, my brother's crazy! He thinks he's a chicken. Then the doc says: why don't you turn him in? And the guy says: I would –but I need the eggs.
>
> Woody Allen

So as a trader, I don't add much social value, but: "Hey, I need the eggs!"...

---

[58] fee.org/ebooks/i-pencil/

I hope that helps (?!).

Before we hit the end of the book, let me cover a few other *self-helpy* lessons I have learned over the years. These soft topics make some people uncomfortable. The more something makes you uncomfortable, the more you should lean into it because that discomfort is probably a signal.

Do the next right thing

Stay away from ethical gray areas. A finance professional whose behavior creeps even a bit into any gray area raises a huge red flag. Most bad behavior will be caught.

Assume that every email you write will be read by regulators and everything you say and write could one day appear on the front page of the Wall Street Journal. If you're not sure, don't send it. Be professional in your communications and never lie. If you're not sure if something is ethical, don't do it. Listen to your conscience.

If you witness behaviors or actions that don't seem right, say something. It can be hard to find the courage, but it will serve you well in the long run. Despite the evil finance archetypes you see in movies and on TV, most of those who succeed in finance are good, hardworking people who are not out to rip anyone off.

If you make a mistake, own it and correct it. Right away.

Trading with courage

You will never succeed in trading if you can't handle discomfort. Losses are a part of the game. Pain is not optional. I wrote in *Alpha Trader* that courage is especially important in fast markets. You can't wait around for the perfect or easy trade. If it's easy, there's no alpha.

A specific aspect of courage that I have realized has huge importance is the ability to come back and take meaningful risk after a huge loss. *This is not the same thing as chasing losses.*

You work at a bank and your max daily loss is $400,000 and you have just put up a streak of five daily losses in a row. You were up $9 million two weeks ago and you're still having a great year, but you're only up $7 million. You are nowhere near your monthly or yearly drawdown limits and you are confident that you're still in synch with markets. The losing streak is more a case of a bad run of variance within the confines of a solid risk management and trading process. You come in to work on day six and there is a great opportunity that looks like a clear 5-star trade.

Do you risk $300,000 like you normally would? This is extremely hard to do. Or do you take the safer approach and just risk $100,000? The trader that can put the same unit of risk on Day 6 after five down days, as they would have on Day 1 of the losing streak, will rebound from drawdown faster and have better outcomes, year after year. Most traders are more likely to take max risk after a winning streak because of the house money effect—and then clam up after a drawdown.

It's critically important to know that the lesson here only applies if your risk-taking on Day 6 is rational and you are emotionally stable after five losing days. Then, you continue your normal process and soon recover from the run of unfortunate variance. On the other hand, if you're angry, breaking your own rules, and foaming at the mouth, you absolutely should not be risking the normal max on Day 6.

Excellent traders can remain rational through both up and downswings and have the courage to take risk whether they are up or down. They also understand the importance of staying alive and will do anything to avoid risk of ruin. It's a tricky balance.

Markets run along a spectrum from fear to greed, and you do too. Think about these questions:

- What is your baseline on the fear to greed spectrum?
- Are you generally somewhat risk-averse or is your default on the side of too-large positions and too many trades?
- What factors move you back and forth along the spectrum?
- Do you take too much risk when you're doing well?
- Do you freeze up when you're in drawdown?
- Do you take too much risk when you first come back from vacation? This was a pattern I noticed in my own trading as I was excited to be back at work and usually came in way too hot on my first day back at the desk.
- What changes can you make to your process to stay near seven or eight on the continuum on the next page?

This scale will help you think about your personal risk appetite and the factors that move it left or right along the spectrum.

Risk appetite scale for traders									
1	2	3	4	5	**6**	**7**	**8**	9	10
Extreme fear		Risk averse			**Sweet spot**			Extreme greed	
Hesitation		Trades too small and reduces risk too much during drawdown			Rational, courageous, calibrated confidence. Comfortable being uncomfortable.			Overtrading, positions too big, out of control, gambling	

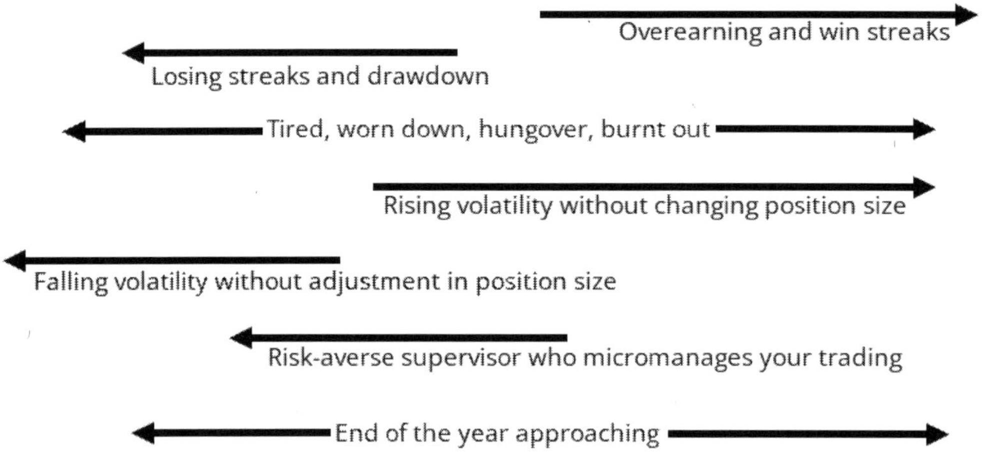

Note: Your risk exposure changes automatically if you do not properly adjust for rising or falling volatility. For example, if you are long 1,000 shares of AAPL and it's realizing 25% vol and then suddenly its volatility goes to 50%; you are now taking twice as much risk without having pressed a single button. This is important. For more on adjusting position size for changes in volatility, see *Alpha Trader*, Chapter 14.

The goal is to stay locked in that 7-8 (out of ten) zone and avoid flying all over the place based on moods and results. If you can treat each day as a unique, positive expected value trial in an endless experiment with infinite trials, you are on the right track.

A rational trader's risk appetite does not go up and down with his P&L.

Build and protect your reputation

> "Your reputation is like a teacup. Once it's broken, it's almost impossible to put back together."
>
> Ben Hunt 2024

One thing that blows my mind as years go by is the number of random connections and actions from the past that have rippled through my life. People remember how you treated them and how you behaved, even 10 or 20 years later. All your actions accumulate in the long run. Be nice to the person who sweeps the floors in your office. Treat the PAs, salespeople and brokers the same way you treat Managing Directors. If nobody wants to work the holiday, put your hand up. If they need someone to stay late, volunteer.

Try to maintain a positive attitude, even at those inevitable moments when everyone else is complaining. Optimism on its own won't get you far, but optimism plus footwork is the recipe for long-run success. An excellent reputation accrues enormous value over time.

The trader with a good P&L and a bad attitude is the first one to get a tap on the shoulder when things go south. The economist who is difficult to work with will not survive for as long as the slightly less intelligent economist who is a great team player. If you are a positive force where you work and your organization has a tough year or two, you'll get a pass. The best hedge against the inevitable ups and downs in finance is to add value in as many ways as possible, above and beyond the basics of your job description.

When I was working as a market maker and would go on a bad trading streak (which happened often enough), there was a running joke: "But he writes a good newsletter!"

It was funny because it was true. My non-P&L related contributions to the business were an excellent hedge for the periods where my P&L was bad. If people generally enjoy working with you, it will open up opportunities for advancement. Treat people with respect, say please and thank you, and never think you are better than anyone else, even if you're making seven figures per year.

Humility

> "It ain't what you don't know that gets you into trouble. It's what you know for sure that just ain't so. "
>
> Mark Twain

Humility in trading starts with radical acceptance of the fact you will be wrong. You will be wrong all the time. It's OK! Once you accept that many of your ideas and trades will not work out, you become less wedded to outcomes and more focused on process. When you are open to the reality that you will often be wrong, you will be significantly less overconfident.

I believe that the confidence vs. accuracy curve in trading and investing looks like this:

Confidence vs. accuracy in trading (estimated)

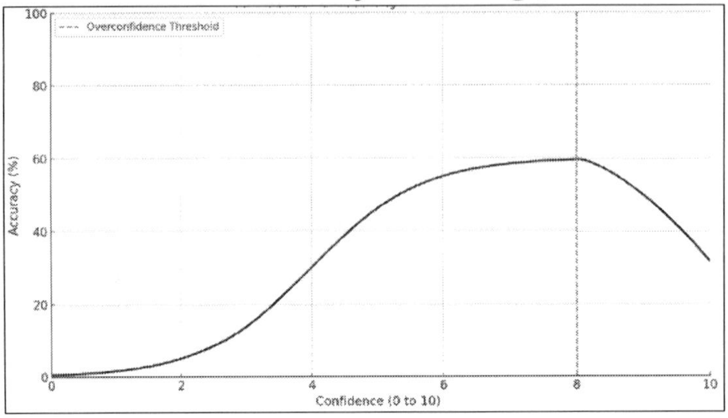

Whenever there is a trade idea where my confidence is so high that I think I should get all my friends on it or I should start a Special Purpose Investment Vehicle or ETF to trade it, it's a bad trade. There is something about a trade being too good that makes it bad. Perhaps any trade that is that perfect must already be known and well-subscribed? I am not sure. I can now recognize my overconfidence in a trade idea and while I may still do the trade, I will do it with tremendous caution and be ready for the alternative hypothesis to play out. I will gameplan all the ways it could go wrong in more detail than usual, whereas in my younger years I would go all-in without considering what might go wrong.

Be humble about your ability to predict the future, even when you think you have copious data supporting your case. Counterintuitively, the more information you have, the worse your decision-making is likely to be. That's right. More information leads to less accurate decisions.

In "Does More Information Lead to Better Informing?" Meliha Handzic concludes:

> The results of the analysis indicate a significant detrimental effect of increased information availability on processing efficiency ... and also show a significant negative effect of increased information availability on decision accuracy.

Davis, Lohse, and Kotteman come to a similar conclusion in a 1994 paper[59]:

> MBA students from an advanced finance course forecasted stock earnings using a computerized information system designed to simulate systems used in practice. Disguised actual company data were presented in three different

[59] Davis and Lohse, "Harmful effects of seemingly helpful information on stock earnings forecasts", (1994).

treatments: baseline information, baseline plus redundant news information, and baseline plus nonredundant news information. The redundant information made subjects significantly more confident in their forecasts compared to the baseline case. The non-redundant information made subjects significantly more confident than both the baseline case and the redundant case. Forecast accuracy, however, was significantly diminished in both the redundant and nonredundant conditions compared to baseline. Thus, the additional news information, whether redundant or non-redundant, had the effect of degrading performance while increasing confidence.

Finally, the OG study on this topic comes from Paul Slovic in 1973[60]. He gave horse racing handicappers the opportunity to predict 40 upcoming races with varying amounts of information for each. Initially, they had just five variables:

- Weight to be carried this race
- Percentage of races in which horse finished first, second, or third
- Weight horse carried in his last race
- Speed rating
- Jockey rating

In other rounds of the experiment, they were given all these variables…This is a screenshot from the original paper, just because I like the font.

```
WEIGHT TO BE CARRIED THIS RACE
1965:   PERCENTAGE OF RACES IN WHICH HORSE FINISHED FIRST,SECOND,OR THIRD
WEIGHT HORSE CARRIED IN HIS LAST RACE
SPEED RATING CORRECTED BY TRACK VARIANT FOR HORSE'S LAST RACE
IS THE JOCKEY ONE OF THE LEADING JOCKEYS IN THIS RACE?
1968:   NUMBER OF STARTS
NUMBER OF DAYS SINCE HORSE'S LAST RACE
NUMBER OF LENGTHS HORSE FINISHED BEHIND LEADER IN LAST RACE
SPEED RATING OF HORSE CORRECTED BY TRACK VARIANT IN NEXT-TO-LAST RACE
SPEED RATING OF HORSE CORRECTED BY TRACK VARIANT ON SECOND-TO-LAST RACE
CLAIMING PRICE THIS RACE
HIGHEST CLASS AT AQUEDUCT THIS SEASON
1967:   PERCENTAGE OF RACES IN WHICH HORSE FINISHED FIRST,SECOND,OR THIRD
RANK IN PACE RATING CORR, FOR WT.: BEST RACE THIS YR, AT "A" AT 6F ON FAST TRACK
CLASS OF HORSE'S LAST RACE
FINISHING POSITION OF HORSE IN LAST RACE
NUMBER OF DAYS SINCE NEXT-TO-LAST RACE
CLASS OF HORSE IN NEXT-TO-LAST RACE
NUMBER OF DAYS SINCE SECOND-TO-LAST RACE
WAS HORSE'S LAST RACE RUN AT AQUEDUCT?
AGE
SEX
HIGHEST CLASS ON HORSE'S PAST PERFORMANCE CHART
HIEST CLASS AT "A" THIS YR AT 6F W/ FINISH 1,2,3,4 OR W/IN 1/2 LENGTH OF LEADER
1968:   NUMBER OF WINS
1966:   TOTAL MONEY WON
1967:   NUMBER OF STARTS
1967:   NUMBER OF WINS
1967:   TOTAL MONEY WON
NUMBER OF RACES IN LAST 21 DAYS
DISTANCE AT WHICH HORSE HAS RACED MOST OFTEN
FASTEST SPEED RATING ON PAST PERFORMANCE CHART FOR RACES OF 6F
DISTANCE OF HORSE'S LAST RACE
NUMBER OF LENGTHS GAINED OR LOST IN THE STRETCH IN LAST RACE
DID HORSE FAIL TO GAIN ON THE LEADER AT ANY CALL IN THE LAST RACE?
DISTANCE OF NEXT-TO-LAST RACE
DISTANCE OF LAST WORKOUT
TIME OF LAST WORKOUT
NUMBER OF DAYS SINCE LAST WORKOUT
IS THE TRAINER ONE OF THE LEADING TRAINERS IN THIS RACE?
```

[60] Paul Slovic, "Behavioral Problems of Adhering to a Decision Policy", (1973).

The results are in the chart below. As the amount of information increased, confidence skyrocketed while accuracy flatlined.

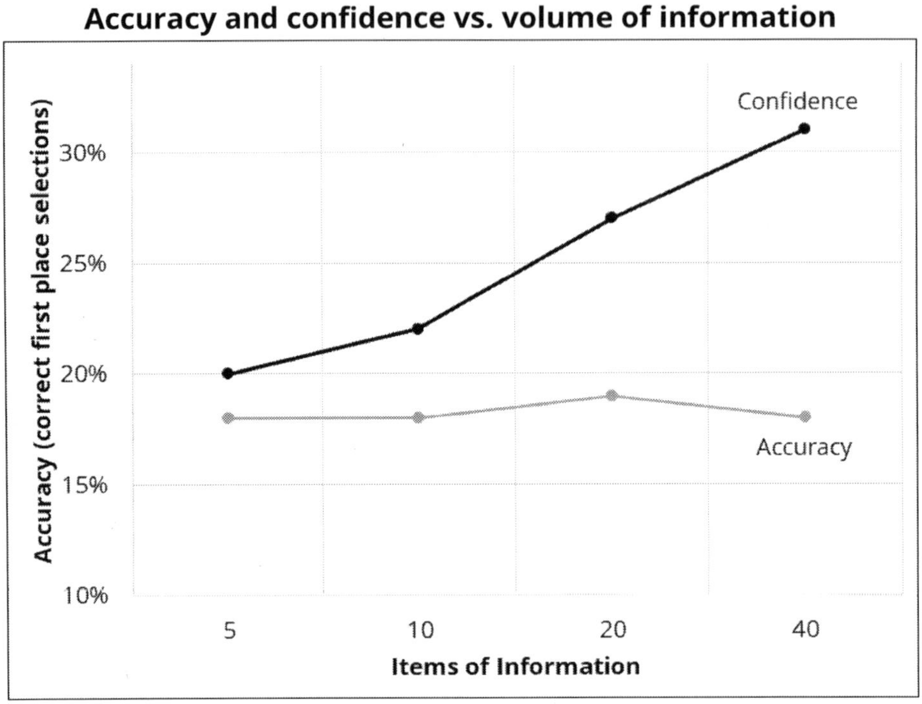

Carefully curate your information feed[61] and be skeptical of overly-complex analysis frameworks. A few well-chosen variables and drivers are just as likely to lead you to good market forecasts as 100 inputs. A smaller list of variables will take you much less time to collect and analyze, and will reduce confusion. **Information overload leads to slower processing, fatigue, distraction and overconfidence.**

That said (as discussed in Chapter 9) don't fall into the trap of trying to predict markets with a single variable.

In the early 2010s, many thought the only thing driving the stock market was the size of the Fed's Balance Sheet. Then, from 2015 to 2020, many people thought the only thing driving the stock market was low interest rates. In 2025, many believe the only thing driving the stock market is high deficits. Nope. It's never that easy.

Reducing your information diet does not mean you starve yourself. It means: choose your inputs carefully and use an appropriately but not overly simple framework to analyze your

[61] For more on curating your information diet, see: www.spectramarkets.com/amfx/its-not-just-x-its-y/

markets. Frameworks that favor minimal but not univariate models have consistently proven to be most effective in the quantitative modeling of markets. This is the spirit of parsimony or **Occam's Razor**:

1. Every added variable increases the chance of error.
2. Every untestable add-on weakens explanatory power.
3. Good models compress reality without distorting it.

In empirical finance and econometrics, the principle of parsimony plays a critical role: models should be as simple as possible, but no simpler. Including only one variable often leads to underfitting, where the model fails to capture the complexity of the underlying data-generating process. Introducing too many variables increases the risk of overfitting.

Markets are usually driven by one or two main stories and two or three main variables. If you can't nail down the few stories and variables driving your market, either there is no clear theme, or you don't understand what's going on.

There is a constant flood of irrelevant information in finance in part because financial media has a scaling problem. 80% of the important, market-moving news and information comes out in 20% of trading days, and the remaining days are mostly noise. But financial media companies and celebrities need to create content 24/7 so they will feature unimportant stories, boost irrelevant themes, and chase meaningless narratives to keep the airwaves, websites and news shows active and followers engaged.

Your job is to discern what is relevant and what is not. This is one of the toughest aspects of trading in the current era. **We have too much information.** Way more than needed to make useful decisions.

An even more radical form of humility is to accept that you don't even know what you think you know. This might sound a bit insane, but it's amazing how often we think we know something and then find out later that what we knew was actually wrong. This excerpt from a 2015 piece by Stephen Duneier captures the essence of this radical acceptance of being wrong.

> One of the fundamental tenets of cognitive psychology is that we essentially have 2 systems at work in our brain. Kahneman calls them "System 1 and System 2", while Thaler and Sunstein refer to them as "Planner and Doer". What you call them isn't nearly as important as recognizing that there is a part of your cognition that is automated, intuitive, and quick to draw conclusions, while the other part is more deliberate, methodical and intellectually demanding. When you read about these abstract characters, you may or may

not agree that they relate to you, but you undoubtedly recognize their existence in others.

In the moment, though, when we are gathering information, interpreting it, processing it, drawing conclusions from it or making decisions based upon it, it is almost impossible for us to recognize whether we are employing mental shortcuts that are likely to result in a systematic error in judgment, ie bias, or we are objectively analyzing the situation, drawing upon our wealth of knowledge and experience to reach a thoughtful conclusion.

So, how was I able to make the leap from someone who had spent years simply studying cognitive science to becoming a practitioner? I owe it all to my mother-in-law and a simple mistake I made on March 24, 1994. I know the exact date because it occurred in the hospital, one day after my first child was born. My mother-in-law asked if I'd like something for lunch and I gave her my order. Forty-five minutes later, she returned, handing me a sandwich and saying, "here's your veal parmigiana hero." My hand automatically jerked away. "I didn't order a veal parmigiana hero," I stated emphatically. She insisted I had and we went back and forth before I finally introduced reason to the rhetoric. I explained that while the veal parmigiana hero had been one of my favorite foods as a kid, after seeing a video years earlier which showed how calves are treated in order to make veal, I had made a conscious decision never to eat veal again. Which is how I knew beyond a shadow of a doubt that I hadn't ordered a veal parmigiana hero this time. She apologized, I skipped lunch and life went on.

A few months later, my wife and I looked through pictures from the birth, as well as video we had taken around that time. That's when my life changed forever. It turns out, someone had been taking video in the room when I gave my lunch order. I saw a person who looked just like me, who sounded just like me say to my mother-in-law, "I'll have a veal parmigiana hero, please." It was like an out-of-body experience. I get chills to this day when I think about it. Immediately, my mind attempted to make sense of it all. "Someone dubbed over my voice." "Someone doctored the tape." "Someone went to a lot of trouble to make me look foolish." The truth, of course, was a whole lot simpler, and there was no getting around it. In that moment, my mind was engaged elsewhere, and that left System 1 or the "Doer" alone to hear the question, interpret it, process it and answer it, all without me even being aware. You see,

> veal occupied a much greater portion of my memory than did eggplant. Avoiding veal was a conscious decision, but on that day my choice had been made unconsciously, even though I was wide awake and conversing.
>
> That was the last time I have ever felt 100% sure about anything that relied on my memory. It's also the moment when I truly understood what Kahneman, Thaler, Sunstein and others meant in all those books.

This is a great example of seeing your own irrational actions. Duneier was lucky to see that video. This is about as radical as you can get in terms of accepting that your view of reality is imperfect and your memory is fallible. There is not a single person in the world who is not flawed. When we admit and accept our flaws, we see the world through more rational and humble eyes.

A note on the word humility: People tend to associate humility with weakness. Part of this might come from negative associations with the word "humiliation." But humiliation is when an outside force makes you humble. This sort of forced humility does reflect weakness. When we embrace a humble mindset without having it forced upon us, we show strength. Ironically, those who are not humble often have humility forced upon them in the form of humiliation. If you are already humble, you are more difficult to humiliate.

And in case you are wondering: The world humble comes from the Latin "humilis" or "on the ground" from the Latin "humus", which means "ground". To be humble is to literally be grounded.

Principle 21: Stay humble.

One last thought on humility.

Yung Pueblo, a writer and speaker known for his reflections on emotional maturity, writes that true humility arises when we stop comparing ourselves to others, because comparison feeds the ego—either by inflating it (when we feel superior) or by deflating it (when we feel inferior). Comparison keeps us stuck in cycles of insecurity and pride.

Humility is alignment with reality, where we understand that everyone is on their own journey and we don't need to rank ourselves against them. One of his core ideas is: "A sign of growth is when you **stop comparing yourself to others and start comparing yourself to your past self**."

Self-awareness

The best antidote to almost every psychological problem is self-awareness. There is nothing wrong with emotions; they're what makes us human. But be aware of your emotions and determine whether they are a help or a hindrance in any given situation. When things are heated on a trading floor, or you are frustrated by a series of bad trades, or you want to scream at someone in an office… Check your mood meter.

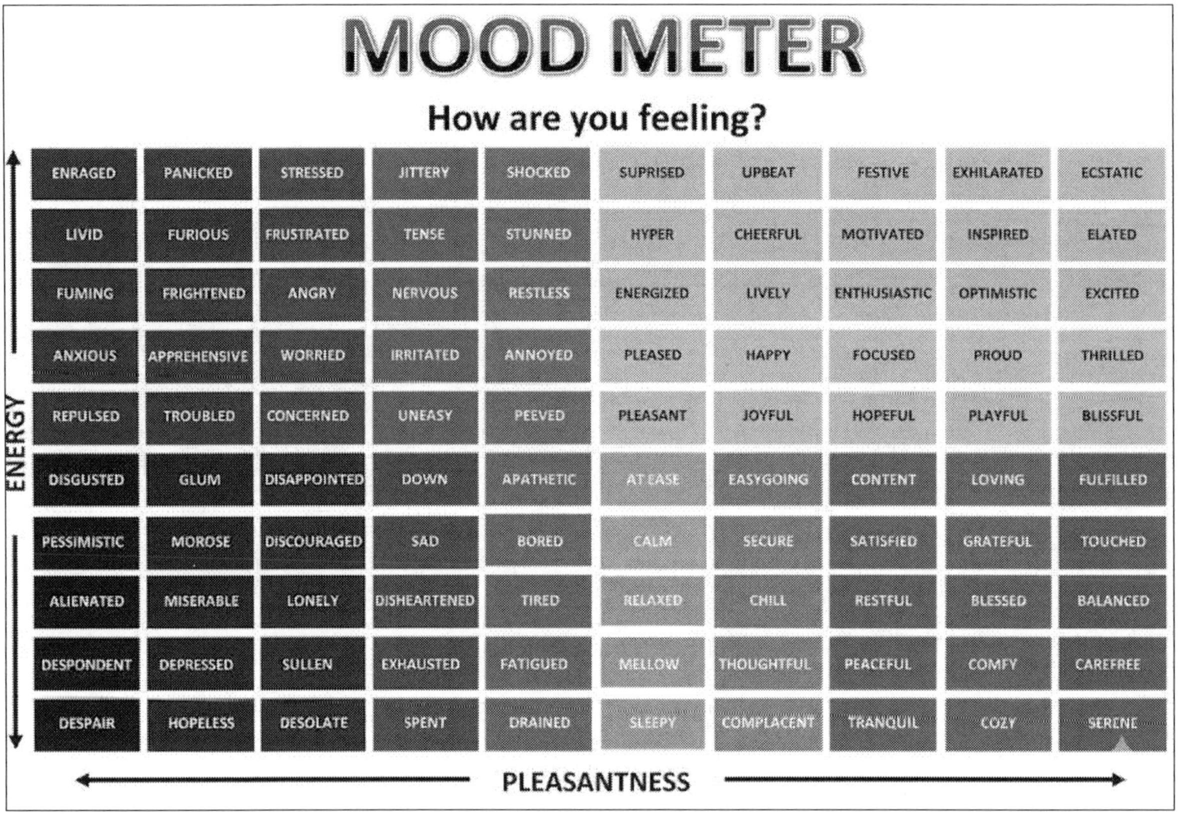

Emotions have a half-life. This is an extremely important idea in and out of finance. I wish someone had taught me this when I was in my 20s. However angry you are about something right now, you will be less angry in two hours. You will be much less angry in 24 hours. This is empirically true.

This is why common sense says never to send an angry email right away. Wait until tomorrow and see if you are still angry. Studies show this consistently and if you think about your own life, you will probably realize that very few emotions stay around very long. This too shall pass.

Here's some great advice Warren Buffett got from Tom Murphy:

> Forty years ago, Tom gave me one of the best pieces of advice I've ever received. He said, "Warren, you can always tell someone to go to hell tomorrow." It's such an easy way of putting it. You haven't missed the opportunity. Just forget about it for a day. If you feel the same way tomorrow, tell them then -- but don't spout off in a moment of anger.

Here's the result of one study:[62] don't worry about the exact numbers. The point is that we are in a permanent state of emotional flux. Emotions come in; emotions go out.

Median Duration of Emotions (in hours)

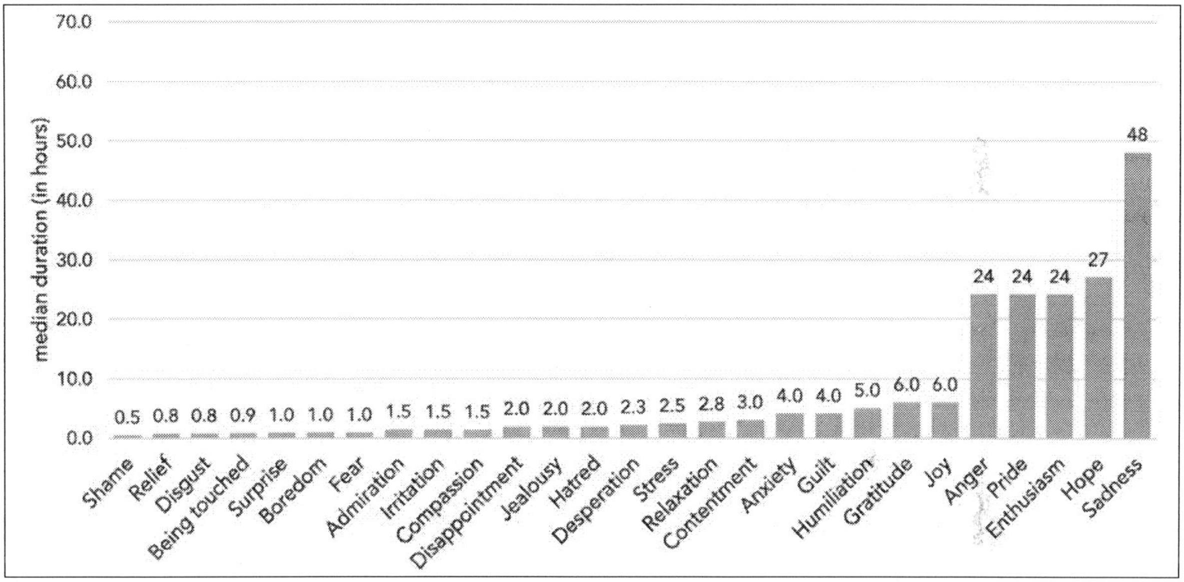

Whether an emotion affects you for 90 seconds or 4 hours isn't the point here. The point is that emotions come and go like waves. Don't make trading or business decisions when you have just been smashed by an emotional wave and you are spinning underwater and you just hit your head on the hard sandy bottom.

When you are triggered, angry, annoyed, or frustrated… Get away from the situation; don't react to it. Once you feel calm and rational, take whatever steps and make whatever decisions are rationally called for in the situation. Screaming at coworkers and smashing phone handsets and keyboards looks cool in movies, but it won't help you in the real world.

---

[62] "Which emotions last longest and why: The role of event importance and rumination", Verdyn (2015)

In 1996, when I was less than one year into trading FX at Citi New York, I was all bummed out about a trade that had gone against me. My boss at the time (Stoney) said to me:

"Hills and valleys, beeper. Hills and valleys."

A few weeks later, I was fist pumping an awesome trade after taking profit and he turns to me and says:

"Hills and valleys, beeper. Hills and valleys."

Simple, sage advice. Don't get too high. Don't get too low.

Note: Stoney called me beeper because I was the only trader who was nice to the brokers and hence I got the nickname: BP (broker's pal) which eventually turned into "beeper." Believe me, befriending the brokers was positive EV optimal metagame, especially if you needed playoff tickets. 😊

Growth is slow and linear

There is a meme that says: If you improve by 1% per day, you will be 37.78 times better after one year. It's a nice thought, but it's wrong.

Personal growth is jumpy and discontinuous, not linear or exponential. T-bill interest in your bank account compounds exponentially and addiction can catch up to the addict in a scary and nonlinear way, but most things we experience as human beings are slow, gradual and more linear.

You cannot say: I am going to increase my pushups by 1% per day, starting with 10 today and keep doing that for five years. That would mean you are doing 770 million pushups at the end of year five! But you can gradually increase the number of pushups you do and get from 10 to maybe 150 pushups.

Learning and advancement works like that, which is why people get bored and frustrated along the way. Each day that you do your best, even when you don't feel like it, is another day you have moved the ball forward another quarter of a yard. There's a meme for that!

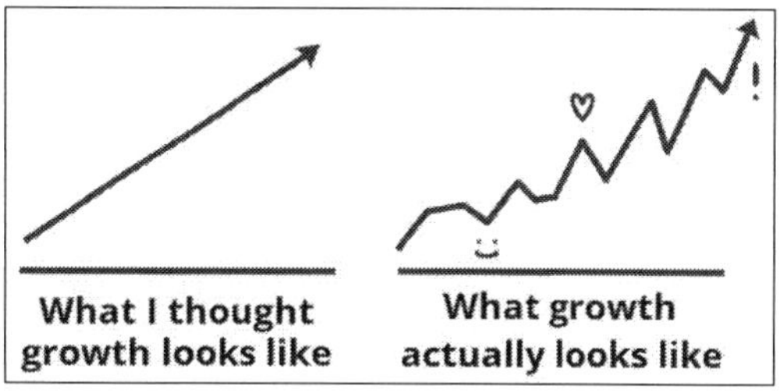

Your actions are cumulative. It's hard to understand this when you are young. If you are less than 30 years old, I promise you that one day you will look back and see the sum of all the little actions you took, and all the right and wrong moves you made and you will understand. Every time you choose to watch TV instead of reading a book, or choose to yell at someone instead of walking away, you make a tiny impact on your reputation, your momentum, and your future self. Keep making the next right move.

Some kids come to Wall Street or The City or Bay Street with visions of Gordon Gekko in their minds and they want to become the most feared trader on the street. In real life, here's what has happened to the three most feared people I have traded against in my career:

1. Convicted of bank fraud. Jailed for 7 years.
2. Convicted and fined for manipulating precious metals prices. Banned.
3. Found guilty of FX market manipulation for his role in pushing around currency markets during an illiquid period. Probation.

Bad actors tend to keep doing bad things until they get caught. You will command more respect by quietly raking in huge P&L than you will by loudly pushing the market or underlings around. This doesn't mean you have to be a people pleaser or a pushover. Just don't be an asshole. It's bad karma and it's bad metagame.

Nice guys finish first

I grew up watching "Wall Street," the movie, and reading *Liar's Poker* and *Reminiscences of a Stock Operator*. Gordon Gekko, the Salomon Brothers bond traders, and Jesse Livermore are all exciting, larger-than-life characters. But while all three of these works motivated countless individuals to choose finance as an occupation, all three are cautionary tales.

You can get ahead by being a sociopath who craves only power and money. But you don't *need* to be that way. And despite examples like this, there are more reliable paths to success. Be a good person who values doing things the right way. Be nice to people, regardless of their status. This is good human behavior, but it also turns out to be optimal career strategy.

Speak positively about others.

Praise in public and criticize in private.

In the short run, you won't always get what you want. Sometimes the less-worthy candidate will get the promotion before you. Sometimes the lucky trader will get a bigger bonus than the skilled trader. Sometimes, the annoying loud-mouth economist will get paid more than the more intelligent one who is great to work with.

Life's not always fair. Play the long game.

Final thoughts on getting rich

One of the scariest moments in life comes after you have been dreaming about a goal for years and years—and then you achieve it. When an Olympian wins gold, they often fall into depression afterwards, because their entire life was focused on one goal and now that the goal has been achieved, they have no idea what comes next[63].

If you've dreamt of enormous wealth your entire life and you achieve it, you might find yourself surprised at how empty it feels. You might double down like Jesse Livermore, instead of taking profit. You may crave the high of chasing the goal, rather than the goal itself.

Life has no finish line; it's a series of experiments and events and milestones and struggles. Some work out; some don't. Wealth offers many benefits, but you might be surprised how little it fills you up when you finally make it. Like I said at the start of the book: there's no point in making life-changing money unless you plan to change your life.

This poem by Kurt Vonnegut about best-selling author Joseph Heller captures it perfectly.

> Joseph Heller, an important and funny writer
> now dead,
> and I were at a party given by a billionaire on Shelter Island.
> I said, "Joe, how does it make you feel to know that our host only yesterday
> ... made more money than your novel 'Catch-22'
> has earned in its entire history?"
>
> Joe said, "I've got something he can never have."
> I said, "What on earth could that be, Joe?"
> Joe said, "... Enough."

---

[63] Check out the documentary: *The Weight of Gold* (2020)

CONCLUSION

Ok, book's over! Thank you for taking the time to read my deeper and wider thoughts on trading and markets. Be courageous, take large and calculated risks, and stay humble.

Have fun. Don't let the ups and downs kill you. Work hard every day. Be nice. Call your mom. She won't live forever.

Forgive yourself. Forgive your enemies. Let go, or be dragged.

And remember: someone out there is wishing for something you already have.

Before you go, check out a recap of the 21 key principles on the next page.

If you can find an edge through some combination of fundamentals, technicals, behavioral analysis and quantitative research, and also stick to these principles… You will be in the top one percent of all traders who have ever tried to conquer markets.

THE 21 PRINCIPLES

1. The way you make money today is not how you will make money tomorrow.
2. When the market does something weird—pay attention.
3. Study your mistakes and they'll pay you back double.
4. Choose family and health over markets.
5. You only need to get rich once.
6. Take the job, but not yourself, seriously.
7. If you think like everyone else, you will perform like everyone else.
8. Live and trade by the wisdom of the Serenity Prayer.
9. There is nothing new under the sun.
10. The most rational trader (not the smartest trader) wins.
11. Good thinkers think about what others are thinking.
12. "It's come too far, too fast!" is not a good reason to put on a trade.
13. Professional traders maximize expected value, not leverage.
14. Avoid risk of ruin first. Maximize returns second.
15. Elite traders don't gamble.
16. Admit what you don't know.
17. An excellent reputation accrues enormous value over time.
18. Match your analysis to your trading time frame.
19. Elite traders are pragmatic, probabilistic, and agnostic.
20. Different views require different structures. Be flexible.
21. Stay humble.

ACKNOWLEDGEMENTS

Thanks to:

Steve Donnelly for your attention to detail and for putting up with your annoying little brother. **Justin Ross**, an excellent coworker and fantastic friend. **Steve Stone** for teaching me more than I realized back when I was Burl Ives. **Sam Rines** for fun and friendship and a fantastic foreword. **Leo Lee** for many useful and deep conversations about risk. **Liam Byrne** for letting me live vicariously through your travels. **Phil Galfond** for your poker wisdom and **Mike Del Vecchio** for yours, too. **Marwan Younes** for being a good friend and solid sounding board for so many years. And **Ryan Scott**, **Trader_XO**, and **TraderSZ** for getting the word out to the crypto peeps.

Matt Gittins for always being there at exactly the right time. In the right way.

Thanks **Dad** for teaching me the difference between right and wrong, even if it took me a while to get it straight. Thanks **Mom** for teaching me how to be a risk taker. Thanks **Adam** for the MTG, conversations, and for being your awesome self all the time. And **Oliver** for being a smart, hardworking, good human being who's fun to hang out with.

Most of all, thank you **Christine** for never giving up. For being the strongest person I know.

RIP Mom. RIP Hooch. RIP Jan. RIP Paul. RIP Harold.

INDEX

Italicized page numbers followed by *g* indicate graphs, charts, or diagrams; *italicized* numbers followed by *p* indicate illustrations.

absorption property, non-ergodicity and, 200

accuracy: confidence and, 188, 189–90, *189g, 190g,* 384–85, *385g*; election betting markets, 83–84; Google's internal markets, 85; LLMs, 63, 70; prediction markets, 79, 82, 108. *See also* confidence

Ackman, Bill, 158, 173

Addiction by Design (Schüll), 141, 142

ADHD, 112, 117. *See also* ADHD, trading and

ADHD, trading and, 112, 113; focus, 113; market noise, 113; patience, 113; reckless impulsivity, 111, 113; record-keeping challenges, 113; solutions, 115–19; stop losses, 117–19, *118g*

adverse selection, 198, 227, 228–30, 245; asymmetric information, 228, 241; avoidance, 231–32; economic outcomes and, 227–41; electronic market makers and, 230; headline risks, 235–37, *237g*; illiquid markets and, 241; loser mentality and, 230–31, 241; psychology of, 237–41, *239g*; securities and, 241; stale/faraway orders, 234–35, *235g,* 241; transaction costs, 232–34, *234g,* 241

Agarwal, Nitin, 222

agency, control and, 27

agnosticism, trader, 295, 397

AI, 18, 62, 63, 238; first use of, 223; for better trading, 63–73; human judgment and, 304; narrative contagion and, 221, 222; speculative bubble, 257, 357; stocks, 357. *See also* LLMs; LLMs, uses of for better trading

AIG, 2008 collapse of, 35

Akerlof, George, 227

Alpha Trader (Donnelly), 3, 18, 19, 25, 54, 65, 80, 95, 116, 119, 123, 128, 181, 188, 194, 226, 250, 255, 267, 277, 334, 350, 353, 373, 381, 383

Amaranth Advisors, 205

am/FX, 3, 94, 170, 210, 223

amygdala, 317–18

anchoring bias, 66, 268; economists and, 89, 92–93, 97; market forecasts and, 277

Antifragile (Taleb), 212, 213

antifragile systems, 212, 214

antifragility, 212

anxiety, trading and, 111, 112, 119–26; managing, 121–23, *121g*; position sizing and, 124–26

apophenia, 372, 373–75, *374p*

Apple, 41–42, *42g*

arbitrage, 6, 24, 49, 86, 88, 100, 103, 106, 114, 257, 308, 347

Archegos Capital, 205–6, *206g*

ARK Innovation ETF, QQQ NASDAQ ETF vs., *36g*

Art of Currency Trading, The (Donnelly), 161, 181, 188, 194

audits, monthly trading, 350–53, 375; forms, 351–52, *352p*; OODA loop and, 350–51, *351p*

AUDUSD, 14, 16, 168–71, *170g, 172g,* 293, 357
Augur, 86

backtesting, 42, 63, 204, 206, 211, 323, 332, 341, 342; LLMs and, 69–70
backwardation, market tilt and, 159–60
Banerji, Gunjan, 144–45
bank research, narrative contagion monitoring and, 223
Bankman-Fried, Sam, 86
Barron's covers: bear markets and, *329g,* 331; bull markets and, 331; bullish skew, 327–32, *328g, 330g*
Bayesian thinking, 207–8, *207g,* 229; in forecasts, 93, 218, 230; non-ergodicity and, 207; weakness of, 207. *See also* probability, trading and
BCOM, 340–41, *340g, 341g*
bear markets, 279, 288; *Barron's* covers and, *329g,* 331
bearish stock market breadth, faulty trading/investing framework of, 293, 323–25, *324g*
Bessembinder, Hendrik, 324
bet sizing, 188–95; confidence and accuracy and, 189–90, *189g, 190g,* 194, 195; *See also* position sizing
bias, 7, 52, 124, 277, 389; *Barron's,* 329; behavioral, 252; *Bloomberg* survey, 98, 101; currency markets, 201; economist surveys, 89; emotional and psychological, 81; in equities, 201; filtering out, 62; financial gurus, 279; forecasters, 219; hedge funds, 307; heuristics and, 305; illusion of control as, 24; information sources, 79; model, 97; personal trading, 262, 309; prediction markets, 88; Wall Street firms, 143. *See also specific types of bias*
bitcoin, 30, 53, 54–55, *54g, 55g,* 89, 95, 146, 222, 334, 337; GameStop announcement about, 234–35, 342–50. *See also* crypto markets; cryptocurrencies
Black Swan, The, (Taleb), 207
Black Wednesday 1992, 10
blockchain technology: Polymarket and, 83; prediction markets and, 86
Bloomberg, 8, 11, 38, 64, 89, 115, 131; monitoring for narrative contagion, 223; TSLA overvaluation and, *294g. See also* Bloomberg survey; magazine cover indicators
Bloomberg survey: bias, 98, 101; for predictions, 97–98, 101, *101g*
bond yields, rising, 322; stock market and, *322g*
Book of Why, The (Pearl & Mackenzie), 168–69, 171
Boyd, John: OODA loop and, 350
breakout trading, 235, 242, 306, 307, 308, 359
Brexit 2016, 10–11
brother-in-law indicator, 56
bubbles, 36, 215; AI speculative, 257, 357; asset price, 34; correlated errors and, 80. *See also* dotcom bubble and crash
Buffett, Warren, 300, 302, 391–92; "too-hard" concept, 256–57. *See also* Buffett Indicator
Buffett Indicator, 300–302, *300g, 301g*
bull markets, 34, 62, 300, 328; *Barron's* and, 327–32, *330g*; narrative contagion and, 221
burnout, trader, 130, 290
BYND, 286–87, *286g, 287g*

calendar management, 320; ADHD and, 116
calendar year-end metagame, 281, *281g*
capitalism, 33, 36; price mechanism, 378–80
career risk, trader, 279–81; managing, 90, 248
Carvana, *289g*
cash flow models, 304
Cassano, Joseph, 35
Chamberlain, Joseph, 33
chaos theory, initial conditions and, 211
chart patterns, 54
ChatGPT, 5, 9, 65, 66–68, *67g*, 72–73, *72g*, 77–78, 362
China, 41, 96, 212, 240, 262, 340; deval of 2015, 41, 126–27, 277
chronocentrism, 30–37, *36g*; COVID-19 and, 34; financial market, 35; recency bias and, 33; remedy, 36
Citigroup, 161, *161g*
Claude, 64, 65
CNBC, 116, 146, 311, 354; market tilt and, 158–59, *159g*
cognitive bias, 317; second-order thinking and, 52
Coinbase, 146, 327; gambling disorder and, 142
concentration, stock market, 323, 324
cone of uncertainty: forecasts and, 220; probabilistic thinking and, 337
confidence: accuracy and, 188, 189–90, *189g*, *190g*, 384–85, *385g*; volume of information and, 384–87, *387g*. *See also* humility, trader
confirmation bias, 30, 81; economists, 89, 95–97; reducing, 129; seasonality trading and, 374
contango, market tilt and, 159–60
continuous improvement, metagame and, 196
contraction, economic, 212, 216, 344; contraction/expansion principle and, 178
control, illusion of in trading, 24–27
convexity, 122, 130, 211, 255; as buying consideration, 355; Sharpe ratio and, 202; short selling and negative, 282, 284, 287, 288; trader understanding of, 208
conviction level, 190, 193, 265, 313; bet sizing and, 195; Kelly criterion and, 194; market tilt and, 158; position sizing and, 188, 194; recording for each trade, 191; risk appetite and, 259; uncertainty and, 244
Copernicus, Nicolaus, 29
correlated errors, 80
correlation: causes of cross-market, 168–72; third variable and, 171. *See also* correlation breakdown
correlation breakdown: as market tell, 160–72, *161g*, *162g*, *163g*, *164g*, *165g*, *170g*, *172g*, 179; persistent, 160, 163–68; temporary, 160–63. *See also* lead/lag trading
CORT, 3–6, *5g*, *6g*
CORZ, 345–47, *346g*
Costanza Trade, 42–44
costs. *See specific trading platforms*; fees; transaction costs
courage, trading and, 268, 317, 381–82, *383g*. *See also* risk
covered call parity, 49

COVID-19 pandemic, 34, 127; fragile restaurants and, 214–15; initial conditions and, 214–15; inverted yield curve and, 297; worker supply and job creation after, 91
Cramer, Jim: "Cramer Bounce," 331; fading trading/investing framework, 327–32, *331g, 332g*
Crash of 1929, 35, 222; Livermore, Jesse, and, 205, 288; short sellers during, 288
crashes, market, 34; correlated errors and, 80; narrative contagion and, 221; short sellers and, 288. *See also specific market crashes*
creativity, 18, 340; Alternative Uses Test and, 22, *22g*; cross-domain exposure and, 21; edge and, 267; increasing, 22; process, 21; research, 22; science of, 21–23
crude oil futures, *179g, 325g, 340g, 341g*; inverted curve, 159–60; price, 303
CRWV, 66–68, *67g*, 232–33, 345, *345g*, 346–47, 349, *349g*, 357–58
crypto markets, 55, 86, 89, 144; gambling disorder and, 145–46; narrative contagion and, 221; as retail sentiment barometer, 296; understanding monetary policy and, 256
crypto trading account, 12, 272
cryptocurrencies, 180, 221; GameStop and, 234–35; meme stocks and, 296, 309; Polymarket and, 100, 103; prediction markets and, 102. *See also* bitcoin
currency markets, 13, 41, 163, 201. *See also* FX markets and trading
cyclical factors, 18, 337–38, 375
CYTK, 64–65, *65g*

Dark Zone, the, 139; machine gambling, 139, 140, 141; trading in, 139–40, 141
data, looking for missing, 338–39, 375; survivor bias and, 338–39
data mining, 364; logical thought process vs., 171; as risky, 70; seasonality and, 374
database analysis, 196–97
Dawkins, Richard, 305
day traders: afterhours trading, 206; "Gap and Trap" and, 42; income, 250–51. *See also* retail day traders, metagame of
Day Trading With Short Term Price Patterns and Opening Range Breakout (Crabel), 178
DBA, 341–42, *341g*
decision-making, amount of information and, 385–88. *See also* decision-making/good thinking, practical frameworks for
decision-making/good thinking, practical frameworks for, 334–39; cyclical factors focus, 337–38; missing data search, 338–39; probabilistic thinking, 334–37
depression, trader, 111, 148
derivatives, 44–46, 86, 256; function, 44, 45; ladder of, 46, 47; trader knowledge of, 256
direct calling process, 13
discipline: poker player, 149; trader, 27, 127, 139, 149, 176, 197, 309
divergent thinking exercises, 21. *See also* second-order thinking
dotcom bubble and crash, 12, 213–14, 256–57, 323, 354; initial conditions of vs. 2022 tech selloff, 213–14
downside support, 4
DraftKings, gambling disorder and, 146–47
Druckenmiller, Stan, 57–59
Drury, Michael, 96

DSM-5 (APA), 110, 111–12; trading and, 112. *See also specific mental health problems*
Duneier, Stephen, 388–90
DWAC, 313–14, *314g*

e-Trade, 146; gambling disorder and, 142
economic collapse of 2023, initial conditions and, 212–13
economics, 95, 96, 211, 378
Economist, The: covers, 56, *56p,* 70–73; magazine cover indicator and, 332
economist surveys, problems with, 89–97; anchoring bias, 89, 92–93, 97; confirmation bias and religiosity, 89, 95–97; herding and clustering, 89, 90–91, *90g,* 97; overreliance on models, 89, 91–92, *91g, 92g,* 97; stale forecasts, 89, 93–95, *94g,* 97
edge, 6, 69, 127, 138, 146, 149, 188, 189, 191, 204, 230, 239, 249, 251, 252, 281, 307–8, 312; catching new narrative early as, 223–24; confidence in one's, 231; finding one's, 20, 62, 267, 396; FX trader, 268; less obvious strategies and, 247; negative, 280; in poker, 195, 311; positive, 281; trader seat as, 265
Efficient Market Hypothesis (EMH), 279, 373; accuracy, 80; reasons for deviation from, 80–82; wisdom of the crowd and, 79–80
egocentrism, 30
election betting markets, 83–84, *84g, 85g*; liquidity, 102; 1916, 83; 2008, 86
Ellis, Charles, 253
emerging markets (EM), 164, 230, 307, 348
emotions, 321, 391–93; as information, *321g*; median duration of, *392g*; Mood Meter, *391g*. *See also* mental capital; mental stamina; polyvagal theory; self-awareness, tilt
Emulex, 269, *270g*
End of History and the Last Man, The (Fukuyama), 33
endowment effect, 66
Enron, *289g*
environment, personal trading, 21–22, 141, 180; ADHD and, 116; creativity and, 21; gambling disorder and, 141; tilt and, 132; Zone, the, and, 116
environment, trading: breakout trading and, 306; initial conditions and, 211; non-ergodic, 208; regime-sensitive models and, 91
Epictetus, 25
equity calls, 208, *250g*
equity markets, 201, 249, 300
equity options, 361–62, *361g, 362g*
ergodic systems, 198, 204, *204g,* 206, *206g, 207g*. *See also* ergodicity
ergodicity, 18, 78, 198, 206, 245; bet sizing and, 203; economic outcomes and, 198–204, *199g, 200g, 201g, 202g, 203g*. *See also* ergodic systems; non-ergodic strategies
ethics, trader/investor, 19, 381
European sovereign debt crisis, initial conditions and, 215
Eurozone Crisis of 2011, 126, 280
EURSEK, 210, *210g,* 281
EURUSD, 228, 240, 242, 310, 311, 319, 336–37, *336g,* 356, *356g*

event traders: making money, 277–78; risk management, 278; successful, 239. *See also* event traders, tips for metagame of
event traders, tips for metagame of, 273–78, *274g, 275g*; bet sizing, 278; automated trading systems, 278; event result prediction, 277; knowledge of catalysts, 276; knowledge of technical levels, 278; listing possible headlines, 276–77; runup trade and, 277; studying past events, 276; trading the aftermath, 277; writing down stop loss, 278
Excellent Sheep (Deresiewicz), 40
execution and tactics, practical frameworks for, 339–55; cutting losing trades, 354–55; monthly trading audits, 350–53; thinking about weird market happenings, 339–50
execution strategy, 264; reevaluating, 24
expected value (EV), 5, 75, 104, 128, 182, 242–43, 244; calculating, 336–37, *336g*; ergodic systems and, 198, 206; maximizing vs. leverage, 77, 397; multiverse thinking and, 242, 245; negative, 127; positive, 76, 197, 199, 200, 205, 206, 311, 348, 361, 383; probability and, 180–81; tradeoff between leverage and positive, 361. *See also* expected value (EV) bets, short-term trading and
expected value (EV) bets, short-term trading and, 76–77
Extraordinary Popular Delusions and the Madness of Crowds (Mackay), 37

fades, *41g*, 75, 183, 240; Cramer's picks, Jim, 331; earnings-day move, 276; falling volatility and, 178; M&A headlines, 39; narratives, 225
false break, 49, 242
family, choosing over markets, 11, 130, 397
FanDuel, gambling disorder and, 146–47
favorite/long shot bias, 88, 105, 147
FCC, 9
Fed Funds futures markets, 82
Federal Reserve: announcements, 242; February 2026 prediction markets paper, 108; impact on stock market, 326–27; inflation and, 216; policy changes and financial markets, 257; rate hikes, 58; trading/investing framework of not fighting, 293, 326–27, *327g*
fees: Coinbase, 146; investing and management, 251, 252; Kalshi, 88–89, 107; securities lending, 347, 348–49; short selling and, 287. *See also* transaction costs
15 Ideas, Frameworks, and Lessons from 15 Years (Hoffstein), 302–3
FIG, 59–60, *60g*
financial crisis of 2008, global, 12, 25, 126, 304; short sellers and, 288
financial markets, history of, 34; books, 37; studying, 36–37
first-derivative thinkers, 40; market success and, 62
first-order thinking, 38, 46, 60; technical analysis and, 56, 58
Fisher, Irving, 35
flat position, 113, 120, 129–30, 142, 260, 262, 277
flexibility: structuring and future, 360; in trader views, 219; trades and, 176
flip-a-coin games, 77–78, 199–200, *199g*, 255, 261
FNM, *Barron's cover* and, 330; 2012 to 2017, *330g*
FOMO, 11, 81, 145, 160, 311

forecasts, economic: bad, 219; biased, 277; crazy, 335; economic outcomes and good, 216–20; economist, 79, 89, 93–95, 97; good, 168, 216–20, *217g,* 245, 295, 387; predicting wrong, 304; prediction markets vs., 82, 88, 101; realistic timeframe, 295
Fortune's Formula (Poundstone), 191
4-7-8 breathing, 123
fragile systems, 212, 214
frameworks. *See* trading/investing frameworks, faulty; trading/investing frameworks, practical
FTX, 86, 87
futures: gold micro, 314; index, 315; interest rate, 201, 311; intraday trading of, 315–16; NASDAQ, 127; natural gas, 202, 205; S&P, 115, 118, *118g,* 261, 325, 353, 354; VIX, 159. *See also* crude oil futures
FX markets and trading, 13, 115, 124, 163, 217, 228, 239, 345, 362, 364
FX rates, 337
FX spot traders, 114, 156, 262, 268; Polymarket and, 107

Gabirol, Solomon, 25
Galfond, Phil, 181, 186
Galileo, 29
Galton, Francis, 79
gambling: addiction process, 140; addictiveness of different types, 141; bad trading as, 127–28, 148, 397; compared with trading and investing, *128g*; preoccupation with, 130. *See also* gambling disorder, trading and
gambling disorder, trading and, 112, 127–48
game selection, 195. *See also* metagame
game theory, 247
GameStop 2021 short squeeze, 73, 285, *285g*; initial conditions and, 214; narrative contagion and, 221. *See also* GME
"Gap and Trap," 42
gap risk, 7, 255, 325; after-hours, 236; avoiding, 357; between market close and open, 325; as buying consideration, 355; cash markets and, 357; central banks and, 325–26; economic data and, 326; events and, 325; liquidity and, 326; trading/investing framework of underestimating/ignoring, 293, 325–26, *325g*; types, 325–26; weekend headline trades and, 7
gaps, 41; close to open, 41; at extremes, 177; fading, 41; as market tell, 176–78, *177g,* 179; stop loss and, 177; Sunday, 41. *See also* gap risk
GBPUSD, 164, *164g,* 363–66, *363g*; FX seasonality, *365g*
Gemini, 3, 5, 65
General Theory of Employment, Interest and Money, The (Keynes), 47–48
geocentrism, 28–29; Aristotle and, 28; Catholic Church and, 29; egocentrism vs., 30; end of, 29; Ptolemy's model of, *28p*
geopolitics, 33; economy and, 168; financial markets and, 257
Gittins, Matt, 361
global macro, 94, 224, 256, 264

GME: crypto/bitcoin announcement, 234–35, *235g, 285g,* 342–50; 2025, *342g, 343g, 344g*. *See also* GameStop 2021 short squeeze
gold, 45, *45g,* 114, 160, 166–67, *166g,* 168, 219, 314–15
good news/bad price, 239; market tell, 155–57, *156g, 157g,* 179
GOOG (Google), 161–62, *162g,* 361–62, *362g*; internal prediction markets, 85–86
Graham, Ben, 302
Greater Fool Theory, 52; speculative memecoin and, 52; wallstreetbets and, 73. *See also* GameStop 2021 short squeeze
guess 2/3 of the average game, 49–52, *51g, 52g*; second-order thinking and, 49–52; speculative memecoin and, 51–52; third-level thinking and, 49–52
Gurung, Inna, 222

Hagakure, 33
Halloween Effect, 367
Handzic, Meliha, 385
Hanson, Robin, 86
hard-to-borrow stocks, underperformance of, 347, *347g, 348g, 349g,* 357–58
Hayek, Friedrich, 85, 378–80
headlines: adverse selection and, 235–37
health: choosing over markets, 11, 397. *See also* environment, personal trading; mental capital; mental stamina
hedge fund managers, tips for metagame of, 258–63, *258g*
Heisenberg's uncertainty principle, 79
heliocentrism, 29
herd: market tells and ignoring, 157; metagame of following, 248, 318; observing, 221; pain of going against, 280, 319. *See also* herding
herding, 81, 251; behavior, 80; Bloomberg and, 101; career risk and, 280; economists and, 89, 90–91, *90g,* 97; emotional arousal and, 222; "looking stupid" risk and, 279; prediction markets and, 97. *See also* herd
heuristics, 305–6, 321; Bayesian belief-updating and, 229; gaze heuristic, 306; problem, 66
high Sharpes, 6, 24, 202, 207; trading headlines as, 308
hindsight bias, 242
history: financial markets, 34, 36–37; prediction markets, 83–87; short selling, 288–90
"homo economicus," 220
house money effect, 153, 382
Housel, Morgan, 317
Howard, Nigel: metagame concept, 247, 248
HTZ, 173–76, *173g, 174g, 176g*
humility, trader, 18, 19, 23, 24, 29, 80, 384–90, *385g, 387g,* 397
Hunt, Ben, 223
Hurricane Katrina, 202, 205
Hwang, Bill, 255
hyperinflation, 217–18, 222

ICO craze, 35
ideas, organic trade, 110
Iguchi, Toshihide, 132, 133
imagination, 22; anxiety and, 120; as asset, 120; lack of, 90, 326; narrative contagion and, 222
income: day traders, 250–51; falling, 248; interest rate hikes and, 213; retail traders, 271; seasonality and, 367–68, *368g*
inflation, 13; central bank and, 212; in Europe, 94; Federal Reserve and, 216, 321; gold and, 314–15; initial conditions and, 216; money printing and, 321; quantitative easing and, 217–18; runaway, 164; steady, 163; stocks and bonds and, 167, *167g*; sudden spike in, 108; 2021–2022 surge, 216. *See also* hyperinflation
information overload, decision-making and, 385–88
initial conditions, 198, 211, 245; central bank policy rate level, 212; chaos theory and, 211; COVID-19 pandemic and, 214–15; economic outcomes and, 198, 211–16; European sovereign debt crisis and, 215; GameStop 2021 saga and, 214; inflation and, 216; market positioning and, 216; microstructure and, 216; monetary policy and, 211–12; state of the economy, 212; 2023 and impending collapse and, 212–13; 2022 tech selloff vs. 2000 dotcom crash and, 213–14
insomnia, trader, 112, 126–27; managing, 127
institutional traders: intraday liquidity and, 271–73; retail traders compared to, 137, *137g*. *See also* institutional traders, metagame of
institutional traders, metagame of, 257–69; hedge fund traders, 258–63, *258g, 259g, 260g*
Interactive Brokers, 87
interest rate futures, 201, 311
interest rates: Federal Reserve hikes in, 58; income and hikes in, 213. *See also* short-term interest rate trading (STIRT)
Intrade, 86
intuition, trader, 114, 125, 304, 339
investing, 36, 49, 128, 355; active vs. passive approaches debate, 251; compared with trading and gambling, *128g*; macro, 313; passive, 316
Irrational Exuberance (Shiller), 37

James, William, 22–23
jellybean experiment, 80, 81, 103; prediction markets and, 82; vs. markets, 82
jeux & stratégie magazine, 49–50, *50p*
journal. *See* trading journal
JPM, 161, *161g*

Kalshi, 87, 104, 311; credit risk and, 105; daily volumes, *87g*; election betting, 103, *103g*; favorite/longshot bias and, 105; fees, 88–89, 107; liquidity and, 103; political bias and, 106; for predictions, 98–102, *98g, 99g*; range of, 108; S&P price range and, *106g*; time value of money and, 106; traditional financial contracts and, 106; vs. Bloomberg survey, 98
Kelly criterion: bet sizing and, 191–93, *191g, 192g,* 194, 195; poker and, 192, 194
Kepler, Johannes: laws of planetary motion, 29

Kernan, Joe, 354
Kerviel, Jérôme, 132, 133
Keynes, John Maynard, 47–48, 224–25, 248, 302; Beauty Contest analogy, 47–49; paradox of thrift, 248
knowledge, trader: admission of limited, 257, 397; insiders with privileged, 81; of leading indicators, 93; from non-financial domains, 20, 109; personal, 20; psychology and market, 111; Theory of Mind (ToM) and, 53
KSS, 74–76, *76g*

law of large numbers, 77, 197; non-ergodicity and, 200
Laws of Trading, The (Lebron), 228–30
lead/lag trading, 114, 160–62, 306. *See also* correlation breakdown
Lebron, Agustin, 228
Ledoux, Alain, 49
Leeson, Nick, 132, 136
Liar's Poker (Lewis), 394
"Liberation Day" April 2025, 126, 165, 275; panic, 209–10. *See also* tariffs, 2025 Trump
limit orders, 198, 265, 278; on halted stock, 5; reducing trading costs with, 241; vs. market orders, 231; when to use, 232–36. *See also* adverse selection
liquid stock, 105; vs. illiquid stock, *105g*. *See also* liquidity
liquidity, 7, 105, 176, 264, 268, 275, 278, 354; after hours, 41; calendar year end and, 281; checking, 101; constraints, 81, 276; election betting (U.S.) and, 102; gap risk and, 326; news and, 237, 275; pre-market opening, 41; prediction markets and, 85, 88, 102–7; retail traders and, 271–73; risk, 255; short squeeze and, 286; speculators and, 380; strategy capacity limit and, 125; volatility and, 326
Livermore, Jesse, 12, 13, 112, 128, 130, 205, 255, 288, 394, 395
LLMs, 3, 8, 18, 62, 63; downsides, 63, 65; reaction to first use of, 223. *See also specific LLMs*; LLMs, uses of for better trading
LLMs, uses of for better trading, 63–73; brainstorming backtesting ideas, 63, 69–70; idea generation, 68; optimizing trade structuring, 63, 66–68, *67g*; quick read on headlines, 63, 64–66, *65g*; unbiased feedback on sentiment, 63, 70–73, *72g*; variance estimating, 187. *See also* AI; ChatGPT; Claude; Gemini
Long-Term Capital Management (LTCM), 205
long-term valuation models, 298, 300. *See also* Buffett Indicator
losing trades, cutting, 354–55, 375; mental capital and, 354; short-term traders and, 355
loss aversion, 81; theory, 260. *See also* risk aversion

MACD, 45; gold and, *45g*
macro investing, 313
magazine cover indicators: *Barron's,* 327–32, *328g, 329g, 330g*; ChatGPT and, 72–73; *Economist, The,* 56, 70–73, *72p*, 332
Man, Play, and Games (Caillois), 377–78
Manias, Panics, and Crashes (Kindleberger), 37
market actions, weird: examples, 339–47, *340g, 341g, 342g, 343g, 344g, 345g, 346g,* 375; thinking about/paying attention to, 8, *8g,* 9, *9g*, 38, 155, 157, 339–50, 375, 397. *See also* tells, market

market capitalization, 291, 294, *294g,* 300, 323
market inefficiencies, 196
market makers, tips for metagame, 263–69
market memory, 28, 36, 37, 390; seasonality and, 371–73, *371g*
market orders, 232, 234, 236, 265; vs. limit orders, 231
markets, financial: basic elements of, 46; global, 172; Keynesian view, 47–48; as self-referential, 79; uncertainty principle, 82; views of, 18. *See also specific types of markets*
Martingale Betting Strategy, 202–3, *203g*
Mauboussin, Michael, 323
mean, 199
mean reversion strategies, market memory and, 373
mediators, correlation and, 169, 171
meditation: ADHD and, 117; mental stamina and, 180
meme stocks, 309; cryptocurrencies and, 296; financial market rules, 257; interest in, 75; narrative contagion and, 221; preferred trading method, 75
memecoin, 35, 147, 271; gambling disorder and, 145–46; Greater Fool Theory and speculative, 52; guess 2/3 of the average game and, 51–52
mental capital: cutting losing trades and, 354; disregard for as trading/investment framework, 293, 308–21, *314g*; importance of, 308; managing, 320–21, *321g*; managing amygdala and, 317–18; managing with time conditions in trades 317; outperformance and, 319; perspective and 320–21; stop losses and, 318, 320; strong bias and, 309; trades consuming, 308–9, 310–11; trades good for, 309–10. *See also* emotions
mental health, trading and. *See* ADHD; ADHD, trading and; anxiety; anxiety, trading and; depression, trading and; *DSM-5*; gambling disorder; gambling disorder, trading and; insomnia, trading and; mental capital; mental stamina
mental stamina, 179–80. *See also* meditation; mental capital; walking
Meriwether, John, 13
Meta, 124, 161–62, *162g*
metacognition, 39
metagame: calendar year-end, 281, *281g*; in chess, 248; event traders, 273–78, *274g, 275g*; following the herd, 248; hedge fund traders, 258–63, *258g, 259g, 260g*; institutional traders, 257–69; market makers, 263–69; meaning of, 246–50, *248g, 250g*; personal, 250–55, *251g, 253g*; player emotions, goals, and motivations in, 247; in pro sports, 248–49; rationality and, 247; retail day traders, 269–73, *270g*; rules and, 247; shifts and rule changes, 249–50; strategies and, 247; in video games, 248
Microsoft internal prediction markets, 86
Mill, John Stuart, 220
Millennium Hedge Fund, 258–59, *259g*
mistakes, trader, 112, 113, 125, 180, 271, 350, 373; admitting, 133; studying own, 10, 397
modeling, 206; quantitative, 388. *See also* models
models: bias, 97; economists and overreliance on 89, 91–92, *91g, 92g,* 97; overreliance on as trading/investment framework, 293, 304–6. *See also* long-term valuation models; modeling; short-term valuation methods

momentum, 62, 79, 173, 315, 332; burnt out, 58; chasing, 24, 236; fades, 75; indicators, 45, 46, 60; labor market, 310; market tilt and, 158; narrative cycle and, 226; strategies, 373. *See also* MACD; momentum stocks; RSI
momentum stocks, 40, 58, 161
monetary policy, 170, 171, 211; inflation and, 216; trader knowledge of, 256. *See also* Federal Reserve
money-making methods, present vs. future, *5g*, 6, *6g*, 397
Mood Meter, *391g*
moving average (MA) filters, 363–64, *363g*, 375
multi-order thinking, 18, 58–60; misconceptions, 60–61. *See also* multiverse thinking; second-order thinking
multiplicative process, non-ergodicity and, 200
multiverse thinking, 241–45, *243g*, *244g*; expected value theory and, 242–43, 245; psychological liberation and, 243; quantum mechanics and, 241; risk management and, 244–45; strong conviction and, 244
Murphy, Tom, 391–92
Musk, Elon, 177

narrative analysis, 225. *See also* narrative contagion; narratives, viral
narrative contagion, 198, 220, 221, *226g*, 245; economic outcomes and, 220–26; features, 222; identifying, 223–26, *226g*; monitoring social media for, 223; relevance, 224–25; second-order thinking and, 225; in social media, 222; storytelling and, 221. *See also* narrative analysis; narrative propagation; narratives, viral
narrative propagation, 18. *See also* narrative contagion
narratives, viral: features, 225. *See also* narrative contagion
news trading, 21, 61, 65–66; second-order thinking and, 61. *See also* headlines
Newton, Isaac: laws of motion and gravitation, 29
NFT madness, 35
Niebuhr, Reinhold, 25. *See also* "Serenity Prayer"
Niederhoffer, Victor, 13, 202, 255
non-ergodic strategies, 205–8; Amaranth Advisors, 205; Archegos Capital, 205–6; Long-Term Capital Management (LTCM), 205; Martingale Betting Strategy, 202–3; real-life examples, 205–8. *See also* Livermore, Jesse; non-ergodic systems; non-ergodicity
non-ergodic systems, 198–99, 202, 204, 208; Bayesian thinking and, 207–8; highly, 205. *See also* non-ergodicity; non-ergodic strategies
non-ergodicity, 199–200, 207; absorption property and, 200; Bayesian thinking and, 207; law of large numbers and, 200; multiplicative process and, 200
nonfarm payroll (NFP) releases, 91–93, *91g*, *92g*, 97–100
NVDA, 40–41, *40g*, 58, 161, 214, 236, 276, 359

obsessive-compulsive disorder (OCD), trading and, 148
Occam's Razor, 388
On the Revolutions of the Celestial Spheres (Copernicus), 29
one trick pony trading/investment framework, 293, 306–8

OODA loop, 350–51, *351p*
optimism, trader, 221, 251, 384
options: mental capital conservation and, 311, 317; short-dated, 75, 272, 358, *359g*, 361–62, *361g*, *362g*; time decay and, 358; trader knowledge of, 256; vs. cash, 356, 357–60, 362. *See also* equity options; options markets
options markets, 208, 249, 358, 359
outcome, process vs., 25, 181, *243g*, *244g*
outperformance, 42, 58, 128, 147, 251, 317, 341, 344, 349; mental discomfort and, 319, 321
overnight index swap (OIS), 82
overtrading, 111, 251, 253; creating barriers to, 119, 140, 141, 142, 147, 148; Wall Street products preying on, 143

pain, trading and, 150, 307, 317; avoiding, 318–19; courage and, 381–83, *383g*; in hedge fund management, 258; loss aversion theory and, 260; risk appetite scale, *383g*; variance and, 188
P&L simulations, 187, *187g*
panics, financial, 221; "Liberation Day" April 2025, 209–10; short selling bans during, 288. *See also* tilt, market
paradox of rationality, 248
paradox of thrift, 248
Paradoxes of Rationality: Theory of Metagames and Political Behavior (Howard), 247
Pareto's Law, gambling disorder and, 143
parsimony, 388
path dependence, 206, 259, 261–62
pattern matching, random, 21
pattern recognition, traders and, 9, 155, 305, 339; Jesse Livermore and, 205
PEGA, 238–39, *239g*
performance coaches for traders, 112, 114, 148, 309
permabears, 219, 311
permabulls, 279, 288
Perscient, monitoring for narrative contagion, 223
personal growth, 393–94
personal metagame, 250–55, *251g*, *253g*; game selection, 250, 252, 254; humility, 250, 384 knowledge of risks, 255; monetary policy knowledge, 256; playing not to lose, 252; playing to win, 254, 255; stock market knowledge, 256; too-hard pile and, 255–57. *See also* retail day trader, metagame of
perspective, 16, 18, 23–24, 52, 263, 320; chronocentrism, 30–37; egocentrism, 30; geocentrism, 28–29. *See also* humility, trader; multiverse thinking; second-order thinking
phone, smart: checking, 126, 130, 131; deleting Twitter app, 141; gambling disorder and, 141; insomnia and, 126; night trading on, 141; push notifications and, 143; turning off at bedtime, 127
Piaget, Jean, 30
pipeline failure, 4
Plotkin, Gabe, 255
poker, professional, 18; markets and, 48, 49; world-class players, 149. *See also* poker, trading and

poker, trading and, 311–12; bet sizing, 188–95; continuous improvement, 196; database analysis and review, 196; decision-making, 197; exploiting market inefficiencies, 196; game selection, 195; mental stamina, 179–80; probability and expected value (EV), 180–81; psychological trap avoidance, 197; self-mastery, 197; tells, 154–79; tight/aggressive, 196; tilt, 150–54; trader talents, 149; ups and downs, 150; variance, 181–88, *187g*. *See also* tells, market
political bias, trader, 88, 106
politics. *See* election betting markets; geopolitics; prediction markets, history of; short selling
Polymarket, 83, 86, 87, 100, *100g*, 101, 103, 104, 311; Bloomberg and, 101, *101g*; credit risk and, 105; election betting, 102, *102g*; favorite/longshot bias and, 105; liquidity and, 102–3; moving before traditional markets, 107; political bias, 106; time value of money and, 106; war betting, *107g*
polyvagal theory, 151–53, *152g*; tilt and, 152–53
Porges, Stephen, 151
position sizing: adapting process over time, 195; anxiety and, 124–26; conviction level and, 188, 195; ergodic personal experience and, 206; Kelly criterion and, 194; multiverse framework and, 244; uncertainty level and, 245; use of basis points for risk units and, 124–25; variance and, 188. *See also* bet sizing; short selling
positive drift, short selling indexes and, 288
pragmatism, trader, 295, 397
prediction markets, 18, 62, 63, 79–82, 88, 101–2, 108; assessing liquidity of, 102–7; clear information and, 88; as early regime shifts/market surprises signal, 88; efficient information aggregation and, 88, 107; Federal Reserve February 2026 paper on, 108; fees, 88; for forecasting, 82, 88; for free information, 89; for trading events in real time, 102–7; jellybean game and, 82; podcast, 107; shortcomings, 88; wisdom of the crowd and, 108. *See also* Kalshi; Polymarket; prediction markets, history of
prediction markets, history of, 83–87; academic interest, 86; ancient, 83; blockchain technology and, 83, 86; first political betting markets, 83–84; institutional phase, 87; Iowa Electronic Markets (IEM), 85; offshore platforms and, 86; post-2000 growth, 86–87; technology and, 85–86; theoretical foundations for, 85–86
predictions, overreliance on models, 304–6
price discovery: capitalism and, 378; friction around, 275; speculators and, 380; tug between opposing views and, 89; waiting for, 177; wisdom of the crowd and, 86
price mechanism, capitalism and, 378–80
price targets, 4; avoiding tweets with crazy, 145
prices, 378; as compressed knowledge signals, 379. *See also* price discovery
principles, trading: 6, 9, 10, 11, 12, 16, 18, 25, 34, 37, 46, 53, 60, 77, 119, 130, 148, 257, 269, 295, 339–50, 362, 384–90, 397
probabilistic thinking, 180–81, 192, 218, 245, 334–37, 375; calculating expected value and, 336–37; cone of uncertainty and, 337; importance of, 295, 397
probability, trading and, 78, 89, 93, 101, 108, 192, 193, 197, 244–45, 336–37; compared to gambling, 127; expected value, 180–81; preparing for low, 277. *See also* Bayesian thinking; Kelly criterion; prediction markets; trading/investing frameworks, practical
Problem of Percentages, 260

process, trading: multiverse thinking and, 242–45, *243g, 244g*; rigorous, 119, 123, 126, 127, 142, 350; vs. outcome, 25, 181, *243g, 244g*
psychology, clinical, 18, 148
Psychology of Intelligence Analysis (Heuer), 190
Pueblo, Yung, 390

QQQ vs. ARK Innovation ETF, *36g*
quantum mechanics, 198, 241; Heisenberg's uncertainty principle, 79. *See also* multiverse thinking

rational traders, 25, 129, 133, 242, 248, 280–81, 350, 382; risk appetite and, 383, *383g*; vs. smartest traders, 37, 397
rationality: human decision-making and, 81; metagame and, 248; rigorous process and, 350. *See also* paradox of rationality; rational traders
Read, Leonard E., 380
recency bias, chronocentrism and, 33
recession, 96, 97, 212, 248, 288; Fed actions and, 326; forecasts of imminent, 219, 221, 306, 334; yield curve inversion and, 218, 297–98, *298g*
Reddit: first-level thinkers and, 56; GameStop saga and, 221; increases in call buying and, 58; monitoring for narrative contagion, 223, 226
regime change/shift, 208, 219, 304, 307, 333; adapting to, 308; correlation breakdown and, 160–68, *161g, 162g, 163g, 164g, 165g*; gold and other metals, 166–67, *166g*; inflation and, *167g*; overreliance on models and, 305; stocks and bonds, 167–68, *167g*; USD and oil, 166
religiosity, biased economic forecasts and, 89, 95–97. *See also* confirmation bias
Reminiscences of a Stock Operator (Lefèvre), 130, 394
reputation, trader, 383–84, 394; lying about errors and, 133; value of excellent, 269, 384, 397
retail day traders, metagame of, 269–73, *270g*; short runway problem, 270–71; trading office and, 273; underfunded problem, 269–70. *See also* day traders; retail traders
retail traders, 249; compared to institutional traders, 137, *137g*; gambling disorder and, 129; prediction markets and, 107; successful, 137; Tesla stock and, 296. *See also* day traders; retail day traders, metagame of
returns, 12–13, 41, *253g, 347g, 348g*; account size and, 272; active managers vs. passive indexes and, 251; automated trading systems and, 278; avoiding risk of ruin and, 119, 326, 358, 397; hedge fund management and, 252; Kelly criterion and gambling, 191–92; lifetime of every stock, 324; overnight, 69; regime shifts and, 308; rigorous process and, 127; selling call spreads and, 75; skew and distribution of, 208; survivor bias and, 338–39. *See also specific companies*; S&P 500
Reuters electronic dealing platform, 13, 14, 89
revenge trading, 111, 132, 133, 151
risk appetite, 221, 259, 281, 334, 382, 383; global, 171; scale, *383g*
risk-averse traders, 113, 120, 382
risk aversion: economic forecasts and, 90. *See also* loss aversion; risk-averse traders
risk management, 18, 257, 281; alignment with self-awareness, 316; banking industry protocols, 133; during personal downs, 131; ergodicity and, 206; mental capital expenditure and, 308, 313–16, 318, 320;

multiverse framework and, 244–45; non-ergodicity and, 207; overreliance on models and, 304–6; poker player, 149; retail trader, 273; rigorous, 117, 124; short selling and, 282; stop losses as tool, 117; trading events and, 278; trading gaps and, 41, *41g*; worst-case scenario, 5. *See also* bet sizing; Livermore, Jesse; position sizing
risk of "looking stupid," 90, 96, 97, 279–80
risk of ruin, 127, 336; avoidance/elimination of, 75, 79, 119, 245, 325, 326, 358, 360, 382, 397; awareness of, 255; Livermore, Jesse, and, 205; retail traders and, 360. *See also* gap risk; gap risk, underestimating/ignoring; risk management
Roaring Kitty, 77, 78
Robinhood, 87; gambling disorder and, 141, 142, 146
robust systems, 196, 212
Rokos Macro Hedge Fund: returns, *258g*
Rounders (film), 154–55
RSI, 45, 69, 340; gold, *45g*; EURSEK, *210g*; market tilt and, 158; skew and, 210–11, *210g*
Rusnak, John, 132, 133
r/wallstreetbets. *See* wallstreetbets (WSB)

"Sally-Anne Test," 53
Salomon Brothers, 394
S&P 500, 41, *41g, 143g, 144g,* 216–17, *217g, 283g, 369g, 370g*
SATS, *8g, 9g*
seasonality, market, 168, 205, 364–75; confirmation bias, 374; critics, 374; equity and, 361, 368–70; in FX, 364–67, *365g, 366g*; household cash flows and, 367–68; market memory and, 371–73, *371g*; median U.S. monthly income, *368g*; probabilistic nature, 366, 375; in stocks, 367–70, *369g, 370g*
second-order thinking, 18, 30, 37, 38, *39g, 40g, 41g,* 42, *42g,* 46–52, 62
Seinfeld (TV show), 42–44
self-awareness, trader, 149, 153, 391–93; emotions duration and, *392g*; gambling disorder and, 133; journaling and, 320; Mood Meter and, *391g*
self-worth, trader, 376–80
selling volume, 75, 306, 307–8
sentiment, 30; extreme, 159; getting unbiased feedback on, 63; using LLMs for unbiased feedback on, 70–79, *72g*. *See also* initial conditions; narrative contagion; prediction markets; skew
"Serenity Prayer," 25, 397
Shantideva, 25
Shiller CAPE ratio, 303, *303g*
shoe-shine indicator, 56
short sellers, 282, 288, 290; medium term, 175. *See also* short selling
short selling, 18, 282–90; adverse events and, 287; burnout from, 290; fees, 287; financial panics and, 288; history, 288–90, *289g*; indexes, 288; long-term trend and, 282, 284; math of, 282–288, *283g, 284g, 285g, 286g, 287g*; negative convexity and, 282, 284, 287, 288; politics and, 282; risk management, 282; stocks, individual, 288. *See also* GameStop 2021 short squeeze
short-term interest rate trading (STIRT), 255–56, 311, 326

short-term trading, 66, 73, 76–77, 148, 276, 345, 355. *See also* initial conditions; lead/lag trading; short-term interest rate trading (STIRT)
short-term valuation methods, 303–4
Silver, Nate, 83
single-product risk, 4
single variable analysis, faulty trading/investing framework of, 293, 321–23, *322g*, 387
skew, 208, 245; economic outcomes and, 208–11, *209g, 210g*; in options markets, 208; RSI and, 210–11; as sentiment indicator, 208
Slingshot Reversal, 49
slippage, 251, 264
Slovik, Paul, 386
"Smarties Test," 53
SNB floor break of 2015, 10
social media: dissing Jim Cramer on, 327, 332; financial gurus, 279; imminent recession anecdotes, 221, 288; monitoring for narrative contagion, 223; narrative contagion in, 222; wisdom of the crowd and, 80. *See also specific social media platforms*; social media traders
social media traders, 73, 77. *See also* wallstreetbets (WSB)
spoofing, 14
stale/faraway orders, 123, 241; adverse selection and, 234–35, *235g*
STIRT. *See* short-term interest rate trading (STIRT)
stop losses, 75, 111, 112, 124, 125, 131, 175, 178, 186, 194, 204–5, 218, 263, 355
storytelling, 220–21; narrative contagion and, 221, 222, 223
strategy: execution, 24, 264; Martingale Betting, 202–3; understanding opponent's, 48
stress, nervous system reaction to, 151–53. *See also* polyvagal theory
structural factors, trade, 18, 337–38
structures: different views and, 362, 397; skillful, 355–62, *356g, 359g, 361g, 362g*, 375
Substack, monitoring for narrative contagion, 223
substance abuse, trading and, 148
survivor bias, missing data and, 338–39
Swiss franc, 292, 297, *299g*; SNB 2015 floor break and, 10
System 1 thinking, 65, 66, 388, 389; impulsive trading and, 114. *See also* first-order thinking
System 2 thinking, 65, 66, 114, 388. *See also* multiverse thinking; second-order thinking

Taleb, Nassim, 202, 207, 208, 212, 213
tariffs, 2025 Trump, 155–56, 163, 164; on Canada, 155–56; on Mexico, 156
tech selloff of 2022, initial conditions vs. dotcom crash of 2000, 213–14
technical analysis, 54, 109, 246, 278, 314; first-order thinking and, 56; magazine covers and, 56; second-order use of, 54–60, *54g, 55g, 60g*; self-fulfilling prophecy and, 54
tells, market, 155–79
tells, poker, 154–55, 175, 179
Theory of Mind (ToM): second-order thinking and, 52–53; tests to measure, 52. *See also* "Sally-Anne Test"; "Smarties Test"; "Unexpected Contents Test"

therapists for traders, 112, 115, 126, 127, 148, 309
theta, options and, 357, 358
thinking: about others' thinking, 46, 53, 397; like yourself vs. others, 18, 397. *See also* first-order thinking; multiverse thinking; second-order thinking; third-order thinking
Thinking, Fast and Slow (Kahneman), 190
Thinking in Bets (Duke), 25, 181
third-order thinking, 47; guess 2/3 of the average game and, 49–52
tilt, 132, 150–54; personal protocol for, 153; pinball and, 150; in poker, 150, 151, 153, 158, 160; polyvagal theory and, 151–53, *152g*; short squeeze and, 286; in trading, 151. *See also* tilt, market; Winner's Tilt
tilt, market, 157–60; characteristics, 158; contango/backwardation shifts and, 159–60; sentiment readings and, 159
time, behavioral vs. statistical, 302–3
time decay, 76; options and, 357, 358
time horizon mismatch, valuation and: as faulty trading/investment framework, 293–304, *294g, 296g, 298g, 299g, 300g, 301g, 303g*
time management methods, ADHD and: Pomodoro technique, 116
time zone bias, 264
TQQQ, 121–22, *121g*
trading coaches, 115, 126, 148, 309
trading floor, 14, 15–16, 153, 197; heated situation on, 391; Winner's Tilt and, 154
Trading in the Zone (Douglas), 138
trading journal, 196; ADHD and, 113; anxiety and, 123; automatic, 153; bet sizing and, 195; goal-setting and, 353; recording emotional state in, 320; *Spectra Markets Trader Handbook,* 116
trading plan, ADHD and, 116
trading styles, regime dependency and, 306–8, 333
trading thesis, 49, 60, 120, 181, 196, 318, 319; view of future as different from present narrative, 61
trading time frame, 143, 172; matching analysis to, 295, 397
Tragedy of the Commons, 248
transaction costs, 81, 118, 232–34, *234g,* 271, 272, 342; as buying consideration, 355; complex structures and, 360; limit orders and, 241; playing to win and, 252; traders and, 251; for transactions at open and close, 349–50. *See also* fees
trending market, 49, 159
trends, 36; "Gap and Trap" and, 42; long-term and short selling, 282, 284; market memory and following, 373
Trump, Donald J., 313, 314; tariffs on Canada, 155–56; tariffs on Mexico, 156; 2024 election, 177
Truss, Liz, 164
TSLA, 24, 29, 46–47, *46g,* 82, 177–78, *177g,* 181, 237, *237g,* 294–98, *294g, 296g,* 311, 335
TSLR, 233–34, *234g*
Twitter, 33, 95, 315; *See also* X

U.S. domestic funds, 251, *251g*
U.S. GDP, 282, 283–84, *284g,* 300, 301

"Unexpected Contents Test," 53
UNF, 38–39, *39g*
University of Michigan Consumer Sentiment Index, 212
Unknown Market Wizards (Schwager), 239, 273
USDCAD, 13, 155–57, *156g, 157g,* 266
USDJPY, 114, 131, *163g, 165g,* 208–9, 211, 239, 273–76, 281, 292, 325, 359, 361, 365–66, *366g;* event traders and, *274g, 275g;* FX seasonality, *365g;* gap risk, 325–26; short-dated options costs in, *361g;* skew, *209g*

valuation, 4, 36, 47–48, 49, 58, 59–60, 333; chronocentrism and, 35; currency, 297; long-term, 298–300, 303; objective, 334; short-term, 303–4; short-term price movement and long-term, 224–25; time horizon mismatch trading/investment framework and, 293–304, *294g, 296g, 298g, 299g, 300g, 301g, 303g*
variance, 181–88, *187g,* 204; law of large numbers and, 77, 199–200; misunderstandings about in poker, 182–85; poker players and, 149; reducing, 185–86; run of bad, 381–82; swings due to, 150; vs. process breakdown, 188; vs. tilt, 188
VIX, 24, *281g,* 307, 308; futures curve, 159
volatility, 59, 60, 75–76, 131, 258, 259, 356, 360
volume, 59, 60, 69, 75; election betting markets and, 83; equity calls and, 250, *250g;* Kalshi, 87, *87g;* Polymarket, 101; profit and, 146; spike with price reversal as market tell, 172–76, *173g, 174g, 176g,* 179; weird market happenings and, 155

walking, 21; ADHD and, 116; anxiety and, 123; gambling disorder and, 132; mental stamina and, 180; poker players and, 153
Wall Street (film), 394
wallstreetbets (WSB), 63, 73–79, *76g, 204g;* Greater Fool theory and, 73; monitoring for narrative contagion, 223; raids, 18, 74, *74g,* 75, 76; traders on, 77, 79; Winner's Tilt and, 154
wealth, trader, 12–13, 78, 324, 395, 397; diversification, 241; investing and, 128
weird market actions. *See* market actions, weird
willpower, gambling disorder and, 130, 142–47, 148
Winner's Tilt, 153–54; as potential reversal indicator, 154
wisdom of the crowd, trading and, 39, 79–82, 89
Wolfers, Justin, 86
Wood, Catherine, 35–36

X: monitoring for narrative contagion, 223. *See also* Twitter
XMSR, 329, *329g*

yield curve inversion, 297–98; COVID-19 and, 297; as recession predictor, 218, 297–98, *298g,* 310

Zitzewitz, Eric, 86
Zone, the, 113, 131, 138–39, 141, 150, 271, 276; characteristics of traders in, 138–39; trading environment and, 116. *See also* Dark Zone, the

ABOUT THE AUTHOR

Brent Donnelly is President of Spectra Markets and the author of *The Art of Currency Trading*, *Alpha Trader*, and *50 Trades in 50 Weeks*. He writes a widely read, highly-respected macro trading daily called **am/FX**.

Over the course of his career, he has been a market maker, trader, and senior manager at some of the top commercial and investment banks in the U.S.A.

Before joining Spectra, Brent was head of G10 Spot Trading at Citi New York and global head of G10 FX Trading at Nomura New York. He was also a portfolio manager at a major hedge fund in Connecticut for three years.

Brent has been trading currencies, FX options, stock index futures, single names, and commodities since 1995. He is a respected macro thinker with the unique perspective of a senior risk taker. His podcast with Alf Peccatiello, *The Macro Trading Floor*, is a must-listen. He has been quoted or featured in the Economist, Epsilon Theory, Real Vision, the Wall Street Journal, Financial Times, Bloomberg, and CNBC.

Brent created and wrote an animated series called "Daft Planet" which aired on TV in Canada, and if all goes well his novel *Ant Farm* will come out in 2027.

Made in United States
Orlando, FL
01 November 2026

89720412R00234